SECOND EDITION

THE *Worship* SOURCEBOOK

SECOND EDITION

# THE *Worship* SOURCEBOOK

FAITH ALIVE®
Christian Resources

CALVIN INSTITUTE OF CHRISTIAN WORSHIP
*for the study and renewal of worship*

BAKER
A DIVISION OF
Baker Book House Co

Calvin Institute of Christian Worship
Grand Rapids, Michigan

Faith Alive Christian Resources
Grand Rapids, Michigan

Baker Books
Grand Rapids, Michigan

*The Worship Sourcebook, Second Edition*
(CD included)

Copublished by

> The Calvin Institute of Christian Worship, 1855 Knollcrest Circle SE, Grand Rapids, MI 49546-4402; phone: (616) 526-6088; e-mail: worship@calvin.edu; website: www.calvin.edu/worship.
>
> Faith Alive Christian Resources, 2850 Kalamazoo Ave. SE, Grand Rapids, MI 49560; phone: (800) 333-8300; website: www.FaithAliveResources.org.
>
> Baker Books, a division of Baker Book House Company, P.O. Box 6287, Grand Rapids, MI 49516; website: www.bakerbooks.com.

Printed in the United States of America.

ISBN 978-1-59255-797-4 (Faith Alive Christian Resources)
ISBN 978-0-8010-1591-5 (Baker Book House)

10 9 8 7 6 5 4 3 2 1

# TABLE OF CONTENTS

*To Emily R. Brink,*
*pastoral leader, theologian,*
*editor, and musician,*

*with gratitude for your global and ecumenical vision,*
*your encouraging spirit,*
*your prayer-shaped hope*
*for the flourishing of Christ's church.*

# PREFACE

## Ancient Wisdom, Multiple Voices, Improvisatory Practice

This book is designed to encourage creative, theologically sound, contextually appropriate worship practices that draw deeply on the rich heritage of Christian worship and respond imaginatively and faithfully to contemporary cultural contexts and ministry challenges. It is a book that gathers several hundred texts appropriate for use in Christian worship, along with teaching notes that describe how a vivid, trinitarian covenantal theology of worship can guide not only the texts that are used but also the way the central practices of worship are embodied.

We are grateful for the enthusiastic response to the book's first edition. We are particularly grateful for the very positive response to the teaching materials found here. The book's users have repeatedly noted that merely using a text from this volume is insufficient for strengthening worship. Rather, the texts become spiritually formative and significant when a congregation experiences them as essential dynamics in the covenantal relationship we are gracefully drawn into by God's Holy Spirit. While individual worshipers do not need to know a detailed theology of worship in order to worship (a grace!), wise, pastoral worship leaders are immensely blessed by growing in knowledge and grace in Christ, by reflecting on worship's deep meaning and purpose, and by refining practices in light of prayerful scriptural study and theological discernment.

We are also grateful for the many users of the first edition who have testified about the power of disciplined improvisation in worship leadership. Broadly speaking, worship in just about any style suffers when it slips into mindless routine that fails to appreciate the formative power of habitual action to shape us as Christian disciples. Worship also suffers from endless innovation that constantly casts about for the latest fad. Between these two extremes lies the wisdom of "disciplined innovation," in which pastoral leaders, like jazz musicians, draw upon ancient patterns and forms and then prayerfully, communally adapt them to address local needs, circumstances, and opportunities.

In contrast to many comparable collections, this volume is not the work of a single author. Rather, it was developed at every step by teams of people. These teams, in turn, looked for ways to include materials in a variety of "registers" of speech, some more formal, some less so. At the same time, this book was not assembled by a denominational task force. It does not bear the imprimatur of a denominational synod or general assembly. It is a collaborative work, designed to feature multiple voices, all reflecting a common appreciation for historic, trinitarian, covenantal worship presented in ways that can be used in a variety of congregations across the ecumenical spectrum.

## Acknowledgments

*The Worship Sourcebook* was borne out of *Reformed Worship*, a quarterly journal of perspectives on and resources for worship (1987-present), and two series of conferences: the Conference on Liturgy and Music (1987-2003) and the Calvin Symposium on Worship (1989-present). The initial outline, structure, and contents of the book were developed by a working group that met in May 2002. We offer special thanks to Joyce Borger for preparing a significant survey of published resources for use at those meetings. Members of the group were Marco Avila, church planter, Passaic, New Jersey; Cindy de Jong, Calvin College, Grand Rapids, Michigan; David Diephouse, Calvin College; Janet Hill, pastoral musician, Grand Rapids, Michigan; Tom Schwanda, Reformed Bible College, Grand Rapids, Michigan; Debra Rienstra, Calvin College; David Vroege, pastor, Halifax, Nova Scotia; and four staff members of the Calvin Institute of Christian Worship: Joyce Borger, Emily Brink, Cindy Holtrop, and John Witvliet; and student assistants Sarah de Young, Rachel Klompmaker, and Carrie Titcombe. During the summer of 2002 Cindy de Jong and Rachel Klompmaker processed the work of that group and continued compiling resources from a growing list (see Acknowledgments, p. 780). Then Emily Brink, Norma de Waal Malefyt, Carrie Titcombe, Howard Vanderwell, and John Witvliet (all staff members of the Institute) formed the main editorial team that began work in the fall of 2002.

In spring 2003, several external reviewers made comments on a draft of the manuscript. We are grateful for insights from Harry Boonstra, Calvin Theological Seminary; Joyce Borger; Robert De Moor, Faith Alive Christian Resources; Brooks Kuykendall, Calvin College; Larry Sibley, Westminster Theological Seminary; Lugene Schemper, Calvin Theological Seminary; and David Vroege. We are also grateful for the review and helpful comments made by members of the *Reformed Worship* Advisory Council and Worship Institute staff: Douglas Brouwer, Wheaton, Illinois; Paul Detterman, Louisville, Kentucky; Sue Imig, Salem, Oregon; George Langbroek, St. Catharines, Ontario; Kathy Smith, Grand Rapids, Michigan; Lisa Stracks, Chicago, Illinois; Mary Sytsma, Wheaton, Illinois; Yvonne Vander Veen, Grand Rapids; and David Vroege. Scott Hoezee supplied additional materials, and Henry

Admiraal prepared the Scripture index. Taken together, these people have served a remarkably diverse group of congregations, large and small, old and new, in a variety of roles, such as pastors, youth group leaders, children's ministry specialists, worship committee members, and pastoral musicians. In the spring, summer, and fall of 2003, several people worked on stylistic and editorial revisions, including Emily Cooper, Paul Faber, Lisa Stracks, and Carrie Titcombe. Particular thanks are due to Emily Cooper of the Institute for her detailed work on copyright permissions.

This second edition was developed in 2012 by Calvin Institute of Christian Worship staff members who worked to draw upon insights gleaned from a wide range of ecumenical, inter-generational programming since its inception in 1997. We are grateful for the insights of Joyce Borger, now editor of *Reformed Worship*; Mark Rice, director of Faith Alive Christian Resources; and Robert Hosack, Baker Books, for their leadership; for revised texts contributed by Mark Charles, Dale Cooper, Neal Plantinga, Bert Polman, Emily Brink, Carrie Steenwyk, Howard Vanderwell, and John Witvliet; and for significant administrative support offered by Institute staff Cindy De Boer and Kristen Verhulst and by student assistants Rachel Adams, Samantha Brondyke, Kyle Erffmeyer, Rebecca Hoeksema, and Kendra Pennings.

We dedicate this book to the work of faithful pastors, worship planners, musicians, artists, and wordsmiths who work each week, often with remarkable generosity, creativity, and resourcefulness, to prepare and lead God-glorifying worship in congregations everywhere.

> Carrie Titcombe Steenwyk,
>     Calvin Institute of Christian Worship,
>     managing editor
>
> John D. Witvliet,
>     Calvin Institute of Christian Worship,
>     executive editor

# PROLOGUE

# PROLOGUE

## I. THE PRACTICE
## OF CHRISTIAN WORSHIP

**Worship's Meaning and Purpose**

Each week Christians gather for worship in mud huts and Gothic cathedrals, in prisons and nursing homes, in storefront buildings and village squares, in sprawling megachurches and old country chapels. In these diverse contexts the style of worship varies greatly. Some congregations hear formal sermons read from carefully honed manuscripts; others hear extemporaneous outpourings of emotional fervor. Some sing music accompanied by rock bands, some by pipe organs, some by drum ensembles, some by rusty old pianos, and some by no accompaniment at all. Some dress in their formal Sunday best, others in casual beach clothes.

Yet for all the diversity of cultural expressions and worship styles, there remain several constant norms for Christian worship that transcend cultures and keep us faithful to the gospel of Christ. Especially in an age that constantly focuses on worship style, it is crucial for all leaders to rehearse these transcultural, common criteria for Christian worship and to actively seek to practice them faithfully. Without attention to these basic norms, the best texts, best music, and best forms for worship can easily become distorted and detract from the gospel of Christ that is the basis for Christian life and hope. Though volumes can be written to probe these transcultural norms, even a brief list is helpful for setting the stage for everything that follows in this book.

1. **Christian worship should be *biblical*.** The Bible is the source of our knowledge of God and of the world's redemption in Christ. Worship should include prominent readings of Scripture. It should present and depict God's being, character, and actions in ways that are consistent with scriptural teaching. It should obey explicit biblical commands about worship practices, and it should heed scriptural warnings about false and improper worship. Worship should focus its primary attention where the Bible does: on the person and work of Jesus Christ as the Redeemer of all creation and the founder and harbinger of the kingdom of God through the work of the Holy Spirit.

2. **Christian worship should be *dialogic* and *relational*.** In worship, God speaks and God listens. By the power of the Holy Spirit, God challenges us, comforts us, and awakens us. And by the prompting of the Holy Spirit we listen and then respond with praise, confession, petition, testimony, and dedication. Scripture constantly depicts God as initiating and participating in ongoing relationships with people. A healthy life with God maintains a balance of attentive listening and honest speech. So does healthy worship. This is why our words matter in worship: they are used by God to speak to us, and they carry our praise and prayer to God.

3. **Christian worship should be *covenantal*.** In worship, God's gracious and new covenant with us in Christ is renewed, affirmed, and sealed. The relationship that God welcomes us into is not a contractual relationship of obligations but a promise-based or covenantal relationship of self-giving love. It is more like a marriage than a legal contract. Worship rehearses God's promises to us and allows for us to recommit ourselves to this covenantal relationship. One question to ask of any worship service is whether it has enabled us to speak to God as faithful and committed covenant partners.

4. **Christian worship should be *trinitarian*.** In worship we address the triune God—Father, Son, and Holy Spirit—one God in three persons, the God of holiness, love, beauty, and power. God is the one who graciously invites our worship and then hears our response. God is the one who perfects and mediates our praise and petitions. God is also the one who helps us comprehend what we hear and prompts us to respond. In worship, then, we are drawn into relationship with God (the Father) through God (the Son) and by God (the Holy Spirit). Worship is an arena in which the triune God is active in drawing us closer, using tangible, physical things like water, bread, and wine; melodies, rhythms, and harmonies; gestures, smiles, and handshakes to nurture and challenge us. In worship we focus our attention on this self-giving God. This God-centered focus also keeps us from the temptation to worship worship itself.

5. **Christian worship should be *communal*.** The gospel of Christ draws us into communal life with other people. Worship is one setting in which we see the church in action and we attempt to demonstrate and deepen the unity, holiness, and witness of the church. Worship is a first-person-plural activity. It is extremely significant in worship that otherwise remarkably different people nevertheless offer praise together, pray together, listen together, and make promises together.

6. **Christian worship should be *hospitable, caring, and welcoming*.** Christian worship must never be self-centered. In worship we pray for the world and offer hospitality to all who live in fear, despair, and loneliness. Public worship sends us out for worshipful lives of service and witness. Worship not only comforts us with the promises of the gospel but also disturbs us (in the best sense) as we realize the significance of fear and brokenness in our world and the world's desperate need for a Savior. Worship stokes the gratitude of our hearts that leads naturally to serving the needs of our broken world.

7. **Christian worship should be *"in but not of" the world*.** Christian worship always reflects the culture out of which it is offered. Patterns of speech, styles of dress, senses of time, rhythms and harmonies of music, and styles of visual symbols vary widely depending on cultural contexts. At the same time, worship must not be enslaved to culture. It must remain prophetic, challenging any dimension of local culture that is at odds with the gospel of Christ.

8. **Christian worship should be *a generous and excellent outpouring of ourselves before God*.** Worship should not be stingy. Like the perfume that anointed Jesus' feet, our worship should be a lavish outpouring of our love and praise to the God who has created and redeemed us. Worship calls for our best offerings. When we practice music, prepare words to speak, set aside gifts of money and time to offer, and ensure that we are rested and ready to give our undivided attention, we are practicing the kind of excellence worthy of our great and gracious God.

9. **Christian worship should be *both expressive and formative*.** It should honestly express what a community already feels and has experienced—imitating the biblical psalms in their vividly honest expressions of praise and lament, thanksgiving and penitence. Yet worship should also stretch us to take to our lips words that we would not come up with on our own that—like the Lord's prayer—will shape new and deeper dimensions of faith and life with God. In this way, words become a tool of Spirit-led discipleship, forming us to be more faithful followers of and witnesses to Jesus Christ.

These norms, which are more illustrative than exhaustive, point to enduring lessons of Christian wisdom drawn from two thousand years of practice and reflection. And because they are so important, these basic norms must not simply reside in introductions to books of resources. They must function habitually in the working imaginations of worship leaders each week. Each week people who are responsible for worship have the joyful task of imagining how worship can be truly biblical, dialogic, covenantal, trinitarian, hospitable, and excellent.

Also important is that these norms come together. Christians need worship that is simultaneously trinitarian and hospitable, covenantal and "in but not of the world." All too often we make choices that, for example, either deepen our theological vision at the expense of hospitality or weaken our theological vision in the name of hospitality.

The resources in this book are available to help congregations embody these norms more fully. The norms become working criteria that help us discern which practices will enhance rather than detract from worship in local contexts. The questions to ask about every resource in this book come right from these norms: Will a given resource make worship in our congregation more biblical? More relational? More trinitarian? More hospitable? More God glorifying? More edifying?

## The Task of Preparing for and Leading Worship

Perhaps you are a member of a worship committee or a worship planning team. Perhaps your church is without a pastor, and you are the one designated to prepare for Sunday worship. Perhaps you are a pastor or seminary student, looking to improve your skills in the area of worship. Perhaps you are a college student, planning worship for a campus ministry center. Maybe you are getting ready to plan a service for the first time. Maybe you are a veteran with many years of experience. Whatever your situation, this book is intended to help you in the important ministry of planning worship.

There is a lot that this book can't do. For one thing, it can't provide the most important qualifications for the role of worship planner: a love of God, a Spirit-prompted desire to worship, a working knowledge of the Bible and Christian theology, and a love for your congregation or community. For another, it can't explain every facet of the planning process for every kind of church—there are simply too many kinds of churches for that. What it does do is provide a range of texts for your use or adaptation, provide basic teaching about key elements and themes in worship, and suggest new ways of approaching particular aspects of worship. For that to be useful, it is important to be clear about the role of worship leaders and planners.

*Worship Planners as Priests and Prophets*

As worship planners, we have the important and terrifying task of placing words of prayer, as well as other words, on people's lips. This happens every time we choose a song or write a prayer. As worship planners, we are like priests as we shape the prayers of God's people. Just as Old Testament priests would represent the people to God, so we help shape the prayers that God's people offer today.

We also have the holy task of being stewards of God's Word. Our choices of which Scripture readings and themes will be featured in worship represent a degree of control over people's spiritual diets, how they feed on the bread of life, the Word of God. As worship planners, we are like prophets as we select which texts and themes from God's Word will be central in public worship. Just as Old Testament prophets declared God's Word, so we also shape how God's written Word is heard in congregations today.

Worship planners are thus called to a task that is part priestly and part prophetic. These roles are formative roles in Christian congregations. They shape people's view of God and the kinds of responses that are appropriate to God. While theologians write the books that shape the theology of the educated Christian, worship leaders plan the services that shape the theology of all God's people.

For these reasons, planning worship is an awesome responsibility. It demands our best attention and efforts. Some make the mistake of thinking that a worship service can be planned in a short phone conversation. Perhaps it can. And it might even be a good service in some sense or in a certain context. The problem is that this approach doesn't do justice to the importance of worship. The question to ask is not "How quickly can we put together this service" but "How can this service faithfully and imaginatively bring this scriptural text alive?" "How can this service invite faithful and meaningful participation of everyone present?" "How can we faithfully and imaginatively serve as prophets and priests for our particular community at worship?"

*The Worship Planner's List of Virtues*

What makes for a good worship planner? What do you need to be an effective priest and prophet in this way? Do you need a willingness to do the job? A large library of resources? A good sense of organization? As important as these qualifications are, they don't go deep enough—at least not for prophets and priests.

Consider the following list of virtues:

- *compassion* for the congregation's needs and concern about how those needs are addressed in worship
- *discernment* about who is gifted to lead worship and in what way

- *cooperativeness* for working on a team of people involved in planning and leading worship
- *knowledge* of God's Word and of which portions of it are especially important for a congregation to hear at a given time, as well as knowledge of the community and its particular pastoral needs
- *wisdom* to understand the psychological and theological issues involved when there is conflict about worship
- *patience* when the congregation is slow to participate fully in certain acts of worship
- *imagination* to generate ideas about which songs, scripts, prayers, and elements will engage a congregation with the power and meaning of a given scriptural theme
- *discipline* to avoid too much or too little innovation. Planning worship is far different from putting on an art fair or writing poetry. When we plan worship, we are planning something for a community's use. No community can sustain endless innovation. No community can truly pray with words that are entirely unfamiliar or are creative for their own sake. Nor can a community thrive if its worship never changes in response to its environment.

These are the kinds of traits that go beyond the mechanics of worship planning to worship's deeper purpose and meaning. Perhaps this list makes you feel inadequate, but remember that none of us has all these virtues naturally. And no one can live up to all these virtues all of the time. But the good news of New Testament living is that these traits are not only ideals that we strive for; they are also gifts that the Holy Spirit gives to a community of believers for building up the church. The first step in worship planning is to pray that the Spirit will nurture these kinds of virtues in you. And for whichever virtues you lack, look to others in your congregation who may share them. Worship planning is deeply enriched through collaboration in preparing for, leading, and reflecting back on worship.

Good resources also play a small but important role. While effective priestly prayer-leadership can arise only out of a life of prayer, even the most effective prayer life cannot prepare us to lead a whole congregation in prayer. We need to learn from others, from worship in other places and times, and—mostly—from Scripture.

This is why we have hymnals and songbooks—collections of sung prayers that help us efficiently draw on the resources of thoughtful Christian worshipers from diverse times and places. Each congregation then adapts hymns and songs for its own use. The choices we make about instrumentation, tempo, volume, and use in worship may make a song or hymn sound very different than it did for the composer or writer.

This is also why we have books of resources for the words we use in worship. Books like this one help us draw on the insights and wisdom of worshipers from diverse times and places. They challenge us to offer our praise and prayer with a wider perspective than any of us can bring individually. And as we do with music, we adapt these words for our own use. We personalize the language by referring to particular needs and concerns in our congregation. We also bring our own tone of voice and emphasis to the words we use.

The resources of this book, then, are provided to help worship planners and leaders of all kinds to fulfill their priestly and prophetic task more faithfully. They are not a substitute for the virtues needed for this important work. And, like sheet music, they remain simply ink on paper until they are brought to life in worship.

When leading prayers in worship, so much depends on the expectations of leaders in the given cultural context. In some cultures, leaders are expected to lead with great feeling. In others, leaders are urged to avoid extreme emotions in order to prevent the impression of coercing a particular affective response. In some contexts, leaders are expected to read prayers that have been thoughtfully scripted ahead of time. In others, leaders are expected to adapt prayers extemporaneously. This book is designed for use in all of these contexts. The challenge for leaders is to sense the expectations of a given community and to lead in a way that does not call attention to itself but invites the congregation into deeper engagement and participation.

**Words in Worship**

Worship is much more than words, of course. And often worship features too many words. We may long for worship that breathes with silence and meditation or for instrumental music that transcends words. Still, worship depends on words. God's revelation to us is given not only in creation but also in words that communicate all we need to know about God, ourselves, and our salvation. Our communal worship is made possible because we have words to speak to each other, to call each other to worship, to speak common prayers, and to encourage each other in the faith.

Yet the words of our worship often don't get the attention that our music does. We often devote hundreds of rehearsal hours to music each year, but very few to selecting how we will speak to each other in worship. Language, like music, is an art to be received and cultivated as a gift from God. Liturgical cliché is not a virtue. As art, language can be immeasurably enhanced by creativity, imagination, and forethought—all of which need not preclude the energy and immediacy of extemporaneous prayer.

Perhaps the largest challenge for the language of worship is that one set of words—usually spoken or prepared by a single person—needs to somehow embrace, express, and elicit the worship of a whole group of people. From the perspective of a worshiper, *public* worship always involves using words that come from someone else. One skill for worshipers to hone is the skill of "learning to mean the words that someone else gives us," whether those are the words of a songwriter or prayer leader. This skill requires a unique mix of humility (submitting ourselves to words given to us by the community of faith), grace (willingness to offer the benefit of the doubt when those words may not have been well chosen), and intention (to actually appropriate those words as our own).

Certainly the ideal is a worship service in which each worshiper in the community is unself-consciously engaged with heart, mind, soul, and will and really means every good word that is spoken or sung. Yet not everyone who sings songs of praise has heart, mind, and will engaged every moment. Not all who speak the Lord's Prayer, for example, are "meaning it" at the moment. And although worshipers' later reports or body language can give us some clues about whether they are meaning it, we never know this with certainty. Some who appear less engaged may actually be deeply engaged. Others who are vigorously participating may be more caught up with the music or beauty of the language than the act of worship itself. The goal for language in worship, as it is for music, is to do everything possible to elicit and express the community's worship in ways that don't unnecessarily get in the way. This is a goal that is never perfectly attainable. But it is also a practice that can be deepened over time. That deepening happens in part through a use of good models. It also is encouraged by reflecting on the goals and criteria of our language. Consider the following three basic goals and criteria for language in worship.

1. **We need words that are faithful to the content of Scripture and the gospel of Christ.** Part of this goal involves speaking in ways that reflect a balanced diet of biblical themes. We need to speak of God as both a mighty sovereign and a tender encourager. We need to speak of Jesus Christ as both Savior and Lord. We need to reflect a balanced piety that stresses that salvation in Christ is intensely personal but that it also extends to creation and culture. We need to speak of the church, the community of believers, as a community called to embrace truth and to extend hospitality, to witness to the gospel of Christ and to work for justice and peace on earth.

   Language about God has been especially contentious in our time. This volume reflects a commitment to focus in on and to draw more intentionally on the wide range of names, metaphors, and images used explicitly in Scripture to shape our language about God. This approach will not satisfy everyone, but we pray that this book will provide a helpful point of departure, especially for congregations having conflicts over language issues.

2. **We need words that members of the congregation can appropriate as their own.** The language of worship should be both accessible and reverent, both understandable and evocative. The language of worship should enable the participation of all members of the body, young and old, brand-new Christians and lifelong believers alike.

   Most churches need to work to enable people to experience worship actively. They also need to work to expand worshipers' participation in corporate prayer. Participation on a deeper level takes time. For example, one congregation intentionally wanted to kneel for prayers of confession and lift their hands during songs of praise. Another wanted to add a response to the Scripture reading ("The Word of the Lord. Thanks be to God.") to allow worshipers to actively respond to the Scripture reading. These patterns of participation cannot be mastered in one service. They must become habits—in the best sense. To accomplish this, every (or nearly every) service must include the same actions.

3. **We need words that both express our experience and form us for a deeper experience.** A healthy prayer life, both private and public, involves two kinds of prayers. First, some prayers are specific, extemporaneous, personal, and immediate. These prayers arise from the honesty of our own experience—for example, "Lord God, help our congregation in this time of great uncertainty and even fear. . . ." Second, some prayers are communal or "given," even "imposed" on us. Think of children learning the Lord's Prayer. They may learn this prayer before they even understand the words, but they grow into it over time, learning to pray it more and more sincerely throughout their entire lives. Think also of an evangelist's invitation: "Pray this prayer with me." Or the practice of praying the Psalms. In all these examples, we can be grateful that our prayer life is not limited to what we can generate from our own thoughts, experiences, and emotions but that we are invited to grow into something bigger than ourselves.

One final note about the words we use in worship and the words contained in this book: words in a book are no more useful than musical notes on a page. Their effectiveness depends on how the words are brought to life through speech. The same prayer, read from a manuscript, book, or bulletin, can be either lifeless or life giving. It all depends on how the words are actually spoken.

This is especially true with respect to words appropriate for children. Children are able to participate in worship much more fully than many churches encourage or allow. For that to happen, the language of worship should be appropriately accessible. This does not mean that words spoken to children should be spoken in a condescending or cutesy way. Even if the words are just right, the tone of voice can make them demeaning. Often church leaders speak to children in far more childish ways than their teachers at school do. What children need is not childish talk but childlike talk—talk that is simple without being simplistic. That's why the designation of some resources in this book as "especially appropriate for children," is by itself insufficient—the words also need to be spoken warmly and with due respect.

### The Order of Worship: Learning from the Wisdom of Christian Practice

Scripture does not mandate a specific order of worship. And having a certain order of worship does not ensure that worship will be authentic, biblical, honest, and alive.

That said, a thoughtful pattern or order of worship is one of the most important things a congregation can have to ensure that the norms of worship (as noted above) are faithfully practiced. A well-thought-out order of worship ensures a balanced diet of worship actions. A regular order of worship protects the congregation from overly zealous or overly creative worship leaders who might impose too much of their own agendas on a worship service. A predictable order of worship gives the congregation something to hang on to, something to expect—especially those people, including children, for whom consistency is an important prerequisite for participation.

Most important, a well-conceived order of worship ensures that the main purposes of worship are carried out. In other words, a thoughtful pattern for worship keeps worship as worship. It protects worship from degenerating into a performance, into entertainment, or into an educational lecture.

For some, an order of worship might feel like a straitjacket, limiting creativity. But consider jazz music. Jazz features spontaneous improvisation. But jazz improvisation works only because the musicians in a jazz combo are following a regular, predictable, repeated chord structure. Without this structure, the music would be chaos. Meaningful spontaneity happens within structure.

Also consider that almost every congregation falls into a predictable order of worship, whether that order is written out or not. Some congregations that protest against written orders of worship and regular structures are, in fact, the most predictable. Even if the order of worship is not printed out, it is best for worship planners and leaders to be aware of their congregation's pattern and why it works the way it does.

It is also important not to confuse structure and style. Congregations in Lagos, Nigeria, and in suburban Kansas City may have different styles of leadership and music because of their cultural differences, but they can have the same structure of worship that arises out of theological reflection.

All of these observations point to the importance of a thoughtful pattern or structure in worship. The following chart outlines a historic pattern of Christian worship. Virtually any element on this chart may be sung as well as spoken. Most often, additional sung responses are added to this list, such as one or more songs of praise after the call to worship, or a doxology after the offering. There may be no single church that uses the exact wording found in this chart, but thousands of churches on many continents use a version of this pattern.

Notice that there's a basic logic or flow to this order. God's words are first, inviting us to worship, and we respond with worship and adoration. God's Word calls us to repent, and we respond by confessing sin and turning toward God for redemption. God's word of assurance leads naturally to thanksgiving. And so on.

Also notice how this pattern reflects the dialogic nature of worship—the sense in which worship is a conversation between God and the gathered community. (Arrows indicate directions in which the conversation flows: from God to the people, from the people to God, and among the people.)

| Gathering | Call to Worship ↓<br>Greeting ↓<br>Prayer of Adoration or Prayer of Invocation ↑<br>Call to Confession ↓<br>Prayer of Confession and Lament ↑ ↔<br>Assurance of Pardon ↓<br>Passing of the Peace ↓ ↔<br>Thanksgiving ↑<br>The Law ↓<br>Dedication ↑ ↔ |
|---|---|
| Proclamation | Prayer for Illumination ↑<br>Scripture Reading ↓<br>Sermon ↓ |
| Response to the Word | Profession of the Church's Faith ↔ ↑<br>Prayers of the People ↑<br>Offering ↑ |
| The Lord's Supper | Declaration of God's Promises and Invitation ↓<br>Prayer of Thanksgiving ↑<br>Breaking of the Bread ↓<br>Communion ↓ ↔<br>Response of Thanksgiving ↑ |
| Sending | Call to Service or Discipleship ↓<br>Blessing/Benediction ↓ |

In sum, there is a theological rationale or logic to this organization of a worship service. Throughout this book, the explanations for each act of worship highlight its meaning and significance.

All of this is better than a "list approach" to an order of service, in which all the actions of worship (praise, intercession, creeds, testimony) are simply listed without regard for how one flows into another. In services like these, the individual actions of worship may be meaningful in themselves. But the same actions would have much more meaning if their context would support them. For example, imagine that a choir is going to sing an arrangement of "Amazing Grace." That music may be meaningful by itself, wherever it is sung. But now picture the hymn being sung at the end of a prayer of confession, following a time of silence. The same music becomes much more powerful and effective because of its context and placement in the flow of the worship service.

This historic order of worship does not, in itself, dictate which style of leadership, music, art, or drama is used to bring the order or structure to life. This same order, with minor variations, is used in thatched huts in Haiti and in large European cathedrals. It is universal enough to be considered classic, the kind of resource from which every pastor and worship leader can learn a great deal.

### The Holy Spirit and the Task of Preparing and Leading Worship

Even with this perspective on the order of worship, books of texts and prayers like this one worry many Christian worshipers and leaders. Prayer books can be—and have been—used by Christians in ways that discourage extemporaneous prayers. They also can be used in ritualistic ways. Texts in books like these may sound false, as if a leader were simply "reading it out of a book" without meaning a word of it. These worries lead some Christians to conclude that "a read prayer is a dead prayer."

All of these concerns are legitimate, for they represent distortions of worship that we should work against. And such concerns are especially pressing in some congregations, whose worship-by-the-book has been lackluster for one reason or another.

But these concerns are not the whole story. Equally problematic are contexts in which a congregation is subject to the imbalanced agendas of a small group of leaders. Equally noticeable are extemporaneous prayers that promise to be unique and pastorally responsive but turn out to be nearly identical week after week, often featuring less diversity in imagery and in pastoral concern than prayer-book prayers. Further, worries about printed prayers can often lead to non-use of appropriate biblical prayers, such as the Psalms, which are certainly among our richest resources for worship to this day.

Both the use of worship resources and the refusal to use them, then, can lead to temptations, problems, and challenges—each of which is mitigated when leaders actively embrace the norms and practice the virtues described above. Perhaps most worrisome, however, is the charge that books like this one squelch the work of the Holy Spirit. Many worry that too many written and published resources leave no room for the Spirit to work in worship. If everything is scripted, where then can the Spirit work?

Note first that using this book does not necessarily mean that worship will be more scripted. Throughout this book, leaders are encouraged to adapt resources for local use or to offer extemporaneous expressions that are in some way derived from the texts here. Several such resources are more like outlines of extemporaneous prayer than complete scripts.

More fundamentally, however, that view of the Spirit's work needs to be challenged and corrected. Christians confess that the Holy Spirit worked through the authors of Scripture to produce both the highly refined poetry of the Psalms as well as the spontaneous sermons of Peter and Paul. While the Holy Spirit led early Christians to speak in tongues, the Spirit of God also brought order out of chaos at creation. If the Spirit works through both order and spontaneity, why do we sometimes limit our language of the Spirit to refer only to the spontaneous? (For example, we might casually say, "Well, we didn't have time to plan worship this week; I guess we will have to have the Spirit lead today," or, "Let's get away from our planned service so that the Spirit can lead.")

As *Authentic Worship in a Changing Culture* (CRC Publications, 1997) makes clear, "We shouldn't link the Holy Spirit with less planning or less formality. The Holy Spirit can be powerfully present in a very highly structured service and can be absent in a service with little structure. Beyond questions of style and formality, the question always before us is this: Does this act of worship bring praise to God through Jesus Christ in the Holy Spirit?" (p. 90). Indeed, the Spirit may well work through the careful preparations of a preacher *as well as* through a gesture or sentence that the preacher hadn't planned on saying. The Spirit may work both through the diligent planning of a worship committee *and* through the spontaneous prayer request or testimony of a worshiper.

How do we know, then, if the Spirit has been active in worship? Ecstasy or solemnity, in itself, doesn't tell us. Neither does spontaneity or carefully scripted planning. The Spirit can use each.

One indicator may be our response to a service. Consider the difference between the following post-service comments: "My, what impressive music today!" versus "Thank you, musician, for helping me pray more deeply today." And "Wasn't that a brilliant sermon?" versus "In this service I encountered the risen Lord." One of the Spirit's main character traits is that of always pointing toward Christ. The Spirit is a witness and an advocate for the person of Jesus. If we leave a worship service comforted and challenged by our faith-filled encounter with Jesus Christ, we can be grateful for the Spirit's work in our hearts.

Clement of Rome wrote some of the first post-New Testament documents we have on Christian faith and living. His writings include this prayer: "O God Almighty, Father of our Lord Jesus Christ: Grant that we may be grounded and settled in your truth by the coming down of the Holy Spirit into our hearts. Reveal to us what we do not yet know. Fill up in us what is wanting. Confirm what we know. And keep us blameless in your service, through Jesus Christ, our Lord. Amen." May God give us grace to pray and to mean words like these as we prepare for worship.

# II. *THE WORSHIP SOURCEBOOK:* A CONTEMPORARY EXPERIMENT BASED ON CLASSICAL MODELS

## Historical Context

This book stands in a long tradition of worship books in the Christian church. The biblical Psalms may well have functioned as a prayer book for the people of Israel. Some of the earliest Christians compiled their advice about forms and patterns of worship into church order documents, the first of which, the *Didache,* dates back perhaps into the first century A.D. Over time, especially in the early medieval period, these documents grew very complex, with detailed instructions about every aspect of worship.

In the Reformation period both Martin Luther and John Calvin called for significant changes to recommended or dictated patterns of worship by simplifying the structure and testing every text by theological criteria. Out of the various Reformation traditions, the Anglican and Lutheran traditions retained the most detailed instructions. The Anglican tradition preserved common patterns and texts for worship in the famous *Book of Common Prayer,* while the Lutherans did so in several editions of service books, adapted for use in each town. The Reformed tradition was also a service book tradition, albeit with far simpler liturgy. In addition to the influence of Huldrych Zwingli's liturgy, Calvin's

Genevan liturgies were adapted for use in Scotland and Hungary, while new liturgies that were developed near Heidelberg, Germany, became influential in the Netherlands. Throughout the early decades of the Reformation, pastors did not create new orders of service for worship each week, as so many do today. Worship was, to the surprise of many contemporary readers, "by the book."

Despite this tradition, most evangelical and even many Reformed and Presbyterian congregations in North America have resisted the use of formal service books and set liturgies. This resistance resulted partly from the influence of Puritan critiques of "by the book" worship, which were much more stringent than critiques offered by Reformers. Other influences included the formation of early Methodist, Baptist, Anabaptist, and other "free church" congregations as well as the spread of North American populism, pragmatism, and revivalism. Congregations in many streams of North American Christianity have long resisted being told how to structure worship and have cherished their ability to respond to their own preferences and sense of what is most effective.

As a result, thousands of North American congregations today owe a great deal both to a two-thousand-year history of service books and to the legacy of North American freedom and populism. In recent years amid remarkable changes in the practice of worship, hundreds of those congregations are looking for new ways to appropriate both of these aspects of their identity. Some efforts go by the names "blended worship," "convergence worship," or even "ancient-future" worship. But despite vast and remarkable growth in contemporary music based on popular styles, many of the best-selling books on worship today are, ironically, studies of worship in the early church, prayer books for formal daily prayer, and books about recovery of the sacraments. Recent innovations under the umbrella of terms like "postmodern worship" and "alternative worship" sometimes feature even greater interest in traditional forms and texts than in the "contemporary worship" of the 1980s and 1990s—though in configurations that elude easy categorization.

**The Nature of This Book**
In light of this history, this book is something of a unique experiment. It is designed to be used by Christians who value free-church, low-church, nonliturgical, evangelical approaches to worship but who also want to learn from and draw on historic patterns of worship. At the same time, the book aims to be useful and instructive to congregations who practice traditional or liturgical worship and who may be looking for ways to adapt it or to rethink its meaning.

The following six rubrics help to explain the nature of this book.

1. **Classical and contemporary.** On the one hand, this book is clearly inspired by classical models. It draws on many texts from historic sources; it features approaches to the various elements of worship that have time-tested value for enhancing participation; and it uses traditional language for the primary elements and main themes in worship. On the other hand, it affirms and enhances the strengths of worship in a more free-church context. It does not mandate one standard service. It provides multiple options so that local leaders are free to adapt and use texts that are pastorally appropriate. It includes examples of fresh new language from sources like the Iona Community in Scotland as well as words of welcome and invitation designed for seekers in contemporary North American culture.

2. **A worship leader's reference book.** This book is designed primarily for people who prepare and lead worship rather than for people in the pew. In this way it is different from the *Book of Common Prayer*, which is designed for all worshipers to follow during the worship service. Further, this book is designed as a reference book rather than as a service book to be used by a minister or leader during the service. In fact, given the number of options under each heading, it could be very difficult to use this book during the service. Most users will likely transfer and adapt the texts in this volume into their own manuscript, set of notes, printed bulletin, or projected resources—perhaps using the CD edition to download texts.

3. **A book for public worship.** This book is more of a liturgical book than a devotional book, though many may find helpful resources for devotional use. It is not designed, then, to look like a collection of "classic Christian prayers." As David Buttrick once observed, "liturgical language is for people to use, not admire." The goal here has been to find texts that are imaginative and evocative without calling much attention to themselves; to use words that are accessible on first hearing; and to find language that is both "fresh" and "contemporary" as well as "classic" and "elegant." Our goal has been to produce a single book that can be used, with appropriate adaptation, to guide the preparations of worship in a wide diversity of congregations. The question to pose about this book is not necessarily "Is this book perfect for us?" but rather "Will this book help to challenge and deepen our worship over time?"

4. **Classic and enduring.** One danger of our time is the production of a vast number of resources, including songs, service outlines, and prayers prepared for temporary or even one-time use. While these certainly can be very helpful, our worship life also needs to be sustained by practices that will last a lifetime. In this context, this book is designed to be more like a "classic"

resource than a merely occasional one. Psalm 95, for example, can function as a beautiful and appropriate call to worship in every culture and in all times. Similarly, we can readily identify a number of scriptural texts that can be inspiring and challenging calls to prayer or assurances of pardon in any age. By compiling a relatively comprehensive set of scriptural resources, we are attempting to provide a useful resource for a generation of leaders.

5. **Multiple options for pastoral application.** The book presents multiple options for each act of worship—sometimes a rather daunting list of options. These are provided so that the book can function in a wide variety of ministry contexts. Nonetheless, it may be very wise for congregations to limit the range of options they use. By presenting multiple options in each section, we do not mean to imply that every option is equally strong—and certainly not for every congregation. In fact, in studying the options of a given section, you may find some texts weaker than others for your particular context. We encourage you to use only the best resources for your congregation.

   Further, there can be significant value in repeating particular prayers or words over time. For example, many congregations regularly use the Apostles' or Nicene Creeds as a response to the sermon or the Lord's Prayer at the end of a congregational prayer. Valuable practices like these can help to make key texts a part of our identity. The repetition is especially important for children! And repetition inevitably entails limitations to the range of options a given congregation will use. So while we present several options for use as statements of faith, for example, it may be wisest to use just a few of them, such as the Apostles' and Nicene Creeds, most of the time.

6. **Ecumenical and evangelical, as well as Reformed and Presbyterian.** This book is designed for use by all biblical, evangelical Christians. Because the volume includes so much Scripture and so many classical resources that transcend time or place, it can be used in many varieties of congregations. Most of the elements of a worship service (Part One) and the themes of the creed and church year (Part Two) are held in common by Christian congregations of various traditions. When Scripture and scriptural themes are at the center of worship, there is much more that unites us than divides us. For this reason, there are remarkable similarities between this book and a variety of other published books of resources, including the *Book of Common Prayer* (Episcopal), the *Methodist Book of Worship* (United Methodist), *Chalice Worship* (Disciples of Christ), and various books used by other evangelical or independent congregations or pastors (such as *Baker's Worship Handbook*).

Still, each Christian tradition speaks with a particular accent. This volume has been prepared by believers from an evangelical and Reformed/Presbyterian branch of Christianity in North America. The Reformed/Presbyterian accent will be very clear at several points. The volume includes texts from confessional documents such as the Heidelberg Catechism, the Belgic Confession, and the Westminster Confession of Faith and Shorter Catechism, as well as more recent documents such as *Our World Belongs to God* (Christian Reformed Church in North America), *Our Song of Hope* (Reformed Church in America), and *A Brief Statement of Faith* (Presbyterian Church, USA). Often these documents are written to highlight distinctives of Reformed/Presbyterian themes. In contrast to many evangelical Christian traditions, confessional accents are strong in the sections on baptism and the Lord's Supper. This book unapologetically presents texts for use for both infant and adult baptism, for example, and assumes the "real, spiritual presence" of Jesus Christ in the sharing of the bread and cup of the Lord's Supper. In contrast to Lutheran tendencies, the volume presents a strong place for the law of God to be read in worship as a natural and fitting response to the gospel, either after the assurance of pardon as a "guide to gratitude" or near the end of worship as an "invitation to discipleship."

This book is also very intentional about being ecumenical *within* the Reformed and Presbyterian traditions. Denominationally approved resources ironically are often developed with little regard for the breadth of practice within the particular denomination's tradition. In contrast, this book intentionally embraces at least part of the spectrum of Reformed and Presbyterian practice. It was prepared primarily by members of the Christian Reformed Church in North America. It includes several synodically approved liturgical texts for use in the Christian Reformed Church and follows guidelines established by the Christian Reformed Church synod for the development of sacramental forms. The volume also draws on approved texts used by the Reformed Church in America and the Presbyterian Church (USA) and especially the Presbyterian *Book of Common Worship*. The volume includes several portions of the Westminster Confession of Faith (Modern English Study Version), perhaps most commonly used today by the Presbyterian Church in America, the Evangelical Presbyterian Church, the Orthodox Presbyterian Church, and the Associate Reformed Presbyterian Church. In addition, large parts of this volume can function as a natural supplement to churches whose worship is regulated by one of the Presbyterian Directories of Worship.

Given the increasing diversity of worship practices and theological traditions within Presbyterian and Reformed denominations, no single volume can pretend to be equally serviceable and appropriate for all. Some congregations may be able to draw exclusively on this volume and use almost any text here.

Others will no doubt use other resources and use only a portion of what is presented here. Whatever the case, we hope that this volume will be at least a reference source for a broad range of congregations and that its effect will be to promote the sharing of texts and resources from various traditions.

### Distinctive Features of This Book

**Scriptural Texts.** For nearly every element of worship this sourcebook features numerous scriptural texts, many more than in comparable volumes. With this feature we hope to encourage the use of more scriptural language in worship. Scriptural texts are from a variety of Bible versions and are referenced as exact quotations, as slight adaptations (noted as "from" a particular text and version), or as paraphrases or quotations coupled with additional phrasing (noted as "based on" a given text). Some other resources also include references to Scripture texts; an index of Scripture references (p. 833) provides complete information as an aid to worship planning.

**Confessional Statements.** This book also includes many confessional statements as liturgical texts. Though originally written to teach doctrine, some catechisms and confessional statements function well as liturgical texts. Often they contain a simple and accessible beauty that is especially appropriate for worship. One goal for worship is to have it work together with a church's educational ministries so that the language of catechetical and confessional teaching becomes familiar in congregational confession and prayer. This does not mean the language of worship should be unnecessarily didactic. In worship, doctrinal texts function not first of all to teach but rather to express the congregation's faith and prayer.

**Congregational Participation.** Many notes and rubrics in this book encourage congregational participation—not only in celebrations of the sacraments or during special seasons such as Advent but also at many points in worship throughout the entire year, as noted by boldfaced type for worshipers to read aloud, usually responsively. This does not imply that every text with boldfaced type can only be used responsively. Leaders may alter boldfacing as they wish to suit the needs and style of their congregation's participation.

**Classic Texts.** This sourcebook also features a variety of classic texts—some that date back hundreds of years and have stood the test of time. Protestants have not often had easy access to remarkable, evangelical prayers from historical sources. Liturgical churches and students of liturgical history will notice that some of these prayers are presented outside of their traditional liturgical context (for example, several prayers are from traditional daily prayer services even though this book includes no section on daily prayer). Our goal has been to place prayers in the context of where they will most likely be useful in a variety of evangelical and Reformed/Presbyterian churches.

**Structure.** The outline of the traditional church year has been subsumed under the structure of the Apostles' and Nicene Creeds. Like the church year, creeds provide a narrative outline of Christ's life on this earth. But they also add important emphases on God's creation, the work of the Spirit, and the life of the church. As a result, these resources are equally useful for a variety of congregations whether they follow the church year or a catechism or another structure that includes the teachings of these creeds. Christ's ascension, for example, is an important biblical event and worship theme regardless of whether a church follows the pattern of the traditional church year.

**Prayers.** One premise of the book is that worship at its best often features a balance of extemporaneous and prepared prayers. In other words, just because this book contains prepared prayers and other texts does not imply that every worship service should feature only prewritten prayers. The goal is not to impose uniformity on worship but rather to provide reliable, trustworthy resources, drawing on the riches of the Christian tradition to help leaders be good stewards of the words they use in worship.

**Resources for Including Children.** Throughout this book many texts are identified as especially appropriate for use with children, though these designations are somewhat arbitrary (many more texts, especially scriptural ones, could be similarly identified). Worship at its best is intergenerational and invites children to be full, conscious, active participants, not just onlookers. The potential for children's participation varies greatly from congregation to congregation, depending on the nature and level of biblical literacy and education programs. Leaders may well need to adapt these texts so that the tone, rhetoric, and content are appropriate for their congregation.

**Resources for Hospitality.** Various texts in this book are designed to extend hospitality to spiritual seekers, guests, and others who do not worship regularly. This language is essentially new to the prayer-book tradition, reflecting the missional context of the church in North America. The presence of these texts emphasizes that hospitality should be a key goal for all worship services. While these resources are more suggestive than exhaustive, we include them in the hope of challenging worship leaders to think about how their words will be heard by people with limited exposure to worship practices.

Several of these features are new to collections of liturgical texts. But we trust that they will become a part of the church's ongoing learning process and growth as practices of worship continue to develop.

### Planning "Traditional" as Well as "Contemporary" Worship

This is a book designed for use by both so-called "traditional" and "contemporary" worship leaders and pastors. Any book of words like this will, by nature, *appear* to be most useful for "more traditional" churches that maintain a fairly detailed order of worship, print out the order of service in a bulletin each week, and use a number of spoken responses or litanies by the congregation. We very much hope that this book will be useful for these churches!

At first glance, this book may not seem a likely resource for leaders of "contemporary worship"—for churches whose worship is led by a worship team, without a detailed order of worship, without printed orders of service, and without congregational responses and litanies. But, in fact, it can be very useful!

First, the book provides texts that leaders, whether lay or ordained, can use or adapt at almost any point in a service. In all services, whether contemporary or traditional, leaders need to find words to call people to worship, to offer a prayer of confession, to prepare people for the reading of Scripture, or to introduce the offering. Often we fall into patterns of speech that are, at best, tired or, at worst, distort the meaning of an action of worship. Having a resource that provides multiple options gives us ways of both testing our own language and of deepening it through the use of additional Scripture texts or other resources.

Second, this volume provides suggestions for leaders who specialize in extemporaneous leadership. Some leaders may have every word printed out, others may lead from a prepared outline, and still others may speak entirely extemporaneously. But even if you lead worship extemporaneously, consider preparing to lead in prayer (or other aspects of worship) by writing your prayers out before leaving the script behind. Extemporaneous or spontaneous prayers often leave us to rely on all-too-familiar phrases and expressions. For example, we might pray, "Be with our missionaries. Be with our friends. Be with our families." Writing a prayer out or adapting another resource forces us to think about our language and to avoid language that becomes monotonous or even meaningless through overuse. Even if you leave your script behind and offer the prayer without notes, a journaling or adaptation exercise will challenge you to use fresh language and consider the balance and vitality of your language.

Third, this sourcebook does not dictate the medium to use in presenting particular resources. In some churches the texts from this book will be printed out in a pastor's or leader's manuscript. In others they will be printed in a bulletin or worship folder. In yet others they will be projected on a large screen for all to see or read. The method of presentation will vary widely from church to church.

Finally, this book provides a structure that can enrich both traditional and contemporary styles. An increasing number of churches that follow contemporary worship models are rethinking the form or structure of their services, trying to find ways to make the structure more balanced and meaningful. There are few better resources for accomplishing this task than the basic structure used by Christian churches for two thousand years. So even if a church doesn't prepare a printed order of service, there is great value in following the basic pattern presented here (gathering and praise, confession and assurance, proclamation of the Word and response, celebration of the sacraments, and concluding blessing), or—at minimum—making sure that each of these elements has a regular, sensible, and natural place in congregational worship.

In sum, this book is designed not to dictate a certain style of music, leadership, or use of multimedia. The goal has been to provide resources that can guide and instruct worship leaders in any style into the better use of God's gift of language.

# III. USING *THE WORSHIP SOURCEBOOK*

## Organization of Resources in This Book

This book offers resources to help worship planners and leaders serve as godly stewards of the gift of language. It includes recommended texts for all typical elements of a worship service, along with seasonal and topical resources for celebrations that many congregations observe each year. It also includes basic teaching pieces on each element of worship.

**Part One** provides resources for each element of weekly public worship, along with teaching notes about the meaning and purpose of each element. Each section is assigned a number for ease of reference and comparison between Parts One and Two of this book. Within each section, each resource is also numbered. In most sections, three numbers are sufficient for identifying each resource: the section number, the subsection number, and the resource number within the subsection.

> For example, resource 1.2.2, a call to worship, is found in section 1 (Opening of Worship), subsection 2 (Call to Worship), under resource number 2.

In sections 6 and 8 on the sacraments (baptism and Lord's Supper), an additional number is included to allow for referencing an additional layer of subheadings within each section.

> For example, resource 8.2.6.2, a prayer for the work of the Holy Spirit, is found in section 8 (Lord's Supper), subsection 2 (Prayer of Thanksgiving), subpart 6 (Prayer for the Work of the Spirit), under resource number 2.

**Part Two** provides resources for common themes taught in ecumenical creeds of the Christian church (such as the Apostles' and Nicene Creeds) and for seasonal celebrations in the traditional Christian year. Sections are labeled alphabetically, and each section includes subdivisions that correspond with the numbered sections of Part One.

> For example, resource E.1.2.2, a call to worship for Christmas, is found in E (Christmas), section 1 (Opening of Worship), subsection 2 (Call to Worship), under resource number 2.

### Getting the Most Out of This Book

Use these guidelines and refer back to them periodically as an aid to getting the most out of this book.

1. Learn the structure of the book. Part Two makes use of the numbering system introduced in Part One, and the headers on each page indicate where you are within the outline of the book.
2. Compare the structure of Part One to the order of worship in your own congregation. Which elements in Part One does your church already include each week? Think about the elements that are written down in a printed order of worship as well as elements that happen regularly even if they aren't formally noted. Consider marking those sections of the book for easy reference.
3. Review your own "worship template," whether it's explicit or implicit. Based on the contents of Part One, what could you do to enhance or deepen

your own congregation's pattern or order of worship? By comparing your practices with the resources in this volume, you may discover that your congregation has been weak in a given area. Think about ways to adapt your approach so that it can be more balanced. Think of ways to introduce changes with clear explanations of what you are doing and why.

4. Discuss your congregation's level of participation in worship with your pastor or other worship leaders. Think about a new habit—or two or three—that your congregation could acquire over time to make worship more participatory. As you introduce changes, be sure also to explain them to the congregation.

5. Review your own approach to leading worship. Should you be spending more time or effort in preparing to lead some aspects of worship? What kinds of notes or manuscript do you have with you as you lead? Would it help to have more (or perhaps fewer) notes?

6. Over time, review the teaching notes in Part One of this book. Consider taking ten minutes at each worship committee or worship planning meeting to study and discuss a set of teaching notes. Do they confirm or challenge your present practices? Would you want to expand the teaching? Could these notes help your congregation to develop more meaningful practices over time?

7. Note that all the prayers end with "Amen" in boldface. The purpose of the "Amen" (which means "this is sure to be") is to invite worshipers to add their voice of assent to the prayer, reinforcing the understanding that the prayer is offered by everyone. Sometimes worship leaders invite the congregation to voice the "Amen" by ending their prayer with the words "And all God's people say . . ." Others might encourage their congregation to spontaneously say "Amen" at the end of every prayer.

## Using the CD for Bulletins and Projection Systems

The CD provided with this book allows easy access to any texts you might wish to use in worship, for special programs, or for educational purposes. Open the *Worship Sourcebook* file on the CD (using Adobe Acrobat® Reader®) and use your computer's search function to locate sections by name or number. For example, to search for Calls to Worship, you can search for "1.2" and then choose from among the search results. If you are looking for texts for a particular season of the Christian year, you could, for example, find options for Advent by searching for "D.1.2," and then compare those selections with options from the Christmas (E.1.2) or Epiphany (F.1.2) sections. Once you select a resource, you can cut and paste for use in a printed bulletin or on a projection system.

For easy identification of Scripture and confessional texts in this book, we've included credit lines immediately following those particular texts.

We recommend that you include those credits when you cut and paste. You may also wish to identify the sources of other items; we did not place credits next to those items, preferring that they be presented without the distraction of numerous and sometimes lengthy credit lines. To identify sources, look up their respective resource numbers (for example, 3.4.8 or A.1.4.1) in the Acknowledgments section, which supplies all necessary source information for resources used in this book. In addition, if you are looking for a prayer from a particular author or collection, you can search and find the author's name or collection title in the Acknowledgments section.

Please note that many of the resources including boldface print (to indicate congregational participation) are presented here in a tight format to save space. When using these resources in bulletins and projection systems, consider adding spaces before and particularly after the boldface lines to make them stand out for use by the participating congregation.

For each resource used we ask that you include the following credit line: "Reprinted by permission from *The Worship Sourcebook,* © 2004, CRC Publications." This notice can appear in small print preferably on the same page on which the resource is reprinted.

To keep records, you'll want to record the resource number (for example, 3.4.8 for resource number 8 in section 3.4) on your worship planning documents and write the date used next to the text in this book.

As much as you are able, use this resource book to God's honor and glory!

John D. Witvliet, director,
Calvin Institute of Christian Worship

# PART ONE

# ELEMENTS OF THE WORSHIP SERVICE

PART ONE

# ELEMENTS OF THE
# WORSHIP SERVICE

The first part of this collection provides basic resources for worship accompanied by brief teaching notes on the meaning and function of each element in worship. The order of these elements will not be the same in every congregation's experience, but the order follows a basic pattern as discussed in the Prologue (p. 24). The nine sections of Part One of this volume are listed in the box on this page.

Part Two of this book is supplemental to Part One. Many texts in Part One can be used for particular themes or occasions treated in Part Two.

It's important to know that the numbering of elements in Part One lays the foundation for the numbering of corresponding elements

in Part Two. For example, within each lettered section (A, B, C . . .) of Part Two, the Call to Worship subsection is labeled A.1.2, B.1.2, and so on to show correspondence with the Call to Worship subsection (1.2) in Part One. Each lettered section in Part Two provides resources for many (though not all) elements of worship; resources for elements of worship that do not appear in Part Two can be found in Part One.

# SECTION 1
# OPENING OF WORSHIP

The opening of an event should set the tone for all that follows—this is just as true for a worship service as for any other event, such as a concert, lecture, workshop, conference, or rally. How an event begins should establish not only its explicit or implicit purpose but also its overall ethos or spirit.

First, the opening actions of a worship service should clearly establish worship's purpose. They should make clear that in worship a congregation is called to listen to God and to respond in faith and prayer. This suggests three kinds of actions—a clear statement of God's invitation to worship, an opportunity for the congregation to respond in praise, and some action that reinforces the public, communal nature of worship.

Second, the opening actions of worship—beginning already with prayers of preparation before worship begins—are important for establishing a prayerful, expectant, humble, and joyous spirit. They should communicate that worship

arises best not out of fear or guilt but out of gratitude. This spirit is conveyed not only in the words that are used but also in the spirit in which are they are spoken.

Though the same fundamental purpose and spirit of worship should characterize the opening of worship services, not every worship service will begin the same way. There will be many different accents—of joy or sorrow, exuberance or humility, for example—depending on the time of year and the pastoral context. That is why even more resources beyond those that follow here are included in Part Two of this book.

# 1.1 PREPARATION FOR WORSHIP

*Worship begins best out of a prayerful spirit. The following texts are for pastors, worship leaders, and others to use as they gather for prayer before the worship service. Often at such times leaders pray spontaneously, without the use of any printed or set prayers. Even so, the following texts may be helpful in suggesting an image, phrase, or petition that can enrich spontaneous prayer. (These texts may also be adapted for the congregation to use—perhaps at home prior to worship, or printed in a service folder, bulletin, or video presentation.) Another aid in preparing for worship is to focus on a song or text that will be featured in the worship service, taking the time to reflect deeply on its meaning and significance.*

1    Fill our worship with grace, Lord Jesus Christ,
      that every thought, word, and deed may be acceptable to you,
      our Rock and our Redeemer. **Amen.**
            —based on Psalm 19:14

2    O God,
      by your power may we, with all the saints,
      comprehend the breadth and length and height and depth
      of the love of Christ that surpasses knowledge,
      so that we may be filled with your fullness. **Amen.**
            —based on Ephesians 3:18-19

3    Almighty God, we pray for your blessing
      on the church in this place.
      Here may the faithful find salvation,
      and the careless be awakened.
      Here may the doubting find faith,
      and the anxious be encouraged.
      Here may the tempted find help,
      and the sorrowful find comfort.
      Here may the weary find rest,
      and the strong be renewed.
      Here may the aged find consolation
      and the young be inspired;
      through Jesus Christ, our Lord. **Amen.**

4    Almighty God,
      to whom all hearts are open,
      all desires known,
      and from whom no secrets are hid:
      Cleanse the thoughts of our hearts
      by the inspiration of your Holy Spirit,
      that we may perfectly love you

and worthily magnify your holy name
through Christ, our Lord. **Amen.**

5  O God, you pour out the Spirit of grace and love.
Deliver us from cold hearts and wandering thoughts,
that with steady minds and burning zeal
we may worship you in spirit and truth. **Amen.**

6  Blessed are you, Lord God, King of the universe.
In your wisdom you have made all creation to worship you.
You call us to worship you now in this time and place,
in unity with prophets, martyrs, and saints from all times and places.

As we prepare for worship, we pray that you will quiet our hearts,
that we may hear your voice in your Word.
We pray that you will stir our hearts,
that we may more faithfully follow Jesus,
and that you will be glorified by the praise and prayers we offer you.

Bless those who lead us in worship with your Spirit.
May our worship today help us to offer our entire lives to you
and unite us with your whole church throughout the world.
We pray this in the name of Jesus Christ,
who with the Father and the Spirit is one God,
blessed forever. **Amen.**

7  This is the day that you have made, Lord.
**Help us to rejoice in it and be glad!**
Remind us of the privileges we enjoy as your people:
**to come to you in these moments,**
**to confess our sins,**
**to receive forgiveness and give it,**
**to pray and sing and listen,**
**to renew our fainting spirits,**
**to rest in all your promises.**
Open our eyes to see you, Lord.
**Open our ears to hear your Word.**
Visit us through your Holy Spirit,
**and help us to celebrate our faith. Amen.**

8  *A text especially mindful of children*

Dear God,
we come to worship you today.
We come to sing, pray, and listen.
You always hear us.
Help us to hear you. **Amen.**

9     Dear God, silence all voices within our minds but your own.
Help us to seek and be able to follow your will.
May our prayers be joined
with those of our sisters and brothers in the faith,
that together we may glorify your name
and enjoy your fellowship forever.
In Jesus' name, **Amen.**

10     Holy God, we pray your blessing
on those who lead us in worship this day,
those who speak and sing and move among us,
those who direct others in singing and playing,
those who have prepared this space with beauty.
We ask that each of them may lead
with a sense of peace and confidence that comes from your Spirit,
so that your truth may be proclaimed faithfully
and we may live up to our calling as the body of Christ.
Through Jesus Christ, our Lord. **Amen.**

11     Loving God, for each one who leads us in worship today,
we pray that they may be so filled with your Spirit
that they will clearly reflect the glory of Christ in all they say and do.
We pray that everyone in this place will know you are with us
and be drawn to bring you all honor and praise. **Amen.**

# 1.2 CALL TO WORSHIP

*The following texts are invitations to worship. Most use scriptural language in which God invites us to offer our worship or in which a leader invites all who are present to offer their praise.*

*One function of the invitation is to express welcome and hospitality. We worship in the joyful context of our renewed relationship with God in Christ. These words may be spoken with a gesture of open embrace and a genuine smile to convey the warmth of God's love.*

*Another function of the invitation is to call the community to the unique activity of worship. The primary activity of the worship service is for worshipers to participate in the gift exchange of worship itself, by hearing God's Word, by offering prayers and praise, and by receiving spiritual nourishment offered at the Lord's table. The call to worship establishes the unique purpose of the worship service and reinforces the "vertical dimension" of worship—an encounter between God and the gathered congregation.*

*The scriptural calls to worship may be preceded by introductory words like these, derived from Jesus' letters to the churches in Revelation 2-3:*

Hear the Word of the Lord.

*or*

Hear what the Spirit is saying to the church.

*After any of the brief scriptural statements in this section, consider adding the following:*

Praise the Lord.
**The Lord's name be praised!**

*or*

O magnify the LORD with me.
**Let us exalt God's name together!**
—from Psalm 34:3, NRSV

*or*

We have gathered to praise our gracious God.
**Praise God, from whom all blessings flow!**

1  Our help is in the name of the LORD,
  **who made heaven and earth.**
    —Psalm 124:8, NRSV

2  We will give thanks to you, O LORD, with our whole heart;
    we will tell of all your wonderful deeds.
  **We will be glad and exult in you;**
    **we will sing praise to your name, O Most High.**
    —from Psalm 9:1-2, NRSV

3  The earth is the LORD's and all that is in it,
    the world, and those who live in it;
  **for he has founded it on the seas,**
    **and established it on the rivers.**
  Who shall ascend the hill of the LORD?
    And who shall stand in his holy place?
  **Those who have clean hands and pure hearts,**
    **who do not lift up their souls to what is false,**
    **and do not swear deceitfully.**
    —Psalm 24:1-4, NRSV

4  Lift up your heads, you gates;
    be lifted up, you ancient doors,
    that the King of glory may come in.
  **Who is this King of glory?**
    The LORD strong and mighty,
    the LORD mighty in battle.
  **Lift up your heads, you gates;**
    **lift them up, you ancient doors,**
    **that the King of glory may come in.**

Who is he, this King of glory?
**The LORD Almighty—
he is the King of glory.**
—Psalm 24:7-10, NIV

5    Let us worship God, our light and our salvation.
**The Lord is the stronghold of our lives.**
We desire to live in God's house
and to seek God in his holy temple.
**We have come with shouts of joy,
to sing and to make music to the Lord.**
Let us worship God in spirit and in truth.
**Teach us your ways and make straight our paths
in this hour of worship and always.**
—based on Psalm 27; John 4:23

6    Clap your hands, all you peoples;
shout to God with loud songs of joy.
**For the LORD, the Most High, is awesome,
a great king over all the earth.**
God has gone up with a shout,
the LORD with the sound of a trumpet.
**Sing praises to God, sing praises;
sing praises to our King, sing praises.**
—Psalm 47:1-2, 5-6, NRSV

7    Make a joyful noise to God, all the earth;
sing the glory of his name;
give to him glorious praise.
**All the earth worships you;
they sing praises to you,
sing praises to your name.**
—Psalm 66:1-2, 4, NRSV

8    There is none like you, O Lord,
nor are there any works like yours.
**All the nations you have made shall come
and bow down before you, O Lord,
and shall glorify your name.**
**For you are great and do wondrous things,
you alone are God.**
—from Psalm 86:8-10, NRSV

9    I will sing of your steadfast love, O LORD, forever;
**with my mouth I will proclaim your faithfulness
to all generations.**
I declare that your steadfast love is established forever;
**your faithfulness is as firm as the heavens.**
You said, "I have made a covenant with my chosen one,

I have sworn to my servant David:
'I will establish your descendants forever,
   and build your throne for all generations.'"
**Praise the Lord!**
   —from Psalm 89:1-4, NRSV

10   It is good to praise the LORD
   and make music to your name, O Most High,
proclaiming your love in the morning
   and your faithfulness at night.
   —Psalm 92:1-2, NIV

11   Come, let us sing for joy to the LORD;
   let us shout aloud to the Rock of our salvation.
**Let us come before him with thanksgiving**
**   and extol him with music and song.**
   —Psalm 95:1-2, NIV

12   Come, let us bow down in worship,
**   let us kneel before the LORD our Maker;**
for he is our God
**   and we are the people of his pasture,**
**   the flock under his care.**
   —Psalm 95:6-7, NIV

13   Come, bow down and worship,
   kneel to the Lord, our Maker.
**This is our God, our shepherd,**
**   we are the flock led with care.**
   —Psalm 95:6-7, TP

14   Sing to the LORD a new song;
**   sing to the LORD, all the earth.**
Sing to the LORD, praise his name;
**   proclaim his salvation day after day.**
   —Psalm 96:1-2, NIV

15   Shout for joy to the LORD, all the earth.
**   Worship the LORD with gladness;**
**   come before him with joyful songs.**
Know that the LORD is God.
   It is he who made us and we are his;
**   we are his people, the sheep of his pasture.**
Enter his gates with thanksgiving
   and his courts with praise;
   give thanks to him and praise his name.
**For the LORD is good and his love endures forever;**
**   his faithfulness continues through all generations.**
   —Psalm 100, NIV

16    Praise the LORD, my soul;
        all my inmost being, praise his holy name.
    **Praise the LORD, my soul,**
        **and forget not all his benefits.**
    Praise the LORD, you his angels,
        you mighty ones who do his bidding,
        who obey his word.
    **Praise the LORD, all his heavenly hosts,**
        **you his servants who do his will.**
    Praise the LORD, all his works
        everywhere in his dominion.
    **Praise the LORD, my soul.**
        —Psalm 103:1-2, 20-22, NIV

17    Our hearts are ready, O Lord,
        our hearts are ready!
    **We will sing and make melody!**
        **We will awaken the dawn!**
    We will give thanks to you, O Lord, among the peoples,
    we will sing praises to you among the nations.
    **For your steadfast love is great above the heavens,**
        **and your faithfulness reaches to the clouds.**
        —based on Psalm 108:1-4

18    Hallelujah!
    Servants of God, praise,
        praise the name of the Lord.
    Bless the Lord's name now and always.
    Praise the Lord's name here and in every place
        from east to west.
        —Psalm 113:1-3, TP

19    This is the day that the LORD has made;
        **let us rejoice and be glad in it.**
        —Psalm 118:24, NRSV

20    Hallelujah!
    Praise! Praise God in the temple, in the highest heavens!
    **Praise! Praise God's mighty deeds and noble majesty.**
    All that is alive, praise!
    **Praise the Lord.**
    **Hallelujah!**
        —Psalm 150:1-2, 6, TP

21    "Come to me, all you who are weary and burdened,
    and I will give you rest.
    Take my yoke upon you, and learn from me;
    for I am gentle and humble in heart,
    and you will find rest for your souls."
        —Matthew 11:28-29, NIV

22    Great and marvelous are your deeds,
        Lord God Almighty.
    **Just and true are your ways,**
        **King of the nations.**
    Who will not fear you, Lord,
        and bring glory to your name?
    **For you alone are holy.**
    **All nations will come and worship before you.**
        —Revelation 15:3-4, NIV

23    Sing a new song to the Lord,
        who has worked wonders,
        whose right hand and holy arm have brought salvation.
    **The Lord has made known salvation;**
        **has shown justice to the nations;**
        **has remembered truth and love for the house of Israel.**
    All the ends of the earth have seen
        the salvation of our God.
    **Shout to the Lord, all the earth,**
        **sing out your joy.**
    Sing psalms to the Lord with the harp,
        with the sound of music.
    **With trumpets and the sound of the horn**
        **acclaim the King, the Lord.**
        —based on Psalm 98:1-6

24    The earth is the Lord's, for he made it:
    **Come, let us adore him.**
    Worship the Lord in the beauty of holiness:
    **Come, let us adore him.**
    The mercy of the Lord is everlasting:
    **Come, let us adore him.**
    Lord, open our lips.
    **And our mouths shall proclaim your praise.**

25    All who thirst, come to the water.
    Come, all who are weary;
    come, all who yearn for forgiveness.
    The Holy Spirit through Jesus Christ has washed over us,
    and our gracious and holy God beckons and blesses us.
    Drink deeply of these living waters.
    **Glory to you, O Lord, glory to you.**

26    Let us worship the eternal God,
    the source of love and life, who creates us.
    **Let us worship Jesus Christ,**
    **the risen one, who lives among us.**

Let us worship the Spirit,
the holy fire, who renews us.
**To the one true God be praise**
**in all times and places,**
**through the grace of Jesus Christ.**

27    God invites us into his healing presence with these words:
      "I am the Lord, who heals you."
      **Diseased, depressed, dysfunctional, defeated,**
      **we come hungering for health that only God can provide.**
      God calls us to bring open eyes, hearing ears,
      and tender hearts turned toward him, the Great Physician.
      **We bow before him in faith and expectancy!**
              —based on Exodus 15:26; Isaiah 6:10

28    God calls us to worship, **and we come,**
      some with laughter and songs of joy.
      God calls us to worship, **and we come,**
      some from a sense of obligation or habit.
      God calls us to worship, **and we come,**
      some with hearts heavy with grief.
      God calls us to worship, **and we come,**
      some with distraction or exhaustion.
      God calls us to worship, **and we come,**
      some with eagerness and enthusiasm.
      God calls us to worship, **and we come,**
      some with stress, loneliness, or depression.
      As God's dearly loved children,
      we bring all our joy and pain, hurt and hope
      **into this place of Spirit-given grace, love, and hope.**

29    The eternal Father,
      who loved us and set us free from our sins,
      who loves us still with that love that will not let us go,
      and who will love us forever,
      calls us to worship him today as the only true lover of our souls.
      The Lord stoops to receive the love of our poor hearts.
      He calls us to remember the depth of his love for us in Christ.
      God seeks our love!

30    The Lord Jesus who calls us to worship him today
      is the same Jesus who refused the temptation
      to worship the evil one.
      Rather than receive the glorious kingdoms of this world,
      he endured the shame of the cross,
      and today is Lord of lords and King of kings.
      Now are gathered in him all the treasures
      of wisdom and knowledge, glory, and power.
      With the saints of all ages we say,

"Worthy is the Lamb, who was slain,
to receive power and wealth and wisdom
and strength and honor and glory and praise!"
—based on Colossians 2:3; Revelation 5:12

31  People of God, worship the living God today!
Remember that out of nothing God created the heavens and earth.
Remember that God raised Jesus
from the powerlessness of death
to the power of his right hand.
Remember that not even the gates of hell
can stand against God's purposes.
Behold your God, who reigns now and forever!

32  Let us worship God.
**"He is our refuge and our fortress,
our God, in whom we trust."**
Let us confess with our mouths, "Jesus is Lord,"
and believe in our hearts that God raised him from the dead.
**"Everyone who calls on the name of the Lord will be saved."**
Let us call upon our true God, believing him in our hearts,
confessing him with our mouths, worshiping him in spirit and in truth.
—based on Psalm 91:2; Romans 10:9, 13

33  "Our help is in the name of the Lord,
who made heaven and earth."
**What did God do to help us?**
God chose the people of Israel to make a new beginning.
**They received God's covenant and prepared the way
for Jesus to come as our Savior.**
Let us worship the God of the covenant, the God of heaven and earth.
—based on Psalm 124:8

34  When Moses gathered the people of Israel, God said,
**"I am the Lord your God,
who brought you out of the land of Egypt,
out of the house of slavery."**
As we gather here today,
let us worship the Lord,
who continues to be our God
and who still brings us out of the places of our bondage.
—based on Exodus 20:1-2

35  In Christ, the God of heaven has made his home on earth.
**Christ dwells among us and is one with us.**
Highest of all creation, he lives among the least.
**He journeys with the rejected and welcomes the weary.**
Come now, all who thirst,
**and drink the water of life.**

Come now, all who hunger,
**and be filled with good things.**
Come now, all who seek,
**and be warmed by the fire of love.**

36 In your wisdom, O God, you call us here to worship you.
**We gather, alive to the Word of God.**
You call us to be fully alive with your life abundant,
ready to listen and respond with heart, soul, strength, and mind.
**We listen, alive to the Word of God.**
You call us to be always watchful for your Word of wisdom,
sometimes startling and unexpected,
sometimes still and quiet,
but always dwelling among us.
**We watch and wait for the Word of God.**

# 1.3 GREETING

*The words of greeting establish the lines of communication in worship. God always comes to us before we come to God. So it is fitting for worship to begin with scriptural words that convey God's greeting to us (historically referred to in some traditions as the "salutation"). The following texts provide several scriptural options, beginning with the classic trinitarian greeting.*

*The posture and gestures of both leader and worshipers can be very important in helping the congregation experience these words of greeting as the communication of God's promise. The leader may raise a hand in blessing over the congregation, and the worshipers may extend their hands or bow their heads to receive God's promise.*

*Any of the following greetings may be introduced with a statement like this:*

Our Lord has called us to worship and now greets us.

## Scriptural Greeting

1 May the grace of the Lord Jesus Christ,
and the love of God,
and the fellowship of the Holy Spirit be with you all.
—2 Corinthians 13:14, NIV

*The congregation may respond with these words:*

> **And also with you.**

or

> **Amen!**

*For an extended greeting, especially in times of significant pastoral concern, consider adding one of the following texts.*

2    See, the Sovereign LORD comes with power,
         and he rules with a mighty arm.
     See, his reward is with him,
         and his recompense accompanies him.
     He tends his flock like a shepherd:
         He gathers the lambs in his arms
     and carries them close to his heart;
         he gently leads those that have young.
             —Isaiah 40:10-11, NIV

3    Look at him! GOD, the Master, comes in power,
         ready to go into action.
     He is going to pay back his enemies
         and reward those who have loved him.
     Like a shepherd, he will care for his flock,
         gathering the lambs in his arms,
     hugging them as he carries them,
         leading the nursing ewes to good pasture.
             —Isaiah 40:10-11, TM

4    You whom I took from the ends of the earth,
         and called from its farthest corners,
     saying to you, "You are my servant,
         I have chosen you and not cast you off";
     do not fear, for I am with you,
         do not be afraid, for I am your God;
     I will strengthen you, I will help you,
         I will uphold you with my victorious right hand.
             —Isaiah 41:9-10, NRSV

5    I am the LORD, I have called you in righteousness,
         I have taken you by the hand and kept you;
     I have given you as a covenant to the people,
         a light to the nations,
         to open the eyes that are blind,
     to bring out the prisoners from the dungeon,
         from the prison those who sit in darkness.
     I am the LORD, that is my name;
         my glory I give to no other,
         nor my praise to idols.
             —Isaiah 42:6-8, NRSV

6    Do not fear, for I have redeemed you;
        I have summoned you by name; you are mine.
    When you pass through the waters,
        I will be with you;
    and when you pass through the rivers,
        they will not sweep over you.
    When you walk through the fire,
        you will not be burned;
        the flames will not set you ablaze.
    For I am the LORD your God,
        the Holy One of Israel, your Savior.
          —Isaiah 43:1-3, NIV

7    Can a mother forget the baby at her breast
        and have no compassion on the child she has borne?
    Though she may forget,
        I will not forget you!
    See, I have engraved you on the palms of my hands;
        your walls are ever before me.
          —Isaiah 49:15-16, NIV

8    "For a brief moment I abandoned you,
        but with deep compassion I will bring you back.
    In a surge of anger
        I hid my face from you for a moment,
    but with everlasting kindness
        I will have compassion on you,"
        says the LORD your Redeemer.
          —Isaiah 54:7-8, NIV

9    The LORD your God is with you,
        the Mighty Warrior who saves.
    He will take great delight in you;
        in his love he will no longer rebuke you,
        but will rejoice over you with singing.
          —Zephaniah 3:17, NIV

10   Grace to you and peace from God our Father and
    the Lord Jesus Christ,
    who gave himself for our sins to set us free
    from the present evil age,
    according to the will of our God and Father,
    to whom be the glory forever and ever. **Amen.**
          —Galatians 1:3-5, NRSV

11   Grace to you and peace from God our Father
    and the Lord Jesus Christ.
          —Philippians 1:2, NRSV

**12**  Grace, mercy, and peace from God the Father
and Christ Jesus our Lord.
—2 Timothy 1:2, NRSV

**13**  May grace and peace be yours in abundance
in the knowledge of God and of Jesus our Lord.
—2 Peter 1:2, NRSV

**14**  Grace, mercy, and peace will be with us
from God the Father and from Jesus Christ,
the Father's Son, in truth and love.
—2 John 3, NRSV

**15**  To those who are called,
who are beloved in God the Father
and kept safe for Jesus Christ:
May mercy, peace, and love be yours
in abundance.
—Jude 1-2, NRSV

**16**  Grace to you and peace from him who is
and who was and who is to come,
and from the seven spirits who are before his throne,
and from Jesus Christ, the faithful witness,
the firstborn of the dead,
and the ruler of the kings of the earth.
—Revelation 1:4-5, NRSV

**17**  *This is one of the simplest of historical greetings, as practiced by Christians in many traditions. It may be used after any of the preceding scriptural greetings.*

The Lord be with you.
**And also with you.**
—based on Ruth 2:4

## Mutual Greeting

*God's words of greeting may be followed by a mutual greeting, in which worshipers extend God's blessing to each other with words such as "Christ's peace be with you." Often called "the passing of the peace," the mutual greeting may also follow the assurance of pardon (see section 2.4) or take place during the celebration of the Lord's Supper (see section 8.2.8). The following words may introduce the mutual greeting.*

As God has greeted us with his peace,
so let us pass the peace of Christ to each other.
*or*
As God has greeted us, so let us greet each other.

## Welcome

*Public worship is an expression of the church's hospitality. Words of welcome make that hospitality explicit. The welcome may be spoken before the call to worship or as an extension of the greeting or mutual greeting. It may also be printed in a bulletin, projected on a screen, or spoken informally by a worship leader.*

*The words spoken should be in keeping with the welcome that guests experience before and after the worship service. In addition to the words of welcome, you may wish to include specific information about the worship service or the worship materials, and offer instructions for guests on how to find additional information about your church or how to meet people after the service.*

18    Welcome in the name of Jesus Christ!
      May each one of us find great joy and spiritual nourishment
      as we worship together today.

19    Welcome to worship today!
      We are all here because of God's hospitality.
      We share the privilege of extending that hospitality to each other.

20    Whether we are old or young,
      whether we are first-time or longtime worshipers,
      whether we come full of doubts or confidence, joy or sorrow,
      in this place we are all family,
      because of what Jesus did for us on the cross.
      Welcome to all of you today!

21    Those who love Jesus and those who are searching, welcome!
      We gather to hear from God, to learn from God, to talk to God.
      Visitors, we are eager to share with you the joy we have in knowing Jesus.
      May we all grow in our knowledge and love of Christ as we worship.

22    If you are spiritually weary and in search of rest,
      if you are mourning and you long for comfort,
      if you are struggling and you desire victory,
      if you recognize that you are a sinner and need a Savior,
      God welcomes you here in the name of Christ.
      To the stranger in need of fellowship,
      to those who hunger and thirst for righteousness,
      and to whoever will come,
      this congregation opens wide its doors
      and welcomes all in the name of the Lord Jesus Christ.

**23**   *For a service including the Lord's Supper*

We welcome to this service those
who have not professed faith in Christ
and who may be hearing the gospel for the first time.
Though you may not be partaking of the sacrament,
it is our privilege to welcome you here.
Perhaps what you experience will raise questions for you.
After the service, we will be eager to talk with you further
about the joy of our life in Christ
and the significance of this celebration in our life together.

# 1.4 OPENING RESPONSES

*The following texts offer the congregation's response to God's words of greeting and promise. Even for leaders who prefer to pray without notes, the following texts can be helpful in suggesting an image, a phrase, or a petition that can enrich and deepen the opening prayer.*

*In many congregations, the first words of praise are sung. It's important for worshipers to sense that these songs or hymns of adoration are prayers—the words of the assembly offered to God. In singing them, worshipers are addressing God just as in spoken or silent prayer.*

*The resources in this section are grouped in three categories: Prayers of Adoration, Prayers of Invocation, and Additional Resources. In most contexts, a worship service might include a single text from only one of these categories, in addition to praise singing. Communities that extend the opening of worship may wish to include several responses, moving from adoration to invocation to a declaration of faith and hope, interspersing songs with some of the texts provided here.*

## Prayers of Adoration

*The primary and most common response during the opening of worship is adoration. Many prayers of adoration, originating as far back as the Old Testament, feature not only praise for attributes of God but also praise for particular actions of God, such as creating the world, providing care and guidance for the people, redeeming the world in Christ, and sending the Holy Spirit. Some scriptural prayers of thanks even resemble brief history lessons, tracing the timeline of God's redemptive actions. Naming particular divine attributes and actions helps our prayers become specific and concrete. This practice also helps us avoid a form of idolatry, in which the "God" we might call to mind when we worship is only a vague "higher power." Such a vague notion of God bears little resemblance to the God revealed in Scripture and seen most clearly in the person of Jesus Christ.*

*These prayers may be introduced with a statement like the following:*

We respond to God's invitation with words of praise.

1   O LORD, God of Israel,
    there is no God like you in heaven above or on earth beneath,
    keeping covenant and steadfast love for your servants
    who walk before you with all their heart.
    Blessed be the LORD,
    who has given rest to his people Israel
    according to all that he promised;
    not one word has failed of all his good promise,
    which he spoke through his servant Moses.
    **The LORD our God be with us,**
    **as he was with our ancestors;**
    **may he not leave us or abandon us,**
    **but incline our hearts to him,**
    **to walk in all his ways,**
    **and to keep his commandments,**
    **his statutes, and his ordinances,**
    **which he commanded our ancestors.**
            —1 Kings 8:23, 56-58, NRSV

2   Praise be to you, LORD,
        the God of our father Israel,
        from everlasting to everlasting.
    **Yours, LORD, is the greatness and the power**
        **and the glory and the majesty and the splendor,**
        for everything in heaven and earth is yours.
    **Yours, LORD, is the kingdom;**
        **you are exalted as head over all.**
    Wealth and honor come from you;
        you are the ruler of all things.
    **In your hands are strength and power**
        **to exalt and give strength to all.**
    Now, our God, we give you thanks,
        and praise your glorious name.
            —1 Chronicles 29:10-13, NIV

3   LORD, our Lord,
        how majestic is your name in all the earth!
    You have set your glory
        in the heavens.
    Through the praise of children and infants
        you have established a stronghold against your enemies,
        to silence the foe and the avenger.
            —Psalm 8:1-2, NIV

4    O God, your constant love reaches to the heavens,
       your faithfulness extends to the skies.
    **Your righteousness towers like the mountains,**
       **your justice is deeper than the sea.**
    All find protection under the shadow of your wings.
    We feast on the abundance you provide.
    **You are the source of all life,**
       **and in your light, we see light.**
       —based on Psalm 36:5-9

5    It is good to praise the LORD
       and make music to your name, O Most High,
    **to proclaim your love in the morning**
       **and your faithfulness at night,**
    to the music of the ten-stringed lyre
       and the melody of the harp.
    **For you make me glad by your deeds, O LORD;**
       **I sing for joy at the works of your hands.**
    How great are your works, O LORD,
       how profound your thoughts!
    **You, O LORD, are exalted forever.**
       —from Psalm 92:1-5, 8, NIV

6    In the midst of the congregation I will praise you.
    Rejoice in the LORD, O you righteous,
       and give thanks to God's holy name!
    **I will extol you, my God and King,**
       **and bless your name forever and ever.**
    **Great is the LORD, and greatly to be praised;**
       **God's greatness is unsearchable.**
       —from Psalm 22:22; 97:12; 145:1, 3, NRSV

7    All glorious God, we give you thanks:
       in your Son, Jesus Christ,
    you have given us every spiritual blessing
       in the heavenly realms.
    You chose us, before the world was made,
       to be your holy people, without fault in your sight.
    You adopted us as your children in Christ.
    You have set us free by his blood;
       you have forgiven our sins.
    You have made known to us your secret purpose,
       to bring heaven and earth into unity in Christ.
    You have given us your Holy Spirit,
       the seal and pledge of our inheritance.
    All praise and glory be yours, O God,
       for the richness of your grace,
       for the splendor of your gifts,
       for the wonder of your love.
       —based on Ephesians 1:3-18

*After these scriptural openings, continue with words of adoration or invocation, as in the following.*

8    **We praise you for creating this world in all beauty,**
     **for redeeming the world through Christ, our Lord,**
     **and for sending us the gift of your Spirit**
     **to encourage, instruct, and sustain us.**
     **We long for your Spirit to work among us now,**
     **to inspire our praise, to challenge us with your truth,**
     **and to equip us for service in your world. Amen.**

9    God, our Creator,
     from nothing you made our world.
     **You formed us, love us,**
     **and give us all that we need.**
     God, our Redeemer,
     you rescued us from sin.
     **You have given us new life**
     **and hope of healing to the world.**
     God, our Comforter,
     you are with us always.
     **You comfort us, renew us,**
     **and guide us into your truth.**
     Almighty God, for your gracious love for us,
     we praise you. **Amen.**

10   God of light and truth,
     you are beyond our grasp or conceiving.
     Before the brightness of your presence
     the angels veil their faces.
     With lowly reverence and adoring love
     we acclaim your glory
     and sing your praise,
     for you have shown us your truth and love
     in Jesus Christ, our Savior. **Amen.**

11   **We praise you, we worship you, we adore you.**
     You hold the heavens in your hand;
     all stars rejoice in your glory.
     You come in the sunrise and the song of morn
     and bless the splendor of the noonday.
     **We praise you, we worship you, we adore you.**
     The stars in their courses magnify you;
     day and night tell of your glory.
     Your peace blows over the earth,
     and the breath of your mouth fills all space.
     **We praise you, we worship you, we adore you.**
     Your voice comes in the thunder of the storm;
     the song of the wind whispers of your majesty.

You satisfy all things living with your abundance,
and our hearts bow at your presence.
**We praise you, we worship you, we adore you.**
Accept us, your children, eternal Father,
and hear our prayer.
Bend over us, eternal Love, and bless us. **Amen.**

12 Creator God,
because you make all that draws forth our praise
and the forms in which to express it,
**we praise you.**
Because you make artists of us all,
awakening courage to look again at what is taken for granted,
grace to share these insights with others,
vision to reveal the future already in being,
**we praise you.**
Because you form your Word among us,
and in your great work embrace all human experience,
even death itself, inspiring our resurrection song,
**we praise you.**
**Yours is the glory. Amen.**

13 You are the Sovereign One, O God, and rightly to be blessed.
Your name shall ever be upon our lips.
You have heard the poor and saved them from trouble.
You have enlightened believers; their faces reflect your radiance.
Aglow with the splendor of your promised redemption,
we gather to worship you, ruler of nations. **Amen.**

14 O God, you summon the day to dawn,
you teach the morning to waken the earth.
**For you the valleys shall sing for joy,**
**the trees of the field shall clap their hands.**
For you the kings of the earth shall bow,
the poor and the persecuted shall shout for joy.
**Your love and mercy shall last forever,**
**fresh as the morning, sure as the sunrise.**
Great is your name.
**Great is your love. Amen.**

15 Mighty God,
we do not yet see the glory you plan for all humankind,
but in faith we do see Jesus.
We thank you for the humility and holiness
in which he lived and died.
We praise you that he freed us from our sin,
that he comforts and strengthens us through our struggles,
and that he gives us courage to follow him.

For this, we now join with all creation and shout for joy:
Holy, holy, holy are you, Lord! **Amen.**

16　Loving God, we have gathered to meet you.
We have come to listen to you,
to seek you, to worship you.
You are the beginning of all things,
the life of all things; you knew us before we were born.
In you we become; in you we live.
Loving God, you are here and everywhere,
around us and within us; you know our inmost thoughts.
In you we hope; in you we live.
You are the source of serenity,
giving peace that is beyond our understanding.
In you we are still; in you we live.
Loving God, we live in you; we worship you.
Loving God, you live in us; we worship you. **Amen.**

17　We give thanks to you, God our Father,
for mercy that reaches out,
for patience that waits our returning,
for your love that is ever ready
to welcome sinners.
**We praise you that in Jesus Christ**
**you came to us with forgiveness,**
**and that, by your Holy Spirit,**
**you move us to repent**
**and receive your love.**
Though we are sinners,
you are faithful and worthy of all praise.
**We praise you, great God,**
**in Jesus Christ, our Lord. Amen.**

18　Our Father,
you are in heaven, high and lifted up,
higher than our highest thoughts.
Holy is your name;
beside you there is no other!
You are God, and you alone!
Receive us into your kingdom—the coming kingdom—
the kingdom of your anointed Son, Jesus, whose name we bear.
Receive us, for we come to you in his name—
we pray in him and with him.
For yours is the kingdom and the power and the glory,
Father, Son, and Holy Spirit, one God, now and forever. **Amen.**
　　　　　—based on Matthew 6:9-10, 13

19   Let us join our voices to praise the spotless Lamb, Jesus Christ,
who has redeemed us from sin and death.
**We, whom he has redeemed,**
**will sing praises and shout for joy this hour;**
because in Christ the Lamb we have redemption through his blood,
the forgiveness of our sins in accordance with the riches of his grace.
**Christ has redeemed us from the curse of the law**
**by becoming a curse for us.**
Let us praise him by saying:
**Worthy is the Lamb, who was slain,**
**to receive power and wealth and wisdom and strength**
**and honor and glory and praise!**
**To him who sits on the throne and to the Lamb**
**we give worship this hour and forever and ever. Amen.**

20   You, O God, are mighty forever.
You cause the wind to blow and the rain to fall.
You sustain the living, give life to the dead,
support the falling, loose those who are bound,
and keep your faith with those who sleep in the dust.
Who is like you, O God of mighty acts?
Praise be to you forever. **Amen.**

21   God our Father,
we call on you like little children because we know
that you love us and care for us like a loving parent.
Because your Son, Jesus, prayed to you as Father,
so we pray this way.
You created us to live with you and to ask for your help and guidance. **Amen.**

*Prayers of adoration especially mindful of children*

22   We are very thankful, God,
that you want us to come and worship you.
We know you are listening to us
when we sing
and when we pray.
And we know that you will bless us
before we leave.
Thank you, God. **Amen.**

23   Loving God,
we come to worship you today.
We come to sing, pray, and listen.
You always hear us.
Help us to hear you. **Amen.**

24 Too often, O God, we pray, "Listen, Lord, for your children are speaking."
   Today help us to pray, "Speak, Lord, for your children are listening."
   Help our ears to hear your Word.
   Help our hearts to trust what you say.
   Help our hands and feet to do what you call us to do. **Amen.**

## Prayers of Invocation

*The following prayers consist mainly of petitions that God will work powerfully through the Spirit during the worship service. These petitions express longing for God as well as deep dependence and humility. Invocations acknowledge that the power in worship is a gift from God rather than a human accomplishment, and they explicitly confess that we approach God only through Christ.*

*The term* invocation *implies that the congregation invokes, or "calls upon," God, but it should never be inferred that we are the ones to invite God into our presence, or that God's presence with us depends on our invoking the Lord. God is present before we begin! Our prayers of invocation celebrate and acknowledge God's presence; they don't produce it.*

25 O gracious and holy God,
   give us diligence to seek you,
   wisdom to perceive you,
   and patience to wait for you.
   Grant us, O God,
   a mind to meditate on you,
   eyes to behold you,
   ears to listen for your Word,
   a heart to love you,
   and a life to proclaim you,
   through the power of the Spirit
   of Jesus Christ, our Lord. **Amen.**

26 O most merciful Redeemer, friend, and brother,
   may we know you more clearly,
   love you more dearly,
   and follow you more nearly,
   day by day. **Amen.**

27 Eternal God,
   you have called us to be members of one body.
   Join us with those who in all times and places
   have praised your name,
   that, with one heart and mind, we may show the unity of your church,
   and bring honor to our Lord and Savior, Jesus Christ. **Amen.**

28 Everlasting God,
   in whom we live and move and have our being:
   You have made us for yourself,

so that our hearts are restless until they rest in you.
Give us purity of heart and strength of purpose,
that no selfish passion may hinder us from knowing your will,
no weakness keep us from doing it;
that in your light we may see light clearly,
and in your service find perfect freedom
through Jesus Christ, our Lord,
who lives and reigns with you and the Holy Spirit,
one God, now and forever. **Amen.**

29   God of grace,
      you have given us minds to know you,
      hearts to love you, and voices to sing your praise.
      Fill us with your Spirit,
      that we may celebrate your glory
      and worship you in spirit and in truth
      through Jesus Christ, our Lord. **Amen.**

30   Eternal Light, **shine into our hearts;**
      eternal Goodness, **deliver us from evil;**
      eternal Power, **be our support;**
      eternal Wisdom, **scatter the darkness of our ignorance;**
      eternal Love, **have mercy upon us,**
      that with all our heart and mind and strength
      we may seek your face
      and be brought by your infinite mercy to your holy presence
      through Jesus Christ, our Lord. **Amen.**

31   God of goodness and grace,
      we long for your presence,
      for the peace your promises bring,
      and for the assurances we have received
      through the gift of your Son.
      **May we, your people,**
      **this day and every day,**
      **have open eyes to see**
      **and open ears to hear**
      **your presence among us.**
      Open us to your Holy Spirit, Lord,
      and prepare us for worship. **Amen.**

32   Praise the Lord.
      **The Lord's name be praised.**
      Great God,
      you have been generous
      and marvelously kind.
      **Give us such wonder, love, and gratitude**
      **that we may sing praises to you**

*69*

**and joyfully honor your name**
**through Jesus Christ, our Lord. Amen.**

33   O God, our guide and guardian,
      you have led us apart from the busy world into the quiet of your house.
      Grant us grace to worship you in spirit and in truth,
      to the comfort of our souls
      and the upbuilding of every good purpose and holy desire.
      Enable us to do more perfectly the work to which you have called us,
      that we may not fear the coming of night,
      when we shall surrender into your hands
      the tasks which you have committed to us.
      So may we worship you not with our lips only at this hour,
      but in word and deed all the days of our lives,
      through Jesus Christ, our Savior. **Amen.**

34   O Lord, our God,
      you are always more ready to give your good gifts to us
      than we are to seek them,
      and you are willing to give more than we desire or deserve.
      Help us so to seek that we may truly find,
      so to ask that we may joyfully receive,
      so to knock that the door of your mercy may be opened to us
      through Jesus Christ, our Savior. **Amen.**

35   Sing praises to God, O you saints,
      and give thanks to God's holy name!
      **We exalt you, O God, for you have restored us to life!**
      We may cry through the night, but your joy comes with the morning.
      **You hear us, O God, and you are gracious in our distress.**
      You turn our mourning into dancing!
      Our souls cannot be silent!
      **O God, our Savior, we give thanks to you forever! Amen.**

36   Almighty and loving God,
      you have given us eyes
      to see the light that fills this room;
      give us the inward vision
      to behold you in this place.
      You have made us feel
      the morning wind upon our limbs;
      help us to sense your presence
      as we bow in worship of you. **Amen.**

37   Lord, open to us the sea of your mercy,
      and water us with full streams
      from the riches of your grace
      and the springs of your kindness.
      Make us children of quietness and heirs of peace;

kindle in us the fire of your love,
and strengthen our weakness by your power
as we become close to you and to each other. **Amen.**

38    O Lord, our God,
      creator of our land,
      our earth, the trees, the animals and humans,
      all is for your honor.
      **The drums beat it out, and people sing about it,**
      **and they dance with noisy joy**
      **that you are the Lord.**
      You also have pulled the other continents out of the sea.
      What a wonderful world you have made out of wet mud
      and what beautiful men and women!
      We thank you for all the beauty of this earth.
      **The grace of your creation is like a cool day between rainy seasons.**
      **We drink in your creation with our eyes.**
      **We listen to the birds' jubilee with our ears.**
      How strong and good and sure your earth smells,
      and everything that grows here.
      We drink in your creation and cannot get enough of it.
      **Bless our land and people.**
      **Prepare us for the service we should render. Amen.**

39    Show us the way to fullness of life, Lord Jesus;
      that our hearts might be filled with joy, hope, and peace, we pray;
      that we might respond to opportunities, we pray;
      that we might be strengthened to face challenges, we pray;
      that we might become the persons we are called to be, we pray;
      that we might learn to respect our sisters and brothers, we pray;
      that we might see the needs of others and give help, we pray. **Amen.**

40    Jesus Christ, you come to transfigure us
      and renew us in the image of God:
      **shine in our darkness.**
      Jesus Christ, light of our hearts, you know our thirst:
      **lead us to the wellspring of your gospel.**
      Jesus Christ, light of the world, you shine in every human being:
      **enable us to discern your presence in each person.**
      Jesus Christ, friend of the poor:
      **open in us the gates of simplicity so that we can welcome you.**
      Jesus Christ, gentle and humble of heart:
      **renew in us the spirit of childhood.**
      Jesus Christ, you send your church to prepare your path in the world:
      **open for all people the gates of your kingdom. Amen.**

**41**  God of all faithfulness,
you have opened the gate of mercy for your people
and are always ready to welcome those who turn to you.
Look on us in your compassion,
that we may gladly respond to your love
and faithfully walk in your way
through Jesus Christ, our Lord. **Amen.**

**42**  Loving God,
we come to you in worship and thanksgiving.
You are greater than we can understand;
**open our eyes that we may see the wonderful truths**
**you have shown to us in Jesus.**
You are more loving than our hearts can respond to;
**help us to give ourselves to you in worship**
**so that we learn what you want us to be.**
You are wiser than we can know;
**still our minds as we worship you**
**so that we can understand the things you are saying to us.**
Loving God, in Jesus
you chose to come to the world in humility.
You chose the path the world saw as foolish.
You used what the world considered weak.
**We worship and adore you. Amen.**

**43**  Lord, our God, we trust your promise
to be among us as we gather.
We come in the name of Christ,
drawn by your Spirit,
eager to hear your Word.
Fill our hearts with your Spirit
and prepare us for faithful service. **Amen.**

**44**  O God, our Father,
you seek men and women, boys and girls,
who will worship you in spirit and in truth;
and so we ask you to inspire
and bless the worship week by week in this church,
in words and music,
prayers and hymns,
psalms and lessons.
Open the hearts and lips of those
who worship you today all over the world,
that all of us may listen with an alert conscience
to the preaching of your Word
and come to receive the bread and cup with true repentance and faith.
We ask this in the name of him
through whom alone our worship is acceptable to you:
our Lord and Savior, Jesus Christ. **Amen.**

45    Christ, in this hour of worship
       lift us out of the routine of our daily lives
       and set us up on your holy mountain.
       Let our worship come from our hearts,
       that it may be genuine.
       Let our praises for you leap from our mouths,
       that we may be alive with faith and joy.
       Make us fresh again! **Amen.**

46    Holy and loving God,
       we come to you,
       with hopes and fears,
       with convictions and doubts,
       with pain and joy.
       By your Spirit,
       **help us to see all things**
       **in the light of your Word,**
       **our Lord Jesus Christ.**
       By your Spirit,
       **help us to pray honestly,**
       **to listen attentively,**
       **to encourage one another warmly.**
       By your Spirit,
       **help us grow in the grace and knowledge**
       **of our Lord and Savior, Jesus Christ,**
       **who with you and the Holy Spirit**
       **lives and reigns forever.**
       **All glory to you, both now and forever! Amen.**

47    With you, gracious God,
       we move into this time of worship,
       grateful that you are never farther
       than the reach of our need and our prayer.
       You who tower over the universe
       are yet intimately present,
       always renewing the face of the earth,
       always renewing the faith of your children.
       Now, in your mercy, make your way past
       all that worries and distracts us
       to lodge in us anew and to center
       our small worship on your great glory. **Amen.**

48    Great and loving God,
       we come before you emptied of all that would distract,
       seeking all that would redeem.
       Let these moments not become so routine
       as to be predictable,
       nor so familiar as to be conventional.

Prepare us for the unexpected.
Open us to the movement of the Holy Spirit
in praise of our Savior. **Amen.**

49   God, our Rock, our refuge, our resting place,
we come to you.
Out of another busy week of work,
out of our struggles to be meaningful in our world,
out of our desire to meet you and know you
as the center of our being,
we come to you, O unmovable Rock of our security. **Amen.**

50   Ever present God,
we thank you for calling us to meet with you today.
We praise you for coming to us long before we first came to you,
for knowing who would be here today,
and for knowing even our motives for coming.
By your Spirit lead and guide us during this service,
to help us hear you when you speak
and to guide our responses with hearts and voices
that rejoice in your presence. **Amen.**

51   Spirit divine, inspire our prayer
and make our hearts your home.
Descend with all your gracious power;
come, Holy Spirit, come!
Come as the light, reveal our need,
and lead us on paths of life.
Come as the fire, cleanse our hearts with purifying flame;
let our whole life be an offering to our Redeemer's name.
Come as the dove, spread your wings of peaceful love;
and let your church on earth become as your church above.
Spirit divine, make this lost world your home.
Come, Holy Spirit, come! **Amen.**
          —based on a hymn by Andrew Reed (1829)

52   O God, who created us in love,
**create us anew in love as we worship you.**
O Jesus Christ, who redeemed this world in love,
**reclaim our hearts as we worship you.**
O Holy Spirit, who moves this world toward its God-appointed end,
**move within us as we worship you. Amen.**

53   O Lord God, how great you are!
On the first day of the week we commemorate
your creation of the world and all that is in it.
**Lord, send forth your Spirit**
**and renew the face of the earth.**
O Lord God, how great you are!

On the first day of the week we commemorate
the resurrection of your Son, Jesus Christ, our Savior, from the dead.
**Lord, create in us a pure heart**
**and renew a steadfast spirit within us.**
O Lord God, how great you are!
On the first day of the week we celebrate in song
the presence of your Holy Spirit in the church
and throughout the whole world. **Amen and Amen!**

54 *A text especially mindful of children*

Dear God,
help us to worship you today.
May we listen carefully, pray honestly, and sing joyfully.
Send your Holy Spirit
so that our words will bring you glory.
Thank you that Jesus makes our worship perfect for you.
Help us remember that when we worship you,
we are part of your family;
we join everyone who loves you
around the world and throughout history.
In Jesus' name we pray. **Amen.**

## Additional Resources

*These additional resources, many drawn from Scripture, are faithful responses to God's words of invitation and promise. Many of them express deep longing for God and hope in God despite difficult circumstances. Each of these responses leads naturally into singing that expresses similar or complementary themes.*

55 Be exalted, O God, above the heavens;
    let your glory be over all the earth.
My heart is steadfast, O God,
    my heart is steadfast;
    I will sing and make music.
**Be exalted, O God, above the heavens;**
    **let your glory be over all the earth.**
    —Psalm 57:5, 7, 11, NIV

56 You, God, are my God,
    earnestly I seek you;
I thirst for you,
    my whole being longs for you,
in a dry and parched land
    where there is no water.
I have seen you in the sanctuary
    and beheld your power and your glory.
Because your love is better than life,

my lips will glorify you.
**I will praise you as long as I live,**
    **and in your name I will lift up my hands.**
—Psalm 63:1-4, NIV

57    I rejoiced with those who said to me,
    "Let us go to the house of the LORD."
—Psalm 122:1, NIV

58    Let us call to mind the reason for our hope:
    Because of the LORD's great love we are not consumed,
        for his compassions never fail.
    They are new every morning;
        great is your faithfulness.
    I say to myself, "The LORD is my portion;
        therefore I will wait for him."
    **The LORD is good to those whose hope is in him,**
        **to the one who seeks him;**
    **it is good to wait quietly**
        **for the salvation of the LORD.**
—from Lamentations 3:21-26, NIV

59    Praise be to the God and Father of our Lord Jesus Christ,
    **who has blessed us in Christ with every spiritual blessing.**
    For he chose us in him before the creation of the world
    **that we might be holy and blameless before God.**
—from Ephesians 1:3-4

60    In holy splendor, we worship the Lord.
    **In God is glory and strength.**
    **The Lord is mighty. God is with us.**
    In torrents and storms, God's peace pervades.
    **In rumbling thunder, God's mighty voice soothes.**
    **The Lord is majestic. God is with us.**
    The whisper of the Lord snaps silence.
    **The unwavering sound persists.**
    **The Lord is awesome. God is with us.**
    As flames being fanned, the presence grows.
    **In its shadow the wilderness pleads.**
    **The Lord is powerful. God is with us.**
    Enthroned, God rules the universe.
    **The peaceful scepter prevails.**
    **God reigns. God is with us.**
    In whirling winds, nature acknowledges glory.
    **The people in the temple rejoice.**
    **It is certain. God is with us.**
—based on Psalm 29

61  We will bless the Lord at all times,
    **God's praise is always on our lips;**
    **in the Lord our souls shall make their boast.**
    The humble shall hear and be glad.
    Glorify the Lord with us.
    Together let us praise God's name.
    **We sought the Lord and were heard,**
    **from all our terrors set free.**
    Look toward God and be radiant;
    let your faces not be ashamed.
    When the poor cry out, the Lord hears them
    and rescues them from all their distress.
    **Taste and see that the Lord is good.**
    **They are happy who seek refuge in God.**
                    —based on Psalm 34:1-8

62  *A text especially mindful of children*

    If today we hear God's voice in our hearts, we must follow it.
    **If today we hear God's voice in our hearts, we must follow it.**
    Come, everyone, let's sing to the Lord.
    Let us tell the world that God has saved us.
    Let us thank him from the bottom of our hearts.
    Let us sing songs of praise to him.
    **If today we hear God's voice in our hearts, we must follow it.**
    Come, let us bow down our heads and pray to God.
    Let us kneel before the God who made us.
    He is our God. We are his people. He loves us.
    **If today we hear God's voice in our hearts, we must follow it.**
    Today if you hear the voice of God in your hearts, follow it.
    Do not grumble or argue the way the people in the desert did
    when everything didn't go the way they expected it to.
    **If today we hear God's voice in our hearts, we must follow it.**
                    —based on Psalm 95

63  **This is the day the Lord has made.**
    **Let us rejoice and be glad in it.**
    Again today we come together to worship—
    the God of creation, of salvation,
    of time and eternity;
    the God of all peoples, of all nations,
    of all conditions of people everywhere.
    **Praise the Lord.**
    **All that is within me,**
    **Praise God's holy name.**
    Praise the Lord and remember all his kindnesses:
    in forgiving our sins;
    in curing our diseases;
    in saving us from destruction;

in surrounding us with love.
**The Lord is full of mercy and compassion.**
**The Lord is slow to anger**
**and willing to give us gifts of love.**
**Praise the Lord!**
**Oh, all that is within me, praise the Lord.**
—based on Psalm 103:1-8; 118:24

64  For rebirth and resilience,
**blessed be God;**
for the spiritually humble,
**glory to God, hallelujah;**
for all who hunger and thirst for justice,
**praise him and magnify him forever;**
for all who are banned for speaking the truth,
**blessed be God;**
for all who triumph over their bitter circumstance
**glory to God, hallelujah;**
for all who risk reputation, livelihood, and life itself
for Christ's sake and the gospel;
**all praise and all glory; this is God's kingdom;**
**praise him and love him forever.**

65  You are the great God—the one who is in heaven.
It is you, shield of truth,
it is you, tower of truth,
it is you, bush of truth,
it is you, who sits in the highest,
**you are the creator of life,**
**you made the regions above.**
The creator who made the heavens also,
the maker of the stars and the Pleiades—
the shooting stars declare it to us.
The trumpet speaks—for us it calls.
You are the hunter who hunts for souls;
you are the leader who goes before us;
you are the great mantle that covers us.
**You are he whose hands are wounded;**
**you are he whose feet are wounded;**
**you are he whose blood is a trickling stream—and why?**
**You are he whose blood was spilled for us.**
For this great price we call,
for your own place we call.

66  God of the past, who has created and nurtured us,
**we are here to thank you.**
God of the future, who is always ahead of us,
**we are here to thank you.**

God of the present, who is here in the midst of us,
**we are here to thank you.**
God of life, who is beyond us and within us,
**we rejoice in your glorious love.**

67  We come to worship God in our need,
**bringing with us the needs of the world.**
We come to God, who comes to us in Jesus,
**and who knows by experience what human life is like.**
We come with our faith and with our doubts,
**we come with our hopes and with our fears.**
We come as we are because it is God who invites us to come,
**and God has promised never to turn us away.**

68  God, who has called you into fellowship
with his Son, Jesus Christ, our Lord, is faithful.
**He is a faithful Lord, keeping his covenant of love**
**to a thousand generations of those who love him**
**and keep his commands.**
His faithfulness reaches to the skies
and continues throughout all generations on into eternity.
**We therefore praise the faithfulness**
**of our Lord Jesus Christ in this assembly, saying,**
**"Great is your faithfulness!**
**We will exalt and praise your name,**
**for in perfect faithfulness you have done marvelous things.**
**Great is your faithfulness to us, O Lord, our God."**

69  Our worship is in the name of the Father,
**the one eternal God in whom we live**
**and move and have our being,**
and of the Son,
**our crucified and risen Lord, Jesus Christ,**
**through whom the love of God**
**is made manifest among us,**
and of the Holy Spirit,
**the Counselor by whom we become**
**the people of God and**
**the church of Jesus Christ.**

70  *A text especially mindful of children*

Lord God,
we love you.
We trust you.
We believe in you.
We know that Jesus loves us and died for us.
We know that you never leave us.
Today, we celebrate together
because of everything you have done for us!

71 **Lord, you are present even before we invoke your presence,**
**your Spirit bestowed at Pentecost promised to us always.**
**So we rejoice in your presence and your promise,**
**and we ask you to move among us as we worship together.**

You know our cares and our concerns;
you know our trials and tribulations;
you know our joys and our sorrows.
And in all that we are, we are nothing without you.

**So today we come to you in worship**
**from a multitude of moments,**
**from a variety of backgrounds,**
**from all walks of living, yet one in the Spirit.**

And we humbly give thanks,
that the promises we count upon
remain true today,
as they have for generation upon generation.

**Your mercies are great and everlasting, O Lord,**
**and we give thanks. Amen.**

72 O Lord, our Lord,
there are many places we could go this morning,
**but we have desired to come to your house.**
There are many voices to which we can listen today,
**but we desire to hear your voice.**
It would be easy to scatter,
**but we have chosen to gather.**
We need to behold your beauty,
**to inquire in your temple,**
to be wrapped in your love,
**and to experience your renewing Spirit.**
Come close, Lord Jesus,
**to fill us and renew us. Amen.**

# SECTION 2
# CONFESSION AND ASSURANCE

Our God longs for honesty and holiness within the promise-based relationship God has established with us in Christ. In a culture that avoids talk of sin and culpability, regular prayers of confession foster honesty and openness in our relationship with God. Just as a marriage cannot flourish without honest confession, so our marriage-like relationship with God cannot flourish unless we freely and honestly express all facets of our life: hopes, fears, sins, desires, thanksgiving, and praise.

Blessed by God's providence, we don't offer our prayers of confession in a spiritual vacuum with a remote hope that some god or higher power will listen and forgive. We confess sin in the context of the covenant Lord's love shown to us through Jesus Christ. We offer our confession as part of a covenantal relationship. For this reason, the confession and assurance part of a worship service is often the most explicitly dialogic, alternating between God's words to us and our words to God. We

confess sin when prompted by God's gracious invitation. Then we hear the strong declaration of God's forgiveness in Christ. And we respond in joyful gratitude with praise and dedication.

The confession part of the service is like a picture of our relationship with God. Participating in this alternating pattern of God's words and our response shapes our faith over time to highlight the tenacity and graciousness of God's covenantal love.

# 2.1 CALL TO CONFESSION

*The call to confession invites us to honest expression within the context of our covenant relationship with God. God's grace comes to us, creating a relationship with us in Christ in which honesty about our sin is welcome and safe. We confess our sin not in order for God to forgive us but because God has forgiven us in Christ. The call to confession, therefore, is a word of grace like the assurance of pardon, not an exercise that shames us into confession.*

*The reading of God's law—the Ten Commandments, the summary of the law from Matthew 22, or a similar text—may also serve as a call to confession. God's law helps us to recognize human sinfulness even as the law provides a trustworthy guide for Christian living (see also section 2.8, Dedication).*

*Most of the texts here are drawn directly from Scripture, helping us hear the call to confession as God's invitation. Any of these texts may be followed by the words*

Let us confess our sin before God and one another.

1   The psalmist testifies:

Happy are those whose transgression is forgiven,
   whose sin is covered.
Happy are those to whom the LORD imputes no iniquity,
   and in whose spirit there is no deceit.
While I kept silence, my body wasted away
   through my groaning all day long.
For day and night your hand was heavy upon me;
   my strength was dried up as by the heat of summer.
Then I acknowledged my sin to you,
   and I did not hide my iniquity;
I said, "I will confess my transgressions to the LORD,"
   and you forgave the guilt of my sin.
Therefore let all who are faithful offer prayer to you.
   —from Psalm 32:1-6, NRSV

2   The psalmist testifies:

Come and hear, all you who fear God,
   and I will tell what he has done for me.
If I had cherished iniquity in my heart,
   the Lord would not have listened.
But truly God has listened;
   he has given heed to the words of my prayer.
Blessed be God,
   because he has not rejected my prayer
   or removed his steadfast love from me.

In the strength of this assurance, let us confess our sins to God.
   —based on Psalm 66:16, 18-20, NRSV

**3**    The psalmist models a transparent faith with these words:

Search me, O God, and know my heart;
    test me and know my thoughts.
See if there is any wicked way in me,
    and lead me in the way everlasting.

We express our longing for God's leading
by our own transparent confession.
     —based on Psalm 139:23-24, NRSV

**4**    "Come now, let us settle the matter,"
    says the LORD.
"Though your sins are like scarlet,
    they shall be as white as snow;
though they are red as crimson,
    they shall be like wool."
     —Isaiah 1:18, NIV

**5**    In repentance and rest is your salvation,
    in quietness and trust is your strength,
    but you would have none of it.
Yet the LORD longs to be gracious to you;
    therefore he will rise up to show you compassion.
For the LORD is a God of justice.
    Blessed are all who wait for him!
     —Isaiah 30:15, 18, NIV

**6**    Our Lord Jesus said:

"'You shall love the Lord your God
with all your heart,
and with all your soul,
and with all your mind.'
This is the greatest and first commandment.
And a second is like it:
'You shall love your neighbor as yourself.'
On these two commandments
hang all the law and the prophets."

As God has instructed us in these great commandments,
and because we have not lived in full obedience,
let us now confess our sins to God,
trusting Christ as our Savior and Lord.
     —based on Matthew 22:37-40, NRSV

**7**    The proof of God's amazing love is this:
While we were sinners, Christ died for us.
Let us therefore approach the throne of grace with boldness,
so that we may receive mercy and find grace to help in time of need.
Trusting in God's faithfulness and compassion,
let us confess our sin before God and one another.
     —based on Romans 5:8; Hebrews 4:16, NRSV

**8**      We know that nothing is able to separate us
from the love of God in Jesus Christ.
Let us in freedom confess the wrong we have done.
      —based on Romans 8:39

**9**      Seeing that we have a great High Priest
who has entered the inmost heaven, Jesus the Son of God,
let us therefore approach the throne of grace with fullest confidence,
that we may receive mercy for our failures
and grace to help in the hour of need.
In the strength of this assurance, let us confess our sins to God.
      —based on Hebrews 4:14, 16

**10**     Since we have confidence
to enter the sanctuary by the blood of Jesus,
by the new and living way that he opened for us
through the curtain (that is, through his flesh),
and since we have a great priest over the house of God,
let us approach with a true heart in full assurance of faith,
with our hearts sprinkled clean from an evil conscience
and our bodies washed with pure water.
      —Hebrews 10:19-22, NRSV

**11**     This is the message we have heard
from him and declare to you:
God is light; in him there is no darkness at all.
**If we claim to have fellowship with him
and yet walk in the darkness,
we lie and do not live out the truth.
But if we walk in the light, as he is in the light,
we have fellowship with one another,
and the blood of Jesus, his Son, purifies us from all sin.**
      —1 John 1:5-7, NIV

**12**     God's Word assures us:

If we say that we have no sin,
we deceive ourselves, and the truth is not in us.
If we confess our sins,
he who is faithful and just will forgive us our sins
and cleanse us from all unrighteousness.

In humility and faith let us confess our sin to God.
      —based on 1 John 1:8-9, NRSV

**13**     The apostle John wrote:

My little children,
I am writing these things to you
so that you may not sin.
But if anyone does sin,

we have an advocate with the Father,
Jesus Christ the righteous;
and he is the atoning sacrifice for our sins,
and not for ours only but also for the sins of the whole world.

In the strength of this assurance,
let us confess our sins to God.
  —based on 1 John 2:1-2, NRSV

14 We cannot come before God
unless we are first honest with ourselves
about who we are,
about the mistakes we make,
and about how well or poorly we care for others.
In this spirit, let us offer our prayers to God.

15 When we see God's beautiful holiness,
we recognize our own lack of holiness.
God is light and truth,
yet we live among shadows and lies.
People of God, let us acknowledge who and whose we are;
let us ask our powerful God to illumine us with grace and truth in Jesus, our Lord.

16 When we gather to praise God,
we remember that we are people
who have preferred our wills to his.
Accepting his power to become new persons in Christ,
let us confess our sin before God and one another.

17 In spite of God's love for us and gift of love to us,
we often act in destructive and hateful ways.
We close our hearts to God and disobey God's law.
Together let us confess our sin.

# 2.2 PRAYERS OF CONFESSION

*The prayer of confession invites us to speak words that are remarkably honest about our own sin, words that do not come naturally in our relationship with God or with our fellow human beings. Such honesty, perhaps more than we could ever generate in our own strength, becomes remarkably liberating when we sense the immensity of God's grace. In this way we can think of the prayer of confession (and of the assurance of pardon that follows) not as an onerous obligation but as a gift of grace.*

*A full prayer of confession acknowledges that our sin is more than an isolated example of bad judgment. We are sinful people, and we live in need of a Savior. Our confession also acknowledges that sin infects not just persons but also societies, institutions, and all of creation. Along with the confession of personal sins, we confess our participation in the structures and institutions in which evil persists.*

*Even as we confess our sin, we are claiming God's promises in Christ, which are sealed in our baptism. Many classical prayers of confession thus feature a decisive turn from honest confession to explicit profession of faith and trust in Christ.*

*The biblical psalms, especially the penitential psalms, model for us the kind of soul-searching honesty and integrity that should mark our prayers of confession. Many of these psalms themselves, either spoken or sung, may serve as prayers of confession today.*

*In preparing a prayer of confession, consider what kind of expression of penitence most compellingly expands on the imagery , metaphors, or keywords in the Scripture readings prominent in the worship service. Also consider incorporating an expectant silence before, during, or after the prayer of confession to allow worshipers to meditate on the poignant words of confession.*

*In some traditions the confession and assurance immediately precede the opening greeting and songs of praise. In others, the confession and assurance follow the sermon or the prayers of the people and immediately precede the Lord's Supper. Either may be appropriate, depending on the pastoral context of the service.*

## Refrains

*The following refrains may be repeated at various appropriate points or at the close of an extemporaneous prayer of confession.*

1  Help us, O God of our salvation,
      for the glory of your name;
   **deliver us, and forgive our sins,**
      **for your name's sake.**
            —Psalm 79:9, NRSV

2  Restore us, O LORD God of hosts;
      **let your face shine, that we may be saved.**
            —Psalm 80:19, NRSV

3  *This simple refrain from the early church, the* Kyrie eleison, *presented here in both Greek and English, expresses both confession and lament and may be spoken or sung at the conclusion of a prayer of confession.*

   **Lord, have mercy.**        *Kyrie eleison.*
   **Christ, have mercy.**       *Christe eleison.*
   **Lord, have mercy.**        *Kyrie eleison.*

**4**   *This simple refrain from the early church is called the* Trisagion, *which roughly means "three times holy." It may be spoken or sung at the conclusion of a prayer of confession.*

**Holy God,**
**holy and mighty,**
**holy immortal One,**
**have mercy on us.**

**5**   *This traditional prayer for forgiveness is called the* Agnus Dei, *which is Latin for "Lamb of God." Though traditionally used in conjunction with the Lord's Supper, it may also be spoken or sung at the conclusion of a prayer of confession.*

**Lamb of God, you take away the sin of the world, have mercy on us.**
**Lamb of God, you take away the sin of the world, have mercy on us.**
**Lamb of God, you take away the sin of the world, grant us your peace.**

## Scriptural Prayers

**6**   Be mindful of your mercy, O LORD,
        and of your steadfast love,
    for they have been from of old.
Do not remember the sins of my youth or my transgressions;
      according to your steadfast love remember me,
    for your goodness' sake, O LORD!
Good and upright is the LORD;
      therefore he instructs sinners in the way.
For your name's sake, O LORD,
      pardon my guilt, for it is great.
Turn to me and be gracious to me,
      for I am lonely and afflicted.
Relieve the troubles of my heart,
      and bring me out of my distress.
Consider my affliction and my trouble,
      and forgive all my sins.
        —Psalm 25:6-8, 11, 16-18, NRSV

*The following three resources draw from two penitential psalms (Ps. 51, 130). Additional texts may draw from the other penitential psalms as well (Ps. 6, 32, 38, 102, 143).*

**7**   Have mercy on me, O God, in your faithful love,
in your great tenderness wipe away my offences;
wash me thoroughly from my guilt,
purify me from my sin.
For I am well aware of my offences,
my sin is constantly in mind.
Against you, you alone, I have sinned,
I have done what you see to be wrong,
that you may show your saving justice when you pass sentence,

and your victory may appear when you give judgment,
remember, I was born guilty,
a sinner from the moment of conception.
But you delight in sincerity of heart,
and in secret you teach me wisdom.
God, create in me a clean heart,
renew within me a resolute spirit,
do not thrust me away from your presence,
do not take away from me your spirit of holiness.
Give me back the joy of your salvation,
sustain in me a generous spirit.
Lord, open my lips,
and my mouth will speak out your praise.
Sacrifice gives you no pleasure,
burnt offering you do not desire.
Sacrifice to God is a broken spirit,
a broken, contrite heart you never scorn.
> —Psalm 51:1-6, 10-12, 15-17, NJB

8  Have mercy on me, O God,
      according to your steadfast love;
   according to your abundant mercy
      blot out my transgressions.
   **Wash me thoroughly from my iniquity,**
      **and cleanse me from my sin.**
   For I know my transgressions,
      and my sin is ever before me.
   **Against you, you alone, have I sinned,**
      **and done what is evil in your sight,**
   **so that you are justified in your sentence**
      **and blameless when you pass judgment.**
   You desire truth in the inward being;
      therefore teach me wisdom in my secret heart.
   **Hide your face from my sins,**
      **and blot out all my iniquities.**
   Create in me a clean heart, O God,
      and put a new and right spirit within me.
   **Do not cast me from your presence,**
      **and do not take your holy spirit from me.**
   > —Psalm 51:1-4, 6, 9-11, NRSV

9  Out of the depths I cry to you, O LORD.
      **Lord, hear my voice!**
   Let your ears be attentive
      to the voice of my supplications!
   **If you, O LORD, should mark iniquities,**
      **Lord, who could stand?**
   But there is forgiveness with you,

so that you may be revered.
**I wait for the LORD, my soul waits,**
    **and in his word I hope;**
**my soul waits for the Lord**
        **more than those who watch for the morning,**
        **more than those who watch for the morning.**
O Israel, hope in the LORD!
    For with the LORD there is steadfast love,
    and with him is great power to redeem.
It is he who will redeem Israel
    from all its iniquities.
—Psalm 130, NRSV

10    O Lord, great God,
    all holy, Father most gracious,
    filled with mercy and steadfast love,
    we are embarrassed to come before you,
    for we have preferred the ways of this world to your ways,
    for we have rebelled against your wisdom
    and we have gotten into trouble,
    for we have rejected your fatherly guidance
    and have gotten lost altogether.
    To you belongs righteousness, O Lord,
    and to us confusion of face.
    O Lord, great God,
    all holy, filled with awe,
    Father, most gracious,
    filled with mercy and steadfast love,
    incline your ear to our troubles.
    Hear us when we pour out our sorrows before you.
    Forgive us,
    not on the ground of our own righteousness,
    but on the ground of your great mercy.
    On the ground of your great mercy
    in the gift of your Son, Jesus Christ.
    It is in his name that we pray,
    for he is our Savior and the mediator of the covenant of grace. **Amen.**
        —based on Daniel 9:4-19

## General Prayers of Confession

11    **Merciful God,**
    **we confess that we have sinned against you**
    **in thought, word, and deed,**
    **by what we have done,**
    **and by what we have left undone.**
    **We have not loved you**
    **with our whole heart and mind and strength.**

We have not loved our neighbors as ourselves.
In your mercy forgive what we have been,
help us amend what we are,
and direct what we shall be,
so that we may delight in your will
and walk in your ways,
to the glory of your holy name.
Through Christ, our Lord. Amen.

12    Almighty and merciful God,
we have erred and strayed from your ways like lost sheep.
We have followed too much
the devices and desires of our own hearts.
We have offended against your holy laws.
We have left undone those things which we ought to have done;
and we have done those things which we ought not to have done.
O Lord, have mercy upon us.
Spare those who confess their faults.
Restore those who are penitent,
according to your promises declared to the world
in Christ Jesus, our Lord.
And grant, O merciful God, for his sake,
that we may live a holy, just, and humble life
to the glory of your holy name. **Amen.**

13    Holy and merciful God,
in your presence we confess
our sinfulness, our shortcomings,
and our offenses against you.
You alone know how often we have sinned
in wandering from your ways,
in wasting your gifts,
in forgetting your love.
Have mercy on us, O Lord,
for we are ashamed and sorry
for all we have done to displease you.
Forgive our sins,
and help us to live in your light
and walk in your ways,
for the sake of Jesus Christ, our Savior. **Amen.**

14    Merciful God,
you pardon all who truly repent and turn to you.
We humbly confess our sins and ask your mercy.
We have not loved you with a pure heart,
nor have we loved our neighbor as ourselves.
We have not done justice, loved kindness,
or walked humbly with you, our God.

Have mercy on us, O God, in your loving-kindness.
In your great compassion,
cleanse us from our sin.
**Create in us a clean heart, O God,
and renew a right spirit within us.
Do not cast us from your presence,
or take your Holy Spirit from us.
Restore to us the joy of your salvation
and sustain us with your bountiful Spirit
through Jesus Christ, our Lord. Amen.**
　　　　—based on Psalm 51:10-12

15　Gracious God,
our sins are too heavy to carry,
too real to hide,
and too deep to undo.
Forgive what our lips tremble to name,
what our hearts can no longer bear,
and what has become for us
a consuming fire of judgment.
Set us free from a past that we cannot change;
open to us a future in which we can be changed;
and grant us grace
to grow more and more in your likeness and image;
through Jesus Christ, the light of the world. **Amen.**

16　Merciful God,
in your gracious presence
we confess our sin and the sin of this world.
Although Christ is among us as our peace,
we are a people divided against ourselves
as we cling to the values of a broken world.
The profit and pleasures we pursue
lay waste the land and pollute the seas.
The fears and jealousies that we harbor
set neighbor against neighbor
and nation against nation.
We abuse your good gifts of imagination and freedom,
of intellect and reason,
and turn them into bonds of oppression.
Lord, have mercy upon us;
heal and forgive us.
Set us free to serve you in the world
as agents of your reconciling love in Jesus Christ. **Amen.**

17　O gracious and gentle and condescending God,
God of peace, Father of mercy, God of all comfort:
we confess before you the evil of our hearts;

we acknowledge that we are too inclined
toward anger, jealousy, and revenge,
to ambition and pride,
which often give rise to discord and bitter feelings
between others and us.
Too often have we thus both offended and grieved you,
O long-suffering Father.
Forgive us this sin and permit us to partake of the blessing
you have promised the peacemakers,
who shall be called the children of God.
Through Jesus Christ, our Lord. **Amen.**

18　Awesome and compassionate God,
you have loved us with unfailing, self-giving mercy,
but we have not loved you.
You constantly call us, but we do not listen.
You ask us to love, but we walk away from neighbors in need,
wrapped in our own concerns.
We condone evil, prejudice, warfare, and greed.
God of grace, as you come to us in mercy,
we repent in spirit and in truth,
admit our sin, and gratefully receive your forgiveness
through Jesus Christ, our Redeemer. **Amen.**

19　Eternal and merciful God,
you have loved us with a love beyond our understanding,
and you have set us on paths of righteousness for your name's sake.
Yet we have strayed from your way;
we have sinned against you in thought, word, and deed,
through what we have done and what we have left undone.
As we remember the lavish gift of your grace
symbolized in baptism, O God,
we praise you and give you thanks that you forgive us yet again.
Grant us now, we pray, the grace to die daily to sin,
and to rise daily to new life in Christ,
who lives and reigns with you,
and in whose strong name we pray. **Amen.**

20　Almighty God, we confess how hard it is to be your people.
You have called us to be the church,
to continue the mission of Jesus Christ to our lonely and confused world.
Yet we acknowledge we are more apathetic than active,
isolated than involved, callous than compassionate,
obstinate than obedient, legalistic than loving.
Gracious Lord, have mercy upon us and forgive our sins.
Remove the obstacles preventing us
from being your representatives to a broken world.
Awaken our hearts to the promised gift of your indwelling Spirit.
This we pray in Jesus' powerful name. **Amen.**

21 Lord, you showed us true humility by becoming one of us,
   **yet too often we practice pride.**
   You cried alongside your friends and for the city of Jerusalem,
   **yet too often we rush past the pain of others and are careless about our cities.**
   You loved those who were weak, despised, or cast out,
   **yet too often we love those who are strong, respected, or popular.**
   You freely forgave and healed,
   **yet too often we hold grudges and cause pain.**
   You lived a perfectly holy life,
   **yet too often we do not yearn for righteousness.**
   You prayed that we who believe in you should be united with each other and you,
   **yet too often we focus on the differences that separate us from other believers.**
   You were mocked, whipped, and even killed for us,
   **yet too often we deny you.**
   You call us to be the salt of the earth and the light of the world,
   **yet too often we blend into or hide from our culture.**
   **Forgive us, Lord, so that we will shine with your glory. Amen.**

22 Often, O holy and righteous God,
       we dare your justice,
       mock your mercy,
       jeer your patience,
       slight your power, and
       show contempt for your love.
   We even say "I'm sorry" insincerely and confess our sin flippantly.
   We plead your help
       to own up carefully to how we have wronged you,
       to admit honestly how we have grieved you,
       to plead penitently for your mercy and pardon.
   We beg your forgiveness through Jesus Christ, our Savior and Lord. **Amen.**
       —based on a prayer by John Bunyan (1628-88)

23 Father, we are sorry for the many times we have left you
   and chosen to satisfy our own selfish desires.
   For the times we have hurt the members of our families
   by refusing to do our share of the family tasks.
   **Father, we have sinned. Forgive us.**
   For the times we were unkind and impatient with those who needed our time and
   concern.
   **Father, we have sinned. Forgive us.**
   For the times we were too weak to stand up for what was right
   and allowed others to suffer because of our cowardice.
   **Father, we have sinned. Forgive us.**
   For the times we refused to forgive others.
   **Father, we have sinned. Forgive us.**

24   O God of shalom,
      we have built up walls to protect ourselves from our enemies,
      but those walls also shut us off from receiving your love.
      Break down those walls.
      Help us to see that the way to your heart
      is through the reconciliation of our own hearts with our enemies.
      Bless them and us,
      that we may come to grow in love for each other and for you,
      through Jesus Christ. **Amen.**

25   Wondrous God,
      who sets suns and moons above us,
      mountains and valleys beneath us,
      and friends and strangers among us:
      how often have we tried to hide from your presence,
      how seldom have we looked for your creating face
      and your fashioning hand!
      **Lord, have mercy upon us.**

      Wondrous God,
      who took upon yourself flesh of our flesh in Jesus our brother,
      and being found in human form made the ultimate disclosure of yourself
      in the face of Jesus Christ:
      how often we have forgotten you,
      how seldom have we really loved and followed you!
      **Christ, have mercy upon us.**

      Wondrous God,
      who pours out freely the Holy Spirit:
      how often have we ignored your promptings,
      how seldom have we asked for your help or accepted your gifts!
      **Lord, have mercy upon us. Amen.**

26   Holy God, we groan at our weaknesses, and we ask forgiveness.
      Your Word is so clear, and your grace is so good.
      But we close our ears to your call,
      and with our perverse pride we foul the gifts you have given us.
      Like your servant Paul, we know what you require of us;
      yet, like Paul, what we do is not the good we want to do,
      and the evil we do not want to do, that evil we keep on doing.
      We mistreat those we love,
      and we dishonor you, the One who made us.
      How long, O Lord, will we continue to ignore your will?
      Yet you provide streams of living mercy;
      you invite us again and again to live renewed lives.
      So we turn once again to the cross,
      to the empty cross, to the stone rolled away,
      to our interceding Lord Jesus Christ seated at your right hand,
      to the gracious gift of your Spirit.

We seek your forgiveness through Jesus Christ, our Savior.
We draw upon your promises,
and we ask once again simply for mercy.
With your Holy Spirit, sanctify us.
Hear our prayer, O Lord, for we ask it in Christ's name. **Amen.**

27    O Lord, our hearts are heavy with the violence of our world,
so much suffering through the ages,
wars and holocausts, genocide and abuse.
We cry on behalf of our violent world:
**Lord, have mercy.**
O Lord, you love and care for us as a parent;
you came to share life with us as a brother.
But we confess we have failed to live as your children
and instead have broken many bonds.
We cry on behalf of our violent world:
**Lord, have mercy.**
O Lord, you have called us to live together in community,
to consider one another as brother and sister,
regardless of ethnicity, economic status, or popularity.
Yet we prejudge one another,
refuse to love one another,
and victimize one another.
We cry on behalf of our violent world:
**Lord, have mercy.**
O Lord, giver of all life,
you fearfully and wonderfully made us
and breathed into our nostrils the breath of life.
Yet we endanger the lives of one another,
abuse the lives of young children among us,
destroy those who are defenseless,
and oppress those who are powerless.
We cry on behalf of our violent world:
**Lord, have mercy.**
**Pardon us through Jesus Christ, our Savior. Amen.**

28    To you, Holy God, we confess our sin
with as much shame and sorrow as we can muster.
We know it won't be enough
because we are on easy terms with our sin.
We confess to you, O God,
that we deceive ourselves about our sin,
and then we deceive ourselves about
whether we deceive ourselves,
slipping and sliding and sidestepping the truth.
O God, you are holy beyond all that we can think or imagine.
You are the source of righteousness,
the overflowing fountain of goodness.

You made us to be like you
in knowledge, righteousness, and holiness.
And yet here we are, so often soiled,
smudged, distracted from your purposes,
and running after the gods of this world.
Please forgive and restore us through Jesus, your Son. **Amen.**

29  O Lord our God, you have searched us and known us.
You know not only what we say, but also what we think.
You know not only what we say, but also what we almost said.
You know how quickly our thoughts rise to praise ourselves
because we are well-off or good-looking or healthy or smart,
boasting of your gifts as if they were our accomplishments.
You know how slowly our thoughts sink to accuse ourselves
even when we have turned our backs on you,
fascinating ourselves with alien gods
whose calling we heed while ignoring your own.
Quickly boasting, slowly accusing, truly we need to repent.
O God, forgive, correct, and heal us through Jesus Christ, our Lord. **Amen.**

30  Merciful God,
for the things we have done that we regret,
**forgive us;**
for the things we have failed to do that we regret,
**forgive us;**
for all the times we have acted without love,
**forgive us;**
for all the times we have reacted without thought,
**forgive us;**
for all the times we have withdrawn care,
**forgive us;**
for all the times we have failed to forgive,
**forgive us.**
For hurtful words said and helpful words unsaid,
for unfinished tasks
and unfulfilled hopes,
**God of all time,**
**forgive us and help us**
**to lay down our burden of regret. Amen.**

31  Forgive us our sins, O Lord.
Forgive us the sins of our youth and the sins of our age,
the sins of our soul and the sins of our body,
our secret and our whispering sins,
our presumptuous and our careless sins,
the sins we have done to please ourselves,
and the sins we have done to please others.
Forgive us the sins that we know,

and the sins that we know not;
forgive them, O Lord,
forgive them all because of your great goodness.
Through Jesus Christ, our Lord. **Amen.**

32   Gracious God,
you have given us the law of Moses and the teachings of Jesus
to direct us in the way of life.
You offer us your Holy Spirit
so that we can be born to new life as your children.
Yet, O God, we confess that the ways of death have a strong attraction
and that we often succumb to their lure.
Give us the vision and courage to choose and nurture life,
that we may receive your blessing. **Amen.**

33   God of birth, God of joy, God of life,
we come to you as a people hungry for good news.
We have been so dead to miracles
that we have missed the world's rebirth.
We have preoccupied ourselves with pleasures
and have overlooked the joy you offer us.
We have been so concerned with making a living
that we have missed the life you set among us.
Forgive us, gracious God.
Open our eyes and our hearts to receive your gift;
open our lips and hands to share it with all humanity
in the name of our Savior, Jesus Christ. **Amen.**

34   For the times we have lied to one another
and the times we have been lied to,
**heal us, Jesus, Savior of the world.**
For the times we have laughed at another's pain
and the times we have been laughed at,
**heal us, Jesus, Savior of the world.**
For the times we have spoken when we should have remained silent
and the times we have remained silent when we should have spoken,
**heal us, Jesus, Savior of the world.**
For the times we have not respected another's freedom
to be different from us,
**heal us, Jesus, Savior of the world.**
For the times we have betrayed a friend
and the times we have been betrayed,
**heal us, Jesus, Savior of the world.**

**O God of heaven and earth,**
**you emptied yourself of your power**
**and became a helpless baby**
**in order that you might heal the sick world.**
**Teach us to empty ourselves of the things**

that destroy us and keep us alone.
Empty us of our jealousy,
of our meanness,
of our fear of others.
For Jesus' sake. Amen.

35  Loving God,
we confess before you and each other
that our lives are not pure and holy
apart from the cleansing we have from the work of Christ.
And we confess that too often Christ in us is hidden by our actions
that wound rather than heal,
that tear down rather than build up.
Open our eyes,
that we may see you in the ones we say we love.
Open our ears,
that we may be quicker to listen than to speak.
Open our mouths
to speak good rather than evil of our neighbors.
Open our hands
in generosity and help us let go of clenched fists.
Open our hearts
to a desire to follow Jesus in full obedience
to your will and your way.
We pray trusting in your forgiveness and
in the power of your Holy Spirit to lead and guide us
in paths of justice and righteousness
for your name's sake. **Amen.**

36  Lord, we cry to you to heal our wounds.
We call to you in distress and plead for your salvation.
We have sinned against your law and failed to do your will;
we confess that we've disobeyed your holy Word.
We pray, purge our lives of selfishness and our hearts of bitterness.
Lead us back to righteousness; save us through Jesus Christ. **Amen.**
—based on a text of Ulrich Zwingli (1529)

37  Eternal God, we confess that often we have failed
to be an obedient church:
we have not done your will;
we have broken your law;
we have rebelled against your love;
we have not loved our neighbors;
we have not heard the cry of the needy.
Forgive us, we pray.
Free us for joyful obedience.
Through Jesus Christ, our Lord. **Amen.**

38 Holy and merciful God,
   for the times we have followed the path of the wicked,
   stood in solidarity with those who were wrong,
   or sat quietly and allowed sin to happen, forgive us.
   Help us to meditate, even delight, in your Word
   so that we will flourish with the fruit of your Spirit. **Amen.**

39 Almighty God,
   so many of King David's psalms show a heart out of tune,
   sighing, crying, and breaking with sorrow,
   yet still clinging to faith in you.
   So too, O Lord, are our hearts.
   In Jesus Christ, you have given us what we need most:
   his cross makes our forgiveness possible,
   and his Spirit tunes our hearts again to sing your praises.
   Humbly we beg your pardon for our sins.
   Eagerly we plead your help
   to enthrone in our hearts David's Son:
   Christ Jesus, King of the universe,
   our Savior and Lord.
   And with King David we declare our trust in your unfailing love. **Amen.**

40 Righteous Father,
   we who own more than we use,
   proclaim more than we experience,
   and request more than we need,
   come asking your forgiveness.
   We seek your salvation, then act like we save ourselves.
   We beg your forgiveness, then repeat our errors.
   We experience your grace, then act defeated.
   We rely on your power, but only in hard times.
   We have become confused and misguided.
   Forgive our every defection.
   Bring us to an unbroken commitment
   and a steady trust,
   through Jesus Christ, who is the way of hope,
   the truth of God,
   and the life of love,
   now and always. **Amen.**

41 Jesus, friend of sinners, your words to your disciples were plain:
   Whatever we did for the least of our brothers and sisters,
   we did for you.
   But have we fed the hungry,
   invited in the stranger,
   clothed those whose garments were thread-bare,
   looked after the sick,
   visited the incarcerated?
   In your mercy, Lord, please forgive us. **Amen.**

42  God of love, in the wrong we have done
    and in the good we have not done,
    we have sinned in ignorance;
    we have sinned in weakness;
    we have sinned through our own deliberate fault.
    We are truly sorry.
    We repent and turn to you.
    Forgive us
    and renew our lives
    through Jesus Christ, our Lord. **Amen.**

43  For self-righteousness that will not compromise,
    and from selfishness that gains by the manipulation of others,
    **forgive us, O God.**
    For the lust of money or power that drives to kill,
    **forgive us, O God.**
    For the arrogance and thoughtlessness
    that abuses your good creation,
    **forgive us, O God.**
    For trusting in the weapons of war
    and mistrusting the councils of peace,
    **forgive us, O God.**
    For hearing, believing, and speaking lies about other nations,
    **forgive us, O God.**
    For suspicions and fears
    that stand in the way of reconciliation,
    **forgive us, O God.**
    For words and deeds that encourage discord,
    perpetuate racist assumptions,
    sexist stereotypes, and classist attitudes—
    for everything that contributes to oppression,
    **forgive us, O God. Amen.**

44  Merciful God,
    you made us in your image,
    with a mind to know you,
    a heart to love you,
    and a will to serve you.
    But our knowledge is imperfect,
    our love inconstant,
    our obedience incomplete.
    Day by day, we fail to grow into your likeness.
    In your tender love, forgive us
    through Jesus Christ, our Lord. **Amen.**

*100*

45  Lord, sometimes our lives have such little focus:
    we have so much to do;
    we possess so much stuff;
    we're driven by the need for still more—
    and it easily seems to control us.
    We're sorry, Lord, for how distracted we've become
    and for losing our way
    without even realizing it.
    Forgive us and help us
    to know that you are the only one we need. **Amen.**

46  God of love and justice,
    we long for peace within and peace without.
    We long for harmony in our families,
    for serenity in the midst of struggle.
    We long for the day when our homes
    will be a dwelling place for your love.
    Yet we confess that we are often anxious,
    we do not trust each other,
    and we harbor violence.
    We are not willing to take the risks
    and make the sacrifices that love requires.
    Look upon us with kindness and grace.
    Rule in our homes and in all the world;
    show us how to walk in your paths,
    through the mercy of our Savior. **Amen.**

47  Holy God, we confess that we have not lived as you have taught us.
    We have put our longing for money, success, or happiness
    above our desire for you and your kingdom.
    We worry about what others will think, what we wear,
    how our reputation can be polished.
    We make idols out of the winning record of a sport team,
    the next promotion at work, the perfect family,
    the cleanliness of our house, or the latest technology.
    We are careless with our words, saying things we don't mean,
    things that are hurtful to our children or friends.
    We are so busy with our lives
    that we forget our every breath depends on you.
    While we waste time on meaningless activities,
    we fail to recognize moments of grace throughout our day.
    We indulge in hateful thoughts against those we feel have offended us,
    and we are indifferent toward the suffering in our own neighborhoods.
    We forget that all people bear your image.
    In an effort to look better, we compare ourselves to others.
    We take advantage of weakness and are passive in the face of injustice.
    For personal gain and reputation, we lie blatantly, and we lie by omission.
    We would rather blame others unjustly than accept fault.

We long for what is not ours and begrudge the blessings of others.
Forgive us for thinking of ourselves before others and before you.
Free us from unreasonable expectations of ourselves and others,
from the need to compete, and from loss of perspective
so that we may glorify you in all we think, say, and do. **Amen.**

48    Our Father, forgive us for thinking small thoughts of you
and for ignoring your immensity and greatness.
Lord Jesus, forgive us when we forget that you rule
the nations and our small lives.
Holy Spirit, we offend you in minimizing your power
and squandering your gifts.
We confess that our blindness to your glory, O triune God,
has resulted in shallow confession,
tepid conviction, and only mild repentance.
Have mercy upon us.
In Jesus' name. **Amen.**

49    There are many times we think we love you well, O God.
But upon hearing your call to love you with all our heart,
and all our mind, and all our strength,
we confess that our love for you is a diluted love,
made insipid and flat by lesser loyalties and a divided heart.
Our love seems pure only for brief moments;
soon our affections are drawn away.
How easily our devotion dies.
Forgive us;
in deep mercy spare us, despite our lost first love for you;
in grace rekindle our love for you
in seeing anew Jesus' love for us. **Amen.**

50    Lord, in your mercy hear our prayer.
We confess that it is still all too easy for us
to sacrifice our convictions for convenience,
your standards for status, your principles for promotion,
your absolutes for our ambition,
our souls for shallow and unsatisfying success.
How easily we are seduced by power, prestige, pleasure,
or possessions—
seduced into violating our integrity or harming our fellowship with you.
From earth's fullest bliss we turn to you again, unfulfilled.
Forgive us our half-hearted devotion and our double-minded spirit.
In the name of him who refused to save himself we pray. **Amen.**

51    God of everlasting love,
we confess that we have been unfaithful
to our covenant with you and with one another.
We have worshiped other gods: money, power, greed, and convenience.

We have served our own self-interest
instead of serving only you and your people.
We have not loved our neighbor as you have commanded,
nor have we rightly loved ourselves.
**Forgive us, gracious God,**
**and bring us back into the fullness**
**of our covenant with you and one another.**
**Through Christ, our Lord. Amen.**

52  God of grace,
we confess that we have elevated
the things of this world above you.
We have made idols of possessions and people
and used your name for causes
that are not consistent with you and your purposes.
We have permitted our schedules to come first
and have not taken the time to worship you.
We have not always honored those who guided us in life.
We have participated in systems
that take life instead of give it.
We have been unfaithful in our covenant relationships.
We have yearned for, and sometimes taken, that which is not ours,
and we have misrepresented others' intentions.
**Forgive us, O God,**
**for the many ways we fall short of your glory.**
**Help us to learn to live together according to your ways**
**through Jesus Christ, our Lord. Amen.**

53  O God, you have shown us the way of life
through your Son, Jesus Christ.
We confess with shame our slowness to learn of him,
our failure to follow him, and our reluctance to bear the cross.
**Have mercy on us, Lord, and forgive us.**
We confess the poverty of our worship,
our neglect of fellowship and of the means of grace,
our hesitating witness for Christ,
our evasion of responsibilities in our service,
our imperfect stewardship of your gifts.
**Have mercy on us, Lord, and forgive us. Amen.**

54  When we have afflicted others,
whether by our own power
or by our silent support of systems
that oppress, enslave, and crush,
**break us, Lord.**
When we have perplexed others
and purposely confused them for our own gain
or driven them to despair,

**break us, Lord.**
When we have persecuted others,
casting them out of our community,
leaving them forsaken and alone,
**break us, Lord.**
When we have struck down others,
casting stones on their dreams and hopes
until they are destroyed,
**break us, Lord.**
Then broken, we carry in our bodies the death of Jesus
so that the life of Jesus may be made visible in our bodies;
**make us, Lord.**
With the power that belongs only to you,
make us into your treasure;
**make us, Lord.**
We are the clay, and you are the potter.
We are the work of your hands;
**make us, Lord.**
Do not be exceedingly angry
and do not remember our iniquity forever.
Now consider, we are all your people.
**Make us, Lord, through Jesus Christ, our Lord. Amen.**

## Prayers for Specific Sins

**55**  *A prayer of confession regarding indifference toward poverty*

O God, in your goodness you "defend the weak"
and "uphold the cause of the poor."
In our unholy carelessness,
we let the poor struggle on their own,
not seeing them, not caring about them, seldom asking about them.
O God, friend of the helpless, you sent
your Son to "proclaim good news to the poor."
But we care much more about those who already have enough
and ignore those who lack even the simplest essentials of life.
Holy judge of all, convict and correct us, we pray. **Amen.**

**56**  *A prayer of confession regarding the sin of racism*

God of all nations, we praise you that in Christ
the barriers that have separated humanity are torn down.
Yet we confess our slowness to open our hearts and minds
to people of other lands, tongues, and races.
Deliver us from the sins of fear and prejudice,
that we may move toward the day
when all are truly one in Jesus Christ. **Amen.**

**57**  *A prayer of confession for cynicism*

Father, you tell us in your Word
that whatever does not proceed from faith is sin.
We confess that we have frequently relaxed our faith.
We have allowed ourselves to become cynical,
and our cynicism has boiled over
with slander, criticism, prayerlessness, and pessimism.
How easily we've allowed ourselves
to crumple under the stresses of our lives.
Forgive us for our smallness of faith.
In your mercy, hear us,
for Jesus' sake. **Amen.**

**58**  *A prayer of confession about self-seeking worship*

Eternal God, you do not change.
You have revealed yourself to us in your Word.
You call us to worship you in spirit and in truth.
But we confess that we often worship
not your true self but who we wish you to be.
We too often ask you to bless what we do
rather than seeking to do what you bless.
Forgive us for seeking concessions
when we should be seeking guidance.
Forgive us when our worship shapes you into what we want
instead of shaping us into what you want.
Help us to meet you here, that we might bow
before your unspeakable majesty
and so live for you now and ever, in Christ. **Amen.**

**59**  *A prayer of confession about inadequate worship*

Lord, you have called us to worship you.
We gladly gather!
As we praise you, though,
our own inadequacy reminds us
of how we have broken our relationship with you.
Because we have sinned against you,
even our worship fails to be what it could.
We often treat it as a show.
We simply go through motions,
failing to recognize that you want to engage us deeply.
Renew us, we pray, according to your steadfast love.
Remind us of your covenant faithfulness
and have mercy on us in the name of Jesus Christ. **Amen.**

**60** *A prayer of confession regarding respect for human life*

Gracious Father, the God of life,
teach us ever more to respect and love all the lives you create.
Forgive us our lack of concern and love for those
who are yet unborn,
who are born with impairments,
who are rejected by their parents.
Teach us to open our hearts and our homes to all your children.
Forgive us when we are negligent and uncaring
for those who are elderly,
for those who are forgotten in nursing homes,
who merely exist in their old age,
who cannot afford medical care,
who suffer from a careless society.
Teach us to open our hearts,
to open our homes and churches,
to visit the lonely,
to bring your love into their lives on this earth.
Through Christ, our Lord. **Amen.**

**61** *A prayer of confession regarding misuse of the body*

Gracious Father and guardian of our lives,
teach us to guard our lives,
to treasure our bodies as temples of the Spirit.
Forgive us our misuse of food and drink,
as we eat too much or not enough,
as we drink without moderation.
Forgive us our undue reliance on drugs
and the abuse that destroys our minds and lives.
Christ Jesus, our great healer, bring healing, we pray,
to our emotions and our bodies,
to our minds and spirits.
In your name, Lord, we pray. **Amen.**

**62** *A prayer of confession regarding broken human relationships*

Almighty God and loving Father,
We thank you for placing us in covenant relationships,
in homes and families and friendships.
Forgive us for taking our vows and promises lightly.
Forgive us for the breakdown of family life,
for misdirected love and for divorces entered lightly,
for failing to give time to our families,
for failing to teach and live by your values,
for neglecting and abusing our children.
Jesus, our heavenly brother,
teach us every day to love and serve,
to cherish and protect those with whom we live.
In your name we pray. **Amen.**

**63**   *A prayer of confession about sexual sins*

Great Creator, we thank you
for the gift and mystery of our bodies.
We thank you for the gift of loving sexual intimacy.
Forgive us the misuse and abuse of that gift.
For taking it too early, with the wrong person,
for replacing love with lust,
for separating concern from self-fulfillment.
Make us pure in love, discerning in passion.
Make us choose commitment over possession.
Christ Jesus, who came to reconcile and restore all relationships,
heal and restore our fragile or broken marriages.
In your name, Lord, we pray. **Amen.**

## Prayers of Confession in Response to Specific Scriptures

**64**   *A prayer based on imagery from the Sermon on the Mount*

Loving God, you call us to be the salt of the earth,
but too often we consider your way to be bland,
and we miss the delight of life filled with flavor
that spreads from us to those around us.
**Forgive us, Lord, and help us be more like Jesus.**
You call us to be the light of the world,
but too often our actions do not bring praise to you.
We make choices that help us blend into our culture
rather than stand out as your people.
**Forgive us, Lord, and help us be more like Jesus.**
You call us to settle matters quickly,
but too often we nurse grudges
and look for ways to settle scores on our own terms.
**Forgive us, Lord, and help us be more like Jesus.**
You call us to go the second mile,
but too often we consider our own convenience first,
passing up opportunities to show love to our neighbor.
**Forgive us, Lord, and help us be more like Jesus. Amen.**

**65**   *A prayer based on Jesus' healing miracles*

Lord Jesus Christ, you came to serve.
As you came to a blind man and gave him sight,
come to us in our darkness
and show us the things we cannot see.
As you came to a man tormented in his mind
and gave him peace and healing,
come to us in our tensions and make us whole.
As you came to Lazarus, who was dead,
and brought him from the grave,
come to us in our deadness and bring us to real life

now with our living Lord.
Lord Jesus Christ, you came not to be served but to serve.
But we see life the other way round:
to get where we do not give,
to exploit whom we have not helped,
to use what we have not earned.
As you came to a dying thief and promised him paradise,
come to us now in forgiveness and give us hope.
In your name, Lord, we pray. **Amen.**

**66** *A prayer based on the teaching of Jesus*

Lord, you said, "If you love me, you will obey what I command."
**Forgive us our lukewarm love and our disobedience.**
Lord, you said, "You may ask for anything in my name."
**Forgive us when we think we need to solve
our own problems.**
Lord, you said, "Do not let your hearts be troubled and do not be afraid."
**We confess that our lives are often consumed
by worry and anxiety.**
Lord, you said, "If you remain in me and I in you,
you will bear much fruit."
**Forgive us our barren lives, Lord.**
Lord, you said, "You must testify, for you have been with me."
**We confess, Lord, that we have been too often silent.**
Lord, you said, "Love each other as I have loved you."
**In this and in so many other ways,
we confess our failures and shortcomings. Amen.**

**67** *A prayer based on the parable of the prodigal son*

O Lord, we would come to you
with the penitence of the prodigal son,
confessing that we have sinned against heaven and in your sight.
Blessed be your name!
You give freely of the bread of life to all who seek your fullness,
and you bestow a father's blessing on every returning wanderer.
We have wandered from you.
We have used the goods you have given us
as though they belonged to us,
forgetting that our life and breath and all things are from you.
Often we have lived as if we had no heavenly Father
to thank for his goodness.
We joined ourselves to the alien of a far country,
but no one gave to us what would feed and nourish us.
We sought food for our wants in earthly pleasures,
but they were only as husks to our souls.
And now we come back crying,
"Why should we perish with hunger,

when there is bread enough in our Father's house to spare?"
Oh, we thank you that we feel our wanderings
and have been inclined to come back to you.
O God, be merciful to all sinners.
Grant us forgiveness. **Amen.**

**68** *This prayer is based on the Beatitudes (Matthew 5:3-10, NLT). One option is to choose
sections especially appropriate to the needs of the congregation or to the theme of the service;
another option is to use one section per service in a series of worship services, each time using the closing three lines of this prayer.*

God blesses those who realize their need for him,
for the kingdom of heaven is given to them.
**But we have been proud in spirit,
inflated with pride in our own self-sufficiency.
We have forgotten how needy we are.**

God blesses those who mourn,
for they will be comforted.
**But we have not mourned over our sins,
instead we have insulated ourselves from those around us,
from their pain, needs, loneliness, and suffering.
We have even hardened ourselves
so that we are unaware that our own lives
cause grief to the Lord.**

God blesses those who are gentle and lowly,
for the whole earth will be their inheritance.
**But we have valued toughness over gentleness.
We have too often chosen to be concerned with ourselves
rather than with our brothers and sisters and neighbors.
Like the prodigal son, we want to satisfy ourselves
rather than our Father.**

God blesses those who are hungry and thirsty for justice,
for they will receive it in full.
**But we have hungered after the pleasures,
prestige, and possessions of this temporal world.
Like Esau, we have despised our birthright
by choosing to satisfy our immediate desires.**

God blesses those who are merciful,
for they will be shown mercy.
**But we have often presided as harsh judges
over the lives of others.
We have been quick to place blame
on anything or anyone but ourselves.
We have avoided obligations to care for
or to help people in need.**

God blesses those whose hearts are pure,
for they will see God.

But we have defiled our hearts
with idols of our own choosing, doubting that
God will keep his Word and his promises.
We continually compromise the truth
by trying to find meaning and security
in our jobs, our friends, our pleasures, our projects—
but not in God.

God blesses those who work for peace,
for they will be called the children of God.
**But we are often at war with one another.**
**In a thousand little ways we demand to be catered to.**
**We seldom esteem others as more important than ourselves.**
**We often create strife by demanding our way**
**rather than by walking in God's Spirit.**

God blesses those who are persecuted
because they live for God,
for the kingdom of heaven is theirs.
**But we have too often retreated**
**from the disapproval of others.**
**We've sought to please the world rather than**
**risking the disapproval of those who need the Messiah.**
**We regard rejection for righteousness**
**as a burden to be borne, rather than**
**an honor to be humbly received.**

Lord, please show us your mercy.
**Lord, have mercy upon us**
**in the name of the Father, Son, and Holy Spirit. Amen.**

## Prayers of Confession Especially Mindful of Children

69   Dear Jesus,
I want to be a Christian in my heart;
**please forgive my disobedience.**
I want to be a Christian in my actions;
**please forgive my bad choices.**
I want to be a Christian in my words;
**please forgive the mean things I say.**
I want to be a Christian in my whole life;
**help me to be more loving to you**
**and to others. Amen.**
            —based on the Afro-American spiritual "Lord, I Want to Be a Christian"

70   Lord, you are a God who keeps promises.
In our prayers and songs we say
that we want to be Christians,
but then we forget our promises.

Our actions do not match up with our words.
We say mean things to other people,
we hurt their feelings,
we think of ourselves first,
and, worst of all, we ignore you.
Lord, forgive us and hear our prayer
for Jesus' sake. **Amen.**

71 Lord, we are like sheep, and we get lost.
We forget the needs of our neighbors
and do not love you above all else.
We need a Savior, so we long for Jesus.
Come, fill our lives, Jesus. **Amen.**

# 2.3 LAMENT

*The biblical psalms feature several remarkable expressions of lament. In these laments, the worshiping community expresses grief and frustration at the brokenness of the world, even in situations in which the community is not directly culpable or blameworthy. These biblical laments witness to God's desire for honesty in worship. No experience in life is too difficult to be brought before God.*

*A lament is an implicit act of faith in which the community of faith turns to God as its only source of hope and comfort. Faith and hope are explicit in Psalm 42, for example, in which the lament "My tears have been my food day and night" leads to a statement of resolute trust: "Hope in God; for I shall again praise him, my help and my God" (vv. 3, 5-6, NRSV).*

*Lament can serve well as an extension of the prayer of confession. As we confess our sin, we also lament that God's kingdom has not yet fully come. Even as confession is followed by assurance of pardon, so lament may be followed, perhaps after a sustained silence, with a confident declaration of God's redemption of the world in Christ.*

*Other texts of lament are provided in section 4.5.*

1 How long, LORD? Will you forget me forever?
    How long will you hide your face from me?
How long must I wrestle with my thoughts
    and day after day have sorrow in my heart?
    How long will my enemy triumph over me?
Look on me and answer, LORD my God.

Give light to my eyes, or I will sleep in death,
and my enemy will say, "I have overcome him,"
and my foes will rejoice when I fall.
**But I trust in your unfailing love;**
**my heart rejoices in your salvation.**
**I will sing the LORD'S praise,**
**for he has been good to me.**
—Psalm 13, NIV

2    As the deer longs for flowing streams,
so my soul longs for you, O God.
My soul thirsts for God,
for the living God.
When shall I come and behold
the face of God?
My tears have been my food
day and night,
while people say to me continually,
"Where is your God?"
These things I remember,
as I pour out my soul:
how I went with the throng,
and led them in procession to the house of God,
with glad shouts and songs of thanksgiving,
a multitude keeping festival.
**Why are you cast down, O my soul,**
**and why are you disquieted within me?**
**Hope in God; for I shall again praise him,**
**my help and my God.**
—Psalm 42:1-6, NRSV

3    O LORD, you have enticed me,
and I was enticed;
you have overpowered me,
and you have prevailed.
I have become a laughingstock all day long;
everyone mocks me.
For whenever I speak, I must cry out,
I must shout, "Violence and destruction!"
For the word of the LORD has become for me
a reproach and derision all day long.
If I say, "I will not mention him,
or speak any more in his name,"
then within me there is something like a burning fire
shut up in my bones;
I am weary with holding it in,
and I cannot.
For I hear many whispering:

"Terror is all around!
Denounce him! Let us denounce him!"
    All my close friends
    are watching for me to stumble.
"Perhaps he can be enticed,
    and we can prevail against him,
    and take our revenge on him."
Why did I come forth from the womb
    to see toil and sorrow,
    and spend my days in shame?
        —Jeremiah 20:7-10, 18, NRSV

4   *This simple refrain from the early church, the* Kyrie eleison, *expresses both confession and lament and may be spoken or sung as a refrain during a prayer of lament.*

| | |
|---|---|
| **Lord, have mercy.** | *Kyrie eleison.* |
| **Christ, have mercy.** | *Christe eleison.* |
| **Lord, have mercy.** | *Kyrie eleison.* |

5   *This simple, classic refrain from the early church, the* Trisagion *("three times holy"), expresses both confession and lament and may be spoken or sung as a refrain during a prayer of lament.*

**Holy God,**
**holy and mighty,**
**holy immortal One,**
**have mercy on us.**

6   *The following congregational lament provides words both for general use and particular circumstances. Use these paragraphs in any combination that is pastorally appropriate.*

[*General*]
Why, Lord, must evil seem to get its way?
We confess that our sin is deeply shameful;
but the wicked are openly scornful—
they mock your name and laugh at our dismay.
**We know your providential love holds true:**
**nothing can curse us endlessly with sorrow.**
**Transform, dear Lord, this damage into good;**
**show us your glory, hidden by this evil.**

[*Imprisonment*]
Why, Lord, must he be sentenced, locked away?
True, he has wronged his neighbor and has failed you.
Yet none of us is innocent or sinless;
only by grace we follow in your way.
**We plead: Repair the brokenness we share.**
**Chastise no more, lest it destroy your creatures.**
**Hear this lament as intercessory prayer,**
**and speak your powerful Word to make us hopeful.**

[*Illness*]
Why, Lord, must she be left to waste away?
Do you not see how painfully she suffers?
Could you not change the curse of this disaster?
Amaze us by your mighty sovereignty.
**We plead: Repair the brokenness we share.**
**Chastise no more, lest it destroy your creatures.**
**Hear this lament as intercessory prayer,**
**and speak your powerful Word to make us hopeful.**

[*Divorce*]
Why, Lord, must broken vows cut like a knife?
How can one wedded body break in pieces?
We all have failed at being pure and faithful;
only by grace we keep our solemn vows.
**We plead: Repair the brokenness we share.**
**Chastise no more, lest it destroy your creatures.**
**Hear this lament as intercessory prayer,**
**and speak your powerful Word to make us hopeful.**

[*Untimely death*]
Why, Lord, did you abruptly take him home?
Could you not wait to summon him before you?
Why must we feel the sting of death's old cruelty?
Come quickly, Lord; do not leave us alone.
**We plead: Repair the brokenness we share.**
**Chastise no more, lest it destroy your creatures.**
**Hear this lament as intercessory prayer,**
**and speak your powerful Word to make us hopeful.**

[*General*]
Why, Lord, must any child of yours be hurt?
Do all our pain and sorrow somehow please you?
You are a God so jealous for our praises—
hear this lament as prayer that fills the earth.
**We plead: Repair the brokenness we share.**
**Chastise no more, lest it destroy your creatures.**
**Hear this lament as intercessory prayer,**
**and speak your powerful Word to make us hopeful. Amen.**

# 2.4 ASSURANCE OF PARDON

*The good news of the gospel is that in Christ we are forgiven! The announcement of this truth is one of the most beautiful moments in worship. Using scriptural words reinforces the truth that our assurance is based on God's words of promise, not merely on our own hopes and desires.*

*Just as confession acknowledges both personal and corporate sin, so also assurance of pardon declares the sure promise that God's grace in Christ redeems not only individuals but also the whole creation.*

*To introduce the promise, use a short phrase that calls attention to the drama and grace of God's assurance, such as "Hear the good news!" or "Hear the Word of the Lord." The heart of the assurance of pardon is the scriptural promise of salvation in Christ.*

*After stating the scriptural promise, consider using words of direct personal application, such as "Believe this gospel and go forth to live in peace," or "Know that you are forgiven, and be at peace," or "Live in the sure hope of Christ's promise." The congregation may also voice their response with a phrase like "Thanks be to God."*

1   *This full example includes (a) a phrase of introduction, (b) the scriptural promise, and (c) brief words of application.*

(a) Hear the good news!
(b) There is no condemnation
    for those who are in Christ Jesus.
    For the law of the Spirit
    of life in Christ Jesus
    has set you free from the law of sin and death.
    Anyone who is in Christ is a new creation.
    The old life has gone;
    a new life has begun.
(c) Know that in Jesus,
    God embraces you, forgives you,
    and strengthens you to live a renewed life.
    **Thanks be to God.**
        —based on Romans 8:1; 2 Corinthians 5:17

*Each of the following scriptural words of assurance may be inserted into the preceding framework.*

2   Happy are those whose transgression is forgiven,
        whose sin is covered.
    Happy are those to whom the Lord imputes no iniquity,
        and in whose spirit there is no deceit.
            —Psalm 32:1-2, NRSV

3  While I kept silence, my body wasted away
      through my groaning all day long.
  For day and night your hand was heavy upon me;
      my strength was dried up as by the heat of summer.
  Then I acknowledged my sin to you,
      and I did not hide my iniquity;
  I said, "I will confess my transgressions to the LORD,"
      and you forgave the guilt of my sin.
            —Psalm 32:3-5, NRSV

4  The LORD is merciful and gracious,
      slow to anger and abounding in steadfast love.
  As a father has compassion for his children,
      so the LORD has compassion for those who fear him.
  For he knows how we were made;
      he remembers that we are dust.
  But the steadfast love of the LORD is from
            everlasting to everlasting
      on those who fear him,
      and his righteousness to children's children,
  to those who keep his covenant
      and remember to do his commandments.
            —Psalm 103:8, 13-14, 17-18, NRSV

5  The LORD is merciful and gracious,
      slow to anger and abounding in steadfast love.
  He will not always accuse,
      nor will he keep his anger forever.
  He does not deal with us according to our sins,
      nor repay us according to our iniquities.
  For as the heavens are high above the earth,
      so great is his steadfast love toward those who fear him;
  as far as the east is from the west,
      so far he removes our transgressions from us.
  As a father has compassion for his children,
      so the LORD has compassion for those who fear him.
            —Psalm 103:8-13, NRSV

6  If you, O LORD, should mark iniquities,
      Lord, who could stand?
  But there is forgiveness with you,
      so that you may be revered.
  O Israel, hope in the LORD!
      For with the LORD there is steadfast love,
      and with him is great power to redeem.
  It is he who will redeem Israel
      from all its iniquities.
            —Psalm 130:3-4, 7-8, NRSV

7    The LORD is faithful in all his words,
        and gracious in all his deeds.
     The LORD upholds all who are falling,
        and raises up all who are bowed down.
            —Psalm 145:13-14, NRSV

8    The LORD builds up Jerusalem;
        he gathers the outcasts of Israel.
     He heals the brokenhearted,
        and binds up their wounds.
     Great is our Lord, and abundant in power;
        his understanding is beyond measure.
            —Psalm 147:2-3, 5, NRSV

9    Come now, let us argue it out,
        says the LORD:
     though your sins are like scarlet,
        they shall be like snow;
     though they are red like crimson,
        they shall become like wool.
            —Isaiah 1:18, NRSV

10   Remember these things, O Jacob,
        and Israel, for you are my servant;
     I formed you, you are my servant;
        O Israel, you will not be forgotten by me.
     I have swept away your transgressions like a cloud,
        and your sins like mist;
     return to me, for I have redeemed you.
            —Isaiah 44:21-22, NRSV

11   Can a woman forget her nursing child,
        or show no compassion for the child of her womb?
     As a mother comforts her child,
        so will I comfort you, says the Lord.
            —from Isaiah 49:15; 66:13, NRSV

12   Surely he has borne our infirmities
        and carried our diseases;
     yet we accounted him stricken,
        struck down by God, and afflicted.
     But he was wounded for our transgressions,
        crushed for our iniquities;
     upon him was the punishment that made us whole,
        and by his bruises we are healed.
     All we like sheep have gone astray;
        we have all turned to our own way,
     and the LORD has laid on him
        the iniquity of us all.
            —Isaiah 53:4-6, NRSV

13  "In a surge of anger
        I hid my face from you for a moment,
    but with everlasting kindness
        I will have compassion on you,"
        says the Lord your Redeemer.
    "I, even I, am he who blots out
        your transgressions, for my own sake,
        and remembers your sins no more."
    "I have swept away your offenses like a cloud,
        your sins like the morning mist.
    Return to me,
        for I have redeemed you."
            —Isaiah 54:8; 43:25; 44:22, NIV

14  I will cleanse them from all the guilt of their sin against me,
    and I will forgive all the guilt of their sin and rebellion against me.
            —Jeremiah 33:8, NRSV

15  I will sprinkle clean water upon you,
    and you shall be clean from all your uncleannesses,
    and from all your idols I will cleanse you.
    A new heart I will give you,
    and a new spirit I will put within you;
    and I will remove from your body the heart of stone
    and give you a heart of flesh.
            —Ezekiel 36:25-26, NRSV

16  How can I give you up, Ephraim?
        How can I hand you over, O Israel?
    How can I make you like Admah?
        How can I treat you like Zeboiim?
    My heart recoils within me;
        my compassion grows warm and tender.
    I will not execute my fierce anger;
        I will not again destroy Ephraim;
    for I am God and no mortal,
        the Holy One in your midst,
        and I will not come in wrath.
            —Hosea 11:8-9, NRSV

17  Who is a God like you, pardoning iniquity
        and passing over the transgression
        of the remnant of your possession?
    He does not retain his anger forever,
        because he delights in showing clemency.
    He will again have compassion upon us;
        he will tread our iniquities under foot.
    You will cast all our sins
        into the depths of the sea.

> You will show faithfulness to Jacob
>> and unswerving loyalty to Abraham,
> as you have sworn to our ancestors
>> from the days of old.
>>> —Micah 7:18-20, NRSV

18  "God so loved the world that he gave his only Son,
so that everyone who believes in him
may not perish but may have eternal life.
Indeed, God did not send the Son into the world
to condemn the world,
but in order that the world might be saved through him."
    —John 3:16-17, NRSV

19  All the prophets testify about Christ
that everyone who believes in him
receives forgiveness of sins through his name.
    —from Acts 10:43, NRSV

20  Through Jesus Christ forgiveness of sins
is proclaimed to you.
In Christ we have redemption through his blood,
the forgiveness of our trespasses,
according to the riches of his grace.
    —from Acts 13:38; Ephesians 1:7, NRSV

21  Since we are justified by faith,
we have peace with God through our Lord Jesus Christ,
through whom we have obtained access to this grace
in which we stand;
and we boast in our hope of sharing the glory of God.
    —Romans 5:1-2, NRSV

22  God demonstrates his own love for us in this:
While we were still sinners, Christ died for us.
Since we have now been justified by his blood,
how much more shall we be saved
from God's wrath through him!
    —Romans 5:8-9, NIV

23  There is now no condemnation
for those who are in Christ Jesus.
    —Romans 8:1, NIV

24  You did not receive a spirit of slavery to fall back into fear,
but you have received a spirit of adoption.
When we cry, "Abba! Father!" it is that very Spirit
bearing witness with our spirit that we are children of God,
and if children, then heirs, heirs of God and joint heirs with Christ.
    —Romans 8:15-17, NRSV

25    What then are we to say about these things?
If God is for us, who is against us?
He who did not withhold his own Son,
but gave him up for all of us,
will he not with him also give us everything else?
Who will bring any charge against God's elect?
It is God who justifies.
Who is to condemn? It is Christ Jesus, who died, yes,
who was raised, who is at the right hand of God,
who indeed intercedes for us.
Who will separate us from the love of Christ?
Will hardship, or distress, or persecution, or famine,
or nakedness, or peril, or sword?
**No, in all these things we are more than conquerors**
**through him who loved us.**
**For I am convinced that neither death, nor life,**
**nor angels, nor rulers,**
**nor things present, nor things to come,**
**nor powers, nor height, nor depth,**
**nor anything else in all creation,**
**will be able to separate us**
**from the love of God in Christ Jesus our Lord.**
        —Romans 8:31-35, 37-39, NRSV

26    When you were dead in trespasses
and the uncircumcision of your flesh,
God made you alive together with Christ,
when he forgave us all our trespasses,
erasing the record that stood against us with its legal demands.
He set this aside, nailing it to the cross.
        —from Colossians 2:13-14, NRSV

27    He himself bore our sins in his body on the cross,
so that, free from sins,
we might live for righteousness;
by his wounds you have been healed.
        —1 Peter 2:24, NRSV

28    This is the message we have heard from God
and proclaim to you,
that God is light and in God there is no darkness at all.
If we walk in the light, as God is in the light,
we have fellowship with one another,
and the blood of Jesus his Son cleanses us from all sin.
        —from 1 John 1:5, 7, NRSV

29    God demonstrates his own love for us in this:
While we were still sinners, Christ died for us.
**For he has rescued us from the dominion of darkness**

and brought us into the kingdom of the Son he loves,
in whom we have redemption, the forgiveness of sins.
Therefore, since we have been justified through faith,
we have peace with God through our Lord Jesus Christ.
—Romans 5:8; Colossians 1:13-14; Romans 5:1, NIV

30   Hear the good news:

This saying is sure and worthy of full acceptance,
that Christ Jesus came into the world to save sinners.
He himself bore our sins
in his body on the cross,
that we might be dead to sin,
and alive to all that is good.

I declare to you in the name of Jesus Christ,
you are forgiven.
**Thanks be to God.**
—based on 1 Timothy 1:15; 1 Peter 2:24

31   Here are words you may trust,
words that merit full acceptance:
Christ Jesus came into the world to save sinners.
To all who confess their sins and resolve to lead a new life,
he says, "Your sins are forgiven."
He also says, "Follow me."
Now to the one who rules all worlds,
immortal, invisible, the only God,
be honor and glory forever and ever.
—based on 1 Timothy 1:15, 17

*The following texts are brief announcements of forgiveness that are summaries of scriptural
themes rather than direct scriptural quotations.*

32   While it is true that we have sinned,
it is a greater truth that we are forgiven
through God's love in Jesus Christ.
To all who humbly seek the mercy of God I say,
in Jesus Christ your sin is forgiven.
**Thanks be to God.**

33   Hear these comforting words:
If you repent and believe in God's redeeming mercy,
your sins are forgiven.
Trust in God's promises and begin anew your life
with God and all people
in the name of Jesus Christ.

34  Christ is our peace;
    those who are divided
    he has made one.
    He has broken down the barriers of separation
    by his death and has built us up
    into one body, with God.
    To all who repent and believe
    he has promised reconciliation.
    So live as people reconciled. **Amen.**

35  God the Creator brings you new life,
    forgives and redeems you.
    Take hold of this forgiveness,
    and live your life in the Spirit of Jesus. **Amen.**

36  Take comfort in the assurance
    that even those things that are hidden from memory,
    or are too deep for our words,
    are not beyond God's forgiving love.
    God, who knows us completely,
    bestows pardon and peace.
    **Thanks be to God.**

37  In the life, death, and resurrection of Jesus,
    we are assured that there is no sin so terrible
    that God cannot forgive,
    no hurt so terrible that God cannot heal.
    God accepts, God forgives, and God sets free.
    Receive the forgiving love of God.
    **Thanks be to God.**

38  The God who challenges us
    is also the God who encourages us.
    The God who confronts us
    is also the God who accepts us.
    Be assured that God is with us even now,
    accepting, guiding, and forgiving.
    **Thanks be to God.**

39  To all who turn from sin in sorrow,
    to all who turn to God in hope,
    this is God's Word of grace:
    We are accepted, we are forgiven, we are loved.
    This gift we have from God.
    **Thanks be to God.**

**40** Hear the good news:
Christ died for us while we were yet sinners;
that proves God's love toward us.
In the name of Jesus Christ, you are forgiven!
**In the name of Jesus Christ, we are forgiven.**
**Glory to God. Amen.**

**41** Through the blood of Christ Jesus, our Lord,
we have redemption, forgiveness of sins.
The riches of God's grace have been poured out upon us.
**Praise be to our God,**
who has chosen and made us his own.
**Praise be to our God,**
who forgives and cleanses us.
**Praise be to our God,**
who blesses us beyond our imagination!

**42** Our God pardons our sins and forgives our disobedience.
Our God does not stay angry forever.
Instead, our God delights to show mercy.
Our God again has compassion on us.
Our God tramples our sins underfoot
and hurls our iniquities into the depths of the sea.
Give thanks to our God, for our God is good!

*The following statements of assurance, drawn from historic confessions of faith, may be used in conjunction with scriptural words of assurance.*

**43** Our Lord Jesus Christ—
truly God and at the same time truly human and truly righteous—
is the mediator who was given to set us completely free
and to make us right with God.
**By the power of his divinity,**
**he bore the weight of God's anger in his humanity,**
**restoring us to righteousness and life.**
—based on Heidelberg Catechism, Q&A's 17-18

**44** We have been made holy
through the sacrifice of the body of Jesus Christ once for all.
**And this is God's gospel promise:**
**To grant us forgiveness of sins and eternal life**
    **by grace**
    **because of Christ's one sacrifice**
    **accomplished on the cross.**
—Hebrews 10:10, NIV; Heidelberg Catechism, Q&A 66

**45** Righteousness from God comes
through faith in Jesus Christ to all who believe.
**By faith I have a wholehearted trust,**
**which the Holy Spirit creates in me by the gospel,**
**that God has freely granted,**
**not only to others but to me also,**
    **forgiveness of sins, eternal righteousness, and salvation.**
    **These are gifts of sheer grace,**
    **granted solely by Christ's merit.**
        —from Romans 3:22, NIV; Heidelberg Catechism, Q&A 21

**46** Your sins are forgiven.
**I believe that God,**
    **because of Christ's atonement,**
**will never hold against me**
    **any of my sins nor my sinful nature,**
    **which I need to struggle against all my life.**
**Rather, in his grace**
    **God grants me the righteousness of Christ**
    **to free me forever from judgment.**
        —based on Heidelberg Catechism, Q&A 56

**47** **By true faith in Jesus Christ,**
**I am righteous before God**
**and heir to life everlasting.**
**Even though my conscience accuses me**
    **of having grievously sinned against all God's commandments,**
    **of never having kept any of them,**
    **and of still being inclined toward all evil,**
**nevertheless, without any merit of my own,**
**out of sheer grace, God grants and credits to me**
**the perfect satisfaction, righteousness, and holiness of Christ,**
    **as if I had never sinned nor been a sinner,**
    **as if I had been as perfectly obedient**
    **as Christ was obedient for me.**
**All I need to do**
**is accept this gift of God with a believing heart.**
        —from Heidelberg Catechism, Q&A's 59-60

*The following words of blessing convey confidence in God's promises to us in Christ. They may be
used after any of the preceding words of assurance. Just as the words of assurance highlight God's
promise of forgiveness, these words of blessing call our attention to God's continued work in us.*

**48** May almighty God,
who caused light to shine out of darkness,
shine in our hearts, cleansing us from all our sins,
and restoring us to the light of the knowledge of God's glory,
in the face of Jesus Christ, our Savior. **Amen.**
        —based on 2 Corinthians 4:6, NIV

49    May the God of mercy,
      who forgives you all your sins,
      strengthen you in all goodness,
      and, by the power of the Holy Spirit,
      keep you in eternal life. **Amen.**

# 2.5 THE PEACE

*Christ's work of reconciliation offers us forgiveness for our sins and the possibility of genuine fel-
lowship and reconciliation in community. Thus, in many Christian traditions, after hearing the
words of assurance, worshipers are invited to share gestures of reconciliation and peace with each
other. (Sharing of the peace may also take place near the beginning of worship or in conjunction
with the Lord's Supper.)*

1    Since God has forgiven us in Christ,
     let us forgive one another.
     The peace of our Lord Jesus Christ be with you all.
     **And also with you.**

2    Hear the teaching of Christ:
         A new command I give you,
             that you love one another as I have loved you.
     The peace of Christ be with you all.
     **And also with you.**
             —based on John 13:34

3    As God has given us peace through Christ,
     so let us pass the peace of Christ to each other.

4    In his abundant grace, God has forgiven us.
     God has freed us from our sin
     and transformed our grief into joy.
     Now we can be at peace with God.
     In gratitude for that great gift,
     let us share God's peace with one another.

# 2.6 Thanksgiving

*God's grace elicits our heartfelt gratitude. We respond to the good news of forgiveness with joyful acclamations of praise! Most often this response is sung (or even shouted) with great joy.*

*An acclamation of thanksgiving may be introduced by the prayer "O Lord, open my lips, and my mouth will declare your praise" (Ps. 51:15). (This is especially appropriate when the earlier portion of Psalm 51 has been used as part of the prayer of confession.) Expressions of thanksgiving may also be introduced with words such as "In gratitude for God's grace, we give thanks now with joy."*

1    Blessed be the LORD, the God of Israel,
        who alone does wondrous things.
    Blessed be his glorious name forever;
        may his glory fill the whole earth.
            **Amen and Amen.**
            —Psalm 72:18-19, NRSV

2    O the depth of the riches and wisdom and knowledge of God!
    How unsearchable are his judgments and how inscrutable his ways!
    **For from him and through him and to him are all things.**
    **To him be the glory forever. Amen.**
            —Romans 11:33, 36, NRSV

3    Worthy is the Lamb that was slaughtered
        to receive power and wealth and wisdom and might
        and honor and glory and blessing!
    You, Lord Jesus Christ, are worthy to take the scroll
        and to open its seals,
    for you were slaughtered
        and by your blood you ransomed for God
        saints from every tribe and language
        and people and nation;
    you have made them to be a kingdom
        and priests serving our God,
        and they will reign on earth.
    **To the one seated on the throne and to the Lamb**
    **be blessing and honor and glory and might**
    **forever and ever! Amen!**
            —from Revelation 5:9-13, NRSV

4    *The Gloria in excelsis ("Glory to God in the highest") is a classic hymn of response at least 1,500 years old. It praises and gives gratitude for God's glory and redemption in Christ. This classic text is also well known in hymnic form as the basis of "All Glory Be to God on High," found in many hymnals.*

Glory to God in the highest,
and peace to God's people on earth.

Lord God, heavenly King,
almighty God and Father,
we worship you, we give you thanks,
we praise you for your glory.

Lord Jesus Christ, only Son of the Father,
Lord God, Lamb of God,
you take away the sin of the world;
have mercy on us.
You are seated at the right hand of the Father;
receive our prayer.

For you alone are the Holy One,
you alone are the Lord,
you alone are the Most High,
Jesus Christ,
with the Holy Spirit,
in the glory of God the Father. **Amen.**

5    *The* Gloria Patri *("Glory to the Father") is more than 1,500 years old, known in all Christian traditions, and usually identified by its Latin name.*

Glory to the Father,
and to the Son,
and to the Holy Spirit,
as it was in the beginning,
is now, and will be forever. **Amen.**

# 2.7 THE LAW

*The movement from confession to forgiveness to thanksgiving invites the natural response of the grateful worshiper to live in a way pleasing to God, according to the commandments and ordinances God has given in Scripture. Throughout the history of the church, theologians have distinguished at least three complementary purposes for the divine commandments recorded in Scripture. Each one suggests a different function for the law in worship, and together they are traditionally called the "three uses of the law."*

- *First, despite pervasive human sinfulness, God's law works to restrain sin in the world. In worship, this suggests the use of the law in preaching, where the preacher specifically calls worshipers to work against sin and evil in society.*

- *Second, God's law convicts us of our own sinfulness and our need for God's forgiveness. In worship, this suggests the use of the law just prior to a prayer of confession.*
- *Third, God's law provides us with a guide for grateful living in response to divine grace. This "third use of the law" was a key teaching of Reformed Christians during the sixteenth-century Reformation. In worship, this suggests the use of the law just after the assurance of pardon; in one of John Calvin's liturgies, the reading of the law was placed after an assurance of pardon. Because of the emphasis on gratitude, the reading of the law—the Ten Commandments, the summary of the law, or another scriptural text giving direction for living—is sometimes called the "guide for grateful living."*

*Any of the following texts may be introduced with a statement like these:*

> As God's forgiven people, how are we to live?
> Hear now the Word of God:

*or*

> We respond to God's forgiveness
> by living our thanks according to God's Word.
> Hear now God's will for our lives:

**1**   God spoke all these words:
"I am the LORD your God.
You shall have no other gods before me.
You shall not make for yourself an idol,
   whether in the form of anything that is in heaven above,
   or that is on the earth beneath,
   or that is in the water under the earth.
You shall not bow down to them or worship them.
You shall not make wrongful use
   of the name of the LORD your God.
Remember the sabbath day, and keep it holy.
Honor your father and your mother.
You shall not murder.
You shall not commit adultery.
You shall not steal.
You shall not bear false witness against your neighbor.
You shall not covet your neighbor's house;
   you shall not covet your neighbor's wife,
   or anything that belongs to your neighbor."
   —from Exodus 20:1-17, NRSV

**2**   Trust in the LORD with all your heart
   and lean not on your own understanding;
in all your ways submit to him,
   and he will make your paths straight.
   —Proverbs 3:5-6, NIV

3   He has told you, O mortal, what is good;
        and what does the LORD require of you
    but to do justice, and to love kindness,
        and to walk humbly with your God?
            —Micah 6:8, NRSV

4   Our Lord Jesus said:
    "'You shall love the Lord your God
    with all your heart,
    and with all your soul,
    and with all your mind.'
    This is the greatest and first commandment.
    And a second is like it:
    'You shall love your neighbor as yourself.'
    On these two commandments
    hang all the law and the prophets."
            —from Matthew 22:37-40, NRSV

5   What is the great and first commandment?
    **Love the Lord your God with all your heart and with all your soul and with all
    your mind.**
    What is the second commandment like it?
    **Love your neighbor as yourself.**
    What does this mean?
    **Love is the fulfilling of the law.**
    To what does this call us?
    **To a life of faith working through love.**
            —based on Matthew 22:37-40

6   Hear the teaching of Christ:
    "A new commandment I give to you,
    that you love one another just as I have loved you."
            —from John 13:34, NRSV

7   I appeal to you therefore, brothers and sisters,
    by the mercies of God,
    to present your bodies as a living sacrifice,
    holy and acceptable to God,
    which is your spiritual worship.
    Do not be conformed to this world,
    but be transformed by the renewing of your minds,
    so that you may discern what is the will of God—
    what is good and acceptable and perfect.
    For by the grace given to me
    I say to everyone among you
    not to think of yourself more highly than you ought to think,
    but to think with sober judgment,
    each according to the measure of faith that God has assigned.
            —Romans 12:1-3, NRSV

8    You heard about Christ and were taught in him
     in accordance with the truth that is in Jesus.
     You were taught, with regard to your former way of life,
     to put off your old self, which is being corrupted by its deceitful desires;
     to be made new in the attitude of your minds;
     and to put on the new self,
     created to be like God in true righteousness and holiness.
     Therefore each of you must put off falsehood
     and speak truthfully to your neighbor,
     for we are all members of one body.
          —Ephesians 4:21-25, NIV

9    Be kind and compassionate to one another,
     forgiving each other, just as in Christ God forgave you.
     Follow God's example, therefore,
     as dearly loved children and walk in the way of love,
     just as Christ loved us and gave himself up for us
     as a fragrant offering and sacrifice to God.
          —Ephesians 4:32-5:2, NIV

10   For you were once darkness,
     but now you are light in the Lord.
     Live as children of light
     (for the fruit of the light consists
     in all goodness, righteousness and truth)
     and find out what pleases the Lord.
     Have nothing to do with the fruitless deeds of darkness,
     but rather expose them.
     It is shameful even to mention
     what the disobedient do in secret.
     But everything exposed by the light becomes visible
     —and everything that is illuminated becomes a light.
          —Ephesians 5:8-13, NIV

11   Be very careful, then, how you live—
     not as unwise but as wise, making the most
     of every opportunity,
     because the days are evil.
     Therefore do not be foolish,
     but understand what the Lord's will is.
     Do not get drunk on wine, which leads to debauchery.
     Instead, be filled with the Spirit,
     speaking to one another with psalms, hymns, and songs from the Spirit.
     Sing and make music from your heart to the Lord,
     always giving thanks to God the Father for everything,
     in the name of our Lord Jesus Christ.
          —Ephesians 5:15-20, NIV

12  Since you have been raised up to be with Christ,
    you must look for the things that are above,
    where Christ is, sitting at God's right hand.
    Let your thoughts be on things above,
    not on things that are on the earth,
    because you have died,
    and now the life you have is hidden with Christ in God.
    But when Christ is revealed—and he is your life—
    you, too, will be revealed with him in glory.
      —Colossians 3:1-4, NJB

13  As the chosen of God, then, the holy people
    whom he loves, you are to be clothed in heartfelt compassion,
    in generosity and humility, gentleness and patience.
    Bear with one another; forgive each other
    if one of you has a complaint against another.
    The Lord has forgiven you; now you must do the same.
    Over all these clothes, put on love, the perfect bond.
    And may the peace of Christ reign in your hearts,
    because it is for this that you were called together in one body.
    Always be thankful.
      —Colossians 3:12-15, NJB

14  If then there is any encouragement in Christ,
    any consolation from love, any sharing in the Spirit,
    any compassion and sympathy, make my joy complete:
    be of the same mind, having the same love,
    being in full accord and of one mind.
    Do nothing from selfish ambition or conceit,
    but in humility regard others as better than yourselves.
    Let each of you look not to your own interests,
    but to the interests of others.
      —Philippians 2:1-4, NRSV

15  Rejoice in the Lord always; again I will say, Rejoice.
    Let your gentleness be known to everyone. The Lord is near.
    Do not worry about anything, but in everything by prayer
    and supplication with thanksgiving
    let your requests be made known to God.
    And the peace of God, which surpasses all understanding,
    will guard your hearts and your minds in Christ Jesus.
    Finally, beloved, whatever is true, whatever is honorable,
    whatever is just, whatever is pure, whatever is pleasing,
    whatever is commendable, if there is any excellence
    and if there is anything worthy of praise,
    think about these things.
    Keep on doing the things that you have learned
    and received and heard and seen in me,
    and the God of peace will be with you.
      —Philippians 4:4-9, NRSV

*The following five resources are responsive readings based on the Ten Commandments.*

**16**    You shall have no other gods before me.
**For from him and through him and to him are all things.**
**To him be the glory forever!**
You shall not make for yourself an idol.
**In Christ we have redemption, the forgiveness of sins.**
**He is the image of the invisible God,**
**the firstborn over all creation.**
You shall not misuse the name of the Lord your God,
for the Lord will not hold anyone guiltless who misuses his name.
**Let us continually offer to God a sacrifice of praise—**
**the fruit of lips that confess his name.**
Remember the Sabbath day by keeping it holy.
Six days you shall labor and do all your work,
but the seventh day is a Sabbath to the Lord your God.
**Let the Word of Christ dwell in you richly**
**as you teach and admonish one another with all wisdom,**
**and as you sing psalms, hymns, and spiritual songs**
**with gratitude in your hearts to God.**
Honor your father and your mother,
so that you may live long in the land
the Lord your God is giving you.
**Children, obey your parents in everything,**
**for this pleases the Lord.**
You shall not murder.
**Be kind and compassionate to one another,**
**forgiving each other, just as in Christ God forgave you.**
You shall not commit adultery.
**You are not your own; you were bought at a price.**
**Therefore honor God with your body.**
You shall not steal.
**Those who have been stealing must steal no longer,**
**but must work, doing something useful with their hands,**
**so that they may have something to share with those in need.**
You shall not give false testimony against your neighbor.
**Instead, speaking the truth in love,**
**we will in all things grow up into him**
**who is the Head, that is, Christ.**
You shall not covet your neighbor's house
or anything that belongs to your neighbor.
**I have learned to be content whatever the circumstances.**

**17**    Hear, O people of God, the law that the Lord speaks
in your hearing this day, that you may know his statutes
and walk according to his ordinances.
**Teach us, O Lord, the grace of your law,**
**and give us life by your Word.**

The God who saved us in Jesus Christ gave this law, saying:
I am the Lord your God! You shall have no other gods before me.
**We will worship the Lord our God and serve only him.**
You shall not make yourself an image of anything to worship it.
**Living no more in bondage to earthly gods,**
**we will worship the Lord our God in spirit and in truth.**
You shall not misuse the name of the Lord.
**We will use the holy name of God with reverence,**
**praising him in everything we do and say.**
You shall observe the Sabbath by keeping it holy,
for in six days you shall labor and do all your work.
**This is the day the Lord has made;**
**let us rejoice and be glad in it.**
You shall honor your father and mother, that you may live long
in the land the Lord your God is giving to you.
**As children we will be obedient to our parents in the Lord;**
**as parents we will correct our children and guide them**
**in the training and instruction of the Lord;**
**we will respect the lawful authorities appointed by God.**
You shall not murder.
**We will be kind and compassionate to one another,**
**forgiving each other, just as in Christ God forgave us.**
You shall not commit adultery.
**We will use our bodies in ways that are holy**
**and honorable, and abstain from immorality and impurity.**
You shall not steal.
**We will do what we can for our neighbor's good,**
**and work faithfully so that we may share with the poor.**
You shall not give false testimony against your neighbor.
**We will speak the truth with our neighbor in love,**
**render judgments that are true and make for peace,**
**and not devise in our hearts any evil against anyone.**
You shall not covet anything that belongs to your neighbor.
**We will be content whatever the circumstances**
**through the strength of Christ within us.**
Thus we must love our neighbor as ourselves.
**For the Lord requires of us to do justice, to love kindness,**
**and to walk humbly with our God. Amen!**

**18**  *These statements drawn from the Heidelberg Catechism summarize biblical teaching based*
*on the Ten Commandments. Choose relevant portions of this text to use in conjunction with*
*Scripture—and perhaps for congregational response.*

This is God's will for our lives:

We must sincerely acknowledge the only true God,
trust him alone, look to him for every good thing
humbly and patiently,
love him, fear him, and honor him
with all our hearts.

We should in no way make any image of God
nor worship him in any other way
than he has commanded in his Word.

We may neither blaspheme nor misuse the name of God
by cursing, perjury, or unnecessary oaths,
nor share in such horrible sins
by being silent bystanders.
Rather, we must use the holy name of God
only with reverence and awe.

On the festive day of rest,
we should regularly attend the assembly of God's people
to learn what God's Word teaches,
to participate in the sacraments,
to pray to God publicly,
and to bring Christian offerings for the poor.
Every day of our lives
the Lord works in us through his Spirit,
and begins already the eternal Sabbath.

We are to honor, love, and be loyal to
our fathers and mothers
and all those in authority over us;
obey and submit to them, as is proper,
when they correct and punish us;
and also be patient with their failings—
for through them God chooses to rule us.

By condemning envy, hatred, and anger
God tells us to love our neighbors as ourselves,
to be patient, peace-loving, gentle,
merciful, and friendly to them,
to protect them from harm as much as we can,
and to do good even to our enemies.

We are temples of the Holy Spirit, body and soul,
and God wants both to be kept clean and holy.
We should therefore thoroughly detest all unchastity
and, married or single, live decent and chaste lives.

God forbids outright theft and robbery,
cheating and swindling our neighbors,
and all greed and pointless squandering of his gifts.

God's will is that we
never give false testimony against anyone,
twist no one's words,
not gossip or slander,
nor join in condemning anyone
without a hearing or without a just cause.
We should love the truth,

speak it candidly,
and openly acknowledge it.
And we should do what we can
to guard and advance our neighbor's good name.

When we live the way of love for God and neighbor,
not even the slightest thought or desire
contrary to any one of God's commandments
should ever arise in our heart.
Rather, with all our heart
we should always hate sin
and take pleasure in whatever is right.

—based on Heidelberg Catechism, Q&A's 94, 96, 99, 103-104, 107-110, 112-113

**19** *A text especially mindful of children*

God gave us the Ten Commandments so that we would know how to live.
God commands us to not have any other gods.
We should not value anything, not money or popularity or success, above God.
**We will love and trust God above all else.**
God commands that we should not make idols.
We should not give more value to anything that people make than to God.
**We will worship only the holy God whom we learn about in the Bible.**
God commands us not to take his name in vain.
We should not curse, swear, or use bad language.
**We will only use the name of God with respect.**
God commands us to keep the Sabbath day holy.
We should not treat the Lord's Day like every other day.
**We will have special times of rest and praise God with his people.**
God commands that we honor our father and mother.
We should not be mean or try to make those in authority,
including our parents, angry.
**We will respect and obey those whom God puts in charge of us.**
God commands that we not kill.
We should not try to hurt other people.
**We will help others in need.**
God commands us not to commit adultery.
We should not think disrespectful thoughts about others.
**We will keep marriage pure.**
God commands us not to steal.
We should not take what does not belong to us.
**We will be honest.**
God commands us not to lie.
We should not say untrue or even hurtful things about others.
**We will build others up with our words.**
God commands us not to covet.
We should not want what others have.
**We will be thankful and content with what we have.**
**We do our best to obey God because we are thankful to God**
**for his many gifts to us.**

**20**  I am the Lord your God,
who brought you out of Egypt,
out of the land of slavery.
You shall have no other gods before me.

**I sincerely acknowledge the only true God,
trust him alone,
look to him for every good thing, humbly and patiently,
and love him, fear him, and honor him with all my heart.
In short, I will give up anything rather
than go against God's will in any way.**

You shall not make for yourself an idol
in the form of anything in heaven above
or on the earth beneath
or in the waters below.

**I will in no way make any image of God
nor worship him in any other way
than he has commanded in his Word.**

You shall not misuse the name of the Lord your God,
for the Lord will not hold anyone guiltless
who misuses his name.

**I will use the holy name of God
only with reverence and awe,
so that I may properly confess him,
pray to him, and praise him
in everything I do and say.**

Remember the Sabbath day by keeping it holy.

**I will regularly attend the assembly of God's people
to learn what God's Word teaches,
to participate in the sacraments,
to pray to God publicly,
and to bring Christian offerings for the poor.
Every day of my life I will rest from my evil ways,
let the Lord work in me through his Spirit,
and so begin already in this life the eternal Sabbath.**

Honor your father and your mother.

**I will honor, love, and be loyal to
my father and mother and all those in authority over me.
I will obey and submit to them, as is proper,
when they correct and punish me;
and I will be patient with their failings—
for through them God chooses to rule us.**

You shall not murder.

**I will not belittle, insult, hate, or kill my neighbor—
not by my thoughts, my words, my look or gesture,**

and certainly not by actual deeds—
and I will not be party to this in others;
rather, I will put away all desire for revenge.
I will not harm or recklessly endanger myself either.

You shall not commit adultery.

**God condemns all unchastity.
I therefore thoroughly detest it
and will live a decent and chaste life.**

You shall not steal.

**I will do whatever I can for my neighbor's good,
treating others as I would like them to treat me,
and I will work faithfully so that
I may share with those in need.**

You shall not give false testimony against your neighbor.

**I will love the truth, speak it candidly,
and openly acknowledge it.
And I will do what I can to guard
and advance my neighbor's good name.**

You shall not covet anything that belongs to your neighbor.

**With all my heart I will always hate sin
and take pleasure in whatever is right.**
—based on Heidelberg Catechism, Q&A's 92, 94, 96, 99, 103-105, 108, 111-113

21    As we are to walk humbly with our God in lives of gratitude,
let us hear again his Word:
God commands us to serve him alone as God,
to serve him according to his Word,
to speak of him only with deep respect and love,
to attend faithfully the assembly of God's people on the day of rest,
and every day to let the Lord work in us through his Spirit;
to respect and cooperate with all God-given authority,
to nurture human life as God's precious gift,
to live purely and joyfully with the gift of sex,
to use the resources of this earth as stewards of God's creation,
to use the gift of speech for promoting the truth in love,
and to exercise purity of heart in all of life.
**May the Spirit of God guide us
to be obedient to this Word. Amen!**

# 2.8 DEDICATION

*The dedication functions much like the "charge" at the end of the service (see section 9), and many texts for these functions are interchangeable. In some traditions, any charge or dedication is reserved for the end of the service as a response to the gospel proclaimed in both Word and sacrament.*

*Any of these lawlike texts may be followed by a congregational response, and in most cases the response is sung. In some congregations the response may come in the form of an offering. The following texts provide examples for dedications that are entirely spoken.*

1   What shall I return to the LORD
        for all his bounty to me?
    **I will lift up the cup of salvation
        and call on the name of the LORD,
    I will pay my vows to the LORD
        in the presence of all his people.
    I will offer to you a thanksgiving sacrifice
        and call on the name of the LORD.
    I will pay my vows to the LORD
        in the presence of all his people,
    in the courts of the house of the LORD,
        in your midst, O Jerusalem.
    Praise the LORD!**
        —Psalm 116:12-14, 17-19, NRSV

2   *The dedication portion of Psalm 51 is especially appropriate in a worship service that incorporates a portion of this psalm into the prayer of confession.*

    **Then I will teach transgressors your ways,
        and sinners will return to you.
    O LORD, open my lips,
        and my mouth will declare your praise.**
        —Psalm 51:13, 15, NRSV

3   **Christ, having redeemed us by his blood,
    is also restoring us
    by his Spirit into his image,
        so that with our whole lives
            we may show that we are thankful to God
                for his benefits,
    so that he may be praised through us,
    so that we may be assured of our faith by its fruits,
    and so that by our godly living
        our neighbors may be won over to Christ.**
        —Heidelberg Catechism, Q&A 86

# SECTION 3
# PROCLAIMING THE WORD

The reading and preaching of God's Word stands at the center of worship and constitutes one of the privileged moments of worship. The words that introduce and respond to the reading and preaching of Scripture are important for helping the congregation to receive them both attentively and gratefully.

# 3.1 PRAYERS FOR ILLUMINATION

*The power of God's Word comes not from the ink and paper of our printed Bibles or from the creative rhetoric of a preacher but from the work of the Holy Spirit. The Spirit has inspired Scripture and now works in the community of faith to use the proclamation of the Word to comfort, challenge, correct, inspire, and deepen the faith and life of God's people.*

*The prayer for illumination explicitly acknowledges the Spirit's work in this part of worship by requesting God's Spirit to act through the reading and preaching of Scripture. This prayer may also acknowledge that we all come to Scripture with varying degrees of faith, trust, and knowledge. The prayer is offered for both the preacher and the listener, for both the speaking and the hearing of the Word. The prayer may be offered by the Scripture reader, by the preacher, by another member of the congregation, or by the entire congregation. The prayer may also be sung.*

*In some congregations the prayer for illumination is offered after the Scripture reading and before the sermon. The most common tradition, however, both historically and ecumenically, is to offer the prayer prior to the reading of Scripture and the preaching. This practice emphasizes that the reading itself, not just the preaching, is made effective by the work of God's Spirit.*

1   Lord God,
let the words of your servant's mouth
and the meditations of our hearts
be pleasing in your sight,
O Lord, our Rock and Redeemer.
Through Christ. **Amen.**
—based on Psalm 19:14, NRSV

2   Lord God,
help us to know your ways;
    teach us your paths.
Lead us in your truth, and teach us,
    for you are the God of our salvation;
    for you we wait all day long.
Through Christ, our Lord. **Amen.**
—based on Psalm 25:4-5, NRSV

3   Teach us your way, O Lord,
    and lead us on a level path.
Teach us, O Lord, to follow your decrees;
    then we will keep them to the end.
Give us understanding, and we will keep your law
    and obey it with all our hearts.
Through Christ, our Lord. **Amen.**
—based on Psalm 27:11, Psalm 119:33-34, NRSV

4   Lord God,
help us turn our hearts to you
    and hear what you will speak,
for you speak peace to your people
    through Christ, our Lord. **Amen.**
—based on Psalm 85:8

5   Lord God,
may your Word be a lamp to our feet
and a light to our path
through Jesus Christ, our Lord. **Amen.**
—based on Psalm 119:105, NRSV

6   Lord Christ,
we believe in you.
Help our unbelief. **Amen.**
—based on Mark 9:24

7  Lord, to whom shall we go?
   You have the words of eternal life!
   Help us now to hear and obey what you say to us today.
   Through Christ, our Lord. **Amen.**
          —based on John 6:68

8  Lord God, we wish to see Jesus.
   By your Spirit's power, give us eyes to see his glory.
   Through Christ we pray. **Amen.**
          —based on John 12:21

9  God of Jesus Christ,
   give us a spirit of wisdom and of revelation in the knowledge of Christ,
   so that the eyes of our hearts might be enlightened.
   Help us to know the hope to which you have called us,
   the riches of the glorious inheritance in the saints,
   and the immeasurable greatness of your power at work in us.
   Through Christ, our Lord. **Amen.**
          —based on Ephesians 1:17-19, NRSV

10  Lord, open our hearts and minds
    by the power of your Holy Spirit,
    that we may hear your Word with joy. **Amen.**

11  Prepare our hearts, O God,
    to hear your Word
    and obey your will.
    Through Jesus Christ, our Lord. **Amen.**

12  Guide us, O God,
    by your Word and Spirit,
    that in your light we may see light,
    in your truth find freedom,
    and in your will discover your peace,
    through Jesus Christ, our Lord. **Amen.**

13  Lord, before this world's days even began,
    your Word was in the beginning,
    and it was with you and it was you.
    The mystery of that brings us to our knees.
    Yet today you allow us to open your Word and know you better.
    So we ask that you would give us eyes to see and ears to hear.
    Give us hearts open to your Spirit as we seek you. **Amen.**

14  O God, our guide,
    set your path clearly before us
    and lead us to follow you willingly
    for the sake of Jesus Christ, our Lord. **Amen.**

15  Living God,
    help us to hear your holy Word with open hearts
    so that we may truly understand;
    and, understanding,
    that we may believe;
    and, believing,
    that we may follow in all faithfulness and obedience,
    seeking your honor and glory in all that we do.
    Through Christ, our Lord. **Amen.**

16  God, source of all light,
    by your Word give light to our lives. **Amen.**

17  Holy Spirit,
    pour out upon us
    wisdom and understanding,
    that, being taught by you in Holy Scripture,
    our hearts and minds may be opened to receive
    all that leads to life and holiness.
    Through Jesus Christ, our Lord. **Amen.**

18  Come, Holy Spirit:
    Inspire our lives with your light and fire.
    Come, Holy Spirit:
    Anoint us with your bounteous spiritual gifts.
    Come, Holy Spirit:
    Speak to us through your timeless Word today.
    We pray in the name of Jesus, our Lord. **Amen.**

19  Our Lord and our God,
    now as we hear your Word, fill us with your Spirit.
    Soften our hearts that we may delight in your presence.
    Sharpen our minds that we may discern your truth.
    Shape our wills that we may desire your ways.
    Through Jesus Christ, our Lord. **Amen.**

20  Lord Jesus Christ, your light shines within us.
    **Let not my doubts nor my darkness speak to me.**
    Lord Jesus Christ, your light shines within us.
    **Let my heart always welcome your love. Amen.**

21  We pray, Lord,
    that you will open the door of our hearts
    to receive you within our hearts.
    Through Jesus Christ, our Lord. **Amen.**

22  *A text especially mindful of children*

Lord God, thank you for giving us the Bible.
Thank you that through reading it
we can learn more about you and learn to love you more.
Send your Spirit to help us understand your Word and to help us grow.
For Jesus' sake, **Amen**.

23  O Lord, you have given us your Word
for a light to shine upon our path.
Grant us so to meditate on that Word,
and to follow its teaching
that we may find in it the light
that shines more and more
until the perfect day.
Through Jesus Christ, our Lord. **Amen.**

24  Lord God,
you have declared that your kingdom is among us.
Open our eyes to see it,
our ears to hear it,
our hearts to hold it,
our hands to serve it.
This we pray in Jesus' name. **Amen.**

25  O God, on earth's first day you caused light to shine out of darkness.
Now flood our hearts with light from your Word.
O Lord Jesus Christ, Son of God,
you are the light of the world.
As we read and speak and listen, shine in and through us, Jesus. **Amen.**

26  Blessed are you, God of all creation.
You spoke in the beginning, and all things came to be.
**You spoke, and your Word came to live with us,**
**full of grace and truth.**
Bless this place where we would hear your voice.
**Bless this place where we would hear your story.**
As we listen, may our ears be attuned to you.
**As the Word is spoken, may you speak to us.**
**May all we hear lead us to you.**
**Through Jesus Christ, our Lord. Amen.**

27  Almighty God, you have spoken to us through your Son.
Let your written Word now be spoken and heard by each of us.
Give us ears to hear and hearts to understand,
that we may not refuse your calling or ignore your voice.
May we all be taught by you through your powerful Word.
Bring our every thought captive to obeying Christ,
to the glory of your holy name. **Amen.**

28  Loving God, you provide for our every need.
    You feed our bodies and our souls,
    yet we hunger to know and love you more and more.
    Nourish us with your Word today.
    Through Jesus Christ and in the power of the Holy Spirit we pray. **Amen.**

29  Eternal God,
    in the reading of the Scripture, may your Word be heard;
    in the meditations of our hearts, may your Word be known;
    and in the faithfulness of our lives, may your Word be shown. **Amen.**

30  O gracious God and most merciful Father,
    you have given us the rich and precious jewel of your holy Word.
    Assist us with your Spirit, that it may be written in our hearts
    to our everlasting comfort,
    to reform us, to renew us according to your own image,
    to build us up into the perfect building of Christ,
    and to increase us in all heavenly virtues.
    Grant this, O heavenly Father, for the same Jesus Christ's sake. **Amen.**

31  Open our eyes, O God:
    **that we may behold wondrous things out of your law.**
    Open our ears, O God:
    **that we may hear what you will speak**
    **to those who turn to you in their hearts.**
    Open our minds, O God:
    **that we may understand what it means**
    **to revere you and to learn of your ways.**
    Open our hearts, O God:
    **that we may grasp the treasures of wisdom and knowledge**
    **hidden in Christ.**
    Open our mouths, O God:
    **that we may proclaim the mystery of the gospel**
    **and speak of it boldly.**

32  Lord, our God,
    in the reading and proclamation of your Word,
    we pray you will illumine our minds and hearts
    so that we may hear and understand your Word,
    know and live according to your Word,
    and become living letters of your Word,
    equipped to follow Jesus
    in every part of our lives,
    by the power of the Holy Spirit,
    through Christ, our Lord, the living Word. **Amen.**

33    Almighty, gracious Father,
         the true understanding of your holy Word helps us to grow
         into the fulness of the salvation you so freely offer in Christ.
         Grant to all of us that our hearts, being freed from worldly affairs,
         may hear and grasp your holy Word with all diligence and faith,
         that we may rightly understand your gracious will,
         cherish it, and live by it with all earnestness, to your praise and honor.
         Through Christ, our Lord. **Amen.**

34    God of all history, thank you for the Bible.
         Through your Word we learn that you love your people dearly,
         and we learn that we are your people.
         Thank you that your Word shapes our identity.
         Thank you that your Word gives us hope for the future.
         As your Word is read and preached,
         send your Spirit so that we can know
         our role in your ongoing work in our world. **Amen.**

35    Blessed you are, Lord, great God,
         for the testimonies of the prophets we bless you.
         For the statutes of the law we bless you.
         For the gospel of Christ and the witness of the apostles
         we bless you, O glorious God.
         Grant to us the Spirit of your glory
         and the brightness of your presence
         that we might read your Word and understand.
         Through Jesus Christ, our gracious Lord. **Amen.**

36    Lord, our God,
         we bless and thank you for the gift of your Word.
         Grant your servant [*name*] both the humility
         and the boldness necessary to preach it.
         Prepare our hearts and lives to be strengthened and changed by it.
         Through Christ, our Lord. **Amen.**

37    Blessed are you, Lord God Almighty, King of the universe.
         In the beginning your Spirit breathed life into the creation,
         and you continue to renew the face of the earth.
         Your Spirit breathed life into the Scriptures,
         and we pray you will continue to speak your Word to us.
         Your Spirit breathes peace and comfort to the whole world,
         and we pray you will enact that among us today.
         Through Christ, our Lord. **Amen.**

# 3.2 Introductions to the Reading of Scripture

*The reading and hearing of Scripture is one of the most important acts of worship. The introduction to the reading should clearly indicate which text is being read and should invite the congregation's careful attention. If worshipers follow the text in pew Bibles, the page number of the reading may be indicated. In congregations in which worshipers listen without reading along, the introduction to the passage may indicate the book and chapter being read, without a listing of verses. To encourage attentiveness to the reading, some congregations invite worshipers simply to listen and then to refer to the written text during the sermon.*

*The following simple phrases announce the specific text.*

1    The Word of the Lord from . . .

2    A reading from the book of . . .

3    The gospel according to . . .

*The following phrases may be added to the announcement of the text to be read. These phrases are designed to alert the congregation that the Bible is no ordinary book and that the reading of the biblical text demands our careful attention.*

4    Listen to the Word of God.

5    Hear what the Spirit is saying to the church.

6    Attend to the wisdom of the Word of God.

7    Let us hear what God is saying to us today.

*Depending on the theme of the service or the context of the congregation's life, the reading may be preceded by a more extended introduction, such as one of the following texts.*

8    For as the rain and the snow come down from heaven,
        and do not return there until they have watered the earth,
     making it bring forth and sprout,
         giving seed to the sower and bread to the eater,
     so shall the word be that goes out from God's mouth.
     It shall not return to God empty, but it shall accomplish God's purpose,
         and succeed in the thing for which God sent it.
            —from Isaiah 55:10-11, NRSV

9    All scripture is inspired by God
     and is useful for teaching, for reproof,
       for correction, and for training in righteousness,
     so that everyone who belongs to God may be proficient,
       equipped for every good work.
        —2 Timothy 3:16-17, NRSV

10   A voice came from the cloud, saying,
     "This is my Son, whom I have chosen; listen to him."
       —Luke 9:35, NIV

# 3.3 RESPONSES TO THE READING OF SCRIPTURE

*Just as a thoughtful introduction to Scripture reading helps to focus the congregation's attention on the Word of God, so too a thoughtful response to the reading of Scripture reinforces that this is no ordinary book. The response helps worshipers to communicate that they receive Scripture as nothing less than God's Word. In some contexts, the response might be followed by a brief moment of silence.*

1    The Word of the Lord.
     **Thanks be to God.**

2    This is the Word of the Lord.
     **Thanks be to God.**

3    The gospel of our Lord Jesus Christ according to _____.
     **Glory to you, O Lord.**

4    The gospel of the Lord.
     **Praise to you, O Christ.**

5    The grass withers
     and the flower fades,
     but the word of the Lord endures forever.
     **Amen.**
       —from 1 Peter 1:24-25, NRSV

6    God's Word is a lamp to our feet,
     and a light to our path.
     **Thanks be to God!**
          —based on Psalm 119:105, NIV

7    May God bless to our understanding
     this reading from the Word.

8    Herein is wisdom.
     **Thanks be to God.**

9    God's Word is full of grace and truth!
     **Thank you, loving God.**

10   *A text especially mindful of children*

     God has spoken to us.
     **Thank you, God, for your Word.**

11   God, we thank you for your Word,
     **the story of your grace.**

# 3.4 CONCLUSIONS OR RESPONSES TO THE SERMON

*The following resources are fitting conclusions or responses to the preaching of God's Word. Some of these resources are acclamations—that is, eager and vigorous expressions of assent and praise. Just as some variation of the phrase "through Christ our Lord" at the end of a prayer communicates that the prayer is offered in the name and through the mediating power of Christ, so too these responses indicate that the sermon is offered on the strength of God's Word and in Jesus' name. Other resources here are prayers, petitions for God's power to help the congregation live out the message they have just heard. Most often these prayers are tailored to particular themes preached in the sermon. After the sermon, a time of silence for personal reflection can also be included before a brief prayer of application.*

*The following resources provide general models for adaptation in a variety of circumstances.*

## Acclamations

1   In the name of the Father, the Son, and the Holy Spirit. **Amen.**

2   O the depth of the riches and wisdom and knowledge of God!
    How unsearchable are his judgments and how inscrutable his ways!
        "For who has known the mind of the Lord?
            Or who has been his counselor?"
        "Or who has given a gift to him,
            to receive a gift in return?"
    **For from him and through him and to him are all things.**
    **To him be the glory forever. Amen.**
        —Romans 11:33-36, NRSV

3   Now to him who by the power at work within us
    is able to accomplish abundantly far more than all we can ask or imagine,
    to him be glory in the church and in Christ Jesus to all generations, forever and
    ever. **Amen.**
        —Ephesians 3:20-21, NRSV

4   Glory to God in the church!
    Glory to God in the Messiah, in Jesus!
    Glory down all the generations!
    Glory through all millennia! Oh, yes!
        —Ephesians 3:21, TM

5   Now to the King eternal,
    immortal, invisible, the only God,
    be honor and glory for ever and ever. **Amen.**
        —1 Timothy 1:17, NIV

6   To Jesus Christ, who loves us
    and freed us from our sins by his blood
    and made us to be a kingdom,
    priests of his God and Father,
    to him be glory and dominion forever and ever. **Amen.**
        —from Revelation 1:5-6, NRSV

7   Blessing and glory and wisdom
    and thanksgiving and honor
    and power and might
    be to our God forever and ever! **Amen.**
        —Revelation 7:12, NRSV

## Prayers

8   Lord God,
    by the power of your Spirit,
    give us strength to live out the message we have heard today.
    Through Christ our Lord. **Amen.**

**9**    Almighty and loving God,
we bless you for the gift of your Word.
We pray now for the grace to believe what we have heard,
and to live in ways that honor you above all.
Through Christ, our Lord. **Amen.**

**10**   O Lord, our God,
you have given to us the glorious gospel of our risen Savior and Master:
Grant that as we joyfully receive the good news for ourselves,
so we may gratefully share it with others,
and ever give glory to you, by whose grace alone we are what we are:
through the same Jesus Christ, our Lord. **Amen.**

**11**   O Lord, we give you our lives.
May our heart, our minds, and our desires be yours.
May our hands and feet and voices
move as you would choose.
May our moments and days
flow in endless praise. **Amen.**
—based on "Take My Life and Let It Be" by Frances R. Havergal (1874)

# 3.5 INTRODUCTIONS TO THE PROFESSION OF FAITH

---

*The following introductions to the profession of faith call attention to the various purposes for the corporate recitation of a scriptural or historic creed.*

**1**    Let us together profess our faith.

**2**    Let us affirm our faith.

**3**    Let us profess the faith of our baptism, as we say:

**4**    Let us join with all the saints in all cultures and ages
in our profession of faith and praise:

**5**    Let us together confess the faith of the church at all times and in all places:

**6**    Let us express our unity with the church of all ages
by professing our faith in the words of [*creed or Scripture*]:

7    Let us join together in love,
and with one heart and one voice
profess the faith of the church
at all times and in all places:

8    Together, we state what our church affirms and believes.
If you are visiting with us today,
we would be happy to explain the joy
we have because of these statements.
Simply ask one of us at the end of the service.

# 3.6 PROFESSION OF OUR CHURCH'S FAITH

*Corporate recitation of a scriptural, historic, or contemporary statement of faith has several possible goals in worship. It is at once*

- *a fitting response to the Word of God as proclaimed.*
- *an expression of the unity in the church across time and space.*
- *a witness to our individual participation in something greater than ourselves.*
- *a summary of the whole gospel to amplify the portion of the gospel preached in a particular service.*
- *a recollection of our baptism and of the faith into which we have been baptized.*
- *an expression of the common faith of the church, whose unity we affirm at the Lord's Supper.*

*Each purpose suggests the value of different kinds of creedal statements, some of which have official status in various denominations. A scriptural profession of faith allows the congregation to respond to the sermon with a text connected to the theme of the sermon; of the many scriptural possibilities, only a few are suggested here as examples. A historic creed, often used at baptism, serves as a reminder of baptismal faith and our connection with the church of all ages. A contemporary statement of faith allows the congregation to connect its faith directly with opportunities and challenges in contemporary culture or to paraphrase other sources with particular attention to the participation of children. Any contemporary statement of faith should be used in such a way that it does not imply that it somehow supersedes the historic statements of faith. Many of these creedal statements may also be sung to musical settings provided in many hymnals and songbooks.*

*The most common tradition is the use of the ecumenical creeds—a statement of what believers in all times and places profess. The use of other historic or contemporary creeds may be appropriate for a given service or theme.*

## Ecumenical Creeds

1   We believe in one God,
    the Father almighty,
    maker of heaven and earth,
    of all things visible and invisible.

And in one Lord Jesus Christ,
    the only Son of God,
    begotten from the Father before all ages,
        God from God,
        Light from Light,
        true God from true God,
    begotten, not made;
    of the same essence as the Father.
    Through him all things were made.
    For us and for our salvation
        he came down from heaven;
        he became incarnate by the Holy Spirit and the virgin Mary,
        and was made human.
    He was crucified for us under Pontius Pilate;
    he suffered and was buried.
    The third day he rose again, according to the Scriptures.
    He ascended to heaven
    and is seated at the right hand of the Father.
    He will come again with glory
    to judge the living and the dead.
    His kingdom will never end.

And we believe in the Holy Spirit,
    the Lord, the giver of life.
    He proceeds from the Father and the Son,
    and with the Father and the Son is worshiped and glorified.
    He spoke through the prophets.
    We believe in one holy catholic and apostolic church.
    We affirm one baptism for the forgiveness of sins.
    We look forward to the resurrection of the dead,
    and to life in the world to come. Amen.
        —Nicene Creed

2   I believe in God, the Father almighty,
    creator of heaven and earth.

I believe in Jesus Christ, his only Son, our Lord,
    who was conceived by the Holy Spirit
    and born of the virgin Mary.
    He suffered under Pontius Pilate,
    was crucified, died, and was buried;
    he descended to hell.
    The third day he rose again from the dead.

He ascended to heaven
and is seated at the right hand of God the Father almighty.
From there he will come to judge the living and the dead.

I believe in the Holy Spirit,
the holy catholic church,
the communion of saints,
the forgiveness of sins,
the resurrection of the body,
and the life everlasting. Amen.
—Apostles' Creed

3   *This question-and-answer format of the Apostles' Creed may be used in baptism and baptismal renewal services.*

Do you believe in God the Father?
I believe in God, the Father almighty,
creator of heaven and earth.

Do you believe in Jesus Christ, the Son of God?
I believe in Jesus Christ, God's only Son, our Lord,
who was conceived by the Holy Spirit,
born of the virgin Mary,
suffered under Pontius Pilate,
was crucified, died, and was buried.
He descended to the dead.
On the third day he rose again;
he ascended into heaven,
he is seated at the right hand of the Father,
and he will come to judge the living and the dead.

Do you believe in God the Holy Spirit?
I believe in the Holy Spirit,
the holy catholic church,
the communion of saints,
the forgiveness of sins,
the resurrection of the body,
and the life everlasting.
—based on Apostles' Creed

## Scriptural Professions of Faith

4   Hear, O Israel: the LORD our God, the LORD is one.
—Deuteronomy 6:4, NIV

5   I know that my Redeemer lives,
and that at the last he will stand upon the earth;
and after my skin has been thus destroyed,
then in my flesh I shall see God.
—Job 19:25-26, NRSV

6    The LORD is my shepherd, I lack nothing.
    **He makes me lie down in green pastures,**
  **he leads me beside quiet waters,**
    **he refreshes my soul.**
**He guides me along the right paths**
    **for his name's sake.**
Even though I walk
    through the darkest valley,
I will fear no evil,
    for you are with me;
your rod and your staff,
    they comfort me.
You prepare a table before me
    in the presence of my enemies.
You anoint my head with oil;
    my cup overflows.
**Surely your goodness and love will follow me**
    **all the days of my life,**
**and I will dwell in the house of the LORD**
    **forever.**
      —Psalm 23


7    God is our refuge and strength,
    a very present help in trouble.
Therefore we will not fear, though the earth should change,
    though the mountains shake in the heart of the sea;
though its waters roar and foam,
    though the mountains tremble with its tumult.
There is a river whose streams make glad the city of God,
    the holy habitation of the Most High.
God is in the midst of the city; it shall not be moved;
    God will help it when the morning dawns.
The nations are in an uproar, the kingdoms totter;
    he utters his voice, the earth melts.
**The LORD of hosts is with us;**
    **the God of Jacob is our refuge.**
Come, behold the works of the LORD;
    see what desolations he has brought on the earth.
He makes wars cease to the end of the earth;
    he breaks the bow, and shatters the spear;
    he burns the shields with fire.
"Be still, and know that I am God!
    I am exalted among the nations,
    I am exalted in the earth."
**The LORD of hosts is with us;**
    **the God of Jacob is our refuge.**
      —Psalm 46, NRSV

8    Lord, you have been our dwelling place
        in all generations.
    **Before the mountains were brought forth,**
        **or ever you had formed the earth and the world,**
        **from everlasting to everlasting you are God.**
          —Psalm 90:1-2, NRSV

9    **This is the good news that we have received, in which we stand,**
    **and by which we are saved, if we hold it fast:**
    **that Christ died for our sins according to the Scriptures,**
    **that he was buried,**
    **that he was raised on the third day,**
    **and that he appeared first to the women,**
    **then to Peter, and to the Twelve, and then to many faithful witnesses.**
    **We believe that Jesus is the Christ, the Son of the living God.**
    **Jesus Christ is the first and the last, the beginning and the end;**
    **he is our Lord and our God.**
          —based on Matthew 16:16; Mark 16:9; John 20:28; 1 Corinthians 15:1-6; Revelation 22:13

10   **We believe there is no condemnation**
    **for those who are in Christ Jesus;**
    **for we know that all things work together for good**
    **for those who love God,**
    **who are called according to God's purpose.**
    **We are convinced that neither death, nor life,**
    **nor angels, nor rulers,**
    **nor things present, nor things to come,**
    **nor powers, nor height, nor depth,**
    **nor anything else in all creation,**
    **will be able to separate us from the love of God**
    **in Christ Jesus our Lord.**
          —from Romans 8:1, 28, 38-39, NRSV

11   **Christ Jesus,**
    **though he was in the form of God,**
        **did not regard equality with God**
        **as something to be exploited,**
    **but emptied himself,**
        **taking the form of a slave,**
        **being born in human likeness.**
    **And being found in human form**
        **he humbled himself**
        **and became obedient to the point of death—**
        **even death on a cross.**
    **Therefore God also highly exalted him**
        **and gave him the name**
        **that is above every name,**
    **so that at the name of Jesus**
        **every knee should bend,**
        **in heaven and on earth and under the earth,**

and every tongue should confess
  to the glory of God:
  Jesus Christ is Lord!
    —from Philippians 2:5-11, NRSV

12  Jesus Christ is the image of the invisible God,
      the firstborn of all creation;
    in him all things in heaven and on earth were created,
      things visible and invisible.
    All things have been created through him and for him.
    He himself is before all things,
      and in him all things hold together.
    He is the head of the body, the church;
      he is the beginning,
      the firstborn from the dead,
    so that he might come to have first place in everything.
    For in him all the fullness of God was pleased to dwell,
    and through him God was pleased to reconcile all things,
      whether on earth or in heaven,
    by making peace through the blood of his cross.
      —from Colossians 1:15-20, NRSV

## Historic Statements of Faith

*The following selections from the Heidelberg Catechism were originally presented in a question-and-answer format. They may easily be adapted as congregational statements of faith, as shown below.*

13  My only comfort in life and in death is
    that I am not my own,
    but belong—
        body and soul,
        in life and in death—
    to my faithful Savior Jesus Christ.
        He has fully paid for all my sins with his precious blood,
        and has set me free from the tyranny of the devil.
        He also watches over me in such a way
        that not a hair can fall from my head
        without the will of my Father in heaven:
        in fact, all things must work together for my salvation.
    Because I belong to him,
    Christ, by his Holy Spirit,
    assures me of eternal life
    and makes me wholeheartedly willing and ready
    from now on to live for him.
      —from Heidelberg Catechism, Q&A 1

14 I believe that the eternal Father of our Lord Jesus Christ,
    who out of nothing created heaven and earth
      and everything in them,
    who still upholds and rules them
      by his eternal counsel and providence,
is my God and Father
    because of Christ the Son.
I trust God so much that I do not doubt
    he will provide whatever I need
      for body and soul,
    and will turn to my good
      whatever adversity he sends upon me
      in this sad world.
God is able to do this because he is almighty God
and desires to do this because he is a faithful Father.
    —from Heidelberg Catechism, Q&A 26

15 I am called a Christian
because by faith I am a member of Christ
and so I share in his anointing.
    I am anointed
    to confess his name,
    to present myself to him as a living sacrifice of thanks,
    to strive with a free conscience against sin and the devil
      in this life,
    and afterward to reign with Christ
      over all creation
      for all eternity.
We call him "our Lord"
because—
    not with gold or silver,
    but with his precious blood—
he has set us free
    from sin and from the tyranny of the devil,
and has bought us,
    body and soul,
to be his very own.
    —from Heidelberg Catechism, Q&A's 32, 34

16 I believe that the Son of God
    through his Spirit and Word,
    out of the entire human race,
    from the beginning of the world to its end,
gathers, protects, and preserves for himself
    a community chosen for eternal life
      and united in true faith.
And of this community I am and always will be
    a living member.
    —from Heidelberg Catechism, Q&A 54

17 I am righteous before God
   only by true faith in Jesus Christ.
   Even though my conscience accuses me
       of having grievously sinned against all God's commandments,
       of never having kept any of them,
       and of still being inclined toward all evil,
   nevertheless,
       without any merit of my own,
       out of sheer grace,
   God grants and credits to me
   the perfect satisfaction, righteousness, and holiness of Christ,
       as if I had never sinned nor been a sinner,
       and as if I had been as perfectly obedient
           as Christ was obedient for me.
   All I need to do
   is accept this gift with a believing heart.
   When I say that through faith alone I am righteous,
   it is not because I please God
       by the worthiness of my faith.
   It is because only Christ's satisfaction, righteousness, and holiness
       make me righteous before God,
   and because I can accept this righteousness and make it mine
       in no other way than through faith.
              —from Heidelberg Catechism, Q&A's 60-61

*The following selections from the Belgic Confession may be used with or without the provided opening questions. The original document is a simple assertion of faith; the questions are added here for congregations accustomed to reciting a profession of faith in question-and-answer format.*

18   What do you believe about God?
     **We all believe in our hearts
     and confess with our mouths
     that there is a single and simple
     spiritual being,
     whom we call God—
         eternal, incomprehensible,
         invisible, unchangeable,
         infinite, almighty;
         completely wise,
         just, and good,
         and the overflowing source of all good.**
              —based on Belgic Confession, Art. 1

19   What do you believe about the work of God?
     **We believe that God—
         who is perfectly merciful
         and also very just—
     sent his Son to assume the nature**

in which the disobedience had been committed,
    in order to bear in it the punishment of sin
    by his most bitter passion and death.

And what do you believe about the work of Jesus Christ?
We believe that Jesus Christ presented himself
in our name before his Father,
to appease his wrath
with full satisfaction
by offering himself
    on the tree of the cross
and pouring out his precious blood
    for the cleansing of our sins,
    as the prophets had predicted.

Why did he endure all this?
He endured all this
for the forgiveness of our sins.

What comfort does this give you?
We find all comforts in his wounds
and have no need to seek or invent any other means
to reconcile ourselves with God
than this one and only sacrifice,
once made,
which renders believers perfect forever.
        —based on Belgic Confession, Art. 20-21

20    What do you believe about your forgiveness?
We believe that our blessedness lies in the forgiveness of our sins
because of Jesus Christ,
and that in it our righteousness before God is contained,
    as David and Paul teach us
    when they declare that person blessed
    to whom God grants righteousness
    apart from works.

How do you come by such forgiveness?
We are justified "freely" or "by grace"
through redemption in Jesus Christ.
And therefore we cling to this foundation,
which is firm forever,
    giving all glory to God,
    humbling ourselves,
    and recognizing ourselves as we are;
    not claiming a thing for ourselves or our merits
    and leaning and resting on the sole obedience of Christ crucified,
    which is ours when we believe in him.

Does this forgiveness give you peace with God?
**This is enough to cover all our sins**
**and to make us confident,**
**freeing the conscience from the fear, dread, and terror**
    **of God's approach,**
**without doing what our first father, Adam, did,**
    **who trembled as he tried to cover himself with fig leaves.**
      —based on Belgic Confession, Art. 23

**21**   What do you believe about the church of Christ?
**We believe and confess**
**one single catholic or universal church—**
    **a holy congregation and gathering**
    **of true Christian believers.**

What binds them all together?
**They await their entire salvation in Jesus Christ,**
**having been washed by his blood,**
**and sanctified and sealed by the Holy Spirit.**

When did this church begin?
**This church has existed from the beginning of the world**
**and will last until the end,**
    **as appears from the fact**
    **that Christ is eternal King**
    **who cannot be without subjects.**

How is this church preserved?
**This holy church is preserved by God**
**against the rage of the whole world,**
    **even though for a time**
    **it may appear very small**
    **in the eyes of humankind—**
    **as though it were snuffed out.**

How big is this church?
**This holy church is not confined,**
**bound, or limited to a certain place or certain persons.**
**But it is spread and dispersed**
**throughout the entire world,**
    **though still joined and united**
      **in heart and will,**
      **in one and the same Spirit,**
      **by the power of faith.**
      —based on Belgic Confession, Art. 27

**22**   What will happen at the end of time?
**When the time appointed by the Lord is come**
**(which is unknown to all creatures)**
**and the number of the elect is complete,**

our Lord Jesus Christ will come from heaven,
    bodily and visibly,
as he ascended,
    with great glory and majesty,
to declare himself the judge
    of the living and the dead.

Will everyone see him when he comes?
All human creatures will appear in person
before the great judge—
    men, women, and children,
    who have lived from the beginning
    until the end of the world.
They will be summoned there
by the voice of the archangel
and by the sound of the divine trumpet.

What about those who have already died? Will they miss it?
All those who died before that time
will be raised from the earth,
    their spirits being joined and united
    with their own bodies in which they lived.

What about those who are still alive?
As for those who are still alive,
they will not die like the others
but will be changed "in the twinkling of an eye"
from "corruptible to incorruptible."

—based on Belgic Confession, Art. 37

*The following selections from the Modern English Study Version (MESV) of the Westminster Confession were offered in 1993 by the Orthodox Presbyterian Church "as a carefully edited and prepared study to the confession itself."*

23    There is only one living and true God,
      who is infinite in being and perfection.
      He is a most pure spirit, invisible,
      with neither body, parts, nor passive properties.
      He is unchangeable, boundless, eternal, and incomprehensible.
      He is almighty, most wise, most holy, most free, and most absolute.
      He works all things according to the counsel of his own unchangeable
      and most righteous will, for his own glory.
      He is most loving, gracious, merciful, long-suffering,
      abundant in goodness and truth, forgiving iniquity, transgression, and sin,
      and he is the rewarder of those who diligently seek him.
      He is also most just and terrifying in his judgments, hating all sin,
      and will by no means acquit the guilty.

—from Westminster Confession (MESV), Chap. II, Sec. 1

24   God—the great creator of all things—
      upholds, directs, disposes, and governs all creatures, actions, and things,
      from the greatest even to the least.
      He exercises this most wise and holy providence
      according to his infallible foreknowledge
      and the free and unchangeable counsel of his own will,
      to the praise of the glory of his wisdom, power,
      justice, goodness, and mercy.
                —from Westminster Confession (MESV), Chap. V, Sec. 1

25   God was pleased, in his eternal purpose,
      to choose and ordain the Lord Jesus, his only begotten Son,
      to be the mediator between God and human beings.
      As the mediator, he is the prophet, priest, and king,
      the head and Savior of the church, the heir of all things,
      and the judge of the world.
      God gave to him, from all eternity,
      a people to be his seed and to be by him, in time,
      redeemed, called, justified, sanctified, and glorified.

      The Lord Jesus, by his perfect obedience and sacrifice of himself—
      which he through the eternal Spirit once offered up to God—
      has fully satisfied the justice of his Father.
      He purchased not only reconciliation but also an everlasting inheritance
      in the kingdom of heaven for all those whom the Father has given to him.
                —from Westminster Confession (MESV), Chap. VIII, Sec. 1, 5

## Contemporary Statements of Faith

*These contemporary statements of faith are intended to complement, not replace, the scriptural or other historic statements included above. These statements of faith also speak to issues and concerns that are unique to our own historical context.*

26   *A text especially mindful of children*

      The Lord is my shepherd.
      He takes care of all my needs.
      **The Lord is my shepherd.**
      **He takes care of all my needs.**
      The Lord watches over me. He takes care of all my needs.
      He gives me a home to live in. He gives me water to drink.
      He gives meaning to my life.
      **The Lord is my shepherd.**
      **He takes care of all my needs.**
      He guides me along the right way.
      Even when I'm walking by myself in a strange place,
      I don't feel scared because I know that the Lord is with me
      to help me and give me courage.
      **The Lord is my shepherd.**

**He takes care of all my needs.**
He gives me food to eat. I always have enough to drink.
He has blessed me with many things.
I will never be able to repay him for his kindness.
**The Lord is my shepherd.**
**He takes care of all my needs.**
—based on Psalm 23

27  As followers of Jesus Christ,
living in this world—
which some seek to control,
and others view with despair—
we declare with joy and trust:
**Our world belongs to God!**
From the beginning,
through all the crises of our times,
until the kingdom fully comes,
God keeps covenant forever:
**Our world belongs to God!**
**God is King: Let the earth be glad!**
**Christ is victor: his rule has begun!**
**The Spirit is at work: creation is renewed!**
**Hallelujah! Praise the Lord!**
—*Our World Belongs to God,* st. 1-2

28  God holds this world with fierce love.
Keeping his promise, he sends Jesus into the world,
pours out the Holy Spirit, and announces the good news:
sinners who repent and believe in Jesus
live anew as members of the family of God—
the firstfruits of a new creation.
**We rejoice in the goodness of God,**
**renounce the works of darkness,**
**and dedicate ourselves to holy living.**
As covenant partners,
set free for joyful obedience,
we offer our hearts and lives to do God's work in the world.
With tempered impatience, eager to see injustice ended,
we expect the Day of the Lord.
**We are confident**
**that the light which shines in the present darkness**
**will fill the earth when Christ appears.**
**Come, Lord Jesus. Our world belongs to you.**
—*Our World Belongs to God,* st. 5-6

*163*

29    Made in God's image
to live in communion with our Maker,
we are appointed earthkeepers and caretakers
to tend the earth, enjoy it,
and love our neighbors.
God uses our skills
for the unfolding and well-being of his world
so that creation and all who live in it may flourish.
Together, male and female,
single and married, young and old—
every hue and variety of humanity—
we are called to represent God,
for the Lord God made us all.
Life is God's gift to us,
and we are called to foster
the well-being of all the living,
protecting from harm
the unborn and the weak,
the poor and the vulnerable.

        *—Our World Belongs to God,* st. 10-11

30    Fallen in that first sin,
we prove each day that apart from grace
we are guilty sinners;
we fail to thank God,
we break God's laws,
we ignore our tasks.
Looking for life without God, we find death;
grasping for freedom outside the law,
we trap ourselves in Satan's snares;
pursuing pleasure, we lose the gift of joy.
In all our striving to excuse or save ourselves,
We stand condemned before the God of truth.
But our world, broken and scarred,
still belongs to God,
who holds it together and gives us hope.

        *—Our World Belongs to God,* st. 14, 17

31    Remembering the promise
to reconcile the world to himself,
God joined our humanity in Jesus Christ—
the eternal Word made flesh.
He is the long-awaited Messiah,
one with us and one with God,
fully human and fully divine,
conceived by the Holy Spirit
and born of the virgin Mary.
Being both divine and human,
Jesus is the only mediator.

He alone paid the debt of our sin;
there is no other Savior.
We are chosen in Christ
to become like him in every way.
God's electing love sustains our hope:
God's grace is free to save sinners who offer nothing
but their need for mercy.
—*Our World Belongs to God*, st. 23, 26

32    The Spirit renews our hearts and moves us to faith,
leads us into truth, and helps us to pray,
stands by us in our need, and makes our obedience fresh and vibrant.
God the Spirit lavishes gifts on the church in astonishing variety—
prophecy, encouragement, healing, teaching, service, tongues, discernment—
equipping each member to build up the body of Christ
and to serve our neighbors.
The Spirit gathers people from every tongue, tribe, and nation
into the unity of the body of Christ.
Anointed and sent by the Spirit,
the church is thrust into the world,
ambassadors of God's peace,
announcing forgiveness and reconciliation,
proclaiming the good news of grace.
Going before them and with them,
the Spirit convinces the world of sin
and pleads the cause of Christ.
Men and women, impelled by the Spirit,
go next door and far away into science and art,
media and marketplace—every area of life,
pointing to the reign of God with what they do and say.
—*Our World Belongs to God*, st. 29-30

33    In our world, where many journey alone, nameless in the bustling crowd,
Satan and his evil forces seek whom they may scatter and isolate;
but God, by his gracious choosing in Christ, gathers a new community—
those who by God's gift put their trust in Christ.
In the new community all are welcome:
the homeless come home, the broken find healing, the sinner makes a new start;
the despised are esteemed, the least are honored, and the last are first.
Here the Spirit guides and grace abounds.
The church is the fellowship of those who confess Jesus as Lord.
She is the bride of Christ, his chosen partner, loved by Jesus and loving him:
delighting in his presence, seeking him in prayer—
silent before the mystery of his love.
Our new life in Christ is celebrated and nourished
in the fellowship of congregations, where we praise God's name,
hear the Word proclaimed, learn God's ways,
confess our sins, offer our prayers and gifts, and celebrate the sacraments.
—*Our World Belongs to God*, st. 34-36

34   The church is a gathering of forgiven sinners called to be holy.
     Saved by the patient grace of God, we deal patiently with others
     and together confess our need for grace and forgiveness.
     Restored in Christ's presence, shaped by his life,
     this new community lives out the ongoing story of God's reconciling love,
     announces the new creation, and works for a world of justice and peace.
     We grieve that the church, which shares one Spirit, one faith, one hope,
     and spans all time, place, race, and language,
     has become a broken communion in a broken world.
     When we struggle for the truth of the gospel
     and for the righteousness God demands, we pray for wisdom and courage.
     When our pride or blindness hinders
     the unity of God's household, we seek forgiveness.
     We marvel that the Lord gathers the broken pieces
     to do his work and that he blesses us still
     with joy, new members, and surprising evidences of unity.
     We commit ourselves to seeking and expressing
     the oneness of all who follow Jesus,
     and we pray for brothers and sisters who suffer for the faith.
          —*Our World Belongs to God*, st. 39-40

35   Joining the mission of God, the church is sent
     with the gospel of the kingdom
     to call everyone to know and follow Christ,
     and to proclaim to all
     the assurance that in the name of Jesus
     there is forgiveness of sin
     and new life for all who repent and believe.
     The Spirit calls all members
     to embrace God's mission
     in their neighborhoods
     and in the world:
     to feed the hungry, bring water to the thirsty,
     welcome the stranger, clothe the naked,
     care for the sick, and free the prisoner.
     We repent of leaving this work to a few,
     for this mission is central to our being.
          —*Our World Belongs to God*, st. 41

36   Our hope for a new creation is not tied to what humans can do,
     for we believe that one day every challenge to God's rule will be crushed.
     His kingdom will fully come, and the Lord will rule.
     Come, Lord Jesus, come.
          —*Our World Belongs to God*, st. 55

37   With the whole creation
     we join the song:
     "Worthy is the Lamb, who was slain,
     to receive power and wealth

and wisdom and strength
and honor and glory and praise!"
He has made us a kingdom of priests
to serve our God,
and we will reign on earth.
God will be all in all,
righteousness and peace will flourish,
everything will be made new,
and every eye will see at last
that our world belongs to God.
Hallelujah! Come, Lord Jesus!

*—Our World Belongs to God, st. 58*

38  In life and in death we belong to God.
Through the grace of our Lord Jesus Christ,
    the love of God, and the communion of the Holy Spirit,
we trust in the one triune God, the Holy One of Israel,
    whom alone we worship and serve.
We trust in Jesus Christ,
    fully human, fully God.
Jesus proclaimed the reign of God:
    preaching good news to the poor and release to the captives,
    teaching by word and deed and blessing the children,
    healing the sick and binding up the brokenhearted,
    eating with outcasts,
    forgiving sinners,
    and calling all to repent and believe the gospel.

*—A Brief Statement of Faith*

39  We trust in God,
    whom Jesus called Abba, Father.
In sovereign love God created the world good
    and makes everyone equally in God's image,
    male and female, of every race and people,
    to live as one community.
But we rebel against God; we hide from our Creator.
Ignoring God's commandments,
we violate the image of God in others and ourselves,
    accept lies as truth,
    exploit neighbor and nature,
    and threaten death to the planet entrusted to our care.
We deserve God's condemnation.
Yet God acts with justice and mercy to redeem creation.
The Spirit justifies us by grace through faith,
    sets us free to accept ourselves and to love God and neighbor,
    and binds us together with all believers
    in the one body of Christ, the church.
The same Spirit who inspired the prophets and apostles

> rules our faith and life in Christ through Scripture,
> engages us through the Word proclaimed,
> claims us in the waters of baptism,
> feeds us with the bread of life and the cup of salvation,
> and calls women and men to all ministries of the church.
> In a broken and fearful world the Spirit gives us courage
>> to pray without ceasing,
>> to witness among all peoples to Christ as Lord and Savior,
>> to unmask idolatries in church and culture,
>> to hear the voices of peoples long silenced,
>> and to work with others for justice, freedom, and peace.
> *—A Brief Statement of Faith*

**40**  *Our Song of Hope is the source for the following set of seven affirmations, which may be used separately or together. The Opening Declaration and Closing Prayer may be used as a frame for any combination of the seven affirmations:*

*Opening Declaration*
We sing to our Lord a new song;
we sing in our world a sure hope:
**Our God loves this world,**
> **God called it into being,**
> **God renews it through Jesus Christ,**
> **God governs it by the Spirit.**
> **God is the world's true hope.**

[*One or more affirmations*]

*Closing Prayer*
**Come, Lord Jesus:**
> **We are open to your Spirit.**
> **We await your full presence.**
> **Our world finds rest in you alone. Amen.**

**41**  *Our hope in the coming of the Lord*

We are a people of hope
> waiting for the return of our Lord.
God has come to us
> through the ancient people of Israel,
> as the true Son of God, Jesus of Nazareth,
> as the Holy Spirit at work in our world.
**Our Lord speaks to us now through the inspired Scriptures.**
**Christ is with us day by day.**

**42** *Our song in a hopeless world*

We know Christ to be our only hope.
We have enmeshed our world in a realm of sin,
    rebelled against God,
    accepted inhuman oppression of humanity,
    and even crucified God's Son.
God's world has been trapped by our fall,
    governments entangled by human pride,
    and nature polluted by human greed.

**43** *Jesus Christ, our only hope*

Our only hope is Jesus Christ.
After we refused to live in the image of God,
he was born of the virgin Mary,
    sharing our genes and our instincts,
    entering our culture, speaking our language,
    fulfilling the law of our God.
Being united to Christ's humanity,
    we know ourselves when we rest in him.
Jesus Christ is the hope of God's world.
In his death, the justice of God is established;
    forgiveness of sin is proclaimed.
On the day of his resurrection,
    the tomb was empty; his disciples saw him;
    death was defeated; new life had come.
God's purpose for the world was sealed.
Our ascended Lord gives hope for two ages.
In the age to come, Christ is the judge,
    rejecting unrighteousness,
    isolating God's enemies to hell,
    blessing the new creation in Christ.
In this age, the Holy Spirit is with us,
    calling nations to follow God's path,
    uniting people through Christ in love.

**44** *Our hope in God's words*

The Holy Spirit speaks through the Scriptures.
The Spirit has inspired Hebrew and Greek words,
    setting God's truth in human language,
    placing God's teaching in ancient cultures,
    proclaiming the gospel in the history of the world.
The Spirit speaks truly what the nations must know,
    translating God's Word into modern languages,
    impressing it on human hearts and cultures.
The Holy Spirit speaks through the church,
    measuring its words by the canonical Scriptures.
The Spirit has spoken in the ancient creeds

and in the confessions of the Reformation.
The Spirit calls the world to bear witness to Christ
    in faithfulness to the Scriptures,
    in harmony with the church of the ages,
    and in unity with all Christ's people.
God's Spirit speaks in the world
    according to God's ultimate Word in Christ.
In every time and place,
    in ancient cities and distant lands,
    in technology and business,
    in art and education,
God has not been without a witness.
The Word has entered where we have failed to go.
In each year and in every place
    we expect the coming of Christ's Spirit.
As we listen to the world's concerns,
    hear the cry of the oppressed,
    and learn of new discoveries,
God will give us knowledge,
    teach us to respond with maturity,
    and give us courage to act with integrity.

**45**   *Our hope in daily life*

As citizens we acknowledge
the Spirit's work in human government
    for the welfare of the people,
    for justice among the poor,
    for mercy toward the prisoner,
    against inhuman oppression of humanity.
We must obey God above all rulers,
    waiting upon the Spirit,
    filled with the patience of Christ.
We pray for the fruits of the Spirit of Christ
    who works for peace on earth,
    commands us to love our enemies,
    and calls for patience among the nations.
We give thanks for God's work among governments,
    seeking to resolve disputes by means other than war,
    placing human kindness above national pride,
    replacing the curse of war with international self-control.
We hear the Spirit's call to love one another
    opposing discrimination of race or sex,
    inviting us to accept one another,
and to share at every level
    in work and play,
    in church and state,
    in marriage and family,
and so fulfill the love of Christ.

As male and female, we look to the Spirit,
who makes us the stewards of life
    to plan its beginning,
    to love in its living,
    and to care in its dying.
God makes us the stewards of marriage
    with its lifelong commitment to love;
    yet God knows our frailty of heart.
The Spirit leads us into truth—
    the truth of Christ's salvation,
    into increasing knowledge of all existence.
The Spirit rejoices in human awareness of God's creation
    and gives freedom to those on the frontiers of research.
We are overwhelmed by the growth in our knowledge.
While our truths come in broken fragments,
    we expect the Spirit to unite these in Christ.

**46** *Our hope in the church*

Christ elects the church
    to proclaim the Word and celebrate the sacraments,
    to worship God's name,
    and to live as true disciples.
He creates this community
    to be a place of prayer,
    to provide rest for the weary,
    and to lead people to share in service.
The Holy Spirit sends the church
    to call sinners to repentance,
    to proclaim the good news
        that Jesus is personal Savior and Lord.
The Spirit sends the church out in ministry
    to preach good news to the poor,
    righteousness to the nations,
    and peace among all people.
The Holy Spirit builds one church,
    united in one Lord and one hope,
    with one ministry around one table.
The Spirit calls all believers in Jesus
    to respond in worship together,
    to accept all the gifts from the Spirit,
    to learn from each other's traditions,
    to make unity visible on earth.
Christ places baptism in the world
as a seal of God's covenant people,
    placing them in ministry,
    assuring them of the forgiveness of sins.
God knows those who are baptized in Jesus' name,
    guiding the church gently to lead us,

calling us back when we go astray,
    promising life amid trials and death.
Christ places the Lord's table in this world.
Jesus takes up our bread and wine
    to represent his sacrifice,
    to bind his ministry to our daily work,
    to unite us in his righteousness.
Here Christ is present in his world
    proclaiming salvation until he comes,
    a symbol of hope for a troubled age.

**47**   *Our hope in the age to come*

God saves the world through Jesus.
Those who call on that name will have life.
Christ's hand reaches out beyond those who say "Lord"
    to the infants who live in the atmosphere of faith,
    even to the farthest stars and planets of all creation.
The boundaries of God's love are not known;
the Spirit works at the ends of the world
    before the church has there spoken a word.
God will renew the world through Jesus,
who will put all unrighteousness out,
    purify the works of human hands,
    and perfect their fellowship in divine love.
Christ will wipe away every tear;
    death shall be no more.
There will be a new heaven and a new earth,
    and all creation will be filled with God's glory.

**48**   We believe in the triune God—Father, Son, and Holy Spirit—
**who gathers, protects, and cares for the church through Word and Spirit.**
We believe in one holy, universal Christian church,
**the communion of saints called from the entire human family.**
We believe that Christ's work of reconciliation is made manifest in the church
**as the community of believers who have been reconciled with God**
**and with one another.**
We believe that this unity is both a gift and an obligation
for the church of Jesus Christ,
**one which the people of God must continually be built up to attain.**
We believe that this unity must become visible so that the world may believe
that hatred among people is sin, which Christ has already conquered.
Anything that threatens this unity may have no place in the church
and must be resisted.
**Together we fight against all that may threaten or hinder this unity.**
Together we celebrate our differences
as opportunities for mutual service within the one visible people of God.
**Together we love each other.**
       —based on Belhar Confession, Art. 1-2

# SECTION 4
# PRAYERS OF THE PEOPLE

One of the central acts of worship is the intercessory prayer. In some churches this is known as the "pastoral prayer," but "congregational prayer" or "prayers of the people" is preferable. This prayer is spoken on behalf of the entire congregation. Calling it the intercessory prayer is also helpful, of course, since that name calls attention to the prayer's primary purpose.

In the intercessory prayer we address God in a special way as priestly intercessors for each other and for the world at large. We pray not just for our own congregation and for the people we know; we also intercede for those in authority, for those suffering oppression, for those who are poor, hungry, or sick, and so on. If this is the only prayer offered during a worship service, it can also appropriately include adoration, confession, and thanksgiving as well as intercession. If those elements are present in other parts of the service (as in this volume), however, then it will usually be

fitting for the prayers of the people to focus mainly on intercession.

The intercessory prayer may include not only words but also periods of silence and sung prayers, such as a refrain or a stanza of a hymn. Prayers may be offered while standing with arms raised (see Ps. 141), kneeling, or seated with hands folded and head bowed. Prayers may be offered from the pulpit, from the communion table, from the baptismal font, or from among the congregation.

Sometimes the pastor or another member of the congregation offers a prayer on behalf of the congregation. At other times everyone prays in unison, or the congregation and leader pray by following a litany. The intercessory prayer may be offered in various ways by a variety of worshipers gathered. Some may be gifted in writing their own prayers. Others may be able to read well, making a prayer written by someone else come alive.

Christian congregations have produced many models, patterns, and habits for structuring prayer.

The best of models feature both disciplined balance (to address a variety of concerns over time) and flexibility (to express the unique circumstances of a given moment). The model most suitable for a congregation's regular worship services will depend mainly on the size of the congregation, the degree of participation that can be achieved, and the expectations of the congregation.

The prayers presented here will, in most circumstances, need to be adapted to include references to specific reasons for thanksgiving and petition. When these written models are freely and discerningly adapted, they serve to broaden and deepen the range and tone of prayers in worship.

# 4.1 INVITATIONS TO PRAYER

*The following simple introductions to prayer emphasize the corporate nature of prayer. They stand in contrast to the familiar phrase "Please join me in prayer," which can imply that the prayer is an individual prayer of the leader to which others are invited to listen.*

1   We offer now our prayers of thanksgiving and intercession.

2   We join our hearts and voices to offer our prayers to God.

3   We pray together now in Jesus' name.

4   We offer our prayers together now, uniting our voices with Christ, who perfects our prayers.

5   Let us join in prayer, offering our praise, thanksgiving, and intercession to God.

6   Let us bring our thanksgiving and concerns before God in prayer.

7    Let us pray for the growth of God's kingdom in our world today.

8    God calls us to be a praying people.
     Let us join in prayer, offering our praise, thanksgiving, and intercession to God.

*Intercessory prayer is a matter of Christian obedience. We pray in response to God's invitation and command. The following texts convey both the privilege and significance of prayer. After each of the following texts, add a phrase of introduction from numbers 1-8 above.*

9    Our help is in the name of the LORD,
     **who made heaven and earth.**
          —Psalm 124:8, NRSV

10   Let all who are faithful
     offer prayer to you;
     at a time of distress,
     the rush of mighty waters shall not reach them.
          —Psalm 32:6, NRSV

11   The Spirit helps us in our weakness;
     for we do not know how to pray as we ought,
     but that very Spirit intercedes with sighs too deep for words.
     And God, who searches the heart,
     knows what is the mind of the Spirit,
     because the Spirit intercedes for the saints according to the will of God.
          —Romans 8:26-27, NRSV

12   Pray in the Spirit at all times
     in every prayer and supplication.
     To that end keep alert and always persevere
     in supplication for all the saints.
          —Ephesians 6:18, NRSV

13   Do not worry about anything,
     but in everything by prayer and supplication
     with thanksgiving let your requests be made known to God.
     And the peace of God, which surpasses all understanding,
     will guard your hearts and your minds in Christ Jesus.
          —Philippians 4:6-7, NRSV

14   First of all, then, I urge that supplications, prayers,
     intercessions, and thanksgivings be made for everyone,
     for kings and all who are in high positions,
     so that we may lead a quiet and peaceable life
     in all godliness and dignity.
     This is right and is acceptable in the sight of God our Savior,
     who desires everyone to be saved
     and to come to the knowledge of the truth.
          —1 Timothy 2:1-4, NRSV

**15** As Christians, we believe that
prayer is the most important part
of the thankfulness God requires of us.
We also believe that God gives his grace and Holy Spirit
only to those who pray continually and groan inwardly,
asking God for these gifts
and thanking God for them.
—from Heidelberg Catechism, Q&A 116

**16** The prayer our Savior taught us begins with the words
"Our Father in heaven."
With this address, Christ aims to stir
in our hearts a childlike awe and trust
because through Christ God has become our Father.
God, our Father, loves us and desires what is best for us.
God, our Father, answers our prayers.
So let us come with reverence and confidence,
trusting in our Father's mercies through Jesus Christ.
—based on Heidelberg Catechism, Q&A 120

**17** God is the one who makes us, loves us, and sustains us.
God is the one who makes, loves, and sustains the world.

**18** Nothing in all creation can separate us from God's love;
we put all our experiences, all our lives, in God's hands.

# 4.2 GATHERING PRAYER REQUESTS

*To live up to its name, the "prayers of the people" should express a broad range of both thanksgiving and petition that reflects the diversity of experience within the congregation. This prayer should also be specific and immediate, expressing the unique circumstances of a congregation at a given time and place. Prayer requests may be gathered in writing prior to a worship service; gathered through a discussion with congregational leaders, worship planners, or a representative group of congregation members; or gathered extemporaneously during the service itself.*

*At times, lists of prayer concerns can become too narrow or self-centered. The following prompting questions can help expand the range of prayer topics suggested by members of the congregation. Leaders may choose to use a representative sample of these or similar questions each time requests are gathered.*

*Praise and Thanksgiving*
- For which divine actions or attributes shall we bless God?
- For which blessings shall we thank God?
- For which aspects of biblical teaching shall we thank God?

*Petitions*
- For which country (or part of the world) shall we pray?
- For which ministry shall we pray?
- For which other congregations shall we pray?
- For which aspects of congregational life shall we pray?
- For which concerns in our town or city shall we pray?
- For which personal concerns shall we pray?
- For which voiceless and powerless persons shall we pray?
- For which spiritual gifts shall we pray?

*See also "Bidding Prayers" (in section 4.4), which invite worshipers to name specific topics as part of the prayer itself.*

# 4.3 PREPARING EXTEMPORANEOUS PRAYERS

*Extemporaneous prayer is a cherished part of worship in many Christian traditions. It allows for the specific circumstances of the community to be named in both thanksgiving and petition and for the emotions of the community to shape the language of prayer. But extemporaneous prayer can become predictable and cliché-ridden over time—just as can the use of set or written prayers. The following resources offer guidance in preparing extemporaneous prayers to help keep the language of such prayers fresh and thoughtful. With this material, prayer leaders can prepare an outline from which they can pray extemporaneously. These resources cover each main part of prayer: addressing God, praising and thanking God, offering petitions and intercessions, and closing (for prayers of confession, see section 2.2).*

### Scriptural Names for Addressing God

*The following scriptural names for God are provided to help leaders preparing to address God in prayer. At its best, a congregation's prayers address God with a full range of biblical imagery that at once grounds our language about God in Scripture and expands our use of language for God beyond our normal patterns of speech. Often the following names are combined in various ways, such as "Almighty, everlasting God" or "Holy God, our provider."*

*Names of Address for God*

Alpha and Omega
(Rev. 1:8; 22:13)

Almighty and loving God
(Gen. 1:1; Ps. 68:1-6)

Almighty God, giver of strength
(Gen. 17:1; Ex. 6:3-8; Ps. 68:4-14)

Creator
(Isa. 43:15; Rom. 1:25; 1 Pet. 4:19)

Everlasting God
(Gen. 21:33; Isa. 40:28)

Faithful God
(Deut. 7:9; 32:4; Ps. 31:5)

Father of compassion and God of all comfort
(2 Cor. 1:3)

Father of mercies
(2 Cor. 1:3)

God, our healer
(Ex. 15:26)

God, our provider
(Gen. 22:14)

God, our peace, *or* God of peace
(Judges 6:24; Heb. 13:20)

God, our purifier
(Ex. 31:13; Lev. 20:8)

God, our righteousness
(Jer. 23:6)

God, our shepherd
(Gen. 49:24; Ps. 23:1; 80:1)

God and Father of Jesus Christ
(Rom. 15:6)

Gracious God
(Jon. 4:2)

Holy God
(Lev. 19:2; Josh. 24:19; Isa. 5:16)

Living God
(Jer. 10:10; 2 Cor. 3:3; 6:16)

Lord
(Gen. 15:2; Ex. 3:14-15; Acts 3:22)

Lord God
(Ps. 68:32; Dan. 9:3)

Lord of hosts
(Josh. 5:14; 1 Sam. 1:3; Ps. 24:10)

Most High God
(Gen. 14:18; Ps. 9:2)

Our Father
(Isa. 64:8; Matt. 6:9; Eph. 1:2)

Redeemer, covenant God
(Ex. 3:14-15; Isa. 49:26)

Refuge
(Ps. 28:8; 46:1; 91:2)

Rock
(2 Sam. 23:3; Hab. 1:12; 1 Cor. 10:4)

Triune God
(derived from 2 Cor. 13:13 [14] and other passages)

*Throughout the history of the Christian church, the primary pattern of praying has been "through Jesus Christ in the Spirit" or "in the name of Jesus in the power of the Holy Spirit," a pattern of address that highlights Jesus' role as mediator and the Spirit's work of prompting and empowering prayer. A secondary pattern of prayer has been to address Jesus or the Holy Spirit directly, a practice based on the theological assertion that Jesus Christ and the Holy Spirit are fully divine persons. The following lists provide a sampling of many possible scriptural names and images for addressing Jesus and the Holy Spirit in prayer.*

*Names of Address for Jesus*

Jesus
(Matt. 1:21)

Christ
(Matt. 1:16; 2:4)

*Any of the following names or titles may be added, such as "Jesus Christ, our bread of life."*

Anointed One
(Ps. 2:2)

Bread of life
(John 6:35)

Bright morning star
(Rev. 22:16)

Cornerstone
(Eph. 2:20; 1 Pet. 2:6-7)

Desire of nations
(Hag. 2:7)

Deliverer
(Rom. 11:26)

Emmanuel
(Matt. 1:23)

Friend of sinners
(Matt. 11:19)

Good shepherd
(John 10:11, 14)

Head of the church
(Col. 1:18)

High Priest
(Heb. 3:1; 4:14)

Holy One of Israel
(Isa. 41:14)

King of kings
(1 Tim. 6:15; Rev. 19:16)

Lamb of God
(John 1:29; 1 Cor. 5:7; Rev. 5:6)

Light of the world
(John 9:5)

Lord of lords
(1 Tim. 6:15; Rev. 19:16)

Master
(Luke 5:5)

Mediator
(1 Tim. 2:5; Heb. 12:24)

Messiah
(John 1:41)

One and Only Son
(John 1:18; 3:16)

Physician
(Matt. 9:12)

Redeemer
(Job 19:25; Isa. 59:20; 60:16)

Savior
(Luke 1:47; 2:11; Titus 3:6)

Servant of God
(Isa. 42:1; 49:5-7)

Son of David
(Matt. 9:27; 15:22)

Son of God
(Matt. 26:63; Luke 1:35)

Son of Man
(Mark 2:10; John 1:51)

Sun of righteousness
(Mal. 4:2)

Teacher
(Mark 10:35; John 20:16)

Wonderful Counselor
(Isa. 9:6)

Way of life
(John 14:6)

Word of God
(John 1:1; Rev. 19:13)

## Names of Address for the Holy Spirit

Advocate
(John 14:16, 26)

Breath of God
(Job 32:8; 33:4; John 20:22)

Comforter
(Acts 9:31; 2 Cor. 1:3-7)

Counselor
(John 14:16, 26)

Creator Spirit
(from Gen. 1:2)

Eternal Spirit
(Heb. 9:14)

Holy Spirit
(Isa. 63:10-11; Luke 3:16; 1 Thess. 4:8)

Spirit of adoption
(Rom. 8:15; Gal. 4:4-7)

Spirit of Christ
(Rom. 8:9; 1 Pet. 1:11)

Spirit of God
(Matt. 3:16; Rom. 8:9; Phil. 3.3)

Spirit of holiness
(Rom. 1:4)

Spirit of truth
(John 15:26; 16:13)

Spirit of wisdom
(Isa. 11:2)

## Actions and Attributes of God

*The following lists cite actions and attributes for which we praise and thank God in prayer. We ground our petitions in God's character by naming particular attributes and actions of God and praising God for them.*

*The following actions or attributes can be included briefly in a form of address to God (such as "Almighty God, you have given us the gift of the Holy Spirit to lead us to Christ") or in an extended prayer of thanksgiving. These lists merely offer suggestions on the many actions and attributes of God we can refer to in prayer.*

## Actions

Gracious God,
you created the world in beauty . . .
you created us in your image and yet more wonderfully restored us
 in Christ . . .
you are re-creating the world in Christ . . .
you revealed yourself to us in Christ . . .
you allow us to glimpse your glory in the face of Christ . . .
you teach, comfort, and challenge us by your Word . . .
you govern this world in power and love . . .
you lead us faithfully . . .
you led your people by fire and cloud . . .
you prepared the way for the coming of your Son . . .
you sent your Son to the world for its salvation . . .
you led the Magi by a star to worship your Son . . .
you anointed Jesus your Son with your Spirit at his baptism . . .
you raised Jesus from the dead through the power of the Spirit . . .
you send us out into the world to make disciples . . .
you sent your Holy Spirit to point us to Christ . . .
you send your Holy Spirit to empower the church . . .
you hear our prayers in Jesus' name . . .
you promise always to be with us . . .
you promise the coming of Christ's kingdom . . .
you alone can bring healing . . .
you alone can bring unity out of dissension . . .
you alone can conquer evil . . .

## Attributes

Gracious God, we praise you as the one who is . . .

| | | |
|---|---|---|
| abundant in truth | good | just |
| almighty | gracious | living |
| beautiful | holy | long-suffering |
| eternal *or* everlasting | incomprehensible | loving |
| ever present | infinite | perfect |
| faithful | invisible | wise |

*For extended expressions of praise, each attribute may be linked with a particular text, a narrative of God's actions in history, or an experience (such as "Gracious Lord, we praise you as the one who was faithful to Abraham and Sarah, Boaz and Ruth, Joseph and Mary, and even to us . . .").*

*Each of these attributes is complementary. Consider pairing attributes that we might otherwise think of as opposites (for example, "We praise you, Lord God, as the one whose justice is expressed in love, and whose love is expressed in justice . . .").*

## Scriptural Openings of Prayer

*Scripture includes many prayers offered by God's people. While these prayers don't speak of specific contemporary needs or concerns, they provide beautiful and faithful language for addressing God. One way to draw from this language is to use a short, responsive verse of Scripture at the beginning of an intercessory prayer.*

1   We pray to you, O Lord;
    you hear our voice in the morning;
    **at sunrise we offer our prayers**
    **and wait for your answer.**
        —based on Psalm 5:2-3

2   **May the words of our mouths**
    **and the meditations of our hearts**
        **be pleasing in your sight,**
    **Lord, our Rock and our Redeemer.**
        —from Psalm 19:14, NIV

3   To you, O LORD, I lift my soul.
    **O God, in you I trust.**
        —from Psalm 25:1-2, NRSV

4   Our prayer is to you, O LORD.
        At an acceptable time, O God,
        in the abundance of your steadfast love, answer us.
        —from Psalm 69:13, NRSV

5   O God, come to our assistance.
    **O Lord, hasten to help us.**
        —based on Psalm 70:1

6   Hear our prayer, O LORD;
    let our cry come to you.
        —from Psalm 102:1, NRSV

7   Let my prayer be counted as incense before you,
    **and the lifting up of my hands as an evening sacrifice.**
        —Psalm 141:2, NRSV

8   Hear my prayer, O LORD;
        give ear to my supplications in your faithfulness;
        answer me in your righteousness.
        —Psalm 143:1, NRSV

## Topics for Petitions

*The following list of topics challenges prayer leaders to think of concerns that should be included regularly in public prayer but may be forgotten in light of a given leader's or congregation's experience. This list can serve well as a checklist over time to ensure that a balanced range of concerns is incorporated in a congregation's prayers.*

*For the Creation*

    Harvest
    Environmental concerns
    Natural disasters
    Seasonable weather
    Restoration

*For the World*

    War
    Injustice
    Hunger
    Disease
    Racial strife
    World governments
    International crisis
    International relief organizations

*For the Nation*

    Courts and judges
    National leaders
    Upcoming elections
    Military personnel
    Lobbyists and advocates for justice and peace

*For the Local Community*

    Local government
    Housing
    Racial strife
    Poverty
    Employment
    Government services
    Schools

*For the Worldwide Church*

    Unity of the church
    Holiness of the church
    Missionaries and mission agencies
    Christian education: schools, colleges, seminaries
    Denominations

Denominational missions and programs
Other Christian traditions

*For the Local Church*

Pastor(s)
Elders and other leaders
Deacons and others who serve
Staff members
Teachers
Stewards of church finances
Musicians and artists
People leaving for service opportunities
Missionaries
All members in their witness in the community
Thanksgiving for faithful service
Local mission
Congregational anniversary
New or remodeled church building
Unity in the congregation

*For Those with Special Needs*

Those who suffer with physical illness, and those who care for them
Those who suffer with mental illness, and those who care for them
Those who have intellectual, emotional, and/or behavioral impairments,
    and those who care for them
Those who are elderly and infirm, and those who care for them
Those who have suffered abuse, and those who support them
Those who suffer with addiction, and those who support them
Those who mourn a death, and those who minister to them
Those who are imprisoned, and those who minister to them
Those who are lonely, and those who support them
Those who are orphaned, and those who care for them
Those who are homeless, and those who care for them
Those who are victims of crime, and those who support them
Those whose needs cannot be spoken
Those who are facing temptations

Those who live as single persons
Those who are about to be married or who are newly married
Those who celebrate a wedding anniversary
Those who struggle with marital difficulties
Those who are divorced and separated
Those whose sexuality is a source of pain

Those who celebrate the birth of a child
Those who long for children
Those who adopt a child or children
Those who are adopted

Those who care for young children
Those who care for elderly or needy parents

Those who are just starting school
Those who are struggling with peer pressure
Those who are trying to choose a college or career path
Those who are leaving home

Those who are unemployed or underemployed
Those who work in business and industry
Those who work in homemaking
Those who work in medicine
Those who work in education
Those who work in agriculture
Those who work in government
Those who work in service to others
Those who are beginning a new career
Those who struggle in their work
Those who are seeking new or different jobs
Those who are retired or anticipating retirement

Those who celebrate baptism
Those who celebrate a renewed faith commitment or profession of faith
Those who struggle with doubts
Those who are persecuted for their faith
Those who seek spiritual renewal
Those with family members and friends who do not have faith

Those who travel
Those who are enjoying leisure or rest
Those who traveled to be present at worship

Those who are new members of the congregation
Those who are departing members of the congregation

## Prayer Refrains

*The following refrains may be used repeatedly throughout an intercessory prayer. Whether the prayer itself is extemporaneous or written out, these refrains enable the congregation to participate by affirming the petitions spoken by the leader.*

9    Lord, in your mercy,
     **hear our prayer.**

10   Let us pray to the Lord.
     **Lord, have mercy.**

11   Gracious God, hear our prayer.
     **And in your love answer.**

12    For your love and goodness,
      **we give you thanks, O God.**

13    God of grace, [*or*] God of all mercies,
      **hear our prayer.**

14    Heavenly Father,
      **hear us as we pray.**

15    O God, hear our prayer,
      **and let our cry come to you.**

16    Holy Spirit, our Comforter,
      **receive our prayer.**

17    Holy Spirit,
      **act through us, we pray.**

18    Healing Spirit,
      **receive our prayer.**

19    Give thanks to the LORD, for he is good.
      **His love endures forever.**
              —Psalm 136:1, NIV

## Concluding Phrases and Prayers

*The closing words of prayer help us to pull back from focusing on our concerns and petitions to survey the large spiritual context in which we pray. Common themes include the mediation of Christ (our prayers are in Jesus' name), the glory of God, the wondrous mystery of the Trinity, and our union in Christ with God's people in all times and all places. The close of the prayer may also be a kind of poetic summary of the grand themes of grace and gratitude in the Christian life.*

*Phrases That Emphasize the Mediating Work of Christ*

20    Through Jesus Christ, our Lord. **Amen.**

21    In Jesus' name. **Amen.**

22    In the strong name of Jesus Christ, our Savior. **Amen.**

23    In the name of Jesus Christ,
      who lives and reigns with you and the Spirit,
      one God, now and forever. **Amen.**

*Ascriptions of Praise*

24    Yours is the kingdom, the power, and the glory,
      now and forever. **Amen.**

25  To you be the glory, now and forever. **Amen.**

26  To your holy name,
with the church on earth and the church in heaven,
we ascribe all honor and glory,
now and forever. **Amen.**

*Concluding Prayers That Emphasize Our Union with Believers in All Times and Places*

27  Loving God,
we offer these prayers,
joining our voices to the great chorus of those
who sing your praise and depend on you alone.
We long for that day when all your children
will live in your peace and praise your name.
Until that day, give us sturdy patience and enduring hope,
rooted only in Jesus, in whose name we pray. **Amen.**

28  Ever-faithful God,
you have knit together as one body in Christ
those who have been your people in all times and places.
Keep us in communion with all your saints,
following their example of faith and life,
until that day when all your saints will dwell together
in the joy of your eternal kingdom.
Through Christ, our Lord. **Amen.**

*Summary Prayers*

29  Almighty God, Father of all mercies,
we, your unworthy servants, give you humble thanks
for all your goodness and loving-kindness
to us and to all whom you have made.
**We bless you for our creation, preservation,
and all the blessings of this life,
but above all for your immeasurable love
in the redemption of the world by our Lord Jesus Christ,
for the means of grace, and for the hope of glory.
And, we pray, give us such an awareness of your mercies
that with truly thankful hearts we may show forth your praise,
not only with our lips, but in our lives,
by giving up ourselves to your service,
and by walking before you
in holiness and righteousness all our days,
through Jesus Christ, our Lord,
to whom, with you and the Holy Spirit,
be honor and glory throughout all ages. Amen.**

30  Almighty God,
you have given us grace at this time with one accord
to make our common supplication to you,
and you have promised through your well-beloved Son
that when two or three are gathered together in his name
you will be in the midst of them.
**Fulfill now, O Lord, our desires and petitions**
**as may be best for us,**
**granting us in this world knowledge of your truth,**
**and in the age to come life everlasting. Amen.**

31  Gracious God,
accept all these prayers offered in Jesus' name,
and give us now the strength to wait patiently for your answer,
and to live faithfully in response to your call.
Through Christ, our Lord. **Amen.**

# 4.4 COMPLETE MODEL OUTLINES AND PRAYERS

*A basic structure for prayers of the people includes an address to God, praise and thanksgiving for who God is and what God has done, intercessions for local and worldwide concerns, and a concluding doxology.*

## Prayer Outlines

*The following text expands upon the basic structure of intercessory prayer, listing particular areas for intercession. Consider printing this outline for your congregation and filling in particular concerns appropriate to the theme of the worship service and concerns of the moment. Worshipers will be able to sense the scope and flow of the prayer, and they may choose a similar outline for their daily personal and family prayers.*

*This outline not only encourages spontaneous prayer but also disciplines that spontaneity to maintain a balanced diet of thanksgiving and petition by encouraging prayer leaders to include references to specific events and concerns in the life of the community.*

**1**    (a)  Address to God

       (b)  Praise and thanksgiving for who God is and what God has done

            (1)  in creating the world

            (2)  in redeeming the world in Christ

            (3)  for specific acts of faithfulness to the present community

            (4)  for the sure promise of the coming kingdom

       (c)  Intercessions for worldwide and local concerns, including

            (1)  the creation and its care, especially . . .

            (2)  the nations of the world, especially . . .

            (3)  the nation and those in authority, especially . . .

            (4)  the community and those who govern, especially . . .

            (5)  the church universal, its mission, and those who minister, especially . . .

            (6)  the local congregation and its ministry, especially . . .

            (7)  those with particular needs, especially . . .

       (d)  Doxology in praise to the triune God,
           in unity with those who praise God in heaven and on earth

*The following model prayer is developed in three parts: praise and thanksgiving, petition, and concluding affirmation and doxology. This model supplies helpful phrases for each section of the prayer and allows the leader to improvise within each section.*

**2**    We praise you, God our creator, for your handiwork
in shaping and sustaining your wondrous creation.
We especially thank you for
    the miracle of life and the wonder of living . . .
    particular blessings coming to us in this day . . .
    the resources of the earth . . .
    gifts of creative vision and skillful craft . . .
    the treasure stored in every human life. . . .

We pray for others, God our Savior,
claiming your love in Jesus Christ for the whole world
and committing ourselves to care for those around us in his name.
We especially pray for
    those who work for the benefit of others . . .
    those who cannot work today . . .
    those who teach and those who learn . . .
    people who are poor . . .
    the church in persecution. . . .

God our creator,
yours is the morning, and yours is the evening.
Let Christ, the sun of righteousness,
shine forever in our hearts
and draw us to the light of your radiant glory.
We ask this for the sake of Jesus Christ, our Redeemer. **Amen.**

## Complete Prose Prayers

*The following examples provide complete prayers developed in the voice of one person or of the community. They can serve as models to be adapted to a congregation's particular needs.*

3   We praise and thank you, O Lord,
    that you have fed us with your Word [*and at your table*].
    Grateful for your gifts and mindful of the communion of your saints,
    we offer to you our prayers for all people.

    God of compassion,
    we remember before you
    the poor and the afflicted,
    the sick and the dying,
    prisoners and all who are lonely,
    the victims of war, injustice, and inhumanity,
    and all others who suffer from whatever their sufferings may be called.
    [*Silence*]

    O Lord of providence
    holding the destiny of the nations in your hand,
    we pray for our country.
    Inspire the hearts and minds of our leaders
    that they, together with all our nation,
    may first seek your kingdom and righteousness
    so that order, liberty, and peace may dwell with your people.
    [*Silence*]

    O God the Creator,
    we pray for all nations and peoples.
    Take away the mistrust and lack of understanding
    that divide your creatures;
    increase in us the recognition that we are all your children.
    [*Silence*]

    O Savior God,
    look upon your church in its struggle upon the earth.
    Have mercy on its weakness,
    bring to an end its unhappy divisions,
    and scatter its fears.
    Look also upon the ministry of your church.
    Increase its courage, strengthen its faith,
    and inspire its witness to all people,
    even to the ends of the earth.
    [*Silence*]

    Author of grace and God of love,
    send your Holy Spirit's blessing to your children here present.
    Keep our hearts and thoughts in Jesus Christ, your Son, our only Savior,
    who has taught us to pray: [*Lord's Prayer*]

**4**    Sovereign God, King of creation,
you are the one who has spread out the expanse of the heavens
and dug the depths of the lakes and seas.
You are the one who has forested the earth
and stocked land and sea with swarms of your creatures.
You called human beings forward to bear your image,
caring for creation, caring for each other, thriving in the light of your love.
We confess to you, holy God, that we have often spoiled your gifts,
abusing creation, ignoring each other, turning our backs on your love.
Because we did not make ourselves,
cannot keep ourselves, and could never forgive ourselves,
we turn to you, our Creator, Savior, and Keeper.
We bring you thanks for Sabbath rest,
for a break from work, for this place and these friends,
for your Word that may be opened and preached into our lives,
for your name on the lips of people we respect.
We thank you, O God, that we may wake refreshed from a night's sleep,
alert to the possibilities of a new day,
ready for your gifts to find and bless us.
We bring you thanks, O God,
for nourishing food and nourishing friends,
for sunny, unspoiled toddlers and for elderly veterans, rich with wisdom.
We give you thanks, O God,
for work to do and energy to do it,
for fine arts and fine artists
in all their beauty and skill.
We give you thanks, O God,
for sports and games, for patriots and heroes, for wonderful things to read.
Even on the rainiest Monday morning of our lives
we have reason to thank you, to bless you, and
to turn our faces toward the radiance of your love.
O God, especially for your grace, for your amazing grace—
so old, so new, always reminding us of our dependence on you,
always healing with your mercy—
for your grace we give you thanks, O God.
Care for our restless world, we pray.
In your mercy, cool our hotspots,
restrain the lawless, and stimulate the imagination of peacemakers.
Defend the weak, heal the sick, and send forth prophets
who preach good news to the poor.
We pray, O God, for the church across the world.
Revive the church, O God, and make us strong
so that we may serve your purposes,
add luster to your reputation,
and bring joy into all the precincts of heaven.
Take into your care, Lord God, those of us who have been betrayed.
Blend in us justice and love that stands like flint against unholy deeds
but also reaches and yearns for unholy persons to become holy.

When we stiffen against your grace, soften us.
When we sag under the weight of our duty, stiffen us.
O God, we did not make ourselves,
cannot keep ourselves,
and could never forgive ourselves.
So we turn to you, our Maker, Provider, and Savior
through Jesus Christ, in whom we pray. **Amen**.

5    O Lord and Father of the household of faith,
we thank you for the gift of faith
worked within us by your Holy Spirit.
We thank you for having called us to yourself,
for consecrating us to your service,
for having set us apart to the sacred ministry of prayer.

O Lord and Father of the household of faith,
we pray for the church
in all her breadth and variety,
gathered out of every nation, family, people, and tongue,
to be a kingdom of priests serving you.
We pray for the church in all the world,
for churches in North America, Europe, and the Middle East,
for churches in Africa, Asia, and Latin America,
for young churches and old churches,
small churches and large churches,
weak churches and strong churches.
Grant to the church true lowliness
and genuine humility where there is pride, unity where there is division.
Grant to her truth where there is error and wisdom where there is folly,
that you might fulfill your purposes for her.

O Lord and Father of the household of faith,
we pray for those stewards to whom you have
entrusted the affairs of your house,
for pastors, elders, deacons, lay leaders, volunteers, and committees.
Give them the spirit of willing service and true humility.
Give them a sense of spiritual devotion.
Give them delight in those whom they serve.
Grant that they may lead your people in the way of Christ,
that thereby we might all enter the land of our heritage.

O Lord and Father of the household of faith,
we pray for all peoples of all nations.
We pray that in every land there might be peace and true justice
(especially in [*country*] and other places of conflict).
Grant that in our own communities
those who are troubled,
those who suffer,
those who are discouraged
might find support in time of need

especially from your church.
Particularly we remember before you
the work done for the troubled, the suffering, and the discouraged
by the deacons in our congregations
and denominational and Christian agencies.

O Lord and Father of the household of faith,
we pray for our nation and
those who lead the nation:
    the president / prime minister and advisors,
    the congress / parliament and the courts,
    the diplomatic corps as they negotiate for peace and justice.
We pray for the leaders of all nations,
that they might know that you have called them
to serve their people in your fear and
for your glory and the good of the peoples.

O Lord and Father of the household of faith,
we pray for those who have special needs.
To all who suffer any sickness or weakness [*especially names(s)*],
    give health and strength.
To all who are disturbed or troubled, give rest and understanding.
To all who are lonely and alienated, give fellowship and love.
To all who grieve and sorrow [*especially name(s)*],
    give comfort and assurance.
To all who are aged and frail, give homes of comfort and safety,
and others to help them, and a willingness to accept help.

All these requests we present to you,
O Father of mercy, in the name of Jesus Christ,
who even now is seated at your right hand to intercede for us
and who will come at the last trumpet to gather us into
his holy city, the Jerusalem that is above,
and toward which we journey even now. **Amen.**

6    Almighty God, gracious Father,
    in the presence of your bounty keep us humble,
    in the presence of all people's needs make us compassionate and caring.

    Give us faith in our praying and love in our serving,
    knowing that by your power
    all may find a new balance in living and a new victory in adversity.

    We pray for all unhappy lives,
    those who are bitter and resentful, feeling life has given them a raw deal,
    those who are sensitive to criticism and quick to take offense,
    those who desire their own way, whatever the inconvenience
        or cost to others.
    May your judgment and mercy be for their healing.

    We pray for those who are lonely,
    who are shy and self-conscious,

who find it hard to make friends;
those who are nervous and timid,
who ever feel themselves strangers in a world they can scarcely understand.
May your presence inspire confidence and ensure companionship.

We pray for those who live with bitter regrets,
for loving relationships brought to ruin,
for opportunities freely given and woefully abused,
for the bitterness of defeat or betrayal at another's hand,
or for failure in personal integrity.
May your grace give new hope to find victory in the very scene of failure.

We pray for all in illness and pain,
weary of the day and fearful of the night.
Grant healing, if it be your will,
and at all times through faith the gift of your indwelling peace.

Bless the company of Christ's folk, the church in every land.
Make her eager in worship,
fearless in proclamation of the gospel, and passionate for caring.

Bless our country. Bless our leaders.
Bless our children and grant us peace within our borders.
Grant us as a nation to be found effective in establishing peace
    throughout the world.

Bless us, each one, in the communion of the saints,
and keep us ever mindful of the great cloud of witnesses that,
following in their steps, as they did in the steps of the Master,
we may with them at the last receive the fulfillment
    promised to your people.
Through Jesus Christ, our Lord. **Amen.**

7    O great God, glorify yourself in all the earth.
Be glorified in creation, be glorified in your church,
be glorified in our worship here this very morning.
Though we are so small and you are so grand,
help us nevertheless to magnify your name.
Help us to make your name and the nature of your grace
larger and easier for people to see.
Help us to live and to worship in such a way
that we become like magnifying glasses
through which our neighbors and coworkers and children and friends
can see you come into focus in ways they may not have seen before.
When people ask for an explanation of the hope we have,
give us the words to answer thoughtfully and well.
When people wonder out loud who Jesus is and why he matters,
help us to reply in words that will echo the sweetness of your gospel.
Help us to magnify your name, O Lord,
so that you may be glorified in all the earth.

Father, ours is a world that could use more glimpses of glory
and fewer glimpses of the hell to which our sin so easily leads.
Ours is a world that needs more of the gentle words of your Son, Jesus,
and fewer angry words shouted by ruthless dictators on platforms
or by husbands who raise both voice and fist against women
    they vowed once to cherish.
We need your glory, Lord God, so that we can aspire to be more like you
and less like the selfish, self-indulgent creatures we have become in our sin.
We need the glory of your grace in a world bent on revenge,
the glory of your truth in a world in love with lies,
the glory of your holiness in a world filled with tawdriness,
the glory of your resurrection life in a world mired in death.
Make us transparent to you so that,
because of your Spirit at work in us,
this world can become a better place,
a more kingdom-like place, a shalom place.

Bless our congregation.
Heal those who are ill;
comfort those who are grieving;
reassure those who feel troubled
and frightened by what the future may hold.
Bless the leadership of our congregation.
Anoint them by your Spirit, and may they really feel that anointing.
As they do sometimes difficult, sometimes joyful, but always holy work,
may they sense your anointing.
Be in the words they speak, the cards they send, the visits they make;
be in the meetings they attend and the committees they work on.
Make each worker in this place a bearer of Pentecost's flame,
warming hearts, providing hope, lending comfort,
and so in all these ways contributing to your glory in this congregation.

Be with all of us as we continue to worship you now
and as we prepare ourselves for the week ahead.
For those of us who need to travel this week—
be it a long trip or many trips across town—grant safety.
For children who climb aboard buses and study at school,
be with them and keep them safe
even as they day by day deepen their awareness
of the world of wonders you have made, Creator God.
For college students writing papers and taking exams,
give them fresh recall of what they have labored so hard to learn.
And for any here today who face an anxious week,
grant extra measures of your Spirit's presence and balm.
For those who worry and who have much to worry about, lend peace.
For those whose worries have led to ulcers, lend healing and calm.
For little children who have been asked to grow up too quickly
because a parent is sick
or because mommy and daddy can't live together any more,

deal gently with these young ones, heavenly Father.
Scoop them up in your divine arms
so that they will know your embrace on those nights
when they find themselves crying into their pillows.

Be also with all the lonely people.
Be with the widow who has been alone for many years
and who we all think has done so well
but who alone knows how much her heart still aches more days than not.
Be with the one who has so long wanted marriage
but who has not found such companionship,
and for whom the years seem to be slipping away.
Be with divorced people who still cannot believe most days
that their fondest dreams for wedded bliss have been shattered
and who now live with both the regret and the loneliness of it all.
Be with those who so wish they could find someone to talk to but cannot,
those who wait for the phone to ring but it stays silent,
those who work so hard on tasks that no one ever mentions or comments on.
Be with those who are hungry for a word of gratitude that never comes,
those who search crowded rooms for a familiar face
but who can never seem to find a friend.
Be with all the lonely people—
be their friend when this world's friends fail,
be their companion when they feel that they walk life's journey alone,
be their word of kindness and hope
when the world seems able only to be gruff and brusque
as it brushes past lives that don't seem to count.

As we continue our worship now, fill us with yourself.
As we sing, lift us ever higher to yourself.
As we give offerings,
be with us as we enter the rhythm of generosity and grace.
As we turn to Word and sacrament, encounter us with your very self.
Be glorified in all we do.
We pray it ever and only in Jesus' precious name. **Amen.**

8    *A prayer during winter*

O God, whom to know is to love,
and whom to love is to find true life,
you have invited us to pray to you,
so this morning we do that
in and through the good and strong name of Christ Jesus, our Lord.
We thank you that we can be here this morning.
We're grateful that you have kept us safe through a week of work,
of travel, of learning, of play.
We thank you that you have protected many of us on snowy and icy roads
even as we remain glad for the blessing of shelter
during winter months and always.
For furnaces that warm us,

for storm windows that provide a buffer between the cold and us,
for sweaters and blankets we can wrap around ourselves,
for coats and mittens to wear when we do go outdoors—
for all these blessings,
and for the money we have to purchase it all in the first place,
we render to you, our Provider God, our thanks and praise.

But we are mindful too of the many people
in this city and elsewhere whose shelters are inadequate,
if they have a roof over their heads at all.
We summon to mind the ill-clad,
those who cannot pay the gas bill,
those whose mittens are threadbare,
and those whose poorly insulated windows whistle when the wind blows.
We cannot be grateful for the ways you provide for most of us, O Lord,
without praying for your providence in the lives of the needy.
In your good name, help your people always
to be reaching out and in so doing
to be the hands and fingers of you, Father God.

This morning we also thank you for this church
and for the many volunteers who every week devote long hours
to lending an ear to the lonely,
to providing a window on your Word to neighborhood children
who need to know that you are love.
When the fruit on this kind of labor seems difficult to see,
may your Spirit distribute bursts of renewed energy and encouragement.
When frustrating and seemingly insoluble problems present themselves,
grant a wisdom and clarity of vision that can help.

We petition for other needs in this place as well, O Lord.
Continue to be with our sick and suffering members
and many others who feel ravaged by the effects of old age.
Sustain family members who grieve silently as they watch helplessly
what appears to be a growing shadow of Alzheimer's disease
    in the mind of a dear person.
Also be especially merciful to our members
who have been living in the presence of that terrible shadow for a long time,
having already bid farewell to one they still love but can no longer reach.

Be too with the many people of this congregation
who suffer in silence as many days as not.
Stand near those who are haunted by bad memories
or who bear the scars of abuse that happened years ago
but still lingers with fresh effects each new morning.
Fortify those who experience panic attacks,
who feel afraid all the time without knowing why.
Lend light to those who pass their days in gloomy clouds of depression.
Signal your love to those who sometimes feel so frustrated at the way
life is turning out that they scarcely know what to do with themselves.

Be with our young children who wither under the taunts of other children,
who poke fun of their weight or their complexion
or their lisp or their off-brand clothing.
Life in this world is not always a picnic, dear God.
Some days are just plain miserable.
The gospel tells us you understand this firsthand through Jesus, our Lord.
Remind us of this compassion and shower us with your love,
especially on days when the love of other people
seems remote or spotty at best.

Yet there are joys too, and we thank you for those gifts.
There are good days too, and we aim our praise for such times
to you first and foremost.
You, O God, have been our help in the past,
and you are our bright hope for years to come.
Your gospel and the holy supper that seals your Word to us
in a new and fresh way is the bright center of our lives.
So bless us in the balance of this service
[and again this evening when we gather for worship once more.]
You have brought us to the blessing of a new morning.
Grant us your presence, and support us all the day long,
until the shadows lengthen and the evening comes,
and the busy world is hushed, and the fever of life is over,
and our work is done.
Then, in your mercy, grant us a safe lodging, and a holy rest,
and peace at the last.
In the Christ, **Amen.**

9    *A prayer during spring*

Lord of creation, in this springtime season
we come to this place this day to praise you.
Your hands, O God, have fashioned whole worlds of wonder.
Today we mark that divine craftsmanship in the budding of the daffodil.
We see colorful crocuses dotting lawns and gardens
and see in this spectacle your very fingerprints.
So often when we touch things,
we leave behind smudgy residues of our sinfulness.
But when you touch the creation, O Father,
you leave behind bright traces of glory.
You dapple the landscape of our lives
with radiant hues of yellow, deep tones of purple,
and flashes of gold as buds push outward on the edge of a branch.

When we open our mouths,
too often we let them gush forth with curses or words said in irritated anger.
When you open your holy mouth, Lord God,
we hear the chorus of the robin's song,
the warble of the goldfinch,
the pure liquid melody of the cardinal.

There is right now so much that is wrong with this world,
so much that causes us anxiety, fear, and deep sadness.
Yet the springtime renewal of life reminds us
that in your hands there is so much that is right.
Help us to see in this spring
not simply a natural cycle that repeats itself each year,
but instead help us to see deeper down
into the dear promise of the gospel itself.
Help us to see in each daffodil
not a fleeting glimpse of beauty that must soon fade away
but an enduring glimpse of the glory you have promised us and all creatures
because of who Jesus Christ is and what he has done.
Help us to find hope in a hopeless age,
peace in a time of war, joy in a world of sorrow,
cause to sing lyrically in a cacophonous era
of shouting, of confusion, and of chaos.

Receive our thanks for all
that is right, good, proper, and radiant with hope.
But hear our petitions for all
that seems wrong, bad, out of joint, and stinking of suffering.
Abide with our sick.
We pray today also that you will comfort our members
whose lives have become what at times seem to be
no more than a series of setbacks and increasing limitations due to old age.
Give stamina to those who have to hear a child say,
"Mom, you can't drive the car anymore," or,
"Dad, we think a move to the nursing section is best for you."
For those who feel their dignity has been stripped,
clothe their spirits with your Spirit,
assuring them that they bear the dignity of being
a child of the great King—a status nothing and no one can remove.
Remind them that nothing can separate them from your love
that is in Christ Jesus, not even old age and the winding down of life.

Be with all in our society who exist
on the dim margins of our collective consciousness.
Provide light for those who so often stumble in the darkness.
Grant healing and proper medical care
for the chronically sick, for the addicted, for the abused.
Help us collectively in church and society
to find food for the hungry, especially for children,
and clothing for the ill-clad.
Give us both the clarity of vision that helps us to see people's needs,
and the wisdom to meet those needs in meaningful and lasting ways.

Bring peace at long last in all places
that for too long have known only war and rumors of war.
Where there is stubborn resolve and tunnel vision
on both sides of this or that divide,

soften hearts and expand vision, O Lord.
Where there is hatred that simmers all the time,
boiling over at times in the form of
a tank smashing the house of the innocent or
a person blowing herself up to kill the innocent,
end this insanity by the sane direction of your Spirit, O God.
Too often we seem to see no way out of various spiraling conflicts.
But we've faced this before, Lord of history.
We prayed for apartheid to end, and it did.
We prayed for the Berlin Wall to fall, and it did.
We prayed for these things,
though we confess we didn't really think we'd live to see the day.
So also we pray for peace
even as we own up to the sneaking suspicion in the back of our minds
that peace seems forever to elude so many parts of this globe.
So surprise us again, Father.
Work through our prayers for a greater justice,
a greater respect for life on all sides,
and a greater peace—all greater than we can even imagine.

Now, O great God, bless us also in the balance of this service,
in our fellowship time and education classes that follow,
in time spent with family this afternoon.
Where we fail to be attentive to the voice of your Spirit,
even as we profess to be focused on you in worship, forgive us.
Still, touch us this day so that we will feel the energy we need
to press on in faithful discipleship in the week ahead.
Lift our sight higher so that we can strive
toward loftier goals in the coming days.
Remind us of your abiding love and grace
so that we can become beacons of love and grace
to coworkers, neighbors, friends, fellow students.
Anoint our eyes to see your image
residing deep within each person we meet.
Anoint our ears to hear the cries
of all who surround us, especially the needy.
Anoint our hands to do gospel work.
Anoint our lips to speak gospel peace
so that in all ways, in all times, in all places, we may glorify you.
In the name of Christ Jesus alone we are so bold to pray this. **Amen.**

## Prayers Based on the Lord's Prayer

*When the disciples asked Jesus to teach them to pray, he did not lecture about the principles of effective prayer. Instead he gave them a model, drawn largely from prayer themes already familiar to devout Jews of the time. The Lord's Prayer remains the model prayer for all Christians. It teaches us that what we ask of God must be rooted in praise and blessing ("hallowed be your name") and must flow out of the most basic of Christian desires—that God's kingdom come and*

*God's will be done. One way to structure intercessory prayer is to follow the outline of the Lord's Prayer, adding appropriate petitions throughout.*

*Note that the wording of the Lord's Prayer may vary in the following texts, depending on the wording found in various Bible versions. You may wish to change the wording in some of these prayers to match your version of choice.*

10  Our Father in heaven, hallowed be your name. . . .
    [*prayers of adoration and thanksgiving*]

    Your kingdom come. Your will be done, on earth as it is in heaven. . . .
    [*prayers of longing for God's shalom*]

    Give us this day our daily bread. . . .
    [*prayers for the needs of the community*]

    Forgive us our debts, as we also have forgiven our debtors. . . .
    [*prayers for interpersonal reconciliation*]

    And do not bring us to the time of trial, but rescue us from the evil one. . . .
    [*prayers for the world and for personal struggles with temptation and evil*]

    For the kingdom and the power and the glory are yours forever. **Amen.**
        —based on Matthew 6:9-13, NRSV

11  *This example includes phrases from the Heidelberg Catechism as extrapolations on each petition of the Lord's Prayer.*

    **Our Father in heaven,**
    **hallowed be your name.**
    Help us to really know you,
    to bless, worship, and praise you
    for all your works
    and for all that shines forth from them:
    your almighty power, wisdom, kindness,
    justice, mercy, and truth.
    Help us to direct all our living—
    what we think, say, and do—
    so that your name will never be blasphemed because of us
    but always honored and praised.

    **Your kingdom come.**
    Rule us by your Word and Spirit in such a way
    that more and more we submit to you.
    Keep your church strong, and add to it.
    Destroy the devil's work;
    destroy every force that revolts against you
    and every conspiracy against your Word.
    Do this until your kingdom is so complete and perfect
    that in it you are all in all.

**Your will be done on earth as in heaven.**
Help us and all people
to reject our own wills
and to obey your will without any back talk.
Your will alone is good.
Help us one and all to carry out the work we are called to,
as willingly and faithfully as the angels in heaven.

**Give us today our daily bread.**
Do take care of all our physical needs
so that we come to know
that you are the only source of everything good,
and that neither our work and worry
nor your gifts
can do us any good without your blessing.
And so help us to give up our trust in creatures
and to put trust in you alone.

**Forgive us our debts,**
**as we also have forgiven our debtors.**
Because of Christ's blood,
do not hold against us, poor sinners that we are,
any of the sins we do
or the evil that constantly clings to us.
Forgive us, just as we are fully determined,
as evidence of your grace in us,
to forgive our neighbors.

**And lead us not into temptation,**
**but deliver us from the evil one.**
By ourselves we are too weak
to hold our own even for a moment.
And our sworn enemies—
the devil, the world, and our own flesh—
never stop attacking us.
And so, Lord,
uphold us and make us strong
with the strength of your Holy Spirit,
so that we may not go down to defeat
in this spiritual struggle,
but may firmly resist our enemies
until we finally win the complete victory.

**For yours is the kingdom and the power**
**and the glory forever.**
We have made all these requests of you
because, as our all-powerful King,
you not only want to,
but are able to give us all that is good;
and because your holy name,

and not we ourselves,
should receive all the praise, forever.
It is even more sure that you listen to our prayer,
than that we really desire what we pray for. **Amen.**
    —based on Heidelberg Catechism, Q&A's 119, 122-129

**12** *A prayer based on the Lord's Prayer and the Psalms*

**Our Father in heaven,**
you indeed are our Father, adopting us into an eternal family.
As an earthly father has compassion on his children,
so you show compassion on those who fear you.
You know how we are made, and remember us in our weakness. [Ps. 103]

**Hallowed be your name.**
You alone are holy, there is none like you;
your glory is above the heavens.
Yet you stoop down to lift up the needy.
We exalt and worship you, for you are holy. [Ps. 113, 99]

**Your kingdom come, your will be done, on earth as it is in heaven.**
In Christ your kingdom has already come,
even though rulers of this earth
gather together against you,
thinking they can thwart your purposes.
They cannot, for you have installed Christ, your Anointed One,
the everlasting, all powerful King over all creation. [Ps. 2]

**Give us this day our daily bread.**
All creatures look to you for their food at the proper time;
when you provide, they are satisfied with good things.
When you hide your face, they are terrified.
Lord, help us be good stewards of the gifts of food you have given us
so that all may have their daily bread. [Ps. 104]

**Forgive us our sins, as we also forgive those who sin against us.**
Blessed are those whose transgressions are forgiven,
whose sin is covered, and who know the joy of forgiveness. [Ps. 32]
As we have been forgiven, help us to become like Christ,
forgiving those who sin against us.

**Save us from the time of trial and deliver us from evil.**
In mercy, O God, answer the prayers of all who are in deep distress.
Hear their cries especially when they are tormented
by those who deny you and act as if you do not care.
At the same time, save us from sinning in our anger.
Let the light of your face shine upon us, O Lord. [Ps. 4]

**For the kingdom, the power, and glory are yours,
now and forever. Amen.**

**Scripture Paraphrase Prayers**

*The following prayers are based on particular scriptural texts. Some are close paraphrases of actual scriptural prayers, such as psalms. Others are new prayers built on an image or a theme from a biblical text. These are provided as models of an approach that may be used in conjunction with any Scripture text.*

13   Lord, our Lord, you are so awesome!
You are beyond what we can imagine possible.
When we take a look at all that you have done and all that you have made,
we wonder why you care for people like us.
You have given us an honorable position on this earth of ours—
to care for the things you have made, to preserve them and maintain them.
You have entrusted living things to us!
Lord, our Lord, the whole earth recognizes how awesome you are!
**Amen.**
      —based on Psalm 8

14   O Lord, we praise you with all our soul.
We praise you for the abundance of grace and mercy
that we unconsciously receive from you in so many different ways.
You overlook our iniquities.
You bring us back to good health.
You save us from evil and inundate us with your love and compassion.

Lord, you provide nourishment and rejuvenation
to our bodies, minds, and souls.
We also know, Lord, that through you,
there will be justice for the suffering of your people.

Thank you for graciously revealing yourself
to your children so long ago,
that we might have the privilege of knowing your will.

We are only deserving of eternal death as a result of our evil ways.
However, rather than eternally condemning your children in anger,
you bestow your unconditional and boundless love on us.
Through your incomprehensible love for us,
you free us completely from the price of our transgressions.

We cherish your compassion
just as a child cherishes the compassion of loving parents.
We know that, without your compassion,
we would be reduced to nothing but dust on this material planet,
alive and growing one day,
then dead and blown away with the wind the next,
fading away even from human memories forever.
Because of your compassion, Lord, we are allowed a life of eternity;
a gift that you have promised even to future God-fearing generations.
Help us and all future generations to hold tightly
to your precious covenant through obedience to your will.

Lord, from your mighty throne you rule over us all.
We call the cherubim that surround you, the seraphim that serve you,
and every believer in your domain to join our souls
in praising your holy name! **Amen.**
        —based on Psalm 103

15  No matter where we are, where we are going, or what we are doing,
we know that we find our help in you, our Lord.
You are the creator and sustainer of all
that has been made and will be made.
And yet, the immensity of creation does not distract you
from caring personally for every person in it.

We know that is true of your care for us too!
You do not daydream or become weary in that care.
We thank you that you not only watch over us with diligence
but that you will guide us so that we will not fall—
so that we won't even stumble.

Whether we are awake or asleep, you are there,
sheltering and protecting us from all that would hurt us.
We know that you watch over all our living—
you have in the past, and we know you are now.
Your promise holds for the future and for eternity,
and we praise and thank you for that. **Amen.**
        —based on Psalm 121

16  Praise the Lord!
Our soul praises you, O Lord.
We will sing praises to you as long as we live.
We will not put our trust in our government or in influential people,
for when they die, their influence and power are gone.

We are blessed because we hope and trust in you,
O God who created the world and everything in it.
You were a faithful God to our spiritual fathers, Abraham, Isaac, and Jacob,
and you remain unchanging and faithful to us in this century
and on to the end of time.

You uphold those of us
who are weighed down with the cares of this world,
and you feed those who are hungry with the bread of life.
You set prisoners free with the assurance that their sins are forgiven
and that you are in control of the events of their lives.
You give sight of understanding to those who are blind in their sin.
You lift up those who are bowed down,
and you love those who are righteous.

You watch over us aliens in a sinful world,
and you are a father to the orphaned and a comforter to the widowed.
You do not allow the plans of the wicked

to flourish or to come to completion.
You will reign forever and for all generations.
Praise the Lord! **Amen.**
—based on Psalm 146

17   Lord Jesus, you are our living head.
Teach us to be your body here on earth—
your hands, your feet, your eyes, and your compassionate heart.
Lord, send the impulses of your love into the sinews of this church.
May your will and thoughts direct us.
Let your hands, through our hands, supply food for our neighbors' hunger.
Let them hear your voice as we visit and talk with them.
Let children come to us and sit in our laps, as they sat in yours.
Without you as our head, Lord, we are lifeless.
We wait for your power, your Word, your instruction.
Fill us with your life and love, Jesus. **Amen.**
—based on 1 Corinthians 12:12-31

## Prayers in Litany Form

*A litany is a prayer led by one person with responses by the congregation. The responses may be extended prose, but they are usually a repeated refrain, such as "Lord, hear our prayer" or "Lord, have mercy upon us." The responses may also be sung. The congregation's response should be clearly introduced by the leader or indicated in a printed order of worship.*

18   Gracious God,
we pray for the faithful all over the world,
that all who love you may be united in your service.
We pray for the church . . .
Lord, in your mercy,
**hear our prayer.**

We pray for the peoples and leaders of the nations,
that they may be reconciled one to another
in pursuit of your justice and peace.
We pray for the world . . .
Lord, in your mercy,
**hear our prayer.**

We pray for all who suffer from prejudice, greed, or violence,
that the heart of humanity may warm with your tenderness.
We pray especially for all prisoners of politics or religion
and for all refugees.
We pray for all who are oppressed . . .
Lord, in your mercy,
**hear our prayer.**

We pray for all in need
because of famine, flood, or earthquake,
that they may know the hope of your faithfulness
through the help of others.
We pray especially for the people of . . .
Lord, in your mercy,
**hear our prayer.**

We pray for the land, the sea, the sky—
for your whole creation, which longs for its redemption.
We pray that we may live with respect for your creation
and use your gifts with reverence.
We pray for the creation . . .
Lord, in your mercy,
**hear our prayer.**

We pray for all who suffer the pain of sickness,
loneliness, fear, or loss,
that those whose names are in our hearts,
in the hearts of others,
or known to you alone,
may receive strength and courage.
We pray for those in need . . .
Lord, in your mercy,
**hear our prayer.**

God of compassion,
into your hands we commend all for whom we pray,
trusting in your mercy now and forever. **Amen.**

19   Let us bring the needs of the church,
the world, and all in need, to God's loving care.
Please respond to the words, "Lord, in your mercy,"
by saying "hear our prayer."

God of heaven and earth,
through Jesus Christ you promise to hear us
when we pray to you in his name.
Confident in your love and mercy
we offer our prayer.
Lord, in your mercy,
**hear our prayer.**

Empower the church throughout the world in its life and witness.
Break down the barriers that divide
so that, united in your truth and love,
the church may confess your name,
share one baptism,
sit together at one table,
and serve you in one common ministry.
Lord, in your mercy,
**hear our prayer.**

Guide the rulers of the nations.
Move them to set aside their fear, greed, and vain ambition
and to bow to your sovereign rule.
Inspire them to strive for peace and justice,
that all your children may dwell secure,
free of war and injustice.
Lord, in your mercy,
**hear our prayer.**

Hear the cries of the world's hungry and suffering.
Give us, who consume most of the earth's resources,
the will to reorder our lives,
that all may have their rightful share of food,
medical care, and shelter,
and so have the necessities of a life of dignity.
Lord, in your mercy,
**hear our prayer.**

Restore among us a love of the earth you created for our home.
Help us put an end to ravishing its land, air, and waters,
and give us respect for all your creatures,
that, living in harmony with everything you have made,
your whole creation may resound in an anthem of praise
to your glorious name.
Lord, in your mercy,
**hear our prayer.**

Renew our nation in the ways of justice and peace.
Guide those who make and administer our laws
to build a society based on trust and respect.
Erase prejudices that oppress;
free us from crime and violence;
guard our youth from the perils of drugs and materialism.
Give all citizens a new vision of a life of harmony.
Lord, in your mercy,
**hear our prayer.**

Strengthen this congregation in its work and worship.
Fill our hearts with your self-giving love,
that our voices may speak your praise
and our lives may conform to the image of your Son.
Nourish us with your Word and sacraments,
that we may faithfully minister in your name
and witness to your love and grace for all the world.
Lord, in your mercy,
**hear our prayer.**

Look with compassion on all who suffer.
Support with your love
those with incurable and stigmatized diseases,
those unjustly imprisoned,

those denied dignity,
those who live without hope,
those who are homeless or abandoned.
As you have moved toward us in love,
so lead us to be present with them in their suffering
in the name of Jesus Christ.
Lord, in your mercy,
**hear our prayer.**

Sustain those among us who need your healing touch.
Make the sick whole [*especially name(s)*].
Give hope to the dying [*especially name(s)*].
Comfort those who mourn [*especially name(s)*].
Uphold all who suffer in body or mind,
not only those we know and love
but also those known only to you,
that they may know the peace and joy of your supporting care.
Lord, in your mercy,
**hear our prayer.**

O God,
in your loving purpose
answer our prayers and fulfill our hopes.
In all things for which we pray,
give us the will to seek to bring them about,
for the sake of Jesus Christ. **Amen.**

20   *The following traditional prayer, based on Eastern Orthodox tradition, is often attributed to
St. John Chrysostom.*

In peace, let us pray to the Lord.
**Lord, hear our prayer.**

For the peace from above,
for the loving-kindness of God,
and for our salvation,
let us pray to the Lord.
**Lord, hear our prayer.**

For the peace of the world,
for the unity of the church of God,
and for the well-being of all peoples,
let us pray to the Lord.
**Lord, hear our prayer.**

For this gathering of the faithful,
and for all who offer here
their worship and praise,
let us pray to the Lord.
**Lord, hear our prayer.**

For all the baptized,
for all who serve in the church,
[*for (names)*],
let us pray to the Lord.
**Lord, hear our prayer.**

For our elected officials,
for the leaders of the nations,
and for all in authority,
let us pray to the Lord.
**Lord, hear our prayer.**

For this city [*town, village, etc.*],
for every city and community,
and for those who live in them,
let us pray to the Lord.
**Lord, hear our prayer.**

For seasonable weather,
and for abundant harvests for all to share,
let us pray to the Lord.
**Lord, hear our prayer.**

For the good earth that God has given us,
and for the wisdom and will to conserve it,
let us pray to the Lord.
**Lord, hear our prayer.**

For those who travel by land, water, or air
[*or through outer space*],
let us pray to the Lord.
**Lord, hear our prayer.**

For those who are aged and infirm,
for those who are widowed and orphaned,
and for those who are sick and suffering,
let us pray to the Lord.
**Lord, hear our prayer.**

For those who are poor and oppressed,
for those who are unemployed and destitute,
for those who are imprisoned and captive,
and for all who remember and care for them,
let us pray to the Lord.
**Lord, hear our prayer.**

For deliverance in times of affliction,
strife, and need,
let us pray to the Lord.
**Lord, hear our prayer.**

Almighty God,
you have given us grace at this time with one accord
to make our common supplication to you,
and you have promised through your well-beloved Son
that when two or three are gathered together in his name
you will be in the midst of them.
**Fulfill now, O Lord, our desires and petitions**
**as may be best for us,**
**granting us in this world knowledge of your truth,**
**and in the age to come life everlasting. Amen.**

21  Lord God,
because Jesus has taught us to trust you in all things,
we hold to his Word and share his plea:
**Your kingdom come, your will be done.**

Where nations budget for war,
while Christ says, "Put up your sword":
**Your kingdom come, your will be done.**

Where countries waste food and covet fashion,
while Christ says, "I was hungry . . . I was thirsty . . .":
**Your kingdom come, your will be done.**

Where powerful governments
claim their policies are heaven blessed,
while Scripture states that God helps the powerless:
**Your kingdom come, your will be done.**

Where Christians seek the kingdom
in the shape of their own church,
as if Christ had come to build
and not to break barriers:
**Your kingdom come, your will be done.**

Where women who speak up for their dignity
are treated with scorn or contempt:
**Your kingdom come, your will be done.**

Where men try hard to be tough,
because they are afraid to be tender:
**Your kingdom come, your will be done.**

Where we, obsessed with being adults,
forget to become like children:
**Your kingdom come, your will be done.**

Where our prayers falter,
our faith weakens,
our light grows dim:
**Your kingdom come, your will be done.**

Where Jesus Christ calls us:
**Your kingdom come, your will be done.**

Lord God,
you have declared that your kingdom is among us.
Open our ears to hear it,
our hands to serve it,
our hearts to hold it.
This we pray in Jesus' name. **Amen.**

**22** Let us pray for the church and for the world.

Grant, almighty God, that all who confess your name
may be united in your truth, live together in your love,
and reveal your glory in the world.
[*Silence*]
Lord, in your mercy,
**hear our prayer.**

Guide the people of this land, and of all the nations,
in the ways of justice and peace,
that we may honor one another and serve the common good.
[*Silence*]
Lord, in your mercy,
**hear our prayer.**

Give us all a reverence for the earth as your own creation,
that we may use its resources rightly in the service of others
and to your honor and glory.
[*Silence*]
Lord, in your mercy,
**hear our prayer.**

Bless all whose lives are closely linked with ours,
and grant that we may serve Christ in them
and love one another as he loves us.
[*Silence*]
Lord, in your mercy,
**hear our prayer.**

Comfort and heal all who suffer in body, mind, or spirit.
Give them courage and hope in their troubles,
and bring them the joy of your salvation.
[*Silence*]
Lord, in your mercy,
**hear our prayer.**

Almighty and eternal God, ruler of all things in heaven and earth,
mercifully accept the prayers of your people
and strengthen us to do your will
through Jesus Christ, our Lord. **Amen.**

## Bidding Prayers

*One type of litany or responsive prayer has traditionally been known as "bidding prayer." In this form of prayer the leader invites, or "bids," worshipers to pray for a particular subject; the worshipers respond with either silent or extemporaneously spoken prayers; then the leader concludes with a brief summary prayer. This pattern may be repeated as many times as appropriate for several topics or subjects of prayer.*

23    Bound together in Christ in the communion of the Holy Spirit,
let us pray with one heart and mind to our God, saying:
God of all mercies,
**hear our prayer.** [*or* **Triune God, hear us.**]

That the love that passes ceaselessly
between the Father and the Son in the fellowship of the Holy Spirit
may renew and deepen the life of each Christian
and draw us all gathered here into your unending life, we pray:
God of all mercies,
**hear our prayer.** [*or* **Triune God, hear us.**]

For the leaders of the church [*especially (names)*]
and for the leaders of nations [*especially name(s)*],
that they may discern ways to overcome divisions and mistrust
and may reflect your unity in every aspect of common life, we pray:
God of all mercies,
**hear our prayer.** [*or* **Triune God, hear us.**]

For our families, our households, and our communities,
that they may be places of communion and mutual support,
which build us up and strengthen us in grace and truth, we pray:
God of all mercies,
**hear our prayer.** [*or* **Triune God, hear us.**]

Thankful for our world that you made through Christ
and renewed in the power of the resurrection,
that we may be wise and careful stewards of creation, we pray:
God of all mercies,
**hear our prayer.** [*or* **Triune God, hear us.**]

In the power of the Spirit,
who joins our prayers to Christ's enduring intercession,
we pray for the sick, the suffering,
and all who stand in need [*especially (names)*].
For healing for all the world we pray:
God of all mercies,
**hear our prayer.** [*or* **Triune God, hear us.**]

[*Here other intercessions may be offered.*]

Gracious God, whom Jesus called Abba, Father,
accept our prayers this day.

By the inner workings of your Spirit, deepen our communion with you,
the source and goal of our life,
and make us more and more signs of your enduring love.
This we pray through Christ, who lives and works
with you and the Holy Spirit, one God, now and forever. **Amen.**

**24**    *The following prayer may be offered in whole or in part.*

Almighty God,
in Jesus Christ you taught us to pray
and to offer our petitions to you in his name.
Guide us by your Holy Spirit,
that our prayers for others may serve your will
and show your steadfast love,
through the same Jesus Christ, our Lord. **Amen.**

Let us pray for the world.

*[Individual prayers may be offered extemporaneously or in silence.]*

God our creator,
you made all things in your wisdom,
and in your love you save us.
We pray for the whole creation.
Overthrow evil powers, right what is wrong,
feed and satisfy those who thirst for justice,
so that all your children may freely enjoy the earth you have made
and joyfully sing your praises,
through Jesus Christ, our Lord. **Amen.**

Let us pray for the church.

*[Individual prayers may be offered extemporaneously or in silence.]*

Gracious God,
you have called us to be the church of Jesus Christ.
Keep us one in faith and service,
breaking bread together
and proclaiming the good news to the world,
that all may believe you are love,
turn to your ways,
and live in the light of your truth,
through Jesus Christ, our Lord. **Amen.**

Let us pray for peace.

*[Individual prayers may be offered extemporaneously or in silence.]*

Eternal God,
you sent us a Savior, Christ Jesus,
to break down the walls of hostility that divide us.
Send peace on earth,
and put down greed, pride, and anger,
which turn nation against nation and race against race.

Speed the day when wars will end
and the whole world will accept your rule,
through Jesus Christ, our Lord. **Amen.**

Let us pray for our enemies.

*[Individual prayers may be offered extemporaneously or in silence.]*

O God,
whom we cannot love unless we love our neighbors,
remove hate and prejudice from us and from all people,
so that your children may be reconciled
with those we fear, resent, or threaten,
and may live together in your peace,
through Jesus Christ, our Lord. **Amen.**

Let us pray for those who govern us.

*[Individual prayers may be offered extemporaneously or in silence.]*

Mighty God,
sovereign over the nations,
direct those who make, administer, and judge our laws—
the president/prime minister
and others in authority among us *[especially (names)]*—
that, guided by your wisdom,
they may lead us in the way of righteousness,
through Jesus Christ, our Lord. **Amen.**

Let us pray for world leaders.

*[Individual prayers may be offered extemporaneously or in silence.]*

Eternal Ruler, hope of all the earth,
give vision to those who serve the United Nations
and to those who govern all countries,
that, with goodwill and justice,
they may take down barriers
and draw together one new world in peace,
through Jesus Christ, our Lord. **Amen.**

Let us pray for the sick.

*[Individual prayers may be offered extemporaneously or in silence.]*

Merciful God,
you bear the pain of the world.
Look with compassion on those who are sick *[especially (names)]*;
cheer them by your Word
and bring healing as a sign of your grace,
through Jesus Christ, our Lord. **Amen.**

Let us pray for those who sorrow.

*[Individual prayers may be offered extemporaneously or in silence.]*

God of comfort,
stand with those who sorrow [*especially (names)*],
that they may be sure that neither death nor life,
nor things present nor things to come,
shall separate them from your love,
through Jesus Christ, our Lord. **Amen.**

Let us pray for friends and families.

[*Individual prayers may be offered extemporaneously or in silence.*]

God of compassion,
bless us and those we love,
our friends and families,
that, drawing close to you,
we may be drawn closer to each other,
through Jesus Christ, our Lord. **Amen.**

[*Other petitions may be added in the same manner.*]

God of all generations,
we praise you for all your servants
who, having been faithful to you on earth,
now live with you in heaven.
Keep us in fellowship with them,
until we meet with all your children
in the joy of your eternal kingdom,
through Jesus Christ, our Lord. **Amen.**

Mighty God,
whose Word we trust,
whose Spirit enables us to pray,
accept our requests
and further those that will bring about your purpose for the earth,
through Jesus Christ, who rules over all things. **Amen.**

25 *After each section of the following prayer, anyone may offer a person's name or a short prayer for someone to whom the situation applies. Each section may be followed by a spoken or sung response like the following:*

Lord, draw near,
**Lord, draw near,**
**draw near and stay.**
*or*
Lord, in your mercy,
**hear our prayer.**

Let us pray for those who need to be
remembered tonight.

Those who have made the news headlines today
because of what they have done or said . . .
[*Response*]

Those who have been brought to our attention
through a meeting or conversation . . .
[*Response*]

Those who are in hospital, in care,
or in a place that is strange to them;
those in whose family, marriage,
or close relationship
there is stress or a break-up . . .
[*Response*]

Those who are waiting for a birth, or a death,
or news that will affect their lives . . .
[*Response*]

Those whose pain or potential
we should not forget to share with God tonight . . .
[*Response*]

Lord, we believe that you hear our prayer
and will be faithful to your promise to answer us.

When our eyes open again,
may they do so not to end our devotions,
but to expect the kingdom,
for Jesus' sake. **Amen.**

**26** *At the end of each section of this prayer, worshipers may say aloud the first names of people
they wish to pray for.*

Eternal God,
whom our words may cradle but never contain,
we thank you for all the sound and silence
and color and symbol
that, through the centuries, have helped
the worship of your church
to be relevant and real.
Here we pause to remember those
who helped us to come to faith,
by singing us songs or telling us stories,
by inviting us in when we felt distant,
by praying for us without being asked.
We name them now.
[*Names mentioned aloud, followed by the response:*]
Jesus, Son of God among us,
**hear our prayer.**

We remember the preachers, the readers,
the musicians, the leaders,
whose sensitivity and skill
have helped us to grow in faith
and to enjoy worshiping you.

We name them now.
[*Names . . .*]
Jesus, Son of God among us,
**hear our prayer.**

We remember those
who encourage people to praise you
outside the sanctuary:
those who teach young children,
those who lead youth groups,
those who take prayers in hospitals,
    in schools,
    in prisons.
We name them now.
[*Names . . .*]
Jesus, Son of God among us,
**hear our prayer.**

We remember people who cannot pray
and who struggle to believe,
or who fear changes in the church
more than in any other area of their lives.
We name them now,
praying that they might be encouraged,
and that love might dispel fear.
[*Names . . .*]
Jesus, Son of God among us,
**hear our prayer.**

And let us pray for the renewal of the church,
beginning with ourselves.
**Reshape us, good Lord,**
**until in generosity,**
**in faith,**
**and in expectation**
**that the best is yet to come,**
**we are truly Christlike.**
**Make us passionate followers of Jesus**
**rather than passive supporters.**

**Make our churches**
**communities of radical discipline**
**and signposts to heaven;**
**then, in us, through us,**
**and—if need be—despite us,**
**let your kingdom come. Amen.**

27   In the brief times following each topic of petition,
     you are invited to name out loud
     or pray in silence for all who have such needs. Let us pray:

     for those who are ill, who face surgeries, and those recovering . . .
     for those who suffer mental and emotional distress . . .
     for those who struggle with addictions . . .
     for those who provide health care . . .

     for those who are lonely, orphans, and displaced . . .
     for those who are poor, hungry, and homeless . . .
     for those who are rich and powerful . . .
     for those who are imprisoned and those who are persecuted . . .
     for those who are unemployed and those who are exploited . . .
     for those who provide social services and counsel . . .

     for those who live in families or as singles . . .
     for those who expect a child or yearn for a child . . .
     for those who provide childcare and education . . .
     for those who labor in business and government . . .
     for those who serve in our armed forces . . .
     for those who work in the sciences, arts, and media . . .
     for those who are leaders in Christian churches throughout the world . . .
     for those who make peace in the world and those who are our enemies . . .

     As we offer these petitions,
     let us remember before God and each other
     how each of us has responsibilities to act upon the prayers we raise.
     May our God hear our prayers
     and gift us with his Spirit to enable us to be faithful followers of Christ. **Amen.**

## Prayers Especially for Children

28   *A prayer especially appropriate for children*

     Loving God:
     We love the beautiful world you have made: the sun and clouds, the seas and
     mountains, plants and animals [include specific items that children suggest].
     We thank you for the Bible: for stories of Abraham and Sarah, Moses and Miriam,
     and especially those about Jesus [include specific items that children suggest].
     We pray today for all whom we love: our parents, teachers, pastors, and friends
     [include specific people that children suggest].
     We pray especially for all who need your help in a special way: [include specific
     items that children suggest].
     We pray today for people we do not know: people who live far away, people who
     cannot leave the hospital or nursing home [include specific items that children
     suggest].
     Help us to grow in your love today, as we pray and worship, as we learn from
     your Word, as we share your love with others [include specific items that children
     suggest].
     We pray in Jesus' name. **Amen.**

**29**  *A prayer especially appropriate for children*

Lord God, thank you for making us part of your family
and for giving us our own families.
Help us to love each other as you love us.
Keep us safe and healthy, and help us to enjoy being with each other.

Thank you for giving us all kinds of people to teach us—
our parents and grandparents,
babysitters and friends,
Sunday school leaders and school teachers,
ministers and many more.
Make them excited about what they teach
and make us all excited about learning more about you.

Lord, we can't even think of all the people who help us each day.
Lead our president/prime minister and government leaders
to make good decisions.
Please keep our firefighters, police officers, and all other people
who work to keep our city safe.
Thank you for these and other strong people who take care of us.

We also pray for people who need help—
for everyone who is sick or scared.
We know you heal better than any doctor on earth.
Give your strength to everyone who is suffering.

We also ask you to bless each of us.
You are the great shepherd who loves us.
Help us to know you will always give us everything we need,
and help us to be happy with what we have.
Continue to watch over us, and teach us to live for you all of the time.
In Jesus' name we pray. **Amen.**

**30**  Loving God,
thank you for everything,
especially the world you have made for us,
the family and friends you give us,
and the love you show us.
Please help sick people feel better,
sad people feel happier,
and angry people feel friendlier.
Help us to grow bigger, stronger,
and more like you every day.
For Jesus' sake, **Amen.**

# 4.5 PRAYERS ON PASTORALLY CHALLENGING TOPICS

*The following specific topics or themes for prayer serve as a sampling of many topics that are especially difficult or neglected.*

## Prayers for Justice and Peace

1    Lover of all humankind,
you call us to be caring and hospitable
toward strangers in our midst.
When brothers and sisters from other countries
flee the difficulties of their land,
help us to welcome and to walk gently with them.
When students and visitors from far away
choose our land as their destination,
help us to respond in kindness to their interests and needs.
[*We pray especially for (names/group/committee) as it extends care and goodwill to (individual/group) at this time.*]
May we care for all our neighbors as for ourselves,
that we may know the blessing of giving. **Amen.**

2    Creator God, convenience and greed have outweighed concern for your world.
Help your beautiful creation not only to survive but thrive.
**We need you, Lord; listen to our call for help.**
Bread of Life, our world is full of people starving for food or attention.
Satisfy their needs with your abundance.
**We need you, Lord; listen to our call for help.**
Great Physician, at times insurance or finances
prohibit the treatment or prevention of disease.
Free the sick from pain, from unanswered questions, and from nights of worry.
**We need you, Lord; listen to our call for help.**
Peacemaker, our world is torn by political and economic turmoil.
May we, and your whole world, rest in your everlasting embrace.
**We need you, Lord; listen to our call for help.**
Help of the helpless, the rich and powerful can't always hear the cries of the weak.
Enable us—whether rich or poor, powerful or powerless—
to bring comfort and relief to those in need.
**We need you, Lord; listen to our call for help.**
O God, you are forgiving and good, full of love for all who call to you.
**You are our God. You alone can renew our world. Amen.**

3    How crooked is our world, O God, and how heavy with sadness:
         the hungry cry out for food; the imprisoned long for freedom;
         the blind want to see; the troubled in heart need relief;
         the alien, the orphaned, and the widow are desperate for help;
         those who stand for what is right want to know their cause is not in vain.
     Show yourself to be God:
         Frustrate the ways of the wicked.
         Sustain the righteous
         and help those who are in need.
     In the name of Jesus Christ and the power of the Holy Spirit. **Amen.**
         —based on Psalm 146

4    As we listen to the world's concerns,
     hear the cry of the oppressed,
     and learn of new discoveries,
     give us knowledge,
     teach us to respond with maturity,
     and give us courage to act with integrity.

     As citizens, we acknowledge the Spirit's work in human government
     for the welfare of the people,
     for justice among the poor,
     for mercy toward the prisoner,
     against inhuman oppression of humanity.
     Help us to obey you above all rulers;
     fill us with the patience of Christ
     as we wait upon the Spirit.
     We pray for the fruit of the Spirit of Christ
     who works for peace on earth,
     commands us to love our enemies,
     and calls for patience among the nations.
     We give thanks for your work among governments,
     seeking to resolve disputes by means other than war,
     placing human kindness above national pride,
     replacing the curse of war with international self-control.

     We hear the Spirit's call to love one another,
     opposing discrimination of race or sex,
     inviting us to accept one another,
     and to share at every level
     in work and play, in church and state,
     in marriage and family, and so to fulfill the love of Christ.
     Enable us to accept that call and be agents of renewal in our work
     through our Lord Jesus Christ. **Amen.**
         —based on *Our Song of Hope*, st. 9-12

5 Father,
  we give our thanks for the men and women
  who go on doing their duty
  in the face of loneliness,
  monotony, misunderstanding, danger.
  We pray for those who serve us in this city at hazard to their lives:
  police and firefighters and all others whose work demands constant risk.
  We pray for soldiers and sailors who at any moment
  are either bored or scared
  but who stay at their post and do what they must.
  Father, bless their courage with the peace that they, and we, are praying for.
  Forgive us, Father, if we ever take for granted what others are doing
  so that we can live in peace and safety.
  Make us the kind of people who appreciate these blessings.
  We expect others to show courage in the line of duty.
  If, once in a while, we must stand up
  and show a little courage of our own,
  help us to set an example by being the kind of people
  Christ has called us to be. **Amen.**

6 Almighty God,
  you have given us this good land as our heritage.
  Help us always to remember your generosity
  and constantly do your will.
  Bless our land with honest industry, sound learning,
  and an honorable way of life.
  Save us from violence, discord, and confusion,
  from pride and arrogance, and from every evil way.
  Defend our liberties and give those whom we have entrusted
  with the authority of government the spirit of wisdom,
  that there might be justice and peace in our land.
  When times are prosperous, let our hearts be thankful;
  in troubled times, do not let our trust in you fail.
  We ask all this through Jesus Christ, our Lord. **Amen.**

7 We pray to you, O Lord, our God and Father,
  because we are encouraged by Jesus Christ,
  your Son and our brother, to do so.
  You have said through the mouth of the prophet:
  "Seek the good of the city and pray for it to the Lord";
  we therefore pray to you today
  for our cities and villages and for the whole land,
  for justice and righteousness, for peace and good order everywhere.
  **Have mercy, Lord, we pray.**
  We pray for those who govern.
  Teach them that you are the ruler of all
  and that they are only your instruments.

Grant them wisdom for their difficult decisions,
a sharp eye for what is essential,
and courage to obey your commandment.
**Have mercy, Lord, we pray.**
We pray for all who, by your ordaining,
are responsible for justice and peace.
We pray for all who continue to seek salvation in violence.
Show terrorists that no blessing rests in violence.
Take the young among them especially into your care
and bring order into their confused thoughts.
Bring murder and kidnapping to an end.
**Have mercy, Lord, we pray.**
We pray for all who are no longer able to sleep in peace
because they fear for their own life
and for the lives of those near and dear to them;
we pray for all who no longer have hope in your kingdom
and for all who are tormented by anxiety or despair.
Grant that they may be blessed
with faithful friends and counselors alongside them
to comfort them with your strengthening gospel and sacrament.
**Have mercy, Lord, we pray.**
Lord, you have the whole wide world in your hands.
You are able to turn human hearts as seems best to you;
grant your grace therefore to the bonds of peace and love,
and in all lands join together whatever has been torn asunder. **Amen.**

8    From many places, O Lord, we gather today,
brought together in this house of worship.
We come from different backgrounds
and even different countries.
Some of us are new to the faith,
while some of us have been on this journey for a long time.
Yet together we praise you for this place of sanctuary
and for a time to praise your holy name.

Still, our hearts are heavy this day, Lord.
Our world groans with the weight of sin;
we cannot comprehend the evils we see around us;
and we cry with those who today mourn the dead.
May we make a difference in the midst of this sorrow;
may your people around the world rise up against evil;
may we be brought to our knees as we call upon your name;
may your kingdom come quickly, Lord. **Amen.**

## Prayers for Healing

**9**    Let us pray, responding to the phrase,
"Jesus Christ, lover of all,"
with the words, "bring healing, bring peace."

Christ our Lord,
long ago in Galilee,
many who were sick and suffering
needed friends to bring them to your side.
Confident of your goodness,
we now bring to you
those who need your healing touch.
We name before you
those who are ill in body,
whose illness is long, or painful,
or difficult to cure,
those who suffer restless days and sleepless nights.
[*Names of specific individuals may be said aloud.*]
Jesus Christ, lover of all,
**bring healing, bring peace.**

We name before you
those who are troubled in mind,
distressed by the past,
or dreading the future,
those who are trapped
and cast down by fear.
[*Names of specific individuals may be said aloud.*]
Jesus Christ, lover of all,
**bring healing, bring peace.**

We name before you
those for whom light has been turned to darkness
by the death of a loved one,
the breaking of a friendship,
or the fading of hope.
[*Names of specific individuals may be said aloud.*]
Jesus Christ, lover of all,
**bring healing, bring peace.**

In silence we name before you
those whose names we may not say aloud.
[*Silence*]
Jesus Christ, lover of all,
**bring healing, bring peace.**

We ask your guidance
for those who are engaged in medical research,
that they may persevere with vision and energy;
and for those who administer

agencies of health and welfare,
that they may have wisdom and compassion.
Jesus Christ, lover of all,
**bring healing, bring peace. Amen.**

10   Most merciful God, you hold each of us dear to your heart.
Hold [*name(s)*] in your loving arms
and tenderly draw them into your love,
together with all who are living with AIDS and HIV infection.
[*Other diseases or suffering of mind, body, or spirit may also be mentioned.*]
Assure them that they are not alone,
and give them the courage and faith for all that is to come.
Strengthen those who care for them and treat them,
and guide those who do research.
Forgive those who have judged harshly,
and enlighten those who live in prejudice and fear.
Nourish those who have lost sight of you,
and heal the spirits of those who are broken.
We pray this in the name of Jesus, who suffered and died,
and then rose from the dead to lead us into new life,
now and forever. **Amen.**

11   Lord Jesus Christ,
we come to you sharing the suffering that you endured.
Grant us patience during this time,
that as we and [*name*]
live with pain, disappointment, and frustration,
we may realize that suffering is a part of life,
a part of life that you know intimately.
Touch [*name*] in his/her time of trial,
hold him/her tenderly in your loving arms,
and let him/her know you care.
Renew us in our spirits,
even when our bodies are not being renewed,
that we might be ever prepared to dwell in your eternal home,
through our faith in you, Lord Jesus,
who died and are alive for evermore. **Amen.**

12   Eternal God, you knew us before we were born
and will continue to know us after we have died.
Touch [*name*] with your grace and presence.
As you give your abiding care,
assure him/her of our love and presence.
Assure him/her that our communion together remains secure,
and that your love for him/her is unfailing.
In Christ, who came to us, we pray. **Amen.**

**13** O Christ, our Lord,
in times past many servants of yours
brought their friends and loved ones to your side,
that they might be blessed and healed.
So today we bring to your attention
those who need your loving touch.
Please look on our faith, small as it is, and send your peace.
**O Lord, bring your healing and your peace!**

We lift up before you
those who suffer from severe physical pain
and those for whom the days are long and the nights seem longer.
**O Lord, bring your healing and your peace!**

For others, Lord, the pain is not of their body,
but of their mind and emotions.
Some are haunted by past failures;
some feel the searing pain of rejection;
some are shackled with fear and depression;
still others are lonely and alone.
**O Lord, bring your healing and your peace!**

We also lift before you
those who are crippled in soul and spirit,
who feel that you have abandoned them
or that they are unloved by you.
**O Lord, bring your healing and your peace!**

We also pray for those who tend the sick,
comfort the dying, care for the poor, and befriend the oppressed.
May their hearts be strong and filled with love and compassion.
When they are weary, infuse the strength of your Spirit.
**O Lord, bring your healing and your peace!**

This we ask in the name of Jesus Christ,
who came to suffer among us
and to care for those who suffer. **Amen.**

**14** Almighty and everlasting God,
who can banish all affliction both of soul and of body,
show forth your power upon those in need,
that by your mercy they may be restored to serve you afresh
in holiness of living, through Jesus Christ, our Lord. **Amen.**

**15** God the Father,
your will for all people is health and salvation;
**we praise and thank you, O Lord.**

God the Son,
you came that we might have life and have it abundantly;
**we praise and thank you, O Lord.**

God the Holy Spirit,
you make our bodies the temple of your presence;
**we praise and thank you, O Lord.**

Holy Trinity, one God,
in you we live and move and have our being;
**we praise and thank you, O Lord.**

Lord, grant your healing grace
to all who are sick, injured, or disabled,
that they may be made whole;
**hear us, O Lord of life.**

Grant to all who seek your guidance,
and to all who are lonely, anxious, or despondent,
a knowledge of your will and an awareness of your presence;
**hear us, O Lord of life.**

Mend broken relationships,
and restore those in emotional distress
to soundness of mind and serenity of spirit;
**hear us, O Lord of life.**

Bless physicians, nurses, and all others who minister to the suffering,
granting them wisdom and skill, sympathy and patience;
**hear us, O Lord of life.**

Grant to the dying peace and a holy death,
and uphold by the grace and consolation
of your Holy Spirit those who are bereaved;
**hear us, O Lord of life.**

Restore to wholeness whatever is broken by human sin,
in our lives, in our nation, and in the world;
**hear us, O Lord of life.**

You are the Lord who does wonders:
**you have declared your power among the peoples.**

With you, O Lord, is the well of life:
**and in your light we see light.**

Hear us, O Lord of life:
**heal us, and make us whole.**
[*A period of silence may follow, with a concluding prayer.*]

16  O God,
the strength of the weak and the comfort of sufferers,
mercifully hear our prayers
and grant to your servant [*name*]
the help of your power,
that his/her sickness may be turned into health
and our sorrow into joy,
through Jesus Christ, our Lord. **Amen.**

## Prayers for Comfort in Grief

17  Eternal God, shepherd of your people,
    we feel the fleeting passage of life,
    and we know how fragile is our existence
    on this tiny planet amid the spinning galaxies.
    We confess with the prophet:
    "All flesh is grass,
    and all its glory is like the flowers of the field.
    The grass withers and the flowers fall. . . ."
    Yet we also confess:
    "The word of our God stands forever."
    Teach us to number our days,
    that we may gain a heart of wisdom.

    We look to you as frightened children look to their mother,
    for you alone can comfort us.
    Have mercy on us, O God.
    See our tears and hear our cries
    and lead us all, as pilgrims,
    through this valley of death's shadow
    into the light of the resurrection
    of Jesus Christ, your Son, our Lord. **Amen.**
        —based on Psalm 90:12; Isaiah 40:6-8

18  Merciful God, you care for your children
    as a shepherd cares for the sheep.
    We lift up [*names*], their parents and friends,
    for your special care today,
    for their loss is so painful
    and their grief threatens to overwhelm them.
    May they find comfort and courage in your unfailing love,
    enough trust to live without answers,
    and deep hope through Jesus Christ, our Lord. **Amen.**

19  God of compassion and love,
    you have breathed into us the breath of life
    and have given us mind and will.
    In our frailty we surrender all life to you from whom it came,
    trusting in your gracious promises,
    through Jesus Christ, our Lord. **Amen.**

20  *A prayer on the loss of a child*

Jesus, Lamb of God,
in your life on earth
you welcomed children in your arms.
And now, reigning in heaven,
you welcome home our dear little one, [*name*].
But our minds and hearts are numb with sorrow.
Our pain is too great to bear.
Surround us too with your loving embrace
so that we will know again that we too are your children. **Amen.**

21  Man of sorrows, you truly are acquainted with grief.
You wept at the tomb of Lazarus.
You cried for the city of Jerusalem.
You anguished in the garden of Gethsemane.
You bore our pain, guilt, and abandonment on the cross.
Thank you for knowing all our pain.
Comfort us with the life-giving presence of your Holy Spirit.
Give us strength to face each struggle.
Give us peace despite our questions.
Give us hope amid our trials.
Give us faith in your never-ending promises. **Amen.**

22  To you, O Lord Jesus Christ, we still pray,
even though we are stricken and terribly hurt.
We still trust you because on Golgotha
you did not hold yourself aloof from suffering
but entered it and were stricken and terribly hurt. **Amen.**

## Prayers of Lament

23  How long, LORD? Will you forget me forever?
How long will you hide your face from me?
How long must I wrestle with my thoughts
and day after day have sorrow in my heart?
How long will my enemy triumph over me?
Look on me and answer, LORD my God.
Give light to my eyes, or I will sleep in death,
and my enemy will say, "I have overcome him,"
and my foes will rejoice when I fall.
**But I trust in your unfailing love;**
**my heart rejoices in your salvation.**
**I will sing the LORD's praise,**
**for he has been good to me.**
—Psalm 13, NIV

24   My God, my God, why have you forsaken me?
      Why are you so far from helping me, from the words
         of my groaning?
O my God, I cry by day, but you do not answer,
      by night, but find no rest.
**Yet you are holy,**
      **enthroned on the praises of Israel.**
**In you our ancestors trusted;**
      **they trusted, and you delivered them.**
**To you they cried, and were saved;**
      **in you they trusted, and were not put to shame.**

But I am a worm, and not human,
      scorned by others, and despised by the people.
All who see me mock me;
      they hurl insults, they shake their heads:
"Commit your cause to the LORD; let him deliver—
      let him rescue the one in whom he delights!"
Yet it was you who took me from the womb;
      you kept me safe on my mother's breast.
On you I was cast from my birth,
      and since my mother bore me you have been my God.
**Do not be far from me,**
      **for trouble is near**
      **and there is no one to help.**
         —from Psalm 22:1-11, NRSV

25   LORD, you are the God who saves me;
      day and night I cry out to you.
May my prayer come before you;
      turn your ear to my cry.
I am overwhelmed with troubles
      and my life draws near to death.
I am counted among those who go down to the pit;
      I am like one without strength.
I am set apart with the dead,
      like the slain who lie in the grave,
whom you remember no more,
      who are cut off from your care.
You have put me in the lowest pit,
      in the darkest depths.
Your wrath lies heavily on me;
      you have overwhelmed me with all your waves.
You have taken from me my closest friends
      and have made me repulsive to them.
I am confined and cannot escape;
my eyes are dim with grief.
I call to you, LORD, every day;
      I spread out my hands to you.

Do you show your wonders to the dead?
    Do their spirits rise up and praise you?
Is your love declared in the grave,
    your faithfulness in Destruction?
Are your wonders known in the place of darkness,
    or your righteous deeds in the land of oblivion?
But I cry to you for help, LORD;
    in the morning my prayer comes before you.
Why, LORD, do you reject me
    and hide your face from me?
From my youth I have suffered and been close to death;
    I have borne your terrors and am in despair.
Your wrath has swept over me;
    your terrors have destroyed me.
All day long they surround me like a flood;
    they have completely engulfed me.
You have taken from me friend and neighbor—
    darkness is my closest friend.
      —Psalm 88, NIV

**26** *The following congregational lament provides words both for general use and for particular circumstances. Use these paragraphs in any combination that is pastorally appropriate.*

[*General*]
Why, Lord, must evil seem to get its way?
We do confess our sin is deeply shameful;
but now the wicked openly are scornful—
they mock your name and laugh at our dismay.
**We know your providential love holds true:**
**nothing can curse us endlessly with sorrow.**
**Transform, dear Lord, this damage into good;**
**show us your glory, hidden by this evil.**

[*Imprisonment*]
Why, Lord, must he be sentenced, locked away?
True, he has wronged his neighbor and failed you.
Yet none of us is innocent or sinless;
only by grace we follow in your way.
**We plead: Repair the brokenness we share.**
**Chastise no more, lest it destroy your creatures.**
**Hear this lament as intercessory prayer,**
**and speak your powerful Word to make us hopeful.**

[*Illness*]
Why, Lord, must she be left to waste away?
Do you not see how painfully she suffers?
Could you not change the curse of this disaster?
Amaze us by your mighty sovereignty.
**We plead: Repair the brokenness we share.**

**Chastise no more, lest it destroy your creatures.**
**Hear this lament as intercessory prayer,**
**and speak your powerful Word to make us hopeful.**

[*Divorce*]
Why, Lord, must broken vows cut like a knife?
How can one wedded body break in pieces?
We all have failed at being pure and faithful;
only by grace we keep our solemn vows.
**We plead: Repair the brokenness we share.**
**Chastise no more, lest it destroy your creatures.**
**Hear this lament as intercessory prayer,**
**and speak your powerful Word to make us hopeful.**

[*Untimely death*]
Why, Lord, did you abruptly take him home?
Could you not wait to summon him before you?
Why must we feel the sting of death's old cruelty?
Come quickly, Lord; do not leave us alone.
**We plead: Repair the brokenness we share.**
**Chastise no more, lest it destroy your creatures.**
**Hear this lament as intercessory prayer,**
**and speak your powerful Word to make us hopeful.**

[*General*]
Why, Lord, must any child of yours be hurt?
Do all our pain and sorrow somehow please you?
You are a God so jealous for our praises—
hear this lament as prayer that fills the earth.
**We plead: Repair the brokenness we share.**
**Chastise no more, lest it destroy your creatures.**
**Hear this lament as intercessory prayer,**
**and speak your powerful Word to make us hopeful. Amen.**

27  God of life, God of comfort:
    alone,
    afraid,
    in fear,
    in loss,
    we cry out:
    "Why, O Lord, why?"
    "How long, O Lord, how long?"
    We cling to you in hope
    even as we grasp for hope.
    So grasp us in your loving embrace
    through Jesus Christ,
    who endured the cross for our sake. **Amen.**

28   O God,
     whose Son knew the agony of being abandoned,
     persecuted, and killed, though he had done no wrong,
     hear the cries of your children who have been imprisoned unjustly.
     We grieve for those who are abandoned
     by their families and former friends.
     While they wait for and then face their day in court,
     give them hope, strength, and justice
     so that they and we together can rejoice in your deliverance,
     singing your praises together. **Amen.**

29   *Each section of this prayer may be followed by a sung refrain, such as "Don't Be Afraid"*
     *(Iona Community) or a* Kyrie eleison.

     O God, your people have always had their fears.
     So we come to you in humility and with honesty, naming our own.
     Lord, we fear the future. What is coming next?
     "Will there be a place for me when I'm done
          with high school or college?" we young people ask.
     "Will there be safe places for our children?" we parents ask.
     "Will I die in peace and with dignity?" we seniors ask.

     Lord, we fear the pain that comes
     with illness and broken bones and aging.
     Some of us wonder how we're going to make it
     through more treatment and medication.
     Some of us wonder how we can possibly face chronic illness.
     Some of us wonder if prayers for healing even reach your throne.
     Physical pain frightens us.

     Lord, as a church, we wonder about our ministries and programs.
     What if they don't "work"?
     What if outreach and faith nurture don't happen?
     We fear the dependence we have to have on your Spirit
     to be the one to breathe life into Christians and non-Christians.

     Lord, we are afraid of people who are different from us:
     those more powerful than us, those poorer than us,
     those of a different color or creed, those smarter than us,
     those with different personalities.
     How do we talk to these people, O God?
     How do we make peace with them?

     Lord, we have acquaintances,
     friends and family members whom we deeply love
     but who do not know you.
     We are afraid for their salvation.

     We admit, O God, that we're fearful of stillness and quiet.
     It seems as if the last thing we want to do
     is slow down and be attentive to you.
     Help us not to shy away from quiet times,

from the simplicity of prayer, Scripture, and your presence.
It seems, O God, that, in the busyness of countless invitations
to parties and activities we are afraid to say no.

And for all those fears for which we cannot name,
we come to you, O God.
Those we cannot name because they're either unknown or unspeakable,
receive them in our silence.

We are fearful so often, O Lord,
because in our encounters with sin and evil
we find ourselves weak and poor.
We thank you so much then, Jesus,
for your actions and for your words—
for love and the promise of nearness,
which are our strength and our riches. **Amen.**

30    We are tired, Lord,
weary of the long night without rest.
We grow complaining and bitter.
We grieve for ourselves
as we grow hardened to the pain of others.
Another death leaves us unmoved.
A widow's tears fall unnoticed.
Our children know only the bitterness
already possessing their parents.
Our violent words explode into violent acts,
bringing destruction without thought or reason.
Lord, have mercy upon us.
Lead us to repentance, that we may forgive and be forgiven. **Amen.**

31    O God, resting place of pilgrims and sojourners,
so many of us are weary.
**Give us rest, O God.**
Our days are heavy with obligations,
and our nights disturbed by worries over them.
**Give us rest, O God.**
We are tired of battling old temptations and besetting sins,
tired by our defeats, and tired from despairing over them.
**Give us rest, O God.**
We are tired from trying to help people
who resist our help.
**Give us—and them—your rest, O God.**
Gracious God, Father of our Lord Jesus Christ,
who welcomed all who were weary and burdened,
inviting us to cast our cares on him,
for his yoke is easy and his burden light,
our hearts are restless until they come to rest in you. **Amen.**

# 4.6 TOWARD EXPRESSING PRAYERS OF, BY, AND FOR ALL GOD'S PEOPLE

*Prayers in worship often convey powerful but unstated assumptions about the range and scope of prayer, and about the breadth and scope of God's redemption in and through the church as the body of Christ. For example, a congregation might pray often for pastors or missionaries but rarely for those who serve God in other ways. A congregation might pray for refugees or immigrants but not indigenous peoples, or vice versa. A congregation might pray for persons with disabilities but not pray as a group of people with a range of abilities and disabilities. A congregation might routinely draw upon biblical language about God's promises to Abraham but not pause to think about its own relationship to those promises, as Jewish or Gentile believers.*

*When churches discover their omissions, assumptions, or insensitivities, there is often a period of difficulties and false starts in learning to grow in awareness, mutual love, and accountability. Some attempts at responding can sound overly didactic or paternalistic. Some can sound ambiguous and tentative. Others may be overly specific or politicized. The context of a particular community will make a large difference in how a given phrase or approach is perceived.*

*The following prayers represent attempts to grow in grace and knowledge by expanding the range of people and concerns named in public prayer. A significant aim of these of prayers is simply to name groups of people and concerns that often are unnamed. Some of these prayers accomplish that by focusing on a single concern. Others list a variety of peoples and needs, leading the congregation to reflect on the variety of experiences, callings, and settings in which people are called to live as disciples of Jesus. These "list-like prayers" can easily be expanded by encouraging the congregation to pause and add specific petitions for each group named.*

*Because these prayers are shaped by local context and culture, it may be wise to discuss them among a group of discerning spiritual leaders and to adapt them to better fit local circumstances. And because this sampling of prayers can only begin the task of learning to express the prayers of the whole church, those discussions may well lead to large categories of concern not mentioned specifically here.*

1    *A prayer for Jewish and Gentile Christians to pray together*

God of the promise,
as members of your body, from every tribe and nation and people,
we pray as one body—
    some of us sons and daughters of Abraham and Sarah, heirs of the promise;
    some of us Gentiles, grafted into the promises to Abraham and Sarah—
all of us fellow citizens,
members of God's household,
built on the foundation of the apostles and prophets,
with Christ Jesus himself as the cornerstone.

May your Spirit continue to build us together to become God's temple (Eph. 2:11-22) through Jesus Christ, our Lord. **Amen.**

2    *A prayer for Jewish and Gentile Christians to pray together*

Lord God,
as you called Melchizedek to serve as "priest of God Most High" (Gen. 14:18),
as you stirred the spirit of King Cyrus of Persia (2 Chron. 36; Ezra 1),
as you caused the queen of Sheba to hear of Solomon's fame (1 Kings 10:1),
as you prompted the Roman centurion to say, "Surely this man was
    the Son of God!" (Mark 15:39),
as you called Magi from the East to worship the Christ-child (Matt. 2),
as you received the prayers and alms of Cornelius the Italian centurion (Acts 10:1-4),
as you called an Ethiopian court official to ask for baptism (Acts 8:27),
as you have called all of us, including those of us
    "who once were far away [but] have been brought near" (Eph. 2:13),
we pray that your Spirit will again be poured out on all peoples,
that people from every tribe and nation and land will rejoice at Christ's appearing.
**Amen.**

3    *A prayer for native and indigenous peoples, immigrants and refugees to pray together*

Triune God—Father, Son, and Holy Spirit—
we come before you as many parts of one body.
You have called us together
from different cultures, languages, customs, and histories:
some of us are indigenous peoples of the land;
some of us are refugees, migrants, or pilgrims—people on the move;
some of us are hosts; some of us are guests;
and many of us are both hosts and guests.
All of us are searching for an eternal place where we can belong.

Creator, forgive us.
The earth is yours, and everything that is in it.
But we forget . . .
In our arrogance we think we own it.
In our greed we think we can take it.
In our ignorance we worship it.
In our thoughtlessness we destroy it.
We forget that you created it
to bring praise and joy to you,
and that you gave it as a gift
for us to steward,
for us to enjoy,
for us to see more clearly your beauty and your majesty.

Jesus, save us.
We wait for your kingdom.
We long for your throne.
We hunger for your reconciliation,

for that day when people from every tribe and language
will gather around you and sing your praises.

Holy Spirit, teach us.
Help us to remember
that the body is made up of many parts.
Each one is unique, and every one is necessary.
Teach us to embrace the discomfort that comes from our diversity
and to celebrate the fact that we are unified not through our sameness
but through the blood of our Lord and Savior, Jesus Christ.

Triune God, we love you.
Your creation is beautiful.
Your salvation is merciful.
Your wisdom is beyond compare.
We pray all this in Jesus' name. **Amen.**

4    *A prayer for home life, in multiple settings and contexts*

Lord, our God,
wherever we live, we need you.
Wherever we live, you call us to serve you.
We pray for all (among us)
    who live alone,
    who live in community, as family or friends,
    who, alone or together, care for children or aging adults,
    who provide foster care,
    who live in college or university housing,
    who live on military bases or camps,
    who live in prisons,
    who live as refugees,
    who live in group homes, nursing homes, or care facilities,
    who are displaced from their homes,
    who live with conflict,
    who do not have a home . . .
        [*add other petitions as appropriate*]

We pray that you will provide for all of your children—
those among us and those around us—
homes of shelter and safety,
communities of loving encouragement and support,
opportunities to live as faithful disciples of Jesus, ministers of Christ's peace. **Amen.**

5    *A prayer for fruitful work and service in all sectors of society*

Lord God,
we pray for all
    who work in business and industry,
    who work in homemaking,
    who work in medicine,
    who work in education,

who work in agriculture,
who work in government,
who work in service to others,
who are beginning a new career,
who struggle in their work,
who struggle to discern your calling,
who are seeking new or different jobs,
who are retired or anticipating retirement,
who are unemployed or underemployed,
whose work is not valued or appreciated,
who are overcommitted.
Give us joy in our work, joy in using gifts and talents we receive from you.
Give us joy in doing all our work to your honor and glory.
Equip us to labor in ways that promote justice and peace.
Equip us to be ministers of your peace in a world that cries for peace,
through Jesus Christ, our Lord. **Amen.**

6    *A prayer for agents of renewal in all sectors of society*

Lord, our God,
help us to be agents of your peace in this [*town, city, township, region*].
We pray for all who work
to provide housing,
to resist racism,
to provide fruitful employment,
to provide safe schools and places of training and learning,
to develop artistic gifts,
to provide health care,
to provide spiritual care,
to bear witness to your love for us in Jesus Christ,
to minister to refugees . . .
    [*add other petitions as appropriate*]

May we, like leaven, be your agents of peace and renewal
so that all your children will flourish and glorify you.
Through Jesus Christ, our Lord, **Amen.**

7    *A prayer for prisoners, victims, and all who love them, serve them, and work with them*

God of justice and mercy,
your grace and truth shine forth through Jesus Christ, our Lord.
In a world clouded by injustice, violence, and revenge,
we pray for the strong work of your Holy Spirit.

May your Spirit bring healing, justice, encouragement, redemption, and hope
to all prisoners—
    those waiting for trial,
    those facing parole boards,
    those who are discouraged,
    those facing long imprisonment,
    those struggling with temptation,

those suffering injustice,
those recently released and trying to readjust to normal life,
those who have given up hope,
those struggling to know the difference between right and wrong . . .
  [*add other petitions as appropriate*]

to families of prisoners—
children missing their parents,
families struggling to make ends meet,
parents who blame themselves,
those filled with fear or loneliness,
those feeling guilty,
those struggling to forgive . . .
  [*add other petitions as appropriate*]

to victims of crime and violence, and to those who love them—
those struggling to return to normal life,
those who no longer feel safe,
those who are angry,
those who need guidance to find help,
those struggling to forgive,
those who help victims take their lives back . . .
  [*add other petitions as appropriate*]

to all judges, lawyers, and lawmakers—
those struggling to discern wise and just courses of action,
those burdened by heavy case loads,
those overwhelmed by a sense of responsibility,
those with insights about ways of strengthening practices of restorative justice . . .
  [*add other petitions as appropriate*]

*to all who work in the prison system —*
those who care for and protect prisoners,
chaplains and others who are ministers of your peace,
social workers and counselors who work with prisoners and their families,
those who feel unsafe,
those who have become apathetic or discouraged . . .
  [*add other petitions as appropriate*]

to all communities and neighborhoods—
those who feel unsafe,
those who do not know how to welcome prisoners back,
police, security guards, and neighborhood watch groups who keep
    communities safe,
those who need to learn to trust again,
those who need to forgive,
those who need to be forgiven . . .
  [*add other petitions as appropriate*]

May your Spirit bring healing, justice,
encouragement, redemption, and hope
to your church in every neighborhood.

We pray for resolve to be ministers of Christ's peace—
    for wisdom to speak and act with truth and grace,
    for justice, peace, healing, and courage in all relationships,
    and for the elimination of prejudice and segregation.

We long for the day, Lord Jesus, when you will return
and when all things will be made new.
With urgency but also with hope we pray:
May your kingdom come. **Amen.**

8    *A prayer for all who suffer from moral injury*

God of justice and mercy,
in the middle of our war-torn world,
in the midst of moral uncertainty, confusion, and disagreement,
we humbly offer our prayers for your justice and mercy.
We pray for all peoples in every nation and culture
who participate in military activities and in the administration of justice.
Teach them—and each of us—the nature of just action and legitimate acts of defense.
We pray especially for those trained to engage in violent action—
    for those who were ordered to engage in violence that turned out not to be just,
    for those who are haunted by guilt and shame for past actions that cannot
        be undone,
    for those who must learn to resist deeply formed habits of retribution . . .
        *[add other concerns as appropriate]*

Through Jesus, may your justice and mercy flow to all the peoples of the world.
Lead us, as your disciples, to be ministers of your peace. In Jesus' name, **Amen.**

9    *A prayer for those affected by cognitive, emotional, relational, physical,*
     *or behavioral impairments and distress*

Loving God, we pray for all who face cognitive, emotional,
relational, physical, or behavioral impairments and distress.
We pray for those who bear pain for loved ones, themselves,
or those in their professional or congregational care.
May all draw strength, wisdom, and hope from you.
We thank you for discoveries of approaches and interventions
that alleviate suffering and promote flourishing.
Embolden us to welcome the many ways in which your care
and healing may come to and through us.
Grant us gratitude for your willingness to enter into our pain,
trust that your faithful love does not depend on our feelings,
grace and hospitality to welcome, compassion to serve faithfully,
strength to bear the weight of confidentiality,
restraint from actions and words that alienate,
wisdom to discern appropriate responses,
fervency in translating our hopes and fears into prayer,
assurance of your abiding love, and hope in your everlasting promises.
Through Jesus Christ we pray. **Amen.**

# SECTION 5
# OFFERING

The offering is a vital part of our response to God and God's Word. It helps us connect our adoration for God with our life of discipleship. The money given at the offering is a token and symbol of our desire to devote our whole selves to God's service in response to God's loving faithfulness to us. It is symbolic of the many other gifts we should return to the Lord: time, possessions, talents, insights, and concern for others. The word *offering* implies something freely given, something presented as a token of dedication or devotion. Everything we have is a gift from God, and our offerings are a way of acknowledging God as the giver. Take care not to refer to this act of worship as the "collection," which can imply that it is gathering money to defray expenses. Quite the contrary—the purpose of the offering is to offer our firstfruits to God, to render to God a sacrifice of praise.

The meaning of the offering may be symbolized by an offertory procession, during which worshipers present their gifts

to God with prayers and songs of gratitude and dedication. In most churches deacons or other appointed persons collect the offerings and present them on the people's behalf. In other churches worshipers who wish to give come forward to bring their gifts. A prayer may be offered either before or after the offering, though it is perhaps most common to begin the offering with an announcement and an invitation to give, and then to close the offering with a prayer of dedication.

The offering may also include other forms of gifts, such as food, clothing, or supplies for a specific need. Congregations might keep a resource bank of members' abilities and spiritual gifts; periodic updates could take place during the offering. Musicians may offer their musical gifts while the rest of the congregation offers monetary gifts. Children may also offer musical gifts or receive the offering, or bring forward signs or symbols of their own gifts to God. Many worship leaders wrestle with when to best make announcements regarding congregational ministries. The time of offering can be appropriate for presenting such announcements about the life of the church, thus demonstrating that the work of the church is not for its own sake but is an offering to the Lord.

The offering as an act of worship has been linked closely with the Lord's Supper throughout the history of the church. In the liturgies of the early church, worshipers brought forward gifts, including bread and wine for use in the Lord's Supper. In some congregations today, as gifts of money are brought forward, one or two members of the congregation bring forward the bread and cup for the celebration of the Lord's Supper. In this practice, care should be taken that prayers or words of explanation do not imply that the Lord's Supper is our offering to God so much as it is God's provision of spiritual nourishment to us. (Some Protestant traditions avoid linking the offering and Lord's Supper to avoid the implication that the Lord's Supper is more about what we do for God than what God does for us.)

# 5.1 INVITATIONS TO THE OFFERING

*The invitation to the offering may be a simple scriptural statement that sets the context for our giving. The invitation reminds us that giving is much more than simply a way to keep the church running! Rather, it is a response of gratitude to God's command, a matter of discipleship within a covenant relationship with God. The invitation may also include a statement about how the gifts will be used and a word of hospitality to visitors that both invites them to participate and ensures that they need not feel compelled to give without understanding more about the church and its ministry.*

1    The earth is the LORD's and all that is in it,
the world, and those who live in it.
      —Psalm 24:1, NRSV

2    Offer to God a sacrifice of thanksgiving,
and pay your vows to the Most High.
      —Psalm 50:14, NRSV

3    Ascribe to the LORD the glory due his name;
        bring an offering, and come into his courts.
    Worship the LORD in holy splendor;
        tremble before him, all the earth.
          —Psalm 96:8-9, NRSV

4    Let us give thanks to the Lord with all our being.
    In the company of the upright,
    let us honor God for the blessings and goodness we have received.
          —based on Psalm 111:1

5    What shall I return to the LORD
        for all his bounty to me?
    I will give what I have promised
        in the presence of all God's people.
          —from Psalm 116:12, 14, NRSV

6    Do not store up for yourselves treasures on earth,
        where moth and rust consume
        and where thieves break in and steal;
    but store up for yourselves treasures in heaven,
        where neither moth nor rust consumes
        and where thieves do not break in and steal.
    For where your treasure is, there your heart will be also.
          —Matthew 6:19-20, NRSV

7    Freely you have received, freely give.
          —Matthew 10:8, NIV

8    Remember the words the Lord Jesus himself said:
    "It is more blessed to give than to receive."
          —from Acts 20:35, NIV

9    I urge you, brothers and sisters, in view of God's mercy,
    to offer your bodies as a living sacrifice, holy and pleasing to God—
    this is your true and proper worship.
          —Romans 12:1, NIV

10    So here's what I want you to do, God helping you:
    Take your everyday, ordinary life—
    your sleeping, eating, going-to-work, and walking-around life—
    and place it before God as an offering.
    Embracing what God does for you is the best thing you can do for him.
          —Romans 12:1, TM

11    The one who sows sparingly will also reap sparingly;
    the one who sows bountifully will also reap bountifully.
    Responding to God's bountiful gifts to us in Christ,
    we have opportunity to share out of our abundance.
          —based on 2 Corinthians 9:6, 8, NRSV

12   Each of you must give as you have made up your mind,
      not reluctantly or under compulsion, for God loves a cheerful giver.
        —2 Corinthians 9:7, NRSV

13   As God's dear children, then, take him as your pattern,
      and follow Christ by loving as he loved you,
      giving himself up for us as an offering
      and a sweet-smelling sacrifice to God.
        —Ephesians 5:1-2, NJB

14   Do good and share what you have,
      for such sacrifices are pleasing to God.
        —from Hebrews 13:16, NRSV

15   How does God's love abide in anyone
      who has the world's goods and sees a brother or sister
      in need and yet refuses to help?
      Dear children, let us love,
      not in word or speech,
      but also in truth and action.
        —from 1 John 3:17-18, NRSV

16   As we come before God with our tithes and offerings,
      let us remember the words of Micah 6:
      What does the Lord require of us?
      To act justly, to love mercy, and to walk humbly with our God.
      Thus we bring our money, gifts, and whole lives as an offering to our God.

17   Give to the Lord the glory due his name;
        bring an offering and come before him.
      **We will sacrifice a thank offering to God**
        **and call on the name of the Lord.**
      **We will fulfill our vows to the Lord,**
        **in the presence of all God's people.**
      Let each of us use whatever gift we have received,
        faithfully sharing God's grace in many forms.
      **Freely we have received; freely we will give.**

18   God has shown us the meaning of generosity
        in the beautiful diversity of creation,
        in the overflowing love of Jesus Christ,
        in the never-ending gift of the Holy Spirit.
      God has abundantly blessed us and called us
        to be a community that honors each other,
        to serve others with joy,
        to share our love and material possessions.
      Let us rejoice in what we have been given
        and in what is ours to give.

19   The willingness to give is a sign of life.
     The fruit tree gives of its fruit,
         and we know it is alive.
     When it no longer gives,
         we know real life has gone out of it.
     The heart that hoards the blessings of God
         is no longer alive with spiritual power.
     To give is to live.

20   Let us be faithful stewards
     of our time, our talents, and our money.
     so that our treasure is in heaven
     and our giving pleases God.

21   With thankfulness we give in gratitude and joy.
     With prayerfulness we give in sacrifice and love.
     With hopefulness we give in commitment to God.

*Several of the preceding invitations present only the context and meaning of the offering; a transition sentence can be added to introduce the offering itself, as in the following three examples.*

22   With joy, we offer our gifts to God
     as a sign of our deep devotion and covenant faithfulness.

23   As recipients of abundant life in Christ,
     we now offer our gifts to God.

24   With gladness, let us present the offerings
     of our life and labor to the Lord.

*The preceding invitations may be followed by further brief explanations as appropriate, such as the following.*

25   Responding to God's invitation,
     we offer our gifts today
     for the work of [*the ministry for which the gifts are designated*].

26   We are very grateful for the presence of visitors with us today.
     We welcome you to participate with us in the ministry of giving
     without any expectation of your monetary gifts.

27   Our offering is an act of worship
     in which we express our gratitude and reliance on God.
     For those of you who are guests with us today, giving is not obligatory.
     We are eager to share with you more about our church and its ministry
     and to invite you to participate with us as you are called by God.

# 5.2 OFFERING PRAYERS

*The offering is about more than just money, and the words of the offering prayer help to make that clear. The offering prayer interprets the action of giving by naming the gifts as a sign of a larger commitment to serve God in the world. This prayer acknowledges that God is the giver of all good gifts and that money itself cannot accomplish good in the world without God's blessing. The prayer can also express specific petitions for the ministry that the money gifts will support. This prayer may be given by a pastor, deacon, or any other member of the congregation.*

1    Praise be to you, LORD,
     the God of our father Israel,
     from everlasting to everlasting.
Yours, LORD, is the greatness and the power
     and the glory and the majesty and the splendor,
     for everything in heaven and earth is yours.
Yours, LORD, is the kingdom;
     you are exalted as head over all.
Wealth and honor come from you;
     you are the ruler of all things.
In your hands are strength and power
     to exalt and give strength to all.
Now, our God, we give you thanks,
     and praise your glorious name. **Amen.**
       —1 Chronicles 29:10-13, NIV

2    Blessed are you, God of all creation;
through your goodness we have these gifts to share.
Accept and use our offerings for your glory
and for the service of your kingdom.
**Blessed be God forever. Amen.**

3    Merciful Father, we offer
with joy and thanksgiving what you have first given us—
our selves, our time, and our possessions—signs of your gracious love.
Receive them for the sake of him who offered himself for us—
Jesus Christ, our Lord. **Amen.**

4    Blessed are you, O Lord our God, maker of all things.
Through your goodness you have blessed us with these gifts.
With them we offer ourselves to your service and dedicate our lives
to the care and redemption of all that you have made,
for the sake of him who gave himself for us—
Jesus Christ, our Lord. **Amen.**

5   Lord God,
we bless you for all your many gifts to us.
We return these gifts as a token of our gratitude,
longing for the conviction and strength
to offer our whole lives to your service.
We pray especially today for your blessing on [*recipient(s) of offering*],
for whom these gifts are designated.
Grant them the wisdom and discernment to be good stewards of these gifts.
We pray that they will be encouraged in their work,
and that their ministry may bear rich fruit in your kingdom.
Through Christ, our Lord. **Amen.**

6   Gracious God,
everything we have comes from you.
You fill us with good things.
Our hearts and lives overflow with your abundance.
With thanksgiving, we bring to you our time, talents, and tithes.
Use these gifts that you have given us
to feed others as we have been fed,
to serve others as we have been served,
and to bless others as we have been blessed,
through Jesus Christ, our Lord. **Amen.**

7   Gracious God, we give our best,
lest in gaining the world we lose life itself.
As a covenant people, we seek to witness to your will and way.
Help us to know more clearly what you would have us do
with the wealth entrusted to our care.
As we contribute to the needs of your people,
we present ourselves as living sacrifices.
Through Christ, our Lord. **Amen.**

8   We are not our own; we belong to you.
You have created us and given us life anew,
O God, our Creator, Savior, and Sustainer.

We extend our arms and open our hands
to present our offerings to you.
We make these gestures to display outwardly
our hearts' overflowing gratitude for all your gifts.

Receive these gifts from us, O Triune God,
and through them bring life and hope to many.
In the name of Jesus through the power of the Holy Spirit. **Amen.**

9   Ever-giving God,
source of all goodness and charity,
your ear is always open to our needs.
**When we cry to you,**
**you are faithful and provide for us.**

With joy we bring our thanksgiving.
**For all your mercies,**
**we return to you from our abundance.**
All that we give, we dedicate to your glory.
**All that we keep, we commit to your care,**
**for we are only stewards of your bounty.**
**Bless what we give and what we keep,**
**for all is your creation. Amen.**

10   Generous God, you have given us life,
a place to live in,
and people to live with.
Open our eyes to each other
and to all our brothers and sisters,
especially the poor, the oppressed, the alienated.
Make us humble enough to help and comfort them,
so that your love and justice and peace may come to them.
We make bold to consecrate ourselves and our gifts
to you and to the service of others,
through Jesus Christ, our Lord. **Amen.**

11   Dear God, wherever we look,
from next door to a world away,
we see the places where your creation groans.
May these gifts be a faithful response to those cries. **Amen.**

12   Almighty God, you have given us everything.
Not only did you create us, but you provide for our every need.
We give thanks to you, Lord, for you are good.
**Your love endures forever.**
When we turned away from you, you reached down to us.
You lifted us up and freed us through the gift of your Son.
We give thanks to you, Lord, for you are good.
**Your love endures forever.**
You are with us always. You watch over our coming and our going.
Your Holy Spirit guides us and leads us every step of our lives.
We give thanks to you, Lord, for you are good.
**Your love endures forever.**
For your abundant grace we give you thanks.
Gratefully we offer the gifts you first gave us.
We give thanks to you, Lord, for you are good.
**Your love endures forever.**
Use our time, our talents, and our tithes for your glory.
May it bless others with hope, peace, and joy. **Amen.**

13   Almighty and most merciful God,
     from you comes every good and perfect gift.
     We give you praise and thanks for all your mercies.
     Your goodness has created us, your bounty has sustained us,
     your discipline has chastened us, your patience has borne with us,
     your love has redeemed us.
     Give us a heart to love and serve you,
     and enable us to show our thankfulness for all your goodness and mercy
     by giving up ourselves to your service
     and cheerfully submitting in all things to your blessed will,
     through Jesus Christ, our Savior. **Amen.**

14   All good things come from you, O God,
     and with gratitude we return to you what is yours.
     You created all that is, and with love formed us in your image.
     When our love failed, your love remained steadfast.
     You gave your only Son, Jesus Christ, to be our Savior.
     All that we are, and all that we have, is a trust from you.
     And so, in gratitude for all your gifts,
     we offer you ourselves, and all that we have,
     in union with Christ's offering for us.
     By your Holy Spirit make us one with Christ, one with each other,
     and one in ministry to all the world,
     through Jesus Christ, our Savior. **Amen.**

15   O Lord our God, the author and giver of all good things,
     we thank you for all your mercies,
     and for your loving care over all your creatures.
     We bless you for the gift of life, for your protection round about us,
     for your guiding hand upon us,
     and for the tokens of your love within us.
     In all these things, O heavenly God,
     make us wise for a right use of your benefits,
     that we may render an acceptable thanksgiving unto you
     all the days of our lives,
     through Jesus Christ, our Lord. **Amen.**

16   O God of all bounty,
     from your hand we have freely received.
     Accept these offerings of your people
     as expressions of our thanks.
     Lovingly remember those who have given,
     enrich the lives of those for whom these gifts are intended,
     and use these gifts to promote goodwill and to bring your kingdom,
     for the sake of our Lord and Savior, Jesus Christ. **Amen.**

17    Almighty God, giver of every good and perfect gift,
        teach us to render to you all that we have and all that we are,
        that we may praise you,
        not with our lips only, but with our whole lives,
        turning the duties, the sorrows, and the joys of all our days
        into a living sacrifice to you,
        through our Savior, Jesus Christ. **Amen.**

18    O Mighty One,
        you have done great things for us,
        and holy is your name.
        Bless all we offer you—
        our selves, our time, and our possessions—
        that through us your grace and favor
        may be made known to all the world,
        for the sake of Jesus Christ,
        our Redeemer. **Amen.**

19    God of wonder,
        we offer you these humble gifts,
        signs of your goodness and mercy.
        Receive them with our gratitude,
        that through us all people may know
        the riches of your love in the Word-made-flesh. **Amen.**

20    God of glory,
        receive these gifts and the
        offering of our lives.
        As Jesus was lifted up from earth,
        draw us to your heart
        in the midst of this world,
        that all creation may be brought
            from bondage to freedom,
            from darkness to light,
            and from death to life,
        through Jesus Christ, our Lord. **Amen.**

21    Giving God, just as we love because you first loved us,
            we give because you first gave to us.
        Out of gratitude we bring gifts of money to be used for your kingdom work.
        With these gifts we also pledge to you our whole selves.
        We give you our bodies as living temples; may we be your hands and feet.
        We give you our minds; may our thoughts support others and glorify you.
        We give you our time; may our presence encourage others.
        We give you our relationships; may our interactions be a light to the world.
        We give you our work; may we always strive to do our best and help others do theirs.
        We give you our play; may our leisure bring joy to many.
        We give you our hopes and our dreams; may our goals reflect your mission.
        Use these gifts, great God, through the power of your Holy Spirit. **Amen.**

22   Our Father in heaven,
as you multiplied the loaves and fish to meet the needs
of those gathered to hear Jesus preach,
take these, our gifts, and maximize their fruitfulness
so that others may have their daily bread
and your will may be done on earth as it is in heaven. **Amen.**

23   In the name and in the spirit of Jesus,
we bring our gifts to you, O God.
Help us to give with them
a ready mind,
a willing spirit,
and a joyful heart. **Amen.**

24   Merciful God, always out to save,
friend of the suffering,
foe of all who cause suffering,
with these gifts we join your greater work in the world,
confident of your final victory
through Jesus Christ. **Amen.**

25   Ever-present God,
with this offering we present also ourselves,
all that we have been,
all that we are,
all that we shall become,
and our resolve to walk in your way.
Accept us and our offering, we pray, for Jesus' sake. **Amen.**

26   God of every good and perfect gift,
our gifts are not always good, and they are always imperfect.
We give, knowing that our motives are mixed
and our mission is unclear.
Still, we offer these efforts with boldness,
knowing that your love is stronger
than our impurities and imperfections.
Through Jesus Christ. **Amen.**

27   *A text especially mindful of children*

Lord, you give us everything that is good—
our homes, our food, our families, and even our lives.
All that we own and all that we are belong to you.
Since you give us so much,
we thank you by sharing our time, talents,
and right now our money with others in need.
Use these gifts to show your love to people
throughout our world in Jesus' name. **Amen.**

28    We bring you these gifts, O God,
       from what we have first received from you.
       Use them, we pray, to enable the ministries of this church
       to flourish as we together serve our neighbors,
       both near and far away,
       by showing love and doing mercy. **Amen.**

29    *A text especially mindful of children*

       Dear God,
       we offer you our praise.
       We offer you our hearts.
       We offer you our money.
       We offer you our lives.
       Thank you for everything you give to us. **Amen.**

30    Gracious God,
       we thank you for gifts that belong
       not to us alone, but to all our sisters and brothers,
       since they too are created in your image.
       Let their need become our need;
       let their hunger become our hunger;
       and grant to us also a portion of their pain,
       so that in sharing ourselves,
       we discover the Christ who walks
       with our brothers and sisters. **Amen.**

31    Generous God,
       we marvel at your lavish gifts to us:
             life and breath,
             food and shelter,
             opportunities for work and play,
             and, most especially, hope and peace in Christ.
       We now pledge ourselves
       to mirror and reflect
       the glory of your self-giving love,
       to continue in the pattern of generosity
       we see perfectly revealed in Christ,
       through whom we pray. **Amen.**

32    We thank you, O God,
       for the gifts of time, talent, and treasure
       that come from you alone;
       for the time of those who have planned
       and those who have practiced
       for this, our time of worship together;
       for the talents of readers, musicians, and authors of hymns;
       for the talents of preachers, presiders, and writers of prayers;
       for this treasure of money earned by your gift of our labor,

so that we might offer it in love to you
for the work of your kingdom. **Amen.**

33    Blessed you are,
      O God and Father of our Lord Jesus Christ.
      Blessed you are forever and ever.
      Yours are the greatness and the power
          and the glory and the majesty!
      Yours are the mercy and patience,
          the loving-kindness, long-suffering,
          and covenant faithfulness!
      Yours is the kingdom, O Lord,
          and you are exalted as head above all.
      In your hand are power and might
          and in your hand it is to make great
          and to give strength to all.

      Prosper these gifts that we have brought you.
      Bless the service we would render you,
          that we may be profitable servants,
          that your kingdom may come,
      for yours is the kingdom, and the power, and the glory.

      Blessed be you, O Father.
      Worship and praise be yours evermore.
      In the name of your Son, our Savior,
      we would serve you now and evermore. **Amen.**
          —based on 1 Chronicles 29:10-13

*The following prayers are appropriate when the offering immediately precedes celebrations of the
Lord's Supper. The prayer should not imply that the Lord's Supper itself is our offering to God as
much as it is God's provision of spiritual nourishment to us. For congregations that receive the
offering after the Lord's Supper, these texts may also be used with minimal adaptations.*

34    I love the LORD, because he has heard
          my voice and my supplications.
      **Because he inclined his ear to me,**
          **therefore I will call on him as long as I live.**
      What shall I return to the LORD
          for all his bounty to me?
      **I will lift up the cup of salvation**
          **and call on the name of the LORD,**
      **I will pay my vows to the LORD**
          **in the presence of all his people.**
      **Praise the LORD!**
          —Psalm 116:1-2, 12-13, 19, NRSV

35  Good shepherd,
     you graciously spread a table before us.
     We offer you these gifts,
     tokens of our grateful hearts.
     Nourish us at the feast of the Lamb,
     that we may proclaim to all the world
     your triumphant love in Jesus Christ, our Lord. **Amen.**

36  As you received the tears of Mary Magdalene,
     the hospitality of Zacchaeus,
     and small coins from the widow,
     accept our earthly gifts and make them holy.
     Give us your heavenly food,
     and make us worthy to be your servants. **Amen.**

37  God of the harvest,
     receive these gifts of the earth
     and human labor with the offering of our hearts.
     Feed us with your bread and cup,
     that we may be signs of your gracious life
     made known in Jesus Christ, our Lord. **Amen.**

38  Creating God,
     all good things come from you:
     food and drink, memory and hope,
     forgiveness of sin, adoption as your children.
     Through your Spirit nourish us with these gifts,
     that we may be signs of your grace in the world.
     With grateful hearts we offer our hearts and lives
     to you, the giver of every good and perfect gift,
     through Jesus Christ, our Lord and Savior. **Amen.**

39  Giver of every good and perfect gift,
     we marvel at your love and care
     for us and for all that you have made.
     **Help us by your Holy Spirit**
     **to lift our hearts to you,**
     **to taste and see that you are good,**
     **and to live lives of abundant generosity,**
     **full of gratitude and grace,**
     **through Jesus, our Lord. Amen.**

# SECTION 6
# BAPTISM

Baptism is a physical, ritual action, mandated by Jesus, through which God acts to nourish, sustain, comfort, challenge, teach, and assure us. A richly symbolic action, the celebration of baptism stirs our imaginations to perceive the work of God and the contours of the gospel more clearly.

As the New Testament unfolds the meaning of baptism, it teaches us that baptism is a single celebration that conveys several layers of meaning. It is at once a sign of the washing away of sin, a sign of our union with Jesus' death and resurrection, a sign of the promise of new birth in Christ, a sign of incorporation in the church, a sign of the promise of the Holy Spirit, and a sign of the covenant and kingdom of God. The celebration of baptism can highlight each of these aspects of the gospel.

Further, the following foundational pastoral principles are especially important to remember in planning a baptism (note parallels with the Lord's Supper—see section 8).

- Baptism is a celebration of God's grace, not of human achievement. It is a means of grace through which God acts to seal the promises of the gospel.

- Baptism is not an end in itself. It always points beyond itself to celebrate God's grace and covenant faithfulness. At the same time, baptism is not incidental or unimportant to God's people. It should be a celebration fitting to the abundant grace of God offered in Christ.

- Baptism is a sign of a covenant relationship. Our relationship with God in Christ is based on God's promises to us, and baptism conveys these promises to us.
- Baptism is deeply personal but never private. It is a communal action of the gathered congregation, which represents the church in all times and places.

Throughout the history of the church (including the present), the greatest problems associated with baptism have developed when one of these foundational claims became distorted or unclear. These themes need to be taught to congregations as well as embodied in how a church celebrates baptism.

Among Christian traditions today, significant differences remain over who should be baptized. The following resources, representing the Reformed tradition, emphasize that baptism is primarily an occasion in which God's covenant promises are signed and sealed, and thus provide for both infant and adult (or believer's) baptism. It is important to note that the essential meaning in baptism is the same for both infant and adult baptism, though adult baptism includes a vow or statement of faith by the candidate for baptism. For this reason, the form, structure, and many of the texts for adult and infant baptism can be the same. In each resource section following,

alternatives are provided for both infant and adult baptism.

Often denominational resources provide a complete service or "form" for baptism. Some congregations follow such forms word-for-word; others ignore them altogether. In either approach it is possible to miss the point of what we do at baptism— and why. The following resources draw on the rich pastoral wisdom that gave rise to traditional baptismal forms and offer several options for use in different contexts. Texts from these resources may be used to create a formal and traditional service. These resources may also be used in a flexible way, in which a pastor delivers part of the liturgy extemporaneously or from memory. Whatever the context, the church's experience over twenty centuries bears witness to the pastoral wisdom of the following elements of baptismal liturgy.

1. A declaration of God's invitation and promises surrounding baptism, through the words of institution and instruction from Scripture. This declaration reinforces both that baptism is an act of obedience and that it conveys God's promises to us. We can celebrate baptism only because of God's prior love.
2. A statement of the church's faith and the specific promises or vows of those being baptized or presenting their children for baptism. Baptism is a sign of participation

in the faith of the church. This action conveys the congregation's participation in the faith of the holy, catholic church in all times and places and the individual ownership or commitment to that faith by those being baptized or, in the case of children's baptism, their parents.

3. A prayer of thanksgiving and petition for the work of the Holy Spirit in and through baptism in the life of the community and of those being baptized. The power in baptism comes not from the water itself but from the Holy Spirit, who seals God's promises to us.

4. The baptism itself, with words of blessing.

5. A welcome into the church and a commitment by the congregation to encourage and support newly baptized members. This support conveys that baptism is a sign of incorporation into the church.

Because baptism is a physical action, consider the following to communicate the celebration of baptism in a multisensory way:

- Use larger rather than smaller fonts to accommodate a more generous use of water.
- Pour the water visibly and audibly into the font from a suitable vessel or pitcher either before or during the prayer of thanksgiving or at the beginning of the baptism.
- Apply the water of baptism as generously as possible. A few nearly hidden drops do not speak as eloquently as water poured from a vessel over a candidate's head or applied generously from a cupped palm.
- Note that the basis for the practice of full immersion is that baptism symbolizes our dying and rising with Christ.

# COMPLETE MODEL LITURGY
# FOR BAPTISM

*The following model liturgy is designed to help leaders visualize the structure of the baptismal celebration. When used in worship, each of the numbered subheadings should be deleted. The pages following this model liturgy offer numerous options for adapting each corresponding sub-section. (For example, see subsection 6.1.1 on page 254 for options to use for Words of Institution, subsection 6.1.2 on pages 254-264 for various Scriptural Promises to use, and so on.)*

## 6.1 God's Invitation and Promises

### 6.1.1 Words of Institution

Hear these words of Jesus, an invitation and a promise offered to us all:

"All authority in heaven and on earth has been given to me. Therefore go and make disciples of all nations, baptizing them in the name of the Father and of the Son and of the Holy Spirit, and teaching them to obey everything I have commanded you. And surely I am with you always, to the very end of the age."
—Matthew 28:18-20, NIV

In obedience to this command, the church baptizes believers and their children.

### 6.1.2 Scriptural Promises

In the sacrament of baptism God gives us a new identity as his people.

In a world that has turned away from its Creator, where anonymity and rootlessness threaten our existence, God calls a people into covenant embrace.

God called Abraham and Sarah, gave them new names, and promised to make of them a new nation through which he would bless all the families of the world.

God cut a covenant into Israel's flesh, carving out a people for himself.

They would light the path home for all humanity.

In the fullness of time, God sent his only Son, Jesus, to be our Savior.

In his death on the cross our old self is dead and buried; in his resurrection we rise to a new life and look forward to a new creation.

When we are baptized in the name of the Father and the Son and the Holy Spirit, the tri-une God seals our adoption as his children and writes his name invisibly on our foreheads.

"You are a chosen people, a royal priesthood, a holy nation, a people belonging to God. . . . Once you were not a people, but now you are the people of God" (1 Peter 2:9-10, NIV).

By baptism we have a new identity in Jesus Christ.

## 6.2 Response of Faith

### 6.2.1 Presentation

[*For infant baptism*] Having heard God's gracious promises to us in Christ, do you desire that [*name*] be baptized?

Parent(s): **We/I do.**

[*For adult baptism*] Having heard God's gracious promises to us in Christ, [*name*], do you desire to be baptized?

Candidate(s) for baptism: **I do.**

### 6.2.2 Profession of Faith/Creed

Do you renounce Satan and all the spiritual forces of evil that rebel against God?

**I renounce them!**

Do you renounce all sinful desires that draw you from the love of God?

**I renounce them!**

Do you turn to Jesus Christ?

**Yes! I trust in him as my Lord and Savior.**

Do you intend to be Christ's faithful disciple, trusting his promises, obeying his Word, honoring his church, and showing his love, as long as you live?

**Yes! God helping me.**

Do you believe in God the Father?

**I believe in God, the Father almighty . . .**

Do you believe in Jesus Christ, the Son of God?

**I believe in Jesus Christ, God's only Son, our Lord . . .**

Do you believe in God the Holy Spirit?

**I believe in the Holy Spirit . . .**
—based on Apostles' Creed

### 6.2.3 Covenant Promises

Will you devote yourself to the church's teaching and fellowship, to the breaking of bread and the prayers?

**I will, with God's help.**
—based on Acts 2:42, NRSV

## 6.3 Prayer of Thanksgiving

We thank you, O God, for our baptism into Christ's death and resurrection. In the beginning your Spirit moved over the waters. . . . In the time of Noah, you destroyed evil in the water of the flood, and by your saving ark you gave a new beginning. In the night of trouble you led Israel through the sea. . . . In the water of the Jordan, our Lord was baptized. . . . In the baptism of Christ's death and resurrection, you have set us free from sin and death and opened up the way to eternal life.

May Christ, who sank deep into death and was raised Lord of life, keep us and our little ones in the grip of his hand. May your Spirit separate us from sin and mark us with a faith that can stand the light of day and endure the dark of night. To you be all honor and glory, dominion and power, now and forever, through Jesus Christ, our Lord. **Amen.**

## 6.4 Baptism

### 6.4.1 Administration

[Name],
I baptize you in the name of the Father,
and of the Son,
and of the Holy Spirit. **Amen.**

### 6.4.2 Blessing

The Lord bless you and keep you.
The Lord be kind and gracious to you.
The Lord look upon you with favor
and give you peace.
**Alleluia! Amen.**
—based on Numbers 6:24-26

## 6.5 Welcome

### 6.5.1 Words of Encouragement and Promise

Brothers and sisters,
we now receive [name(s)] into Christ's church.
I charge you to nurture and love [them] and to assist [them] to be Christ's faithful disciple(s).

**With joy and thanksgiving, we now welcome you into Christ's church, for we are all one in Christ. We promise to love, encourage, and support you and to help you know and follow Christ.**

### 6.5.2 Intercessory Prayer

[*At the baptism of children, the minister may lay hands on those receiving baptism while saying the following.*]

Gracious God and heavenly Father, we thank you that you make us new persons in Jesus Christ through grace alone.

We pray for [name(s)]. Bless and strengthen [them] daily with the gift of your Holy Spirit. Unfold to [them] the riches of your love.

Deepen [their] faith. Keep [them] from the power of evil.

Enable [them] to live a holy and blameless life until your kingdom comes.

[*After withdrawing hands, the minister may continue as follows.*]

Look with kindness on [these parents]. Let [them] always rejoice in the gift you have given [them]. Grant [them] the presence of your Holy Spirit, that [they] may bring up [these children] to know you, love you, and serve you and [their] neighbor, through Jesus Christ, our Lord. **Amen.**

# 6.1 GOD'S INVITATION AND PROMISES

*Baptism begins with God's gracious invitation. Thus, in many congregations, the presentation of candidates for baptism is preceded by a clear declaration of both God's mandate for baptism and God's gracious promises offered to us in Christ. In most contexts, the primary purpose of this action is to offer a declaration of God's gracious invitation and promises rather than to offer instruction about baptismal theology. Even so, this declaration will carry with it a powerful message about the meaning of baptism. All of these words of invitation and promise may appropriately be spoken while the minister stands by the baptismal font.*

## 6.1.1 Words of Institution

*The service of baptism may be opened with a brief statement of intent, such as the following.*

> Hear these words of Jesus,
> an invitation and a promise offered to us all:

*or*

> Congregation of our Lord Jesus Christ:
> Let us hear our Lord's command concerning the sacrament of holy baptism.
> After he had risen victorious from the grave, Jesus said to his disciples:
>
> "All authority in heaven and on earth has been given to me.
> Therefore go and make disciples of all nations,
> baptizing them
> in the name of the Father and of the Son and of the Holy Spirit,
> and teaching them to obey everything I have commanded you.
> And surely I am with you always, to the very end of the age."
> —Matthew 28:18-20, NIV

> In obedience to this command, the church baptizes believers and their children.

## 6.1.2 Scriptural Promises

*Baptism is a celebration that conveys several layers of meaning. It is at once a sign of the washing away of sin, a sign of our union with Jesus' death and resurrection, a sign of the promise of new birth in Christ, a sign of incorporation in the church, a sign of the promise of the Holy Spirit, and a sign of the covenant and kingdom of God. The following resources incorporate several of the central biblical texts about baptism, for declaring God's promises to the congregation and for serving as summary statements that draw together several scriptural themes.*

*Scriptural Texts*

**1**    God said to Abram:
"I will establish my covenant between me and you,
and your offspring after you throughout their generations,
for an everlasting covenant,
to be God to you and to your offspring after you."
—from Genesis 17:3, 7, NRSV

**2**    But now thus says the LORD,
he who created you, O Jacob,
he who formed you, O Israel:
Do not fear, for I have redeemed you;
I have called you by name, you are mine.
—Isaiah 43:1-2, NRSV

**3**    The days are surely coming, says the LORD,
when I will make a new covenant
with the house of Israel and the house of Judah.
It will not be like the covenant that I made with their ancestors
when I took them by the hand to bring them
out of the land of Egypt—
a covenant that they broke,
though I was their husband, says the LORD.
But this is the covenant that I will make with the house of Israel
after those days, says the LORD:
I will put my law within them, and I will write it on their hearts;
and I will be their God, and they shall be my people.
No longer shall they teach one another,
or say to each other, "Know the LORD,"
for they shall all know me,
from the least of them to the greatest, says the LORD;
for I will forgive their iniquity, and remember their sin no more.
—Jeremiah 31:31-34, NRSV

**4**    I will sprinkle clean water on you,
and you shall be clean from all your uncleannesses,
and from all your idols I will cleanse you.
A new heart I will give you,
and a new spirit I will put within you;
and I will remove from your body the heart of stone
and give you a heart of flesh.
I will put my Spirit within you,
and make you follow my statutes
and be careful to observe my ordinances.
You shall live in the land that I gave to your ancestors,
and you shall be my people, and I will be your God.
—from Ezekiel 36:25-28, NRSV

5     To all who received him, who believed in his name,
he gave power to become children of God, who were born,
not of blood or of the will of the flesh or of the will of man,
but of God.
        —John 1:12-13, NRSV

6     Peter said to them,
"Repent, and be baptized
every one of you in the name of Jesus Christ
so that your sins may be forgiven;
and you will receive the gift of the Holy Spirit.
For the promise is for you, for your children,
and for all who are far away,
everyone whom the Lord our God calls to him."
        —Acts 2:38-39, NRSV

7     Do you not know that all of us
who have been baptized into Christ Jesus
were baptized into his death?
Therefore we have been buried with him by baptism into death,
so that, just as Christ was raised from the dead
by the glory of the Father,
so we too might walk in newness of life.
        —Romans 6:3-4, NRSV

8     All who are led by the Spirit of God are children of God.
For you did not receive a spirit of slavery to fall back into fear,
but you have received a spirit of adoption.
When we cry, "Abba! Father!"
it is that very Spirit bearing witness with our spirit
that we are children of God,
and if children, then heirs, heirs of God and joint heirs with Christ—
if, in fact, we suffer with him so that we may also be glorified with him.
        —Romans 8:14-17, NRSV

9     Just as the body is one and has many members,
and all the members of the body, though many,
are one body, so it is with Christ.
For in the one Spirit we were all baptized into one body—
Jews or Greeks, slaves or free—
and we were all made to drink of one Spirit.
        —1 Corinthians 12:12-13, NRSV

10     As many of you as were baptized into Christ
have clothed yourselves with Christ.
There is no longer Jew or Greek,
there is no longer slave or free,
there is no longer male and female;
for all of you are one in Christ Jesus.
        —Galatians 3:27-28, NRSV

11  There is one body and one Spirit,
    just as you were called to the one hope of your calling,
    one Lord, one faith, one baptism,
    one God and Father of all,
    who is above all and through all and in all.
        —Ephesians 4:4-6, NRSV

12  In him also you were circumcised with a spiritual circumcision,
    by putting off the body of the flesh in the circumcision of Christ;
    when you were buried with him in baptism,
    you were also raised with him through faith in the power of God,
    who raised him from the dead.
        —Colossians 2:11-12, NRSV

13  When the goodness and loving kindness
    of God our Savior appeared, he saved us,
    not because of any works of righteousness that we had done,
    but according to his mercy,
    through the water of rebirth and renewal by the Holy Spirit.
    This Spirit he poured out on us richly through Jesus Christ our Savior,
    so that, having been justified by his grace,
    we might become heirs according to the hope of eternal life.
    The saying is sure.
        —Titus 3:4-8, NRSV

14  You are a chosen race, a royal priesthood,
    a holy nation, God's own people,
    in order that you may proclaim
    the mighty acts of him who called you
    out of darkness into his marvelous light.
    Once you were not a people,
        but now you are God's people;
    once you had not received mercy,
        but now you have received mercy.
        —1 Peter 2:9-10, NRSV

## Summary Paragraphs

*The following resources draw together several scriptural themes about baptism.*

15  Our gracious God has always desired
    to hold his people in a covenant embrace.
    The LORD declares over and over,
    "I will be their God, and they shall be my people."
    Pursuing this deep desire,
    God called Abraham and Sarah to trust in him
    and gave a covenant sign to show that they belonged to him.
    In baptism God now claims us in Christ,

marks us as his own people,
and seals our membership in God's covenant community, the church.
Baptism is the covenant sign that God frees us
from the power of sin and death,
uniting us with Jesus Christ in his death and resurrection.
By water and the Holy Spirit we are washed clean from sin.
God's grace in baptism calls us to give ourselves to him
in trust, love, and obedience.

*The following paragraph may be included at the baptism of infants.*

From the beginning,
God graciously has included our children in his covenant.
All God's promises are for them as well as for us.
We are to teach them that they have been set apart
by baptism as God's own children
so that as they grow older they may respond to him
in personal faith and commitment.

16  In the sacrament of baptism
God gives us a new identity as his people.
In a world that has turned away from its creator,
where anonymity and rootlessness threaten our existence,
God calls a people into covenant embrace.
God called Abraham and Sarah, gave them new names,
and promised to make of them a new nation
through which he would bless all the families of the world.
God cut a covenant into Israel's flesh, carving out a people for himself.
They would light the path home for all humanity.
In the fullness of time, God sent his only Son, Jesus, to be our Savior.
In his death on the cross our old self is dead and buried;
in his resurrection we rise to a new life and look forward to a new creation.
When we are baptized
in the name of the Father and the Son and the Holy Spirit,
the triune God seals our adoption as his children
and writes his name invisibly on our foreheads.
>   "You are a chosen people, a royal priesthood,
>   a holy nation, God's special possession. . . .
>   Once you were not a people,
>   but now you are the people of God" (1 Pet. 2:9-10, NIV).
By baptism we have a new identity in Jesus Christ.

17  By baptism God assures us that he will be with us always.
When, in the beginning,
the deep dark waters churned,
God's Spirit hovered over them.
When, in Noah's day,
the waters engulfed everything and destroyed the world,

God saved his faithful people, whom he loved.
When, in Egypt, Pharaoh's army hotly pursued Israel to the sea,
God parted the waters and led his people through to safety.
When, in the dead of night on Galilee's raging sea
Jesus' disciples feared for their lives,
he called, "It is I; do not fear."
Time and again, God saved our drowning ancestors,
and he promises also to rescue us.
For Christ, our Savior,
went down into the depths of hell
and rose up victorious from them.
Therefore, we receive God's baptismal promise,
trusting that he will rescue us from the dark depths of sin and death
and bring us to safe shore and firm ground.

**18**  Let us hear the promises of God, which are confirmed in baptism.

The Lord made this great promise to Abraham:
    "I will establish my covenant as an everlasting covenant
    between me and you and your descendants after you
    for the generations to come, to be your God
    and the God of your descendants after you" (Gen. 17:7, NIV).

In later years, though Israel was unfaithful,
God renewed his promise through the prophet:
    "'This is the covenant I will make with the people of Israel
        after that time,' declares the LORD.
    'I will put my law in their minds
        and write it on their hearts.
    I will be their God,
        and they will be my people.
    No longer will they teach their neighbor,
        or say to one another, "Know the LORD,"
    because they will all know me,
        from the least of them to the greatest,' declares the LORD.
    'For I will forgive their wickedness
        and will remember their sins no more'" (Jer. 31:33-34, NIV).

In the fullness of time God came in Jesus Christ
to give pardon and peace through the blood of the cross,
the "blood of the covenant, which is poured out for many
for the forgiveness of sins" (Matt. 26:28, NIV).

After Jesus had risen from the dead, the apostles proclaimed:
    "Repent and be baptized, every one of you,
    in the name of Jesus Christ for the forgiveness of your sins.
    And you will receive the gift of the Holy Spirit.
    The promise is for you and your children and for all who are far off—
    for all whom the Lord our God will call" (Acts 2:38-39, NIV).

Anticipating the fulfillment of God's promises, Paul assures us,
"If we died with him,
we will also live with him;
if we endure,
we will also reign with him" (2 Tim. 2:11-12, NIV).

These are the unfailing promises of our Lord to those who are baptized.

**19**  *This text may be used independently or in conjunction with number 18 above.*

Let us recall the teaching of Scripture concerning the sacrament of baptism.

The water of baptism signifies the washing away of our sin by the
blood of Christ and the renewal of our lives by the Holy Spirit.
It also signifies that we are buried with Christ.
From this we learn that our sin has been condemned by God,
that we are to hate it and to consider ourselves as having died to it.
Moreover, the water of baptism
signifies that we are raised with Christ.
From this we learn that we are to walk with Christ in newness of life.
All this tells us that God has adopted us as his children:
"Now if we are children, then we are heirs—
heirs of God and co-heirs with Christ" (Rom. 8:17).

Thus in baptism God seals the promises he gave
when he made his covenant with us, calling us and our children
to put our trust for life and death in Christ our Savior,
deny ourselves, take up our cross, and follow him in obedience and love.

God graciously includes our children in his covenant,
and all his promises are for them as well as for us.
Jesus himself embraced little children and blessed them,
and the apostle Paul said that children of believers are holy.
So, just as children of the old covenant received the sign of circumcision,
our children are given the sign of baptism.
We are therefore always to teach our little ones
that they have been set apart by baptism as God's own children.

**20**  Sacraments are holy signs and seals for us to see.
They were instituted by God so that by our use of them
he might make us understand more clearly
the promise of the gospel
and might put a seal on that promise.

And what is God's gospel promise?
**To forgive our sins and give us eternal life**
**by grace alone**
**because of Christ's one sacrifice**
**finished on the cross.**

How does baptism
remind you and assure you
that Christ's one sacrifice on the cross
is for you personally?
**In this way:**
**Christ instituted this outward washing**
**and with it gave the promise that,**
**as surely as water washes away dirt from the body,**
**so certainly his blood and his Spirit**
**wash away my soul's impurity,**
**in other words, all my sins.**

What does it mean
to be washed with Christ's blood and Spirit?
**To be washed with Christ's blood means**
**that God, by grace, has forgiven my sins**
**because of Christ's blood**
**poured out for me in his sacrifice on the cross.**
**To be washed with Christ's Spirit means**
**that the Holy Spirit has renewed me**
**and set me apart to be a member of Christ**
**so that more and more I become dead to sin**
**and increasingly live a holy and blameless life.**

*The following paragraph may be included at the baptism of infants.*

Should infants too be baptized?
**Yes. Infants as well as adults**
**are in God's covenant and are his people.**
**They, no less than adults, are promised**
**the forgiveness of sins through Christ's blood**
**and the Holy Spirit who produces faith.**
**Therefore, by baptism, the mark of the covenant,**
**infants should be received into the Christian church**
**and should be distinguished from the children of unbelievers.**
**This was done in the Old Testament by circumcision,**
**which was replaced in the New Testament by baptism.**
—from Heidelberg Catechism, Q&A's 66, 69-70, 74

21  What does baptism signify?
**By it we are received into God's church**
**and set apart from all other people and alien religions,**
**that we may wholly belong to him**
**whose mark and sign we bear.**
**Baptism also witnesses to us**
**that God, being our gracious Father,**
**will be our God forever.**

What else does it mean?

> Baptism signifies to us that just as water washes away
> the dirt of the body when it is poured on us
> and also is seen on the bodies of those who are baptized
> when it is sprinkled on them,
> so too the blood of Christ does the same thing internally,
> in the soul, by the Holy Spirit.
>
> Should our children be baptized too?
> Yes, we believe our children ought to be baptized
> and sealed with the sign of the covenant,
> as little children were circumcised in Israel
> on the basis of the same promises
> made to our children.
> Christ has shed his blood no less
> for washing the little children of believers
> than he did for adults.
>
> Is the significance of baptism, then, similar to circumcision?
> Yes, baptism does for our children
> what circumcision did for the Jewish people.
> That is why Paul calls baptism
> the "circumcision of Christ."
>
> —from Belgic Confession, Art. 34

22  Obeying the word of our Lord Jesus,
    and confident of his promises,
    we baptize those whom God has called.

   In baptism, God claims us
   and seals us to show that we belong to God.
   God frees us from sin and death,
   uniting us with Jesus Christ in his death and resurrection.

   By water and the Holy Spirit,
   we are made members of the church, the body of Christ,
   and joined to Christ's ministry of love, peace, and justice.

   Let us remember with joy our own baptism
   as we celebrate this sacrament.

23  Christ is present with us in this sacrament.
    It is he himself who baptizes us,
    and by the Spirit of Pentecost
    he brings us into his church.

   Baptism is a sign of dying to sin
   and rising to new life in Christ.

   By water and the Holy Spirit,
   God claims us as his own,
   washes us from sin,
   and sets us free from the power of death.
   Here we know

that we are made one with Christ
crucified and risen,
members of his body,
called to share his ministry in the world.

In this sacrament,
the love of God is offered to each one of us.
Though we cannot fully understand it or explain it,
we are called to accept that love
with the openness and trust of a child.
In baptism [*name*] is assured of the love that God has for him/her,
and the sign and seal of the Holy Spirit is placed upon him/her.

**24** *The following statements include confession and assurance and can be placed in that part of the worship service.*

[*Call to Confession*]
Before we celebrate baptism,
let us hear what the law of God requires of us,
that it may convince us of our sin and incite us to seek his mercy.
Christ teaches this in summary:
"'Love the Lord your God with all your heart
and with all your soul and with all your mind.'
This is the first and greatest commandment.
And the second is like it: 'Love your neighbor as yourself.'
All the Law and the Prophets
hang on these two commandments" (Matt. 22:37-40, NIV).

[*Prayer of Confession*]
**We confess to you, our God, and before one another
that we have sinned greatly, in thought, word, and deed.
We have offended your holiness.
We have failed to love our neighbor.
We have followed the devices of our own hearts
and have spurned the promptings of your Spirit.
Through our own fault, we have deserved your judgment.
O Lord God, Lamb of God, Son of the Father,
who takes away the sin of the world,
have mercy on us and hear our prayer. Amen.**

[*Assurance of Pardon*]
Let us hear the promises of God, which are confirmed in baptism.

The Lord made this great promise to Abraham:
"I will establish my covenant as an everlasting covenant
between me and you and your descendants after you
for the generations to come, to be your God
and the God of your descendants after you" (Gen. 17:7, NIV).

In later years, though Israel was unfaithful,
God renewed his promise through the prophet:
"'This is the covenant I will make with the people of Israel

after that time,' declares the LORD.
'I will put my law in their minds
    and write it on their hearts.
I will be their God,
    and they will be my people.
No longer will they teach their neighbor,
    or say to one another, "Know the LORD,"
because they will all know me,
    from the least of them to the greatest,' declares the LORD.
'For I will forgive their wickedness
    and will remember their sins no more'" (Jer. 31:33-34, NIV).

In the fullness of time God came in Jesus Christ
to give pardon and peace through the blood of the cross,
the "blood of the covenant, which is poured out for many
for the forgiveness of sins" (Matt. 26:28, NIV).

After Jesus had risen from the dead, the apostles proclaimed:
    "Repent and be baptized, every one of you,
    in the name of Jesus Christ for the forgiveness of your sins.
    And you will receive the gift of the Holy Spirit.
    The promise is for you and your children and for all who are far off—
    for all whom the Lord our God will call" (Acts 2:38-39, NIV).

Anticipating the fulfillment of God's promises, Paul assures us,
    "If we died with him,
        we will also live with him;
    if we endure,
        we will also reign with him" (2 Tim. 2:11-12, NIV).

These are the unfailing promises of our Lord to those who are baptized.

# 6.2 RESPONSE OF FAITH

*After hearing God's promises, worshipers—including the candidates for baptism or the parents of young children—respond by declaring their faith and trust in the triune God. This is the church's answer to God's promises in the dialogue between God and God's people that expresses a covenant relationship.*

### 6.2.1 Presentation

*The pastor may invite the candidate for baptism, or the parent(s) of a young child about to be baptized, to stand and respond to God's promises. To communicate the communal nature of baptism, a sponsor, a mentor, or an elder in the community may present the candidate for baptism, either informally or with a sentence such as "on behalf of the council [or board, consistory, session] of the congregation, I present [name] for baptism." The presentation, profession of faith, and baptismal vows can flow quite seamlessly; each is the response of the congregation and the candidates for baptism to the declaration of God's promises.*

### For the baptism of infants

1   Having heard God's gracious promises to us in Christ,
    do you desire that [*name*] be baptized?
    **We/I do.**

2   In presenting your child for baptism,
    you announce your love for Jesus Christ,
    your eagerness to participate in the life of Christ's body, the church,
    and your commitment to live as Christ's disciples in the world.
    With joy, we celebrate together the gift of God's grace in Christ.

3   Who presents [*name*] for baptism?
    **We/I do.**

### For the baptism of adults and older children

4   Having heard God's gracious promises to us in Christ, [*name*], do you desire to be
    baptized?
    **I do.**

5   In presenting yourself for baptism,
    you announce your love for Jesus Christ,
    your eagerness to participate in the life of Christ's body, the church,
    and your commitment to live as Christ's disciple in the world.
    With joy, we celebrate together the gift of God's grace in Christ.

### For the baptism of adults and their children

6   [*To each adult*]
    Having heard God's gracious promises to us in Christ,
    [*name*], do you desire to be baptized?
    **I do.**

    And do you desire that your children be baptized?
    **We/I do.**

### 6.2.2 Profession of Faith/Creed

*Baptism is always celebrated in the context of the faith of the church, and candidates are baptized into the church and its faith. This is why a statement of the church's faith may precede individual promises, vows, and testimonies. The church's faith is prior and primary; we come as individuals into something larger than ourselves.*

*The church's faith may be expressed through a historic creed or through renunciations and a creed. The combination of renunciations and creed is a balanced statement of saying no to Satan and yes to the triune God; it bears witness that the Christian life involves both dying and rising with Christ; it also indicates our desire to "be genuinely sorry for sin and more and more to hate and run away from it" and to live in "wholehearted joy in God through Christ" (Heidelberg Catechism, Q&A's 89-90).*

### *Introductions*

1     With all God's people throughout time and space,
   let us together profess our faith in the triune God.

2     [*For infant baptism*]
   Since you are presenting these children for baptism,
   we ask you, before God and his people,
   to reject sin and to profess your faith in Jesus Christ.

   [*For adult baptism*]
   Since you have responded by God's grace
   to the call of the gospel to believe and be baptized,
   we ask you, before God and his people,
   to reject sin and to profess your faith in Jesus Christ.

3     In presenting your child for baptism,
   desiring that he/she may be grafted into Christ
   as a member of his body, the church,
   do you receive the teaching of the Christian faith,
   which we confess in the Apostles' Creed?

### *Renunciations*

*The following texts are slightly different translations of renunciations that were used in the early church.*

4     Do you renounce Satan and all the spiritual forces of evil
   that rebel against God?
   **I renounce them!**
   Do you renounce all sinful desires
   that draw you from the love of God?
   **I renounce them!**
   Do you turn to Jesus Christ?
   **Yes! I trust in him as my Lord and Savior.**

272

Do you intend to be Christ's faithful disciple,
trusting his promises, obeying his Word,
honoring his church, and showing his love,
as long as you live?
**Yes, God helping me.**

5   Trusting in the gracious mercy of God,
    do you turn from the ways of sin
    and renounce evil and its power in the world?
    **I do.**
    Do you turn to Jesus Christ
    and accept him as your Lord and Savior,
    trusting in his grace and love?
    **I do.**
    Will you be Christ's faithful disciple,
    obeying his Word and showing his love?
    **I will, with God's help.**

6   Do you renounce all evil
    and powers in the world
    that defy God's righteousness and love?
    **I renounce them.**
    Do you renounce the ways of sin
    that separate you from the love of God?
    **I renounce them.**
    Do you turn to Jesus Christ
    and accept him as your Lord and Savior?
    **I do.**
    Will you be Christ's faithful disciple,
    obeying his Word and showing his love,
    to your life's end?
    **I will, with God's help.**

7   Beloved of God,
    I ask you before God and Christ's church
    to reject evil,
    to profess your faith in Christ Jesus,
    and to confess the faith of the church.
    Do you renounce sin and the power of evil in your life and in the world?
    **I renounce them.**
    Who is your Lord and Savior?
    **Jesus Christ is my Lord and Savior.**
    Will you be a faithful member of this congregation
    and, through worship and service,
    seek to advance God's purposes
    here and throughout the world?
    **I will, and I ask God to help me.**

*Creeds*

*The Apostles' Creed was originally developed as a baptismal document. It was given to candidates for baptism as a summary of the faith into which they were being baptized. It may be spoken by the entire congregation or by individual candidates for baptism.*

8    I believe in God, the Father almighty,
        creator of heaven and earth.

I believe in Jesus Christ, his only Son, our Lord,
    who was conceived by the Holy Spirit
    and born of the virgin Mary.
    He suffered under Pontius Pilate,
    was crucified, died, and was buried;
    he descended to hell.
    The third day he rose again from the dead.
    He ascended to heaven
    and is seated at the right hand of God the Father almighty.
    From there he will come to judge the living and the dead.

I believe in the Holy Spirit,
    the holy catholic church,
    the communion of saints,
    the forgiveness of sins,
    the resurrection of the body,
    and the life everlasting. Amen.
        —Apostles' Creed

9    *This interrogatory form of the creed may be spoken by the entire congregation or by individual candidates for baptism.*

Do you believe in God the Father?
I believe in God, the Father almighty,
creator of heaven and earth.

Do you believe in Jesus Christ, the Son of God?
I believe in Jesus Christ, God's only Son, our Lord,
who was conceived by the Holy Spirit,
born of the virgin Mary,
suffered under Pontius Pilate,
was crucified, died, and was buried.
He descended to the dead.
On the third day he rose again;
he ascended into heaven,
he is seated at the right hand of the Father,
and he will come to judge the living and the dead.

Do you believe in God the Holy Spirit?
I believe in the Holy Spirit,
the holy catholic church,
the communion of saints,
the forgiveness of sins,

**the resurrection of the body,**
**and the life everlasting.**
—based on Apostles' Creed

## Testimonies

*Following the church's statement of faith, candidates for baptism, parent(s) of children about to be baptized, or sponsors, mentors, or elders may offer a personal testimony of faith. This beautifully emphasizes that faith is both corporate and personal.*

## 6.2.3 Covenant Promises/Vows

*The following words express personal, covenantal promises of the baptismal candidates or parents. Generally, the vows offered are of two types. The first has to do with what the parents or candidates for baptism believe—whether they affirm central tenets of the Christian faith. The second has to do with what the parents or candidates for baptism promise—to commit themselves to ongoing Christian discipleship. In some congregations, the second vow is delayed until after the baptism itself, to convey that the promise of discipleship is offered in response to God's gracious action in Christ. In any case, care should be taken to stress that baptism is a celebration of God's grace, not of human achievement.*

*The first three vows below ask parents or candidates both what they believe and what they promise to do.*

1    *A vow of beliefs and actions for parents at the baptism of infants*

Since you have presented [*name(s)*] for baptism,
we ask you the following questions before God and his people.

Do you profess your faith in Jesus Christ as your Lord and Savior
and affirm the promises of God made to you and your children in his Word?
**We/I do.**

Do you promise to instruct [*name(s)*]
by word and example, with the help of the Christian community,
in the truth of God's Word,
and in the way of salvation through Jesus Christ?
Do you promise to pray for [*them*] and teach [*them*] to pray?
Do you promise to nurture [*them*]
within the body of believers, as citizens of Christ's kingdom?
**We/I do, God helping us/me.**

2    *A vow of beliefs and actions for the baptism of adults or older children*

[*Name(s)*], will you stand now
and in the presence of God and his people
respond to the following questions:

Do you believe that Jesus Christ is the Son of God sent to redeem the world,
do you love and trust him as the one who saves you from your sin,
and do you with repentance and joy embrace him as Lord of your life?

275

**I do.**
Do you believe that the Bible is the Word of God,
revealing Christ and his redemption,
and that the confessions of this church faithfully reflect this revelation?
**I do.**
Do you promise to do all you can, with the help of the Holy Spirit,
to strengthen your love and commitment to Christ
by sharing faithfully in the life of the church,
honoring and submitting to its authority;
and do you join with the people of God
in doing the work of the Lord everywhere?
**I do.**

3    *A vow of beliefs and actions for the baptism of adults and their children. This vow may also function at a service in which adults make public profession of their faith and have their children baptized.*

[*Name(s)*], will you stand now
and in the presence of God and his people
respond to the following questions:

Do you believe that Jesus Christ is the Son of God sent to redeem the world,
do you love and trust him as the one who saves you from your sin,
and do you with repentance and joy embrace him as Lord of your life?
**I do.**
Do you believe that the Bible is the Word of God,
revealing Christ and his redemption,
and that the confessions of this church faithfully reflect this revelation?
**I do.**
Do you promise to do all you can, with the help of the Holy Spirit,
to strengthen your love and commitment to Christ
by sharing faithfully in the life of the church,
honoring and submitting to its authority;
and do you join with the people of God
in doing the work of the Lord everywhere?
**I do.**

Do you promise to instruct [*name(s)*]
by word and example, with the help of the Christian community,
in the truth of God's Word,
and in the way of salvation through Jesus Christ?
Do you promise to pray for [*them*] and teach [*them*] to pray?
Do you promise to nurture [*them*]
within the body of believers, as citizens of Christ's kingdom?
**We/I do, God helping us/me.**

*The following questions apply to the second type of vow, asking what parents or candidates prom-ise to do. These questions are designed not to stand alone but to follow a creedal profession of faith.*

**4**   Will you be a faithful member of this congregation,
      share in its worship and ministry
      through your prayers and gifts,
      your study and service,
      and so fulfill your calling to be a disciple of Jesus Christ?
      **I will, with God's help.**

**5**   Will you devote yourself to the church's teaching and fellowship,
      to the breaking of bread and the prayers?
      **I will, with God's help.**
            —based on Acts 2:42, NRSV

# 6.3 PRAYER OF THANKSGIVING

*The prayer of thanksgiving at baptism offers thanks for God's covenant faithfulness in the past and requests God's continuing work through the Holy Spirit in the life of the candidate for bap-tism and the congregation. In an apt parallel with traditional prayers at the Lord's Supper, any of these prayers may also be preceded by the following words.*

The Lord be with you.
**And also with you.**
Let us give thanks to the Lord our God.
**It is right to give our thanks and praise.**

**1**   *The following outline points out the various parts of a baptismal prayer.*

   A.  Address of God
   B.  Praising God for covenant faithfulness
       to Noah, Abraham, David, and the new covenant in Christ
   C.  Remembering with gratitude God's reconciling acts such as
       the cleansing and rebirth through the flood in Noah's day,
       the exodus through the waters of the Red Sea,
       Jesus' baptism in the Jordan River,
       Jesus' death and resurrection
   D.  Praying for the work of the Holy Spirit
       to make the water a sign and seal of redemption and rebirth
       for the gathered community,
       to make baptism a sign of witness to the world,

to give the congregation unity in Christ,
to equip the church for faithfulness
    E.   Concluding doxology of praise

**2**    Father in heaven,
we pray that you will never destroy us in our sin as with the flood,
but save us as you saved believing Noah and his family,
and spare us as you spared the Israelites who walked safely through the sea.

We pray that Christ,
who went down into the Jordan and came up to receive the Spirit,
who sank deep into death and was raised up Lord of life,
will always keep us and our little ones in the grip of his hand.

We pray, O holy Father, that your Spirit
will separate us from sin and openly mark us with a faith
that can stand the light of day and endure the dark of night.

Prepare us now, O Lord,
to respond with glad hope to your promises
so that we and all entrusted to our care
may drink deeply from the well of living water.
We pray in the name of Jesus Christ, our Lord. **Amen!**

**3**    We thank you, O God,
for our baptism into Christ's death and resurrection.
In the beginning your Spirit moved over the waters,
and you created everything that is—seen and unseen.
In the time of Noah
you destroyed evil in the water of the flood,
and by your saving ark you gave a new beginning.
In the night of trouble
you led Israel through the sea,
out of slavery into the freedom of the promised land.
In the water of the Jordan
our Lord was baptized by John and anointed by your Spirit.
In the baptism of Christ's death and resurrection,
you have set us free from sin and death
and opened up the way to eternal life.

May Christ, who sank deep into death
and was raised Lord of life,
keep us and our little ones in the grip of his hand.
May your Spirit separate us from sin
and mark us with a faith
that can stand the light of day and endure the dark of night.

To you be all honor and glory,
dominion and power, now and forever,
through Jesus Christ, our Lord. **Amen.**

4    Blessed are you, O God, maker and ruler of all things.
     Your voice thundered over the waters at creation.
     You water the mountains and send springs into the valleys
     to refresh and satisfy us and all living things.
     Through the waters of the flood you carried those in the ark to safety.
     Through the sea you led your people Israel from slavery to freedom.
     In the wilderness you nourished them with water from the rock,
     and you brought them across the river Jordan to the promised land.
     By the baptism of his death and resurrection, your Son, Jesus,
     has carried us to safety and freedom.
     The floods shall not overwhelm us, the deep shall not swallow us up,
     for Christ has brought us over to the land of promise.
     He sends us to make disciples,
     baptizing in the name of the Father, and of the Son, and of the Holy Spirit.
     Pour out your Holy Spirit,
     wash away sin through the cross of Christ,
     clothe the baptized with Christ,
     and claim your daughters and sons,
     no longer Jew or Greek, no longer slave or free, no longer male or female,
     but one with all the baptized in Christ Jesus,
     who lives and reigns with you in the unity of the Holy Spirit,
     one God, now and forever. **Amen.**

5    Blessed are you, gracious God,
     creator of the universe, ruler of heaven and earth.
     You are the source of light and life for all creation.
     In your goodness you give us the sign of water.
     **Glory to you forever and ever.**
     [*or* **Blessed be God forever and ever.**]
     At the beginning your Spirit was at work,
     brooding over the waters of creation's birth,
     bringing forth life in all its fullness.
     Through the gift of water
     you nourish and sustain all living things.
     **Glory to you forever and ever.**
     [*or* **Blessed be God forever and ever.**]
     In the time of Noah, you destroyed the wicked
     and cleansed the earth through the waters of the flood.
     By the pillar of cloud and fire,
     you led Israel through the waters of the Red Sea
     out of slavery to freedom in the promised land.
     **Glory to you forever and ever.**
     [*or* **Blessed be God forever and ever.**]
     In the waters of the river Jordan,
     Jesus was baptized by John and
     anointed by the Holy Spirit.
     He is the never-failing spring,
     who has promised that all who thirst can come to the living water.

**Glory to you forever and ever.**
[*or* **Blessed be God forever and ever.**]
By the baptism of his own death and resurrection,
he set us free from bondage to sin and death
and opened to us the joy and freedom of everlasting life.
As he suffered for us,
the piercing of his side brought forth water and blood.
**Glory to you forever and ever.**
[*or* **Blessed be God forever and ever.**]
That we might live no longer for ourselves,
but for him who died and rose for us,
Christ sent the Holy Spirit,
his own first gift for those who believe.
He sends us out to proclaim the gospel to all nations,
baptizing them
in the name of the Father and of the Son and of the Holy Spirit.
**Glory to you forever and ever.**
[*or* **Blessed be God forever and ever.**]
Therefore, saving God,
we bless you for the water with which you bless us.
We pray that [*name(s)*],
coming to the waters of life,
will live in your grace,
sharing in the death and resurrection of Jesus.
Send your Holy Spirit upon us,
that all who are gathered under this sign
may be one in Christ.
**Glory to you forever and ever.**
[*or* **Blessed be God forever and ever.**]
We give you praise and honor and worship
through your Son, Jesus Christ, our Lord,
in the unity of the Holy Spirit, now and forever.
**Glory to you forever and ever.**
[*or* **Blessed be God forever and ever.**]
**Amen.**

# 6.4 BAPTISM

*The baptism itself is primarily the physical act of sprinkling, pouring, or immersing the candidate in water. The words that accompany this physical action convey its meaning with direct and joyful simplicity, emphasizing how baptism is an act by which God signs and seals the promises of the gospel to us.*

## 6.4.1 Administration

*The water may be poured into the font at this time, if this was not done earlier in the service.*

*Invitation*

1   *The following (optional) words of invitation and promise are appropriate for infant or adult baptism.*

[*Name*],
for you Jesus Christ came into the world:
for you he lived and showed God's love;
for you he suffered the darkness of Calvary
    and cried at the last, "It is finished";
for you he triumphed over death
    and rose in newness of life;
for you he ascended to reign at God's right hand.
All this he did for you, [*name*],
before you knew anything of it.
And so the Word of Scripture is fulfilled:
"We love because God loved us first."

2   *The following (optional) words of invitation are for use in infant baptism.*

Our Lord said, "Let the little children come to me,
and do not hinder them,
for the kingdom of heaven belongs to such as these."
        —from Mark 10:14, NIV

*Baptism*
*These words are spoken as the baptism is administered.*

3   [*Name*],
I baptize you in the name of the Father,
and of the Son,
and of the Holy Spirit. **Amen.**
        —based on Matthew 28:19

## 6.4.2 Blessing

*The minister may place a hand on the head of each person baptized or make a sign of the cross on each one's forehead, with the following words of blessing.*

1   The LORD bless you and keep you;
the LORD make his face to shine upon you,
    and be gracious to you;
the LORD lift his countenance upon you,
    and give you peace.
**Alleluia! Amen.**
        —from Numbers 6:24-26, NRSV

2  May the God of peace himself
   sanctify you entirely;
   and may your spirit and soul and body
   be kept sound and blameless
   at the coming of our Lord Jesus Christ.
   **Alleluia! Amen.**
   —from 1 Thessalonians 5:23, NRSV

3  [*Name*], child of the covenant,
   in baptism you are sealed with the Holy Spirit
   and marked as Christ's own. **Amen.**

4  O Lord, uphold [*name*] by your Holy Spirit.
   Give him/her the spirit of wisdom and understanding,
   the spirit of counsel and might,
   the spirit of knowledge and the fear of the Lord,
   the spirit of joy in your presence,
   both now and forever. **Amen.**

# 6.5 WELCOME

*The welcome is the congregation's natural response to God's grace. Worshipers welcome those baptized as members of Christ's body and promise to encourage, support, teach, challenge, and comfort them as integral members of the community of faith.*

## 6.5.1 Words of Encouragement and Promise

*The welcome stresses the corporate nature of baptism. The welcome may include promises of the congregation offered in response to God's gracious promises sealed in baptism. The congregation's promises may be spoken by any committed member of the body of Christ, young or old, member of the congregation, or guest. Occasionally, to stress the communal nature of the worldwide body of Christ, these words of welcome may be introduced by the following:*

   Some of us will have the privilege of encouraging
   [*name(s)*] often, over the course of many years.
   Others of us may not be able to do so.
   Yet we all speak words of promise and welcome,
   speaking on behalf of Christ's whole church, in time and space,
   and committing ourselves to live lives of Christian encouragement,
   wherever God calls us.

*Any of the following texts may be used after "the passing of the peace" or an appropriate song or hymn.*

1    Brothers and sisters,
     we now receive [*name(s)*] into Christ's church.
     Do you welcome [*them*] in love,
     and do you promise to pray for, encourage,
     and help nurture [*them*] in the faith?
     **We do, God helping us.**

2    Brothers and sisters,
     we now receive [*name(s)*] into Christ's church.
     I charge you to nurture and love [*them*]
     and to assist [*them*] to be Christ's faithful disciple(s).
     **With joy and thanksgiving,**
     **we now welcome you into Christ's church;**
     **for we are all one in Christ.**
     **We promise to love, encourage, and support you**
     **and to help you know and follow Christ.**

3    [*Name(s)*] have been received
     into the one holy catholic and apostolic church through baptism.
     God has made [*them members*] of the household of God,
     to share with us the priesthood of Christ.
     Let us welcome the newly baptized.
     **With joy and thanksgiving**
     **we welcome you into Christ's church**
     **to share with us in his ministry,**
     **for we are all one in Christ.**

4    You who are gathered here
     represent the whole church, the church catholic.
     Word and sacrament bring you
     the joy of Christ's presence in your midst.
     They also bring you responsibilities
     as Christ's people in this place.
     Do you welcome [*name(s)*],
     and do you renew your commitment,
     with God's help,
     to live before all God's children
     in a kindly and Christian way,
     and to share with them
     the knowledge and love of Christ?
     **We do.**
     **We will nurture one another in faith,**
     **uphold one another in prayer,**
     **and encourage one another in service.**

5    Friends in Christ,
     this child of God is now received into the holy catholic church.
     See what love the Father has given us,
     that we should be called children of God!
          —based on 1 John 3:1, NRSV

*In some congregations the second part of the baptismal vow is delayed until after the baptism itself, to convey that our promise of discipleship is offered in response to God's gracious action in Christ. If the second vow is heard now, the following texts may be used to complete the vows.*

6    *A vow for infant baptism*

     On the strength of God's gracious love for us,
     and in solidarity with this Christian congregation,
     do you promise to instruct [*these children*]
     by word and example, with the help of the Christian community,
     in the truth of God's Word,
     and in the way of salvation through Jesus Christ?
     Do you promise to pray for [*them*] and teach [*them*] to pray?
     Do you promise to nurture [*them*]
     within the body of believers as citizens of Christ's kingdom?
     **We/I do, God helping us/me.**

7    *A vow for adult baptism*

     On the strength of God's gracious love for us,
     and in solidarity with this Christian congregation,
     will you be a faithful member of this congregation,
     share in its worship and ministry
     through your prayers and gifts,
     your study and service,
     and so fulfill your calling to be a disciple of Jesus Christ?
     **I will, with God's help.**

8    *A vow for adult baptism*

     On the strength of God's gracious love for us,
     and in solidarity with this Christian congregation,
     will you devote yourself to the church's teaching and fellowship,
     to the breaking of bread and the prayers?
     **I will, with God's help.**
          —based on Acts 2:42, NRSV

## 6.5.2 Intercessory Prayer

*The following prayers ask for God's ongoing blessing for those who are baptized as well as for the entire congregation. These prayers may be offered at the conclusion of the baptism or may be incorporated into the prayers of the people (see section 4) at another point in the service.*

1     [*At the baptism of children, the minister may lay hands on those receiving baptism while saying the following.*]

Gracious God and heavenly Father,
we thank you that you make us new persons in Jesus Christ
through grace alone.
We pray for [*name(s)*].
Bless and strengthen [*them*] daily
with the gift of your Holy Spirit.
Unfold to [*them*] the riches of your love.
Deepen [*their*] faith.
Keep [*them*] from the power of evil.
Enable [*them*] to live a holy and blameless life
until your kingdom comes.

[*After withdrawing hands, the minister may continue as follows.*]

Look with kindness on [*these parents*].
Let [*them*] always rejoice in the gift you have given [*them*].
Grant [*them*] the presence of your Holy Spirit,
that [*they*] may bring up [*these children*]
to know you, love you, and serve you and [*their*] neighbor,
through Jesus Christ, our Lord. **Amen.**

2     *A prayer for children's baptism*

Lord our God, forever faithful to your promise,
we thank you for assuring us again
that you will forgive us and receive us as children in Christ.
Grant wisdom and love to [*the parents*] and to us all
as we carry out the vows we have just made.
We pray that you will guide our little ones throughout their lives.
Enable them to respond in faith to the gospel.
Fill them with your Spirit and make their lives fruitful.
Give them strength to endure trials.
And when Christ returns, let them celebrate with all the people of God
your greatness and goodness forever in the joy of your new creation. **Amen.**

3     *A prayer for adult baptism*

Our Father in heaven,
we thank you for Jesus Christ,
for the new life given in him,
and for the one faith, one hope, and one baptism
that your people have shared through the ages.
We rejoice that [*name(s)*] are now one with your church
and that we may receive [*them*] as members of this congregation.
Guide [*them*] in the Christian way and sustain us all
in the fellowship and service of our Lord. **Amen.**

**4**  *A prayer for newly baptized infants and children*

Ever-living God,
in your mercy you promised to be not only our God
but also the God of our children.
We thank you for receiving [*name(s)*] by baptism.
Keep [*them*] always in your love.
Guide [*them*] as [*they grow*] in faith.
Protect [*them*] in all the dangers and temptations of life.
Bring [*them*] to confess Jesus Christ as [*their*] Lord and Savior
and to be his faithful [*disciples*] to [*their*] life's end,
in his name. **Amen.**

**5**  *A prayer for parents of newly baptized children*

Gracious God, giver of all life,
we pray for [*name(s)*].
Give [*them*] wisdom and patience
to guide [*their children*] in the way of Jesus Christ
and the faith of the church.
Let your peace and joy dwell in [*their*] home,
that [*their*] family life may be instructed by faith,
sustained by prayer, and governed by love.
Strengthen [*them*] in [*their*] own baptism,
that [*they*] may rejoice as [*children*] of God,
and serve you faithfully,
in the name of Jesus Christ. **Amen.**

**6**  *A prayer for the newly baptized and new members*

Merciful God, you call us by name
and promise to each of us your constant love.
Watch over your servant(s), [*name(s)*],
deepen [*their*] understanding of the gospel,
strengthen [*their*] commitment to follow the way of Christ,
and keep [*them*] in the faith and communion of your church.
Increase [*their*] compassion for others,
send [*them*] into the world in witness to your love,
and bring [*them*] to the fullness of your peace and glory,
through Jesus Christ, our Lord. **Amen.**

**7**  *A prayer for families*

Loving God,
you nurture and guide us like a father and mother.
We pray for the families of this congregation
and for all Christian families everywhere.
Give them strength to honor you in their homes
and to love and serve each other.
Help all who have been baptized in your name
to live in peace and unity

as sisters and brothers in the household of faith,
and to serve others in the name of Jesus Christ. **Amen.**

8    O God, as a mother comforts her children,
you strengthen, sustain, and provide for us.
We come before you with gratitude
for the gift of [*this child*],
for the joy that has come into this family,
and for the grace with which you surround them
and all of us.
As a father cares for his children,
so you continually look upon us
with compassion and goodness.
Pour out your Spirit.
Enable your servants to abound in love,
and establish our homes in holiness,
through Jesus Christ, our Lord. **Amen.**

9    *A prayer for a newly baptized adopted child*

Gracious God, in your love and mercy you have adopted us
as your children through Jesus Christ.
From the riches of your grace,
bless this child [*name*] with knowing you as Father,
living a new life in Christ,
and developing the gifts of your Spirit.
Help us all to nurture this child [*name*] as a citizen of your kingdom,
as together we wait with all of creation
for the final coming of your perfect kingdom
in a new heaven and a new earth.
In the name of Christ we pray. **Amen.**

10   *A prayer offered by the parents of a newly baptized child*

Our loving God, thank you for the amazing gift of our child.
Even more, thank you that this child is your child.
Thank you for loving [*name*] more than we do.
Thank you that he/she belongs to you forever.
Thank you for your family, the church,
and for the promises our church made to love [*name*] and teach [*name*] about you.
Help them and us to guide [*name*], encourage [*name*], and challenge [*name*].
Bless [*name*] as he/she grows;
may he/she know and love you more with each new day.
Give him/her your wisdom and grace
so that he/she will learn about and serve you, others, and your world.
In the power of your Holy Spirit, through Jesus Christ, our Lord, we pray. **Amen.**

**11**   *A prayer to be led by an older sibling of a newly baptized child*

God, our Father,
thank you for giving our family my younger brother/sister.
Thank you for loving us
and showing us your love through [*name's*] baptism today.
Thank you for the gift of your Son, Jesus Christ,
who makes us part of your family
with Christians all over the world.
We ask that you will help us
to know more about Jesus every day
and to remember how great you are
and how much you love us. In Jesus' name, **Amen.**

**12**   *A prayer to be led by an older sibling of a newly baptized child*

Thank you, O God, for creating [*name*]
and for placing her/him in our family as my younger brother/sister.
She/he is a precious gift to me.
By baptism, you show all of us,
    my parents and me,
    my church family,
    and the whole world too,
that [*name*] is even more precious to you.
With this water you promise that
    you will be [*name's*] heavenly Father,
        caring for and protecting her/him every day;
    you will be [*name's*] Savior; because Jesus gave his life for [*name*],
        you will welcome her/him eagerly into your family;
    you will give [*name*] strength to trust and obey you;
        your Holy Spirit will be Jesus' presence and power to her/him.
Help me every day
    to love [*name*]
    and to help her/him
        to know you,
        to have faith and hope in you,
        and to please you always.
In Jesus' name I pray. **Amen.**

# SECTION 7
# PROFESSION OF FAITH AND REMEMBRANCE OF BAPTISM

Baptism establishes our ultimate identity in Christ, a sense of identity that is expressed and further formed through our habits of prayer, worship, and service. At its best, our worship each week reminds us of our baptismal identity. As John Calvin affirmed, "we must realize that at whatever time we are baptized, we are once for all washed and purged for our whole life. Therefore, as often as we fall away (i.e., newly committed sins into which we fall after baptism), we ought to recall the memory of our baptism and fortify our mind with it, that we may always be sure and confident of the forgiveness of sins" (*Institutes of the Christian Religion*, 4.15.3). As we worship, we hear again God's gracious promises, remember that we live in union with Christ, and renew our own commitment to Christ. In worship and life, we practice what it means to daily die to sin and rise with Christ to newness of life.

What a gift this is in the context of contemporary culture! In an age

in which people long for a sense of belonging, affirming baptism rehearses that we belong to Christ and to the body of Christ, the church. In an age of individualism, baptism affirms our inclusion as members of Christ's body. In an age that tends to evaluate people on their achievements, baptism affirms that our identity in Christ is a gift that does not depend on our own efforts.

**Multiple Occasions**

There are many occasions when our focus on baptismal identity is especially important. Some of these are moments in the lives of *individuals*, such as when they profess their faith publicly, return to the life of the church after a time of estrangement, or join a congregation. Public celebrations of "milestone moments" (see Josh. 4:21-24) promise to reinforce baptismal identity, convey the church's love for each individual, and express a warm invitation to deeper participation in the life of faith. Others are moments in the life of an entire *congregation*, such as when it celebrates an anniversary, faces a crisis or difficult decision, welcomes a new pastor, or dedicates a new ministry or building. All such occasions, and many others, are fitting times for individuals or congregations to intentionally and explicitly remember baptism, claim again the promises of God in Christ, and renew the commitment to baptismal living.

To underscore the link with baptism, these public affirmations of baptism might be led from the baptismal font. In some traditions, water is poured into a font or sprinkled on the congregation as a reminder of baptism.

**Profession of Faith**

Public profession of faith is an especially important milestone for expressing gratitude for the work of the Holy Spirit in the lives of individual believers. Public profession of faith affirms what was already signed and sealed at baptism. It is an opportunity for individuals to give account of the hope that they have in Christ (1 Pet. 3:15). It marks a time at which a believer is ready for new responsibilities and roles in the life of the church. It offers rich opportunities to express communal gratitude for the work of God in the lives of his children. The opportunity for public profession of faith is a gift, then, both for individuals and for the church.

There is no single age which the church mandates for public profession of faith. Indeed, in God's sovereign grace, congregations have witnessed profound professions of faith by believers 8 and 88 years of age. While professions of faith may arise out of individual initiative, congregations need not passively wait for individuals to step forward. Rather, congregations should eagerly and sensitively invite children and youth to take the significant step of publicly professing their faith. For many generations, a public profession of faith has served as a rite of passage from childhood into adolescent or adult faith. It serves as a natural occasion for challenging youth to consider the claims of Christ, to give voice to the faith, and to celebrate and affirm their God-given gifts.

Profession of faith is a significant milestone in the lifelong journey of discipleship. Congregations should not view profession of faith as a "graduation" from church-based education programs but rather a time of renewed commitment to learning and service as a part of the congregation.

**Not Rebaptism**

It is important to note that the resources in this section are *not* liturgies for rebaptism. Rebaptizing can convey three false impressions: (1) that God's promises were not really given in one's original baptism, and (2) that the church or denomination in which a given member was originally baptized is not a legitimate part of Christ's body, and (3) that personal experience is the sole barometer of the presence of God. For these reasons, churches in many cultural contexts have responded to requests for rebaptism by planning for public celebrations of *affirmation* of baptism.

These celebrations offer praise and thanks for the sovereign grace of God, providing a memorable, visible, and public milestone for both the congregation and the individual.

These liturgies, therefore, should be celebrated so as to communicate both that they are connected to the church's celebration of baptism and that they do not repeat baptism. Services that include remembrance of baptism should also be intentional about welcoming not only those who have a baptism to remember but also those who do not. In fact, the main goal of the remembrance of baptism should be to proclaim the gospel so directly, sincerely, and enthusiastically that spiritual seekers will more eagerly anticipate their own baptism.

The following resources include materials for both individual profession of faith and general congregational use.

# COMPLETE MODEL LITURGY FOR PROFESSION OF FAITH

*The following model liturgy is designed to help leaders visualize the structure of the profession of faith celebration. When used in worship, each of the numbered subheadings should be deleted. The pages following this model liturgy offer numerous options for adapting each corresponding section. (For example, see section 7.1 on pages 288-290 for options to use for the Introduction, section 7.2 on pages 290-293 for choices to use in the Declaration of God's Promises, and so on.)*

## 7.1 Introduction

*[For individual professions of faith]*

Congregation of our Lord Jesus Christ:
Today we are privileged to welcome those who wish to confess their faith in Christ as Lord and Savior.

When they were baptized, God made clear his claim on them as his own, and they were received into the church.

Now they wish publicly to accept and confirm what was sealed in their baptism, confess their faith in the Lord Jesus, and offer themselves to God as his willing servants.

We thank God for having given them this desire and pray that as we now hear their confession, God's Spirit will strengthen all of us for continued service in Christ's kingdom.

*[General congregational use]*

Brothers and sisters in Christ,
we are united by a common faith in Jesus Christ.

The power at work in this community does not come from our own strength but from God's Spirit working in us.

Claiming God's promises, we remember again God's gracious love for us and recommit ourselves to joyful life together in Christ.

## 7.2 Declaration of God's Promises

Through baptism God gave us a gracious sign of love and hope in Christ.

Hear again the promises God has made to us in Christ.

Baptism is the sign and seal of God's promises to this covenant people.

In baptism God promises by grace alone to forgive our sins, to adopt us into the body of Christ, the church, to send the Holy Spirit daily to renew and cleanse us, and to resurrect us to eternal life.

This promise is made visible in the water of baptism. Water cleanses, purifies, refreshes, sustains; Jesus Christ is living water.

Through baptism Christ calls us to new obedience: to love and trust God completely, to forsake the evil of the world, and to live a new and holy life.

Yet, when we fall into sin, we must not despair of God's mercy or continue in sin, for baptism is the sign and seal of God's eternal covenant of grace with us.

## 7.3 Profession of Faith

*[Spoken to either an individual or the congregation]*

I invite you now to remember God's promise, to turn away from all that is evil, and to reaffirm your faith in Jesus Christ and your commitment to Christ's church.

Do you renounce Satan and all the spiritual forces of evil that rebel against God?

**I renounce them!**

Do you renounce all sinful desires that draw you from the love of God?

**I renounce them!**

Do you turn to Jesus Christ?

**Yes! I trust in him as my Lord and Savior.**

Do you intend to be Christ's faithful disciple, trusting his promises, obeying his Word, honoring his church, and showing his love, as long as you live?

**Yes! God helping me.**

Do you believe in God the Father?

**I believe in God, the Father almighty,
creator of heaven and earth.**

Do you believe in Jesus Christ, the Son of God?

**I believe in Jesus Christ, God's only Son,
    our Lord,
who was conceived by the Holy Spirit,
born of the virgin Mary,
suffered under Pontius Pilate,
was crucified, died, and was buried.
He descended to the dead.
On the third day he rose again;
he ascended to heaven,
he is seated at the right hand of the Father,
and he will come to judge the living and
    the dead.**

Do you believe in God the Holy Spirit?

**I believe in the Holy Spirit,
the holy catholic church,
the communion of saints,
the forgiveness of sins,
the resurrection of the body,
and the life everlasting.**

—based on Apostles' Creed

You have publicly professed your faith.
Will you devote yourself
to the church's teaching and fellowship,
to the breaking of bread and the prayers?

**I will, with God's help.**

—based on Acts 2:42, NRSV

## 7.4 Prayers of Thanksgiving, Blessing, and Dedication

The Lord be with you.

**And also with you.**

Let us give thanks to the Lord our God.

**It is right to give our thanks and praise.**

We give you thanks, O holy and gracious God,
for the gift of water.

In the beginning of creation your Spirit moved
over the waters.

In the waters of the flood you destroyed evil.
You led the children of Israel through the sea
into the freedom of the promised land. In the
river Jordan, John baptized our Lord and your
Spirit anointed him.

By his death and resurrection Jesus Christ, the
living water, frees us from sin and death and
opens the way to life everlasting.

**We have put on Christ. In him we have been
baptized. Alleluia! Alleluia!**

We thank you, O God, for the gift of baptism.

In the waters of baptism you confirm to us that
we are buried with Christ in his death, raised
to share in his resurrection, and are being
renewed by the Holy Spirit.

Pour out upon us and on your whole church
the gift of your Holy Spirit, so that all who
have passed through the waters of baptism
might be dead to sin and alive to God in Christ
Jesus.

To God be all honor and glory, dominion and
power, now and forever, through Jesus Christ
our Lord, in whose name we are bold to pray:

**Our Father in heaven . . .**

## 7.5 Welcome and Encouragement

[*In services for individuals*]

In the name of our Lord Jesus Christ,
we now welcome you to all the privileges of
full communion.

We welcome you to full participation in the
life of the church, to its responsibilities, its joys,
and its sufferings.

**Thanks be to God!
We promise you our love, encouragement,
and prayers.**

## 7.6 Call to Service and Blessing

[*Individual name(s) or name of the congregation*]:

Remember your baptism and be thankful.
You are disciple(s) of Jesus Christ.
Live in love, as Christ loved us
and gave himself for us.
Rejoice always; pray without ceasing;
give thanks in all circumstances;
for this is the will of God in Christ Jesus for you.
The peace of God, which passes all under-
standing, keep your heart and your mind in
Christ Jesus.

**Amen.**

# 7.1 Introduction

*The liturgy begins with a warm, simple statement of purpose. The introduction should point to the significance and meaning of the celebration and should set a celebrative and welcoming tone. The following sample texts should be adapted to particular situations as needed.*

## 7.1.1 Individual Professions of Faith

1    Congregation of our Lord Jesus Christ:
Today we are privileged to welcome
those who wish to confess their faith in Christ as Lord and Savior.
When they were baptized, God made clear his claim on them as his own,
and they were received into the church.
Now they wish publicly to
accept and confirm what was sealed in their baptism,
confess their faith in the Lord Jesus,
and offer themselves to God as his willing servants.
We thank God for having given them this desire
and pray that as we now hear their confession,
God's Spirit will strengthen all of us for continued service in Christ's kingdom.

2    [*Name(s)*] are presented by the elders
for the reaffirming of the baptismal covenant
into which they were baptized.
They now desire to profess publicly their faith
and to assume greater responsibility
in the life of the church
and God's mission in the world.
We rejoice that you now desire to declare your faith
and to share with us in our common ministry.

3    *For baptism and profession of faith*

The elders of [*name of congregation*] have welcomed these persons
who appeared before them and made profession of their Christian faith.
[*Name(s)*] come before us now
to make public this profession of faith
and to receive the sacrament of baptism.
And [*name(s)*] have been baptized into the body of Christ.
In making public this profession of faith,
they affirm the meaning of their baptism.

## 7.1.2 Reaffirmation of Faith

*The following text may be used or adapted for several occasions, such as for a person returning to the church, for persons marking growth in their Christian life, or for those being commissioned for service in a particular role or ministry.*

1    Brothers and sisters,
     from time to time we experience a new beginning in our faith journey,
     when the Holy Spirit breaks into our lives to inspire us, to lead us,
     and to deepen our commitment to Christ.
     Today, we praise the Lord
     for what has been happening in [*name*]'s life.

## 7.1.3 Welcome of New Members

*The following introduction may be used to welcome new members into a congregation.*

1    Brothers and sisters,
     we praise God for the life and witness of [*name(s)*].
     We are grateful that they desire to join our congregation
     and to share with us in our work of worship, witness, and fellowship.
     What unites us is nothing less than our common identity in Christ.
     We celebrate our unity and receive these new members with joy.

## 7.1.4 Remembrance of Baptism

*The following introductions may be used for services remembering baptism for the whole congregation.*

1    Brothers and sisters in Christ,
     we are united by a common faith in Jesus Christ.
     The power at work in this community
     does not come from our own strength
     but from God's Spirit working in us.
     Claiming God's promises,
     we remember again God's gracious love for us
     and recommit ourselves to joyful life together in Christ.

2    Brothers and sisters in Christ,
     we worship today in the context of a very significant event
     in the life of our congregation:
     [*explanation, as appropriate, of circumstances*].
     At this important time, we need to claim again God's promises to us.
     We need to recommit ourselves to service in Christ.
     We need to place our only hope and trust in God
     and pray for the work of God's Spirit in our midst.

Baptism is a sign of God's faithful covenant promises,
under which we live as a congregation each day.
Let us remember now our baptism and be thankful.

# 7.2 DECLARATION OF GOD'S PROMISES

*Services of baptismal remembrance and profession of faith are like echoes of baptism. Like baptism, the focus is primarily on God's grace and how it makes possible the renewal of our faith. Thus a clear declaration of God's promises confirmed in Christ is at the center of baptismal renewal. The following texts provide several options for the use of Scripture texts that memorably convey God's promises to us. In most contexts, they can be proclaimed with little, if any, commentary. (See also any of the scriptural promises for baptism in section 6.1). The following declarations can be introduced by words such as these:*

Hear again the gracious promises of God,
and know that all of God's promises
are brought to completion through Jesus Christ!

*or*

Through baptism God gave us
a gracious sign of love and hope in Christ.
Hear again the promises God has made to us in Christ.

## 7.2.1 Scriptural Promises

1     While we were still weak,
at the right time Christ died for the ungodly.
Indeed, rarely will anyone die for a righteous person—
though perhaps for a good person someone might actually dare to die.
But God proves his love for us
in that while we still were sinners Christ died for us.
Much more surely then, now that we have been justified by his blood,
will we be saved through him from the wrath of God.
For if while we were enemies,
we were reconciled to God through the death of his Son,
much more surely, having been reconciled, will we be saved by his life.
       —Romans 5:6-10, NRSV

2   If Christ is in you,
though the body is dead because of sin,
the Spirit is life because of righteousness.
If the Spirit of him who raised Jesus from the dead dwells in you,
he who raised Christ from the dead will give life
to your mortal bodies also through his Spirit that dwells in you.
So then, brothers and sisters,
we are debtors, not to the flesh, to live according to the flesh—
for if you live according to the flesh, you will die;
but if by the Spirit you put to death the deeds of the body, you will live.
For all who are led by the Spirit of God are children of God.
For you did not receive a spirit of slavery to fall back into fear,
but you have received a spirit of adoption.
When we cry, "Abba! Father!"
it is that very Spirit bearing witness with our spirit
that we are children of God,
and if children, then heirs, heirs of God and joint heirs with Christ—
if, in fact, we suffer with him so that we may also be glorified with him.
       —Romans 8:10-17, NRSV

3   Just as the body is one and has many members,
and all the members of the body, though many, are one body,
so it is with Christ.
For in the one Spirit we were all baptized into one body—
Jews or Greeks, slaves or free—
and we were all made to drink of one Spirit.
Now you are the body of Christ
and individually members of it.
       —1 Corinthians 12:12-13, 27, NRSV

4   As many of you as were baptized into Christ
have clothed yourselves with Christ.
There is no longer Jew or Greek,
there is no longer slave or free,
there is no longer male or female;
for all of you are one in Christ Jesus.
       —Galatians 3:27-28, NRSV

5   We are what God has made us,
created in Christ Jesus for good works,
which God prepared beforehand
to be our way of life.
       —from Ephesians 2:10, NRSV

6   You are citizens with the saints
and also members of the household of God,
built upon the foundation of the apostles and prophets,
with Christ Jesus himself as the cornerstone.
In him the whole structure is joined together

and grows into a holy temple in the Lord;
in whom you also are built together spiritually
into a dwelling place for God.
—Ephesians 2:19-22, NRSV

7   There is one body and one Spirit,
just as you were called to the one hope of your calling,
one Lord, one faith, one baptism,
one God and Father of all,
who is above all and through all and in all.
—Ephesians 4:4-6, NRSV

8   You were taught,
with regard to your former way of life,
to put off your old self,
which is being corrupted by its deceitful desires;
to be made new in the attitude of your minds;
and to put on the new self,
created to be like God in true righteousness and holiness.
—Ephesians 4:22-24, NIV

9   You are a chosen race, a royal priesthood,
a holy nation, God's own people,
in order that you may proclaim the mighty acts
of the one who called you out of darkness
into God's marvelous light.
—from 1 Peter 2:9, NRSV

## 7.2.2 Summary Paragraphs

*The following paragraphs draw together various scriptural themes about baptism. They may be used in place of or alongside one of the preceding scriptural promises.*

1   Through baptism God gave us
a gracious sign of love and hope in Christ.
Hear again the promises God has made to us in Christ.

Baptism is the sign and seal of God's promises
to this covenant people.
In baptism God promises by grace alone
    to forgive our sins,
        to adopt us into the body of Christ, the church,
        to send the Holy Spirit daily to renew and cleanse us,
        and to resurrect us to eternal life.
This promise is made visible in the water of baptism.
Water cleanses, purifies, refreshes, sustains;
Jesus Christ is living water.
Through baptism Christ calls us to new obedience:
    to love and trust God completely,

> to forsake the evil of the world,
>     and to live a new and holy life.
> Yet when we fall into sin,
> we must not despair of God's mercy or continue in sin,
> for baptism is the sign and seal
> of God's eternal covenant of grace with us.

# 7.3 PROFESSION OF FAITH

*The church's faith may be expressed either through a historic creed or through renunciations and a creed. The combination of renunciations and creed is a balanced statement of saying no to Satan and yes to the triune God; it bears witness that the Christian life involves both dying and rising with Christ; it also indicates our desire to "be genuinely sorry for sin and more and more to hate and run away from it" and to live in "wholehearted joy in God through Christ" (Heidelberg Catechism, Q&A's 89-90).*

## 7.3.1 Introductions

*For individual professions of faith*

1     I invite you now to remember God's promise,
      to turn away from all that is evil,
      and to reaffirm your faith in Jesus Christ
      and your commitment to Christ's church.

2     Now, as you publicly declare your faith,
      we ask you to reject sin,
      to profess your faith in Christ Jesus,
      and to confess the faith of the church,
      the faith in which you were baptized.

*For welcoming new members*

3     We ask you now to declare your faith
      before God and Christ's church
      that we may rejoice together and
      welcome you as brothers and sisters in Christ.

*For general congregational use*

4    Sisters and brothers in Christ,
     our baptism is the sign and seal
         of our cleansing from sin
         and of our being grafted into Christ.
     Through the birth, life, death, and resurrection of Christ,
     the power of sin was broken
     and God's kingdom entered our world.
     Through our baptism we were made citizens of God's kingdom
     and freed from the bondage of sin.
     Let us celebrate that freedom and redemption
     through the renewal of the promises made at our baptism.
     I ask you, therefore, once again
         to reject sin,
         to profess your faith in Christ Jesus,
         and to confess the faith of the church,
             the faith in which we were baptized.

5    The faith we together affirm today
     is the faith of the whole church, throughout time and space.
     With all God's people, let us profess our faith in the triune God.


## 7.3.2 Renunciations

*For additional formulations of renunciations, see resources for baptism (section 6.2.2).*

1    Do you renounce Satan and all the spiritual forces of evil
     that rebel against God?
     **I renounce them!**
     Do you renounce all sinful desires
     that draw you from the love of God?
     **I renounce them!**
     Do you turn to Jesus Christ?
     **Yes! I trust in him as my Lord and Savior.**
     Do you intend to be Christ's faithful disciple,
     trusting his promises, obeying his Word,
     honoring his church, and showing his love,
     as long as you live?
     **Yes! God helping me.**

## 7.3.3 Creeds

1   I believe in God, the Father almighty,
       creator of heaven and earth.

   I believe in Jesus Christ, his only Son, our Lord,
       who was conceived by the Holy Spirit
       and born of the virgin Mary.
       He suffered under Pontius Pilate,
       was crucified, died, and was buried;
       he descended to hell.
       The third day he rose again from the dead.
       He ascended to heaven
       and is seated at the right hand of God the Father almighty.
       From there he will come to judge the living and the dead.

   I believe in the Holy Spirit,
       the holy catholic church,
       the communion of saints,
       the forgiveness of sins,
       the resurrection of the body,
       and the life everlasting. Amen.
           —Apostles' Creed

2   Do you believe in God the Father?
   I believe in God, the Father almighty,
   creator of heaven and earth.

   Do you believe in Jesus Christ, the Son of God?
   I believe in Jesus Christ, God's only Son, our Lord,
   who was conceived by the Holy Spirit,
   born of the virgin Mary,
   suffered under Pontius Pilate,
   was crucified, died, and was buried.
   He descended to the dead.
   On the third day he rose again;
   he ascended to heaven,
   he is seated at the right hand of the Father,
   and he will come to judge the living and the dead.

   Do you believe in God the Holy Spirit?
   I believe in the Holy Spirit,
   the holy catholic church,
   the communion of saints,
   the forgiveness of sins,
   the resurrection of the body,
   and the life everlasting.
       —based on Apostles' Creed

*301*

### 7.3.4 Personal Vows

*A personal vow is especially appropriate in remembrance of baptism services marking an occasion in which individuals are professing their faith, returning to the church, or joining a congregation.*

*For profession of faith*

1    [*Name(s)*], will you stand now
and in the presence of God and his people
respond to the following questions:

Do you believe that Jesus Christ is the Son of God sent to redeem the world,
do you love and trust him as the one who saves you from your sin,
and do you with repentance and joy embrace him as Lord of your life?
**I do.**

Do you believe that the Bible is the Word of God,
revealing Christ and his redemption,
and that the confessions of this church faithfully reflect this revelation?
**I do.**

Do you accept the gracious promises of God sealed to you in your baptism
and do you affirm your union with Christ and his church,
which your baptism signifies?
**I do.**

Do you promise to do all you can, with the help of the Holy Spirit,
to strengthen your love and commitment to Christ
by sharing faithfully in the life of the church,
honoring and submitting to its authority;
and do you join with the people of God
in doing the work of the Lord everywhere?
**I do.**

*For profession of faith, returning to the church, or joining a congregation*

2    You have publicly professed your faith.
Will you devote yourself to the church's teaching and fellowship,
to the breaking of bread and the prayers?
**I will, with God's help.**
      —based on Acts 2:42, NRSV

3    You have publicly professed your faith.
Will you be a faithful member of this congregation,
share in its worship and ministry
through your prayers and gifts,
your study and service,
and so fulfill your calling to be a disciple of Jesus Christ?
**I will, with God's help.**

*For profession of faith, if those being received also have children who will be baptized*

4     Will you promise
      to instruct these children
      in the truth of God's Word,
      in the way of salvation through Jesus Christ;
      to pray for them,
      to teach them to pray, and
      to train them in Christ's way
      by your example,
      through worship,
      and in the nurture of the church?
      **I will, and I ask God to help me.**

### 7.3.5 Personal Testimony

*The person celebrating profession of faith or remembrance of baptism may give a brief witness to an experience of Christ or a new beginning in faith, or the pastor or another person may outline briefly the experiences that have brought the person to make this witness.*

# 7.4 PRAYERS OF THANKSGIVING, BLESSING, AND DEDICATION

---

*For professions of faith or other celebrations in the lives of individuals. Any of these prayers may be accompanied by the laying on of hands, a vivid way of embodying blessing, encouragement, calling, and a sense of mutual dependence on the Holy Spirit.*

1     Lord, our God,
      we thank you for your Word and Spirit,
      through which we know Jesus Christ as Lord and Savior.
      May those who confessed your name today
      never cease to wonder at what you have done for them.
      Help them to continue firmly in the faith,
      to bear witness to your love,
      and to let the Holy Spirit shape their lives.
      Take them, good Shepherd, into your care
      that they may loyally endure opposition
      they may face as they serve you.
      May we, with all your children,

live together in the joy and power of your Holy Spirit.
We ask this, Lord Jesus, in the hope of your coming. **Amen.**

2    Gracious God, by water and the Spirit
you claimed us as your own,
cleansing us from sin and giving us new life.
You made us members of your body, the church,
calling us to be your servants in the world.
Renew in [*name(s)*] the covenant you made in [*their*] baptism.
Continue the good work you have begun in [*them*].
Send [*them*] forth in the power of your Spirit
to love and serve you with joy
and to strive for justice and peace in all the earth,
in the name of Jesus Christ, our Lord. **Amen.**

3    Almighty God, thank you for your never-failing love for [*name(s)*].
Moment by moment you work in [*their*] lives.
Pour out your Spirit on [*name*(s)].
Give [*them*] your wisdom and understanding.
Comfort [*them*] and instruct [*them*].
May [*their*] lives overflow with your lavish joy
both now and forevermore. **Amen.**

4    Defend, O Lord, your servant(s), [*name(s)*],
with your heavenly grace,
that [*they*] may continue yours forever
and daily increase in your Holy Spirit more and more,
until [*they*] come to your everlasting kingdom. **Amen.**

5    Ever-living God,
guard [*these*], your servant(s), with your protecting hand
and let your Holy Spirit be with [*them*] forever.
Lead [*them*] to know and obey your Word,
that [*they*] may serve you in this life
and dwell with you forever in the life to come,
through Jesus Christ, our Lord. **Amen.**

*For persons joining a congregation*

6    Holy God,
we praise you for calling us to be a servant people
and for gathering us into the body of Christ.
We thank you for choosing to add to our number
brothers and sisters in faith.
Together may we live in your Spirit
and so love one another
that we may have the mind of Jesus Christ, our Lord,
to whom we give honor and glory forever. **Amen.**

*For persons returning to the church after a time of estrangement or nonparticipation for an extended time*

7    Faithful God,
     you work in us and for us,
     even when we do not know it.
     When our path has led us away from you,
     you guide us back to yourself.
     We thank you for calling your servant(s), [*name(s)*],
     to the fellowship of your people.
     Renew in [*them*] the covenant you made in [*their*] baptism.
     By the power of your Spirit,
     strengthen [*them*] in faith and love,
     that [*they*] may serve you with joy,
     to the glory of Jesus Christ, our Lord. **Amen.**

8    Faithful God,
     in baptism you claimed us,
     and by your Spirit you are working in our lives,
     empowering us to live a life worthy of our calling.
     We thank you for leading [*name(s)*]
     to this time and place of reaffirming the covenant
     you made with [*them*] in [*their*] baptism.
     Establish [*them*] in your truth,
     and guide [*them*] by your Spirit,
     that, together with all your people,
     [*they*] may grow in faith, hope, and love,
     and be faithful [*disciples*] of Jesus Christ,
     to whom, with you and the Holy Spirit
     be honor and glory, now and forever. **Amen.**

9    Covenant God,
     we push you away, but you never let us go.
     We turn away from you and even try to run away from you.
     But you never let us go.
     You seek us out when we are far from you
     and draw us back to your waiting arms.
     You never let us go.
     Hold us tight, almighty God.
     Embrace us with your never-ending love.
     Never let us go, for Jesus' sake. **Amen.**

*For an entire congregation*

10   The Lord be with you.
     **And also with you.**
     Let us give thanks to the Lord our God.
     **It is right to give our thanks and praise.**
     We give you thanks, O holy and gracious God, for the gift of water.

In the beginning of creation your Spirit moved over the waters.
In the waters of the flood you destroyed evil.
You led the children of Israel through the sea
into the freedom of the promised land.
In the river Jordan, John baptized our Lord
and your Spirit anointed him.
By his death and resurrection Jesus Christ, the living water,
frees us from sin and death and opens the way to life everlasting.
[*acclamation, spoken or sung*]
**We have put on Christ. In him we have been baptized. Alleluia! Alleluia!**

We thank you, O God, for the gift of baptism.
In the waters of baptism you confirm to us
that we are buried with Christ in his death,
raised to share in his resurrection,
and are being renewed by the Holy Spirit.
[*repeat acclamation*]

Pour out upon us and on your whole church the gift of your Holy Spirit,
so that all who have passed through the waters of baptism
might be dead to sin and alive to God in Christ Jesus.
[*repeat acclamation*]

To God be all honor and glory, dominion and power, now and forever,
through Jesus Christ our Lord, in whose name we are bold to pray:
**Our Father in heaven . . .**

11  We praise you this day, O Lord,
for the gift of water.
Water quenches. Water washes.
Water gives life.

We praise you this day, O Lord,
for your power over water,
for separating the water to create dry ground,
for saving Noah while the flood destroyed evil,
for leading your people through the parted waters of the Red Sea,
for giving us the living water, Christ, whom you claimed as your Son at his baptism.

We praise you this day, O Lord,
for the gift of baptism,
a sign of our union with Jesus' death and resurrection,
a sign of the washing away of our sins.

We praise you this day, O Lord,
for your promises made visible in baptism,
your covenant seal, placed upon us,
given as a sign of our new life in you.

We praise you this day, O Lord,
that through the gift of your Son,

we have been adopted as your covenant children,
part of the family of God.

We praise you this day, O Lord,
for the gift of adoption,
for the grafting together
that formed this new family.

Help us remember our baptism into Jesus' death and resurrection.
Help us remember our adoption as your children.
Help us remember our brothers and sisters in Christ,
brought together from around the world in your covenant love.

We praise you, great God, that in Christ there is neither east nor west. **Amen.**

12  The Lord be with you.
    **And also with you.**
    Let us give thanks to the Lord our God.
    **It is right to give our thanks and praise.**

    Eternal God of all grace and mercy,
    after calling your people into existence,
    you have always blessed them with signs of your presence.

    From the beginning
    you have given your promises of loving care
    and have been forever faithful to those promises.

    When your people were in bondage,
    you did not hesitate to rescue them through the sea
    and lead them into the land of your promise.

    And we praise you most of all for sending your Son, Jesus Christ,
    born of the virgin Mary, baptized in the waters of the Jordan,
    and anointed by your Holy Spirit.

    We praise you for his gracious ministry
    of teaching, healing, and comforting,
    and for his death and resurrection in victory.

    We praise you that through his death and resurrection
    you set us free from the bondage of sin and death.
    You give us baptism as a sign of the cleansing and rebirth
    we have through our Lord Jesus Christ.

    And we rejoice that you are renewing us by your Spirit,
    leading us to be ambassadors of your love,
    until that day when your kingdom will fully come.
    To you be all glory, now and forever. **Amen.**

# 7.5 WELCOME AND ENCOURAGEMENT

*A welcome and congregational affirmation is especially appropriate at remembrance of baptism services that mark an occasion in which individuals are professing their faith, returning to the church, or joining a congregation.*

*For individual professions of faith*

1    In the name of our Lord Jesus Christ
     we now welcome you to all the privileges of full communion.
     We welcome you to full participation in the life of the church,
     to its responsibilities, its joys, and its sufferings.
         "May the God of peace,
         who through the blood of the eternal covenant
         brought back from the dead our Lord Jesus,
         that great Shepherd of the sheep,
         equip you with everything good for doing his will,
         and may he work in us what is pleasing to him,
         through Jesus Christ, to whom be glory
         for ever and ever. **Amen.**" (Heb. 13:20-21, NIV).
     **Thanks be to God!**
     **We promise you our love, encouragement, and prayers.**

*For new members who are joining a congregation*

2    [*Name(s)*], by publicly professing their faith,
     have expressed their intention to continue in the covenant
     God made with them in their baptism.
     Let us welcome them as they join with us
     in the worship and mission of the church.
     **With joy and thanksgiving, we welcome you**
     **to share with us in the ministry of Christ,**
     **for we are all one in him.**

3    Welcome our brothers and sisters in Christ.
     **Joyfully we receive you.**
     **Join with us as we give witness in the world to the good news,**
     **for we are all one in Christ Jesus.**
     **Alleluia.**

4    Welcome to this congregation and its worship and ministry.
     The peace of Christ be with you.
     **And also with you.**

*For general use at professions of faith, occasions of welcome, or other significant moments in the lives of individuals.*

5    By the Holy Spirit,
     all who believe and are baptized receive a ministry
     to witness to Jesus as Savior and Lord,
     and to love and serve those with whom they live and work.
     **We are ambassadors for Christ,**
     **who reconciles and makes whole.**
     **We are the salt of the earth;**
     **we are the light of the world.**

6    Do you promise to love, encourage, and support [*name(s)*]
     by teaching the gospel of God's love,
     by being an example of Christian faith and character,
     and by giving the strong support of God's family
     in fellowship, prayer, and service?
     **We do.**

# 7.6 CALL TO SERVICE AND BLESSING

*Baptismal remembrance appropriately ends with an invitation to Christian discipleship and a final word of God's blessing. The choice of these texts may be personalized to the context of the occasion. For additional texts that can be used in this setting, see section 9.*

## 7.6.1 Call to Service

1    Know therefore that the LORD your God is God;
     he is the faithful God,
     keeping his covenant of love
     to a thousand generations
     of those who love him and keep his commands.
          —Deuteronomy 7:9, NIV

2    God has told you what is good;
     and what does the LORD require of you
     but to do justice, and to love kindness,
     and to walk humbly with your God?
          —from Micah 6:8, NRSV

3    Lead a life worthy of the calling to which you have been called,
     with all humility and gentleness,
     with patience, bearing with one another in love,
     making every effort to maintain
     the unity of the Spirit in the bond of peace.
             —Ephesians 4:1-3, NRSV

4    [*Individual name(s) or name of the congregation*]:
     You are disciple(s) of Jesus Christ.
     Live in love, as Christ loved us
     and gave himself for us.
     Rejoice always; pray without ceasing;
     give thanks in all circumstances;
     for this is the will of God in Christ Jesus for you.
     The peace of God, which passes all understanding,
     keep your heart and your mind in Christ Jesus. **Amen.**
             —based on Ephesians 5:2; Philippians 4:7; 1 Thessalonians 5:16-18, NRSV

5    *This response may be used independently or after any of the preceding scriptural texts.*

     Remember your baptism and be thankful.
     In the name of the Father and of the Son and of the Holy Spirit.
     **Amen.**

## 7.6.2 Blessing

1    The LORD bless you and keep you;
     the LORD make his face to shine upon you,
         and be gracious to you;
     the LORD lift up his countenance upon you,
         and give you peace. **Amen.**
             —Numbers 6:24-26, NRSV

2    The peace of our Lord Jesus Christ be with you.
     **And also with you.**

*The blessing may be followed by "the passing of the peace," or mutual greeting (see section 1.3).*

SECTION 8

# THE LORD'S SUPPER

The Lord's Supper is a physical, ritual action, mandated by Jesus, through which God acts to nourish, sustain, comfort, challenge, teach, and assure us. A richly symbolic act, the celebration of the Lord's Supper nourishes our faith and stirs our imaginations to perceive the work of God and the contours of the gospel more clearly.

As the New Testament unfolds the meaning of the feast, it describes the Lord's Supper as a single celebration that conveys several layers of meaning. First, the Lord's Supper is a celebration of memory and hope. We remember all that God has done for us, especially in Christ. The Lord's Supper is a thankful remembrance of the entire life and ministry of Christ: his participation in the creation of the world; his birth at Bethlehem; his teaching and miracles; his suffering, death, resurrection, and ascension; his sending of the Spirit; and his second coming and final reign. Significantly we remember not only the actual events (past and future), but espe-

cially how those events give us an identity, how they transform us and all creation.

The Lord's Supper is also a celebration and proclamation of Jesus' real, spiritual presence with us, of the forgiveness offered to us through Christ's work on the cross, and of the ongoing spiritual nourishment he provides us. It is also a celebration of the unity of Christ's body, the church, as well as a meal of hope, of anticipating the heavenly feast of Christ's coming kingdom. The Lord's Supper is linked to nearly every aspect of the gospel!

This means that the Lord's Supper is appropriate in a worship service based on any scriptural theme during any season of the year. The particular theme or season will likely suggest which dimension of the Lord's Supper can be highlighted. During Advent the celebration may highlight our expectation of Christ's coming kingdom. During Holy Week it may emphasize the significance of Christ's suffering and death. During Eastertide the Lord's Supper may be a feast of celebration for Christ's victory. As a result, in addition to this complete section of Lord's Supper resources, supplemental texts for celebrating the supper are provided in various sections of Part Two of this book.

This sacrament's multiple layers of meaning are conveyed in part by the different names for the celebration. "Lord's Supper" conveys that Jesus himself is host of the supper and that we celebrate this feast in obedience to Christ. "Communion" highlights the intimate union we experience with both Christ and fellow believers. "Eucharist" (based on the Greek word for "thanksgiving") names this feast as a meal of gratitude, just as the last supper was, for Jesus and his disciples, a meal of thanksgiving.

Whatever the particular theme of the service or season, it's especially important to underscore the following pastoral themes in celebrations of the Lord's Supper (note here the various parallels with baptism—see section 6). Throughout the history of the church, including the present day, the greatest problems associated with the Lord's Supper have developed when one or more of these foundational claims have become distorted or unclear.

- The Lord's Supper is a celebration of God's grace, not human achievement. It is a means of grace through which God acts to seal the promises of the gospel. The power of the celebration does not lie in our ability to think hard about Jesus' death and our sin, but in the way God's Spirit uses the celebration to nourish and sustain us. The Lord's Supper is a gift!

- The Lord's Supper is not an end in itself. It always points beyond itself to celebrate God's grace and covenant faithfulness. This does not mean the physical aspects of the celebration are incidental or unimportant. The Lord's Supper should be a celebration fitting to the abundant grace of God offered in Christ.

- The Lord's Supper is a sign of a covenantal relationship. Our relationship with God in Christ is based on promises. That's why the celebration of the Lord's Supper fittingly begins with a clear statement of God's invitation and promises and continues with a robust prayer of thanksgiving and hope.

- The Lord's Supper is deeply personal, but never private. It is a communal action of the gathered congregation, which represents the church in all times and places.

Worshipers need to be taught these themes and how to incorporate them in celebrating the Lord's Supper.

Often denominational resources provide a complete service or "form" for the Lord's Supper. Some congregations follow such forms word-for-word; others ignore them altogether. In either approach it is possible to miss the point of what we do at the Lord's Supper—and why. The following resources draw on the rich pastoral wisdom that gave rise to traditional Lord's Supper forms and offer several options for use in different contexts. Texts from these resources may be used to design a formal and traditional service. These resources may also be used in a flexible way, in which a pastor offers part of the liturgy extemporaneously or from memory. Whatever the context, the church's experience over twenty centuries bears witness to the pastoral wisdom of the following elements of the Lord's Supper liturgy:

1. A declaration of God's invitation and promises surrounding the Lord's Supper, through the words of institution and instruction from Scripture. This declaration reinforces both that the Lord's Supper

is an act of obedience and that it conveys God's promises to us. We are able to celebrate the Lord's Supper only because of God's prior love to us.

2. A prayer of thanksgiving and petition for the work of the Holy Spirit in and through the Lord's Supper. The prayer of thanksgiving makes the celebration a memorial that recalls God's specific action in history. The prayer for the Holy Spirit's action emphasizes that the power in the Lord's Supper does not come from the bread and cup but from the Holy Spirit, who unites us with Christ through the celebration.

3. The physical preparation of the elements, along with gracious words of invitation.

4. The communion itself.

5. A response of thanksgiving or prayer.

These actions correspond to four verbs contained in the gospel accounts of the last supper. Jesus took bread, gave thanks, broke it, and gave it to his disciples. So we take bread, announcing that it is God's gift to us. We give thanks for all God's faithfulness to us. We break the bread, with gestures of hospitality. We offer it to the gathered community in love. These actions correspond to each main heading in the model liturgy on the following pages and, in turn, to the contents of this entire section on the Lord's Supper.

# Complete Model Liturgy for the Lord's Supper

*The following model liturgy is designed to help leaders visualize the structure of the Lord's Supper celebration. When used in worship, each of the numbered subheadings should be deleted. The pages following this model liturgy offer numerous options for adapting each corresponding section. (For example, see section 8.1 on pages 310-317 for options to use for the Declaration of God's Invitation and Promises, section 8.2 on pages 317-340 for Great Prayer of Thanksgiving options, and so on.) Several parts of this liturgy may be sung, and hundreds of musical settings are available, especially for acclamations of praise and memorial acclamations in the Great Prayer of Thanksgiving section (see pp. 319-320, 323).*

## 8.1 Declaration of God's Invitation and Promises

Hear the words of the institution of the Holy Supper of our Lord Jesus Christ:

The Lord Jesus, on the night of his arrest, took bread, and after giving thanks to God, he broke it, and gave it to his disciples, saying, "Take, eat. This is my body, given for you. Do this in remembrance of me."

In the same way he took the cup, saying, "This cup is the new covenant sealed in my blood, shed for you for the forgiveness of sins. Whenever you drink it, do this in remembrance of me."

Every time you eat this bread and drink this cup, you proclaim the saving death of the risen Lord until he comes.

With thanksgiving, let us offer God our grateful praise.

—based on 1 Corinthians 11:23-26

## 8.2 Great Prayer of Thanksgiving

*The prayer can be spoken as one continuous prayer; the numbered subdivisions are noted here simply to clarify the structure.*

### 8.2.1 Opening

The Lord be with you.

**And also with you.**

Lift up your hearts.

**We lift them up to the Lord.**

Let us give thanks to the Lord our God.

**It is right for us to give thanks and praise.**

### 8.2.2 Thanksgiving for the Work of God in Creation

With joy we praise you, gracious God, for you created heaven and earth, made us in your image, and kept covenant with us—even when we fell into sin. We give you thanks for Jesus Christ, our Lord, who by his life, death, and resurrection opened to us the way of everlasting life. Therefore we join our voices with all the saints and angels and the whole creation to proclaim the glory of your name.

### 8.2.3 Acclamation of Praise

[*sung or spoken*] **Holy, holy, holy Lord, God of power and might, heaven and earth are full of your glory. Hosanna in the highest. Blessed is he who comes in the name of the Lord. Hosanna in the highest.**

—based on Psalm 118:26; Isaiah 6:3

### 8.2.4 Thanksgiving for the Work of Christ

We give thanks to God the Father that our Savior, Jesus Christ, before he suffered, gave us this memorial of his sacrifice, until he comes again.

At his last supper, the Lord Jesus took bread, and when he had given thanks, he broke it and said, "This is my body, which is for you; do this in remembrance of me."

In the same way, he took the cup after supper and said, "This cup is the new covenant in my blood; do this in remembrance of me."

For whenever we eat this bread and drink this cup, we proclaim the Lord's death until he comes.

—based on 1 Corinthians 11:23-26

### 8.2.5 Memorial Acclamation

Therefore we proclaim our faith
as signed and sealed in this sacrament:

[*sung or spoken*]
**Christ has died,**
**Christ is risen,**
**Christ will come again.**

### 8.2.6 Prayer for the Work of the Spirit

Lord, our God, send your Holy Spirit so that this bread and cup may be for us the body and blood of our Lord Jesus Christ. May we and all your saints be united with Christ and remain faithful in hope and love.

Gather your whole church, O Lord, into the glory of your kingdom.

### 8.2.7 The Lord's Prayer

We pray in the name of Jesus, who taught us to pray:

**Our Father in heaven . . . Amen.**

### 8.2.8 Passing of the Peace

Thanks be to God: Christ makes us one.
The peace of Christ be with you all.

**And also with you.**

## 8.3 Preparing the Bread and Cup

[*breaking the bread*] The bread that we break is a sharing in the body of Christ.

**We who are many are one body, for we all share the same loaf.**

[*pouring the cup*] The cup for which we give thanks is a sharing in the blood of Christ.

**The cup that we drink is our participation in the blood of Christ.**

## 8.4 Communion

### 8.4.1 Invitation

Congregation of Jesus Christ, the Lord has prepared his table for all who love him and trust in him alone for their salvation.
All who are truly sorry for their sins, who sincerely believe in the Lord Jesus as their Savior, and who desire to live in obedience to him as Lord are now invited to come with gladness to the table of the Lord.

The gifts of God for the people of God.

### 8.4.2 Distribution

[*as the bread is shared*]

The body of Christ, given for you.

**Thanks be to God.**

[*as the cup is shared*]

The blood of Christ, shed for you.

**Thanks be to God.**

## 8.5 Response of Praise and Prayer

### 8.5.1 Acclamation

Praise the Lord, O my soul;
**all my inmost being, praise his holy name.**
Praise the Lord, O my soul,
**and forget not all his benefits—**
who forgives all your sins
**and heals all your diseases,**
who redeems your life from the pit
**and crowns you with love and compassion.**
Worthy is the Lamb, who was slain,
**to receive power and wealth**
**and wisdom and strength**
**and honor and glory and praise!**

—Psalm 103:1-4; Revelation 5:12, NIV

### 8.5.2 Prayer

Loving God, we thank you that you have fed us in this sacrament, united us with Christ, and given us a foretaste of the heavenly banquet in your eternal kingdom.

Send us out in the power of your Spirit to live and work to your praise and glory for the sake of Jesus Christ, our Lord. **Amen.**

# 8.1 Declaration of God's Invitation and Promises

*The Lord's Supper opens with God's invitation and promises by way of the words of institution (if not used later in the liturgy), a summary of scriptural teaching about the supper, and a statement of invitation. The following resources provide texts for each of these three categories. (Note: Almost every possible combination of these three elements may be found in the published orders of celebration of various traditions.)*

*Whatever the practice in a given congregation, the following tenets are most important: (1) that the liturgy convey that God is the one who invites us to the table and (2) that through the celebration of the Lord's Supper God offers to seal the promise of the gospel to us.*

## 8.1.1 Words of Institution

*The Lord's Supper may begin with God's gracious invitation—the biblical mandate to celebrate the Lord's Supper. Placing the words of institution at the beginning of the celebration of the Lord's Supper emphasizes that we celebrate the feast as an act of obedience.*

*In some congregations the words of institution are included later, within the prayer of thanksgiving, as one of the acts of God for which we give particular thanks (see section 8.2). In such cases, the opening declaration of God's invitation and promises either begins with a summary of scriptural teaching (see 8.1.2) or moves straight into the invitation (see 8.1.3).*

1    Hear the words of the institution
     of the Holy Supper of our Lord Jesus Christ:

The Lord Jesus, on the night of his arrest, took bread,
and after giving thanks to God,
he broke it, and gave it to his disciples, saying,
"Take, eat. This is my body, given for you.
Do this in remembrance of me."

In the same way he took the cup, saying,
"This cup is the new covenant sealed in my blood,
shed for you for the forgiveness of sins.
Whenever you drink it,
do this in remembrance of me."

Every time you eat this bread and drink this cup,
you proclaim the saving death of the risen Lord until he comes.

With thanksgiving, let us offer God our grateful praise.
          —based on 1 Corinthians 11:23-26

**2**    Hear the words of the institution
of the Holy Supper of our Lord Jesus Christ:

Jesus said to his disciples,
"I have eagerly desired to eat this Passover with you before I suffer.
For I tell you, I will not eat it again until it finds fulfillment
in the kingdom of God."

After taking the cup, he gave thanks and said,
"Take this and divide it among you.
For I tell you I will not drink again of the fruit of the vine
until the kingdom of God comes."

And he took bread, gave thanks and broke it,
and gave it to them, saying,
"This is my body given for you;
do this in remembrance of me."
In the same way, after the supper he took the cup, saying,
"This cup is the new covenant in my blood,
which is poured out for you."
                    —based on Luke 22:15-20, NIV

**3**    Friends, this is the joyful feast of the people of God!
People will come from east and west,
from north and south,
and sit at table in the kingdom of God.
When our risen Lord was at table with his disciples,
he took the bread, and blessed and broke it,
and gave it to them.
Then their eyes were opened and they recognized him.
This is the Lord's table.
Our Savior invites those who trust him
to share the feast that he has prepared.
                    —based on Luke 13:29; 24:30-31

**4**    Hear the words of the institution
of the Holy Supper of our Lord Jesus Christ:

The Lord Jesus, on the night he was betrayed, took bread,
and when he had given thanks, he broke it and said,
"This is my body, which is for you;
do this in remembrance of me."

In the same way, after supper he took the cup, saying,
"This cup is the new covenant in my blood;
do this in remembrance of me."

For whenever you eat this bread and drink this cup,
you proclaim the Lord's death until he comes.
                    —based on 1 Corinthians 11:23-26, NIV

5　Now let us hear the story of how this sacrament began.
　　On the night on which Jesus was betrayed,
　　he sat at supper with his disciples.
　　While they were eating, he took a piece of bread,
　　said a blessing, broke it, and gave it to them with the words,
　　"This is my body, which is for you.
　　Do this to remember me."
　　Later he took the cup, saying,
　　"This cup is God's covenant,
　　sealed with my blood.
　　Drink from it, all of you, to remember me."
　　**So now, following Jesus' example and command,**
　　**we take this bread and this cup,**
　　**the ordinary things of the world,**
　　**which Christ will use for extraordinary purposes.**
　　**And as he said a prayer before sharing,**
　　**let us do so too.**

> —based on 1 Corinthians 11:23-26

## 8.1.2 Summary of Scriptural Teaching

*In some congregations, the celebration of the Lord's Supper begins with a summary of scriptural teaching about the feast. This summary may also follow the words of institution (unless the words of institution are used at a later point in the liturgy). The point of this summary is to declare clearly and memorably God's multiple promises offered through the supper. In some congregations this section is omitted, especially if the same scriptural themes are prominent in the sermon or in other parts of the service.*

1　With these words Christ has commanded me and all believers
　　to eat this broken bread and to drink this cup
　　in true faith and in the confident hope of his return in glory.
　　**In this supper God declares to us**
　　**that all our sins are completely forgiven**
　　**through the one sacrifice of Jesus Christ,**
　　**which he himself accomplished on the cross once for all.**
　　He also declares to us
　　that the Holy Spirit grafts us into Christ,
　　who with his true body
　　is now in heaven at the right hand of the Father
　　where he wants us to worship him.

> —from Heidelberg Catechism, Q&A's 75, 80

2　Our Savior Jesus Christ
　　has ordained and instituted the sacrament of the Holy Supper
　　to nourish and sustain those who are already regenerated
　　and ingrafted into his family, which is his church.
　　Christ has instituted

an earthly and visible bread as the sacrament of his body
and wine as the sacrament of his blood.
**Just as truly as we take and hold the sacraments in our hands**
**and eat and drink it with our mouths,**
**by which our life is then sustained,**
**so truly we receive into our souls, for our spiritual life,**
**the true body and true blood of Christ, our only Savior.**
**We receive these by faith, which is the hand and mouth of our souls.**
This banquet is a spiritual table
at which Christ communicates himself to us with all his benefits.
**By the use of this holy sacrament**
**we are moved to a fervent love of God and our neighbors.**
    —from Belgic Confession, Art. 35

3    God meets us in the sacraments, communicating grace to us
by means of water, bread, and wine.
In baptism, whether of the newly born or newly converted,
God reminds and assures us of our union with Christ in covenant love,
the washing away of our sin, and the gift of the Holy Spirit—
expecting our love and trust in return.
In the Lord's Supper, Christ offers his own crucified body and shed blood
to his people, assuring them a share in his death and resurrection.
By the Holy Spirit, he feeds us with his resurrection life
and binds us to each other as we share one loaf and cup.
**We receive this food gladly, believing, as we eat,**
**that Jesus is our life-giving food and drink**
**and that he will come again**
**to call us to the wedding feast of the Lamb.**
    —from *Our World Belongs to God*, st. 37-38

4    Beloved in the Lord Jesus Christ,
the Holy Supper that we are about to celebrate
is a feast of remembrance, of communion, and of hope.
We come in remembrance
that our Lord Jesus Christ was sent of the Father into the world
to assume our flesh and blood
and to fulfill for us all obedience to the divine law,
even to the bitter and shameful death of the cross.
By his death, resurrection, and ascension
he established a new and eternal covenant of grace and reconciliation,
that we might be accepted of God and never be forsaken by him.
We come to have communion with this same Christ,
who has promised to be with us always, even to the end of the world.
In the breaking of the bread he makes himself known to us
as the true heavenly bread that strengthens us unto life eternal.
In the cup of blessing he comes to us as the vine,
in whom we must abide if we are to bear fruit.

We come in hope,
believing that this bread and this cup
are a pledge and foretaste of the feast of love
of which we shall partake when his kingdom has fully come,
when with unveiled face we shall behold him,
made like unto him in his glory.
**Since by his death, resurrection, and ascension,**
**Christ has obtained for us the life-giving Spirit,**
**who unites us all in one body,**
**so are we to receive this supper in true love,**
**mindful of the communion of saints.**

5    Christ calls the bread his body
and the cup his blood,
or the new covenant in his blood.
**Christ has good reason for these words.**
**He wants to teach us that**
    **just as bread and wine nourish the temporal life,**
    **so too his crucified body and poured-out blood**
    **are the true food and drink of our souls for eternal life.**
**But more important,**
**he wants to assure us, by this visible sign and pledge,**
    **that we, through the Holy Spirit's work,**
        **share in his true body and blood**
        **as surely as our mouths**
        **receive these holy signs in his remembrance,**
**and that all of his suffering and obedience**
**are as definitely ours as if we personally**
**had suffered and made satisfaction for our sins.**
—from Heidelberg Catechism, Q&A 79

## 8.1.3 Invitation

*The words of invitation emphasize that we come to the Lord's table in response to the invitation from Jesus himself. The church simply echoes God's own invitation; our hospitality mirrors the hospitality God shows us in Christ.*

1    O taste and see that the LORD is good;
happy are those who take refuge in him.
—Psalm 34:8, NRSV

2    Jesus said, "Come to me,
all you who are weary and are carrying heavy burdens,
and I will give you rest.
Take my yoke upon you, and learn from me;
for I am gentle and humble in heart,
and you will find rest for your souls."
—from Matthew 11:28-29, NRSV

3    From east and west, from north and south,
     people will come and take their places
     at the banquet in the kingdom of God.
          —based on Luke 13:29

4    Jesus said,
     "I am the bread of life.
     Whoever comes to me will never be hungry,
     and whoever believes in me will never be thirsty."
          —from John 6:35, NRSV

5    Brothers and sisters in Christ,
     the gospels tell us that on the first day of the week,
     the day on which our Lord rose from the dead,
     he appeared to some of his disciples
     and was made known to them
     in the breaking of bread.
     Come, then, to the joyful feast of our Lord.

6    He was always the guest.
     In the homes of Peter and Jairus,
     Martha and Mary,
     he was always the guest.
     At the meal tables of the wealthy,
     where he pled the cause of the poor,
     he was always the guest.
     Upsetting polite company,
     befriending isolated people,
     welcoming the stranger,
     he was always the guest.
     But here, at this table,
     he is the host.

     Those who wish to serve him
     must first be served by him.
     Those who want to follow him
     must first be fed by him.
     Those who would wash his feet
     must first let him make them clean.

     For this is the table
     where God intends us to be nourished;
     this is the time when Christ can make us new.

     So come, you who hunger and thirst for a deeper faith,
     for a better life, for a fairer world.
     Jesus Christ, who has sat at our tables,
     now invites us to be guests at his.

7    Come to this table:
         you who have much faith,
         and you who would like to have more;
         you who have been to this sacrament often,
         and you who have not been for a long time;
         you who have tried to follow Jesus,
         and you who have failed.
     Come. It is Christ who invites us to meet him here.

8    Congregation of Jesus Christ,
     the Lord has prepared his table for true believers.
     If you are sorry for your sins
     and sincerely follow Jesus Christ as your Savior and Lord,
     you are invited to come with gladness to this table of the Lord.

9    Congregation of our Lord Jesus Christ,
     the Lord has prepared his table for all who love him
     and trust in him alone for their salvation.
     All who are truly sorry for their sins,
     who sincerely believe in the Lord Jesus as their Savior,
     and who desire to live in obedience to him,
     are now invited to come with gladness
     to the table of the Lord.

10   Professing members in good standing of a church
     in which Jesus Christ is professed as Lord and Savior
     are warmly invited to join with us in the celebration
     of the Lord's Supper.

11   *The following invitation offers meditational prayers for use by persons who have not been
     baptized, have not made profession of faith, or choose not to participate for reasons of con-
     science. The invitation may be printed or spoken.*

     We welcome all baptized Christians who are sorry for their sin, love Jesus, and de-
     sire to serve him to join us in the celebration of the Lord's Supper. To others among
     us: we are deeply grateful you are with us; we are eager to share with you the joy of
     knowing Jesus and of living together as Jesus' disciples. We warmly invite you to
     reflect on and pray the following prayers.

     *A prayer for people searching*
     Search me, O God, and know my heart;
     test me and know my anxious thoughts.
     See if there is any offensive way in me,
     and lead me in the way everlasting.
     Through Christ, our Lord. Amen.
         —based on Psalm 139

*A prayer of belief*

All-powerful God, I am sinful. Nothing I can do can save me. I turn away from my sin, and I flee to you. I need you. I need the life-giving death and resurrection of Jesus. Send me your Spirit so that I can be made new. Thank you for offering me forgiveness. Thank you for taking the punishment I deserved. Thank you for loving me more than I could possibly imagine. Amen.

# 8.2 GREAT PRAYER OF THANKSGIVING

*The prayer of thanksgiving has a long tradition that dates back to the early church and reflects the influence of Jewish prayer patterns, including those of Passover prayers. This prayer is often called the "Great Prayer of Thanksgiving" because, like a creed, it sums up the entire teaching of the Christian faith, offering thanksgiving to God for everything from creation to our anticipation of the full coming of God's kingdom.*

*The prayer usually consists of two parts. The first part is a rhapsodic, thankful remembrance of all God's works of redemption, from creation to new creation. This part of the prayer often sounds like a psalm or a creed as it rehearses the scope of salvation history. In many traditional forms this part of the prayer is itself divided into two parts: thanksgiving for creation, ending with a song of praise based on Isaiah 6:3, "Holy, holy, holy" (the* Sanctus*); and thanksgiving for the work of Christ, ending with a memorial, spoken or sung, such as "Christ has died, Christ is risen, Christ will come again."*

*The second part consists of a prayer that God's Spirit will work in and through the present celebration to accomplish the purposes of the Lord's Supper, which are to nourish, encourage, and strengthen the church. Sometimes this is called a prayer of consecration or* epiclesis *(Latin for "to call upon").*

*Overall, the prayer has an explicitly trinitarian shape: thanksgiving and remembrance of God the Father, thanksgiving and remembrance for Jesus Christ, and prayer for the present work of the Holy Spirit. Several texts are provided here for each section of the prayer, followed by several additional complete prayers (see 8.2.9). Though the terminology for various parts of the prayer can vary from one Christian tradition to another, we'll use the following terms here:*

- 8.2.1 Opening
- 8.2.2 Thanksgiving for the Work of God in Creation
- 8.2.3 Acclamation of Praise ("Holy, holy, holy . . .")
- 8.2.4 Thanksgiving for the Work of Christ
- 8.2.5 Memorial Acclamation ("Christ has died, Christ is risen, Christ will come again.")
- 8.2.6 Prayer for the Work of the Spirit

- 8.2.7 The Lord's Prayer
- 8.2.8 Passing of the Peace

*Additional alternatives are included in Part Two of this book under various themes of the Christian faith.*

## 8.2.1 Opening

1   *This traditional opening is sometimes called the* Sursum corda *(Latin for "Lift up your hearts").*

The Lord be with you.
**And also with you.**
Lift up your hearts.
**We lift them up to the Lord.**
Let us give thanks to the Lord our God.
**It is right for us to give thanks and praise.**

2   As the Lord Jesus,
the same night in which he was betrayed,
took bread and offered thanksgiving to God,
so too we now offer to God our thanks and praise.

## 8.2.2 Thanksgiving for the Work of God in Creation

*"Preface" is the traditional name given to this section of the prayer of thanksgiving. Additional options appropriate to the theme of the season are provided in Part Two of this book.*

1   *This text is from a fourth-century liturgy used in the city of Alexandria.*

It is truly right to glorify you, Father,
and to give you thanks,
for you alone are God, living and true,
dwelling in light inaccessible from before time and forever.

Fountain of all life and source of all goodness,
you made all things and fill them with your blessing;
you created them to rejoice in the splendor of your radiance.

Countless throngs of angels stand before you
to serve you night and day,
and, beholding the glory of your presence,
they offer you unceasing praise.
Joining with them,
and giving voice to every creature under heaven,
we glorify your name
and lift our voices in joyful praise:
**[Holy, holy, holy . . . ]**

2    Generous God, overflowing fountain of good,
you who lived from all eternity in trinitarian abundance
and yet made room for creatures, creating life
through the mediating Son and the hovering Spirit,
pouring out value on all that you made—

You honored us human beings with the breath of your life,
making us in your image and likeness,
to care for the earth in stewardship and love,
to live together in hospitality and zest
as a daily reminder of your trinitarian abundance.

You crowned us with virtue and honor
and are now renewing us in your image through the work of your Son.
Magnificent you are, strong God, giver of splendors.

You bless inside a world of curses.
You heal inside a world of wounds.
You save inside a world bent on being lost.

We thank, praise, and honor you,
generous God, overflowing fountain of good,
through Jesus Christ, our Lord. **Amen.**

3    With joy we praise you, gracious God,
for you created heaven and earth,
made us in your image, and kept covenant with us—
even when we fell into sin.
We give you thanks for Jesus Christ, our Lord,
who by his life, death, and resurrection
opened to us the way of everlasting life.
Therefore we join our voices
with all the saints and angels and the whole creation
to proclaim the glory of your name.

### 8.2.3 Acclamation of Praise

*By far the most common and traditional acclamation of praise is drawn from Isaiah 6:3: "Holy, holy, holy . . ." (the* Sanctus*). The text is usually paired with Psalm 118:26: "Blessed is he who comes in the name of the Lord" (the* Benedictus*).*

*Most often this acclamation is sung; hymns and other settings of this text are available in nearly every musical style. Other acclamations, including those drawn from songs and hymns of praise, may also be used.*

1    **Holy, holy, holy Lord,
God of power and might,
heaven and earth are full of your glory.
Hosanna in the highest.**

> **Blessed is he who comes in the name of the Lord.**
> **Hosanna in the highest.**

2   **Holy, holy, holy! Lord God Almighty!**
    **All thy works shall praise thy name**
    **in earth and sky and sea.**
    **Holy, holy, holy! Merciful and mighty!**
    **God in three persons, blessed Trinity!**

### 8.2.4 Thanksgiving for the Work of Christ

*The outpouring of thanksgiving continues with explicit remembrances of the work of Jesus Christ. We thank God for Jesus' birth, life, death, resurrection, ascension, and second coming. This prayer of thanksgiving leads naturally to the exclamation "Christ has died, Christ is risen, Christ will come again."*

*The following prayer texts draw from a variety of Scripture passages, perhaps most notably 1 Corinthians 11:23-26, which itself ties in closely with Luke 22:19-20 and other gospel accounts.*

*Additional options appropriate to the theme of the season are provided in Part Two of this volume.*

1   *This text is from a fourth-century liturgy used in the city of Alexandria.*

    We acclaim you, holy God, glorious in power;
    your mighty works reveal your wisdom and love.
    You formed us in your own image,
    giving the whole world into our care
    so that, in obedience to you, our creator,
    we might rule and serve all your creatures.
    When our disobedience took us far from you,
    you did not abandon us to the power of death.
    In your mercy you came to our help,
    so that in seeking you we might find you.
    Again and again you called us into covenant with you,
    and through the prophets you taught us to hope for salvation.

    Almighty God, you loved the world so much
    that in the fullness of time you sent your only Son to be our Savior.
    Incarnate by the Holy Spirit, born of the virgin Mary,
    he lived as one of us, yet was without sin.
    To the poor he proclaimed the good news of salvation;
    to prisoners, freedom; to the sorrowful, joy.
    To fulfill your purpose, he gave himself up to death
    and, rising from the grave, destroyed death
    and made the whole creation new.

    And that we might live no longer for ourselves
    but for him who died and rose for us,
    God sent the Holy Spirit,
    God's first gift for all who believe,

to complete God's work in the world,
and to bring to fulfillment the sanctification of all.

When the hour had come for him to be glorified
by you, his heavenly Father,
having loved his own who were in the world,
he loved them to the end:
at supper with them he took bread,
and after giving thanks to you,
he broke it and gave it to his disciples, saying,
"Take, eat. This is my body, which is given for you.
Do this for the remembrance of me."
After supper he took the cup, saying,
"This cup is the new covenant sealed in my blood,
shed for you and for all for the forgiveness of sins.
Whenever you drink it,
do it for the remembrance of me."

Holy God, we now celebrate this memorial of our redemption.
Recalling Christ's death and his descent among the dead,
proclaiming his resurrection and ascension to your right hand,
awaiting his coming in glory,
and offering to you, from the gifts you have given us,
this bread and this cup,
we praise you and we bless you.
**We praise you, we bless you,
we give thanks to you,
and we pray to you, Lord, our God.**

2   Holy God, you are mighty in power yet abounding in mercy.
While our world was marred with sin,
so much so that we had no hope of redemption,
you made a covenant with your people.
You promised to renew your creation.
You promised to give hope amid the sorrow,
healing in place of sickness, wholeness in place of emptiness.

You stepped into our darkness in the person of Jesus Christ.
Our Lord and Savior lived among us.
He, God before the beginning of time,
willingly came to live at a specific place in a specific time.
He came quietly to a young unwed mother
through the power of your Holy Spirit.
He experienced our human joys and sorrows.
The Lord of the universe became a helpless boy.
He ate, he drank, he grew.
He was like us but without sin.

Then the King of kings showed us how to live.
He healed the sick, cared for the least of society, and took time for children.

He forgave sins and performed miracles.
He loved, and he served.
He gave up his very life for his friends.
He died the excruciating, disgraceful death of a criminal for us.
Yet you raised him out of the tomb.
He triumphed over death so that we too may live.

On the night before our Lord died, he ate with his disciples.
As we so often do, Jesus began with prayer.
He took the bread and the cup, and he shared them with his friends,
saying, "This is my body given for you. This cup is poured out for you.
My body and my blood are given for the forgiveness of your sins.
Do this in remembrance of me."

So, loving God, we do, in obedience to your command,
eat the bread and drink from the cup.
As we do, we remember with awe and gratitude
the life, death, and resurrection of our Lord Jesus Christ,
King of all, Savior, Anointed One.

We rejoice that your great love through our Redeemer's sacrifice has set us free
and given us hope for a future with you.

Until our Lord Jesus returns to establish his kingdom without end,
we will joyfully proclaim his death and resurrection.

3    We give thanks to God the Father
     that our Savior, Jesus Christ, before he suffered,
     gave us this memorial of his sacrifice,
     until he comes again.

At his last supper, the Lord Jesus took bread,
and when he had given thanks, he broke it and said,
"This is my body, which is for you;
do this in remembrance of me."

In the same way,
he took the cup after supper and said,
"This cup is the new covenant in my blood;
do this in remembrance of me."

For whenever we eat this bread and drink this cup,
we proclaim the Lord's death until he comes.

## 8.2.5 Memorial Acclamation

*The memorial is essentially a short creed, a summary of the work of Christ that we remember and proclaim at the Lord's Supper.*

1    **We shall do as our Lord commands.**
     **We proclaim that our Lord Jesus**
     **was sent by the Father into the world,**

that he took upon himself our flesh and blood,
and bore the wrath of God against our sin.
We confess that he was condemned
to die that we might be pardoned,
and suffered death that we might live.
We proclaim that he is risen to make us right with God
and that he shall come again in the glory of his new creation.
This we do now and until he comes again.

2    Therefore we proclaim our faith
as signed and sealed in this sacrament:
[*sung or spoken*]
**Christ has died,**
**Christ is risen,**
**Christ will come again.**

3    Praise to you, Lord Jesus:
**Dying, you destroyed our death;**
**rising, you restored our life.**
**Lord Jesus, come in glory.**

4    We profess our union with Christ
in his life, death, and resurrection.
We offer our thanks while
we yearn for the coming Supper of the Lamb.

5    Christ is the bread of life:
**When we eat this bread and drink this cup,**
**we proclaim your death, Lord Jesus,**
**until you come in glory.**

## 8.2.6 Prayer for the Work of the Spirit

*The prayer continues with the petition that God's Spirit will work in and through the present celebration to accomplish the purposes of the Lord's Supper, which are to nourish, encourage, and strengthen the church.*

1    Heavenly Father, show forth among us
the presence of your life-giving Word and Holy Spirit,
to sanctify us and your whole church through this sacrament.
Grant that all who share the body and blood of our Savior, Jesus Christ,
may be one in him and may remain faithful in love and hope.
And as this grain has been gathered from many fields into one loaf
and these grapes from many hills into one cup,
grant, O Lord, that your whole church may soon be gathered
from the ends of the earth into your kingdom.

2    Send your Holy Spirit upon us, we pray,
that the sharing of the bread that we break
and the cup that we bless
may be for us the communion of the body and blood of Christ.
Grant that, being joined together in him,
we may attain to the unity of the faith
and grow up in all things into Christ, our Lord.
And as this grain has been gathered from many fields into one loaf,
and these grapes from many hills into one cup,
grant, O Lord, that your whole church
may soon be gathered from the ends of the earth
into your kingdom.
Even so, come, Lord Jesus!

3    Living God,
send your Holy Spirit upon us
as we share your heavenly meal;
nourish us with your grace
so that we are strengthened
to do your work in this world;
unite us with you so that we are renewed;
and join us with your covenant people
throughout time and space
so that all divisions will be healed.
May we gratefully and joyfully remember that Jesus, our Savior,
lived, died, and rose to give us new life
and make us new creations in him.
May we live in the hope
we discover through Jesus Christ, our Lord. **Amen.**

4    God of all power, send your Holy Spirit upon us,
that in sharing the bread we may share in the body of Christ,
that in sharing the cup we may share in his blood.
Grant that, being joined together in Christ Jesus,
we may become united in faith
and in all things become mature in the one who is our head.

5    Creator God, be present
with your life-giving Word and Holy Spirit,
that we and your entire church
may be called out and made whole through this supper.
Grant that all who share
the communion of the body and blood of your Son may be united in him.
And may we all remain faithful in love and hope
until we feast joyfully with Christ at the coming of the kingdom.

6    Lord, our God, send your Holy Spirit
     so that this bread and cup may be for us
     the body and blood of our Lord Jesus Christ.
     May we and all your saints be united with Christ
     and remain faithful in hope and love.
     Gather your whole church, O Lord,
     into the glory of your kingdom.

*Any of the preceding prayers may end with the following acclamation.*

   [*sung or spoken*]
   **Through him, with him, in him,**
   **in the unity of the Holy Spirit,**
   **all honor and glory are yours,**
   **Almighty Father, now and forever. Amen.**

## 8.2.7 The Lord's Prayer

*Any of the preceding prayers may be followed by the Lord's Prayer. The petition "your kingdom come" particularly points to our anticipation of Christ's kingdom in all its fullness, a key dimension of the Lord's Supper. You may wish to introduce the Lord's Prayer with words like these:*

   We pray in the name of Jesus,
   who taught us to pray:

1    **Our Father who art in heaven,**
     **hallowed be thy name.**
     **Thy kingdom come.**
     **Thy will be done,**
     **on earth as it is in heaven.**
     **Give us today our daily bread.**
     **Forgive us our debts,**
     **as we forgive our debtors.**
     **And lead us not into temptation,**
     **but deliver us from evil,**
     **for thine is the kingdom,**
     **and the power,**
     **and the glory, forever. Amen.**

2    **Our Father in heaven,**
     **hallowed be your name,**
     **your kingdom come,**
     **your will be done,**
     **on earth as it is in heaven.**
     **Give us today our daily bread.**
     **Forgive us our sins**
     **as we forgive those who sin against us.**
     **Save us from the time of trial**

**and deliver us from evil.**
**For the kingdom, the power, and the glory are yours**
**now and forever. Amen.**

## 8.2.8 Passing of the Peace

*The passing of the peace is a fitting part of the communion liturgy, calling attention to the communal aspect of the feast. Following these introductions, members of the congregation may greet each other with phrases such as "Christ's peace be with you" or "Christ's peace to you." Other examples of the passing of the peace are found in sections 1.3 and 2.5.*

1     Thanks be to God: Christ makes us one.
      The peace of Christ be with you all.
      **And also with you.**

2     *This introduction is in the form of a prayer, which may be used at the conclusion of the*
      *prayer of thanksgiving.*

      Lord Jesus Christ, you told your apostles,
      "Peace I leave with you; my peace I give to you."
      Grant us always this peace and guide us
      toward the perfect unity of your kingdom for ever.
      **Amen.**
      Let us give one another a sign of reconciliation and peace.
          —based on John 14:27

3     *This text may also be used after communion.*

      On the evening of the first Easter Day,
      when the disciples were together
      behind locked doors for fear,
      Jesus came and stood among them.
      "Peace be with you!" he said;
      then he showed them his hands and his side.
      On seeing the Lord,
      the disciples were overjoyed.
      Jesus said again, "Peace be with you!"

      In the joyful presence of our risen Lord,
      let us give one another a sign of peace.

      The peace of Christ be with you always!
      **And also with you.**
          —based on John 20:19-21

## 8.2.9 Additional Complete Prayers

*Readers familiar with the Bible will notice that the following prayer texts draw from a variety of Scripture passages, perhaps most notably Psalm 118:26; Isaiah 6:3; Matthew 6:9-13; Luke 22:19-20; and 1 Corinthians 11:23-26.*

1   *This outline is provided as a guide for praying the Great Prayer of Thanksgiving extemporaneously. The most common congregational responses, which may be sung or spoken, are included in boldface in brackets.*

[*Address of God*]
Thankful praise to God, and remembrance of all God's works:
for God's work in creation and providence, and in covenant history;
for the witness of the prophets;
for God's steadfast love in spite of human failure;

[*Acclamation of Praise, such as "Holy, holy, holy . . ."*]

for the ultimate gift of Christ—
his birth, life, ministry, suffering, death, resurrection, ascension,
his present intercession for us and
the promise of his coming again—
as well as the gift of the sacrament, which Christ instituted.
[*May include the words of institution,
if not used as part of the invitation.*]

[**Memorial Acclamation, such as "Christ has died,
Christ is risen, Christ will come again."**]

The Holy Spirit is called upon
to lift all who share in the feast into Christ's presence;
to make the breaking of the bread and sharing of the cup
a participation in the body and blood of Christ;
to unite us in communion with the risen Christ
and with all God's people in heaven and on earth;
to nourish us with the body of Christ so that we may mature
into the fullness of Christ;
to keep us faithful as Christ's body,
representing Christ in witness and ministry in the world,
in anticipation of the fulfillment of the kingdom Christ proclaimed.

[**Lord's Prayer**]

[**Closing doxology and Amen**]

2    Lift up your hearts.
     **We lift them up to the Lord.**
     Let us give thanks to the Lord our God.
     **It is right for us to give thanks and praise.**

     **It is our joy and our peace,**
     **at all times and in all places**
     **to give thanks to you,**
     **holy Father,**
     **almighty, everlasting God,**
     **through Christ, our Lord.**

     We bless you for your continual love and care for every creature.
     We praise you for forming us in your image
          and calling us to be your people.
     We thank you that you did not abandon us
          in our rebellion against your love,
     but sent prophets and teachers to lead us into the way of salvation.
     Above all we thank you for sending Jesus, your Son,
     to deliver us from the way of sin and death
          by the obedience of his life,
          by his suffering upon the cross,
          and by his resurrection from the dead.
     We praise you that he now reigns with you in glory
          and ever lives to pray for us.
     We thank you for the Holy Spirit,
          who leads us into truth,
          defends us in adversity,
          and out of every people unites us into one holy church.

     Therefore with the whole company of saints in heaven and on earth
     we worship and glorify you, God most holy, and we sing with joy.
     [*sung or spoken*]
     **Holy, holy, holy! Lord God Almighty!**
     **All thy works shall praise thy name**
     **in earth and sky and sea.**
     **Holy, holy, holy! Merciful and mighty!**
     **God in three persons, blessed Trinity!**

     We give thanks to God the Father
     that our Savior, Jesus Christ, before he suffered,
     gave us this memorial of his sacrifice until he comes again.
     The Lord Jesus, on the night when he was betrayed, took bread,
     and when he had given thanks, he broke it and said,
     "This is my body, which is for you; do this in remembrance of me."
     In the same way, he took the cup after supper, saying,
     "This cup is the new covenant in my blood;
     do this, whenever you drink it, in remembrance of me."
     For whenever you eat this bread and drink this cup,
     you proclaim the Lord's death until he comes.

**We shall do as our Lord commands.**
**We proclaim that our Lord Jesus**
**was sent by the Father into the world,**
**that he took upon himself our flesh and blood**
**and bore the wrath of God against our sin.**
**We confess that he was condemned**
**to die that we might be pardoned,**
**and suffered death that we might live.**
**We proclaim that he is risen to make us right with God**
**and that he shall come again in the glory of his new creation.**
**This we do now, and until he comes again.**

Heavenly Father, show forth among us
the presence of your life-giving Word and Holy Spirit,
to sanctify us and your whole church through this sacrament.
Grant that all who share the body and blood of our Savior, Jesus Christ,
may be one in him and may remain faithful in love and hope.
And as this grain has been gathered from many fields into one loaf
and these grapes from many hills into one cup,
grant, O Lord, that your whole church may soon be gathered
from the ends of the earth into your kingdom.
Now, as our Savior Christ has taught us, we pray:

**Our Father in heaven . . .**

3     The Lord be with you.
**And also with you.**
Lift up your hearts!
**We lift them up to the Lord.**
Let us give thanks to the Lord our God.
**It is right for us to give thanks and praise.**

Holy and right it is, and our joyful duty
to give thanks to you at all times and in all places,
O Lord, our Creator, almighty and everlasting God!
You created heaven with all its hosts and the earth with all its plenty.
You have given us life and being,
and you preserve us by your providence.
But you have shown us the fullness of your love
in sending into the world your Son, Jesus Christ,
the eternal Word, made flesh for us and for our salvation.
For the precious gift of this mighty Savior who has reconciled us to you,
we praise and bless you, O God.
With your whole church on earth and with all the company of heaven
we worship and adore your glorious name.

[*sung or spoken*]
**Holy, holy, holy Lord,**
**God of power and might,**
**heaven and earth are full of your glory.**
**Hosanna in the highest!**

**Blessed is he who comes in the name of the Lord.**
**Hosanna in the highest!**

Most righteous God,
we remember in this supper
the perfect sacrifice offered once on the cross
by our Lord Jesus Christ
for the sin of the whole world.

In the joy of his resurrection
and in the expectation of his coming again,
we offer ourselves to you as holy and living sacrifices.
Together we proclaim the mystery of the faith.
[*sung or spoken*]
**Christ has died,**
**Christ is risen,**
**Christ will come again.**

Send your Holy Spirit upon us, we pray,
that the bread we break
and the cup we bless
may be to us the communion of the body and blood of Christ.
Grant that, being joined together in him,
we may attain to the unity of the faith
and grow up in all things into Christ, our Lord.

And as this grain has been gathered from many fields into one loaf,
and these grapes from many hills into one cup,
grant, O Lord, that your whole church
may soon be gathered from the ends of the earth
into your kingdom.
Even so, come, Lord Jesus!

4   *This prayer is designed to provide a balance of familiar, set texts and extemporaneous*
    *prayers. When the service is printed for the congregation, omit the suggestions indicated in*
    *brackets.*

The Lord be with you.
**And also with you.**
Lift up your hearts.
**We lift them up to the Lord.**
Let us give thanks to the Lord our God.
**It is right for us to give thanks and praise . . .**

[*A prayer of thankful remembrance for God's work*
*in creation and redemption*]

. . . Therefore we praise you,
joining our voices with choirs of angels
and with all the faithful of every time and place,
who forever sing to the glory of your name:

[*sung or spoken*]
**Holy, holy, holy Lord,**
**God of power and might,**
**heaven and earth are full of your glory.**
**Hosanna in the highest.**

**Blessed is he who comes in the name of the Lord.**
**Hosanna in the highest.**

[*The prayer continues with a thankful recalling of the acts*
*of salvation in Jesus Christ, including the gift of the sacrament*
*(which may include the words of institution if not otherwise used),*
*and ending with the following.*]

Remembering your mighty acts in Jesus Christ,
we take from your creation this bread and this wine
and joyfully celebrate his dying and rising,
as we await the day of his coming.
With thanksgiving we offer our very selves to you
to be a living and holy sacrifice
dedicated to your service.

Great is the mystery of faith:
[*sung or spoken*]
**Christ has died,**
**Christ is risen,**
**Christ will come again.**

[*The Holy Spirit is called upon by means of*
*the following or similar words.*]

Gracious God,
pour out your Holy Spirit upon us
and upon these your gifts of bread and wine,
that our sharing of the bread we break
and the cup we bless
may be the communion of the body and blood of Christ.

[*Petitions are offered, that we may*
    *be made one with the risen Christ and with all God's people;*
    *be united with all the faithful in heaven and on earth;*
    *be nourished with the body and blood of Christ;*
    *receive new life and mature into the fullness of Christ;*
    *remain faithful as Christ's body in ministry in the world;*
    *have hope in the promise of Christ's kingdom fulfilled.*]

[*The prayer concludes with doxological praise by means of*
*the following or similar words.*]

[*sung or spoken*]
**Through Christ, with Christ, in Christ,**
**in the unity of the Holy Spirit,**
**all glory and honor are yours, almighty God,**
**now and forever. Amen.**

**5**   *This text is based on one of the earliest prayers of thanksgiving from the early church, often attributed to Hippolytus (c. A.D. 215).*

The Lord be with you.
**And also with you.**
Lift up your hearts.
**We lift them up to the Lord.**
Let us give thanks to the Lord our God.
**It is right for us to give thanks and praise.**

We give you thanks, O God,
through your beloved servant, Jesus Christ,
whom you have sent in these last times
as Savior and Redeemer and messenger of your will.
He is your Word, inseparable from you,
through whom you made all things
and in whom you take delight.

You sent him from heaven into the virgin's womb,
where he was conceived and took flesh.
Born of the virgin by the power of the Holy Spirit,
he was revealed as your Son.
In fulfillment of your will he stretched out his hands in suffering
to release from suffering those who place their trust in you,
and so won for you a holy people.

He freely accepted the death to which he was handed over
in order to destroy death and to shatter the chains of the evil one;
to trample underfoot the powers of hell
and to lead the righteous into light;
to fix the boundaries of death
and to manifest the resurrection.

And so he took bread, gave thanks to you, and said,
"Take, and eat; this is my body, given for you."
In the same way he took the cup, saying,
"This is my blood, shed for you.
When you do this, do it for the remembrance of me."

Remembering therefore his death and resurrection,
we set before you this bread and cup,
thankful that you have counted us worthy
to stand in your presence and serve you as your priestly people.

We ask you to send your Holy Spirit
upon the offering of the holy church.
Gather into one all who share these holy mysteries,
filling them with the Holy Spirit and confirming their faith in the truth,
that together we may praise you and give you glory,
through your servant, Jesus Christ.

Through him all glory and honor are yours, almighty Father,
with the Holy Spirit in the holy church
now and forever. **Amen.**

6    The Lord be with you.
     **And also with you.**
     Lift up your hearts.
     **We lift them up to the Lord.**
     Let us give thanks to the Lord our God.
     **It is fitting for us to give thanks.**

     **It is right and fitting, our joy and our salvation,**
     **that we should at all times and in all places**
     **give thanks to you, almighty, everlasting God,**
     **through Christ, our Lord:**
     by whom you made the world and all things living and beautiful.
     We bless you for your continual love and care for every creature.
     We praise you for forming us in your image
     and calling us to be your people.
     **We thank you that you did not abandon us**
     **in our rebellion against your love,**
     **but sent prophets and teachers to lead us**
     **into the way of salvation.**
     Above all we thank you for sending Jesus
     to deliver us from the way of sin and death
          by the obedience of his life,
          by his suffering upon the cross,
          and by his resurrection from the dead.
     We praise you that he now reigns with you in glory
     and ever lives to pray for us.
     **We thank you for the Holy Spirit,**
          **who leads us into truth,**
          **enables us to witness to our Lord with joy,**
          **and out of every people unites us into one holy church.**
     **Therefore with the whole company of saints in heaven and on earth**
     **we worship and glorify you, God most holy,**
     **and we sing with joy:**
     [*sung or spoken*]
     **Holy, holy, holy Lord,**
     **God of power and might,**
     **heaven and earth are full of your glory.**
     **Hosanna in the highest.**

     **Blessed is he who comes in the name of the Lord.**
     **Hosanna in the highest.**

     We give thanks to God
     that our Savior, Jesus Christ, before he suffered,
     gave us this memorial of his sacrifice, until his coming again.
     For on the night of his arrest he took bread,

and after giving thanks to God, broke it and said,
"This is my body, which is for you; do this as a memorial of me."
In the same way he took the cup after supper and said,
"This cup is the new covenant sealed by my blood.
Whenever you drink it, do this as a memorial of me."

**Your death, O Christ, we proclaim.**
**Your resurrection we declare.**
**Your coming we await.**
**Glory be to you, O Lord.**

Creator God, show forth among us
the presence of your life-giving Word and Holy Spirit,
to sanctify us and your whole church through this sacrament.
Grant that all who share the communion
of the body and blood of our Savior, Jesus Christ
may be one in him and remain faithful in love and hope.
And as this grain has been gathered from many fields into one loaf,
and these grapes from many hills into one cup,
grant, O Lord, that your whole church may soon be gathered
from the ends of the earth into your kingdom.
**To God our Maker, to Christ our Lord, and to the Holy Spirit**
**be honor and glory now and forever. Amen.**

7    The Lord be with you.
**And also with you.**
Lift up your hearts.
**We lift them up to the Lord.**
Let us give thanks to the Lord our God.
**It is right for us to give thanks and praise.**

It is indeed right, for you made us,
and before us you made the world we inhabit,
and before the world you made the eternal home
in which, through Christ, we have a place.

All that is spectacular and all that is plain
    have their origin in you;
all that is lovely and all who are loving
    point to you as their fulfillment.

And grateful as we are for the world we know
and the universe beyond our knowing,
we particularly praise you, whom eternity cannot contain,
for coming to earth and entering time in Jesus.

For his life, which informs our living,
for his compassion, which changes our hearts,
for his clear speaking, which contradicts our generalities,
for his disturbing presence, his innocent suffering, his fearless dying,
his rising to life and breathing forgiveness, we praise you and worship him.

Here too our gratitude rises for the promise of the Holy Spirit,
who even yet, even now, confronts us with your claims
and attracts us to your goodness.

Therefore we gladly join our voices
to the song of the church on earth and in heaven:

[*sung or spoken*]
**Holy, holy, holy Lord,**
**God of power and might,**
**heaven and earth are full of your glory.**
**Hosanna in the highest.**

**Blessed is he who comes in the name of the Lord.**
**Hosanna in the highest.**

And now, lest we believe
that our praise alone fulfills your purpose,
we fall silent and remember him who came
because words weren't enough.

Setting our wisdom, our will, our words aside,
emptying our hearts, and bringing nothing in our hands,
we yearn for the healing, the holding, the accepting,
the forgiving that Christ alone can offer.

[*Silence*]

Merciful God, send now, in kindness,
your Holy Spirit to make our sharing in this bread and cup
a sharing in Christ's body and blood.

And let that same Spirit rest on us,
converting us from the patterns of this passing world,
until we conform to the shape of him whose food we now share. **Amen.**

8    The Lord be with you.
**And also with you.**
Lift up your hearts.
**We lift them up to the Lord.**
Let us give thanks to the Lord our God.
**It is right for us to give thanks and praise.**

It is indeed right; it is our duty and our joy,
at all times and in all places, to give you thanks and praise,
holy Father, heavenly King, almighty and eternal God.

We give thanks that in the creation of the world,
when you laid the earth's foundation and set its cornerstone in place,
the morning stars sang in chorus and the angels of God all shouted for joy.
By the power of your Spirit you made the universe;
by the might of your Word you gave us life.

We give thanks that in the new creation,
when you gave your Son to raise us up again,
since we and all our human race had fallen,
you claimed us for your own people,
that we might proclaim the glorious deeds
of him who has called us out of darkness into his marvelous light.
By the life of your Spirit you fill the hearts of the faithful,
by the light of your Word you give us strength and love.

Therefore, with your people of all places and times
and with the whole company of heaven
we proclaim your greatness and sing your praise in the angels' song:

[*sung or spoken*]
**Holy, holy, holy Lord,**
**God of power and might,**
**heaven and earth are full of your glory.**
**Hosanna in the highest.**

**Blessed is he who comes in the name of the Lord.**
**Hosanna in the highest.**

In tune with all the heavenly hosts,
we here on earth acknowledge your glory
and give you thanks that in the fullness of time
you sent your Son to be our Savior.

We bless you for his incarnation among us,
his holy birth, his perfect life on earth,
his suffering for us, and his triumph over death;
for his ascension to your right hand and his gift of the Holy Spirit;
and for the promise of his coming again.

Remembering his work and passion
and pleading his eternal sacrifice,
we follow his example and obey his command.

Send down your Holy Spirit to bless us
and these your gifts of bread and wine,
that the bread we break
may be for us the communion of the body of Christ,
and the cup of blessing we bless
may be the communion of the blood of Christ;
that we, receiving them, by faith
may be made partakers of his body and blood,
with all his benefits, to nourish us and help us grow in grace,
to the glory of your most holy name.

And here we offer and present to you our very selves
to be a living sacrifice, dedicated and fit for your acceptance,
through Jesus Christ, our Lord.

[*sung or spoken*]
**Through him, with him, in him,**
**in the unity of the Holy Spirit,**
**all honor and glory are yours,**
**almighty Father, now and for ever. Amen.**

9   The Lord be with you.
**And also with you.**
Lift up your hearts.
**We lift them up to the Lord.**
Let us give thanks to the Lord our God.
**It is right for us to give thanks and praise.**

Father of mercy and God of all comfort,
we acknowledge you to be the Lord,
and at all times we honor your greatness and glory.
First, because you created us in your own image and likeness,
but chiefly because you freed us from the enslavement of sin
through your only Son.

You gave him in love to be made man,
like us in all things except sin,
that by his death and resurrection
he might bring again life to the world.

Lord, we are not able, in our dullness,
to understand the breadth and length
and height and depth of your love,
but, true to the commandment of Jesus Christ, our Lord,
we come to this table, which he has left to us,
to be used in remembrance of his death until he comes again.

Here we declare and witness before the world that
by him alone we have received liberty and life,
by him alone you claim us as children and heirs,
by him alone we have access to your favor, freely shown,
by him alone we are raised into your spiritual kingdom,
there to eat and drink with you and the Son
at that most joyful table of eternal life.

In this present time we on earth
have communion with you in heaven.
But in the time to come we shall be raised to that endless joy
prepared for us before the foundation of the world was laid.

We acknowledge that we have received these inestimable gifts
by your free mercy and grace, through your only Son, Jesus Christ.
Moved by your Holy Spirit, we, your congregation,
give you all thanks, praise, and glory for ever and ever. **Amen.**

**10**  The Lord be with you.
**And also with you.**
Lift up your hearts.
**We lift them up to the Lord.**
Let us give thanks to the Lord our God.
**It is right for us to give thanks and praise.**

It is right for us to give thanks and praise,
O Lord, our God, sustainer of the universe.
At your command all things came to be.
By your will, the vast expanse of space,
galaxies, suns, the planets in their courses,
and this fragile earth, our island home,
were all created and have their being.

You brought forth the human race
and blessed us with memory, reason, and skill.
You made us the stewards of creation,
but we turned against you
and betrayed your trust.

Yet your mercy is like a spring that never fails.
You yourself, in Christ your Son, come to deliver us:
you redeem us in your love and pity;
you create new heavens and a new earth
where the cry of distress is heard no more.

Therefore we praise you,
joining with the heavenly chorus
and with those in every generation
who have looked to you in hope,
to proclaim with them your glory
in their unending hymn:

[*sung or spoken*]
**Holy, holy, holy Lord,**
**God of power and might,**
**heaven and earth are full of your glory.**
**Hosanna in the highest.**

**Blessed is he who comes in the name of the Lord.**
**Hosanna in the highest.**

Gracious God,
we recall the death of your Son, Jesus Christ,
we proclaim his resurrection and ascension,
and we look with expectation for his coming as Lord of all the nations.

We who have been redeemed by him
and made a new people by water and the Spirit
now bring you these gifts.
Send your Holy Spirit upon us
and upon this bread and wine,

that we who eat and drink at this holy table
may share the life of Christ, our Lord.

Pour out your Spirit upon the whole earth
and bring in your new creation.
Gather your church together
from the ends of the earth into your kingdom,
where peace and justice are revealed,
that we, with all your people
of every language, race, and nation,
may share the banquet you have promised.

[*sung or spoken*]
**Through Christ, with Christ, in Christ,**
**all honor and glory are yours for ever. Amen.**

11  *This prayer features language marked by simplicity and designed for use with children.
Whether the congregation welcomes children who have made profession of faith to full communion or children participate by watching, they are in either case participating members of
the worshiping community.*

The Lord be with you.
**And also with you.**
Lift up your hearts.
**We lift them up to the Lord.**
Let us give thanks to the Lord our God.
**It is right for us to give thanks and praise.**

Loving God, you made this world marvelous for us to enjoy.

You gave Jesus to be our Savior and friend and to bring us to you.

You sent your Spirit to make us one family in Christ.

For these gifts of your love we thank you,
and we join with angels and saints in this joyful hymn of praise:

[*sung or spoken*]
**Holy, holy, holy Lord,**
**God of power and might,**
**heaven and earth are full of your glory.**
**Hosanna in the highest.**

**Blessed is he who comes in the name of the Lord.**
**Hosanna in the highest.**

For your kindness to us and your goodness to all, we give you thanks.

We thank you that you showed your love by sending your Son,
who gave his life for us, and rose again from death,
and lives to pray for us for ever.

We thank you that he has taken away all that separates us from you
and has made us friends with you and with one another.

We thank you that he has brought us together at this table,
to strengthen us by his love.

Send your Holy Spirit
on us and these your gifts of bread and wine,
that we may know Christ's presence, real and true,
and be his faithful followers, showing your love for the world.

[*sung or spoken*]
**Through Christ, with Christ, in Christ,**
**in the unity of the Holy Spirit,**
**all glory and honor are yours,**
**almighty Father, for ever. Amen.**

# 8.3 PREPARING THE BREAD AND CUP

*The following texts are provided for use as the bread is broken and cup is poured just before the communion. This action is often called "breaking of the bread," or "fraction."*

1    *The questions in this text may also be spoken as statements (see section 8.3 of model liturgy on p. 309).*

Is not the bread that we break
a sharing in the body of Christ?
**We who are many are one body,**
**for we all share the same loaf.**

Is not the cup for which we give thanks
a sharing in the blood of Christ?
**The cup that we drink**
**is our participation in the blood of Christ.**

**Holy Father, in thanks for the sacrifice of Jesus Christ,**
**in the joy of his resurrection,**
**in the hope of his coming again,**
**we present ourselves a living sacrifice**
**and come to the table of our Lord.**

2    *These words of preparation include the scriptural words of institution for use in liturgies that do not include them earlier.*

We celebrate this feast in obedience to Christ's example and mandate.

[*as the minister breaks the bread*]
The Lord Jesus, on the night of his arrest, took bread,
and after giving thanks to God,

he broke it, and gave it to his disciples, saying,
"Take, eat. This is my body, given for you.
Do this in remembrance of me."

[*as the minister lifts or pours the cup*]
In the same way he took the cup, saying,
"This cup is the new covenant sealed in my blood,
shed for you for the forgiveness of sins.
Whenever you drink it,
do this in remembrance of me."

Every time you eat this bread and drink this cup,
you proclaim the saving death of the risen Lord
until he comes.
          —based on 1 Corinthians 11:23-26

**3**   *The following prayer is a traditional congregational response that may be spoken or sung
after the breaking of the bread. It is often called the* Agnus Dei *(Latin for "Lamb of God").*

**Lamb of God, who takes away the sin of the world, have mercy on us.**
**Lamb of God, who takes away the sin of the world, have mercy on us.**
**Lamb of God, who takes away the sin of the world, grant us your peace.**
**Amen.**

# 8.4 COMMUNION

---

*At the center of the Lord's Supper celebration is the action of sharing the bread and the cup. At
this point, gestures, movement, and even facial expressions communicate the meaning of the supper, along with simple, direct words of promise and welcome.*

## 8.4.1 Invitation

*This invitation is intended to complement the invitation offered at the beginning of the Lord's
Supper celebration (see 8.1.3); it need not repeat what was said there.*

**1**   Blessed are those who hunger and thirst for righteousness,
        for they will be filled.
          —Matthew 5:6, NRSV

2    Jesus said,
     "I am the bread of life.
     Whoever comes to me will never be hungry, and
     whoever believes in me will never be thirsty."
          —from John 6:35, NRSV

3    Come, then, for all is ready.
     **I am not worthy that you should come under my roof;**
     **but speak one word only, Lord, and I shall be healed.**
     Blessed is the one who comes in the name of the Lord.
     **I shall receive the bread of heaven.**
     **I shall drink the cup of salvation.**
          —based on Psalm 118:26; Luke 7:6-7

4    Hear the words of our Savior:
     "Come to me, all you who labor and are heavy laden,
     and I will give you rest.
     Take my yoke upon you, and learn from me,
     for I am gentle and humble in heart,
     and you will find rest for your souls."
     Come, then, for all is ready.
     **We come not because we ought, but because we may,**
     **not because we are righteous, but because we are penitent,**
     **not because we are strong, but because we are weak,**
     **not because we are whole, but because we are broken.**
          —based on Matthew 11:28-29

5    Come, then, for all is ready.
     Christ was raised to life,
     death is swallowed up,
     victory is won. Alleluia!
     **Therefore let us keep the feast. Alleluia!**

6    Congregation of Jesus Christ,
     the Lord has prepared his table for all who love him
     and trust in him alone for their salvation.
     All who are truly sorry for their sins,
     who sincerely believe in the Lord Jesus
     as their Savior,
     and who desire to live in obedience to him as Lord
     are now invited to come with gladness
     to the table of the Lord.

*Any of the preceding invitations may be followed by one of these declarations.*

7    The gifts of God for the people of God.

8    The gifts of God for the people of God.
     Take them in remembrance that Christ died for you
     and feed on him in your hearts by faith, with thanksgiving.

*348*

## 8.4.2 Distribution

*Several distribution methods are appropriate for the celebration of the Lord's Supper, depending on the worship space and the particular needs and expectations of a congregation. The following three patterns are the most common:*

1. *Worshipers come forward to receive the bread and cup individually from a pastor, elder, or other leader.*
2. *Worshipers come forward to form a circle in which they pass the bread and cup to one another.*
3. *Servers distribute the bread and cup to the congregation where they are seated. Worshipers partake together at the invitation of the pastor.*

*Depending on the mode of distribution, the following words may be spoken by the pastor to the congregation, by servers to individual worshipers, or by members to one another.*

*Children may be invited to come forward with their parents or guardians to partake and/or to receive a blessing. A pastor, elder, or other leader may welcome them with a simple, direct blessing, such as "Jesus loves you," "Jesus died and rose for you," or "God made you and loves you."*

*The distribution of the bread and cup may be accompanied by silent meditation, instrumental music, congregational singing, or the reading of Scripture. The Scripture and music that accompany the celebration may rehearse the whole gospel of Christ, from creation to new creation, and may vary from season to season, depending on the theme of the service and the needs of the congregation. While the Lord's Supper proclaims Jesus' death "until he comes," Jesus invites us to "remember" him at the supper (1 Cor. 11:24-26). Thus we remember and celebrate all the works of Christ: his participation in creation; his birth; his teaching and miracles; his suffering, death, resurrection, and ascension; his sending of the Spirit; and his coming again. "Christ the Lord Is Risen Today" and "When I Survey the Wondrous Cross" are thus equally appropriate songs at the Lord's Supper—as are many, many more!*

1   [*when the people are ready to eat the bread*]
    Take, eat, remember, and believe
    that the body of our Lord Jesus Christ
    was given for the complete forgiveness of all our sins.

    [*when the people are ready to drink the cup*]
    Take, drink, remember, and believe
    that the precious blood of our Lord Jesus Christ
    was shed for the complete forgiveness of all our sins.

2   Take and eat.
    This is the body of Christ, which is [*given*] for you.
    Do this, remembering him.

    This cup is the new covenant
    sealed by Christ's blood,
    which was shed that the sins of many
    might be forgiven.
    Drink from it, all of you.

3    [*as the bread is shared*]
     The body of Christ, given for you.
     **Thanks be to God.**

     [*as the cup is shared*]
     The blood of Christ, shed for you.
     **Thanks be to God.**

4    [*as the bread is shared*]
     The body of Christ, the bread of heaven.
     **Thanks be to God.**

     [*as the cup is shared*]
     The blood of Christ, the cup of salvation.
     **Thanks be to God.**

# 8.5 RESPONSE OF PRAISE AND PRAYER

*The natural response to celebrating the Lord's Supper includes both joyful praise and prayers of thanksgiving and dedication. Some congregations include both an acclamation and a prayer. Other congregations choose one or the other, depending on the context and the themes of the service.*

## 8.5.1 Acclamation

1    Praise the LORD, my soul;
         **all my inmost being, praise his holy name.**
     Praise the LORD, my soul,
         **and forget not all his benefits—**
     who forgives all your sins
         **and heals all your diseases,**
     who redeems your life from the pit
         **and crowns you with love and compassion.**
         —Psalm 103:1-4, NIV

2    Now to him who by the power at work within us
     is able to accomplish abundantly far more than all we can ask or imagine,
     to him be glory in the church and in Christ Jesus to all generations,
     forever and ever.
         —Ephesians 3:20-21, NRSV

3    To Jesus Christ, who loves us
     and freed us from our sins by his blood,
     and made us to be a kingdom,
     priests serving his God and Father,
     to him be glory and dominion forever and ever.
          —from Revelation 1:5-6, NRSV

4    Worthy is the Lamb, who was slain,
     **to receive power and wealth and wisdom and strength
     and honor and glory and praise!**
          —Revelation 5:12, NIV

## 8.5.2 Prayer

1    Now, Master,
     you are letting your servants go in peace as you promised;
     for our eyes have seen the salvation
     that you have made ready in the sight of the nations;
     a light of revelation for the Gentiles
     and glory for your people Israel.
     Through Christ, our Lord, **Amen.**
          —based on Luke 2:29-32, NJB

2    O Lord, our God, we give you thanks
     for uniting us by baptism in the body of Christ
     and for filling us with joy in the eucharist.
     Lead us toward the full visible unity of your church,
     and help us to treasure all the signs of reconciliation you have granted us.
     Now that we have tasted the banquet
     you have prepared for us in the world to come,
     may we all one day share together
     the inheritance of the saints in the life of the heavenly city.
     **Through Jesus Christ, our Lord,
     who lives and reigns with you in the unity of the Holy Spirit,
     ever one God, world without end. Amen.**

3    Lord God,
     in deep gratitude
     for this moment, this meal, these people,
     we give ourselves to you.

     Take us out to live as changed people
     because we have shared the living bread
     and cannot remain the same.

     Ask much of us, expect much from us,
     enable much by us, encourage many through us.

So, Lord, may we live to your glory,
both as inhabitants of earth
and citizens of the commonwealth of heaven. **Amen.**

4    We thank and praise you, Jesus Christ,
for these gifts of bread and wine,
signs of your great sacrifice for us
and, by your Spirit's presence and power,
a means for us to commune with you.

We eat this bread and drink this cup
to refresh our hearts,
to strengthen our faith,
and to rouse our hope
that soon we shall take our places at your heavenly banquet
to eat and drink with you and all you have redeemed.

For all your gifts, we bless you, Lord.
Above all, your heavenly food,
pardoning grace, and life-giving Word
motivate us to sing that you are good. **Amen.**
—based on "Yes, God Is Good" by John Hampden Gurney (1862)

5    *This prayer is designed for congregational participation without a printed text. Each short line spoken by the leader may be repeated by the congregation.*

We bless you, O God,
for gifts of bread and cup,
for sustaining us in hope,
every day of our lives.
We pray for your strength
to prepare us now for your service
as we offer to you
lives of witness and worship
in the world you have made.
Through Christ, our Lord. **Amen.**

6    Gracious God,
we thank you for the love
that brings us food from heaven,
gives us the life of your dear Son,
and assures us that we belong
to the company of all his faithful people
in heaven and on earth.

Grant that, strengthened by this fellowship
and by the power of his Holy Spirit,
we may continue his work in the world,
until we come
to the glory of your eternal kingdom;

through the same Jesus Christ,
your Son, our Lord. **Amen.**

7   Glory to God the Father,
who brought back from the dead
our Lord Jesus Christ
and crowned him with glory and honor.

Glory to God the Son,
who lives to plead our cause
at the right hand of God
and who will come again
to make all things new.

Glory to God the Holy Spirit,
who brings us the taste
of the good Word of God
and the power of the age to come.

**Amen! Praise and glory and wisdom,
thanksgiving and honor,
power and might be to our Lord for ever! Amen.**

8   Lord, you have put gladness in our hearts;
you have satisfied our hunger with good things.
In giving all, you have not withheld from us
your own dear Son.
**How can we withhold anything from you,
our Lord and our God?
Renew us day by day with the gift of your Spirit,
that we may give ourselves completely to your service
and walk with joy in the footsteps
of Jesus Christ, our Lord. Amen.**

9   Loving God,
we thank you that you have fed us in this sacrament,
united us with Christ,
and given us a foretaste of the heavenly banquet
in your eternal kingdom.
Send us out in the power of your Spirit
to live and work to your praise and glory
for the sake of Jesus Christ, our Lord. **Amen.**

10  You have fed us, Lord, and we are grateful.
Allow us to respond this day, and in the days to come,
with hearts made ready,
eyes made open,
hands made strong,
and feet made willing

to do your will in this place,
and in all the places to which you call us. **Amen.**

11   Most gracious God,
we are in awe of your great gifts to us,
experienced here at this table.
You have given your Son that we might live,
you have fed our spirits with bread and wine,
you have made us one body with all your children.
We are renewed today
in our commitment to loving service.
We leave here to build your kingdom in this world,
and we ask that your love will shape our love,
that we may reach to others
as Jesus Christ has reached to us.
Hear us, accept our thanks,
and continue to walk with us.
In the name of him who gave himself for us, **Amen.**

12   Eternal God,
you have graciously accepted us
as living members of your Son, our Savior, Jesus Christ,
and you have fed us with spiritual food
in the sacrament of his body and blood.
Send us now into the world in peace,
and grant us strength and courage
to love and serve you with gladness and singleness of heart,
through Christ, our Lord. **Amen.**

13   Loving God,
you graciously feed us
with the bread of life and the cup of eternal salvation.
May we who have received this sacrament
be strengthened in your service;
we who have sung your praises
tell of your glory and truth;
we who have seen the greatness of your love
see you face to face in your kingdom.
For you have made us your own people
by the death and resurrection of your Son, our Lord,
and by the life-giving power of your Spirit. **Amen.**

14   Loving God,
you have given us a share in the one bread and the one cup
and made us one with Christ.
Help us to bring your salvation and joy to all the world.
We ask this through Christ, our Lord. **Amen.**

15 O God,
   you have so greatly loved us,
   long sought us,
   and mercifully redeemed us.
   Give us grace,
   that in everything we may yield
   ourselves, our wills, and our works,
   a continual thank-offering to you,
   through Jesus Christ, our Lord. **Amen.**

16 God of grace,
   you renew us at your table with the bread of life.
   May this food strengthen us in love
   and help us to serve you in each other.
   We ask this in the name of Jesus, the Lord. **Amen.**

17 God of all hope,
   we bless and thank you
   for nourishing us with Christ, the bread of life.
   Help us to live free from all desires
   for anything else that promises to satisfy.
   Strengthen us now to offer this bread
   to all who hunger.
   Through Jesus Christ, the living bread, **Amen.**

18 O amazing God, you come into our ordinary lives
   and set a holy table among us,
   filling our plates with the bread of life
   and our cups with salvation.
   Send us out, O God, with tenderheartedness
   to touch an ordinary everyday world
   with the promise of your holiness. **Amen.**

19 Generous God,
   you have given yourself to us and made us yours.
   You prepared a table before us,
   led us to it, and fed us abundantly.
   Thank you, great God, for your life-giving gifts.
   Thank you for uniting us with you and with each other,
   for giving us new life and new hope,
   and for preparing us to live as your people.
   May our lives joyfully display our hope in you.
   In the power of your Holy Spirit we pray. **Amen.**

20 Most holy and loving God:
   For being present among us,
   **we thank you!**
   For making us one with you,
   **we thank you!**

For enabling us to know you more,
**we thank you!**
For feeding us with your bread of life,
**we thank you!**
For uniting us with your people,
**we thank you!**
For the reminder of your covenant promises,
**we thank you!**
For this sign of forgiveness,
**we thank you!**
For the time to express our gratitude,
**we thank you!**
For the promise of a future together,
**we thank you! Amen.**

21  Loving, glorious, gracious God,
you have fed us at your table.
In your mercy you have nourished us,
and we are grateful.
This day, in this time and place,
we connect through the centuries
with the church everlasting,
those who before us broke bread and took the cup.
Help us now, as we leave this place,
to continue the work of the holy catholic church,
to practice the communion of the saints,
and, with hearts and souls refreshed, to seek your will.
Help us, now that we have been fed,
to feed those who are hungry,
invite in the stranger,
and visit the imprisoned.
You have met us where we are, O Lord,
and filled our needs yet again.
May we do the same for all of your children;
may we leave this place to love abundantly.
May we love you with all our hearts.
May we love our neighbors as ourselves.
In Christ's name we pray. **Amen.**

# SECTION 9
# CLOSING OF WORSHIP

The close of a worship service depends a great deal on the theme and development of the particular service. Some services end in celebration, others in quiet contemplation. Some end in a confident call to discipleship, others in a quiet prayer for God's comfort. This section begins with invitations to discipleship, prayers for blessing, and acclamations of praise—all of which are intended to be followed by a blessing.

# 9.1 SENDING

## Call to Service/Discipleship

*Worship does not end when we leave a worship service. A clear call to discipleship reminds us that our worship continues through obedient and grateful living. Like the offering, this call reminds us that our worship must bear fruit in our witness. Having come together to meet God as the children of God, we go out with the mandate to promote God's rule in the world. This challenge can be given any of several names, such as exhortation, call to commitment, charge to the people, call to service, and commissioning. The call to discipleship should convey two important convictions. First, we live in faithful service not so that God will love us, but because God has loved us first. Second, we live by the power of the Spirit and thus do not need to rely on our own strength.*

*Because of these convictions, a call to service should always be followed by a blessing. Scripture gives us not only the call to obedience but also the promise of God's presence to sustain us.*

*The call to discipleship may be introduced by words like these:*

> As you prepare to leave this place,
> hear now God's invitation to a life of Christian discipleship.

*or*

> Hear now this call to service.

1  God has shown you what is good.
   And what does the Lord require of you?
   To act justly and to love mercy
   and to walk humbly with your God.
   —from Micah 6:8, NIV

2  Someone asked Jesus,
   "Teacher, which is the greatest commandment in the Law?"
   Jesus replied:
   " 'Love the Lord your God
   with all your heart
   and with all your soul
   and with all your mind.'
   This is the first and greatest commandment.
   And the second is like it:
   'Love your neighbor as yourself.'
   All the Law and the Prophets hang on these two commandments."
   —from Matthew 22:36-40, NIV

3  Jesus said:
   " 'Love the Lord your God
   with all your passion and prayer and intelligence.'
   This is the most important, the first on any list.
   But there is a second to set alongside it:
   'Love others as well as you love yourself.'
   These two commands are pegs;
   everything in God's Law and the Prophets hangs from them."
   —Matthew 22:37-40, TM

4  Go therefore and make disciples of all nations,
   baptizing them
   in the name of the Father and of the Son and of the Holy Spirit,
   and teaching them to obey everything that I have commanded you.
   And remember, I am with you always, to the end of the age.
   —Matthew 28:19-20, NRSV

5  Keep alert,
   stand firm in your faith,

*358*

be courageous, be strong.
Let all that you do be done in love.
—1 Corinthians 16:13-14, NRSV

6   Lead a life worthy of the calling
    to which you have been called,
    with all humility and gentleness,
    with patience, bearing with one another in love,
    making every effort to maintain the unity of the Spirit
    in the bond of peace.
    There is one body and one Spirit,
    just as we were called to the one hope of our calling,
    one Lord, one faith, one baptism,
    one God and Father of all,
    who is above all and through all and in all.
    —from Ephesians 4:1-6, NRSV

7   As God's own,
    clothe yourselves with compassion,
    kindness, and patience,
    forgiving each other
    as the Lord has forgiven you,
    and crown all these things with love,
    which binds everything together in perfect harmony.
    —based on Colossians 3:12-14

8   Whatever you do, in word or deed,
    do everything in the name of the Lord Jesus,
    giving thanks to God the Father through him.
    —Colossians 3:17, NRSV

9   Go forth in the name of the Lord.
    This is God's charge:
    We should believe in the name of his Son, Jesus Christ,
    and love one another, just as he commanded us.
    —based on 1 John 3:23, NRSV

10  Go in peace to love and serve the Lord.

11  We leave from here to bear witness to Christ
        in faithfulness to the Scriptures,
        in harmony with the church of the ages,
        and in unity with all Christ's people.
        —from *Our Song of Hope*, st. 7

12  Go in peace, in the knowledge of God's power.
    Go in confidence, in the knowledge of God's strength.
    Go in joy, in the knowledge of God's love.

13  Go into the world:
    dance, laugh, sing, and create.
    **We go with the assurance of God's blessing.**
    Go into the world:
    risk, explore, discover, and love.
    **We go with the assurance of God's grace.**
    Go into the world:
    believe, hope, struggle, and remember.
    **We go with the assurance of God's love.**
    **Thanks be to God!**

14  Go forth, remembering who you are
    and to whom you belong.

15  God be in your head and in your understanding.
    God be in your eyes and in your looking.
    God be in your mouth and in your speaking.
    God be in your heart and in your thinking.
    God be at your end and at your departing.

16  Let us go forth in the name of Christ.
    **Thanks be to God.**

17  Go in peace to love and serve the Lord.
    **Thanks be to God.**

18  Let us go forth into the world,
    rejoicing in the power of the Spirit.
    **Thanks be to God.**

19  Let us bless the Lord.
    **Thanks be to God.**


*The following texts include both a call to discipleship and a benediction.*

20  As you have been fed at this table, go to feed the hungry.
    As you have been set free, go to set free the imprisoned.
    As you have received, give.
    As you have heard, proclaim.
    And the blessing that you have received
    from Father, Son, and Holy Spirit
    be always with you. **Amen.**

21  Go in peace as the reaffirmed church of Jesus Christ.
    **We go to be his body in a broken world.**
    May the grace of God and the love of Christ go with you. **Amen.**

**22**  Let mutual love continue.
Do not neglect to show hospitality to strangers,
for by doing that some have entertained angels without knowing it.
Remember those who are in prison,
as though you were in prison with them.
Be content with what you have.
And remember that God has promised,
"I will never leave you or forsake you."
—from Hebrews 13:1-3, 5, NRSV

**23**  Go out into the world in peace:
have courage;
hold on to what is good;
return no one evil for evil;
help the suffering;
honor all;
love and serve the Lord,
rejoicing in the power of the Holy Spirit.
**With God's help we will.**
And the blessing of God Almighty,
the Father, the Son, and the Holy Spirit,
be upon you, and remain with you forever. **Amen.**
—based on 1 Corinthians 16:13; 1 Thessalonians 5:13-22; 1 Peter 2:17

**24**  As you leave the sanctuary today,
may you know the hope to which God has called you,
experience the riches of his glorious inheritance in the saints,
and trust his incomparably great power for us who believe. **Amen.**
—based on Ephesians 1:18-19

**25**  *For evening worship*

Watch now, dear Lord, with those who watch or weep tonight,
and give your angels charge over those who sleep.
Tend your sick ones, Lord Christ,
rest your weary ones, bless your dying ones,
soothe your suffering ones, pity your afflicted ones,
shield your joyous ones, and all for your love's sake.
**And may the God of hope fill us with all joy and peace in believing,
that we may abound in hope by the power of the Holy Spirit. Amen.**
—based on Psalms 3-5; 121; 130; Romans 15:13

## Acclamations/Doxologies

*A doxology is a "word of praise" for God's glory and goodness. In a sense, a doxology is what all worship should be. A focused act of praise is especially appropriate to draw worship to a close, as a concluding joyful burst of adoration. Most often, a doxology or acclamation will be sung.*

26    Blessed be the LORD, the God of Israel,
      from everlasting to everlasting. **Amen and Amen.**
        —Psalm 41:13, NRSV

27    Blessed be the LORD, the God of Israel,
        who alone does wondrous things.
      Blessed be his glorious name forever;
        may his glory fill the whole earth.
          **Amen and Amen.**
        —Psalm 72:18-19, NRSV

28    Praise be to the LORD, the God of Israel,
        from everlasting to everlasting.
      Let all the people say, **"Amen!"**
      **Praise the LORD.**
        —Psalm 106:48, NIV

29    Oh, the depth of the riches and wisdom and knowledge of God!
      How unsearchable are his judgments and how inscrutable his ways!
        "For who has known the mind of the Lord?
          Or who has been his counselor?"
        "Or who has given a gift to him,
          to receive a gift in return?"
      **For from him and through him and to him are all things.**
      **To him be the glory forever. Amen.**
        —from Romans 11:33-36, NRSV

30    Now to him who by the power at work within us
      is able to accomplish abundantly far more
      than all we can ask or imagine,
      to him be glory in the church and in Christ Jesus
      to all generations, forever and ever. **Amen.**
        —Ephesians 3:20-21, NRSV

31    Now to the King eternal,
      immortal, invisible, the only God,
      be honor and glory for ever and ever. **Amen.**
        —1 Timothy 1:17, NIV

32    To him who is able to keep you from falling
      and to present you before his glorious presence
      without fault and with great joy—
      to the only God our Savior
      be glory, majesty, power, and authority,
      through Jesus Christ our Lord,
      before all ages, now and forevermore! **Amen!**
        —Jude 24-25, NIV

33  To Jesus Christ, who loves us
and freed us from our sins by his blood
and made us to be a kingdom,
priests serving his God and Father,
to him be glory and dominion forever and ever. **Amen.**
      —from Revelation 1:5-6, NRSV

34  Blessing and glory and wisdom
and thanksgiving and honor
and power and might
be to our God forever and ever! **Amen.**
      —Revelation 7:12, NRSV

## Closing Prayers

*A closing prayer expresses gratitude for the gift of worship and requests God's blessing as the congregation departs.*

35  Almighty God,
be gracious to us and bless us
    and make your face to shine upon us,
that your way may be known upon earth,
    your saving power among all nations.
Empower all the peoples to praise you, O God,
    that the nations may be glad and sing for joy.
For you judge the peoples with equity
    and guide the nations upon earth.
Enable all the peoples to praise you, O God,
    for the earth has yielded its increase
    and you, our God, have blessed us.
We ask that you will continue to bless us
    so that all the ends of the earth will revere you. **Amen.**
      —based on Psalm 67, NRSV

36  Now, Master, you are letting your servants go in peace
as you promised;
for our eyes have seen the salvation
that you have made ready in the sight of the nations;
a light of revelation for the Gentiles
and glory for your people Israel.
Through Christ, our Lord. **Amen.**
      —based on Luke 2:29-32, NJB

37  Grant, O Lord,
that what has been said with our lips we may believe in our hearts,
and that what we believe in our hearts we may practice in our lives,
through Jesus Christ, our Lord. **Amen.**

**38**   O Creator and Mighty God,
you have promised strength for the weak,
rest for the laborers, light for the way,
grace for the trials, help from above,
unfailing sympathy, undying love.
O Creator and Mighty God,
help us to continue in your promise. **Amen.**

**39**   *A text mindful of children*

Lord, we have worshiped you and felt your love.
Lord, as we leave this worship place,
and go to schools, to homes, and to work,
bless us and be near us,
so that we may feel your presence in all we do. **Amen.**

**40**   Grant us, Lord God,
the vision of your kingdom,
forgiveness and new life,
and the stirring of your Spirit,
so that we may share your vision,
proclaim your love,
and change this world
in the name of Christ. **Amen.**

**41**   Almighty God, our heavenly Father, the privilege is ours
to be called to share in the loving, healing, and reconciling mission
of your Son, Jesus Christ, our Lord, in this age and wherever we are.
Since without you we can do no good thing,
    may your Spirit make us wise;
    may your Spirit guide us;
    may your Spirit renew us;
    may your Spirit strengthen us
so that we will be
    strong in faith;
    discerning in proclamation;
    courageous in witness;
    persistent in good deeds.
This we ask through the same Jesus Christ, our Lord. **Amen.**

**42**   God the Sender, **send us,**
God the Sent, **come with us,**
God the Strengthener of those who go, **empower us,**
**that we may go with you**
**and find those who will call you**
**Father, Son, and Holy Spirit. Amen.**

43   Grant to us, O Lord,
      to know that which is worth knowing,
      to love that which is worth loving,
      to praise that which pleases you most,
      to esteem that which is most precious unto you,
      and to dislike whatsoever is evil in your eyes.
      Grant us true judgment to distinguish things that differ
      and above all to search out and do what is well pleasing to you,
      through Jesus Christ, our Lord. **Amen.**

44   With you, wondrous God, we move from this time of worship.
      Thank you for calling us to worship you and for accepting
      our praises as a fragrant offering, an acceptable sacrifice, pleasing to you.
      Thank you, O God, that your Word came to us in power,
      inspired by your Holy Spirit.
      Thank you for nourishing us with your Word and Spirit
      and strengthening us with your grace for the days ahead.
      Thank you for listening to prayers that rose to you from humble hearts.
      Thank you for surrounding us with brothers and sisters in Jesus Christ
      who love us, share our triumphs and disappointments,
      and support us in times of need.
      Thank you that our offering may provide relief
      for those who suffer in poverty of body or spirit.
      In the week ahead, O God, may we turn each moment of joy into praise,
      and may we cling to your promise in times of suffering.
      Guide us, O God, so that we can obey you.
      Make your light shine through us
      so that others will see our good deeds and glorify you.
      Fill our lives with love for you, O God,
      and for the world that so desperately needs its Savior, in whom we pray. **Amen.**

45   Loving God,
      together we have heard you speak to us,
      welcoming us, forgiving us,
      teaching us, challenging us.
      And we have responded to you
      with praise and confession,
      listening to your Word,
      praying in thanksgiving and intercession,
      and committing ourselves to you anew.
      It has been good to be together.

      As we prepare to leave this place,
      we await your blessing
      so that we may be comforted
      by the assurance that you will
      be with us during the coming week.
      Continue to speak to us as we seek your face.
      Guide us by your Holy Spirit.

Keep us close to you, we pray,
in every aspect of our daily lives,
that we may seek your honor and glory
wherever we are and in whatever we do.
We pray, anticipating your blessing,
for we pray in the name of Jesus,
our Savior and Lord. **Amen.**

46   Bless to us, O God,
the doors we open,
the thresholds we cross,
the roads that lie before us.
Go with us as we go,
and welcome us home. **Amen.**

47   Tender and compassionate God,
you long to gather us in your arms as a hen gathers her chicks.
Draw us to yourself in love,
surround us with your grace,
and keep us in the shelter of your wings
so that in our time of testing we may not fall away. **Amen.**

48   Lord, dismiss us with your blessing;
fill our hearts with joy and peace.
Let each of us, your love possessing,
triumph in redeeming grace.
As we depart, we give you thanks
for your gospel's joyful sound.
May the fruits of your salvation
flourish in our hearts and lives,
that we may bring glory to you
and be found faithful to your truth. In Christ, **Amen.**
—based on "Lord, Dismiss Us with Your Blessing" by John Fawcett (1773)

# 9.2 BLESSING/BENEDICTION

*The greeting from God at the beginning of a service and God's blessing at the end of the service frame the entire worship liturgy. Just as we begin with God's gracious invitation, so we end with God's promise to always be with us. In the benediction the dialogue of worship shifts from the people's response to God's parting words. The words of benediction (a Latin word meaning "to speak well" or "to speak a good word") are intended to bring a blessing.*

*Of all of the actions that are part of the "sending," the blessing, or benediction, is arguably the most important and the least understood. It is so important because it sends worshipers on their way with a parting word of God's grace and blessing. This is much more fitting to the Christian gospel than ending either with a command, which can imply that the Christian life is only about working hard to earn God's favor, or with merely a well-wish, which fails to convey the beauty and power of God's promise to go with us. Yet the benediction is often misunderstood in these ways, such that it is turned into a command, a well-wish, or simply a farewell. The following resources provide many benedictions that appropriately convey God's grace and blessing.*

*In many communities, the benediction is spoken only by the pastor, and it includes the raising of hands in a gesture of blessing. In such contexts, when an ordained pastor is not available, the following texts may be adapted in two ways. First, the second-person pronouns may be changed to first-person (for example, "May the God of hope fill you . . ." may be changed to "May the God of hope fill us . . ."). Alternatively, a leader may introduce words of benediction directly from Scripture by saying, for example, "Hear the word of the Lord from Romans 15:13."*

*Worshipers may respond with words or gestures to indicate their acceptance of God's blessing (for example, by voicing an audible "Amen" or by holding out their hands as a sign of receiving God's blessing). Some congregations respond to the blessing with "the passing of the peace" as a way of extending God's blessing to each other and beginning a time of congregational fellowship (see Mutual Greeting in section 1.3).*

## Scriptural Blessings

*The blessing may be introduced by such words as*

> People of God, hear now these words of blessing.

*or*

> As you prepare to leave, gratefully hear now God's word of blessing.

*Any blessing may be concluded by the following:*

> Alleluia!
> **Alleluia! Amen!**

*or*

> Bless the Lord.
> **The Lord's name be praised.**

1    The LORD bless you and keep you;
     the LORD make his face to shine upon you
          and be gracious to you;
     the LORD turn his face toward you
          and give you peace.
               —Numbers 6:24-26, NIV

**2**    May the God of hope
      fill you with all joy and peace in believing,
      so that you may abound in hope
      by the power of the Holy Spirit.
          —Romans 15:13, NRSV

**3**    The grace of the Lord Jesus Christ,
      the love of God,
      and the communion of the Holy Spirit
      be with all of you.
          —2 Corinthians 13:13, NRSV

**4**    May the grace of Christ, which daily renews us,
      and the love of God, which enables us to love all,
      and the fellowship of the Holy Spirit, which unites us in one body,
      make us eager to obey the will of God until we meet again,
      through Jesus Christ, our Lord.
          —based on 2 Corinthians 13:13 [14]

**5**    The peace of God,
      which passes all understanding,
      keep your hearts and minds
      in the knowledge and love of God,
      and of God's Son, Jesus Christ, our Lord;
      and the blessing of God Almighty,
      the Father, the Son, and the Holy Spirit,
      remain with you always.
          —based on Philippians 4:7

**6**    The grace of our Lord Jesus Christ be with you all.
          —2 Thessalonians 3:18, NIV

**7**    May the God of peace
      himself sanctify you entirely;
      and may your spirit and soul and body be kept sound
      and blameless at the coming of our Lord Jesus Christ.
          —1 Thessalonians 5:23, NRSV

**8**    May God himself,
      the God who makes everything holy and whole,
      make you holy and whole,
      put you together—spirit, soul, and body—
      and keep you fit for the coming of our Master, Jesus Christ.
      The one who called you is completely dependable.
      If he said it, he'll do it!
          —1 Thessalonians 5:23-24, TM

9    May our Lord Jesus Christ himself and God our Father,
who loved us and by his grace
gave us eternal encouragement and good hope,
encourage your hearts and strengthen you
in every good deed and word.
>    —2 Thessalonians 2:16-17, NIV

10    The God of peace,
who brought back from the dead our Lord Jesus,
the great shepherd of the sheep,
by the blood of the eternal covenant,
make you complete in everything good
so that you may do God's will,
working among us that which is pleasing in God's sight,
through Jesus Christ, to whom be the glory forever and ever!
>    —from Hebrews 13:20-21, NRSV

## Additional Blessings

*In some contexts benedictions are limited to only the preceding biblical texts. In other contexts, words of blessing combine various Scripture passages, draw on varied sources, or are spoken extemporaneously.*

11    The peace of God, which passes all understanding,
keep your hearts and minds in the knowledge and love of God,
and of his Son, Jesus Christ, our Lord;
and the blessing of God Almighty,
the Father, the Son, and the Holy Spirit,
be among you and remain with you always.

12    May the love of God surround you,
the wisdom of Christ guide you,
and the power of the Holy Spirit encourage you
as you joyfully proclaim:
Our world belongs to God!

13    May you, people of God, know that
God our Father made you and guides your every step;
Jesus Christ gave his life for you and brings you new life;
the Spirit keeps you in the Lord's presence and empowers you to serve.
May almighty God continue to bless you and move you to give thanks. **Amen.**

14    The love of God the Father, the faithful creator,
the peace of Christ, the wounded healer,
the joy of the challenging Spirit,
the hope of the Three in One
surround and encourage you
today, tonight, and forever.

15 May our Lord Jesus Christ,
   the one who came with grace and truth,
   also fill your hearts with grace and truth,
   as you serve him in the days ahead.
   And may the joy of the Lord—Father, Son, and Holy Spirit—
   be your strength. **Amen.**

16 May the love of God enfold us.
   **May the grace of God uphold us.**
   May the power of God set us free
   **to love and serve all God's people.**
   Now to God, who by the means of the power working in us
   is able to do so much more than we can ask or even think,
   to God be the glory in the church and in Christ Jesus for all times,
   for ever and ever.

17 May God the Father bless you,
   God the Son heal you,
   God the Holy Spirit give you strength.
   May God the holy and undivided Trinity
   guard your body, save your soul,
   and bring you safely to his heavenly country,
   where he lives and reigns for ever and ever.

18 As you leave this place this day,
   may God's love sustain you,
   and may you love those who surround you.
   May God's Spirit empower you,
   and may you empower all those you meet.
   May God's joy fill your hearts,
   and may this joy overflow
   to the ends of the earth for God's glory,
   now and forever. **Amen.**

19 May the grace of God,
   freely given through Christ, our Lord,
   and sufficient for all our needs,
   and may the fellowship of the Holy Spirit,
   who testifies with our spirit
   that we are God's children,
   guide and sustain us this day
   and forever. **Amen.**

20 May the blessing of God,
   the giver of every good and perfect gift;
   and of Christ, who summons us to service;
   and of the Holy Spirit, who inspires generosity and love,
   be with us all.

21    The grace of Christ attend you,
the love of God surround you,
the Holy Spirit keep you
now and forevermore.

22    May God go before you to lead you.
May God go behind you to guard you.
May God go beneath you to support you.
May God go beside you to befriend you.
Do not be afraid.
Let the blessing of God—the Father, the Son, the Holy Spirit—
come upon you today and settle in around you.
Do not be afraid.
Go in peace to love and serve the Lord. **Amen.**

23    May the omniscient God give you knowledge,
the omnipotent God give you power,
the omnipresent God give you a presence that blesses—
so that you may share God with the world. **Amen.**

# CENTRAL THEMES OF THE CHRISTIAN FAITH

# CENTRAL THEMES OF THE CHRISTIAN FAITH

This second part of *The Worship Sourcebook* provides texts on central themes of the Christian faith. These themes are highlighted in the ecumenical creeds of the church and in traditional observances of the Christian year. Whether a congregation follows the Christian year or organizes its worship calendar by means of a creed, a catechism, the *Revised Common Lectionary,* or some other pattern, the goal for each congregation should be to ensure that worship covers the subject matter of the whole Christian faith over time in a balanced way.

The chart on this page shows how the central themes of the Christian year fit neatly into the structure of the Nicene Creed while also providing the outline of Part Two of this book.

Part Two of this sourcebook is supplemental to Part One. Many texts in Part One can be used for particular themes or occasions treated in Part Two.

It's important to know that in Part Two the numbering of ele-

ments of worship builds on the numbering used throughout Part One. For example, within each lettered section (A, B, C . . .) of Part Two, the Call to Worship subsection is labeled A.1.2, B.1.2, and so on to show correspondence with the Call to Worship subsection (1.2) in Part One. Each lettered section in Part Two provides resources for many (though not all) elements of worship; resources for elements of worship that do not appear in Part Two can be found in Part One.

Part Two also includes a new feature: each lettered section offers a list of Scripture texts and statements of faith appropriate for preaching and for developing liturgical texts on that section's theme. For additional reference, see the chart "Central Themes in Statements of Faith" (p. 822), which offers an overview regarding themes in Part Two as taught in the Belgic Confession, the Heidelberg Catechism, the Canons of Dort, the Westminster Confession of Faith, *Our Song of Hope,* and *Our World Belongs to God.*

Also new in Part Two is a subsection 10, titled Suggested Scripture Readings. Since the earliest days of the church, Christians have found it helpful to read passages from different parts of the Bible in the same worship service. This practice reflects one of the central principles of biblical interpretation, namely, that Scripture interprets Scripture. It helps congregations sense the unity of the Bible. It also helps worshipers sense the unique angle of a given text, as it contributes to a service focused on a particular event in the history of redemption or a particular scriptural theme or topic. The following combinations of readings might be read back to back without interruption, or the readings might be interspersed with a brief prayer, a spoken meditation, or an appropriate song.

# SECTION A
# CREATION

The church confesses that God is the maker of heaven and earth and of all things within them. This conviction about origins has great implications for the way we view the world around us. We care for this world, we see beauty in it, we recognize God's glory expressed in it, we aim to protect it, and we grieve when it is abused and damaged. The church also confesses that God has created all human beings in his own image. Male and female, old and young, strong and weak—all carry the stamp of God's image as moral, ethical, and spiritual beings called into a unique covenant relationship with their creator. This conviction leads us to view each human being as having God-given dignity and being worthy of respect, care, and honor.

These convictions have implications for our corporate worship. The worshiping community needs to give praise and thanks for the creation; to express grief and pain at the abuse, pollution, and corruption of what God has created; and

to offer prayers for God's blessing on the seasons and on our faithful use of provisions God makes available through the creation. In our corporate worship we also need to affirm human efforts to carry out God's command to exercise obedient supervision over all God has created; to seek wisdom in our tasks of creative efforts; and to seek discipline in our work of being caretakers.

In certain seasons this worship takes on a special urgency. At times during the church year we have opportunity to affirm the value of life and to support and encourage those who are burdened with the weaknesses of life in a fallen world. In spring we ask for God's blessing on a growing season. In fall we give thanks for harvest times. And in times of national and world crisis and concern we call on God corporately for aid and direction. These concerns may be the focus of an entire service or may be components in a service that also includes other themes.

---

**Scriptures and Statements of Faith Applying to the Theme of Creation**

*The following texts are particularly appropriate for sermons or for supplemental liturgical use.*

| | | |
|---|---|---|
| Genesis 1 | Psalm 95:1-7 | Isaiah 51:12-16 |
| Genesis 2 | Psalm 104 | Romans 1:16-25 |
| Deuteronomy 4:32-39 | Psalm 139:13-16 | Romans 8:19-22 |
| Job 38-39 | Psalm 148 | Ephesians 1:3-10 |
| Psalm 8 | Isaiah 42:5-9 | Colossians 1:15-23 |
| Psalm 19:1-6 | Isaiah 43:1-7 | 1 Timothy 4:4-5 |
| Psalm 33 | Isaiah 45:7-8 | Revelation 4:11 |

Belgic Confession, Art. 2, 12, 14-15
Heidelberg Catechism, Q&A's 6, 9
Canons of Dort, Pt. III/IV, Art. 1
Westminster Confession, Chap. IV, Sec. 1-2
*Our Song of Hope*, st. 2
*Our World Belongs to God*, st. 7-11, 13-17

---

# A.1 OPENING OF WORSHIP

---

**A.1.2 Call to Worship** (see also section 1.2)

1   Praise the LORD!
    **Praise the LORD from the heavens;**
        **praise him in the heights!**
    Praise him, all his angels;
        praise him, all his host!
    **Praise him, sun and moon;**
        **praise him, all you shining stars!**

Praise him, you highest heavens,
   and you waters above the heavens!
**Let them praise the name of the LORD,**
   **for he commanded and they were created.**
He established them for ever and ever;
   **he fixed their bounds, which cannot be passed.**
Praise the LORD from the earth,
   you sea monsters and all deeps,
**fire and hail, snow and frost,**
   **stormy wind fulfilling his command!**
Mountains and all hills,
   fruit trees and all cedars!
**Wild animals and all cattle,**
   **creeping things and flying birds!**
Kings of the earth and all peoples,
   princes and all rulers of the earth!
**Young men and women alike,**
   **old and young together!**
Let them praise the name of the LORD,
   for his name alone is exalted;
   **his glory is above earth and heaven.**
He has raised up a horn for his people,
   praise for all his faithful,
   **for the people of Israel who are close to him.**
**Praise the LORD!**
   —Psalm 148, NRSV

2   God is King: Let the earth be glad!
**Christ is victor: his rule has begun!**
The Spirit is at work: creation is renewed!
**Hallelujah! Praise the Lord!**
   —from *Our World Belongs to God*, st. 2

3   Who is this God whom we have come to worship?
**God is the creator of all.**
The creator of birds and trees, wind and sea?
**God is the creator of all things seen and unseen.**
Then let us worship the God of creation,
**the God of all things great and small.**

4   *A text especially mindful of children*

This is the day that the Lord has made;
**let us rejoice and be glad in it.**
God made the bright, warm sunshine and the freezing-cold snow.
**Let us rejoice and be glad in it.**
God made the little tiny flowers and the great big pine trees.
**Let us rejoice and be glad in it.**
God made the peaceful ponds and the crashing waves.

**Let us rejoice and be glad in it.**
God made the cornfields and the rocky mountains.
**Let us rejoice and be glad in it.**
God made the creeping caterpillars and kicking kangaroos.
**Let us rejoice and be glad in it.**
God made you, and God made me.
**Let us rejoice and be glad in it.**
Come, let us praise God for making all things good!

### A.1.4 Opening Responses (see also section 1.4)

*Prayers of Adoration*

1   We praise you, God almighty,
    for the power you have shown in creating the world.
    We thank you for your love in redeeming us from sin
    and in creating us anew in Christ.
    Grant us strength in this life to honor you, Lord God,
    both in worship and in witness, for Jesus Christ's sake. **Amen.**

2   O God, our heavenly Father,
    we thank you for the wonderful way our bodies are made.
    We praise you for each breath we take, each step we take;
    for the gift of sight and the power to read;
    for the minds that can observe and store up what they see.
    We thank you for hands that are skillful in doing work,
    and for all the creative arts within us.
    Above all, we praise you that our bodies are the temples of your own Spirit
    and that we are made in your image.
    Father, we give you praise, through Christ our Lord. **Amen.**

3   Creator God,
    you made all that is, both seen and unseen.
    You made us in your image, both male and female,
    that we might reflect your goodness, wisdom, and love.
    As we gather around your Word [*and table*] this day,
    may our faith be renewed, that we may serve you. **Amen.**

*The following four prayers of adoration are parallel in structure and focus on the gifts of life, water, soil, and air, respectively. These prayers were inspired by Brian Wren's hymn "Thank You, God, for Water, Soil, and Air."*

4   How magnificent for us to ponder, triune God of grace,
    how your Word spoke creation into being,
    how your Spirit breathed life into every living creature.
    Receive now our praise in concert
    with the symphony of praise

sung by trees and fields on earth,
and saints and angels in heaven—
all offered through Jesus Christ, our Lord. **Amen.**

5    Creator God,
whose Spirit moved over the face of the waters;
who gathers the seas into their places
and directs the courses of the rivers;
who sends rain upon the earth,
that it should bring forth life:
We praise you for the gift of water.
Create in us such a sense of wonder and delight
in this and all your gifts
that we might receive them with gratitude,
care for them with love,
and generously share them with all your creatures,
to the honor and glory of your holy name. **Amen.**

6    Creator God,
who lifted up the mountains and formed the dry land;
whose hands shaped us out of the dust of the earth;
who formed the soils and made this earth
a place of beauty and abundance:
We give you thanks for the gift of soil.
Create in us such a sense of wonder and delight
in this and all your gifts
that we might receive them with gratitude,
care for them with love,
and generously share them with all your creatures,
to the honor and glory of your holy name. **Amen.**

7    Creator God,
who set the stars in their places
and directs the courses of the planets;
who robed this earth with a thin garment of air,
making it a haven of beauty and life;
who breathed into each of us the breath of life:
We thank you for the gift of air.
Create in us such a sense of wonder and delight
in this and in all your gifts
that we might receive them with gratitude,
care for them with love,
and generously share them with all your creatures,
to the honor and glory of your holy name. **Amen.**

8    On this day of rest and gladness,
we praise you, God of creation,
for the dignity of work and the joy of play,

for the challenge of witness
and the invitation to delight at your table.
Renew our hearts through your Sabbath rest,
that we might be refreshed
to continue in your work
of restoring the world to wholeness. **Amen.**

**9** *A prayer especially mindful of children*

O Lord, our Lord,
how majestic is your name in all the earth!
Everything we see reminds us of your power and glory
because you made everything out of nothing.
You made the sun and the moon,
you made the land and the sea,
you made the birds and the fish and all the animals,
and you made us to love you and take care of your creation.
We praise you for all your gifts
and for helping us take care of your world.
Thank you for your creativity and your love.
O Lord, our Lord,
how majestic is your name in all the earth! **Amen.**
—based on Psalm 8

## Prayers of Invocation

**10** We gather in your presence, King of the universe,
to acclaim your great salvation.
You have done marvelous things.
You rescued your people from sin and death,
through the mighty work of Jesus, your Son.
You send missionaries to the ends of the earth.
You raise up prophets to witness to justice.
You reveal your righteousness to the nations.
Send forth your Spirit, Lord;
**renew the face of the earth.**

The whole earth rejoices.
Waves crash over waves in echoes of praise.
Rivers proclaim your goodness as they cascade against their beds.
Mountains, standing together as a chorus, declare your faithfulness.
Wind whispering through the leaves makes music to you.
Creatures of all shapes and sizes join in the song.
Into this glorious harmony
send forth your Spirit, Lord;
**renew the face of the earth.**

We too raise our voices, almighty God.
With all the earth, we shout for joy.

We burst into jubilant song
for the marvelous things you have done.
For your faithfulness, for your love, for your salvation,
for the promise of your return in glory,
we make music to you, our Lord and King.
While we wait for your coming,
send forth your Spirit, Lord;
**renew the face of the earth. Amen.**
     —based on Psalm 98; 104:30

## Additional Resources

**11**   At the beginning of time and space,
God gave us a world.
**And God filled it with the useful—**
with granite, with gravity, with grapes.
**And God gave us minds and hands**
**to engineer the granite,**
**to probe the forces of gravity,**
**to squeeze the grapes.**

At the beginning of time and space,
God gave us a world.
**And God filled it with the beautiful—**
with marble, with molds, with marigolds.
**And God gave us compassion and imagination**
**to shape the marble into sculptures,**
**the molds into medicines,**
**the marigolds into tapestries of yellow and bronze.**

At the beginning of time and space,
God gave us a world.
**And God filled it with the comic—**
with croaking bullfrogs, with the buoyancy of water,
with duck-billed platypuses.
**And God gave us, as imagebearers of God,**
**a sense of humor and different ways of seeing**
**in order to delight in the world.**

At the beginning of time and space,
God gave us a world.
**And God filled it with mystery—**
with living cells and dying stars,
with black holes and the speed of light,
with human beings.
**And God gave us dominion over the earth,**
**to till it and to nurture it with curiosity and creativity.**

At the beginning of time,
God gave us a world.
**Let us give praise and thanksgiving to God, our Creator.**

12    In you, infinite God, we live and move and have our being.
You have been our dwelling place throughout all generations.
Before the mountains were born
or you brought forth the whole world,
from everlasting to everlasting you are God.
**We praise and adore you, everlasting God.**

But we are creatures of dust who return to dust.
In the morning you wake us up into the thunder of life.
In the evening you sweep us away in the sleep of death.
We are only mortals, mere transients in the world.
Our days quickly pass, and we fly away.
**We bow before you, everlasting God.**

Our times are in your hands, because
from everlasting to everlasting you are God.
So teach us to number our days,
that we may gain a heart of wisdom.
**We need your guidance, everlasting God.**

You could condemn us with just cause.
Because of our sin, you could consume us with your anger,
yet you surround us with compassion.
Your unfailing love is all we need.
**We thank you, everlasting God.**

May we sing for joy all our days.
Bless our work and our lives
so that they may testify to your glory.
**We worship you, everlasting God,
through Jesus Christ, our Lord. Amen.**
            —based on Psalm 90

13    Creator God,
we praise you for this world.
As we continue to learn more of the vastness of your cosmos
and the smallest particles of each atom,
we stand in awe that you created all things
in a great harmonious design.
Open our eyes and ears that we may take delight
in the beauty and variety of sky and sea,
of desert and mountain, of plants and flowers,
of birds and fish, of creatures large and small,
and of humankind, the crown of your creation.
We praise you for the world you made, maintain,
and give to us to care for and enjoy. **Amen.**

# A.2 CONFESSION AND ASSURANCE

## A.2.1 Call to Confession (see also section 2.1)

1 Made in God's image
to live in loving communion with our Maker,
we are appointed earthkeepers and caretakers
to tend the earth, enjoy it,
and love our neighbors.
God uses our skills
for the unfolding
and well-being of his world
so that creation
and all who live in it may flourish.
**Yet often we neglect our task.**
**Recalling our task leads us to confess our sin**
**and to yearn for God's forgiveness.**
—from *Our World Belongs to God*, st. 10

2 When humans deface God's image,
The whole world suffers:
**We abuse the creation or idolize it.**
**We are estranged from our Creator, from our neighbor,**
**from our true selves, and from all that God has made.**
Therefore let us confess our sins.
—from *Our World Belongs to God*, st. 15

## A.2.2 Prayers of Confession (see also section 2.2)

1 Lord God, you have provided for us
a creation filled with food and water,
a universe rich with energy and resources,
and charged us to have dominion over all you have created.
But we confess that we have often spoiled your gifts,
we have put material possessions ahead of everything else,
and we have abused the environment you have provided for us.
Forgive us, Lord, and make us better stewards of your creation.
We pray through Christ, our Lord. **Amen.**

2 God of all creation:
**On the first day you made day and night.**
Forgive us for taking for granted the dependable patterns of your world.
Open our eyes to see the beauty of the cosmos you created as our home.
**On the second day you made the sky.**

Forgive us for polluting the air.
Help us see how best to restore and renew your creation.
**On the third day you made the seas and plants.**
Forgive us for spoiling the seas.
Give us resolve to change our hurtful habits.
**On the fourth day you made the sun and moon.**
Forgive us for failing to pause in praise of their splendor.
Open our lips so that we will sing your praise.
**On the fifth day you made swarms of living creatures.**
Forgive us for seeing their value only in terms of serving our interests.
Give us new opportunities to delight in their beauty and diversity.
**On the sixth day you made humankind in your image.**
Forgive us for denying dignity to all your people.
Work through us until all know their worth as your creatures.
**On the seventh day you rested.**
Forgive us for failing to take joy in our rest.
Help us enter your rhythm of rest, even in this day of worship.
Through Christ, our Lord, firstborn of all creation. **Amen.**

3     Creator God, we confess that all too often
we have ignored and denied your lordship of the land entrusted to us
by assuming the right to do with it as we please,
by taking more from it than we have returned to it,
by taking for granted its productivity,
by denying justice to many who have labored on the land,
by wanting food for less than it costs to produce.

We confess that material values, rather than kingdom realities,
have often determined our relationships.
We have indulged our appetites with little consideration for others.
We have been more interested in our neighbor's land than in our neighbor.
We have harbored bitterness and resentments
because of economic problems.
We are not reconciled to some who have hurt us,
even members of your body.

**Lord of the church, have mercy on us.**
**Grant us peace with you and with each other in Christ. Amen.**

4     *A prayer especially mindful of children*

Great God, you made this world good,
but we don't take very good care of it.
We waste water on long showers
and leave the refrigerator door open.
We forget to turn off the light when we leave the room.
We use more than we need,
and we don't always recycle.
Forgive us, God, and help us care for your creation. **Amen.**

5    Creator God,
     breathing life into our being,
     you gave us the gift of life.
     You placed us on this earth
     with its minerals and waters,
     flowers and fruits,
     living creatures of grace and beauty!
     You gave us the care of the earth.
     Today you call us:
     "Where are you; what have you done?"
     [*Silence*]
     We hide in utter shame, for we are naked.
     We violate the earth and plunder it;
     we refuse to share the earth's resources;
     we seek to own what is not ours, but yours.
     **Forgive us, Creator God, and reconcile us to your creation.**

     O God of love,
     you gave us the gift of peoples—
     of cultures, races, and colors,
     to love, to care for, to share our lives with.
     Today you ask us:
     "Where is your brother, your sister?"
     [*Silence*]
     We hide ourselves in shame and fear.
     Poverty, hunger, hatred, and war rule the earth;
     the refugees, the oppressed, and the voiceless cry to you.
     **Forgive us, O God of love,**
     **and reconcile us to yourself and to one another.**
     **Teach us, O Creator God of love,**
     **that the earth and all its fullness are yours,**
     **the world and those who dwell in it.**
     **Call us yet again to safeguard the gift of life,**
     **through Christ, our Lord. Amen.**

6    O God,
     the earth is full of your creatures;
     in wisdom you have made us all,
     and you have delivered us into one another's care,
     asking that we love one another as you first loved us.
     But we have fostered discord rather than unity,
     contempt rather than respect, ignorance rather than love.
     Communities, peoples, creatures, lands, seas—
     they have been set apart, or torn apart, or driven apart,
     by conflicting claims and thoughtless ambitions.
     You know our works and our thoughts, Lord.

So do this day as you have promised:
Gather together all our tribes and tongues, and restore us to harmony.
Reconcile us in your spirit of peace, and from new moon to new moon,
and from sabbath to sabbath, all flesh shall worship your name. **Amen.**

7 God of all creation,
you loved us into being,
yet we often flee our rightful place in your creation.
We confess that we exploit the gifts you place around us
and dominate the richness of the natural order.
Forgive our greedy grasping.
We confess our part in the devastation of our planet home,
mirrored in the violence of cities,
and the brokenness of hearts.

Forgive and restore us, O God.
Nurturing God, remind us of other ways to live
and of a place called home,
where creation reflects your goodness
and each thing lives in balance with all others.
Come and find us, set us right again,
and take us home. **Amen.**

## A.2.4 Assurance of Pardon (see also section 2.4)

1 Hear the good news of the gospel about our life in Christ:
   There is therefore now no condemnation
   for those who are in Christ Jesus.
   For the law of the Spirit of life in Christ Jesus
   has set you free from the law of sin and of death.
Hear the good news of the gospel about all of creation:
   I consider that the sufferings of this present time
   are not worth comparing
   with the glory about to be revealed to us.
   For the creation waits with eager longing
   for the revealing of the children of God;
   for the creation was subjected to futility,
   not of its own will
   but by the will of the one who subjected it,
   in hope that the creation itself
   will be set free from its bondage to decay
   and will obtain the freedom of the glory of the children of God.
         —based on Romans 8:1-2, 18-21, NRSV

2 Our world, broken and scarred, still belongs to God,
**who holds it together and gives us hope.**
With the whole creation we join the song:
**"Worthy is the Lamb, who was slain, to receive power and wealth
and wisdom and strength and honor and glory and praise!"**

He has made us a kingdom of priests to serve our God,
**and we will reign on earth.**
God will be all in all, righteousness and peace will flourish,
**everything will be made new, and every eye will see at last**
**that our world belongs to God. Hallelujah! Come, Lord Jesus!**
—from *Our World Belongs to God*, st. 17, 58

# A.3 PROCLAIMING THE WORD

## A.3.1 Prayers for Illumination (see also section 3.1)

1   Lord God,
    at the beginning of time your Spirit moved over the waters.
    So send your Spirit to us now to open our hearts and minds
    to receive the re-creating power of your Word.
    Through Christ, **Amen.**

## A.3.6 Profession of Our Church's Faith (see also section 3.6)

1   Grateful for advances in science and technology,
    we participate in their development,
    fostering care for creation and respect for the gift of life.
    We welcome discoveries that prevent or cure diseases
    and that help support healthy lives.
    **We commit ourselves to honor all God's creatures**
    **and to protect them from abuse and extinction,**
    **for our world belongs to God.**
    —from *Our World Belongs to God*, st. 50-51

2   **We believe in God, the Father almighty,**
    **maker of heaven and earth.**
    **We believe that God's love is powerful beyond measure.**
    **God not only preserves the world, God continually attends to it.**
    **God commands us to care for the earth in ways**
    **that reflect God's loving care for us.**
    **We are responsible for ensuring that the earth's gifts**
    **are used fairly and wisely,**
    **that no creature suffers from the abuse of what we are given,**
    **and that future generations may continue to enjoy**
    **the abundance and goodness of the earth in praise to God.**
    **Entrusting ourselves wholly to God's care,**

we receive the grace to be patient in adversity,
thankful in the midst of blessing,
courageous when facing injustice,
and confident that no evil may afflict us
that God will not turn to our good.

# A.4 PRAYERS OF THE PEOPLE

### A.4.4 Complete Model Outlines and Prayers (see also section 4.4)

*Prayer Outlines*

1   *The following is a guide for extemporaneous prayers. The pattern provides a suggested text
for the opening and closing of each part of the prayer and calls for extemporaneous prayers of
thanksgiving, petition, and intercession.*

Creator God,
we praise you for creating a world filled with beauty and variety.
We thank you for revealing yourself
through the beauty of a flower and the power of a storm.
Today we particularly marvel at the beauty of . . .
    for your work in the world, especially . . .
    for evidence of your presence in the church and local community . . .
    for creating humanity in your image and
    for our task as caretakers of this world and all it contains.

Yet we come before you, acknowledging that
we have failed in our task as stewards of this world.
Along with creation we look forward to the new creation.
As we wait, we pray that we may be greater imagebearers of you,
as evidenced in
    our care of creation, especially . . .
    our work toward peace and reconciliation in our world,
        especially . . .
    our government and all who lead . . .
    the church worldwide and particularly the work of . . .
    the ministry of this church as we . . .
    in our love and care for persons who have particular needs,
        especially . . .

We offer these prayers in the name of our creating God,
Father, Son, and Holy Spirit,
who with all creation we worship now and through eternity. **Amen.**

*Complete Prose Prayers*

2    Lord, you make a pink flower from a gray seed,
an ear from a kernel,
a carrot from a seed the size of a pinhead,
an oak tree from an acorn.
You have programmed your soil to provide food for your plants,
wooden trees to make apples, feathered hens to lay eggs,
grass-eating cows to give milk.
And you, grand Creator, you have us take care of your grand creation.

In your mercy, Lord, send rain to water our crops and gardens.
Let your sun shine on our fields so that seeds will produce abundantly,
so that vines and stalks and trees will hang heavy with fruit and grain.
And Lord, let your grace be as rich to our cattle as it is to us;
let it keep our hogs free of disease,
our hens laying eggs, and our cows giving milk.
May our animals be fertile;
may our lambs and calves and pigs frolic in your green pastures
so that even in their play we may see your grace.

Help us to live on your good earth—
preserving and caring for the life and soil you bless,
ever thankful that for our good
you gave your laws of nature and your law of love.
Help us for our good and your glory to see those laws as you see them
and as the psalmist saw them—as good and perfect, pleasant to think about.

And Lord, teach us to share the abundance you have given us,
never gloating in our excess
but always giving our first bushels to feed the hungry in your name.
Enlighten our hearts, Lord,
so that our thank-yous ever rise in a crescendo to your throne.
See and hear us through the blood of your Son, Jesus. **Amen.**

3    Lord, you saw the wheel in your mind
before we saw it roll on your good earth.
You put iron in the bowels of your earth
and imagined the great girders
that would hold up bridges over land and sea.
You heard the motor in your mind before we revved it up on our roads.
You saw the computer chip before we harnessed it in our offices
and the laser before we discovered how to use it
for blasting mines or for performing delicate surgery.
Now bless our hands as we manipulate the machines we have made.
Teach us how to use them wisely so that we will not be used by them.
Bless our grinding and polishing, our honing and hammering.
Let our demands for precise and careful work be as rigorous as yours
so that we may rest as safely in our cars and planes as in your arms.
Help us in all this, Lord, with joy and thanks,

to see your upholding hand, great creator of metal and mountain,
master artist of sunset and rainbow.
May we not sit on foam rubber without feeling your grace
or read by a lightbulb without feeling a current of thankfulness
for your marvelous creation running through our veins.
Hear our prayer for your Son's sake. **Amen.**

4    God of beauty and of justice,
we pray for the earth—
for restoration of soil, air, and water.
We pray for all people you have created—
for restoration of dignity and hope.
We pray for our nation and community—
for restoration of our sense of responsibility in service.
We pray even for ourselves—
for restoration of our resolve to love you and the world you made.
Through Christ, our Lord. **Amen.**

5    The heavens declare your glory, great God.
Thank you for the works of your hands,
for the moon and the stars,
for the birds in the sky, and the fish in the sea.
Thank you for crowning us with glory and honor
and for making us rulers over the works of your hands.
Help us to care for your creation.
May we respect the land and animals
as we use resources carefully and gratefully.
Thank you too, God our Father, for creating humanity in your image,
for knitting us together in our mother's wombs.
Thank you for knowing us so intimately
that you know when a hair falls from our heads.
May our love for others reflect your love for us.
Help us to feed the hungry, shelter the homeless,
support the sick, and comfort the lonely. In Jesus' name, **Amen.**

*Prayers in Litany Form*

6    For the earth and the gift of good land,
**we give thanks, O Lord.**
For the anticipation of a new growing season,
**we give thanks, O Lord.**
For those who labor on the farm and in the marketplace,
**we give thanks, O Lord.**
For the abundance of food and the opportunities to share,
**we give thanks, O Lord.**
For the delight of eating and the challenge of self-denial,
**we give thanks, O Lord.**

O God, our help, we lift up our hearts for the needs of your people:
to those who continue to be burdened with financial problems,
**give strength, O Lord.**
To those who have lost their land or livelihood,
who have experienced the pain of displacement,
**give hope, O Lord.**
To those serving people who are troubled and discouraged,
**give wisdom, O Lord.**
To those who are strong and have prospered,
**give humility, O Lord.**
To those seeking to be open to your gifts and calling,
**give us grace to be patient in suffering**
**and sensitive to the pain of others.**
**Help us to be faithful to that which you have committed to us**
**so that we may realize your kingdom where we are.**
**Through Jesus Christ, who taught us to pray,**
**saying, "Our Father . . ."**

# A.9 CLOSING OF WORSHIP

## A.9.1 Sending (see also section 9.1)

*Closing Prayers*

1    *A prayer especially mindful of children*

God, our creator,
thank you for all that you have made,
and help us remember every day
always to take care of your world
for Jesus' sake. **Amen.**

## A.9.2 Blessing/Benediction (see also section 9.2)

1    May God, the Father of our Lord Jesus Christ,
who is the source of all goodness and growth,
pour his blessing upon all things created,
and upon you, his children,
that you may use them to his glory and the welfare of all peoples.

# A.10 SUGGESTED SCRIPTURE READINGS

**1**  *Creation as the work of Father, Son, and Holy Spirit*

Genesis 1-2: God created, and it was good
Proverbs 8:12-13: The wisdom of God in the beginning
Colossians 1:15-19: All things were created through the Son
John 1:1-4: The Word at creation
Psalm 104: The Spirit in creation

**2**  *Hymns of praise about creation*

Psalm 8: How majestic is God's name in all the earth
Psalm 19: The heavens declare the glory of God
Psalm 24: The earth is the LORD's, and everything in it
Psalm 65: The earth is filled with awe at God's wonders
Psalm 96: Sing to the LORD, all the earth
Psalm 148: All creation sings praise

**3**  *Creation care*

Genesis 2:15-18: Naming the animals
Genesis 9:9-10: Covenant with Noah and every living creature
Psalm 65: God cares for the land
2 Chronicles 7:13-14: God will heal the land
Romans 8:19-23: Hope for glory

**4**  *God will provide*

Job 12:7-16: God is in control

**5**  *In the beginning*

Genesis 1: In the beginning God created
Psalm 102:24-28: In the beginning God laid the foundations
Proverbs 8:22-31: In the beginning was Wisdom
Isaiah 40:21-31: In the beginning was the Creator
John 1:1-5: In the beginning was the Word
Colossians 1:15-19: In the beginning was Christ, the firstborn
1 John 1: In the beginning was the Word of Life
Revelation 21:1-8: The beginning and the end

# SECTION B

# PROVIDENCE

The God who created the world is not absent from it; God remains actively and covenantally engaged with creation. The church professes that God "still upholds and rules" the creation by his eternal providence (Heidelberg Catechism, Q&A 26). God's involvement in creation includes the power of preservation, by which he holds all created things in existence, and the power of supervision, by which God guides all people and events to the purposes he has intended.

This profession leads naturally to two responses, both of which need to be expressed in worship. First, God's providence inspires our gratitude. We give thanks that God is on the throne, holding our world in his hands. We bless and thank God for all the good gifts given to us and to all creation. Second, God's providence calls for our trust and confidence. Even in times of suffer-

ing, disappointment, and tragedy, we can be patient and trust that God still guides all things, though we may not always perceive God's purposes. Both thanks and trust may be expressed in worship by means of songs, professions, prayers, offerings, and more.

These themes of thanksgiving and trust are especially appropriate for times of new beginnings, such as the marking of a new calendar or church year.

---

**Scriptures and Statements of Faith Applying to the Theme of Providence**

*The following texts are particularly appropriate for sermons or for supplemental liturgical use.*

| | | |
|---|---|---|
| Genesis 9:8-17 | Psalm 104 | Acts 14:8-18 |
| Genesis 45:1-20 | Psalm 107 | 2 Corinthians 9:8-15 |
| Job 38-42 | Psalm 147:1-11 | Ephesians 1:1-14 |
| Psalm 69:30-36 | Matthew 6:25-34 | Philippians 4:4-7 |
| Psalm 103 | John 6:5-14, 35, 48-51 | 1 Timothy 2:1-4 |

Belgic Confession, Art. 13
Heidelberg Catechism, Q&A's 1, 27-28
Westminster Confession, Chap. V, Sec. 1-7
*Our World Belongs to God*, st. 4-5, 12

---

# B.1 OPENING OF WORSHIP

---

## B.1.2 Call to Worship (see also section 1.2)

1    Bless the LORD, O my soul,
       and all that is within me,
       bless his holy name.
    Bless the LORD, O my soul,
       and do not forget all his benefits—
    who forgives all your iniquity,
       who heals all your diseases,
    who redeems your life from the Pit,
       who crowns you with steadfast love and mercy,
    who satisfies you with good as long as you live
       so that your youth is renewed like the eagle's.
       —Psalm 103:1-5, NRSV

2    O give thanks to the LORD, for he is good;
       for his steadfast love endures forever.
    Let the redeemed of the LORD say so,
       those he redeemed from trouble
    and gathered in from the lands,
       from the east and from the west,

from the north and from the south.
Some wandered in desert wastes,
    finding no way to an inhabited town;
hungry and thirsty,
    their soul fainted within them.
Then they cried to the LORD in their trouble,
    and he delivered them from their distress;
he led them by a straight way,
    until they reached an inhabited town.
**Let them thank the LORD for his steadfast love,**
    **for his wonderful works to humankind.**
**For he satisfies the thirsty,**
    **and the hungry he fills with good things.**
    —Psalm 107:1-9, NRSV

**3**    *A call to worship especially mindful of children*

God makes the sun rise and set.
**He is faithful from generation to generation.**
God makes summer and winter come and go.
**He is faithful from generation to generation.**
God helps plants grow and flowers bloom.
**He is faithful from generation to generation.**
God gives us food to eat, places to live, and people to love us.
**He is faithful from generation to generation.**
God is always with us.
**He is faithful from generation to generation.**
God keeps his promises to us.
**He is faithful from generation to generation.**
Let us praise our faithful God.

## B.1.4 Opening Responses (see also section 1.4)

*Prayers of Adoration*

**1**    Loving God,
    you created heaven and earth out of nothing.
    You uphold and rule heaven and earth
    by your eternal counsel and providence.
    We give you praise, almighty God.

God of eternity,
    you not only created each of us,
    but you sustain and form each of us
    with your Holy Spirit.
    We worship you, Creator God.

You provide whatever we need for body and soul.
You guide us and guard us.

We trust in you, God, our Maker; Jesus, our Mediator;
Holy Spirit, our Comforter.

As we turn toward the promise of a new year,
allow us to look back and to look ahead,
to see the places in the past
where your promises have upheld us,
and to look to an unknown future
with confidence and trust in you.
In the strong name of Christ we pray. **Amen.**

## Additional Resources

2    Almighty and ever present God,
     you uphold heaven and earth and all creatures.
     All things come from your generous hand:
     You send the nourishing rain, the refreshing wind,
     the warming sun, the blustering snow.
     You make buds appear, flowers bloom,
     fruit grow, and harvests mature.
     Through each day of our lives,
     whether in sickness or health,
     prosperity or poverty, joy or sorrow,
     you are in control.
     Help us to be patient when things go against us,
     thankful when things go well,
     and always confident that nothing
     could ever separate us from your love.
     For your unending faithfulness, we thank and praise you.
     To you be glory, now and forever. **Amen.**
          —based on Heidelberg Catechism, Q&A's 27-28

3    God of new beginnings,
     you wipe away our tears
     and call us to care for one another.
     Give us eyes to see your gifts,
     hearts to embrace all creation,
     and hands to serve you every day of our lives.
     We ask this in the name of Jesus. **Amen.**

4    God of our life, through all the circling years, we trust in you.
     In all the past, through all our hopes and fears, your hand we see.
     **With each new day, when morning lifts the veil,**
     **we own your mercies, Lord, which never fail.**

God of the past, our times are in your hand; with us abide.
Lead us by faith to hope's true promised land; be now our guide.
**With you to bless, the darkness shines as light,**
**and faith's fair vision changes into sight.**

God of the coming years, through paths unknown we follow you.
When we are strong, Lord, leave us not alone; our refuge be.
**Be for us in life our daily bread,**
**our heart's true home when all our years have sped. Amen.**

5    For all the possibilities ahead in this new year,
     make us thankful, O Lord.
     Give us wisdom, courage, and discernment
     in the face of so much chaos, despair, and fear.
     Help us to see how, in our circumstances,
     we can contribute toward peace, faith, and love.
     And give us the will to translate our desires into action. **Amen.**

# B.2 CONFESSION AND ASSURANCE

**B.2.2 Prayers of Confession** (see also section 2.2)

1    As we draw to the close of this year
     and claim the year ahead, our Father,
     we need to confess to you those pieces of the past
     that persist in pulling us backward.
     Through admitting our failures and sharing our sin,
     we would like to put away those things
     that nibble and nag, de-energize and depress.
     With boldness, then, and a certain measure of embarrassment,
     we admit to squandering time and talent,
     good intentions and better ideas,
     opportunities for growth and occasions for grace.
     We admit that we have most often taken care of ourselves
     while others have stood in line.
     We have defined our interests carefully and our goals precisely,
     using energy and expertise gainfully
     to the detriment of family, friends, community, and church.

We agonize with memories that sit heavily
and images that cause us to blush
and ask that you would grant us your forgiveness
as we confess our individual regrets and remorse in silence. . . .
Through Jesus Christ, our Lord, **Amen.**

2    *A prayer especially mindful of children*

Loving Father, we confess that
sometimes we think we can do things all by ourselves
and sometimes we are worried about things.
We forget that you give us everything we have
and that you make us who we are.
Please forgive us for thinking about ourselves first.
Please forgive us for not trusting you to take care of us.
Thank you for always loving us
even when we forget that we need you.
In Jesus' name, **Amen.**

## B.2.4 Assurance of Pardon (see also section 2.4)

1    The LORD works vindication
        and justice for all who are oppressed.
He made known his ways to Moses,
        his acts to the people of Israel.
The LORD is merciful and gracious,
        slow to anger and abounding in steadfast love.
**He will not always accuse,**
        **nor will he keep his anger forever.**
**He does not deal with us according to our sins,**
        **nor repay us according to our iniquities.**
For as the heavens are high above the earth,
        so great is his steadfast love toward those who fear him;
**as far as the east is from the west,**
        **so far he removes our transgressions from us.**
As a father has compassion for his children,
        so the LORD has compassion for those who fear him.
**For he knows how we were made;**
        **he remembers that we are dust.**
As for mortals, their days are like grass;
        they flourish like a flower of the field;
for the wind passes over it, and it is gone,
        and its place knows it no more.

But the steadfast love of the LORD is from everlasting
      to everlasting
  on those who fear him,
    and his righteousness to children's children,
to those who keep his covenant
    and remember to do his commandments.
      —Psalm 103:6-18, NRSV

# B.4 PRAYERS OF THE PEOPLE

## B.4.4 Complete Model Outlines and Prayers (see also section 4.4)

*Prayer Outlines*

1    *The following is a guide for extemporaneous prayers. The pattern provides a suggested text for the opening and closing of each part of the prayer and calls for extemporaneous prayers of thanksgiving, petition, and intercession.*

Lord of heaven and earth,
we praise and thank you for upholding and ruling all creation
by your eternal providence:
    for your sustaining hand in creation . . .
    for providing leaders in government . . .
    for church leaders . . .
    for the way in which you have worked in this church . . .
    for the riches you have lavished upon each one of us . . .
    and for the great gift of your Son, through whom we are redeemed.

As our sovereign God holding our world and our lives in your hands,
we intercede on behalf of
    the nations of the world . . .
    those whom you have put in government . . .
    our community and those who serve in it . . .
    your church, that it may expand your kingdom, especially in . . .
We ask that your powerful hands may be evident in the lives of . . .
And in all circumstances may we have the faith
to hold on to your promise that you will work things out for our good,
even when we see no good.

We pray this in the name of the Father, Son, and Holy Spirit, one God,
to whom belongs the kingdom, the power, and the glory forever. **Amen.**

*Prayers in Litany Form*

**2**    Eternal God,
a thousand years in your sight are but as yesterday.
They pass as quickly as one night's watch.
Whatever the significance of this new year,
yesterday morning was the same as the dawning of every day
since you first created life and light and proclaimed it all "very good."
We acknowledge your lordship over the world you have made
and over the creatures you have placed in it.
We acknowledge your lordship over us—
feeble creatures who vainly strive to be masters of the universe
you made and over which you still rule.
We are very impressed with our technology—
indeed, it is very impressive—
but our inventions are made with the brains and skills
and the knowledge and zeal that you impart.
As we move further into this new year,
we affirm with confidence your lordship in the future,
based on our conviction that you have been Lord from the beginning.
We are sure of nothing as we face the future,
except that you remain Lord of the world
that you created and that you still love.
**You have filled us with the light of your Word,**
**made flesh in Jesus Christ.**
**Let the light of faith shine in all we do,**
**that the one who is from everlasting to everlasting—**
**yet who was born among us and lived with us—**
**may continue to inspire the thoughts of our hearts**
**and the actions of our lives.**

As you have led us in days past, so guide us now and always,
that our hearts may learn to choose your will
and our new resolves be strengthened.
Help us to face the future with confidence,
knowing that you have guided and led your people through the eons past,
and knowing also that you are a personal God,
concerned not just with the mighty forces of wind and weather
and of the destiny and fate of nations
but also with the joys and sorrows that characterize our lives.
**You have filled us with the light of your Word,**
**made flesh in Jesus Christ.**
**Let the light of faith shine in all that we do,**
**that the one who is from everlasting to everlasting—**
**yet who was born among us and lived with us—**
**may continue to inspire the thoughts of our hearts**
**and the actions of our lives.**

Bless especially this day those who are in need:

the people we do not know, whose hope for the future
is not buoyed by the experience of blessing in the past,
who have not known healing, or faith, or prosperity,
and who have no hope.
Bless also those known to us who need
to sense your healing presence today—
especially [*name(s)*] and others whom we name silently.
You have been our God in ages past,
and we know that you will continue to be our God in years to come.
So wrap us in your arms of love,
as together at the beginning of this new day, this new year,
we join in the church's ancient prayer: **Our Father . . .**

# B.5 OFFERING

## B.5.2 Offering Prayers (see also section 5.2)

1    *A prayer especially mindful of children*

Lord,
you have given us so many gifts in the past year.
We thank you for watching over us and guiding us.
Thank you for your faithfulness
and for promising never to leave us.
Now we offer to you what you have given us;
use us and our gifts to help others know about you
for Jesus' sake. **Amen.**

2    Generous God, each moment is a gift from you.
You give us all that we have.
In gratitude, we offer our time, talents, and tithes.
May they bless others as we have been blessed.
In Jesus' name we pray. **Amen.**

# B.9 CLOSING OF WORSHIP

**B.9.1 Sending** (see also section 9.1)

*Closing Prayers*

1   Lord of time and new beginnings,
    give us good judgment to know what new things to do for you this year,
    and grant us the inner strength to finish each job we begin;
    so may we fully know the joy of doing your will;
    so may your kingdom come on earth—
    through Jesus Christ, our Lord. **Amen.**

2   Eternal God, as we leave this place, guide our feet.
    As our steps take us into an unknown future,
    give us confidence in your faithfulness.
    Help us see opportunities to serve and to love.
    Support us with your love
    so that we can work with you and rest in you. **Amen.**

3   Covenant God, your Word tells us of your faithfulness in the lives of your people,
    and we have seen your faithfulness in our lives.
    May we confidently live in the peace and hope that come from being your children
    so that we may share your love with others. For Jesus' sake, **Amen.**

# B.10 SUGGESTED SCRIPTURE READINGS

1   *Testimonies about God's providence*

    Genesis 24: Finding Rebekah
    Genesis 45:1-11; 50:19-21: Through Joseph, God provides food in famine
    Deuteronomy 8:1-18: God's leading in the wilderness
    1 Samuel 2:1-10: Hannah's song
    Psalm 31: Our times are in God's hands
    Psalm 121: The LORD watches over us
    Job 12: God's sovereign providence over every nation
    Matthew 6:25-33: Do not worry

# THANKSGIVING

When Israel was preparing for a new life in the promised land, God gave them the instruction, "Celebrate the Feast of Harvest with the firstfruits of the crops you sow in your field" (Ex. 23:16). Thanksgiving celebrations were an important part of the people's worship before God. Throughout history, worshiping communities have set aside certain times and days as events of special thanksgiving to God. These events are an acknowledgment that God, as creator, is also the provider of all the bounty of life.

In addition, churches are encouraged to schedule multiple times of thankful worship as determined by their experiences. When special blessings are experi-

enced, when fervent prayers have been answered, when times of prosperity come, or when God has led and protected through times of trial or uncertainty, the church does well to gather in thankful worship before God.

---

**Scriptures and Statements of Faith Applying
to the Theme of Thanksgiving**

*The following texts are particularly appropriate for sermons or for supplemental liturgical use.*

| | | |
|---|---|---|
| Exodus 15:1-21 | Psalm 116:1-7, 12-19 | Colossians 2:6-7 |
| Deuteronomy 8:3-20 | Psalm 145:13-21 | Colossians 4:2 |
| Psalm 95:1-5 | Jonah 2:7-9 | 1 Timothy 4:4 |
| Psalm 100 | Luke 17:11-19 | |

Heidelberg Catechism, Q&A's 86, 116
Canons of Dort, Pt. III/IV, Art. 15
*Our World Belongs to God*, st. 6, 44

---

# C.1 OPENING OF WORSHIP

---

**C.1.2 Call to Worship** (see also section 1.2)

1   Let the nations be glad and sing for joy,
         for you judge the peoples with equity
         and guide the nations upon earth.
     **Let all the peoples praise you, O God;**
         **let all the peoples praise you.**
     The earth has brought forth its increase;
         God, our God, has blessed us.
     **Let all the peoples praise you, O God;**
         **let all the peoples praise you.**
             —from Psalm 67:4-6, NRSV

2   Come, let us sing for joy to the LORD;
         **let us shout aloud to the Rock of our salvation.**
     Let us come before him with thanksgiving
         **and extol him with music and song.**
     For the LORD is the great God,
         **the great King above all gods.**
     In his hand are the depths of the earth,
         **and the mountain peaks belong to him.**

The sea is his, for he made it,
**and his hands formed the dry land.**
Come, let us bow down in worship,
**let us kneel before the LORD our Maker;**
for he is our God
**and we are the people of his pasture,**
**the flock under his care.**
—Psalm 95:1-7, NIV

3    *Young children are often taught to memorize Psalm 100. Consider inviting one or more children to recite it as a call to worship.*

Shout for joy to the LORD, all the earth.
    Worship the LORD with gladness;
    come before him with joyful songs.
Know that the LORD is God.
    It is he who made us, and we are his;
    we are his people, the sheep of his pasture.
Enter his gates with thanksgiving
    and his courts with praise;
    give thanks to him and praise his name.
For the LORD is good and his love endures forever;
    his faithfulness continues through all generations.
—Psalm 100, NIV

4    O give thanks to the LORD, call on his name,
**make known his deeds among the peoples.**
Sing to him, sing praises to him;
**tell of all his wonderful works.**
Glory in his holy name;
**let the hearts of those who seek the LORD rejoice.**
He is the LORD our God;
his judgments are in all the earth.
**He is mindful of his covenant forever,**
**of the word that he commanded,**
**for a thousand generations.**
—Psalm 105:1-3, 7-8, NRSV

5    All together now—applause for God!
    Sing songs to the tune of his glory,
    set glory to the rhythms of his praise.
Say of God, "We've never seen anything like him!"

Take a good look at God's wonders—
    they'll take your breath away.
He converted sea to dry land;
    travelers crossed the river on foot.
    Now isn't that cause for a song?

Bless our God, O peoples!
—Psalm 66:1-3, 5-6, 8, TM

**6**   Our help is in the name of our God,
who made heaven and earth. **Amen.**

Sing to the Lord with thanksgiving.
Make music upon the harp.
How good it is to celebrate God's presence
and sing praise throughout each day!
**How good it is to sing praise and give honor to our God!**

Our God rebuilds the people of earth.
The wandering ones are gathered together,
the brokenhearted are healed, the hungry are fed,
the prisoners are freed, the blind are given sight,
the lonely are befriended.
**How good it is to sing praise and give honor to our God!**

All of nature sings aloud the goodness of God—
clouds, rain, grass, creatures great and small.
Our God creates and sustains our world
with his ever-growing, never-ending love.
**How good it is to sing praise and give honor to our God!**

Grace and peace be yours in abundance
through the knowledge of God and of Christ Jesus, our Lord. **Amen.**
—based on Psalm 147; 2 Peter 1:2

## C.1.4 Opening Responses (see also section 1.4)

*Prayers of Adoration*

**1**   Father in heaven, we give you thanks for life
and for all of the experiences that life brings us.
We give you thanks for joy, hope, peace, and answered prayers,
but we also give you thanks in our trials, sorrows, and pain.
We give thanks for our land,
for the beauty of the landscape,
for the riches it provides for our living,
for the people and cultures among us.
Above all things, we give thanks for our hope in Christ,
the life and freedom that will ultimately be ours.
Teach us to cherish all your gifts.
Teach us also to use all these resources
for the good of society and for glory to you.
Through Jesus Christ, our Lord. **Amen.**

**2**   Great God, King of the universe,
dwelling beyond all worlds and stars
and yet intimately present to human hearts,
you who shine with purity and glory,

lighting up ranks of angels and archangels,
you give martyrs their comfort and saints their heavenly rest.
We praise and thank you.

Gracious God, lover of the world,
you are the one willing to suffer so that we might be healed,
willing to stoop to us in our misery,
so that we might stand tall as loved sons and daughters.
You have served us even when we were unwilling to serve you,
and longed for us even when we had ignored you.
Surely you are a surprising God
and a God of amazing grace.
We praise and thank you.

Nothing we do makes you seek us less;
nothing we do makes you seek us more.
You seek us with all the passion of a lover,
and so we praise and thank you. **Amen.**

3    Gracious God,
your heart abounds with goodness,
and your hand pours out abundance.
**We praise you for the continuous cycle
of seedtime and harvest
and the order of nature.
We bless you for the beauty of autumn
and its generous yield.
We thank you that you are mindful of us
and supply our needs.**
Accept our thanksgiving and our praise
for the cycle of life
and for all the joys of living. **Amen.**

4    *A prayer especially mindful of children*

Loving God,
you take care of all our needs
and love us more than we can imagine.
You have given us everything,
and we always need you.
Thank you for never leaving us.
Thank you for guiding us as we worship you
and for speaking to us through Jesus, our Lord. **Amen.**

*Prayers of Invocation*

5   Give us, our Father, a sense of your presence
    as we gather now for worship.
    Grant us gratitude as we remember your goodness,
    penitence as we remember our sins,
    and joy as we remember your love.
    Enable us to lift up our hearts
    in humble prayer and fervent praise,
    through Jesus Christ, our Lord. **Amen.**

6   Almighty God,
    Lord of heaven and earth,
    in you we live and move and have our being.
    You are the one who does good to all people,
    making your sun to rise on the evil and on the good
    and sending rain on the just and on the unjust.
    Favorably behold us your servants, who call upon your name,
    and send us your blessing from heaven, giving us fruitful seasons,
    and satisfy us with food and gladness.
    May both our hearts and our mouths be continually filled
    with your praise, giving thanks to you in your holy church,
    through Jesus Christ, our Lord. **Amen.**

7   Lord our God,
    love began with you
    and has filled our cup to overflowing.
    In the abundance of your countless gifts
    give us your grace to fill others' lives with love,
    that we may more nearly be worthy
    of all you have given us.
    We ask this in the name of Jesus, the Lord. **Amen.**

*Additional Resources*

8   *The response (in boldface) may be sung by the congregation, using the tune* KREMSER.

    Praise is due to you, O God, in Zion,
    and to you shall vows be performed.
    Happy are those whom you choose and bring near to live in your courts.
    We shall be satisfied with the goodness of your house, your holy temple.

    **We praise you, O God, our Redeemer, Creator;
    in grateful devotion our tribute we bring.
    We lay it before you, we kneel and adore you;
    we bless your holy name, glad praises we sing.**

By awesome deeds you answer us with deliverance,
O God of our salvation;
you are the hope of all the ends of the earth and of the farthest seas.
You silence the roaring of the seas, the crashing of their waves,
the tumult of the peoples.
Those who live at earth's farthest bounds are awed by your signs.

**We worship you, God of our fathers and mothers;**
**through life's storm and tempest our guide you have been.**
**When perils o'ertake us, you never forsake us.**
**And with your help, O Lord, our battles we win.**

You visit the earth and water it, you greatly enrich it;
the river of God is full of water.
You provide the people with grain, for so you have prepared it.
You crown the year with your bounty;
your wagon tracks overflow with riches.

**With voices united our praises we offer;**
**our songs of thanksgiving to you we now raise.**
**Your strong arm will guide us, our God is beside us.**
**To you, our great Redeemer, fore'er be praise!**
        —based on Psalm 65

9   Let us give thanks to the Lord,
    our rock, our fortress, and our deliverer.
    Let us remember his mercy, for he is gracious and compassionate.
    **We thank you for calling us to faith in Christ,**
    **for putting your Spirit within us,**
    **for giving us the mind of Christ,**
    **for gathering us into your church.**

    We thank you, Lord, for extending your grace to us,
    for calling us to a life of gratitude,
    for calling us to service in your kingdom.
    **Thanks be to God!**

    Let us give thanks to the Lord,
    for he satisfies the thirsty, he fills the hungry with good things,
    and he heals the afflicted. Let us celebrate his abundant goodness.
    **We thank you, gracious Father,**
    **that you provide for all our needs,**
    **for the food on our tables,**
    **for the clothes on our bodies,**
    **for the beds we sleep in,**
    **and for the dwellings that shelter us.**

    We praise you for all your gifts that go beyond our basic needs,
    for the things that make our work easier,
    for the conveniences of modern life,
    for the beauty and pleasure that you bring into our lives.
    **Thanks be to God! Amen.**

10 Let us give thanks to the Lord for the people he has given us.
For parents and grandparents, for sons and daughters,
for brothers and sisters, for husband and wife,
for all those who reflect to us the human dimension of your love,
**we give you thanks, O Lord.**
For neighbors and colleagues, for friends both far away and nearby—
for all those who share the joys and sorrows of our daily lives,
**we give you thanks, O Lord.**
For those who serve us in restaurants, in repair shops, in stores,
in schools, in hospitals—
for all those who make our lives more comfortable,
**we give you thanks, O Lord.**
For the family of God, for the church universal,
and for those who worship with us and minister to us in this church,
**we give you thanks, O Lord.**
For those who are weak and destitute,
for those who need protection and support,
for those who need healing and nurturing,
for all those to whom we minister,
**we give you thanks, O Lord. Amen.**

11 Great God of our lives,
for all that is gracious in our lives,
revealing the image of Christ,
**we give you thanks.**
For our daily food and drink,
our homes and families, and our friends,
**we give you thanks.**
For minds to think and hearts to love and hands to serve,
**we give you thanks.**
For health and strength to work, and leisure to rest and play,
**we give you thanks.**
For all valiant seekers after truth, liberty, and justice,
**we give you thanks.**
For the great mercies and promises given to us in Christ Jesus our Lord;
to you, O God, be praise and glory. **Amen.**

12 Gracious God,
for your creation and your care for it,
for your Son and our salvation,
for your Spirit and your care for us,
for your abundant, boundless gifts,
we thank you.
In Jesus' name, **Amen.**

# C.2 CONFESSION AND ASSURANCE

## C.2.2 Prayers of Confession (see also section 2.2)

1    Loving God, we gather today, rich in blessing,
     somehow believing that we merit the wealth and comforts we enjoy.
     Forgive us, our God, for comfortably closing our eyes
     to the faces of the poor that stare blankly in our direction.
     **Lord, have mercy on us.**
     With bellies full of grain and meat,
     we offer token gestures to the hungry in our world
     and we feel we have done enough.
     Forgive us, God, for keeping a distance between "us" and "them,"
     for closing our ears to the cries of the hungry.
     **Christ, have mercy on us.**
     With hands tightly clasping our treasures on earth,
     we cannot reach out to our oppressed brothers and sisters around this world.
     Forgive us for clinging to our own possessions rather than to you.
     Unite us with hearts of thanksgiving,
     that we may work to ensure freedom and justice for all.
     **Lord, have mercy on us.**

2    *A prayer especially mindful of children*

     Holy God, you have given us many good gifts.
     Today we thank you for all of them,
     but we also confess that sometimes
     we love those gifts more than we love you.
     We confess wanting more and more things:
     food, clothes, toys, and money.
     Forgive us for not being content and thankful.
     Forgive our selfishness.
     Help us to love you more than everything else.
     We pray in Jesus' name. **Amen.**

3    Almighty God, giver of every good and perfect gift,
     forgive us for ignoring your gifts, misusing your gifts,
     even abusing your gifts.
     We repent of our feelings of entitlement,
     of our lack of generosity, of our ingratitude.
     Forgive us, we pray, for Jesus' sake. **Amen.**

# C.4 Prayers of the People

**C.4.4 Complete Model Outlines and Prayers** (see also section 4.4)

*Prayer Outlines*

1 *The following is a guide for extemporaneous prayers. The pattern provides a suggested text for the opening and closing of each part of the prayer and calls for extemporaneous prayers of thanksgiving, petition, and intercession.*

> God of all good gifts,
> we come before you today with praise in our hearts
> and thanksgiving on our lips.
> We thank you for
>> the creation and the wonders of this world, especially . . .
>> our nation . . .
>> the community . . .
>> our work . . .
>> opportunities to learn . . .
>> this church . . .
>> the riches of our lives . . .
>> and the greatest gift of all, given through your Son,
>> our Savior and Redeemer.
>
> Knowing that you desire to bless us with all good things,
> we offer these intercessions:
>> for [*world events*] . . .
>> for the nations of the world . . .
>> for this nation and our government . . .
>> for our community and those in authority over it . . .
>> for the church universal, its mission, and those who minister . . .
>> for the churches of this community . . .
>> for our church in its ministry to . . .
>> for persons whom we know with particular needs, especially . . .
>
> We pray this in the name of the triune God,
> Father, Son, and Holy Spirit,
> to whom all thanks and praise are due. **Amen.**

*Complete Prose Prayers*

2 Almighty God,
> do take care of all our physical needs
> so that we come to know
> that you are the only source of everything good

and that neither our work and worry
nor your gifts can do us any good without your blessing.
And so help us to give up our trust in creatures
and trust in you alone.
Through Jesus Christ, our Lord. **Amen.**

—from Heidelberg Catechism, Q&A 125

3  Loving God:
**Thank you for our eyes.**
Teach us to see your world
and each other as you do;
give us eyes of compassion
and love for each other and for your world.
**Thank you for our ears.**
Make us quick to listen to what you are saying to us,
and also quick to listen to each other.
**Thank you for our minds.**
Help us to develop the mind of Christ;
we ask for your wisdom as we make decisions.
**Thank you for our voices.**
May we always speak the truth in love
and sing your praises with joy. **Amen.**

4  We thank you, God, for this amazing day;
for the true dream of a cloud-filled sky,
for the cool embrace of a comforting breeze,
for everything that is natural,
everything that is alive,
everything that is part of your dynamic creation.

We thank you, God,
for the phenomenon that we know as life.
We experience life as joy at the birth of a child;
as love when we find others who share with us;
as exhilaration of victory in sporting events,
    academic debate, business ventures;
as fulfilling satisfaction when we achieve;
as confusion and disappointment when others fail us;
as anxiety and pain when illness intervenes;
as fear and hurt when death takes someone we love.

We acknowledge the complex rhythms
that make life different for each of us,
but we are brought together by a community of faith
that interweaves us with one another,
individuals bound by a common purpose
and circles of concern.

We give thanks for this spirit of humanity.
In all we do and experience, O God,
teach us first to love, for love is most precious.
Love knows no limit to its endurance,
no end to its trust, no fading of its hope.
It outlasts anything, and it stands when all else has fallen.

When we love, it is easier to speak;
it is easier to listen;
it is easier to play;
it is easier to work;
it is easier to cry;
it is easier to laugh.

Teach us that love is the truest of all seasons;
give us the desire and willingness to share its beauty.
Teach us that of all the music of this earth,
that which reaches the farthest into heaven
is the beating of a loving heart.

Now, O God, in the quiet of this moment,
we pray for a reawakening of our senses to this day.
Open our minds to all that is ours—
to imagination, to understanding,
to a sense of peace, to constant singing.
And when this day is done,
give us hope for another day,
to experience your enduring love.
For all that we are, this is our prayer. **Amen.**

—based on 1 Corinthians 13

5    Mighty God of mercy,
we thank you for the resurrection dawn,
bringing the glory of our risen Lord, who makes every day new.
Especially we thank you for
    the beauty of your creation . . .
    the new creation in Christ and all gifts of healing and forgiveness . . .
    the sustaining love of family and friends . . .
    the fellowship of faith in your church . . .
Merciful God of might,
renew this weary world, heal the hurts of all your children,
and bring about your peace for all in Christ Jesus, the living Lord.
Especially we pray for
    those who govern nations of the world . . .
    the people of countries where there is strife or warfare . . .
    all who work for peace and international harmony . . .
    the church of Jesus Christ in every land . . .
**Amen.**

6    Almighty God,
thank you for the intricate
life-sustaining world you created.
Make us good caregivers.
Help us share the wealth of resources
that you lavishly share with us.
Thank you for the salvation made possible to us
through the life, death,
and resurrection of our Lord Jesus Christ.
Following our Lord's example,
help us love the unloved and serve the lowly.
Thank you for the gifts of your Holy Spirit:
the comfort, the encouragement, and the formation
that we experience as evidence of the Spirit in us.
Grow in us an unquenchable desire for you.
Transform us. Make us new in you.
May we daily grow to be more like you.
In Jesus' name we pray. **Amen.**

7    Almighty and merciful God,
from whom comes all that is good,
we praise you for all your mercies:
     for your goodness that has created us,
     your grace that has sustained us,
     your wisdom that has challenged us,
     your patience that has borne with us,
     and your love that has redeemed us.
Help us to love you and all your children
and to be thankful for all your gifts,
by serving you and delighting to do your will.
In Jesus' name we pray. **Amen.**

8    God, giver of all good,
you continually pour your benefits upon us.
Age after age the living wait upon you and find
     that your faithfulness has no end,
     that your care is unfailing.
We praise you that the mystery of life
is a mystery of infinite goodness.
We praise you
     for the order and constancy of nature,
     for the beauty and bounty of the earth,
     for day and night, summer and winter,
     seedtime and harvest,
     for the varied gifts of loveliness that every season brings.
We give you thanks
     for all the comfort and joy of life,
     for our homes, for our friends,
     and for all the love, sympathy, and goodwill of all people.
**Amen.**

*Prayers in Litany Form*

**9**   Give thanks to the Lord, who is good.
**God's love is everlasting.**
Come, let us praise God joyfully.
**Let us come to God with thanksgiving.**

For the good world:
for things great and small, beautiful and awesome,
for seen and unseen splendors,
**thank you, God.**

For human life:
for talking and moving and thinking together,
for common hopes and hardships shared from birth until our dying,
**thank you, God.**

For work to do and strength to work:
for the comradeship of labor,
for exchanges of good humor and encouragement,
**thank you, God.**

For marriage:
for the mystery and joy of flesh made one,
for mutual forgiveness and burdens shared,
for secrets kept in love,
**thank you, God.**

For family:
for living together and eating together,
for family amusements and family pleasures,
**thank you, God.**

For children:
for their energy and curiosity,
for their brave play and startling frankness,
for their sudden sympathies,
**thank you, God.**

For the young:
for their high hopes,
for their irreverence toward worn-out values,
for their search for freedom,
for their solemn vows,
**thank you, God.**

For growing up and growing old:
for wisdom deepened by experience,
for rest in leisure,
for time made precious by its passing,
**thank you, God.**

For your help in times of doubt and sorrow:
for healing our diseases,
for preserving us in temptation and danger,
**thank you, God.**

For the church into which we have been called:
for the good news we receive by Word and sacrament,
for our life together in the Lord,
**we praise you, God.**

For your Holy Spirit,
who guides our steps and brings us gifts of faith and love,
who prays in us and prompts our grateful worship,
**we praise you, God.**

For your Son Jesus Christ,
who lived and died and lives again for our salvation:
for our hope in him,
for the joy of serving him,
**we thank and praise you, eternal God,**
**for all your goodness to us.**
Give thanks to the Lord, who is good.
**God's love is everlasting. Amen.**

10  **Make a joyful noise to the Lord, all the lands!**
　　　**Serve the Lord with gladness!**
　　　**Come into his presence with singing!**

For all the times we laughed till our sides ached;
for all the times we were troubled
　　and friends we didn't know we had
　　sprang up from nowhere and ministered to us;
for all the times we could have chosen evil over good, but didn't;
for all the times we could have been hurt, but weren't;
for all the times we could have died suddenly and unprepared, but didn't.
O Lord, we thank you.

**Know that the Lord is God!**
　　　**It is he that made us, and we are his;**
　　　**we are his people, and the sheep of his pasture.**

For the sheer wonder of our creation, preservation, and redemption;
for the privilege of prayer, the gift of the Spirit, and the gifts of the Spirit;
for the everlasting arms beneath us,
　　the watchful eye above us,
　　the friends around us,
　　and the trust within us;
O Lord, we thank you.

**Enter his gates with thanksgiving,**
　　　**and his courts with praise!**
　　　**Give thanks to him, bless his name!**

For our churches,
    and all things good and godly they have done and been;
for all their saints whom we have laid to rest;
and for their little children,
    who shall one day lay our bodies to rest
    and carry on in our stead;
O Lord, we thank you.

**For the Lord is good.**

For seedtime and harvest and food enough;
for every good night's sleep and every good day's work;
for every good friend and every grand sunset;
for warm memories of the past
    and the promise of an eternal tomorrow;
for eyes to see beauty,
    ears to hear a bird's songs,
    hands to hold someone else's hands,
    and someone else's hands to hold;
O Lord, we thank you.

**His steadfast love endures forever
and his faithfulness to all generations.**

For all persons whose love for us is unconditional,
    and in whose presence we can drop all pretense,
    be ourselves,
    and know that we shall be accepted;
for the one who calls us long distance
    and the one who calls us darling,
    and the one who calls us Dad or Mom;
for the one who shall one day call us into eternity;
O Lord, we thank you.

**What shall we render to the Lord for all his bounty to us?**
We will offer to him the sacrifice of thanksgiving. **Amen.**
      —based on Psalm 100; 116:12, 17

11   Gracious God,
    you supply us with blessings beyond our deserving.
    We thank you for your creation
        and every sign of your presence within it,
    for your everlasting grace and forgiveness,
    for the risen Lord, who has gone before us
        and calls us to follow him.
    **We thank and praise you, O Lord our God.**
    For our homes and our loved ones,
    for work to do, and strength to do it,
    for moments of gladness that sparkle our day,
    **we thank and praise you, O Lord our God.**

For our faith and all that sustains it,
for all whose lives and examples have persuaded us
    that the journey is worth the taking,
for your caring discipline that keeps our faith pure,
**we thank and praise you, O Lord our God.**
For the depths of the sea where our falseness lies buried,
for the guiding comfort of your Holy Spirit,
for the powerful promise of life everlasting,
**we thank and praise you, O Lord our God,**
**for yours is the glory forever. Amen.**

12   Let us give thanks to God our Creator
for all the blessings we share this day.
For all of those who have gone before, people strong and brave,
willing to put their lives on the line for the causes they believe in,
we give you thanks.
**Grant us, our God, the courage**
**to step out in faith for that which is true and right.**

For freedom of speech and of the press,
for the avenues open to expressing ourselves,
for opportunities to effect change,
we give you thanks.
**We pray for those who are voiceless victims of unjust governments.**

For fertile soil, abundant rain, and seasons of refreshment,
we give you thanks.
**We pray for those whose land is parched and whose wells are dry.**

For our families, friends, and the church,
who provide us with food and drink for our journey,
we give you thanks.
**We pray for those who are hungry and tired,**
**hopeless and wandering, finding no place to rest.**

For strong bodies and minds,
for opportunities that encourage us to grow
and become more the servants of thanksgiving you call us to be,
we give you thanks.
**We pray for the sick,**
**as well as for the stagnant who are unwilling to dream or change.**

Help us, O God, to be responsible stewards of your blessings,
people who care for the earth and all its people.
Keep us connected with all humanity,
even though miles and cultures tend to separate us.
**May we always respond to your call**
**with a true spirit of thanksgiving. Amen.**

**13**   Give thanks to God, all the earth; praise God's holy name.
Let us give thanks to God
for ballot boxes, newspaper editorials, and open borders,
**for all the freedoms we enjoy.**
Let us give thanks to God for diplomats, treaties, and compromise,
**for peace in a world of war.**

Let us give thanks to God
for police officers, streetlights, and concerned neighbors,
**for safety from fear and harm.**
**Give thanks to God, all the earth; praise God's holy name.**

Let us give thanks to God for St. Paul and St. Priscilla,
St. Francis and St. Claire, Martin Luther,
Martin Luther King, and Mother Teresa,
**for all Christians who ran the race before us.**
Let us give thanks to God for the Scriptures,
for creeds and confessions,
for the songs and hymns of God's people,
**for all good things in our heritage of faith.**
Let us give thanks to God for a good creation,
a redeeming Son, and a transforming Spirit,
**for all the benefits of our salvation.**
**Give thanks to God, all the earth; praise God's holy name.**

Let us give thanks to God for purple and orange sunsets,
bright red flowers, great gray elephants, and the vast blackness of space,
**for all the wonders, God, of your creative mind.**
Let us give thanks to God for Mozart, Michelangelo, and Milton,
for pianos, paintbrushes, and pencils,
**for all the wonders of our creative minds, made in your image, O Lord.**
**Give thanks to God, all the earth; praise God's holy name.**

Let us give thanks to God for Thanksgiving turkey,
mashed potatoes, cranberry sauce, and pumpkin pie,
**for the abundance of food that sustains our bodies.**
Let us give thanks to God for soft beds, warm fires,
familiar chairs, and open windows,
**for the abundant comfort of our homes.**
Let us give thanks to God for cars that run,
brand-new sneakers, and long, hot showers,
**for God's goodness that flows above and beyond our needs.**
**Give thanks to God, all the earth; praise God's holy name.**

Let us give thanks to God for aggressive immune systems,
for running cross-country, and for sound sleep,
**for the strength and health of our bodies.**
Let us give thanks to God for crossword puzzles,
learning foreign languages, and plane geometry,
**for healthy, strong minds.**
**Give thanks to God, all the earth; praise God's holy name.**

Let us give thanks to God for pesky little brothers, wise grandmothers,
favorite uncles, and loving parents,
**for the families that shaped our lives.**
Let us give thanks to God for surprise phone calls,
funny birthday gifts, and long talks late at night,
**for friends who stick with us as the years go by.**
Let us give thanks to God for men and women
with dark skin and light skin, freckles and curls,
pug noses and beards, graceful limbs and ample laps,
**for all the beautiful diversity of people, all over the world,**
**who make up one family of God, bound together in Christ.**
**Give thanks to God, all the earth; praise God's holy name.**
**Give thanks to God, all the earth; praise God's holy name. Amen.**

14   Almighty God, we thank you for creating the universe,
for making us in your image as the crown of your creation,
for sending us your Son, Jesus, to reveal yourself to us,
and for preparing a place for us to live with you forever.
**Thank you, Christ, that you are before us and behind us.**

We thank you for giving us a world vast in resources,
for enabling us to explore your world and its cultures,
for making us part of your redemption story,
and for prodding us to reflect to you all the glory of your creation.
**Thank you, Christ, that you are beneath us and above us.**

We thank you for your mighty power that works salvation:
you called us to a life set apart for you,
you saved us from the corrupting ways of sin,
and you brought us new life through your Son, Jesus, the Messiah.
**Thank you, Christ, that you are on our right and on our left.**

We thank you that you've called us to be servant-leaders in your world,
to be your agents of reconciliation, comfort, and healing,
and to live your gospel in our work, play, and worship
through the power and guidance of your Holy Spirit.
**Thank you, Christ, that you are with us when we rest and when we rise.**

Lord God, we thank you for the gifts of your Holy Spirit
that enable us to love each other, to act justly and love mercy,
and to live with joy, kindness, and gentle patience.
May each moment bring you glory.
**Thank you, Christ, that you are in our hearts and in our minds.**

Thank you for giving us a vision for a renewed heaven and earth,
where tears of pain and terrors of death are no more,
where all sorrow and suffering will cease,
and where the redeemed of the Lord and all creation will praise you forever.
**Thank you, Christ, that you are in us and ever with us. Amen!**
    —based on a prayer attributed to St. Patrick (5th century)

15   Caring God,
       we thank you for your gifts in creation:
       for your world, the heavens that tell of your glory;
       for our land, its beauty and resources;
       for the rich heritage we enjoy.
       **We pray for those who make decisions about the resources of the earth,**
           **that we may use your gifts responsibly;**
       **for those who work on land and sea, in city and in industry,**
           **that all may enjoy the fruits of their labors**
           **and marvel at your creation;**
       **for artists, scientists, and visionaries,**
           **that through their work we may see creation afresh.**

       [*Silence*]

       We thank you for giving us life;
       for all who enrich our experience.
       **We pray for all who through their own or others' actions**
           **are deprived of fullness of life;**
       **for prisoners, refugees, those differently able, and all who are sick;**
       **for those in politics, medical science,**
           **social and relief work, and for your church;**
       **for all who seek to bring life to others.**

       [*Silence*]

       We thank you that you have called us to celebrate your creation.
       **Give us reverence for life in your world.**
       We thank you for your redeeming love;
       **may your Word and sacrament**
       **strengthen us to love as you love us.**

       [*Silence*]

       God, our Creator, bring us new life.
       Jesus, Redeemer, renew us.
       Holy Spirit, strengthen and guide us. **Amen.**

# C.5 OFFERING

## C.5.1 Invitations to the Offering (see also section 5.1)

1   He who supplies seed to the sower and bread for food
     will supply and multiply your seed for sowing
     and increase the harvest of your righteousness.

You will be enriched in every way for your great generosity,
which will produce thanksgiving to God through us;
for the rendering of this ministry not only supplies the needs of the saints
but also overflows with many thanksgivings to God.

**In joy, we offer our gifts now to God.**

—based on 2 Corinthians 9:10-11, NRSV

## C.5.2 Offering Prayers (see also section 5.2)

1    All good things come from you, O God,
and with gratitude we return to you what is yours.
You created all that is, and with love formed us in your image.
When our love failed, your love remained steadfast.
You gave your only Son, Jesus Christ, to be our Savior.
All that we are and all that we have
are a trust from you.
And so, in gratitude for all your gifts,
we offer you ourselves and all that we have,
in union with Christ's offering for us.
By your Holy Spirit make us one with Christ,
one with each other,
and one in ministry to all the world,
through Jesus Christ, our Savior. **Amen.**

# C.9 CLOSING OF WORSHIP

## C.9.1 Sending (see also section 9.1)

*Closing Prayers*

1    Almighty and gracious Father,
we give you thanks
for the fruits of the earth in their season,
and for the labors of those who harvest them.
Make us, we pray, faithful stewards of your great bounty,
in the provisions for our necessities
and the relief of all who are in need,
to the glory of your name,
through Jesus Christ, our Lord,
who lives and reigns with you and the Holy Spirit,
one God, now and forever. **Amen.**

### C.9.2 Blessing/Benediction (see also section 9.2)

1      May God the Creator fill you with gratitude for your creation.
       May God the Savior fill you with gratitude for your salvation.
       May God the Comforter fill you with gratitude for your new life.

2      Almighty God, the one who created the world and everything in it,
         the one who came to die for you, the one who lives within you,
       loves you now and always, will never leave you or forsake you,
       and holds you tight as you leave this place.
       With a grateful heart, go in peace.

3      May our great God, the source of all good things,
       shower you with his abundant blessings
       so that your hearts overflow with endless gratitude.

# C.10 SUGGESTED SCRIPTURE READINGS

1     *Psalms of thanksgiving*

       Psalm 95:1-7: Let us come before him with thanksgiving
       Psalm 100: Enter his gates with thanksgiving
       Psalm 107: Thanks for God's provision
       Psalm 136: Thanks for God's love and faithfulness
       Psalm 147: Thanks that God is in control

2     *Guide for grateful living*

       Acts 17:22-31: No other gods
       Isaiah 44:6-11: No idols
       Hebrews 13:15-19: Honor God's name
       Luke 6:1-11: Remember the Sabbath
       Ephesians 6:1-9: Honor your father and mother
       1 John 3: Do not murder
       John 8:4-11: Do not commit adultery
       Ephesians 4:17-32: Do not steal
       Colossians 3:1-17: Do not bear false witness
       Matthew 6:19-24: Do not covet

# SECTION D
# ADVENT

The great proclamation "The Word became flesh and made his dwelling among us" (John 1:14) assures us that God has entered into human history through the incarnation of the Son. The season of Advent, a season of waiting, is designed to cultivate our awareness of God's actions—past, present, and future. In Advent we hear the prophecies of the Messiah's coming as addressed to us— people who wait for the second coming. In Advent we heighten our anticipation for the ultimate fulfillment of all Old Testament promises, when the wolf will lie down with the lamb, death will be swallowed up, and every tear will be wiped away. In this way Advent highlights for us the larger story of God's redemptive plan.

A deliberate tension must be built into our practice of the Advent season. Christ has come, and yet not all things have reached completion. While we remember Israel's waiting and hoping and we give thanks for Christ's birth, we also anticipate his second coming at the end of time. For this reason Advent began as a penitential season, a time for discipline and intentional repentance in the confident expectation and hope of Christ's coming again.

The Advent season includes the four Sundays preceding Christmas. Worship on these

Sundays should be designed to help people see the tension between celebrating and hoping. Special attention should be given to visual displays in the worship space. The liturgical colors for Advent are purple and deep blue, and rough and coarse textures are common. An Advent wreath with four candles and a Christ candle can heighten the sense of anticipation. Many Scripture lessons also suggest other visual symbols to communicate the intent of the season.

## Scriptures and Statements of Faith Applying to the Theme of Advent

*The following texts are particularly appropriate for sermons or for supplemental liturgical use.*

| | | |
|---|---|---|
| Genesis 3:8-15 | Isaiah 12:2-6 | Luke 1 |
| Genesis 22:1-8 | Isaiah 35 | Luke 3:1-6 |
| Numbers 24:17 | Isaiah 40:1-11 | Luke 3:7-18 |
| 2 Samuel 7 | Isaiah 61:1-4, 8-11 | Luke 21:25-36 |
| Psalm 25 | Isaiah 64:1-9 | John 1:6-8, 19-28 |
| Psalm 40 | Jeremiah 23:5-6 | Romans 1:1-7 |
| Psalm 42 | Jeremiah 33:14-16 | Romans 13:11-14 |
| Psalm 72 | Micah 5:2-5 | Romans 15:4-13 |
| Psalm 80 | Zephaniah 3:14-20 | Romans 16:25-27 |
| Psalm 85 | Haggai 2:4-9 | 1 Corinthians 1:3-9 |
| Psalm 89 | Malachi 3:1-4 | Philippians 1:3-11 |
| Psalm 122 | Matthew 1:18-25 | Philippians 4:4-7 |
| Psalm 126 | Matthew 3:1-12 | 1 Thessalonians 3:9-13 |
| Psalm 146 | Matthew 11:2-11 | 1 Thessalonians 5:16-24 |
| Isaiah 2:1-5 | Matthew 24:36-44 | Hebrews 10:5-10 |
| Isaiah 7:10-16 | Mark 1:1-8 | James 5:7-10 |
| Isaiah 11:1-10 | Mark 13:24-37 | 2 Peter 3:8-15 |

Belgic Confession, Art. 10, 18
Heidelberg Catechism, Q&A's 29-36
Westminster Confession, Chap. VIII, Sec. 2
*Our Song of Hope,* st. 1-2
*Our World Belongs to God,* st. 5, 23

# D.1 Opening of Worship

**D.1.2 Call to Worship** (see also section 1.2)

1    In days to come
         the mountain of the LORD's house
     shall be established as the highest of the mountains,
         and shall be raised above the hills;
     all the nations shall stream to it.
         Many peoples shall come and say,
     **"Come, let us go up to the mountain of the LORD,**
         **to the house of the God of Jacob;**
     **that he may teach us his ways**
         **and that we may walk in his paths."**
     For out of Zion shall go forth instruction,
         and the word of the LORD from Jerusalem.
     He shall judge between the nations,
         and shall arbitrate for many peoples;
     they shall beat their swords into plowshares,
         and their spears into pruning hooks;
     nation shall not lift up sword against nation,
         neither shall they learn war any more.
     **O house of Jacob,**
         **come, let us walk in the light of the LORD!**
              —Isaiah 2:2-5, NRSV

2    A voice cries:
     "In the wilderness prepare the way of the Lord,
     make straight in the desert a highway for our God."
     As we worship today,
     let us prepare to welcome God's dramatic work in our midst,
     in our hearts, in our community, and in all of creation.
     Let us worship God.
              —based on Isaiah 40:3, NRSV

3    Blow the trumpet in Zion;
     sound the alarm on my holy hill.
     Let all who live in the land tremble,
     for the day of the Lord is coming.
     It is close at hand.
     Come, let us worship God.
              —based on Joel 2:1, NIV

429

4    You know what time it is,
     how it is now the moment for you to wake from sleep.
     For salvation is nearer to us now
     than when we became believers;
     the night is far gone, the day is near.
     Let us then lay aside the works of darkness
     and put on the armor of light.
     Come, let us worship God.
            —based on Romans 13:11-12, NRSV

5    Rejoice in the Lord always.
     **I will say it again: Rejoice!**
     Let your gentleness be evident to all.
     **The Lord is near.**
     We rejoice in the hope of Christ's coming.
     Let us worship God!
            —based on Philippians 4:4-5, NIV

6    I wait for the Lord, my soul waits,
     and in his Word I hope.
     My soul waits for the Lord
     more than those who watch for the morning.
     **There is no darkness with you, O Lord.**
     O Israel, hope in the Lord!
     For with the Lord there is steadfast love,
     and with him is plenteous redemption.
     **There is no darkness with you, O Lord.**
     Glory to the Father and to the Son and to the Holy Spirit.
     **There is no darkness with you, O Lord.**
            —based on Psalm 130:5-7

7    We gather in preparation
     **for good news is about to be proclaimed.**
     We gather in expectation
     **for joy is about to explode in our midst.**
     We gather in celebration
     **for we are those people who have said**
          **yes to the manger,**
          **yes to love enfleshed,**
          **yes to the one incarnate for others,**
          **yes to the wholeness of God.**
     With preparation and in expectation, let us celebrate!

8    The mighty God summons the earth
     from the rising of the sun to the place where it sets.
     **Our God comes and will not be silent.**
     **God calls, and we respond to his love.**
     The heavens declare God's righteousness.
     **We tell out God's glories!**

Offer up to God your thanksgiving.
**And our God will hear us, save us, and stay with us forever.**
—based on Psalm 50:1-3, 6

9   The Lord has done great things for us!
**And we are filled with joy!**
Our God has turned our weeping into singing,
**our tears into songs of joy!**
O Christ of God, come anew in our hearts this day,
**and remain in us forever.**
—based on Psalm 126

10   Our souls magnify the Lord!
**Our spirits rejoice in God our Savior!**
The mighty One has done great things for us!
**Holy is God's name!**
Let us worship God.
**For God is our Maker and our Redeemer;**
**from generation to generation God gives mercy.**
—based on Luke 1:46-50

11   Show us your unfailing love, O God, our Savior,
**and grant us your salvation.**
Listen to what the Lord our God says:
**He promises peace to his people,**
**who are his beloved saints.**
The Lord will indeed give what is good.
**Righteousness goes before him**
**and prepares the way for his steps.**
May the Lord make his holy face to shine upon us
in this time of Advent worship.
May we see God's face and so know peace. **Amen.**
—based on Psalm 85:7-13, NIV

12   The Lord whom you seek shall suddenly come to his temple;
the messenger of the covenant in whom you delight.
Behold, he is coming. Rejoice greatly! Shout in triumph!
**Our King is coming; the righteous Savior,**
**who shall speak peace to the nations.**

13   *A text especially mindful of children*

Let us praise our Lord Jesus Christ.
**Alleluia! Jesus is coming!**
At Christmas Jesus came as a baby.
**Alleluia! Jesus is coming!**
He came to be like us because he loves us.
**Alleluia! Jesus is coming!**
He came to save us from our sin.
**Alleluia! Jesus is coming!**

He died, rose from the dead, and lives in heaven.
He will come again because he loves us.
**Alleluia! Jesus is coming!**
We praise Jesus, who came as a baby
and will come again at the end of time.
**Alleluia! Jesus is coming!**

### D.1.3 Greeting (see also section 1.3)

1    The Lord be with you.
**And also with you.**
As we enter this season of Advent,
may the love of God the Father, and the grace of Jesus the Son,
and the fellowship of the Holy Spirit be and abide with us all.
**Amen!**

### D.1.4 Opening Responses (see also section 1.4)

*Along with prayers of adoration and invocation and additional resources, this section includes resources for Advent candle lighting (see p. 432).*

*Prayers of Adoration*

1    Lord God Almighty,
King of glory and love eternal,
you are worthy at all times to receive adoration, praise, and blessing;
we praise you now for sending your Son, our Savior, Jesus Christ,
for whom our hearts wait, and to whom,
with you and the Holy Spirit, one God,
be honor and dominion, now and for ever. **Amen.**

2    Father, all-powerful and ever-living God,
we do well always and everywhere to give you thanks
through Jesus Christ, our Lord.
When he humbled himself to come among us as a man,
he fulfilled the plan you formed long ago
and opened for us the way to salvation.
Now we watch for the day,
hoping that the salvation promised us will be ours
when Christ our Lord will come again in his glory.
And so, with all the choirs of angels in heaven
we proclaim your glory and join in their unending hymn of praise:
[*Sing a setting of "Glory to God" (the* Gloria*).*]

3    Blessed are you, Lord our God, ruler of the universe,
for you have kept us in life, sustained us,
and brought us to this holy season. **Amen.**

**4**  *A prayer especially mindful of children*

> King of glory, you are God.
> You are powerful.
> You rule the entire world.
> We praise you because you are so great.
> But you became a baby.
> You were tiny and weak.
> You were just like us.
> We praise you because you came,
> and we look forward to when you will come again.
> In your name we pray. **Amen.**

## Prayers of Invocation

**5**  O send out your light and your truth;
>    let them lead me;
> let them bring me to your holy hill
>    and to your dwelling.
> **Then I will go to the altar of God,**
>    **to God, my exceeding joy;**
> **and I will praise you with the harp,**
>    **O God, my God.**
> Why are you cast down, O my soul,
>    and why are you disquieted within me?
> **Hope in God; for I shall again praise him,**
>    **my help and my God. Amen.**
>    —from Psalm 43:3-5, NRSV

**6**  God of Israel,
> with expectant hearts
> we your people await Christ's coming.
> As once he came in humility,
> so now may he come in glory,
> that he may make all things perfect
> in your everlasting kingdom.
> For he is Lord for ever and ever. **Amen.**

**7**  Father in heaven,
> our hearts desire the warmth of your love,
> and our minds are searching for the light of your Word.
> Increase our longing for Christ, our Savior,
> and give us the strength to grow in love,
> that the dawn of his coming
> may find us rejoicing in his presence
> and welcoming the light of his truth.
> We ask this through Christ, our Lord. **Amen.**

**8**    Faithful God, we wait for you to come.
We know that you will
because you already have
and because you promised to return.
While we wait, send your Spirit
so that we may grow in grace.
Prepare us for your coming, Lord. **Amen.**

**9**    The Lord is glorious and exalted.
**Lord, shine in our hearts and lives.**
God's people are often in distress and sorrow.
**Lord, show your might and deliver us from evil.**
We sometimes do not feel the Lord's presence.
**O Lord, let your face again shine on us.**
The Lord was the shepherd of his people Israel.
**Lord, lead us in our way and guide us in our walk.**
In this Advent season we stand on tiptoe—
**Immanuel, invade our lives. Amen.**
        —based on Psalm 80:1-7

**10**    Covenant God,
you heard your people yearning for a Savior.
Thank you for sending your Son so long ago.
We now rehearse your promise
that Christ will come again,
that death and suffering will end
and every tear will be wiped away.
Come, Lord Jesus, come.
As you fulfilled Israel's hopes long ago,
so we long for all these promises to be fulfilled. **Amen.**

**11**    God of all hope and joy,
open our hearts in welcome,
that your Son, Jesus Christ, at his coming
may find in us a dwelling prepared for him,
who lives and reigns with you and the Holy Spirit,
one God now and forever. **Amen.**

**12**    If our lives are dry and parched,
**Lord, send the living waters of your Spirit
to revive us, to enliven us,
to bring forth new life.
Immanuel, come quickly.**

If our times are empty and barren,
**Lord, grant us a rich harvest,
send us home with sheaves of blessing,
fill us with your abundance,
and teach us to share the harvest with others.
Immanuel, come quickly.**

If our bodies are weary and heavy laden,
**Lord, fill us with laughter;**
**give us shouts of joy;**
**envelop us with your gladness.**
**Immanuel, come quickly.**

If our lives are small and trivial,
**Lord, make us see great things;**
**enlarge our vision;**
**widen our borders.**
**Immanuel, come quickly.**
—based on Psalm 126

13   O God, whose will is justice for the poor
and peace for the afflicted,
let your herald's urgent voice
pierce our hardened hearts
and announce the dawn of your kingdom.
Before the Advent of the one who baptizes
with the fire of the Holy Spirit,
let our complacency give way to conversion,
oppression to justice,
and conflict to acceptance of one another in Christ.
We ask this through him whose coming is certain,
whose day draws near:
your Son, our Lord Jesus Christ,
who lives and reigns with you and the Holy Spirit,
one God, forever and ever. **Amen.**

## Additional Resources

14   In this Advent season of waiting on the Lord,
**we trust in the Lord's goodness.**
**We rely on his mercy.**
**We find shelter in his steadfast love.**
In this Advent season of waiting on the Lord,
**we walk in the Lord's way.**
**We follow his example of love.**
**We keep our covenant promises.**
In this Advent season of waiting,
**Lord, forget our sins.**
**Remember your love.**
**Remember each one of us.**
**Remember your people everywhere.**
In this Advent season of waiting,
**Lord, we wait for your salvation.**
**We wait for your leading.**
**We wait for your coming.**
—based on Psalm 25:1-10

**15**   O Lord Jesus Christ,
whose first coming brought joy to your waiting people,
keep us in faith and hope
as we eagerly await your coming again. **Amen.**

**16**   All-powerful God,
increase our strength of will for doing good,
that Christ may find an eager welcome at his coming
and call us to his side in the kingdom of heaven,
where he lives and reigns with you and the Holy Spirit,
one God, for ever and ever. **Amen.**

**17**   In the psalms of David,
in the words of the prophets,
in the dream of Joseph,
your promise is spoken, eternal God,
and takes flesh at last
in the womb of the virgin.
May Emmanuel find welcome in our hearts,
take flesh in our lives, and be for all peoples
the welcome advent of redemption and grace.
We ask this through him whose coming is certain,
whose Day draws near;
your Son, our Lord Jesus Christ,
who lives and reigns with you and the Holy Spirit,
one God, for ever and ever. **Amen.**

**18**   Above the clamor of our violence
your Word of truth resounds,
O God of majesty and power.
Over nations enshrouded in despair
your justice dawns.
Grant your household
a discerning spirit and a watchful eye
to perceive the hour in which we live.
Hasten the advent of that day
when the weapons of war shall be banished,
our deeds of darkness cast off,
and all your scattered children gathered into one.
We ask this through him whose coming is certain,
whose day draws near:
your Son, our Lord Jesus Christ,
who lives and reigns with you and the Holy Spirit,
one God, forever and ever. **Amen.**

**19**   Father of our Lord Jesus Christ,
ever faithful to your promises
and ever close to your church:
the earth rejoices in hope of the Savior's coming

and looks forward with longing
to his return at the end of time.
Prepare our hearts and remove the sadness
that hinders us from feeling the joy and hope
that his presence will bestow,
for he is Lord for ever and ever. **Amen.**

20  Lord of hope,
as night workers long for the sunrise,
we long for the coming of Christ.
In our worship today we yearn for your Spirit
to give us a glimpse of your glory,
that one day we will see in full,
when all will be made new,
through Christ, our Lord, our light. **Amen.**

21  O God,
you have given us the sure promise that Jesus will return to judge the earth.
Make us ready, we pray, for his royal coming,
that we may consider daily what sort of people we ought to be,
and be found faithful servants waiting and working for our Master's return.
Grant in your mercy that many may be won for him before he comes,
and make us bold in our witness until that day,
whether he comes at midnight, or at dawn, or in the daytime.
For his name's sake. **Amen.**

22  God of power and mercy,
you call us once again to celebrate the coming of your Son.
Remove those things that hinder love of you,
that when he comes,
he may find us waiting in awe and wonder for him
who lives and reigns with you and the Holy Spirit,
one God, now and forever. **Amen.**

23  In anticipation we gather.
**With expectation we wait.**
We gather to watch for the coming of the good news
into our world and into our lives.
**We wait to see the fullness of God's vision.**
O God, open the doors to our hearts,
that this year we may have room for the birth of Jesus.
**O God, as we marvel over all that you are doing,**
**overwhelm us with so much wonder**
**that words of praise spring forth from our lips!**
In this time of waiting, let true worship begin in our hearts.
**Let our praises rise up to the heavens!**
**Let our celebrations spread new hope over a tired world!**
**Let us gather together all our dreams and lives**
**to worship our God! Amen.**

24  God of timeless grace,
     you fill us with joyful expectation.
     Make us ready for the message that prepares the way,
     that with uprightness of heart and holy joy
     we may eagerly await the kingdom of your Son, Jesus Christ,
     who reigns with you and the Holy Spirit, now and forever. **Amen.**

25  God of hope,
     you call us from the exile of sin
     with the good news of restoration;
     you build a highway through the wilderness;
     you come to us and bring us home.
     Comfort us with the expectation of your saving power,
     made known to us in Jesus Christ, our Lord. **Amen.**

26  We are a people of hope
     waiting for the return of our Lord.
     God will renew the world through Jesus,
     who will put all unrighteousness out,
     purify the works of human hands,
     and perfect our fellowship in divine love.
     Christ will wipe away every tear;
     death shall be no more.
     There will be a new heaven and a new earth,
     and all creation will be filled with God's glory.
                    —from *Our Song of Hope* st. 1, 21

## Advent Candle Lighting

*The lighting of Advent candles dramatically depicts the growing expectation we have for the coming of Christ, the light of the world. This action most often functions as a call to worship, but it can also function as a response to the assurance of pardon or to the sermon.*

*The traditional Advent wreath has four purple candles (lit on the four Sundays of Advent) grouped around a white Christ candle (lit on Christmas Day). The main symbolism portrayed by the wreath is the growing intensity of light as the candle lighting includes an additional candle each worship day and as anticipation builds for the celebration of Christ's second coming.*

*Some congregations attribute particular meaning to individual candles, associating them with peace, joy, love, and light; with Mary, Joseph, the shepherds, and the Magi; or with other related aspects of Christ's coming. These associations may be helpful for a congregation at a particular time, but they are not in any way necessary to a worshipful celebration. Similarly, a tradition calling for the third candle to be pink is not especially important. It is based on a medieval tradition in which the second to last Sunday of Advent (and Lent) accented Christian joy in the middle of a penitential season.*

*The following resources offer readings to accompany the lighting of the Advent candles for each particular Sunday during Advent. Lighting the Advent candles and reading associated texts provides a fine opportunity to involve a variety of adults and children in leading worship.*

**27**  *A series of readings from Isaiah*

Jesus said, "I am the light of the world;
the one who follows me will not walk in darkness but have the light of life."
**We light this candle [*these candles*] as a sign of the coming light of Christ.**

[*on the First Sunday of Advent and at each successive lighting*]
The people who walked in darkness
    have seen a great light;
those who lived in a land of deep darkness—
    on them light has shined.
            —Isaiah 9:2, NRSV

[*on the Second Sunday of Advent and at each successive lighting*]
I will lead the blind
    by a road they do not know,
by the paths they have not known
    I will guide them.
I will turn the darkness before them into light,
    the rough places into level ground.
These are the things I will do
    and I will not forsake them.
            —Isaiah 42:16, NRSV

[*on the Third Sunday of Advent and at each successive lighting*]
The LORD says to his servant,
"It is too light a thing that you should be my servant
    to raise up the tribes of Jacob
    and to restore the survivors of Israel;
I will give you as a light to the nations,
    that my salvation may reach to the end of the earth."
            —from Isaiah 49:6, NRSV

[*on the Fourth Sunday of Advent and at each successive lighting*]
Then your light shall break forth like the dawn,
    and your healing shall spring up quickly;
your vindicator shall go before you,
    the glory of the LORD shall be your rear guard.
            —Isaiah 58:8, NRSV

[*on the eve of Christmas or on Christmas Day*]
Arise, shine; for your light has come,
    and the glory of the LORD has risen upon you.
For the darkness shall cover the earth,
    and thick darkness the peoples;
but the LORD will arise upon you,
    and his glory will appear over you.

Nations shall come to your light,
    and kings to the brightness of your dawn.
        —Isaiah 60:1-3, NRSV

[*on each occasion the candle lighting is concluded as follows.*]
Come, Lord Jesus, our light and our salvation.
**Let us walk in the light of the Lord.**

28  *Another series of readings from Isaiah*

We light [*these candles*] as a sign of the coming light of Christ.
**Advent means coming.**
**We are preparing for the full coming of God's kingdom:**

[*on the First Sunday of Advent and at each successive lighting*]
The nations shall beat their swords into plowshares,
    and their spears into pruning hooks;
nation shall not lift up sword against nation,
    neither shall they learn war any more.
        —from Isaiah 2:4, NRSV

[*on the Second Sunday of Advent and at each successive lighting*]
The wolf shall live with the lamb,
    the leopard shall lie down with the kid,
the calf and the lion and the fatling together,
    and a little child shall lead them.
        —Isaiah 11:6, NRSV

[*on the Third Sunday of Advent and at each successive lighting*]
The wilderness and the dry land shall be glad,
    the desert shall rejoice and blossom;
like the crocus it shall blossom abundantly,
    and rejoice with joy and singing.
        —Isaiah 35:1-2, NRSV

[*on the Fourth Sunday of Advent and at each successive lighting*]
The Lord will give you a sign.
Look, the young woman is with child
and shall bear a son,
and shall name him Immanuel ("God is with us").
        —from Isaiah 7:14, NRSV

[*on the eve of Christmas or on Christmas Day*]
The people who walked in darkness
    have seen a great light;
those who lived in a land of deep darkness,
    on them light has shined.
        —Isaiah 9:2, NRSV

[*on each occasion the candle lighting is concluded as follows.*]
Let us walk in the light of the Lord.

**29**  [*on the first Sunday of Advent and at each successive lighting*]
We light [*these candles*] as a sign of the coming light of Christ.
**In the wilderness prepare the way of our Lord,**
**make straight in the desert a highway for our God.**
      —based on Isaiah 40:3, NRSV

[*on the second Sunday of Advent and at each successive lighting*]
The Lord will give you a sign.
A young woman is with child and shall bear a son.
**And they shall name him Immanuel,**
**which means "God is with us."**
      —from Isaiah 7:14; Matthew 1:23, NRSV

[*on the third Sunday of Advent and at each successive lighting*]
Every valley shall be lifted up
and every mountain and hill be made low;
**the uneven ground shall become level,**
**and the rough places a plain.**
      —Isaiah 40:4, NRSV

[*on the fourth Sunday of Advent and at each successive lighting*]
Then the glory of the LORD shall be revealed,
**and all the people shall see it together,**
**for the mouth of the LORD has spoken.**
      —Isaiah 40:5, NRSV

[*on the eve of Christmas or on Christmas Day*]
The Word became flesh and lived among us,
**and we have seen his glory,**
the glory as of a father's only son, full of grace and truth.
      —John 1:14, NRSV

**30**  *This resource involves only one verse of Scripture; each week a phrase from Isaiah 9:6 is added. The various candles are lit just before the various names for the coming Messiah are read. On Christmas Day all of the candles can be lit before the reading of the entire text.*

For to us a child is born,
to us a son is given,
and the government will be on his shoulders.
And he will be called
[*week 1*]      Wonderful Counselor,
[*week 2*]      Mighty God,
[*week 3*]      Everlasting Father,
[*week 4*]      Prince of Peace.

We light [*these candles*] as a sign
of our waiting and hope for the coming Christ.
      —based on Isaiah 9:6, NIV

**31** *This resource involves simply repeating Isaiah 11:1-3 and pausing to light the candles at a different point in the reading each time.*

A shoot will come up from the stump of Jesse;
from his roots a Branch will bear fruit.
[*week 1*]     The Spirit of the Lord will rest on him—
[*week 2*]     the Spirit of wisdom and of understanding,
[*week 3*]     the Spirit of counsel and of power,
[*week 4*]     the Spirit of knowledge and of the fear of the Lord—
[*Christmas*]  and he will delight in the fear of the Lord.

We light [*these candles*] as a sign
of our waiting and hope for the coming Christ.
> —based on Isaiah 11:1-3, NIV

**32** *This resource involves simply repeating Isaiah 61:1-3 and pausing to light the candles at a different point in the reading each time.*

The spirit of the Lord God is upon me,
because the Lord has anointed me;
[*week 1*]     he has sent me to bring good news to the oppressed,
[*week 2*]     to bind up the brokenhearted,
                   to proclaim liberty to the captives
                   and release to the prisoners;
[*week 3*]     to proclaim the year of the Lord's favor
                   and the day of vengeance of our God;
[*week 4*]     to comfort all who mourn;
                   to provide for those who mourn in Zion—
[*Christmas*]  to give them a garland instead of ashes,
                   the oil of gladness instead of mourning,
                   the mantle of praise instead of a faint spirit.
                   They will be called oaks of righteousness,
                   the planting of the Lord, to display his glory.

We light [*these candles*] as a sign
of our waiting and hope for the coming Christ.
> —based on Isaiah 61:1-3, NRSV

**33** *This resource for two readers (or two groups of readers) focuses on the symbols of darkness and light.*

[*First Sunday of Advent*]
Reader 1:  In the beginning when God created the heavens and the earth,
                   the earth was a formless void
                   and darkness covered the face of the deep.
Reader 2:  A wind from God swept over the face of the waters.
                   Then God said, "Let there be light,"
Reader 1:  and there was light. And God saw that the light was good.
Reader 2:  God separated the light from the darkness.
                   God called the light Day, and the darkness he called Night.
                   **And there was evening and there was morning,
                   the first day.**
> —from Genesis 1:1-5, NRSV

[*Second Sunday of Advent*]
Reader 1:  The LORD is my light and my salvation;
                 whom shall I fear?
Reader 2:  The LORD is the stronghold of my life;
                 of whom shall I be afraid?
Reader 1:  I believe that I shall see the goodness of the LORD
                 in the land of the living.
Reader 2:  Wait for the LORD;
                 be strong, and let your heart take courage.
                 **Wait for the LORD!**
           —from Psalm 27:1, 13-14, NRSV

[*Third Sunday of Advent*]
Reader 1:  The people who walked in darkness have seen a great light.
Reader 2:  Those who lived in a land of deep darkness—
                 on them has light shined.
Reader 1:  A shoot shall come out from the stump of Jesse,
                 and a branch shall grow out of his roots.
Reader 2:  And the Spirit of the LORD shall rest on him.
                 **His delight shall be in the fear of the LORD.**
           —from Isaiah 9:2; 11:1-3, NRSV

[*Fourth Sunday of Advent*]
Reader 1:  We wait for light, and lo! there is darkness;
                 for brightness, but we walk in gloom.
Reader 2:  Arise, shine; for your light has come,
                 and the glory of the LORD has risen upon you.
Reader 1:  For darkness shall cover the earth,
                 and thick darkness the peoples.
Reader 2:  But the LORD will arise upon you,
                 and nations shall come to your light.
Reader 1:  The sun shall no longer be your light by day,
                 nor for brightness shall the moon give light to you by night.
                 **For the LORD will be your everlasting light**
                 **and your God will be your glory.**
           —from Isaiah 59:9; 60:1-3, 19, NRSV

[*Eve of Christmas or Christmas Day*]
Reader: 1:  In the beginning was the Word, and the Word was with God,
                  and the Word was God.
Reader 2:  He was in the beginning with God.
                 All things came into being through him.
Reader 1:  In him was life, and the life was the light of all people.
Reader 2:  The light shines in the darkness,
                 and the darkness did not overcome it.

Reader 1:  The true light, which enlightens everyone,
was coming into the world.
**And the Word became flesh and lived among us,**
**and we have seen his glory,**
**the glory as of a father's only son,**
**full of grace and truth.**
—from John 1:1-5, 9, 14, NRSV

**34**  *In this resource each week of Advent is associated with a particular virtue (hope, love, joy, peace).*

[*First Sunday of Advent, after lighting the first Advent candle*]
Prepare the way of the Lord.
We light this candle in hope,
the hope of our coming Savior, Jesus.
**Prepare, then, the way of the Lord.**

[*Second Sunday of Advent, after lighting the second Advent candle*]
Prepare the way of the Lord.
We light this candle in love,
the love that Jesus, our Savior, has for us.
**Prepare, then, the way of the Lord.**

[*Third Sunday of Advent, after lighting the third Advent candle*]
Prepare the way of the Lord.
We light this candle in joy,
the joy that we have in Jesus, our Savior.
**Prepare, then, the way of the Lord.**

[*Fourth Sunday of Advent, after lighting the fourth Advent candle*]
Prepare the way of the Lord.
We light this candle in peace,
the peace that Jesus, our Savior, gives to the world.
**Prepare, then, the way of the Lord.**

[*Christmas reading, after lighting the Christ candle*]
Joy to the world, the Lord is come!
We light this candle because Jesus, the light of the world,
was born on this day,
and he brightens all things.
**Joy to the earth, the Savior reigns!**

**35**  *Each reading in this resource focuses on a significant Advent theme (contemplation, holiness, social justice, rejoicing, incarnation).*

[*First Sunday of Advent*]
The Advent wreath is a circle with no beginning and no end.
It is a symbol of God's unending love and faithfulness.
**The prophet Isaiah said, "The Lord himself will give you a sign:**
**the virgin will be with child and will give birth to a son,**
**and will call him Immanuel."**

The angel Gabriel said to Mary, "Greetings you who are highly favored!
The Lord is with you."
**We rejoice that we too have found favor with God.**
God's mercy extends to those who fear him from generation to generation.
    —based on Isaiah 7:14; Luke 1:28, NIV

[*Second Sunday of Advent*]
The Advent wreath is a circle with no beginning and no end.
It is a symbol of God's unending love and faithfulness.
**Its light reminds us of Jesus, the light of the world.**
**In him was life, and the life was the light of all people.**
**The light shines in the darkness,**
**and the darkness did not overcome it.**
Once you were darkness, but now in the Lord you are light.
Live as children of light.
**If we walk in the light as he himself is in the light,**
**we have fellowship with one another,**
**and the blood of Jesus his Son cleanses us from all sin.**
We are all children of light and children of the day;
we are not of the night or of darkness.
**Jesus said, "Everyone who believes in me**
**should not remain in the darkness."**
    —based on John 1:4-5; 12:46; Ephesians 5:8; 1 Thessalonians 5:5; 1 John 1:7, NRSV

[*Third Sunday of Advent*]
The Advent wreath is a circle with no beginning and no end.
It is a symbol of God's unending love and faithfulness.
**Isaiah the prophet calls us to prepare for the coming of Jesus**
**by making straight all that is crooked.**
A voice cries out: "In the wilderness prepare the way of the Lord,
make straight in the desert a highway for our God.
**Then the glory of the Lord shall be revealed,**
**and all people shall see it together,**
**for the mouth of the Lord has spoken."**
Let us prepare for Jesus, the Christ,
who is anointed by God to bring good news to the oppressed,
to bind up the broken-hearted,
to proclaim liberty to the captives and release to the prisoners.
**For as a garden causes seeds to grow,**
**so the Lord God will cause righteousness and praise**
**to spring up before all the nations.**
    —based on Isaiah 40:3, 5; 61:1, 11, NRSV

[*Fourth Sunday of Advent*]
The Advent wreath is a circle with no beginning and no end.
It is a symbol of God's unending love and faithfulness.
**The shepherds were the first to hear**
**the joyful announcement of Christ's birth—**
**the good news of great joy for all the people.**

Upon seeing the baby Jesus, the shepherds
spread the word concerning what had been told them about this child,
and all who heard it were amazed.
**We have also heard this wonderful news.**
**We welcomed the message with the joy given by the Holy Spirit.**
Though we have not seen Jesus, we love him;
and even though we do not see him now, we believe in him.
**And we are filled with an expressible and glorious joy.**
    —based on Luke 2:10, 17-18; 1 Thessalonians 1:6; 1 Peter 1:8, NIV

[*Eve of Christmas or Christmas Day*]
The Advent wreath is a circle with no beginning and no end.
It is a symbol of God's unending love and faithfulness.
**Jesus Christ is the brightest revelation of God's love.**
**He is the image of the invisible God, the firstborn over all creation.**
Christ Jesus, who, being in very nature God,
did not consider equality with God something to be grasped,
**but made himself nothing, taking the very nature of a servant,**
**being made in human likeness.**
The Word became flesh and made his dwelling among us.
We have seen his glory,
**the glory of the One and Only, who came from the Father,**
**full of grace and truth.**
    —based on John 1:14; Philippians 2:5-7; Colossians 1:15, NIV

# D.2 CONFESSION AND ASSURANCE

### D.2.1 Call to Confession (see also section 2.1)

1    Prepare the way of the Lord!
     Let us make our confession to God.

### D.2.2 Prayers of Confession (see also section 2.2)

1    O that you would tear open the heavens and come down,
          so that the mountains would quake at your presence—
     as when fire kindles brushwood
          and the fire causes water to boil—
     to make your name known to your adversaries,
          so that the nations might tremble at your presence!
     When you did awesome deeds that we did not expect,

you came down, the mountains quaked at your presence.
From ages past no one has heard,
   no ear has perceived,
no eye has seen any God besides you,
   who works for those who wait for him.
You meet those who gladly do right,
   those who remember you in your ways.
But you were angry, and we sinned;
   because you hid yourself we transgressed.
We have all become like one who is unclean,
   and all our righteous deeds are like a filthy cloth.
We all fade like a leaf,
   and our iniquities, like the wind, take us away.
There is no one who calls on your name,
   or attempts to take hold of you;
for you have hidden your face from us,
   and have delivered us into the hand of our iniquity.
Yet, O Lord, you are our Father;
   we are the clay, and you are our potter;
   we are all the work of your hand.
Do not be exceedingly angry, O Lord,
   and do not remember our iniquity forever.
**Restore us, we pray, through the coming of our Lord Jesus,**
**in whom we place our hope and trust. Amen.**
    —based on Isaiah 64:1-9, NRSV

2    *A prayer especially mindful of children*

Lord God, our lives are filled with sin.
We forget our neighbor's needs
and do not love you above all else.
We need a Savior.
Help us to be ready for Jesus in our own hearts.
O come, O come, Savior of the world. **Amen.**

3    O promised Christ:
We are a world at war.
Our peace depends on your coming.
We are a sinful people.
Our pardon depends on your coming.
We are full of good intentions but weak at keeping promises;
our only hope of doing God's will
is that you should come and help us do it.
Lord Christ, Word made flesh,
our world waits
for your peace,
for your pardon,
and for your grace.
Even so: come, Lord Jesus. **Amen.**

**4**    Arise, shine: for your light has come.
**O God, we live as if the light**
**had never defeated the darkness in the world or in us.**
And the glory of the Lord has risen upon you.
**We confess that we ignore the Christ**
**you sent to be among us, to be in us.**
For behold, darkness shall cover the earth,
and thick darkness the peoples;
but the Lord will arise upon you, and his glory will be seen upon you.
**We've kept the birth of your Son confined to the Christmas season**
**and do not yearn for his birth each moment in our waiting hearts.**
And nations shall come to your light,
and kings to the brightness of your rising.
**Lord, you came to us in the fullness of time.**
**Forgive us for not opening our eyes to your coming.**
**It's time that we prepare for your coming.**
**Let the earth ring with song. Let the light break forth.**
**Let us all rejoice in the miracle of love.**
**Let Christ come into the fullness of our time. Amen.**
        —based on Isaiah 60:1-3

**5**    Lord Christ,
we confess our willingness to be loved
but also our reluctance to love.
We confess our readiness to accept your forgiving love
but also our refusal to forgive.
We confess our eagerness to grasp your offer of redeeming love
but also our resistance to follow you without question.
In this Advent time, forgive us our failure
to respond as we should.
Come to us anew, and by your grace, assist us to receive you
with joy, as the shepherds;
with gratitude, as Simeon;
with obedience, as Mary;
with love, as you have loved us.
Even so: come, Lord Jesus. **Amen.**

**6**    Merciful God,
always with us, always coming:
We confess that we do not know
how to prepare for your Advent.
We have forgotten how to hope in miracles;
we have ignored the promise of your kingdom;
we get distracted by all the busyness of this season.
Forgive us, God.
Grant us the simple wonder of the shepherds,
the intelligent courage of the Magi,
and the patient faith of Mary and Joseph,

that we may journey with them to Bethlehem
and find the good news of a child born for us.
Now, in the quiet of our hearts,
we ask you to make us ready for his coming. **Amen.**

7   Lord, we have not kept watch for you.
    We have occupied ourselves with our own concerns.
    We have not waited to find your will for us.
    We have not noticed the needs of the people around us.
    We have not acknowledged the love that has been shown to us.
    Forgive us for our lack of watchfulness.
    Help us to wait to know your will.
    Help us to look out for the needs of others.
    Help us to work and watch for your coming. **Amen.**

8   While we ask, Lord, for the most meaningful Advent season ever,
    we sadly confess having done so little with so much.
    Forgive us Lord,
    for not bending the knee,
    for not reading your Word,
    for not searching our hearts,
    for not facing our sins.
    Forgive us according to your tender mercies, O God!
    Grant that when Christmas morning breaks for us this year,
    we may have a fresh sense of your presence
    and a renewed resolve to live to the praise of Christ's glory. **Amen.**

9   Almighty God,
    you who shaped out of nothing all that is,
    forgive us for returning empty-handed.
    You who called forth light,
    forgive our preference for the dark!
    You who sent John to be a voice crying,
    forgive our unwillingness to say anything at all!
    Create in us clean hearts, O God,
    and renew a right spirit within us.
    Through Jesus Christ our Lord. **Amen.**

10  God of salvation, in Christ you have done great things—
    our hearts are filled with joy.
    By your power you lifted us out of the wasteland of sin
    and brought us with joy and laughter into your kingdom.
    Salvation is your gift to us.
    But we confess that often we try to replace your gift with our own efforts.
    We try to complete what is already perfect;
    we try to add to what is already full;
    we try to earn what we already have.
    Forgive us for our foolishness.

Help us to focus on your grace.
Help us to live grateful lives in return.
For Jesus' sake alone, **Amen.**
  —based on Psalm 126

11  O God,
    you give us your good news
    and call us into a new covenant relationship with you.
    Help us to prepare the way of the Lord Jesus Christ.
    Let the valleys be lifted up!
    **Draw us away from degrading thoughts and actions,**
    **and lift from us depressions and worry.**
    [*Silent prayer*]

    Through humble people, prepare your world, O God.
    Let the mountains be leveled off!
    **End our pride and take away our arrogance:**
    **save us from false hope and unwarranted presumption.**
    [*Silent prayer*]

    Through faithful people, prepare your world, O God.
    Let the crooked be made straight!
    **Forgive our sin, and pardon our wrongdoing;**
    **defeat evil and overcome the power of death.**
    [*Silent prayer*]

    Through saved people, prepare your world, O God.
    Let the rough be made smooth!
    **Help us grow in understanding,**
    **and give us wisdom to discern that which is good and true.**
    [*Silent prayer*]

    Through sanctified people, prepare your world, O God.
    Let all people see the salvation of our God.
    **Redeem your world, and make all things new,**
    **and bring us into your holy and perfect presence,**
    **now and for all eternity.**
    [*Silent prayer*]

    Keep us humble and faithful.
    Save us and sanctify us, O God.
    **For the sake of Jesus Christ, your Son, our Lord. Amen.**

12  It is Advent. It is the season in which we prepare our hearts
    to welcome Christ, who is the bringer of all peace.
    We confess to you the ways in which
    we block the peace of Christ in our lives.
    **God of peace, hear our prayer.**
    The rushing and scurrying to get things done,
    **we confess to you, O God of peace.**
    The worry about the little details,

we confess to you, O God of peace.
The financial burdens we put on ourselves,
we confess to you, O God of peace.
The impatience and irritability we feel and take out on one another,
we confess to you, O God of peace.
The bickering and quarreling we get into because we are too busy,
we confess to you, O God of peace.
Though we make ourselves less than peaceful at this time of the year,
your peace is always there for us.
Instill within us your peace, O God.
When we feel overwhelmed,
instill within us your peace, O God.
When we are filled with worry,
instill within us your peace, O God.
When we become irritable,
instill within us your peace, O God.
When the guilt of our ways threatens to overcome us,
help us to remember that we are forgiven in Christ.
Instill within us your peace, O God.
Instill within us your peace, O God.
Instill within us your peace
and help us to make choices that bring us closer to you.
Help us to be more peaceful
so that we may spread Christ's peace and love to others. **Amen.**

13    If we look at our own lives,
       **we must confess the mixture of giving and selfishness,**
       **our waiting on the Lord turned to an endless rush,**
       **our missing the mark of Advent.**
       Lord, forgive our frantic ways and misplaced efforts.
       But we can also trust in God,
       **who still brings us salvation,**
       **who still supplies us strength,**
       **who hears our songs of gratitude,**
       **who accepts our joyful praise.**
       Let us all draw water from the wells of salvation.
       Let us shout it in church and in town:
       **The Lord's great name will still be praised.**
       **His saving deeds support our lives.**
       **His greatness still astounds us.**
       **The Holy One of Israel is among us.**
       **Praise the Lord and sing for joy.**
           —based on Isaiah 12

14    O Holy Child of Bethlehem,
       descend to us, we pray.
       Cast out our sin and enter in;
       be born in us today.

## D.2.4 Assurance of Pardon (see also section 2.4)

1    Surely God's salvation is at hand for those who fear him,
        that his glory may dwell in our land.
    Steadfast love and faithfulness will meet;
        righteousness and peace will kiss each other.
    Faithfulness will spring up from the ground,
        and righteousness will look down from the sky.
    The Lord will give what is good,
        and our land will yield its increase.
    Righteousness will go before him
        and will make a path for his steps.

    In Christ, God's salvation is at hand, and righteousness has come.
    **Thanks be to God!**
        —based on Psalm 85:9-13, NRSV

2    Comfort, comfort my people, says your God.
    Your sins are pardoned.
    The penalty is paid.
    **Thanks be to God.**
        —based on Isaiah 40:1-2

3    The days are surely coming, says the Lord,
    when I will fulfill the promise I made
    to the house of Israel and the house of Judah.
    In those days and at that time I will cause
    a righteous Branch to spring up for David;
    and he shall execute justice and righteousness in the land.
    In those days Judah will be saved and Jerusalem will live in safety.
    And this is the name by which it will be called:
    "The Lord is our righteousness."

    People of God: Jesus Christ, our Lord,
    whose coming we announce in this season, is our righteousness.
    In Christ, we are made right with God.
    **Thanks be to God!**
        —based on Jeremiah 33:14-16, NRSV

4    Sing aloud, O daughter Zion;
        shout, O Israel!
    Rejoice and exult with all your heart,
        O daughter Jerusalem!
    The LORD has taken away the judgments against you,
        he has turned away your enemies.
    The king of Israel, the LORD, is in your midst;
        you shall fear disaster no more.
    On that day it shall be said to Jerusalem:
    Do not fear, O Zion;
        do not let your hands grow weak.

The LORD, your God, is in your midst,
  a warrior who gives victory;
he will rejoice over you with gladness,
  he will renew you in his love;
he will exult over you with loud singing.
    —Zephaniah 3:14-18, NRSV

5    See, I am sending my messenger to prepare the way before me,
     and the Lord whom you seek will suddenly come to his temple.
     The messenger of the covenant in whom you delight—
     indeed, he is coming, says the Lord of hosts.
     But who can endure the day of his coming,
     and who can stand when he appears?
     For he is like a refiner's fire and like fullers' soap;
     he will sit as a refiner and purifier of silver,
     and he will purify the descendants of Levi
     and refine them like gold and silver,
     until they present offerings to the Lord in righteousness.
     Then the offering of Judah and Jerusalem will be pleasing to the Lord
     as in the days of old and as in former years.

     The messenger of the Lord has come in Christ.
     In Christ, we present offerings to the Lord in righteousness!
     Thanks be to God for his lavish grace!
       —based on Malachi 3:1-4, NRSV

6    As we hear the ancient prophecies of the coming of the Messiah,
     we long for the day when death will be swallowed up
     and every tear will be wiped away.
     As we wait expectantly
     for Christ's promised return,
     we live in the assurance of God's gracious forgiveness.

7    Almighty God, by whose providence
     our Savior, Jesus Christ, came among us in great humility,
     will sanctify you with the light of his blessing and set you free from all sin.

8    Jesus, the long-expected Savior, was born to set us free.
     He releases us from our fears and sins
     and helps us find our rest in him.
     Jesus delivers us from the way of sin and death.
     Yet he remains the desire of people in every nation,
     and he will direct us into the ways of his kingdom.
     And so, with hopeful hearts, we call to him:
     **Come now, long-expected Jesus,**
     **come again to rule in our hearts. Amen.**
       —inspired by Charles Wesley (1744)

# D.3 Proclaiming the Word

## D.3.1 Prayers for Illumination (see also section 3.1)

1  Make us to know your ways, O LORD;
       teach us your paths.
   Lead us in your truth, and teach us,
       for you are the God of our salvation;
       for you we wait all day long. **Amen.**
       —from Psalm 25:4-5, NRSV

2  Creator God,
   you remind us that the darkness of ignorance and doubt
   cannot overcome your life-giving Word.
   May your Holy Spirit, who first inspired these words of Scripture,
   shine your light and once again awaken us
   to the hearing and living of this radiant truth.
   In Jesus' name, **Amen.**

3  God of love and power,
   you are revealed to us in your Word,
   in accounts of prophecy and fulfillment
   that direct our attention to Jesus Christ.
   Illumine us now as we hear your Word proclaimed,
   that we may open our hearts to him,
   yearn for his coming in glory,
   and serve him with joy. **Amen.**

4  God of the universe, revealed to us in Holy Scripture
   through the writings of the prophets and the preaching of John the Baptist,
   you have called us to prepare our hearts for your visitation.
   Ready us now to hear your Word and to respond as faithful servants,
   to the glory of Christ. **Amen.**

5  Gracious God,
   sometimes we see your hand in little events,
   and sometimes we see it in the broad sweep of history.
   Stir our hearts, that we might be people of hope;
   help us seek you in your Word;
   and keep us from growing weary as we wait—
   that we may not miss the glory of your appearing.
   Even so, come quickly, Lord Jesus. **Amen.**

6   O God, our beginning and end,
    by whose command time runs its course:
    bless our impatience,
    perfect our faith,
    and, while we await
    the fulfillment of your promises,
    grant us hope in your Word. **Amen.**

7   *A prayer especially mindful of children*

    Immanuel, as we wait for your return,
    help us see your glory and love
    through the reading and preaching of your Word.
    We pray in your name. **Amen.**

## D.3.6 Profession of Our Church's Faith (see also section 3.6)

1   As followers of Jesus Christ,
    living in this world—
    which some seek to control,
    and others view with despair—
    we declare with joy and trust:
    **Our world belongs to God!**

    Remembering the promise
    to reconcile the world to himself,
    God joined our humanity in Jesus Christ—
    the eternal Word made flesh.
    **He is the long-awaited Messiah,
    one with us and one with God,
    fully human and fully divine,
    conceived by the Holy Spirit
    and born of the virgin Mary.**

    We long for that day when our bodies are raised,
    the Lord wipes away our tears,
    and we dwell forever in the presence of God.
    We will take our place in the new creation,
    where there will be no more death or mourning or crying or pain,
    and the Lord will be our light.
    Come, Lord Jesus, come.

    **With the whole creation we join the song:
    "Worthy is the Lamb, who was slain,
    to receive power and wealth and wisdom and strength
    and honor and glory and praise!"
    He has made us a kingdom of priests to serve our God,
    and we will reign on earth.
    God will be all in all,
    righteousness and peace will flourish,**

everything will be made new,
and every eye will see at last
that our world belongs to God.
Hallelujah! Come, Lord Jesus!
—from *Our World Belongs to God*, st. 1, 23, 56, 58

2   In love you came to a stable in Bethlehem
to become one with us.
In love you walked the plains and hills of Galilee and Judea
to teach us how to live.
In love you were nailed on a cross on Calvary
to bear away our sin.
In love you rose from a tomb in Joseph's garden
to defeat death's power over us.
In love you ascended beyond the clouds
to be our reigning Lord.
You came to love us so that we need never feel
unloved, deserted, alone, condemned.

3   Our only hope is Jesus Christ.
After we refused to live in the image of God,
he was born of the virgin Mary,
sharing our genes and our instincts,
entering our culture, speaking our language,
fulfilling the law of God.
Being united to Christ's humanity,
we know ourselves when we rest in him.

Come, Lord Jesus:
We are open to your Spirit.
We await your full presence.
Our world finds rest in you alone.
—*Our Song of Hope*, st. 3, closing prayer

4   We are called as pilgrim followers of Jesus Christ
to steer our lives carefully in this world,
lest we lose our way and mar our leader's name.
We give thanks for generations of saints
who walked the way before us.
Their strong profession and bold obedience
are gifts to us, a tradition to guide us.
As we seek to follow our Lord in the time and place marked out for us,
we depend on God's help alone:
  Keep us, we pray, from the disobedient perils
  of cementing ourselves in the past
  and of chasing after fads in the present.
  Help us to take heart from our faith's ancestors,
  to live intentionally for our faith's heirs,
  and to delight and honor you. **Amen.**

# D.4 PRAYERS OF THE PEOPLE

## D.4.4 Complete Model Outlines and Prayers (see also section 4.4)

*Prayer Outlines*

1   *The following is a guide for extemporaneous prayers. The pattern provides a suggested text for the opening and closing of each part of the prayer and calls for extemporaneous prayers of thanksgiving, petition, and intercession.*

God, our hope,
we rejoice that you became flesh and made your dwelling among us,
even as we long for your return.
As we wait, our hearts overflow with gratitude:
    for the beauty of creation . . .
    for your work in the world . . .
    for signs of peace and reconciliation . . .
    for our community and its leaders . . .
    for your work accomplished through your church, especially for . . .
For all these reasons and so much more we give you praise.

As we celebrate the first coming of your Son as a helpless child,
we also yearn for his return,
for the day in which there will be no more sorrow, pain, or death.
Today we remember in prayer:
    the nations of the world . . .
    those in authority . . .
    the needs of the community . . .
    the church universal, its mission, and those who minister . . .
    the local congregation and its ministry, especially . . .
    those with particular needs . . .
We offer these prayers in the name Jesus Christ, our source of hope. **Amen.**

*Complete Prose Prayers*

2   *A prayer for the first Sunday in Advent*

God of the future, you are coming in power to bring all nations and all peoples under the rule of your lordship through Jesus Christ. We know about, believe in, and hope for that future advent of the kingdom because we know about, believe in, and find as the source of all hope your first advent in Bethlehem. As we enter into this new season today, help us to be expectant people. Bend our thoughts and aspirations beyond the moment, beyond what we can see in front of us at any given time. Although we want to do our daily tasks well and to your glory right now, help us to be people who also look ahead, who peer around various cosmic corners, and who know that the ultimate things of existence in this universe are the things that have been secured for us through Jesus and that are real already now in the kingdom he established.

In Advent we sing about our having open hearts for you to enter in. May we, by the grace of your Spirit, be open indeed, Father. Make us open to the ways your kingdom can influence our decision making at work, at school, and at home. Make us open toward others, enabling us to see each and every person we meet as Jesus in our midst. Make us open to opportunities to serve others, to serve your whole creation out of devotion to you and to your Son, who showed us what true service is all about when he came down into a virgin's womb to salvage the universe you fashioned in the beginning.

As people whose hearts are open indeed, we make petition this morning for your needy world. This Advent season sees once again a world of war and rumors of war, a world of violence and terrorism that strikes the unsuspecting. It is easy, O God, for us to see why this world needs saving, but sometimes it is not so easy to believe that in Christ it has already been saved. Beyond the glitter and goodwill and cozy warmth of the Christmas season, Father, help us as Christians to find in Jesus' birth long ago a true reason for hope in this present moment. And then lead us to be workers for peace, bearers of shalom, agents of healing in this world gone mad.

Here in this place, you see the needs and hurts of our members during this new holiday season. Stand close to anyone here this morning who struggles. Be with the college student who is worried about exams or who frets about various issues that may crop up when he or she travels home for Christmas. Be with the parent here today who has real cause for alarm over the course a child's life seems to be taking. Lift the clouds of depression from those who wrestle so mightily with their emotions. Minister to those who have chronic pain and give them some relief, we pray. Lead to a better time those who are unemployed right now, who are worried about family finances, and who wonder what the new year may hold. Grant that the coming weeks and months will hold new and good and wonderful things for those seeking a meaningful outlet for the gifts you have given to them.

You alone see us as we are, Lord God, and so we beg for you to nurture us according to our needs, to minister to us according to our hurts, to heal us in all those places where you see that we are broken or sick.

But despite whatever happens in our lives or whatever is going on at this present moment in our various hearts and minds, still we do adore you, God of wonder and God of glory. We worship you; we lay our hearts open before you. So as we come to you at your table in a little while, come also to us by your Spirit. Our hearts are open. Be born in us anew this day so that every day we may spread the increase of your peace. In Jesus, the Prince of Peace, we pray. **Amen.**

3    To God we pray, "Your kingdom come!"
     Come bring your purpose near
     to make the force of evil fade,
     your goodness to appear
     as righteousness, a rolling stream
     to quench a thirsty land,
     the waiting season spent at last:
     your kingdom close at hand!

To God we pray, "Your kingdom come!"
Come as a marriage feast
in which the first and honored guests
shall be the last and least;
come lift the poorest of the poor
up to your finest ranks,
the hungry fed, the naked clothed,
the downcast filled with thanks!

To God we pray, "Your kingdom come!"
Come with your gift of growth;
you scatter seed upon the ground,
mix leaven in the loaf!
What's sown in secret, soon reveal
to claim your harvest's goal,
till we attain your lasting aim:
the leavening of the whole!

To God we pray, "Your kingdom come!"
Come grant your unity.
You seek and tend the wayward ones
to form community,
so that the lost may enter in
your good and holy place,
and find their joy is centered in
a heavenly embrace!

To God, we pray, "Your kingdom come!"
Come claim creation wide;
then shall the power of evil break,
and sin no more divide.
Your love shall launch a lasting reign
as earth's old ills are healed;
by mercy, justice, peace anew,
in perfect joy revealed! **Amen.**

4    Eternal God,
for whom all people wait and search,
even when they don't realize it,
we cry out today for a live and present Word from you.
As our season of discontent approaches the day of your coming,
we pray that you would speak to us in the graceful ways that you know best.

Open our eyes that have been closed by fear and blinded by self-pity,
that we may see you even in the anxieties and uncertainties
that beset our days and threaten to overwhelm us like a cloud of darkness.

Help us to see that amid the hustle and bustle
of this holiday time—the crowded stores and rude shoppers,
the impatient drivers, the frayed generosity—
you have become incarnate,

sanctifying the smallest tasks of love, generosity, and kindness
that we are enabled by your grace to perform.

We think of the needs of others at this time, O Lord,
and we are embarrassed by our selfishness.
May the answer to our prayers begin with us to redeem the times.
Bring to all those who are in need the alleviation of their poverty
or comfort for their minds and spirits.
Enable us to do what we can to help them—
to share our own happiness and prosperity,
to provide a listening ear or friendly word,
to do errands or acts of kindness.
But let us not be content so long as conditions exist
that foster human distress from generation to generation
through the repetition of ignorance, filth, and disease.

We pray that the promise of your birth—
that peace shall be on earth—
may soon be fulfilled,
both in our troubled hearts and in our troubled world.
Come to us, Lord, for we need your presence in our own lives.
We pray especially for those dear to us who are sick, or troubled,
or unsure, or near the hour of their death.
Comfort, comfort your people, and fill each heart with your love.

We pray for the world into which you came
and which you still love.
Touch us anew with the hope that is the heritage
of those who love you and trust your promises.

Through Jesus Christ, who is the joy of those who are happy
and the comfort of those who mourn,
as we join the church in the family prayer:
**Our Father . . .**

*Prayers in Litany Form*

5    Remember your church, O Christ;
     send your Spirit of unity, courage, and holiness.
     **Come to us in power, O Christ.**

     By shedding your blood, you have purified us;
     keep us ready to welcome the Day of your coming.
     **Come to us in power, O Christ.**

     Call from among us bearers of your presence;
     may they go to the far ends of the earth
     as tokens of your friendship and signs of your light.
     **Come to us in power, O Christ.**

Give joy to all your faithful servants;
may they follow you all the days of their life.
**Come to us in power, O Christ.**

Nurture within us your Spirit of love;
may we never close our hearts to any of our sisters and brothers.
**Come to us in power, O Christ.**

Bring to an end the divisions between Christians;
gather us in one visible communion.
**Come to us in power, O Christ.**

Have mercy on all who suffer persecution for your name's sake;
uphold them by your strong Spirit,
that they may remain true to you in all their trials.
**Come to us in power, O Christ.**

Comfort all who are suffering in their hearts or in their bodies;
give them health and peace to sing of your power.
**Come to us in power, O Christ.**

We pray for all who are leading the nations;
give them a sense of what is right,
that they may work toward peace and fullness of life for all.
**Come to us in power, O Christ.**

Give eternal rest to all who are dying;
may the light that never sets shine upon them.
**Come to us in power, O Christ. Amen.**

*The following two resources are based on the "O" Antiphons, a traditional Advent prayer that is probably most familiar through the hymn "O Come, O Come, Immanuel." Portions of these prayers may be used in particular Advent services or all together in an extended time of intercessory prayer.*

6    O Immanuel,
     child of promise and sign of hope,
     you come from a distance far beyond our reach,
     yet are closer to us than we are to ourselves:
     remain with us in our own days of expectation,
     that we may give birth to what is just, true, beautiful, and good—
     through the name of Jesus Christ, our Lord,
     who with the Father and the Holy Spirit,
     abides with us, one God now and forever. **Amen.**

     O Wisdom,
     your words uttered in the beginning
     generated a world of beauty and goodness,
     giving purpose and value to each creature;
     instruct us in the way of prudence,
     that we may nurture the world with justice and joy.

Help us to resist evil and to obey you,
so that we may walk in your ways and
the beauty of your creation may flourish—
through the one whom we know as the Wisdom of the ages,
even Christ, our Lord. **Amen.**

O Lord of might,
master of the universe and ruler of the house of Israel,
your mighty acts have rescued remnants of your people
from the midst of slavery, exile, war, and holocaust:
raise your scepter over us, that your saving rule
may be extended to all people in all places—
for the sake of him who we know as Lord of all,
even Jesus, the Christ. **Amen.**

O Root of Jesse,
you reach deep down into the darkness of the earth
and stir the world's longings for deliverance and hope:
raise up within our own lives
a spirit of courage and strength, of wisdom and insight,
that we may do your work for the coming of your kingdom—
through the merits of the one we know as the beginning of the ages,
even Christ, our Lord. **Amen.**

O Key of David and throne of glory,
you open the way to the future and no one closes;
you close the way to the past and no one opens.
Release us and all your people from the oppressions of the past,
that we may face the future with boldness and purpose—
through the merits of the Son of David, Jesus Christ, our Lord. **Amen.**

O Rising Dawn,
you shine with warm brightness and clean freshness,
chasing the fearsome shadows of the night away:
enlighten the lives of your people with visions of shalom
until you bring all things into the harmony of your kingdom—
for the sake of him we call the light of the world, Christ, our Lord. **Amen.**

7    O Wisdom,
Divine Speech,
Eloquent Word of God,
as you spoke to call forth
the creation of this cosmos,
speak again:
Show us the way of life through your coming.
Maranatha. **Come, Lord Jesus.**

O Adonai,
Ruler and Sovereign of your covenant people, Israel,
as you appeared to Moses in the burning bush
and gave him your law at Sinai,

462

come to us in all your saving power.
Maranatha. **Come, Lord Jesus.**

O Root of Jesse,
as you rise as a sign for all the peoples,
and call forth the worship of all the nations,
come quickly to deliver us from sin and death.
Maranatha. **Come, Lord Jesus.**

O Key of David,
scepter over the house of Israel, your covenant people,
you open our hearts, our lives, our futures.
Set free all who are imprisoned,
all those who live in the valley of the shadow of death.
Maranatha. **Come, Lord Jesus.**

O Radiant Dawn,
Sun of righteousness, so full of splendor:
shine your radiance on all
who live in the shadows,
groping for life and light.
Maranatha. **Come, Lord Jesus.**

O Ruler of all nations,
Lord of all time and space,
you hold humanity together.
As you lovingly formed us from the dust of the earth,
lovingly reform, save, and renew us, we pray.
Maranatha. **Come, Lord Jesus.**

O Immanuel,
our Lord and lawgiver,
our hope and desire,
come mightily to save us;
our trust is in you.
Maranatha. **Come, Lord Jesus.**
*[After a brief silence, the leader concludes:]*

Promise-keeping God,
we rejoice in your faithfulness.
Our hearts overflow with hope
as we express our longing for the advent of our Lord.
Prepare us to receive, honor, and follow him,
our Messiah, the King of kings and Lord of lords.
**Amen.**

## D.4.5 Prayers on Pastorally Challenging Topics (see also section 4.5)

*Prayers of Lament*

1   *This prayer of corporate lament and intercession uses short phrases of text, silence, and portions of the familiar Advent hymn "O Come, O Come, Immanuel." Prayer leaders should rewrite the intercessions to express the particular needs and concerns of a local congregation. The prayer concludes with words of assurance from Isaiah 11, followed by the refrain "Rejoice! Rejoice!" which is purposefully held back until the end of the prayer.*

Lord God,
we long for the coming of your kingdom in Jesus Christ, our Lord.
We lament before you the signs
that your kingdom has not come in fullness.
We lament signs of brokenness in the community of nations.
[*Silence*]

We lament that Christians are persecuted
because they profess the name of Jesus.
[*Silence*]

[*All sing*]
"O come, O King of nations, bind
in one the hearts of all mankind.
Bid all our sad divisions cease,
and be yourself our King of peace."

We lament the broken relationships
that bring such pain to many we know.
[*Silence*]

We lament that many of our friends and coworkers
have chosen to ignore or disown the gospel of Christ.
[*Silence*]

[*All sing*]
"O come, O come, Immanuel,
and ransom captive Israel
that mourns in lonely exile here
until the Son of God appear."

We lament racism that plagues our community.
[*Silence*]

We lament the physical and emotional abuse
of children and spouses in our homes.
[*Silence*]

[*All sing*]
"O come, O Bright and Morning Star,
and bring us comfort from afar!
Dispel the shadows of the night
and turn our darkness into light."

*[Reading from Isaiah 11:1-9]*

With resolute hope, despite our sadness,
we sing with the angels and all the people of God:

*[All sing]*
"Rejoice! Rejoice! Immanuel
shall come to you, O Israel."

# D.5 OFFERING

## D.5.2 Offering Prayers (see also section 5.2)

**1**   *A prayer especially mindful of children*

What can I give him, poor as I am?
If I were a shepherd, I would bring a lamb.
If I were a wise man, I would do my part.
Yet what I can, I give him, give him my heart.

**2**   O Mighty One,
you have done and are doing great things for us,
and holy is your name.
Bless all we offer you—ourselves, our time, and our possessions—
that through us your grace and favor
may be made known to all the world,
for the sake of Jesus Christ, our Redeemer. **Amen.**

**3**   God of hope,
you gave your Son to free a lost world.
You give your Spirit to comfort and encourage.
You give us hope for a future
free of pain, sorrow, and tears.
You promise us a future with you.
In gratitude, we bring you our time, talents, and tithes.
May our gifts be used so that many others will taste and see
the goodness of knowing you.
In Jesus' name we pray. **Amen.**

# D.8 THE LORD'S SUPPER

## D.8.2 Great Prayer of Thanksgiving (see section 8.2)

*D.8.2.2 Thanksgiving for the Work of God in Creation (see also section 8.2.2)*

**1**   *This prayer offers thanks for the work of God in creation and may be included in the complete Prayer of Thanksgiving as found in section 8.2 of this book.*

With joy we praise you, gracious God,
for you have created heaven and earth,
made us in your image, and kept covenant with us—
even when we fell into sin.
We give you thanks for Jesus Christ, our Lord,
whose coming opened to us the way of salvation
and whose triumphant return we eagerly await.
Therefore we join our voices
with all the saints and angels and the whole creation
to proclaim the glory of your name.

*D.8.2.4 Thanksgiving for the Work of Christ (see also section 8.2.4)*

**1**   *This prayer offers thanks for the work of Jesus Christ and may be included in the complete Prayer of Thanksgiving as found in section 8.2 of this book.*

You are holy, O God of majesty,
and blessed is Jesus Christ, your Son, our Lord.
You sent him into this world
to satisfy the longings of your people for a Savior,
to bring freedom to the captives of sin,
and to establish justice for the oppressed.
He came among us as one of us,
taking the lot of the poor,
sharing human suffering.
We rejoice that in his death and rising again,
you set before us the sure promise of new life,
the certain hope of a heavenly home
where we will sit at table with Christ, our host.

**D.8.5 Response of Praise and Prayer** (see also section 8.5)

*D.8.5.2 Prayer (see also section 8.5.2)*

1    Strengthen us, O God, in the power of your Spirit
     to bring good news to the poor
     and lift blind eyes to sight,
     to loose the chains that bind
     and claim your blessing for all people.
     Keep us faithful in your service
     until Christ comes in final victory
     and we shall feast with all your saints
     in the joy of your eternal realm.
     Through Christ, with Christ, in Christ,
     in the unity of the Holy Spirit,
     all glory and honor are yours, almighty God,
     now and forever. **Amen.**

# D.9 CLOSING OF WORSHIP

**D.9.1 Sending** (see also section 9.1)

*Call to Service/Discipleship*

1    In gratitude to God, empowered by the Spirit,
     let us strive to serve Christ in our daily tasks
     and to live holy and joyful lives,
     even as we watch for God's new heaven and new earth,
     praying: Come, Lord Jesus!
          —from *A Brief Statement of Faith*

2    Be on guard! Be alert!
     You do not know when that time will come.
     It's like a man going away:
     He leaves his house and puts his servants in charge,
     each with his assigned task,
     and tells the one at the door to keep watch.
     Therefore keep watch because you do not know
     when the owner of the house will come back—
     whether in the evening, or at midnight,

or when the rooster crows, or at dawn.
If he comes suddenly, do not let him find you sleeping.
What I say to you, I say to everyone: "Watch!"
—Mark 13:33-37, NIV

3   Besides this, you know what time it is,
    how it is now the moment for you to wake from sleep.
    For salvation is nearer to us now
    than when we became believers;
    the night is far gone, the day is near.
    Let us then lay aside the works of darkness
    and put on the armor of light.
    —Romans 13:11-12, NRSV

4   In accordance with his promise,
    we wait for new heavens and a new earth,
    where righteousness is at home.
    Therefore, beloved, while you are waiting for these things,
    strive to be found by him at peace, without spot or blemish;
    and regard the patience of our Lord as salvation.
    —2 Peter 3:13-15, NRSV

## *Acclamations/Doxologies*

5   May Jesus Christ be praised!
    May he judge your people with righteousness,
        and your poor with justice.
    May the mountains yield prosperity for the people,
        and the hills, in righteousness.
    **For he defends the cause of the poor of the people**
        **and gives deliverance to the needy.**

    May he live while the sun endures,
        and as long as the moon, throughout all generations.
    May he be like rain that falls on the mown grass,
        like showers that water the earth.
    In his days may righteousness flourish
        and peace abound, until the moon is no more.
    May he have dominion from sea to sea.
    May all kings fall down before him,
        all nations give him service.
    **For he delivers the needy when they call,**
        **the poor and those who have no helper.**
    **He has pity on the weak and the needy,**
        **and saves the lives of the needy.**
    **From oppression and violence he redeems their life;**
        **and precious is their blood in his sight.**

May his name endure forever,
    his fame continue as long as the sun.
May all nations be blessed in him.
**May Jesus Christ be praised!**
      —based on Psalm 72, NRSV

6    Blessed be the LORD, the God of Israel,
      who alone does wondrous things.
    Blessed be his glorious name forever;
      may his glory fill the whole earth.
        **Amen and Amen.**
      —Psalm 72:18-19, NRSV

## Closing Prayers

7    Eternal God,
    you taught us that the night is far spent and the day is at hand.
    Keep us awake and alert, watching for your kingdom,
    and make us strong in faith,
    so that when Christ comes in glory to judge the earth,
    we may joyfully give him praise
    who lives and reigns with you and the Holy Spirit,
    one God, now and forever. **Amen.**

8    O King of nations,
    your reign spreads through all the lands,
    you defend the cause of the poor
    and plead for the wretched of the earth.
    Fashion us into an obedient people,
    that we may spread the good news
    of your reign of perfect peace and justice,
    until all creation will finally rejoice in your perfect will,
    until all bend the knee to the King of kings and Lord of lords,
    in whose name we pray, even Jesus Christ, your Son and our Savior. **Amen.**

9    Lord, in these days of trials and troubles,
    help us to keep our lamps trimmed and burning.
    Though the bridegroom may tarry,
    help us stay awake through the night
    so that on that day and hour we do not know,
    we might find the door opened for us,
    and greet our Lord with praise and adoration,
    as he welcomes us to eternal life with him. **Amen.**
      —based on Matthew 25:1-13

**D.9.2 Blessing/Benediction** (see also section 9.2)

1    Isaiah says,
> "The root of Jesse shall come,
>> the one who rises to rule the Gentiles;
>
> in him the Gentiles shall hope."

May the God of hope fill you with all joy and peace in believing,
so that you may abound in hope by the power of the Holy Spirit.
>> —Romans 15:12-13, NRSV

2    May the Lord make you increase and abound in love
for one another and for all,
just as we abound in love for you.
And may he so strengthen your hearts in holiness
that you may be blameless before our God and Father
at the coming of our Lord Jesus with all his saints.
>> —1 Thessalonians 3:12-13, NRSV

3    May the God of peace himself sanctify you entirely;
and may your spirit and soul and body
be kept sound and blameless
at the coming of our Lord Jesus Christ.
The one who calls you is faithful,
and he will do this.
>> —1 Thessalonians 5:23-24, NRSV

4    God the Father, who loved the world
so much that he sent his only Son,
give you grace to prepare for eternal life.
God the Son, who comes to us as Redeemer and Judge,
reveal to you the path from darkness to light.
God the Holy Spirit, by whose working
the virgin Mary conceived the Christ,
help you bear the fruits of holiness. **Amen.**

# D.10 SUGGESTED SCRIPTURE READINGS

1    *Songs of Advent*

    1 Samuel 2:1-10: Song of Hannah
    Exodus 15:1-19: Song of Moses and Miriam
    Luke 1:67-79: Song of Zechariah
    Luke 1:46-55: Song of Mary
    Luke 2:13-15: Song of Angels
    Luke 2:28-32: Song of Simeon

# SECTION E
# CHRISTMAS

At Christmas, we remember and celebrate the nativity of Christ and the mystery of the incarnation. Whereas during Advent we anticipate the fulfillment of the Old Testament prophecies of the Messiah, at Christmas we identify with the angels who proclaimed, "Glory to God in the highest"; with the shepherds, who were afraid but nevertheless offered worship; and with Mary, who pondered the meaning of these events in her heart (Luke 2:13-20).

The spirit of the worship service and the visuals of the worship space change dramatically from the Fourth Sunday of Advent to the celebration of Christmas. White, yellow, and gold are the colors of Christmas, and many visual symbols and images—angels, candles, the star of peace, shepherds, the manger, and so on—come to mind. Christmas carols have their own built-in spirit of celebration.

The Christmas season extends from December 25 through January 5 and includes at least

one and usually two Sundays. Celebrating Christmas as a season helps us both to enter into the meaning of the incarnation more fully than celebrating a single day and to focus on additional Scripture texts that explore the meaning of Christmas beyond the familiar words of Luke 2.

Though North American culture considers Christmas the most important day of the Christian year, we must be careful to see the significance of Christmas in the light of all that follows, particularly Easter. In fact, Christmas is the first in a series of celebrations (Christmas, Epiphany, the baptism of our Lord, and the transfiguration of Jesus) that affirm the identity of Jesus as not only fully human but also fully divine. If the intervening weeks between these celebrations focus on the remarkable content of Jesus' teaching and the relationships he established with his disciples, these four events anchor the church's reflection on the meaning of Jesus' life for our understanding of God and of the coming kingdom. Together, these celebrations prepare us for the journey toward the cross and the empty tomb.

---

### Scriptures and Statements of Faith Applying to the Theme of Christmas

*The following texts are particularly appropriate for sermons or for supplemental liturgical use.*

| | | |
|---|---|---|
| Psalm 97 | Jeremiah 31:7-14 | Ephesians 2:13-18 |
| Psalm 98 | Matthew 1:18-2:23 | Titus 2:11-14 |
| Psalm 147 | Luke 2 | Titus 3:4-7 |
| Psalm 148 | John 1:1-18 | Hebrews 1:1-12 |
| Isaiah 52:7-10 | Galatians 4:4-7 | Hebrews 2:10-18 |
| Isaiah 61:10-62:12 | Ephesians 1:3-14 | 1 John 4:13-16 |
| Isaiah 63:7-9 | | |

Belgic Confession, Art. 18-19
Heidelberg Catechism, Q&A's 35-36
Westminster Confession, Chap. VIII, Sec. 2-3
*Our Song of Hope*, st. 3
*Our World Belongs to God*, st. 23

# E.1 Opening of Worship

**E.1.2 Call to Worship** (see also section 1.2)

1   The people walking in darkness
      have seen a great light;
    **on those living in the land of the shadow of death**
      **a light has dawned.**

    Jesus Christ is our life and light.
    In his name and in his power, let us worship God!
          —based on Isaiah 9:2, NIV

2   *A text especially mindful of children*

    All God's people—
    Boys and girls, women, men:
    **Come and worship!**
    Shepherds, Magi, saints, and angels:
    **Come and worship! Come and worship!**
    All who need the Savior, all who long for comfort:
    **Come and worship, come and worship Christ, the newborn King!**

3   Let us go, in heart and mind, to see what has come to pass.
    Let us go with the shepherds:
    **Let us go to find the Savior!**
    Let us go with the wise ones:
    **Let us go to find God's promise, born for us!**
    Let us go with the poor and humble:
    **Let us go to find our King, born in a lowly manger.**
    Let us go with all the world, with all the peoples of the nations.
    Come, let us worship; come, let us adore him:
    **Christ the Lord!**

4   Lift up your hearts in prayer:
    lift up your voices in praise.
    Let your eyes rise in expectation
    and your hands in exultation,
    for the Lord has drawn near
    and dwells among us.
    **We lift them up. Amen.**

5   God is here! The Messiah has come!
    We open our eyes to see him and lift our hearts to worship him.
    We have come to exalt the name of Jesus, our Savior and King,
    and to bring glory to God the Father.

In our worship we demonstrate the mind of Christ
in declaring to God that he is the supreme authority in our lives.
We bow before him in submission to our Lord and King.
**Come, worship the Lord!**

### E.1.4 Opening Responses (see also section 1.4)

*In addition to these resources, see also the Advent candle-lighting resources (pp. 432-440), which include suggested texts for Christmas.*

## Prayers of Adoration

1    *A prayer especially mindful of children*

Jesus, Son of the living God, splendor of the Father, eternal light.
**Lord, we praise you!**
Jesus, King of glory, sun of justice, son of the virgin Mary.
**Lord, we praise you!**
Jesus, Wonderful Counselor, everlasting Lord, Prince of Peace.
**Lord, we praise you!**
Jesus, gentle and humble of heart, our help and our refuge.
**Lord, we praise you!**
Jesus, God of peace, friend of all, source of life and of holiness.
**Lord, we praise you!**
Jesus, brother of the poor, goodness without measure, unending wisdom.
**Lord, we praise you!**
Jesus, good shepherd, true light, our way and our life.
**Lord, we praise you! Amen.**

2    Everlasting God,
your Son is the light of the world.
Your Son is the way, the truth, and the life.
Lead us by your light and truth.
Looking for Jesus, let us find him.
Looked for by Jesus, we are found first. **Amen.**

3    Almighty God,
you wonderfully created
and yet more wonderfully restored
the dignity of human nature.
In your mercy, by the power of the Holy Spirit,
grant that we may share the divine life of Jesus Christ,
who humbled himself to share our humanity
and who now lives and reigns with you and the Holy Spirit,
one God, now and forever. **Amen.**

4    All glory to you, great God,
for the gift of your Son,
light in darkness and hope of the world,

whom you sent to save us.
With singing angels
let us praise your name
and tell the earth his story,
that all may believe, rejoice, and bow down,
acknowledging your love
through Jesus Christ, our Lord. **Amen.**

5    God of glory,
your splendor shines from a manger in Bethlehem
into the darkness of human night.
Open our eyes to Christ's presence in the shadows of our world
so that we, like him, may become beacons of your justice
and defenders of all for whom there is no room. **Amen.**

6    Come and stand amazed, you people,
see how God is reconciled!
See his plans of love accomplished,
see his gift, this newborn child.
See the Mighty, weak and tender,
see the Word who now is mute.
See the Sovereign without splendor,
see the Fullness destitute;
the Beloved, whom we covet,
in a state of low repute.

See how humankind received him;
see him wrapped in swaddling bands,
who as Lord of all creation
rules the wind by his commands.
See him lying in a manger
without sign of reasoning;
Word of God to flesh surrendered,
he is wisdom's crown, our King.
See how tender our Defender
at whose birth the angels sing.

O Lord Jesus, God incarnate,
who assumed this humble form,
counsel me and let my wishes
to your perfect will conform.
Light of life, dispel my darkness,
let your frailty strengthen me;
let your meekness give me boldness,
let your burden set me free;
let your sadness give me gladness,
let your death be life for me. **Amen.**

7  Glory be to God in the highest,
   and on earth peace, goodwill toward those he favors.
   For unto us is born a Savior, who is Christ the Lord.
   We praise you, we bless you, we glorify you,
   we give thanks unto you for this greatest of your mercies,
   O Lord God, heavenly King, God the Father almighty.
   O Lord, the only begotten Son, Jesus Christ.
   O Lord God, Lamb of God, Son of the Father,
   who was made human to take away the sins of the world,
   have mercy upon us and turn us from our iniquities.
   You who were made manifest to destroy the works of the devil,
   have mercy upon us and enable us to renounce and forsake them.
   You who are the great advocate with the Father, receive our prayer. **Amen.**

### Prayers of Invocation

8  O Immanuel,
   O Wisdom from on high,
   O Lord of might,
   O Branch of Jesse's stem,
   O Key of David,
   O Bright and Morning Star,
   O King of nations,
   We rejoice and are glad
   on this bright Christmas morning,
   for truly you have come,
   full of grace and truth.
   Even now, come into our hearts again.
   Show us the path of knowledge.
   Comfort us in our mourning.
   Save us from our sin.
   Open wide our way to heaven.
   Turn our darkness into light.
   End our sad divisions
   and be our King of peace,
   so that every creature in heaven and on earth
   will join in a chorus of praise,
   and shout with joy to you, our Lord. **Amen.**

9  *A prayer especially mindful of children*

   Be near us, Lord Jesus, we ask you to stay
   close by us forever and love us, we pray.
   Immanuel, we invite you to draw near and dwell with us.
   Surround us with your tender, caring presence,
   that what we say and do in worship
   might prepare us to live forever with you in heaven.
   In your powerful name we pray. **Amen.**

10   We pray, O Lord, purify our hearts,
      that they may be worthy to become your dwelling place.
      Let us never fail to find room for you,
      but come and abide in us, that we also may abide in you,
      who were born into the world for us,
      you, who live and reign,
      King of kings and Lord of lords, now and for evermore. **Amen.**

11   O God, our Father, creator of the universe,
      whose Son, Jesus Christ, came to our world,
      pour your Holy Spirit upon your church,
      that all people of our world,
      being led through the knowledge of your truth to worship you,
      may offer the gold of intellect,
      the frankincense of devotion,
      and the myrrh of discipline
      to him who, with you and the Holy Spirit,
      lives and reigns for ever, one God, world without end. **Amen.**

## Additional Resources

12   *A prayer especially mindful of children*

      He came as a baby in a manger.
      **O come, let us adore him.**
      He came in a lowly stable.
      **O come, let us adore him.**
      Shepherds brought their worship.
      **O come, let us adore him.**
      Angels sang his praise.
      **O come, let us adore him.**
      Magi brought their gifts.
      **O come, let us adore him.**
      What shall we do?
      **O come, let us adore him, Christ, the Lord! Amen.**

13   Emmanuel, God with us,
      you are our heart's delight.
      Because of your amazing love,
      you came to earth,
      you became one of us,
      you reached out to us while we were lost,
      you rescued us from death,
      you brought us salvation.
      Your love is so high and wide and deep
      that it, and only it, could reach this suffering world.
      You came to bring an end to our sadness,
      to dry our tears, to still our fears, to give us hope.

In deep gratitude we praise you.
We worship you for dwelling among us. **Amen.**

14   You came in the fullness of time, O Savior,
     emptying yourself for us.
     Your incarnation foreshadowed, O Savior,
     that you would be obedient unto death.
     Therefore God has given you, O Savior,
     a name that is above all names:
     we confess you are Christ the Lord!
              —based on Philippians 2:5-11

15   O God, our loving Father,
     help us rightly to remember the birth of Jesus,
     that we may share in the songs of the angels,
     the gladness of the shepherds,
     and the worship of the Magi.
     May the Christmas morning make us happy to be your children,
     and the Christmas evening bring us to our beds with grateful thoughts,
     forgiving and forgiven, for Jesus' sake. **Amen.**

16   O God, you have caused this holy night [*day*]
     to shine with the brightness of the true light.
     Grant that we, who have known the mystery of that light on earth,
     may also enjoy him perfectly in heaven,
     where with you and the Holy Spirit he lives and reigns,
     one God, in glory everlasting. **Amen.**

17   O God, who made this most hallowed night
     resplendent with the glory of the true light;
     grant that we who have known the mysteries of that light on earth
     may enter into the fullness of his joys in heaven. **Amen.**

18   Let your goodness, Lord, appear to us,
     that we, made in your image, may conform ourselves to it.
     In our own strength we cannot imitate
     your majesty, power, and wonder;
     nor is it fitting for us to try.
     But your mercy reaches from the heavens,
     through the clouds, to the earth below.
     You have come to us as a small child,
     but you have brought us the greatest of all gifts,
     the gift of eternal love. **Amen.**

19   God of power and might,
     in this bleak midwinter
     we humbly offer our praise to you.
     The coming of your Son
     breaks our night

like the coming of the dawn.
This sun of righteousness
warms our faith
and stokes our hope
that one day your kingdom
will fully come in grace and truth. **Amen.**

20    O Lord, our God,
as we celebrate again the festival of Christmas,
we ask you to make us humble and loving like Jesus,
who did not come to be served but to serve,
and who said that it is better to give than to receive,
so that in his name
we may devote ourselves to the care
and service of all who are in need.
We ask this through the same Jesus Christ, our Lord. **Amen.**

21    God of love,
open the hearts and minds of many this Christmastime
to the good and saving news of Jesus Christ,
that all whose lives are insecure, or empty, or aimless,
may find in the one born at Bethlehem all they need today—
and much more besides. For his name's sake, **Amen.**

22    Good Christian friends, rejoice!
Today your Lord comes
in love and power,
in grace and truth,
offering hope and peace.
**Christ is born today! Alleluia!**
This promised one,
mighty, though small,
is our hope, our strength, and our life.
**Christ is born to save! Alleluia!**
In hope, let us worship God. Alleluia! **Amen.**

23    Almighty and everlasting God,
you have stooped to raise fallen humanity.
Grant that we who have seen your glory revealed in our human nature,
and your love made perfect in our weakness,
may daily be renewed in your image
and conformed to the pattern of your Son,
Jesus Christ, our Lord. **Amen.**

24    You surprised a world, O God,
by coming not in clashing thunder or flashing lights
but in the quiet and simple splendor of a child's radiant face.
Help us to understand this mystery of love beyond all loves,
that we may be led to a new kind of love:

a love that loves not by what we can get but in what we can give,
a love that counts not who is worthy to receive
but, beyond our human calculations, is showered freely on all.
Show us the way of Bethlehem's child,
that in seeing, we may believe,
and in believing, we may learn again how to love. **Amen.**

25    Lord Jesus, you were a refugee in Egypt
when your family fled for fear of death.
Move us by your Spirit to welcome the stranger
who seeks asylum in our midst,
that our nation may be filled with your justice and peace,
and no one in need may be denied. **Amen.**

# E.2 CONFESSION AND ASSURANCE

### E.2.1 Call to Confession (see also section 2.1)

1    Today we celebrate that Jesus, our Lord,
came to earth as a human, just like us but without sin.
He came so that we who sin may be freed from sin.
With the peace that comes from knowing Jesus came,
let us confess our sins and be forgiven.

### E.2.2 Prayers of Confession (see also section 2.2)

1    God of love,
all year long we pursue power and money,
yet you come in weakness.
All season long we covet great material gifts,
when you alone offer what is lasting.
Through the work of this Lord Jesus,
who comes among us full of grace and truth,
forgive us,
heal us,
correct us.
Then open our lips,
that we may sing your praise with the angels,
and remake our lives,

that we may witness to your transforming love.
Through Christ, our Lord. **Amen.**

2   O God, in the beginning you spoke,
    and creation was born, the object of your loving care.
    In the fullness of time you spoke,
    and the Word became flesh, Jesus, gift of your love.
    We wonder at the miracle of creation;
    we stand in awe before the mystery of the incarnation.
    Forgive us earthbound creatures, feeble in faith,
    empty of hope, lacking in love.
    This year let the miracle and mystery of Christmas happen for us again.
    We wait upon you with ready hearts, O God,
    through Jesus Christ, our Lord. **Amen.**

3   O God, we need Christ to renew our commitment.
    **We confess that our lack of faith has made us fearful.**
    May your angels sing again to us of peace for body and soul.
    **We acknowledge that we have foolishly let our desires
    lead us astray.**
    May your star once more set our course firmly in your direction.
    **We have turned our faith into a lifeless ritual.**
    May your manger call us again to expressions of love and devotion.
    **We have carefully kept our gifts
    and have not freely given our goods and our hearts to you.**
    May the Magi show us the spirit of giving.
    **Lord, may your Spirit linger in our hearts
    and bring renewal in our lives. Amen.**

4   Generous God,
    you give us the greatest gift of all, yourself,
    but often we find it hard to take notice;
    we are caught up with our own gifts, given and received.
    **Forgive us, generous God,
    for the casual way we treat your gift of love.
    Cast out our sin and enter in,
    be born in us today.**

5   Holy God, you sent a star
    to guide the Magi to the child Jesus.
    We confess that we have not followed the light of your Word.
    We have not searched for signs of your love in the world
    or trusted your good news to be good.
    We have failed to praise your Son's birth
    and refused his peace on earth.
    We have expected little
    and hoped for less.
    Forgive our doubt

and renew in us all fine desires,
that we may watch and wait
and once more hear the glad story of our Savior,
Jesus Christ, the Lord. **Amen.**

6    When we allow darkness to overcome the light,
     **forgive us, Lord.**
     When we reduce Christmas to plastic and tinsel,
     **have mercy on us, Father.**
     When hardness of heart keeps us from seeing and hearing and touching,
     **let your grace consume us, O God.**
     When the wars around us are of no concern,
     **forgive us, Lord, and move us to compassion for those who suffer.**
     When our caring is not extended to action,
     **move us to seek justice for our brothers and sisters.**
     **We come to confess our sinfulness before you and before each other.**
     **We are but dust without your love. Remove all barriers that divide us,**
     **and let there be no obstacle to our love for you and for one another.**
     **Amen.**

7    Almighty God who inhabits eternity
     but dwells with those who are of a humble and contrite spirit:
     before you and our Lord Jesus Christ
     we confess our sins.
     We have ignored the presence of your Spirit.
     We have failed to look for the return
     of our Savior and Judge.
     We have been blind to your coming
     in the suffering of the hungry, the exiled,
     the destitute, the sick, and the imprisoned.
     In your great goodness
     put away our offenses
     and cleanse us from our sin, for Jesus' sake. **Amen.**

## E.2.4 Assurance of Pardon (see also section 2.4)

1    Break forth together into singing,
         you ruins of Jerusalem;
     for the Lord has comforted his people,
         he has redeemed Jerusalem.
     The Lord has bared his holy arm
         before the eyes of all the nations;
     and all the ends of the earth shall see
         the salvation of our God.

     People of God, through the coming of Jesus Christ,
     whose birth we celebrate,
     the Lord has comforted and redeemed us too!

In Christ we receive the salvation of our God.
Glory to God in the highest!
      —based on Isaiah 52:9-10; Luke 2:14, NRSV

2    Go through, go through the gates,
         prepare the way for the people;
      build up, build up the highway,
         clear it of stones,
         lift up an ensign over the peoples.
      The Lord has proclaimed to the end of the earth:
         Say to daughter Zion, "See, your salvation comes;
      his reward is with him,
         and his recompense before him."
      They shall be called, "The Holy People,
         The Redeemed of the Lord";
      and you shall be called, "Sought Out,
         A City Not Forsaken."

      People of God, in Jesus Christ you are a holy people,
      the redeemed of the Lord.
      Praise God, from whom all blessings flow!
         —based on Isaiah 62:10-12, NRSV

3    She will give birth to a son,
      and you are to give him the name Jesus,
      because he will save his people from their sins.
         —Matthew 1:21, NIV

4    I bring you good news that will cause great joy for all the people.
      Today in the town of David a Savior has been born to you;
      he is the Messiah, the Lord.
         —Luke 2:10-11, NIV

5    To all who did receive him,
      to those who believed in his name,
      he gave the right to become children of God.
         —John 1:12, NIV

6    God has caused light to shine in our hearts,
      the light that is knowledge of the glory of God
      in the face of Jesus Christ.
         —based on 2 Corinthians 4:6

7    When the fullness of time had come,
      God sent his Son, born of a woman, born under the law,
      in order to redeem those who were under the law,
      so that we might receive adoption as children.
         —Galatians 4:4-5, NRSV

8    The saying is sure and worthy of full acceptance,
     that Christ Jesus came into the world to save sinners.

     In Christ, we are forgiven! Thanks be to God!
          —based on 1 Timothy 1:15, NRSV

9    The grace of God has appeared, bringing salvation to all.
          —Titus 2:11, NRSV

10   When the goodness and loving kindness
     of God our Savior appeared,
     he saved us, not because of any works of righteousness
     that we had done, but according to his mercy,
     through the water of rebirth and renewal by the Holy Spirit.
     This Spirit he poured out on us richly through Jesus Christ our Savior,
     so that, having been justified by his grace,
     we might become heirs according to the hope of eternal life.
          —Titus 3:4-7, NRSV

11   The Lord's grace is sure.
     God has looked with favor upon his people
     and has redeemed them.
     God has raised up a mighty savior
     from the house of David.
     God spoke through the prophets of old
     so that we would be saved from our enemies
     and from the hand of all who hate us.
     God has shown mercy and has remembered his promises.
          —based on Luke 1:68-72

12   In the past God spoke to our ancestors
     through the prophets at many times and in various ways,
     but in these last days he has spoken to us by his Son,
     whom he appointed heir of all things,
     and through whom also he made the universe.
     The Son is the radiance of God's glory
     and the exact representation of his being,
     sustaining all things by his powerful word.
     After he had provided purification for sins,
     he sat down at the right hand of the Majesty in heaven.
          —Hebrews 1:1-3, NIV

# E.3 PROCLAIMING THE WORD

**E.3.1 Prayers for Illumination** (see also section 3.1)

1    Mighty God,
the shepherds of old were full of your praises,
saying that all they had heard and seen
was mirrored by what they had been told.
Move among us now with your Holy Spirit,
that we too might hear and experience
the wonder and joy of the living Word
as we seek to welcome the written Word into our lives.
In Jesus' name, **Amen.**

2    O Christ, the prophets foretold your coming,
the poor longed to see you.
The heavens celebrated your birth;
the apostles, the martyrs, and the faithful down though the ages
repeated the song of the angels.
Your church praises you in every human language,
for she has seen your salvation.
Son of God, you humbled yourself and became a servant,
raising us up to share in your glory.
We were in darkness and you have given us
light and strength, peace and joy.
Lead us according to your loving will;
make us a people who follow you in holiness.
Give us generous hearts to hear your Word,
and produce in us abundant fruit,
through the power of your Spirit. **Amen.**

**E.3.6 Profession of Our Church's Faith** (see also section 3.6)

1    In the beginning was the Word,
and the Word was with God, and the Word was God.
**He was in the beginning with God.**
All things came into being through him,
and without him not one thing came into being.
**What has come into being in him was life,**
**and the life was the light of all people.**
The light shines in the darkness,
**and the darkness did not overcome it.**

The true light, which enlightens everyone, was coming into the world.
**He was in the world, and the world came into being through him;**
**yet the world did not know him.**
He came to what was his own,
**and his own people did not accept him.**
But to all who received him, who believed in his name,
he gave power to become children of God,
**who were born, not of blood or of the will of the flesh**
**or of the will of man, but of God.**
And the Word became flesh and lived among us,
**and we have seen his glory, the glory as of a father's only son,**
**full of grace and truth.**

> —John 1:1-5, 9-14, NRSV

2 I believe the Word was in the form of God
and did not count equality with God
a thing to be grasped.
He emptied himself,
took the form of a servant,
and was born in our own likeness.
I believe he humbled himself
and became obedient unto death.
I believe God has highly exalted him
and bestowed on him the name
that is above every name.
I believe that at the name of Jesus
every knee shall bow,
every knee in heaven and on earth and under the earth.
I believe that every tongue will confess
that Jesus Christ is Lord
to the glory of God the Father. **Amen.**

> —based on Philippians 2:6-11

3 We declare to you what was from the beginning,
what we have heard, what we have seen with our eyes,
what we have looked at and touched with our hands,
concerning the word of life—
this life was revealed, and we have seen it and testify to it,
and declare to you the eternal life
that was with the Father and was revealed to us—
we declare to you what we have seen and heard
so that you also may have fellowship with us;
and truly our fellowship is with the Father
and with his Son Jesus Christ.
We are writing these things so that our joy may be complete.

> —1 John 1:1-4, NRSV

4    As followers of Jesus Christ,
living in this world—
which some seek to control,
and others view with despair—
we declare with joy and trust:
**Our world belongs to God!**
Our world, fallen into sin,
has lost its first goodness,
but God has not abandoned the work of his hands:
**our Maker preserves this world, sending seasons, sun, and rain,**
**upholding all creatures, renewing the earth,**
**promising a Savior, guiding all things to their purpose.**
Remembering the promise to reconcile the world to himself,
God joined our humanity in Jesus Christ—
the eternal Word made flesh.
**He is the long-awaited Messiah,**
**one with us and one with God,**
**fully human and fully divine,**
**conceived by the Holy Spirit**
**and born of the virgin Mary.**
Being both divine and human,
Jesus is the only mediator.
**He alone paid the debt of our sin;**
**there is no other Savior.**
Jesus Christ rules over all.
To follow the Lord is
to serve him wherever we are,
without fitting in,
light in the darkness,
salt in a spoiling world.
       —from *Our World Belongs to God,* st. 1, 4, 23, 26, 43

5    I believe in one Lord Jesus Christ,
the only begotten of the Father before all worlds;
God of God, Light of light,
very God of very God;
begotten, not made,
being of one substance with the Father,
by whom all things were made.
Who, for us and our salvation,
came down from heaven,
and became incarnate by the Holy Spirit of the virgin Mary,
and was made man.
       —from Nicene Creed

6    We believe that Jesus Christ,
according to his divine nature,
is the only Son of God—

eternally begotten,
not made or created,
for then he would be a creature.
He is one in essence with the Father; coeternal;
the exact image of the person of the Father
and the "reflection of God's glory,"
being like the Father in all things.
Jesus Christ is the Son of God
not only from the time he assumed our nature
but from all eternity,
as the following testimonies teach us
when they are taken together.
Moses says that God created the world;
and John says that all things were created through the Word,
which he calls God.
The apostle says that God created the world through the Son.
He also says that God created all things through Jesus Christ.
And so it must follow
that the one who is called God, the Word, the Son, and Jesus Christ
already existed before creating all things.
Therefore the prophet Micah says
that Christ's origin is "from ancient days."
And the apostle says that the Son has "neither beginning of days nor end of life."
So then, he is the true eternal God, the Almighty,
whom we invoke, worship, and serve.

—Belgic Confession, Art. 10

7    We confess that God fulfilled the promise
made to the early fathers and mothers
by the mouth of the holy prophets
when he sent the only and eternal Son of God
into the world at the time appointed.
The Son took the "form of a slave"
and was made in "human form,"
truly assuming a real human nature,
with all its weaknesses, except for sin;
being conceived in the womb of the blessed virgin Mary
by the power of the Holy Spirit,
without male participation.
And Christ not only assumed human nature
as far as the body is concerned
but also a real human soul,
in order to be a real human being.
For since the soul had been lost as well as the body,
Christ had to assume them both to save them both together.
In this way Christ is truly our Immanuel—
that is: "God with us."

—from Belgic Confession, Art. 18

**8** Why is he called God's "only begotten Son"
when we also are God's children?
**Because Christ alone is the eternal, natural Son of God.**
**We, however, are adopted children of God—**
**adopted by grace through Christ.**
—Heidelberg Catechism, Q&A 33

**9** What does it mean that he
"was conceived by the Holy Spirit
and born of the virgin Mary"?
**That the eternal Son of God,**
**who is and remains true and eternal God,**
**took to himself, through the working of the Holy Spirit,**
**from the flesh and blood of the virgin Mary,**
**a truly human nature**
**so that he might become David's true descendant,**
**in all things like us except for sin.**
—from Heidelberg Catechism, Q&A 35

**10** How does the holy conception
and birth of Christ benefit you?
**He is our mediator,**
**and, in God's sight,**
**he covers with his innocence and perfect holiness**
**my sinfulness in which I was conceived.**
—Heidelberg Catechism, Q&A 36

**11** We believe that the Son of God, the second person of the Trinity,
being truly and eternally God, of one substance and equal with the Father,
did, when the fullness of time had come, take upon himself human nature,
with all its essential properties and common frailties, yet without sin.
He was conceived by the power of the Holy Spirit
in the womb of the virgin Mary, and of her substance.
In this way, two whole natures, the divine and the human,
perfect and distinct, were inseparably joined together in one person
without being changed, mixed, or confused.
This person is truly God and truly man,
yet one Christ, the only mediator between God and man.
In his human nature, united to the divine nature, the Lord Jesus
was set apart and anointed with the Holy Spirit beyond measure,
having in him all the treasures of wisdom and knowledge.
In him the Father was pleased to have all fullness dwell, so that—
being holy, blameless, and undefiled, full of grace and truth—
he might be completely equipped
to fulfill the office of a mediator and guarantor.
He did not take this office to himself but was called to it by his Father,
who put all power and judgment into his hand
and commanded him to execute it.
—from Westminster Confession (MESV), Chap. VIII, Sec. 2-3

**12**   *A text especially mindful of children*

> **Jesus is our Savior!** He gave his life to rescue us.
> **Jesus is our Shepherd!** He leads our lives and keeps us safe.
> **Jesus is our Friend!** He listens to us; he shares our joys and our sadness.
> **Jesus is our Prophet!** He speaks God's promises to us;
>     he declares God's commands.
> **Jesus is our Priest!** He pleads our cause daily.
> **Jesus is our King!** He guards and keeps us in the freedom he won for us.
> **Jesus is our Lord!** He protects us—in life and in death we belong to him.
> **Jesus is our Life!** He conquered death for us.
>     Risen with him, we enjoy new life.
> **Jesus is our Way!** He guides us to his kingdom.
> **Jesus is our End!** Soon we will be with him,
>     and we will worship him forever and ever.
> As we celebrate Christmas, the birthday of Jesus,
> we rejoice that Jesus came to save us,
> and we look forward to the day
> when we will join all who love him
> and crown him Lord of all.

**13**   Our only hope is Jesus Christ.
>   After we refused to live in the image of God,
>   he was born of the virgin Mary,
>   sharing our genes and our instincts,
>   entering our culture, speaking our language,
>   fulfilling the law of our God.
>   Being united to Christ's humanity,
>   we know ourselves when we rest in him.
>   Jesus Christ is the hope of God's world.
>                   —*Our Song of Hope*, st. 3-4

# E.4 PRAYERS OF THE PEOPLE

## E.4.4 Complete Model Outlines and Prayers (see also section 4.4)

*Prayer Outlines*

**1**   *The following is a guide for extemporaneous prayers. The pattern provides a suggested text for the opening and closing of each part of the prayer and calls for extemporaneous prayers of thanksgiving, petition, and intercession.*

Incarnate God,
with the angels we sing and glorify your name,
thankful for all that you have given us:
> for your presence in the world . . .
> for our nation . . .
> for our community and its leaders . . .
> for the witness of your church celebrating around the world . . .

But today we are especially grateful for the gift of your Son, who gave up his heavenly home for a manger and a cross so that we might experience redemption, a gift that neither spoils nor fades.

With the angels we also desire peace on earth, a peace that is broader and deeper than the end of war. We pray for the restoration of this world, for the growth of your kingdom, for reconciliation, healing, and renewal. We bring before you our prayers for
> the nations of the world, especially . . .
> our nation and those in authority . . .
> our community and those who govern it . . .
> the church universal, its mission, and those who minister . . .
> the local congregation and its ministry, especially . . .
> those with particular needs on this holy day . . .

Make your incarnate presence known in each situation, and may we as your servants be vessels of your peace.

We pray this in the name of the one who became flesh and dwelt among us, Jesus Christ, our Lord. **Amen.**


*Complete Prose Prayers*

2    *The following prayer may be led by two people, with one reading the texts from Scripture (in quotations) and the other reading the other portions.*

"This is what will prove it to you: you will find a baby,
wrapped in strips of cloth and lying in a manger."

Eternal God, we bow before the mystery of your incarnation.
You have chosen weakness to confound the strong
and poverty to send the rich empty away.
We remember the millions in our world today
who are hungry, who receive no hospitality—
all with whom your Son has become one by being born in a manger.
[*Silence*]

"Blessed be the Lord our God,
for he has visited and redeemed his people."
The angel of the Lord appeared in a dream to Joseph and said,
"Herod will be looking for the child in order to kill him.
So get up, take the child and his mother and escape to Egypt."
Joseph got up, took the child and his mother and left during the night.

Merciful God, we call upon you
for all who have fled their homes in the darkness of night.
We remember the millions in our world who have been made refugees,
who have sought asylum in lands not their own,
who are displaced, homeless, landless, or lost—
all whose experience you have made your own in the life of your Son.
[*Silence*]

"He has stretched out his mighty arm
and scattered the proud with all their plans."
Herod gave orders to kill all the boys in Bethlehem
and its neighborhood who were two years old and younger.
In this way what the prophet Jeremiah had said came true:
"A sound is heard in Ramah, the sound of bitter weeping.
Rachel is crying for her children;
she refuses to be comforted, for they are dead."

Loving God, our hearts are heavy
with the sufferings of this world.
We remember the many victims of political power and greed:
the innocent killed in war and violence,
all those who are tortured or put to death,
those who languish in prison and camps,
those missing or taken hostage—
all whose lot your Son shared by being born when Herod was king.
[*Silence*]

"He has brought down mighty rulers from their thrones,
and lifted up the lowly."
And Mary said: "I am the Lord's servant;
may it happen to me as you have said."

Gracious God, you placed yourself in the care of Mary
to show to the world your will to save.
Give us grace to follow her example:
to become instruments of your grace,
servants of your will, and channels of your love.
May it happen to us as you have willed.
[*Silence*]

"My soul magnifies the Lord,
and my spirit rejoices in God, my Savior."

O God of peace, you fill our hearts with hope at every Christmastide,
for we remember again that this is the world you have loved.
May hope, peace, and joy fill our hearts this night. **Amen.**

    —based on Matthew 2:13-14, 16-18; Luke 1:38, 46-47, 51-52, 68; 2:12

*Prayers in Litany Form*

3    All the ends of the earth
     have seen the salvation of our God. Alleluia!
     **Shout to the Lord, all the earth. Alleluia!**
     O Christ, splendor of God's eternal glory,
     the mighty Word, sustaining the universe:
     Renew our lives by your presence.
     **Lord, have mercy.**
     O Christ, born into the world in the fullness of time
     for the liberation of all creation:
     Release all into your promised freedom.
     **Lord, have mercy.**
     O Christ, begotten of the Father before all time,
     born in a stable at Bethlehem:
     May your church be a sign of hope and joy.
     **Lord, have mercy.**
     O Christ, truly God and truly human,
     born to a people in fulfillment of their expectations:
     Fulfill our desires in you.
     **Lord, have mercy.**
     O Christ, born of the virgin Mary,
     child of wonder and splendor,
     Mighty God of all ages, Prince of Peace:
     May the whole world live in peace and justice.
     **Lord, have mercy.**

# E.5 OFFERING

### E.5.2 Offering Prayers (see also section 5.2)

1    *A prayer especially mindful of children*

     What can I give him, poor as I am?
     If I were a shepherd, I would bring a lamb.
     If I were a wise man, I would do my part.
     Yet what I can, I give him,
     give him my heart.

2     God of wonder, we offer you these humble gifts,
signs of your goodness and mercy.
Receive them with our gratitude,
that through us all people may know
the riches of your love in the Word-made-flesh. **Amen.**

3     Gracious God,
you have shown your great love for your children
by using commonplace things for your purpose—
water to mark your children,
bread and wine to feed and nourish us ordinary people to be disciples,
a child in a manger to announce your grace.
Take these commonplace things,
these gifts of paper and metal and the lives that stand behind them.
Bless and use them to proclaim your gracious love,
for we offer them in the name of Jesus, the Lamb of God. **Amen.**

# E.8 THE LORD'S SUPPER

## E.8.2 Great Prayer of Thanksgiving (see section 8.2)

*E.8.2.2 Thanksgiving for the Work of God in Creation (see also section 8.2.2)*

*The following prayers offer thanks for the work of God in creation and may be included in the complete Prayer of Thanksgiving as found in section 8.2 of this book.*

1     With joy we praise you, gracious God,
for you have created heaven and earth,
made us in your image, and kept covenant with us—
even when we fell into sin.
We give you thanks for Jesus Christ, our Lord,
who came among us as the Word made flesh
to show us your glory, full of grace and truth.
Therefore we join our voices
with all the saints and angels and the whole creation
to proclaim the glory of your name.

2    O God, in the sending of your Son, Jesus,
     to be born of Mary,
     your Word became flesh,
     and we have seen a new and radiant vision of your glory.
     His name is above every name,
     the Prince of Peace and Savior of all.
     In him we have been brought out of darkness
     into your marvelous light.

## E.8.2.4 Thanksgiving for the Work of Christ (see also section 8.2.4)

1    *This prayer offers thanks for the work of Jesus Christ and may be included in the complete
     Prayer of Thanksgiving as found in section 8.2 of this book.*

     This feast for which we gather remembers Jesus' birth, life, death, and resurrection.
     This feast for which we gather proclaims the good news of forgiveness.
     This feast for which we gather nourishes us with Jesus' own life.
     This feast for which we gather celebrates the sure hope we have of Jesus' coming.
     Come to the joyful feast of the Lord.

     We serve a majestic God,
     whose compassion moved him
     to send his only Son
     from heaven to earth.
     This Son, born in a stable,
     lived and worked among us.
     He taught, he healed,
     he served, and he loved.
     This Son loved so much
     that he died for us, rose for us, and lives for us.
     He ascended to heaven,
     where he is our mediator,
     interceding with the Father on our behalf.
     Before that he broke bread with his disciples
     and simply said:
     "Do this in remembrance of me."
     And he took a cup and drank and simply said:
     "This is a new covenant."
     Therefore, in remembrance and in celebration,
     we eat the bread and drink from the cup.
     We proclaim our Lord's death and life until he returns.

# E.9 CLOSING OF WORSHIP

**E.9.1 Sending** (see also section 9.1)

*Call to Service/Discipleship*

1   The grace of God has appeared, bringing salvation to all,
    training us to renounce impiety and worldly passions,
    and in the present age to live lives
    that are self-controlled, upright, and godly,
    while we wait for the blessed hope and the manifestation
    of the glory of our great God and Savior, Jesus Christ.

    Live now in the power of Christ, to the praise of his name!
        —based on Titus 2:11-13, NRSV

2   Go now into the world,
    carrying Christmas with you into everyday life.
    Open the inn within you and make room for that gift of gifts,
    even our Lord Jesus Christ. **Amen.**

*Closing Prayers*

3   O God, you have caused this holy night [*day*]
    to shine with the brightness of the true light:
    Grant that we, who have known the mystery of that light on earth,
    may also enjoy him perfectly in heaven,
    where with you and the Holy Spirit he lives and reigns,
    one God, in glory everlasting. **Amen.**

4   God of all grace,
    you who have sent your Son to be our Redeemer,
    to give light in our darkness,
    pardon for our sins,
    and hope in our turmoil,
    accept now our hearty thanks
    for your Word (and for this sacrament).
    We have met our Savior here;
    we know your promises are true,
    and our hearts have been nourished.
    Send us forth to live obediently
    until we gather here again in his name. **Amen.**

5   Almighty God, you have poured upon us
    the new light of your incarnate Word:
    Grant that this light, enkindled in our hearts,
    may shine forth in our lives,
    through Jesus Christ, our Lord,
    who lives and reigns with you
    in the unity of the Holy Spirit,
    one God, now and for ever. **Amen.**

6   O God, you make us glad in the yearly festival
    of the birth of your only Son, Jesus Christ:
    Grant that we, who joyfully receive him as our Redeemer,
    may with sure confidence
    behold him when he comes to be our Judge,
    who lives and reigns with you and the Holy Spirit,
    one God, now and forever. **Amen.**

## E.9.2 Blessing/Benediction (see also section 9.2)

1   The joy of the angels,
    the eagerness of the shepherds,
    the perseverance of the Magi,
    the obedience of Joseph and Mary,
    and the peace of the Christ child be yours this Christmas.
    And the blessing of God almighty, Father, Son, and Holy Spirit,
    be upon you and remain with you always. **Amen.**

2   Jesus is the Word made flesh in our midst.
    May his incarnation fill your hearts with joy and peace.
    **O Lord, give us peace.**
    Jesus is the promised Savior, born of Mary.
    May his birth among us renew your hope.
    **O Lord, give us hope.**
    Jesus is the King of kings and the Lord of lords.
    May the gift of his presence bring forth rejoicing.
    **O Lord, give us joy.**
    Almighty God, Father, Son, and Holy Spirit,
    bless you now and forever. **Amen.**

3   May God, who sent his angels
    to proclaim the glad news of the Savior's birth,
    fill you with joy and make you heralds of the gospel. **Amen.**

4   May Jesus Christ, the sun of righteousness,
    who comes with healing in his wings,
    fill you with the joy and peace that passes all understanding.
    The blessing of God almighty, Father, Son, and Holy Spirit,
    be upon you and remain with you always. **Amen.**

# E.10 SUGGESTED SCRIPTURE READINGS

*The following readings provide several alternatives for lessons and carols services that trace the unfolding drama of salvation throughout the Old Testament and through the account of Jesus' birth at the beginning of the New Testament.*

1   *The coming Savior*
    Genesis 3:8-19: Promise of a Savior
    Genesis 22:13-18: The Lord will provide
    Isaiah 9:2-7: The promised child will reign
    Isaiah 11:1-9: The Spirit of the Lord will rest on him
    Luke 1:26-38: You are to call him Jesus
    Luke 2:1-7: The time came for the baby to be born
    Luke 2:8-16: Glory to God in the highest
    Matthew 2:1-12: We saw his star and have come to worship
    John 1:14: The Word became flesh

2   *A "Pentecostal" Christmas: the Holy Spirit's role in the Christmas drama*
    Genesis 1; Psalm 104:24-34: The Spirit forms and renews creation
    Genesis 3:8-15; Psalm 51:1-2, 10-15: People pray for the Spirit
    Isaiah 63:11-14; 2 Corinthians 3:7: The Spirit leads
    Isaiah 42:1-9: Prophet foretells Anointed One who would receive God's Spirit
    Isaiah 11:1-10: Prophet tells of *shalom*
    Luke 1:39-45; Matthew 1:18-21: Mary is with child by the Holy Spirit
    Luke 2: Birth of Jesus of Nazareth
    Luke 2:25-34; Titus 3:4-8: Holy Spirit reveals the Redeemer to Simeon
    John 1:1-4, 14; Galatians 4:4-7: Sending of the Son and the Spirit

3   *When justice and peace embrace—singing psalms at Christmas*
    Genesis 3:8-15; Psalm 51: Penitence
    Psalms 42-43: Lament and waiting
    Psalm 80: The Shepherd God protects and disciplines the sheep
    Psalm 63:1-7; Psalm 66: God's salvation leads us to peace and joy
    Psalm 24: The King of Glory comes, full of truth and grace
    Psalm 72: The Kings of the earth pay tribute to the Prince of Peace
    Psalm 85:8-13; John 1:1-4, 14: When justice and peace embrace

4   *Linking Jesus' birth and saving death*
    Genesis 3:8-15: God's redemptive promise anticipates Christ's death and conquest
    Isaiah 9:6-7: The prophet's promise hails the coming kingdom of peace
    Isaiah 53: The promise of a suffering Lord
    Psalm 110; Jeremiah 23:5-6: The promise of a risen and royal Savior
    Isaiah 35: The promise of Christ's coming kingdom
    Luke 2:1-7: The birth of one whose death brings life
    Luke 2:8-14: The angels praise the Lamb of God
    Matthew 2:1-12: The Magi's gifts foreshadow Christ's death and resurrection
    Philippians 2: Christ's birth, death, and resurrection lead to praise

# SECTION F
# EPIPHANY

Often the content of our Christmas celebration is shaped by what we do with the weeks following Christmas. Churches that observe Christmas as a stand-alone event may find it difficult to get past the sentimentality of seeing a cute, mild-natured baby in the manger. But the incarnation involves much more than the drama of Christmas itself; it brings a vision of God's glory to the nations of the world.

Our word *epiphany* comes from a Greek word meaning "manifestation or appearance," and in church history this word has become closely associated with the revelation of Christ in connection with the visit of the Magi. Epiphany has been observed throughout much of the Western church as occurring on January 6, but because most churches do not mark Epiphany with a mid-week service, the celebration of this special day is often associated with the nearest Sunday. In recent years many churches have worked to recover a full celebration that

begins at Christmas and ends at Epiphany twelve days later.

In the traditional celebration of the Christian year, the Sundays after Epiphany do not constitute a special season in the same way as do Advent and Lent. However, some congregations do celebrate this period as "Epiphany season," focusing on the teaching and healing ministry of Christ. Some of the resources in this section are applicable for use in that extended approach to observing Epiphany. Whether or not congregations follow a traditional lectionary for the weeks after Epiphany (making use of the traditional color green), these weeks can be a time to focus on Jesus' ministry so that, from Christmas onward, worshipers grow in awareness of the significance of Jesus' entire life.

The visual appearance of the worship space during Epiphany maintains the textures and colors of Christmas (white, yellow, and gold) to communicate that this season is a time of joy and light.

---

**Scriptures and Statements of Faith Applying to the Theme of Epiphany**

*The following texts are particularly appropriate for sermons or for supplemental liturgical use.*

| | | |
|---|---|---|
| Psalm 72 | Luke 13:22-30 | Ephesians 3:1-12 |
| Isaiah 49:5-7 | John 8:12 | Titus 2:11-14 |
| Isaiah 60 | Romans 15:5-13 | Revelation 21:22-26 |
| Matthew 2:1-12 | 2 Corinthians 4:4-6 | |

Belgic Confession, Art. 19
*Our World Belongs to God*, st. 24

---

# F.1 OPENING OF WORSHIP

---

### F.1.2 Call to Worship (see also section 1.2)

1    The heavens are telling the glory of God;
        and the firmament proclaims his handiwork.
    Day to day pours forth speech,
        and night to night declares knowledge.
    There is no speech, nor are there words;
        their voice is not heard;
    yet their voice goes out through all the earth,
        and their words to the end of the world.

The glory of God echoes throughout the world.
Let us praise the name of the Lord.
  —based on Psalm 19:1-4, NRSV

2  Give the king your justice, O God,
    and your righteousness to a king's son.
  May he judge your people with righteousness,
    and your poor with justice.
  **May the mountains yield prosperity for the people,**
    **and the hills, in righteousness.**
  May he defend the cause of the poor of the people,
    give deliverance to the needy,
    and crush the oppressor.
  **May he live while the sun endures,**
    **and as long as the moon, throughout all generations.**
    —Psalm 72:1-5, NRSV

3  O sing to the LORD a new song,
    for he has done marvelous things.
  His right hand and his holy arm
    have gotten him victory.
  The LORD has made known his victory;
    he has revealed his vindication in the sight of the nations.
  He has remembered his steadfast love and faithfulness
    to the house of Israel.
  All the ends of the earth have seen
    the victory of our God.
    —Psalm 98:1-3, NRSV

4  Arise, shine, for your light has come,
    and the glory of the LORD rises upon you.
  See, darkness covers the earth
    and thick darkness is over the peoples,
  but the LORD rises upon you
    and his glory appears over you.
  Nations will come to your light,
    and kings to the brightness of your dawn.
    —Isaiah 60:1-3, NIV

5  *A text especially mindful of children*

  Arise, shine, for your light has come!
  **The glory of the Lord has risen upon us.**
  Let us praise the Lord together.
  **The sun shall no longer be our light by day,**
  **nor will the brightness of the moon shine on us,**
  for the Lord will be our light,
  and our God will be our glory.

**The Lord will be our everlasting light,**
**and our days of sorrow will end.**
Come, let us sing to our light and salvation!
—based on Isaiah 60

6   The Christ child is born!
    All you who would find him,
    prepare for a journey, as determined as the Magi.
    All you who would praise him,
    come with the faith to follow but a star.
    All you who would worship him,
    come with humility to the child
    who shows forth the immeasurable riches of God.
    —based on Matthew 2:1-12

7   Long ago, God spoke to our ancestors through the prophets;
    **now God has spoken to us by a Son.**
    God made the world through the Son,
    who has been appointed heir of all things
    and the perfect reflection of God's glory.
    **The Son is the exact representation of God's being,**
    **sustaining all things by his powerful Word.**
    Praise God for the gift of the Son.
    **We welcome the light of the world!**
    —based on Hebrews 1:1-3

8   O come, let us worship the Lord
    and consider what wondrous things God has done:
    **The Magi who study the heavens follow a guiding star!**
    O come, let us worship the Lord
    and consider what wondrous things God has done:
    **The peoples who live in the shadows see a glorious light!**
    O come, let us worship the Lord
    and consider what wondrous things God has done:
    **The Christ who embodies the Word unveils the hidden plan,**
    making us joint heirs of the promise of salvation through the gospel!
    **O come, let us worship the Lord,**
    **for God has done wondrous things!**

9   The mystery from which true godliness springs is great—come and see!
    Jesus Christ appeared in the flesh,
    **was vindicated by the Spirit,**
    was seen by angels,
    **was preached among the nations,**
    was believed on in the world,
    **was taken up in glory.**
    May all the ends of the earth
    see the salvation of our God.
    —based on 1 Timothy 3:16; Isaiah 52:10

10    Give the king your justice, O God,
      **that he may rule your people righteously
      and the poor with justice.**
      In his time will righteousness flourish;
      there shall be abundance of peace till the moon shall be no more.
      **He shall rule from sea to sea,
      and from the river to the ends of the earth.**
      Come, let us worship God.

11    *A text especially mindful of children*

      May the light of God's love push back the darkness.
      **We come to the light from the four corners of the earth,
      from the north, from the south,
      from the east, and from the west.**
      But we are all one in Jesus Christ.
      **We come from many nations and many cultures.**
      But we are all one in Jesus Christ.
      **We come seeking the light that guides us to life.**
      But we are all one in Jesus Christ.
      **Let us lift up our many voices and praise the God of all people.**

## F.1.4 Opening Responses (see also section 1.4)

*Prayers of Adoration*

1    Almighty Lord God,
     you gave your Son, Jesus Christ, to be the light of the world:
     We praise and magnify your holy name that in him
     you have revealed the wonder of your saving love to all people.
     With those of old who brought their tribute to his feet,
     confessing him as King of heaven and earth,
     we now present the worship of our grateful hearts,
     asking you to give us grace to give ourselves to you,
     through the same Jesus Christ, our Lord. **Amen.**

2    God, you have made yourself known,
     but in a most amazing way,
     coming in weakness, in a tiny baby;
     you covered your glory and hid your greatness.
     **God of mystery and surprise, we praise you.**
     God, you have made yourself known,
     but in a most amazing way,
     in a dirty poor stable no one else wanted;
     you hid your wealth and infinite riches.
     **God of mystery and surprise, we praise you.**
     God, you have made yourself known,
     but in a most amazing way,

born to humble working people,
hidden in a simple life,
and yet announced in the stars of heaven and visited by kings.
**God of mystery and surprise, we praise you. Amen.**

*Prayers of Invocation*

3    Perfect Light of revelation,
     as you shone in the life of Jesus,
     whose Epiphany we celebrate,
     so shine in us and through us,
     that we may become beacons of truth and compassion,
     enlightening all creation
     with deeds of justice and mercy. **Amen.**

4    O God,
     you spoke your Word
     and revealed your good news in Jesus, the Christ.
     Fill all creation with that Word again
     so that by proclaiming your joyful promises to all nations
     and singing of your glorious hope to all peoples,
     we may become one living body,
     your incarnate presence on the earth. **Amen.**

5    Everlasting God,
     you brought the nations to your light
     and kings to the brightness of your rising.
     Fill the world with your glory,
     and show yourself to all the nations,
     through him who is the true light
     and the bright morning star,
     Jesus Christ, your Son, our Lord,
     who lives and reigns with you and the Holy Spirit,
     one God, now and forever. **Amen.**

6    O God who quickens the faith that brought Magi from the east,
     who kindles the hope that brought captives from exile,
     and who inspires the love that brings strangers together,
     let the light that shone in the darkness shine upon us.
     Let it shine within us, that it might refine our divided hearts.
     Let it shine around us, that it might illumine
     the way that leads to our neighbors.
     And let it shine above us, that it might reveal
     the Christ who manifests your presence. **Amen.**

7    God of Advent, of waiting and hoping,
keep our hearts expectant, ready for your coming among us.
God of Christmas, of celebration and rejoicing,
make our hearts glad with the joy nothing can take from us.
God of Epiphany, of hiding and making known,
fill our hearts with wonder at the revelation of your glory
that we have seen in Christ, our Lord. **Amen.**

## Additional Resources

8    *A prayer especially mindful of children*

Father,
you revealed your Son to the nations
by the guidance of a star.
Lead us to your glory in heaven
by the light of faith.
We ask this through our Lord Jesus Christ, your Son,
who lives and reigns with you and the Holy Spirit,
one God, for ever and ever. **Amen.**

9    *A prayer especially mindful of children*

Eternal God,
by a star you led Magi to the worship of your Son.
Guide the nations of the earth by your light,
that the whole world may see your glory,
through Jesus Christ, our Lord,
who lives and reigns with you and the Holy Spirit,
one God, now and forever. **Amen.**

10    O God, our Father, creator of the universe,
whose Son, Jesus Christ, came to our world,
pour your Holy Spirit upon your church,
that all the people of our world,
being led through the knowledge of your truth to worship you,
may offer the gold of intellect,
the frankincense of devotion,
and the myrrh of discipline
to him who with you and the Holy Spirit
lives and reigns for ever, one God, world without end. **Amen.**

11    Almighty Father,
in the glorious incarnation of your Son, Jesus Christ,
you have sent a new light into the world;
give us grace, that we may so receive the same light
into our hearts as to be guided
by it into the way of everlasting salvation,
through the same Jesus Christ, our Lord. **Amen.**

12  O God,
    by the leading of a star you manifested
    your only Son to the peoples of the earth:
    Lead us, who know you now by faith, to your presence,
    where we may see your glory face to face,
    through Jesus Christ, our Lord, who lives and reigns
    with you and the Holy Spirit, one God, now and for ever. **Amen.**

13  God, whom we gather to worship,
    gave Jesus, born in Bethlehem,
    as the fulfillment of the promise to his people,
    the children of Abraham.
    God called persons of another tradition,
    the Magi, to seek out Jesus and to worship him.
    Yes, God, maker of heaven and earth,
    so loved the world—and each person in it—
    that he gave his only Son so that whoever believes in him
    shall not perish but have everlasting life.
    Come, let us worship God.

14  Gracious God, you led the Magi by a star and brought them to Jesus.
    Lead us to Jesus, and help us to worship you.
    Help us to offer you gifts of abundance and gratitude.
    Show us the lengths that you go to draw us close.
    Help us to see how your light shines in every corner of the world,
    leading people of every tribe, language, and nation
    to offer homage to the one light of the world,
    our Lord Jesus Christ. **Amen.**

# F.2 CONFESSION AND ASSURANCE

### F.2.1 Call to Confession (see also section 2.1)

1   The light has come into the world,
    and people loved darkness rather than light
    because their deeds were evil.
    Let us confess our sin to God.
            —based on John 3:19, NRSV

## F.2.2 Prayers of Confession (see also section 2.2)

1    God of the Bethlehem star,
everyone is searching for your light
shining in the face of Christ.
The Magi sought Christ simply to worship him.
But Herod sought him to appease his jealous anger.
We confess that our motives in seeking Jesus are not pure.
We do not come simply to worship:
we come to Christ, asking his benefits of reassurance, health, wealth;
asking him to fulfill the hundred petitions
for not-so-important requests that we heap before him.
But the Magi sought first the kingdom.
Help us, God, to follow their example,
putting our own need in perspective,
worshiping the Christ in love, content to be in your presence,
and laying our gifts before you.
Then may we journey, trusting that your goodness and light
will accompany us all the days of our life. **Amen.**
      —based on Matthew 2:1-16; 6:33

2    O God, our guide,
who once used a star to lead people to Christ,
we confess our poor sense of direction.
We let ourselves become confused, easily distracted, and lose our way.
We fail to follow the signs you provide.
Forgive our waywardness, O God.
Lead us to the Christ so that we may follow his way to you. **Amen.**

3    God of grace,
you have given us Jesus,
the light of the world,
but we choose darkness
and cling to things that hide the brightness of your love.
Immersed in ourselves, we have not risen to new life.
Baptize us with your Spirit,
that, forgiven and renewed,
we may preach your Word to the nations
and tell of your glory shining in the face of Jesus Christ,
our Lord and our light forever. **Amen.**

4    *A prayer especially mindful of children*

Jesus, the Magi saw you,
we see you in the Bible,
and the whole world can see you in creation.

As we see you,
we also look at ourselves
and see that we do not always obey you.
Forgive us for not following you.
Free us from our sin for Jesus' sake. **Amen.**

5    Eternal Light,
     **shine in our hearts;**
     Eternal Goodness,
     **deliver us from evil;**
     Eternal Power,
     **be our support;**
     Eternal Wisdom,
     **scatter the shadows of our ignorance;**
     Eternal Compassion,
     **have mercy on us,**
     **that with heart and mind**
     **and soul and strength**
     **we may seek your face**
     **and be brought by your infinite mercy**
     **to the Holy Presence,**
     **through Jesus Christ, our Savior. Amen.**

6    Almighty and merciful God,
     we confess that we have sinned
     against you and one another
     in both our actions and our inactions.
     We recognize that in Jesus Christ our light has come,
     yet often we choose to walk in shadows and ignore the light.
     Gracious God, forgive our sins and remove from us
     the veil of darkness that shrouds our lives.
     Illumined by your Word and sacrament,
     may we rise to the radiance of Christ's glory. **Amen.**

7    God of light,
     we have been so blind when truth has been so clear.
     When we could have looked ahead, we fell behind.
     When we could have viewed the wider picture, we saw only a part.
     When we could have sensed the Spirit leading, we missed the way.
     Forgive our dim apprehension of love's clear leading.
     Give us faith that trusts when it cannot see,
     through the light that lingers when all else fails,
     even the bright Morning Star of our faith,
     Jesus Christ, the Savior. **Amen.**

**F.2.4 Assurance of Pardon** (see also section 2.4)

1   The true light that gives light to everyone was coming into the world.
    Yet to all who did receive him, to those who believed in his name,
    he gave the right to become children of God.
        —John 1:9, 12, NIV

2   This is the message we have heard from him and proclaim to you,
    that God is light and in him there is no darkness at all.
    If we say that we have fellowship with him
    while we are walking in darkness,
    we lie and do not do what is true;
    but if we walk in the light as he himself is in the light,
    we have fellowship with one another,
    and the blood of Jesus his Son cleanses us from all sin.
        —1 John 1:5-7, NRSV

# F.3 PROCLAIMING THE WORD

**F.3.1 Prayers for Illumination** (see also section 3.1)

1   Lord God of the nations,
    we have seen the star of your glory rising in splendor.
    The radiance of your incarnate Word
    pierces the night that covers the earth
    and signals the dawn of justice and peace.
    May his brightness illumine our lives
    and invite all nations to walk as one in your light
    even now as your Word is read and proclaimed.
    We ask this through Jesus Christ, your Word made flesh,
    who lives and reigns with you and the Holy Spirit
    in the splendor of eternal light, God forever and ever. **Amen.**

2   God of light and life,
    open our eyes as well as our ears,
    so that we may not only hear your Word preached today
    but then see your Word lived out in our lives and in your world,
    through Christ, our Lord, the light of the world. **Amen.**

3    Shine your truth into our lives, O God,
     sharpening our awareness of your abundant gifts
     and attuning us to the signs by which you would lead us.
     As heirs of your promise,
     we seek to be guided by your eternal purposes,
     that the church may make your wisdom known,
     through Christ. **Amen.**

4    Guide us, O God,
     by your Word and Spirit,
     that in your light we may see light,
     in your truth find freedom,
     and in your will discover your peace,
     through Jesus Christ, our Lord. **Amen.**

5    We pray, Lord, as you shine the light of your Word on us,
     that your glory will rise upon us by the power of your Spirit.
     Darkness may cover the earth and thick darkness the peoples,
     but, we pray, rise upon us, that your glory may appear to the world.
     Nations will come to the light of your Word,
     and peoples will be drawn to the brightness of your coming.
     Help us, Lord, to lift our eyes to you, to hear you speak,
     and to listen with open hearts to your gospel.
     Empower us to respond to your Word with obedience,
     and help us to be your shining lights in the universe.
     We pray in the name of Christ, the light of the world. **Amen.**
          —based on Isaiah 60:1-4a

6    *A prayer especially mindful of children*

     Our Lord and our God,
     now as we hear your Word,
     fill us with your Spirit.
     Soften our hearts that we may see your ways.
     Fill us with your light.
     Through Jesus Christ, our Lord, **Amen.**

7    We praise you, O God,
     for the sun of righteousness rises
     with healing in its wings.
     May the warm and healing rays of the light,
     our Lord Jesus Christ,
     soften, heal, and transform us
     through the power of your Holy Spirit
     as your Word is proclaimed today. **Amen.**
          —based on Malachi 4:2

# F.4 PRAYERS OF THE PEOPLE

**F.4.4 Complete Model Outlines and Prayers** (see also section 4.4)

*Prayer Outlines*

1   *The following is a guide for extemporaneous prayers. The pattern provides a suggested text for the opening and closing of each part of the prayer and calls for extemporaneous prayers of thanksgiving, petition, and intercession.*

God of light,
we praise you as the one who shows your glory
to the nations in the coming of Jesus Christ!
We thank you for reflections of your glory
in our world and in our community:
>    for your work in creation, especially . . .
>    for your work in the world, especially . . .
>    for your work in the church and local community . . .

Help us to see these signs of glory as signs of your coming kingdom.
We long for the fullness of that kingdom. Come, Lord Jesus.

In light of your love, we offer our petitions to you now,
coming to you in the name and power of Jesus Christ.
Today, we pray for
>    the creation and its care, especially . . .
>    the nations of the world, especially . . .
>    our nation and its leaders, especially . . .
>    our community and those who govern, especially . . .
>    the church universal, its mission, and those who minister, especially . . .
>    our local congregation and its ministry, especially . . .
>    people with particular needs, especially . . .

We offer these prayers in the strong name of Jesus Christ,
our light and our salvation. **Amen.**

*Complete Prose Prayers*

2   God of new beginnings, as we conclude the recent holiday season and celebrate now your Epiphany, we recognize that we are even now forging ahead into a new year. As we look back on the year gone by, we see so many things: things that grieve us, things that cause us to rejoice, things that surprise us in ways both good and bad, things that concern us. For our congregation, O Lord, any given year is often a time of highs and lows, of births and of deaths, of exciting opportunities and of unfulfilled hopes. Yet you are the faithful God who stays with us in and through it all. When we ascend into heights of joy, you are there to receive the words of

*511*

praise that gush from our lips. When we descend into valleys of shadow, death, fear, and uncertainty, you are there to hold our hand in the darkness and to assure us that we are not alone. When we walk level paths as we go about ordinary tasks, you walk with us, gracing the fruit of our hands with your own sacred benediction.

We confess, Father, that because we do not always behave the way we desire for ourselves, there are times when your abiding presence makes us squirm, when the brilliance of your light makes us scurry for cover. We are ashamed of some of the things we do as you walk alongside us, of some of the thoughts we entertain in the deep places of our hearts (places that are, even so, not hidden from you). Yet in your grace you continue to stick with us, so we find your faithful constancy as our companion in joys and sorrows to be a source of relief, of assurance, of repose. Thank you for being with us through the many turns and twists our paths took last year.

And now as we enter a new year, bathed in the sacred light of Epiphany, we sense anew how much we need your providential presence. We know that in past months loved ones have suddenly died, precious jobs were suddenly terminated, illnesses that we did not even remotely suspect were diagnosed—and suddenly all of life changed. We did not see any of those things coming, O God, and we do not have eyesight that can penetrate the months ahead in this new month and year. All we can do is petition you for mercy and strength to face what is to come. But we pray too that you will keep us in good health, in perfect safety, and in the knowledge that we are loved by you and also by family and friends.

We need that sense of love, O God, because we know there are so many around us in life who lack this awareness. So many are lonely. So many endured the holiday season with only a grim determination to help them keep getting out of bed in the morning. They had no parties to attend, received no Christmas cards in the mail, had few if any for whom to buy gifts (or from whom to receive them). The lonely among us are often also the invisible among us. But you see them, and by the goading and prompting of your Spirit, you can enable us to see them as well. Minister to them, and help us to minister to those who find the cosmos a barren and cold place. Befriend the friendless, swaddle in love the unloved, take compassion on the bereft, the childless, the lonely—and do all of that, O God, through us and through the love, friendship, and compassion we ourselves proffer to this community.

Hear us as we pray, sacred Father. For any here this morning who feel so constricted by doubt, anger, or grief that they cannot pray, assure them that we, along with many others, are praying for them. Bless us in the balance of this service even as you have already blessed us and graced us by your presence as we together glorify you in our worship. Through Christ Jesus, the light of Epiphany, the light of the world, we pray, **Amen.**

3 God of glory, we seek your glory:
the richness that transforms our drabness into color
and brightens our dullness with vibrant light,
your wonder and joy at the heart of all life.
God of incense, we offer you our prayer:
our spoken and unspeakable longings, our questioning of truth,
our search for your mystery deep within.

God of myrrh, we cry out to you in our suffering:
the pain of all our rejections and bereavements,
our baffled despair at undeserved suffering,
our rage at continuing injustice.
And we embrace you, God-with-us,
in our wealth, in our yearning, in our anger and loss. **Amen.**

4    O Jesus, light of the world,
come into the dark places of this earth.
You bring a light from God that only you can shed.
Light eternal, your light shines in the darkness,
and the darkness does not overcome it.
We bring to you the darkness of our world
in war, starvation, cruelty, and exploitation.
We bring to you the darkness of our earth,
damaged and defaced by pollution.
We bring to you the darkness of our nation,
beset with conflict of race and class, religion and politics.
We bring to you the darkness of our relationships,
people not looking, not speaking, not listening, not forgiving.
We bring to you the darkness of our own souls,
hidden closets we have not visited or cleaned out for years.
O Jesus, light of the world, be a morning star above for us,
a radiance within, the shining all around that lets us live in love.
Only then shall we be reflectors of your brightness
and give glory to God in heaven. **Amen.**

*Prayers in Litany Form*

5    Let us pray for the church and for the world.
Grant, almighty God,
that all who confess your name may be united in your truth,
live together in your love, and reveal your glory in the world.
[*Silence*]
Lord, in your mercy,
**hear our prayer.**

Guide the people of this land,
and of all the nations, in the ways of justice and peace,
that we may honor one another and serve the common good.
[*Silence*]
Lord in your mercy,
**hear our prayer.**

Give us all a reverence for the earth as your own creation,
that we may use its resources rightly
in the service of others and to your honor and glory.
[*Silence*]
Lord in your mercy,
**hear our prayer.**

Comfort and heal all those who suffer in body, mind, or spirit;
give them courage and hope in their troubles,
and bring them the joy of your salvation.
[*Silence*]
Lord, in your mercy,
**hear our prayer, through Jesus Christ, our Lord. Amen.**

6    God has called us out of darkness
into the glorious light of the Son.
Let us therefore pray for those who do not yet know the light
and for all those in need of our prayers,
saying, "Lord, hear our prayer."
For the church and its ministry to the world,
and for all those who bring the gospel of Jesus Christ to the nations,
let us pray to the Lord.
**Lord, hear our prayer.**
[*Silence*]

For the nations of the world and their leaders,
for all those in authority [*especially . . .* ],
and for an end to war and oppression,
let us pray to the Lord.
**Lord, hear our prayer.**
[*Silence*]

For those who have not heard the good news of salvation,
for those who have heard but have not believed,
and for those who have forsaken their faith,
let us pray to the Lord.
**Lord, hear our prayer.**
[*Silence*]

For those who are lonely and destitute,
for victims of injustice and discrimination,
for those who are unloved and forgotten,
let us pray to the Lord.
**Lord, hear our prayer.**
[*Silence*]

For those who are sick in body, mind, and spirit,
for those who are hungry and homeless,
for those who are dying or bereaved,
and for all those in need of our prayers [*especially . . .* ],
let us pray to the Lord.
**Lord, hear our prayer.**
[*Silence*]

For the saints who have gone before us in the faith
and are now at rest [*especially . . .* ],
we give thanks to the Lord.
And for all the saints on earth
who surround us in a great fellowship of love,

let us pray to the Lord.
**Lord, hear our prayer.**

Loving God, hear the prayers of your faithful people
and guide our thoughts and actions,
so that your will may be done and your name glorified,
through Jesus Christ, our Lord. **Amen.**

7    All the ends of the earth
have seen the salvation of our God. Alleluia!
**Shout to the Lord, all the earth. Alleluia!**
With joy let us pray to our Savior,
the Son of God, who became one of us.

O Christ,
let your gospel shine in every place
where the Word of life is not yet received.
Draw the whole creation to yourself,
that your salvation may be known through all the earth.
God of all mercies,
**hear our prayer.**
O Christ, Savior and Lord,
extend your church to every place.
Make it a place of welcome for people of every race and tongue.
God of all mercies,
**hear our prayer.**
O Christ, Ruler of rulers,
direct the work and thoughts of the leaders of nations,
that they may seek justice
and further peace and freedom for all.
God of all mercies,
**hear our prayer.**
O Christ, Master of all,
support of the weak and comfort of the afflicted,
strengthen the tempted and raise the fallen.
Watch over the lonely and those in danger.
Give hope to the despairing
and sustain the faith of the persecuted.
**The grace of God be with us all. Amen.**

[*After a brief silence, the leader concludes the litany.*]
O Christ, light made manifest as the true light of God,
gladden our hearts on the joyful morning of your glory,
call us by our name on the great Day of your coming,
and give us grace to offer,
with all the hosts of heaven,
unending praise to God,
in whom all things find their ending,
now and ever. **Amen.**

8    Let us praise God for the
manifestation of the Christ in his mission on earth.
Let us praise God for the Magi from the east,
who were sent to Bethlehem
to teach us to honor him
and to offer our gifts.
**We praise you, O God.**
Let us praise God for the multitudes around the world
who are today using the resources of their customs and cultures
in developing new forms of worshiping the Christ.
**We praise you, O God.**
Let us praise God for all those
who are presenting themselves to be baptized in the name of Christ
and for all the parents who are bringing their children to the water of Christ.
**We praise you, O God.**
Let us praise God for the manifestation of Christ in our own time
when the thirsty are given something to drink and the hungry are fed.
**We praise you, O God.**
Let us pray for Christ's continuing epiphany
among all who long for his presence.
For your manifestation among all who long for truth
and are educated and wise in this world,
for those who conduct research and those who teach,
for those who study the stars
and those who give counsel to kings and rulers,
**we seek your grace, O wisdom of God.**
For your epiphany among all who are open
to your presence in the water and the wine,
and especially among those who have seen your star
but have not yet heard your name,
**we seek your grace, O Savior of the nations.**
For your epiphany
among all who are suffering for the cause of righteousness,
for all who are in prison,
for those who are oppressed,
and for those who are hungry, thirsty, and homeless,
**we seek your grace, O Son of God.**
For your manifestation of your glory
in the course of our daily lives,
in our homes, our schools, our workplaces,
and our facilities for play and entertainment,
**we seek your grace, O Lamb of God.**
**In your name, Amen.**

9    Where ignorance, self-love, and insensitivity
have fractured life in community,
**give us your light, O God of love.**
Where injustice and oppression

have broken the spirit of peoples,
**give us your light, O God of freedom.**
Where hunger and poverty, illness and death
have made life an unbearable burden,
**give us your light, O God of grace.**
Where suspicion and hatred, conflict and war
have challenged your goodness,
**give us your light, O God of peace.**
Eternal God,
remove the blindness of the nations and peoples
so that they may walk in the light of love;
remove the ignorance and stubbornness of nations and peoples
so that they may drink from the fountains of your goodness. **Amen.**

# F.5 OFFERING

**F.5.2 Offering Prayers** (see also section 5.2)

1   Bright Morning Star,
    your light has come,
    and your birth, O Jesus,
    has overwhelmed us with joy.
    Like the Magi of long ago,
    may we be drawn to you
    and offer you such gifts as we are able. **Amen.**

2   *A prayer especially mindful of children*

    Lord, you were born in a simple stable
    and received gifts from the Magi.
    Please accept our gifts of money today,
    for we also love you
    and want to serve you with them. **Amen.**

3   Emmanuel, God with us,
    the Magi followed the star to find you.
    Amazed, they gave gifts.
    We too are amazed by your presence among us,
    by the gift that you are to us.
    With joyful hearts, we bring you our gifts
    of time, of money, of ourselves.
    Use these and us to serve you and your world. **Amen.**

4    O God,
     from whom come all the good things we enjoy,
     we offer our gifts as the Magi did who opened costly treasures before Jesus.
     We give in response to your generosity,
     identifying with your pity and compassion
     for victims of violence, poverty, and oppression.
     May all who are in need
     experience the unsearchable riches of Christ
     and the gift of the Holy Spirit
     even as their physical needs are met.
     May we be coworkers with Christ,
     whose sacrifice bought our redemption. **Amen.**

# F.8 THE LORD'S SUPPER

## F.8.1 Declaration of God's Invitation and Promises (see also section 8.1)

*F.8.1.3 Invitation (see also section 8.1.3)*

1    Brothers and sisters in Christ,
     the gospel tells us that God, by the leading of a star,
     manifested the Savior to the peoples of the earth,
     and, by the power that enabled Christ
     to change water into wine, made known his glory to the disciples.
     Come then to the joyful feast of the Lord and be transformed.

## F.8.2 Great Prayer of Thanksgiving (see section 8.2)

*F.8.2.2 Thanksgiving for the Work of God in Creation (see also section 8.2.2)*
*The following prayers offer thanks for the work of God in creation and may be included in the complete Prayer of Thanksgiving as found in section 8.2 of this book.*

1    With joy we praise you, gracious God,
     for you have created heaven and earth,
     made us in your image, and kept covenant with us—
     even when we fell into sin.
     We give you thanks for Jesus Christ, our Lord,
     who came as the light of the world
     to show us your way of truth in parables and miracles.

Therefore we join our voices
with all the saints and angels and the whole creation
to proclaim the glory of your name.

2    We thank you, God, for sending a star
to guide the wise ones to the Christ child.
But, even more, we praise you for signs and witnesses
in every generation that lead us to Christ.
We thank you for the covenant made first with Israel—
promising to be Israel's light and salvation.
You made Israel your people and promised that through them
all the peoples of the world would be blessed.

We thank you for prophets who declared your Word,
for priests who made sacrifices for the sins of many,
and for kings and rulers who ruled with justice,
lifted up the poor and needy,
and defended the people from their enemies.

With the apostles, prophets, and martyrs;
with all those through the ages who have loved the Lord Jesus Christ;
and with all who strive to serve him on earth here and now,
we join our voices in offering praise
to the God of loving power and powerful love.

### F.8.2.4 Thanksgiving for the Work of Christ (see also section 8.2.4)

*The following prayers offer thanks for the work of Jesus Christ and may be included in the complete Prayer of Thanksgiving as found in section 8.2 of this book.*

1    In sending Christ, the light of the world,
you revealed your glory to the nations.
You sent a star to guide seekers of wisdom to Bethlehem,
that they might worship Christ.
Your signs and witnesses in every age
lead people from every place to worship him.
We praise you that in him we become your children,
baptized into your service.

2    God of wisdom, with gratitude and love
we remember your mighty acts.
You created a world that was good.
You gave us this earth to enjoy.
You trusted us to share with you in caring for it.
And when we sinned, you still did not abandon us
but made covenant with our ancestors.
You called your people to yourself,
led them from slavery to freedom,
gave them the law to obey, prophetic teaching to follow,
and songs of hope to sing.

Then, God of unending grace,
you sent your Son, Christ Jesus, born of a woman,
to be the glory of your people Israel, a light to shine in the darkness.
To this light came travelers from the east,
those already wise seeking higher wisdom.
Finding greater wisdom in a young child than they had ever known,
they offered their precious gifts.
This child of Mary and Joseph was indeed the Son of God,
the one who revealed your glory, transforming sin to goodness,
disease to health, despair to hope, sorrow to joy, and death to life.
Yet he too knew sorrow and death,
bearing upon himself the sin of the world at Calvary:
betrayed, deserted, crucified.
And on the night in which he was betrayed,
he took bread and blessed it, gave thanks and broke it,
shared it with his companions, and said,
"This is my body, which is for you.
Take, eat, do this in remembrance of me."
In the same manner, he took the cup, blessed it, and said,
"Drink from this, all of you.
This cup is the new covenant in my blood;
do this, as often as you drink it, in remembrance of me."
God of wisdom and light, send your Holy Spirit upon us
and upon this bread and wine.
As we come together to eat at your table,
we offer ourselves to you
in praise and thanksgiving for your mighty acts.

3    With the coming of Jesus,
the covenant with Israel was expanded and confirmed.
Through Christ, the gates of salvation have been thrown open.
Just as the Magi were welcomed at the cradle of the Christ child,
so God welcomes all strangers and those in need
into the covenant of blessing.
Jesus Christ offered food to the hungry and water to the thirsty,
shelter to the wanderer and justice to the oppressed,
friendship to the lonely and kinship to the faithful.
Jesus forgave sins, preached good news,
and filled all people with the hope of new life.

Jesus took upon himself the full consequences of our sinfulness—
even the agony of abandonment by God—
in order that we might be spared.
But our Lord could not be held by the power of death.
Jesus appeared to his followers,
triumphant from the grave, in newness of life.
He has shown us his hands and feet in order
that we might know that the one who was crucified
is the Lord and Savior of the world.

# F.9 Closing of Worship

## F.9.1 Sending (see also section 9.1)

*Call to Service/Discipleship*

1    The light of God's purposes has shone upon us.
Carry that light into another week.
**The star of God's promises that led us to worship
now leads us to serve in God's world.**
When we have met God in the light,
we cannot dwell comfortably in the shadows.
**We cannot enjoy our abundance and wealth
without thanksgiving and generous sharing.**
The glory of God shines on you today.
Others will see your radiance and rejoice with you.
**We seek God's peace that we may share it,
God's wisdom that we may live by it,
in Christ's name.**
Amen. **Amen.**

2    Our risen Lord declares:
**"All power belongs to me in heaven and on earth."**
Our risen Lord commands:
**"In my name go and make disciples, baptizing and teaching in my name."**
Our risen Lord assures us:
**"I am with you always."**
We belong forever to our risen Lord;
**we depart in his name.**

*Acclamations/Doxologies*

3    Now to God who is able to strengthen you
according to my gospel and the proclamation of Jesus Christ,
according to the revelation of the mystery
that was kept secret for long ages but is now disclosed,
and through the prophetic writings is made known to all the Gentiles,
according to the command of the eternal God,
to bring about the obedience of faith—
to the only wise God, through Jesus Christ,
to whom be the glory forever! **Amen.**
        —Romans 16:25-27, NRSV

*Closing Prayers*

4　God of goodness and grace,
　　with you is the fountain of life,
　　and in your light we see light.
　　Now may we leave this place,
　　ready to serve the risen Savior. **Amen.**

5　As sages from the east offered you their best,
　　**so may we honor you, O Christ,**
　　**with our highest visions and finest energies.**
　　As you turned the water to wine at Cana,
　　**so come to your church**
　　**and teach us to change human tears to joyful song.**
　　As you were baptized to fulfill all righteousness,
　　**so may your church humbly do your will.**
　　As you gave light to those who followed you on earth,
　　**so be our light as we follow you**
　　**on city streets or country roads.**
　　**Be revealed among us in power, in Word, in sacrament,**
　　**and in places where we live and work.**
　　**Glory be to you, O Christ, now and forever. Amen.**

6　O God, who in Jesus Christ
　　called us out of darkness into marvelous light,
　　enable us always to declare your wonderful deeds,
　　thank you for your steadfast love,
　　and praise you with heart, soul, mind, and strength,
　　now and forever. **Amen.**

7　God of blazing light,
　　through the power of the cross you shattered our darkness,
　　scattering the fears that bind us
　　and setting us free to live as your children.
　　Give us courage and conviction,
　　that we may joyfully turn and follow you
　　into new adventures of faithful service,
　　led by the light that shines
　　through Jesus Christ, our Savior. **Amen.**

## F.9.2 Blessing/Benediction (see also section 9.2)

1　May the light of the glorious gospel of Christ
　　shine in our hearts, transform our lives,
　　and brighten the world.

　　And the blessing of God almighty,
　　Father, Son, and Holy Spirit,
　　rest upon you always. **Amen.**

2    In response to what we have heard
and to what we know ourselves to be,
let us begin anew.
**We have been called to participate in his mission.**
The Lord has laid upon us the responsibility for his world.
**Let us offer ourselves
to him and to that world, which is his own.**
The Lord be with you.
**And also with you.**
Go in peace. Amen.
**Amen.**

3    May Christ, the Son of God,
be manifest in you,
that your lives may be a light to the world;
and the blessing of God Almighty,
the Father, the Son, and the Holy Spirit,
be among you and remain with you always. **Amen.**

4    As we leave this service of worship,
let us go as the Magi left the infant Jesus,
rejoicing on our way that we have seen the living Lord,
ready to return to our daily life and work,
spreading the good news of Jesus the Christ.
Receive now these words of promise and blessing
from our Lord Jesus Christ:
Remember, "I am with you always, to the end of the age."
"Peace I leave with you; my peace I give to you.
Do not let your hearts be troubled.
Do not be afraid.
I am the light of the world.
Whoever follows me will never walk in darkness
but will have the light of life.
As the Father has loved me, so I have loved you.
Abide in my love."
Thanks be to God.
And let all God's people say:
**Amen.**
      —from Matthew 28:20; John 14:27; 15:8; 8:12

5    Almighty God has given each of us everything we need
to see our lives as a sheer gift from his hand:
      The Father has created us and sustains our lives daily;
      the Son has paid for our sins and brought us new life;
      the Spirit keeps us in our Savior's love
      and empowers us to live for him.

All glory be to the triune God,
      the Father, Son, and Holy Spirit.

May his name be honored and adored,
    now and forevermore.

Beloved children of God:
May the Lord direct your hearts into God's love for you,
    and keep you in his peace.
May you receive strength
        to grow in faith, hope, and love,
        to live with joy and delight,
and to give God thanks and praise. **Amen.**

# F.10 SUGGESTED SCRIPTURE READINGS

**1**  *All nations shall be blessed!*

Genesis 12:1-3: All people will be blessed
1 Chronicles 16:8-36: Declare God's deeds among all the peoples
Psalm 47: The kings of the earth belong to God
Psalm 67: May all nations praise God
Psalm 96: Declare his glory among the nations
Psalm 117: Praise the Lord, all nations
Isaiah 12:4-6: Make known among the nations what God has done
Isaiah 42:1-9: He will bring justice to the nations
Isaiah 60:1-3: Nations will come to your light
Matthew 2:1-12: Magi worship
Romans 15:8-13: Rejoice, you Gentiles
Philippians 2:1-11: Every knee should bow
Revelation 5: The blood of the Lamb for people from every nation

**2**  *Shining stars*

Genesis 22:1-18: All nations will be blessed
Numbers 24:1 A star will come out of Jacob
Psalm 8: The Creator cares for humanity
Psalm 136: God's love endures forever
Matthew 2:1-12: We saw his star
Philippians 2:12-18: Shine like stars in the sky
Revelation 22:12-17: Jesus is the bright Morning Star

## SECTION G

# BAPTISM OF OUR LORD

The baptism of Jesus is one of the most theologically profound events in the gospel narratives. When the Father spoke, "This is my Son, whom I love; with him I am well pleased" (Matt. 3:17), the divine sonship of Christ was announced in a vivid, dramatic way. The event gives us a picture of the Trinity, with the Father's gift of the Spirit to the Son.

Congregations may wish to commemorate Jesus' baptism on the Sunday after Epiphany. Recently many churches have recognized that jumping from Christmas to Lent and Easter

without attending to key events in Jesus' life can impoverish our understanding of Jesus' identity and mission.

---

**Scriptures and Statements of Faith Applying to the Theme of Jesus' Baptism**

*The following texts are particularly appropriate for sermons or for supplemental liturgical use.*

| | | |
|---|---|---|
| Genesis 1:1-5 | Isaiah 49:1-7 | Acts 8:14-17 |
| Psalm 2 | Matthew 3:13-17 | Acts 10:34-48 |
| Psalm 29 | Mark 1:4-11 | Acts 19:1-7 |
| Isaiah 11:2 | Luke 3:15-17, 21-22 | Hebrews 1 |
| Isaiah 42:1-9 | John 1:32-34 | Hebrews 5:1-9 |
| Isaiah 43:1-7 | | |

Heidelberg Catechism, Q&A's 31-32

# G.1 OPENING OF WORSHIP

## G.1.2 Call to Worship (see also section 1.2)

1   Sing to the LORD, praise his name;
    **proclaim his salvation day after day.**
Declare his glory among the nations,
    **his marvelous deeds among all peoples.**
      —Psalm 96:2-3, NIV

2   Ascribe to the LORD the glory of his name,
    **worship the LORD in holy splendor.**
The voice of the LORD is over the waters;
    **the God of glory thunders,**
    **the LORD, over mighty waters.**
The voice of the LORD is powerful;
    **the voice of the LORD is full of majesty.**
      —Psalm 29:2-4, NRSV

3   God said, "This is my Son, with whom I am pleased."
**But this one has no splendor, no beauty we would fancy.**
"This is my child, in whom I take delight."
**But this one carries the load of a servant,**
**not the scepter of a king.**
"This is my child, whom I have called."
**But this one demands justice from all earth's nations;**
**his words shall judge our own.**
"This is my child, whom I uphold."
**But this one would release the dungeon's prisoners;**
**he would set the captives free.**
"This is my child, whose hand I hold."
**But this one is a man of sorrows; he is no stranger to grief.**
"This is my child; I give him to you."
**Surely this child will bear our suffering on his shoulders**
**and carry our rejection in his heart.**
**Wounded for our transgressions,**
**he will be cut off from the land of the living.**
**Like sheep we have gone astray;**
**like a lamb he shall be led to the slaughter.**
**And still our God declares it:**
**"This is my beloved child, with whom I am well pleased.**
**Listen to him."**
      —based on Isaiah 53; Matthew 3:17; 17:5

4    God anointed Christ to console the afflicted.
     **Come, let us worship the Lord our Comforter!**
     God anointed Christ to emancipate the enslaved.
     **Come, let us worship the Lord our liberator!**
     God anointed Christ to bind up the wounded.
     **Come, let us worship the Lord our healer!**
     God anointed Christ to deliver the troubled.
     **Come, let us worship the Lord our Savior!**

5    All who thirst, come to the water
     and drink deeply of these living streams.
     Come, all who are weary;
     come, all who yearn for forgiveness.
     Our gracious God beckons and blesses us.
     Let us give praise for new life in Christ.

## G.1.4 Opening Responses (see also section 1.4)

*Prayers of Adoration*

1    God of majesty and light,
     you hold the whole world in your hand.
     So we give you our great praise
     that in Jesus Christ all people may see your glory.
     We thank you for revealing Jesus to be your Son
     and for claiming our lives in baptism to be his glad disciples.
     By your Spirit, may peace descend upon us,
     that we may follow him with grateful hearts.
     Take us and all we have to be useful in your service,
     God of all nations,
     in the gracious name of Jesus Christ, your Son,
     by the power of your Holy Spirit,
     now and forever. **Amen.**

*Prayers of Invocation*

2    Lord God, gracious and merciful,
     you anointed your beloved Son with the Holy Spirit
     at his baptism in the Jordan,
     and you consecrated him prophet, priest, and king.
     Pour out your Spirit on us again
     that we may be faithful to our baptismal calling,
     ardently desire the communion of Christ's body and blood,
     and serve the poor of your people and all who need your love,
     through Jesus Christ, your Son, our Lord,
     who lives and reigns with you in the unity of the Holy Spirit,
     ever one God, world without end. **Amen.**

3     Eternal God,
      at the baptism of Jesus in the river Jordan
      you proclaimed him your beloved Son
      and anointed him with the Holy Spirit.
      Grant that all who are baptized into his name
      may keep the covenant they have made
      and boldly confess him as Lord and Savior;
      who with you and the Holy Spirit lives and reigns,
      one God, in glory everlasting. **Amen.**

4     Glory be to you, O God,
      whom we worship in awe and wonder.
      You are the author of all beginnings
      and all that is pronounced "good."
      In you both day and night have purpose,
      both calm and storm have meaning.
      Open the eyes of our imagination,
      that we may be ready to receive your gifts
      and discern your activity in our midst.
      In the name of Jesus,
      in whose baptism we too are baptized. **Amen.**

### Additional Resources

5     God of grace and glory,
      you call us with your voice of flame
      to be your people, faithful and courageous.
      As your beloved Son
      embraced his mission in the waters of baptism,
      inspire us with the fire of your Spirit
      to join in his transforming work.
      We ask this in the name of our Savior, Jesus Christ,
      who lives and reigns for ever and ever. **Amen.**

6     Holy God,
      you sent your Son to be baptized among sinners,
      to seek and save the lost.
      May we, who have been baptized in his name,
      never turn away from the world
      but reach out in love to rescue the wayward,
      by the mercy of Christ, our Lord,
      who lives and reigns with you and the Holy Spirit,
      one God, now and forever. **Amen.**

7     Let us give thanks to the Lord our God.
      **It is right to give our thanks and praise.**
      God of heaven and earth,
      you call us to come in humility before you,

bringing the offering of our very selves.
As you revealed Jesus to be your Son
in his baptism at the hand of John,
so you claimed our lives in baptism,
that we might die to sin
and be raised with him to new life.
By your Spirit,
confirm in our hearts the witness
that Christ is Savior of the world and our Lord.
**Accept all we have and are, O God,**
**in the service of Jesus Christ,**
**and strengthen us with your Spirit's power,**
**now and forever. Amen.**

8    Your voice, O God,
is powerful and majestic,
strengthening and blessing your people with peace.
By your Spirit help us to hear today
the majesty and blessing of your voice. **Amen.**
—based on Psalm 29:6, 11

# G.2 Confession and Assurance

### G.2.2 Prayers of Confession (see also section 2.2)

1    God of all mercy,
in our baptisms you have marked us as your own;
you have given us a new identity
and made us part of the body of Christ.
In doing so, you have called us to rise to new life
and to live together in community.
However, we have not been faithful to your call.
We have forged our own identity
and held to destructive habits.
We confess we have failed to welcome others,
broken bonds we have had with brothers and sisters,
and served ourselves more than you.
Forgive us, we pray, for the sake of Christ, our Savior. **Amen.**

529

2     Creator of all worlds,
      we confess to sporadic beliefs and inconsistent faithfulness.
      Before the mystery of the universe
      our minds cannot grasp a God who embraces infinity.
      In the face of natural disasters and cruel inhumanity
      we doubt that love reigns.
      Between our own actions and the best we know
      we see a wide gap that we cannot bridge.
      O God, reclaim us and help us to reclaim our baptism;
      we need your healing, forgiving, transforming Spirit. **Amen.**

3     Merciful God,
      in baptism you grafted us into the body of Christ,
      promising us forgiveness of sin and newness of life.
      But we fail to live as forgiven people.
      We keep destructive habits and hold grudges.
      We allow our past to hold us hostage
      and are reluctant to welcome newness.
      In your loving-kindness
      have mercy on us and free us from sin.
      Remind us of the promises you have made to us in baptism
      so that we may live as your people,
      claimed in the waters of promise. **Amen.**

## G.2.4 Assurance of Pardon (see also section 2.4)

1     You did not receive a spirit of slavery to fall back into fear,
      but you have received a spirit of adoption.
      When we cry, "Abba! Father!"
      it is that very Spirit bearing witness
      with our spirit that we are children of God,
      and if children, then heirs, heirs of God and joint heirs with Christ.

      Praise God that in the power of the Spirit
      we are joint heirs with Christ!
      We see the love of God at Christ's baptism.
              —based on Romans 8:15-17, NRSV

2     Friends, hear the good news!
      Though we are unworthy,
      we are granted God's favor in Jesus Christ
      and are baptized into the church of his beloved Son.
      Friends, believe the good news!
      **In Jesus Christ, we are forgiven.**

# G.4 PRAYERS OF THE PEOPLE

## G.4.4 Complete Model Outlines and Prayers (see also section 4.4)

*Prayer Outlines*

1   *The following is a guide for extemporaneous prayers for services that remember Jesus'
    baptism. The pattern provides a suggested text for the opening and closing of each part of the
    prayer and calls for extemporaneous prayers of thanksgiving, petition, and intercession.*

Triune God,
at Jesus' baptism, when the heavens opened and the Spirit descended,
you declared that he is your beloved Son.
Your voice continues to echo throughout the world
whenever Christ is declared the Savior and Lord of all.
Today we come, thankful for his lordship, as evidenced in
    nations that . . .
    government leaders who . . .
    communities that . . .
    the church worldwide . . .
    our own church as it . . .

We also come with great thanksgiving for our own baptism, which has united us
with Christ so that we may not only be saved but also share in his mission.

But sometimes the task is disheartening. In our discouragement remind us that you
are Lord. And, as our only Lord, we pray that you hear our prayers on behalf of
    the nations of the world, especially . . .
    our nation and those in authority . . .
    this community and those who serve it . . .
    the church universal, its mission, and those who
        minister, especially . . .
    those with particular needs . . .

We look forward to the day when all voices will join with yours
in declaring Christ as your Son, our Savior and Lord.
For to you belong all glory, honor, and praise. **Amen.**

*Complete Prose Prayers*

2   O Lord Jesus Christ, Son of God,
you emptied yourself of heaven's riches
and came to share our lot.
You made yourself poor
so that by your poverty we might become rich.
Perfect in purity, you submitted to baptism,

like any sinner in need of cleansing.
So many today need your tender care.
Tend your prisoners, lonely and abandoned.
Tend your addicts, trapped by lethal hungers.
Tend your prostitutes, hard used by the lust of strangers.
Tend your refugees, footsore, threadbare, humiliated by their loss.
Tend your unemployed and underpaid,
your lonely ones, your depressed ones, your wretched ones.
O Lord Jesus Christ, welcome our brothers and sisters
whose calling this day is to die.
Escort them by a party of angels into your radiance
and enlighten them with the rays of your love.
O Lord Jesus Christ, you who were baptized like any sinner,
love us sinners and intercede for us in the hour of our need. **Amen.**


*Prayers in Litany Form*

3    In the waters of baptism, we were called to be God's children
and to minister to one another.
Let us therefore pray for ourselves, for one another,
and for all those in need of our prayers, saying:
"Lord, in your mercy, hear our prayer."

Let us pray for the church,
that it may stand fast in the one faith to which it has been called.
[*Silence*]
Lord, in your mercy,
**hear our prayer.**

Let us pray for the world,
that our conflicts may cease and that peace may reign in this new year.
[*Silence*]
Lord, in your mercy,
**hear our prayer.**

Let us pray for all Christians who have been baptized
into the one family of faith, that our lives may reflect the forgiveness
and love that were first shown us.
[*Silence*]
Lord, in your mercy,
**hear our prayer.**

Let us pray for all who are blind to the injustices of our world,
that their eyes may be opened and they may work
for an end to oppression and injustice.
[*Silence*]
Lord, in your mercy,
**hear our prayer.**

Let us pray for the sick [*especially . . .* ],
that their sickness may be turned to health
and they may once again join us in our work and worship.
[*Silence*]
Lord, in your mercy,
**hear our prayer.**

[*Here other intercessions may be offered.*]

Let us give thanks for the faithful who have gone before us,
that we may follow the example of their lives
and be reunited with them in the joy of everlasting life.
[*Silence*]
Lord, in your mercy,
**hear our prayer.**

Omniscient God,
you know our thoughts and needs better than we ourselves.
Accept the prayers that we now offer
and strengthen us to do your will,
through Jesus Christ, our Lord. **Amen.**

# G.8 THE LORD'S SUPPER

## G.8.2 Great Prayer of Thanksgiving (see section 8.2)

### G.8.2.2 Thanksgiving for the Work of God in Creation (see also section 8.2.2)

*The following prayer offers thanks for the work of God in creation and may be included in the complete Prayer of Thanksgiving as found in section 8.2 of this book.*

1    In being baptized by John in Jordan's waters,
    Jesus took his place with sinners,
    and your voice proclaimed him as your Son.
    Like a dove, your Spirit descended on him,
    anointing him as the Christ,
    to bring good news to the poor
    and proclaim release to the captives,
    to restore sight to the blind
    and free the oppressed.
    We praise you that in our baptism
    we are joined to Christ
    and, with all the baptized,
    are called to share his ministry.

## G.8.2.4 Thanksgiving for the Work of Christ (see also section 8.2.4)

*The following prayer offers thanks for the work of Christ and may be included in the complete Prayer of Thanksgiving as found in section 8.2 of this book.*

1   You are holy, O God of majesty,
    and blessed is Jesus Christ, your Son, our Lord,
    in whom you have revealed yourself,
    our light and our salvation.
    Baptized in Jordan's waters,
    Jesus took his place with sinners,
    and your voice proclaimed him your beloved.
    Your Spirit anointed him
    to bring good news to the poor,
    to proclaim release to the captives,
    to restore sight to the blind,
    to free the oppressed.
    He lived among us in power and grace,
    touching broken lives with your healing peace.
    By the baptism of his suffering, death, and resurrection,
    you gave birth to your church
    and made with us a new covenant
    by water and the Spirit.

2   O God, as you once claimed us in the Spirit's waters
    and number us among your own beloved,
    give us power to do your work,
    to show your love,
    and to live holy and joyful lives.
    Keep us faithful in your service
    until Christ comes in final victory
    and we shall feast with all your saints
    in the joy of your eternal realm.
    Through Christ, with Christ, in Christ,
    in the unity of the Holy Spirit,
    all glory and honor are yours, almighty God,
    now and forever. **Amen.**

# G.9 CLOSING OF WORSHIP

**G.9.1 Sending** (see also section 9.1)

*Closing Prayers*

1    Spirit of God, you who joined with Mary
to send Jesus into the world,
send us forward into the hours and days ahead,
equip us with power to love what is right and want it,
to know what is right and do it,
to see what is already right and join it.
Make us good citizens of the kingdom,
longing for justice, doing justice, joining hands with the just. **Amen.**

**G.9.2 Blessing/Benediction** (see also section 9.2)

1    God the Father, who sent his Spirit upon his Son,
bless you with the presence of his Spirit.
Jesus, who received the Spirit and manifested the Father,
abide in you and make you a manifestation of his life.
And God the Spirit, who came upon Christ in the fullness of power,
empower you to live a life of faith.
To the glory of God, Father, Son, and Holy Spirit. **Amen.**

2    The peace of God, known in this sanctuary,
will go with you, empowering you to meet adversity.
**We carry God's peace into a troubled world,**
**seeking to be peacemakers wherever we go.**
The blessing of God, who touched believers' lips
and set them free to sing praises,
will lift you up each day to use your gifts.
**We carry God's blessing into our daily lives**
**and dare to share the riches entrusted to us.**
The strength of God, seen in wind and fire,
will set you ablaze with vitality and purpose.
**We commit ourselves anew to live by God's will**
**as it is revealed to us day by day. Amen.**

3    May the Holy Spirit of God,
who at Jordan's riverside
descended upon the Father's well-loved Son, Jesus Christ,
and empowered him to obey God's will,
now rest upon you.

May the Spirit give you courage and strength
   to turn away from sin,
   to obey God's will,
   and to proclaim the coming reign of God.

May the triune God, the Father, Son, and Holy Spirit,
bless you and keep you always. **Amen.**

# G.10 SUGGESTED SCRIPTURE READINGS

1    *Voice of God*

    Exodus 19:1-19: God speaks to Moses
    Deuteronomy 5: God commands out of fire
    1 Kings 19:9-13: God speaks in a gentle whisper
    Job 37:1-13: God's voice thunders
    Psalm 29: The voice of the Lord is powerful and majestic
    Matthew 3:13-17; Mark 1; or Luke 3:21-22: God speaks at Jesus' baptism
    Matthew 17:1-7; Mark 9:2-8; or Luke 9:28-36: God speaks at the transfiguration
    John 10:1-18: The voice of the shepherd
    Acts 10:9-23: God speaks to Peter
    Acts 26:13-18: God speaks to Saul
    Hebrews 1: God speaks in many ways

# SECTION H
# TRANSFIGURATION

Jesus' transfiguration is traditionally celebrated on the Sunday before Ash Wednesday. At the transfiguration the glory of God in the person of Jesus was revealed to Peter, James, and John. In this glory we glimpse the glory Jesus would receive at the completion of his redemptive work. The spirit and colors of the worship space at this time should aim to reflect Christ's glory, so the suggested color for celebrating is white.

Transfiguration, like Christmas, Epiphany, and Baptism of our Lord, affirms the identity of Jesus as not only fully human but also fully divine. Just as the transfiguration prepared Jesus for his passion and death, so our observance of his transfiguration prepares us for our Lenten journey toward the cross and the empty tomb.

---

### Scriptures Applying to the Theme of Jesus' Transfiguration

*The following texts are particularly appropriate for sermons or for supplemental liturgical use.*

| | | |
|---|---|---|
| Exodus 24 | Psalm 50:1-6 | Luke 9:28-36 |
| Exodus 34:29-35 | Psalm 99 | 2 Corinthians 3:12-4:6 |
| 1 Kings 19:1-18 | Matthew 17:1-3 | 2 Peter 1:16-21 |
| 2 Kings 2:1-12 | Mark 9:2-12 | 1 John 3:2 |
| Psalm 2 | | |

# H.1 OPENING OF WORSHIP

## H.1.2 Call to Worship (see also section 1.2)

1   The Lord is Sovereign; let the people tremble in awe.
    **God is enthroned upon the cherubim; let the earth shake.**
    The Lord is great in Zion and is high above all peoples.
    **Proclaim the greatness of the Lord our God,**
    **and worship God upon the holy mountain.**
        —based on Psalm 99:1-3

2   *A text especially mindful of children*

    Great is the Lord—
    **exalted among the nations.**
    Mighty is the Lord—
    **King of heaven and earth.**
    Holy is the Lord—
    **beyond our understanding.**
    Let us worship our God and King!

## H.1.4 Opening Responses (see also section 1.4)

*Prayers of Adoration*

1   Holy God, mighty and immortal,
    you are beyond our knowing,
    yet we see your glory in the face of Jesus Christ,
    whose compassion illumines the world.
    Transform us into the likeness of the love of Christ,
    who renewed our humanity through his life, death, and resurrection—
    the same Jesus Christ, our Lord,
    who lives and reigns with you and the Holy Spirit. **Amen.**

2   God of power and wonder,
    we are awestruck by the glory of your presence.
    We rejoice at what we can see;
    we marvel at what we cannot see.
    You dazzle us with your brightness;
    you overshadow us as with a great cloud.
    Loving, protecting, challenging, nurturing,
    you strengthen and transform us.
    May we love and serve you in all that we are and do.
    Glory be to you. **Amen.**

**3**   *A prayer especially mindful of children*

> Jesus, today we celebrate your transfiguration.
> You remind us that you are powerful and holy.
> We cannot completely understand you,
> but you do teach us that you are our God and you love us.
> We praise you, holy Lord!
> We glorify you, almighty King!
> We exalt you, Son of God!
> Thank you for showing us who you are.
> In your name we pray. **Amen.**

*Additional Resources*

**4**   O God of the covenant,
> the cloud of your splendor and the fire of your love
> revealed your Son on the mountain heights.
> Transform our lives in his image,
> write your law of love on our hearts,
> and make us prophets of your glory,
> that we may lead others into your presence. **Amen.**

**5**   God of glory and mercy,
> before his death in shame your Son went to the mountaintop
> and you revealed his life in glory.
> Where prophets witnessed to him,
> you proclaimed him to be your Son,
> but he returned to die among us.
> Help us to face evil with courage,
> knowing that all things, even death,
> are subject to your transforming power.
> We ask this through Christ, our Lord. **Amen.**

**6**   Lord Jesus Christ,
> on the mountaintop Peter, James, and John
> looked upon the majesty of your glory,
> and from the mystery of a cloud
> they heard a voice declaring you to be God's Son.
> Though we do not live on mountaintops,
> grant that we too may glimpse your glory.
> In the mundane predictability of our life,
> may there be moments
> when sight gives way to insight
> and the paths of earth
> become the road to heaven. **Amen.**

# H.2 CONFESSION AND ASSURANCE

**H.2.2 Prayers of Confession** (see also section 2.2)

1    Eternal God,
     we confess that we do not expect and long for
     the transforming power of your love
     to work miracles in these hard hearts of ours.
     Yet we secretly long for a rescue, an escape, a miracle,
     to relieve us of the responsibilities and the challenges you set before us.
     Healing Spirit, renew our confidence in your power
     and in the power of love to change our lives,
     and give us courage to be the fully responsible persons
     Christ calls us to be. **Amen.**

2    Most amazing God, the mystery of your radiance surrounds us.
     Like the disciples of Jesus,
     we confess our unease with transcendent mystery.
     Faced with your splendor, we do not take time
     for attentive silence as Jesus did,
     but we evade the holy with stammering and busyness—
     anything to avoid your power.
     We also confess those times when we are at ease with holiness,
     absorbed in prayer and thought but so in love with your love
     that we neglect those in need.
     As Jesus descended into the valley
     to work among the poor of the earth,
     so direct us to our responsibilities.
     Such is the mystery of your love, O God,
     which both overwhelms and attracts us.
     Have mercy upon us and forgive us.
     Free us to love and serve in equal measure. **Amen.**

3    Almighty God, we enter your presence humbly,
     aware that we approach you from a world
     that chooses to walk in darkness, apart from you.
     Each one of us has ignored and even denied
     the enlightening power of Jesus Christ.
     We confess now our sins to you, God of power and might.
     Penetrate our darkness by the power of Christ's light,
     that we may live in the joy of knowing and loving you and each other.
     [*Silent prayer of confession*]

     We pray through Jesus Christ, our Lord. **Amen.**

4     Eternal God, we confess that we have praised you with our lips
but have not glorified you with our lives.
Have mercy on us, we pray,
for our weak faith that fades under pressure,
for our quick enthusiasm that just as quickly dies,
for the hopes we proclaim but do not pursue.
Forgive us, Lord God, and give us new trust in your power,
that we may live for justice and tell of your loving-kindness
by our acts as by our words, through Jesus Christ, our Lord. **Amen.**

5     God of transfiguration,
you meet us in the ordinary
as well as the extraordinary moments of life.
We seek you in the valleys and on the mountaintops.
Yet we admit that too often our eyes are blind to your presence,
too often our ears are deaf to your call.
When you reach out to us
through the cries of the hungry and homeless,
too often our hearts shrink from your touch.
Forgive us, we pray,
and set us free to love and serve. **Amen.**

6     God of compassion,
in Jesus Christ we behold your transforming light,
yet we continue to live in darkness.
Preoccupied with ourselves,
we fail to see your work in the world.
We speak when we should listen;
we act when we should reflect.
Empower us to live in your light
and to walk in your ways
for the sake of him who is the light of the world,
Jesus Christ, our Lord and Savior. **Amen.**

## H.2.4 Assurance of Pardon (see also section 2.4)

1     Now the Lord is the Spirit,
and where the Spirit of the Lord is, there is freedom.
And all of us, with unveiled faces,
seeing the glory of the Lord as though reflected in a mirror,
are being transformed into the same image
from one degree of glory to another,
for this comes from the Lord, the Spirit.

In Jesus Christ we are forgiven and transformed!
Praise be to God!
—based on 2 Corinthians 3:17-18, NRSV

# H.3 PROCLAIMING THE WORD

### H.3.1 Prayers for Illumination (see also section 3.1)

1    Holy God,
     you revealed to the disciples
     the everlasting glory of Jesus Christ.
     Grant us, who have not seen and yet believe,
     the gift of your Holy Spirit,
     that we may boldly live the gospel
     and shine with your transforming glory
     as people changed and changing
     through the redeeming presence of our Savior. **Amen.**

2    Lord Jesus,
     your majesty surpasses all
     that your disciples could have imagined.
     Your goodness exceeds all that we think or understand.
     As your Word is proclaimed today,
     open our minds and hearts
     to perceive your majesty and goodness more fully
     and to respond in joy. **Amen.**

# H.4 PRAYERS OF THE PEOPLE

### H.4.4 Complete Model Outlines and Prayers (see also section 4.4)

*Prayer Outlines*

1    *The following is a guide for extemporaneous prayers for services that remember Jesus' trans-*
     *figuration. The pattern provides a suggested text for the opening and closing of each part of*
     *the prayer and calls for extemporaneous prayers of thanksgiving, petition, and intercession.*

     Jesus Christ,
     glorified and risen Lord,
     though you could have stayed on the mountain,
     you chose to descend, knowing the agony that lay ahead to bring our salvation.
     We thank you for your redemption, that can be seen even now in

creation . . .
the nations of the world . . .
world leaders . . .
our nation . . .
our community . . .
the church universal . . .
our church . . .
the life of . . .
our own lives . . .

Yet knowing that many in this world
are not willing to acknowledge you as God and Savior,
or are unable to pray,
we offer these prayers on their behalf:
for creation and its care . . .
for the nations of the world . . .
for our nation and its leaders . . .
for our community and those who govern . . .
for the church universal, its mission, and those who minister . . .
for this local congregation and its ministry . . .
for persons with particular needs . . .

We pray in the name of Jesus Christ,
our glorified and risen Lord. **Amen.**

## Prayers in Litany Form

2    The Word of God calls us
to see that all the places and occasions of the world,
even places of sorrow and death,
are transfigured by the presence of the glory of God in Christ Jesus.

Let us now call to mind all who are in any need
and commend them to God's transforming care, saying,
"O merciful God, hear our prayer."

For those who are alone,
for widows and widowers and orphans,
and for the divorced,
O merciful God, **hear our prayer.**

For the imprisoned,
for those whose only home is the streets,
and for those caught in addiction,
O merciful God, **hear our prayer.**

For the hungry,
for those who cannot feed their children,
and for the unemployed,
O merciful God, **hear our prayer.**

For refugees,
for victims of warfare,
and for those held in poverty by racial discrimination,
O merciful God, **hear our prayer.**

For the people of our nation, our city, and our community,
O merciful God, **hear our prayer.**

For artists and writers
and for all who think on the edge of society,
O merciful God, **hear our prayer.**

For preachers and teachers of the light-bearing Word of Christ,
O merciful God, **hear our prayer.**

For the church and its leaders,
formed by the life-giving Word of Christ,
O merciful God, **hear our prayer.**

For this assembly, feeding on the Word of Christ,
O merciful God, **hear our prayer.**

[*Here other intercessions may be offered.*]

With Moses and Elijah and all the people of God,
with the church throughout the ages bearing witness
to the great light of God shining in dark places,
we commend to you all for whom we pray,
O merciful God, through Jesus Christ, our Lord. **Amen.**

## Bidding Prayers

3    O God, as your Son drew apart to be in prayer with you,
we offer our prayers for the transformation of the world and the church.

[*Prayers of the People, concluding with the following:*]

You revealed your glory and presence
in your beloved Son, Jesus the Christ.
In receiving our prayers, reveal the glory and presence
of your Spirit alive in the world today,
free us from all doubts,
and empower us to act as a transfigured people. **Amen.**

# H.8 THE LORD'S SUPPER

**H.8.2 Great Prayer of Thanksgiving** (see section 8.2)

*H.8.2.4 Thanksgiving for the Work of Christ (see also section 8.2.4)*

*The following prayer offers thanks for the work of Christ and may be included in the complete Prayer of Thanksgiving as found in section 8.2 of this book.*

1    On the holy mountain
the divine glory of the incarnate Word was revealed.
From the heavens your voice proclaimed your beloved Son,
who is the fulfillment of the law and the prophets.
We rejoice in the divine majesty of Christ,
whose glory shone forth even when confronted with the cross.

2    In splendor and majesty
your Word was revealed,
the hope of Israel,
transfigured in glory.
In splendor and majesty
he set his face toward Jerusalem,
choosing the way of suffering and death
that would be majestically transfigured
into the way of life and hope.

# H.9 CLOSING OF WORSHIP

**H.9.1 Sending** (see also section 9.1)

*Closing Prayers*

1    O God, before the passion of your one and only Son
you revealed his glory upon the holy mountain:
Grant to us that we,

beholding by faith the light of his countenance,
may be strengthened to bear our cross
and be changed into his likeness from glory to glory,
through Jesus Christ, our Lord,
who lives and reigns with you and the Holy Spirit,
one God, for ever and ever. **Amen.**

**H.9.2 Blessing/Benediction** (see also section 9.2)

*Scriptural Blessings*

1    The Lord bless you and keep you;
     the Lord make his face shine upon you
          and be gracious to you;
     the Lord turn his face toward you
          and give you peace.
     **Alleluia! Amen.**
               —based on Numbers 6:24-26, NIV

*Additional Blessings*

2    May the glory of Christ, our King, be revealed in your life,
     may his Spirit surround you in the mystery of God,
     and may God transform your coming and your going.

3    May our covenant God encompass you
     with the mysterious power of the Spirit of God
     and transform you to become more and more like Christ.

# H.10 SUGGESTED SCRIPTURE READINGS

1    *Mountains and glory*
     Exodus 34:29-35: Moses experiences God's glory on Mount Sinai
     1 Kings 19:8-14: Elijah encounters God's presence on Mount Horeb
     Psalm 125: God's presence is compared with the mountains surrounding Jerusalem
     Matthew 5: Jesus preaches on a mountain
     2 Corinthians 3:7-18: God's glory transforms
     2 Peter 1:16-18: Peter's eyewitness account of the transfiguration

# ASH WEDNESDAY

Ash Wednesday is the first day of Lent. By the fourth century the Western church had determined that the Lenten period of fasting and renewal should correspond to Christ's forty-day fast (Matt. 4:2), and, by counting forty days back from Easter (excluding Sundays, which remain "feast" days), arrived at the Wednesday seven weeks before Easter. At one time Lent was primarily viewed as a period during which converts prepared for baptism on Easter Sunday, but later the season became a general time of penitence and renewal for all Christians. Thus Ash Wednesday became the day that marked the beginning of the Lenten renewal.

The aim of Ash Wednesday worship is threefold: to meditate on our mortality, sinfulness, and need of a savior; to renew our commitment to daily repentance in the Lenten season and in all of life; and to remember with confidence and gratitude that Christ has conquered death and sin. Ash Wednesday worship, then, is filled

with gospel truth. It is a witness to the power and beauty of our union with Christ and to the daily dying and rising with Christ that this entails.

The imposition of ashes is often a central part of the worship service. Ashes have a long history in biblical and church traditions. In Scripture ashes or dust symbolize frailty or death (Gen. 18:27), sadness or mourning (Esther 4:3), judgment (Lam. 3:16), and repentance (Jon. 3:6). Some traditions also have considered ash a purifying or cleansing agent. All these images are caught up in the church's use of ashes as a symbol appropriate for Lent. In Christ's passion we see God's judgment on evil; in our penitence we express sorrow and repentance for our sins; in our rededication we show that we are purified and renewed. The ashes, which often are the burnt residue of the previous year's palms from Palm Sunday, are often mixed with a little water and carried in a small dish. As the leader goes from worshiper to worshiper, or as worshipers come forward, the leader dips a finger in the moist ash and makes a cross on each person's forehead (the "imposition"), saying words such as "Remember that you are dust and to dust you shall return," or, "Consider yourself dead to sin and alive in Jesus Christ."

In some contexts, the imposition of ashes may be a barrier to thoughtful Lenten worship because of its newness or because it may be misunderstood. Most important is that worshipers rend their hearts (Joel 2:13). Decisions about whether or how to practice the imposition of ashes should always be made contextually, understanding how the symbol will be perceived within a particular community and cultural context.

---

**Scriptures and Statements of Faith Applying to the Theme of Ash Wednesday**

*The following texts are particularly appropriate for sermons or for supplemental liturgical use.*

| | | |
|---|---|---|
| Psalm 51 (and other penitential psalms: 6, 32, 38, 102, 130, 143) | Psalm 103 | Matthew 6:1-6, 16-21 |
| | Psalm 139:23-24 | Matthew 11:28-29 |
| | Joel 2:12-17 | 2 Corinthians 5:20-6:2 |
| Psalm 90 | Matthew 5:6 | 1 Peter 1-2:3 |

Heidelberg Catechism, Q&A's 3-11, 88-89

---

# I.1 OPENING OF WORSHIP

---

## I.1.2 Call to Worship (see also section 1.2)

1  Our help is in the name of the LORD,
    **who made heaven and earth.**

Why are you cast down, O my soul,
　　and why are you disquieted within me?
**Hope in God; for we shall praise him,**
　　**our help and our God.**
　　　—from Psalm 42:5; 124:8, NRSV

2　Brothers and sisters in Christ,
　every year at Easter,
　during the time of the "Christian Passover,"
　we celebrate our redemption
　through the death and resurrection of our Lord Jesus Christ.
　Lent is a time to prepare for this celebration
　and to practice with discipline daily repentance,
　our daily dying and rising in union with Christ.
　We begin this season
　by acknowledging our need for repentance
　and for the mercy and forgiveness
　proclaimed in the gospel of Jesus Christ.

## I.1.4 Opening Responses (see also section 1.4)

*Prayers of Invocation*

1　O Lord, open my lips,
　　**and my mouth will declare your praise.**
　You do not delight in sacrifice, or I would bring it;
　　**you do not take pleasure in burnt offerings.**
　The sacrifices of God are a broken spirit;
　　**a broken and contrite heart,**
　　**O God, you will not despise. Amen.**
　　　—from Psalm 51:15-17, NIV

2　Lord, you have been our dwelling place
　　in all generations.
　Before the mountains were brought forth,
　　or you had formed the earth and the world,
　　from everlasting to everlasting you are God.
　**Teach us, Lord, to count our days**
　　**that we may gain a wise heart.**
　**Satisfy us in the morning with your steadfast love,**
　　**so that we may rejoice and be glad all our days.**
　**Through Christ, our Lord. Amen.**
　　　—based on Psalm 90, NRSV

3    Lord, our God, you are full of compassion.
As we enter this season of Lent,
send your Spirit so that we may
grow more and more aware of our need for a Savior,
turn away from our sinful habits regularly and genuinely,
resist temptations great and small,
and remember with confidence
that our Lord Jesus conquered sin and death. **Amen.**

## *Additional Resources*

4    Merciful God,
we come to you today realizing
that we are not how you want us to be.
Help us let go of our past,
that we may turn toward you and live again the life of faith.
Help us call out our fear and hatred, our anger and self-pity.
Lift the burden they place on our shoulders.
Help us set aside our guilt and enter a season of healing.
As we pray and fast today, help us become simple people,
that we may see you plainly.
As we wear the mark of ashes,
rekindle the sign of hope within our eyes.
Let us draw near to you now. **Amen.**

5    Covenant God of love and mercy,
we come to you at the beginning of these forty days,
remembering how Jesus fasted and prayed
for forty days in the wilderness.
We remember how he steadfastly set his face toward Jerusalem,
obedient in living and dying, even through death on a cross.
We too would walk these next forty days in humble obedience,
following our Savior, Jesus Christ,
in our everyday lives
at home, at work, and in your world.
Prepare us anew, we pray,
to keep our hearts and minds fixed on Jesus,
ready and willing from now on to live for him. **Amen.**

6    Faithful and loving God,
as we walk this Lenten journey,
help us to choose the path of obedience and life.
Help us to see clearly the way ahead
and to be confident that your commands
are sweeter than honey, more valuable than gold. **Amen.**

# I.2 CONFESSION AND ASSURANCE

## I.2.1 Call to Confession (see also section 2.1)

1   Our congregation invites you
    to observe this season of Lent
    through self-examination and penitence,
    prayer and fasting,
    reading and meditating on the Word of God,
    and works of love and witness.

    Let us bow before God, our Creator and Redeemer,
    and confess our sin.

2   Lent is a journey of deepening reflection and renewal,
    an opportunity to make new commitments in faith.
    We prepare for the journey
    by setting aside burdens that would weigh us down.
    Let us turn to God and confess our sin.

3   Genuine repentance involves two things:
    the dying-away of the old self and the coming-to-life of the new.
    The dying-away of the old self is to be genuinely sorry for sin,
    to hate it more and more, and to run away from it.
    The coming-to-life of the new self
    is wholehearted joy in God through Christ
    and a delight to do every kind of good as God wants us to.

    Together, as Christ's body, we now confess our sin
    and express our longing to live in joyful obedience to God.
    —based on Heidelberg Catechism, Q&A's 88-90

## I.2.2 Prayers of Confession (see also section 2.2)

1   Have mercy on me, O God,
        according to your unfailing love;
    **according to your great compassion
        blot out my transgressions.**
    Wash away all my iniquity
        **and cleanse me from my sin.**
    Surely you desire truth in the inner parts;
        **you teach me wisdom in the inmost place.**
    Create in me a pure heart, O God,
        and renew a steadfast spirit within me.

> Do not cast me from your presence
> or take your Holy Spirit from me.
> Restore to me the joy of your salvation
> and grant me a willing spirit, to sustain me. Amen.
>> —from Psalm 51:1-2, 6, 10-12, NIV

2    *A prayer especially mindful of children*

Lord God, it is hard to think that we will die someday.
We dream, make plans, and talk about what we'll do in the near future.
We don't always think about what you want.
Instead, we make choices that we think are good for us.
But we are only here because you take care of us.
We confess that we forget we need you all the time.
We confess that sometimes we make choices that aren't what you want.
We don't know what is best for our lives.
Holy God, we are sorry for our sin.
Help us to remember we live because of you.
Help us to do what you want us to do
through Jesus, our Lord. **Amen.**

## I.2.4 Assurance of Pardon (see also section 2.4)

1    Surely he has borne our griefs and carried our sorrows.
He was wounded for our transgressions
and bruised for our iniquities.
Upon him was the chastisement
that makes us whole,
and with his stripes we are healed.
He will feed his flock like a shepherd
and gather the lambs in his arms.
>> —based on Isaiah 40:11; 53:4-5

2    God so loved the world that he gave his only Son,
so that everyone who believes in him
may not perish but may have eternal life.
>> —John 3:16, NRSV

*The following resource may be used after either of the preceding texts.*

3    May God the Father, who does not despise the broken spirit,
    give us contrite hearts.
May Christ, who bore our sins in his body on the tree,
    heal us by his wounds.
May the Holy Spirit, who leads us into all truth,
    speak words of pardon and peace.

# I.4 PRAYERS OF THE PEOPLE

**I.4.4 Complete Model Outlines and Prayers** (see also section 4.4)

*Prayer Outlines*

1    *The following is a guide for extemporaneous prayers. The pattern provides a suggested text for the opening and closing of each part of the prayer and calls for extemporaneous prayers of thanksgiving, petition, and intercession.*

God of new birth,
we praise you for being the giver of life and the victor over death,
    for the evidence of new life we see in creation . . .
    for our baptism, a sign of our union with Christ
        in his death and resurrection . . .
    for the promise of the coming kingdom . . .

God of new birth,
we acknowledge that all of life is sustained by you, so we pray
    for creation and its care . . .
    for the nations of the world, especially . . .
    for our nation and those in authority . . .
    for this community and its leaders . . .
    for the church universal, its mission, and those who minister . . .
    for our local church and its ministry . . .
    for persons with particular needs . . .

We pray all these things in the name of the triune God,
the giver and sustainer of life. **Amen.**

*Imposition of Ashes*

*The imposition of ashes is essentially an act of prayer and meditation and thus is included in this section of prayer resources.*

2    We begin our journey to Easter with the sign of ashes.
This ancient sign speaks of the frailty and uncertainty of human life,
calls us to heartfelt repentance,
and urges us to place our hope in God alone.

Almighty God,
you have created us out of the dust of the earth.
May these ashes remind us of our mortality and penitence
and teach us again that only by your gracious gift
are we given everlasting life
through Jesus Christ, our Savior.
**Amen.**

*[Worshipers are invited to come forward to receive the imposition of ashes. During the imposition, suitable hymns or psalms may be sung, or worshipers may keep silence. A worship leader marks the forehead of each person with the ashes, using the following words.]*

Remember that you are dust,
and to dust you shall return.
> —from Genesis 3:19, NRSV

*[or]*

Consider yourself dead to sin
and alive to God in Jesus Christ.
> —from Romans 6:11, NRSV

*After all who desire the imposition of ashes have received them, the following prayer may be said.*

3     Gracious God, out of your love and mercy
you breathed into dust the breath of life,
creating us to serve you and our neighbors.
**In this season of repentance,**
**restore to us the joy of our salvation**
**and strengthen us to face our mortality,**
**that we may reach with confidence for your mercy,**
**in Jesus Christ, our Lord,**
**who lives and reigns with you and the Holy Spirit,**
**one God, now and forever. Amen.**

# I.9 CLOSING OF WORSHIP

## I.9.1 Sending (see also section 9.1)

*Closing Prayers*

1     *A prayer especially mindful of children*

Jesus Christ,
we want always to remember
that you love us, died for us, and rose from the dead for us.
In the next weeks, help us to remember,
and help us trust in you more and more. **Amen.**

2    God of compassion,
     through your Son, Jesus Christ,
     you reconciled your people to yourself.
     Following his example of prayer and fasting,
     may we obey you with willing hearts
     and serve one another in holy love through Jesus Christ. **Amen.**


## I.9.2 Blessing/Benediction (see also section 9.2)

1    The God of peace himself sanctify you entirely;
     and may your spirit and soul and body be kept sound and blameless
     at the coming of our Lord Jesus Christ.
     The one who calls you is faithful, and he will do this. **Amen.**
          —from 1 Thessalonians 5:23-24, NRSV

2    May God the Father, who does not despise the broken spirit,
          give you a contrite heart.
     May Christ, who bore our sins in his body on the tree,
          heal you by his wounds.
     May the Holy Spirit, who leads us into all truth,
          speak to you words of pardon and peace. **Amen.**

3    May God, who by his power
     raised from the dead our Lord Jesus Christ,
     hold you in his love,
     surround you with his presence,
     give you grace for every need,
     and present you whole and holy
     in the day of Jesus Christ. **Amen.**

4    May the Lord of all compassion
     satisfy you in the morning with his steadfast love,
     so that you may rejoice and be glad all your days.
     May the favor of the Lord our God be upon you,
     and may the work of your hands prosper. **Amen.**
          —from Psalm 90:13-17

5    Hear these words of promise from your God:
     "Those who love me, I will deliver;
     I will protect those who know my name.
     When they call to me, I will answer them;
     I will be with them in trouble,
     I will rescue them and honor them.
     With long life will I satisfy them,
     and show them my salvation." **Amen.**
          —from Psalm 91:14-16

6    Penitent and forgiven,
     may you step forward from this hour
     in the assurance that God is
     ever old, ever new, always hidden, always present.
     May you step forward now in the blessed assurance
     that you can never step out of God's abiding love. **Amen.**

# I.10 SUGGESTED SCRIPTURE READINGS

1    *Ashes*

     Genesis 18:16-33: Abraham pleads for Sodom
     2 Samuel 12:1-24: David cries for his son
     Esther 4: Wailing for the Jews
     Psalm 102: A cry for help and a declaration of confidence
     Isaiah 61: Crown of beauty in place of ashes
     Daniel 9:1-19: Daniel's prayer of repentance
     Jonah 3: Nineveh cries out to God
     Malachi 4: Judgment and promise

2    *Call to repent*

     2 Chronicles 6:37-38: God's people are challenged to turn to God
     Isaiah 55: Come, all who are thirsty
     Ezekiel 14:6: God calls Ezekiel to preach repentance
     Joel 2:12-17: Rend your hearts
     Matthew 3:1-6: John the Baptist calls for repentance
     Matthew 4:12-17: Jesus begins to preach
     Mark 6:6-13: Jesus' disciples preach a message of repentance
     Luke 13:1-9: Repent and bear fruit
     John 1:14-15: Jesus calls listeners to repent
     Acts 2:38-41: Repent and be baptized
     Acts 3:19-26: Peter calls for repentance
     Revelation 2:5, 16, 21-22: New Testament churches are called to repent

# SECTION J
# LENT

The death and resurrection of Jesus Christ are at the heart of the Christian gospel, and Good Friday and Easter are two of the most significant celebrations of the Christian year. Lent is a season of preparation and repentance during which we anticipate Good Friday and Easter. Just as we carefully prepare for big events in our personal lives, such as a wedding or commencement, Lent invites us to make our hearts ready for remembering Jesus' passion and celebrating Jesus' resurrection.

The practice of a forty-day preparation period began in the Christian church during the third and fourth centuries. The number *forty* carries biblical significance based on the forty years Israel spent in the wilderness and Jesus' forty-day fast in the wilderness. The forty days of Lent begin on Ash Wednesday and continue through holy week, not counting Sundays (which are reserved for celebratory worship). In practice, many congregations choose to

focus Sunday worship on the themes of repentance and renewal.

As a period of preparation, Lent has historically included the instruction of persons for baptism and profession of faith on Easter Sunday; the calling back of those who have become estranged from the church; and efforts by all Christians to deepen their piety, devotion, and readiness to mark the death and resurrection of their Savior. As such, the primary focus of the season is to explore and deepen a "baptismal spirituality" that centers on our union with Christ rather than to function only as an extended meditation on Christ's suffering and death.

The traditional color for the season is purple. Some congregations choose to highlight the contrast between Lent and Eastertide (the period from Easter to Ascension Day or Pentecost or Trinity Sunday) by omitting the singing of "Alleluia" during the Lenten season, and yet other congregations stress that all the Sundays of Lent are "little Easters" and thus may appropriately feature Easter-like praise.

---

### Scriptures and Statements of Faith Applying to the Theme of Lent

*For a complete list of lectionary texts for Lent, see page 825. The following texts, which focus on three main dimensions of Lenten spirituality, are especially appropriate for supplemental liturgical use.*

*Penitential psalms:*
Psalms 6, 32, 38, 51, 102, 130, 143

*The importance of heartfelt repentance:*
Psalm 50
Isaiah 1
Joel 2:12-17
Matthew 6:1-6, 16-21

*Baptismal spirituality and unity with Christ:*
Romans 6:1-14; 8:12-17
2 Corinthians 1:21-22; 4:1-16; 5:20-6:2
Galatians 2:19-21; 3:27-29
Ephesians 2:4-20; 4:1-6
Colossians 2:9-3:7
Titus 3:4-8

Belgic Confession, Art. 21
Heidelberg Catechism, Q&A's 37-39
Canons of Dort, Pt. II, Art. 2-5, 8
Westminster Confession, Chap. VIII, Sec. 4; Chap. XV, Sec. 1-6
*Our World Belongs to God,* st. 24-26

# J.1 OPENING OF WORSHIP

### J.1.1 Preparation for Worship (see also section 1.1)

1    Holy and loving God,
     as we worship you today,
     we long for your Spirit to both comfort and challenge us,
     to help us become more holy and more loving.
     In a world that does not understand repentance,
     we pray for new understanding, humility, patience, and discipline
     that will help us die to sin and live for Jesus. **Amen.**

2    Lord God,
     in this season of Lent
     we look forward to our remembrance of Jesus' death
     and our celebration of his resurrection.
     We pray that your Spirit will renew in us today
     our anticipation for these events
     and our awareness that Jesus' death and resurrection
     are a sure source of hope and life.
     In the power of Jesus' name we pray. **Amen.**

### J.1.2 Call to Worship (see also section 1.2)

1    Let us worship God, who has done great things.
     **We rejoice in our God, who made a way**
     **through the desert of this world.**
     Let us worship God, who has caused streams of mercy
     to flow in the wasteland.
     **We are the people God has formed through Christ;**
     **we worship him, and we rejoice!**
     Let us worship God in spirit and in truth.
     **We praise God for the grace that has saved us.**
     **Alleluia! We rejoice!**
          —based on Isaiah 43:19-21

2    Let us worship God,
     who reconciled us to himself through Christ.
     **We are new creations;**
     **the old has gone, the new has come!**
     Let us worship God as Christ's ambassadors.
     **Through us and through our worship**
     **may we announce the good news to all.**

Let us worship God in spirit and in truth.
**Praise God! We are reconciled, redeemed, renewed!**
—based on John 4:24; 2 Corinthians 5:17-21

3   Let us worship God,
    for whom our souls thirst and our bodies long.
    **Listen, listen to me,**
    **and your soul will delight in the richest of fare.**
    We have come to hear the Word God has sent.
    **God's Word will not return empty**
    **but will accomplish through us his holy purpose.**
    Let us worship God in spirit and in truth.
    **Then we will go out with joy and be led forth in peace;**
    **the mountains and the hills will sing;**
    **the trees of the field will clap their hands.**
    —based on Isaiah 55:2, 11-12; John 4:24

4   Let us fix our eyes on Jesus,
    the author and perfecter of our faith,
    who for the joy set before him endured the cross,
    scorning its shame, and sat down at the right hand of God.
    Let us consider him who endured such opposition from sinful people,
    so that we will not grow weary and lose heart.
    —from Hebrews 12:2-3, NIV

5   Let us contemplate Jesus the Lord:
    Instead of the joy meant for him,
    he endured the cross, disregarding its disgrace.
    **We worship you, Lord.**
    O Jesus Christ, born in humility
    to confound the proud and to raise the humble:
    **We worship you, Lord.**
    You lived among us, healing the sick,
    proclaiming good news to the poor and freedom to prisoners.
    **We worship you, Lord.**
    You came to unbind the chains of every slavery,
    O friend of the humble, bread of hungry hearts.
    **We worship you, Lord.**
    Jesus, full of patience and goodness,
    you showed forgiveness and kindness to the very end.
    **We worship you, Lord.**
    Jesus, gentle and humble of heart,
    you call to yourself all who are weary and burdened.
    **We worship you, Lord.**
    Jesus, you came into the world to serve and to give your life;
    you were betrayed for money, dragged before judges,
    and nailed to a cross.
    **We worship you, Lord.**

Jesus, Lord of the universe,
by your resurrection from the dead you are alive at the Father's side,
and there you prepare a place for us.
**We worship you, Lord.**

6    Come to the Lord, who is rich in grace;
approach our God, who is full of mercy.
**We will praise God with all our heart
and glorify the name of the Most High forever.**

7    The trumpet of the Lord sounds, calling us to examine our souls,
**for we have not only met temptation, we have felt its grip.**
The trumpet of the Lord sounds, calling us to mend our ways,
**for we have not only committed sin, we have felt its sting.**
The trumpet of the Lord sounds, calling us to rend our hearts,
**for we have not only witnessed forgiveness, we have felt its power.**
**O come, let us worship the Lord!**

8    The day of the Lord is coming! The day of the Lord is near!
**The time is fulfilled! The reign of God is at hand!**
O people, repent! Believe in the gospel!
**Come, let us turn and follow the Lord!**

## J.1.4 Opening Responses (see also section 1.4)

*Prayers of Adoration*

1    O Christ, Savior, like the seed fallen to the ground,
you suffered death.
United to you, our lives will bear much fruit.
**We praise you, Lord.**
O Christ, you went down to the lowest point of the human condition;
you remain close to all who are abandoned.
**We praise you, Lord.**
In your love you took upon yourself our sins;
innocent, you accepted death to free us from death.
**We praise you, Lord.**
By your love you conquered evil and hatred,
and you live forever at the Father's side.
**We praise you, Lord.**
You listen to us in your goodness, and you visit us in our misfortune;
fill our hearts to overflowing by revealing to us the light of your face.
**We praise you, Lord. Amen.**

*Prayers of Invocation*

2    All-knowing and all-caring God,
      we gather this day drained by another week.
      We are like a parched desert, empty and in need of replenishment.
      Visit us with your presence, saturate us with your Spirit,
      and bathe us in your streams of living water,
      that our lives might acknowledge and worship you
      to the praise and honor of Jesus Christ. **Amen!**
          —based on John 4:13-14; 7:37-38

3    O God, in creation you fashion us in your image,
      in Christ you reveal to us your love,
      through the Holy Spirit you welcome us into the fellowship of believers;
      we bow in gratitude before you.
      We constantly distort your image, but still you restore it.
      We daily betray your love, but still you extend it.
      We often disrupt fellowship, but still you bless it.
      Come unto us at this time and in this place, O Lord,
      that your image in us might be revealed, your love for us returned,
      and our fellowship in Christ renewed. **Amen.**

4    From Bethlehem to Nazareth,
      from Jordan to Jericho,
      from Bethany to Jerusalem,
      from then to now,
      **come, Lord Jesus.**
      To heal the sick,
      to mend the brokenhearted,
      to comfort the disturbed,
      to disturb the comfortable,
      to cleanse the temple,
      to liberate faith from convention,
      **come, Lord Jesus.**
      To carry the cross,
      to lead the way,
      to shoulder the sin of the world
      and take it away,
      **come, Lord Jesus.**
      Today,
      to this place,
      to us,
      **come, Lord Jesus. Amen.**

5    Gracious God,
      out of your love and mercy
      you breathed into dust the breath of life,
      creating us to serve you and our neighbors.

Call forth our prayers and acts of tenderness
and strengthen us to face our mortality,
that we may reach with confidence for your mercy
in Jesus Christ, our Lord,
who lives and reigns with you and the Holy Spirit,
one God, now and forever. **Amen.**

6    Journey with us, O holy God,
as we begin [*continue*] our way to the cross.
Sharpen our focus, that our attention
may center more on you than ourselves.
Lead us through the shadows of darkness and prepare our hearts,
that we might be a people of prayer,
ready to perceive and respond to your Son and our Savior, Jesus Christ.
In his name we pray. **Amen.**

7    Lord God,
we gather in this place
not because we are deserving of your love
and not because we have lived faithfully before your face.
We gather here because you have called us.
You loved us before we could love you.
You have given your Son for our salvation.
For this we join all creation
in blessing you, praising you, thanking you.
Holy, holy, holy, Lord God Almighty!
You are great, and greatly to be praised.
As we offer our praise,
we long for you to mold us in the image of your Son,
whose death and resurrection give us hope.
Through the power of the Holy Spirit. **Amen.**

8    Lord Jesus, we walk with you
through the valley of the shadow of death.
**Let us find our life in you, O Lord.**
Banished from the Garden of Eden for our rebellion,
**we long for the garden of Paradise.**
O Lord, you are the Christ.
**Remember us in your kingdom.**
We come to hear you speak of your love for us.
**You have the words of eternal life. Amen.**

9    God of all hope,
we gather today so deeply aware
of the world's grief and pain—and our own.
Comfort us, we pray, with the sure knowledge
that our Lenten journey culminates in Easter joy. **Amen.**

# J.2 CONFESSION AND ASSURANCE

## J.2.1 Call to Confession (see also section 2.1)

1    The sacrifice acceptable to God is a broken spirit;
     a broken and contrite heart, O God, you will not despise.
          —Psalm 51:17, NRSV

2    Search me, O God, and know my heart;
          **try me and know my thoughts.**
     See if there is any wicked way in me,
          **and lead me in the way everlasting.**
          —Psalm 139:23-24, NRSV

3    Is not this the fast I choose:
          to loose the bonds of injustice;
          to share your bread with the hungry;
          to bring the homeless poor into your house;
          to clothe the naked?
     Then your light shall break forth like the dawn,
     and your healing shall spring up quickly.

     Having heard these promises, let us confess our sins.
          —based on Isaiah 58:6-8, NRSV

4    For a brief moment I abandoned you,
          but with great compassion I will gather you.
     In overflowing wrath for a moment
          I hid my face from you,
     but with everlasting love I will have compassion on you,
          says the Lord, your Redeemer.

     Let us confess our sins to almighty God.
          —based on Isaiah 54:7-8, NRSV

5    Seek the Lord while he may be found,
          call upon him while he is near;
     let the wicked forsake their way,
          and the unrighteous their thoughts;
     let them return to the Lord, that he may have mercy on them,
          and to our God, for he will abundantly pardon.

     Trusting ourselves to the grace of God,
     let us confess our sins before God and one another.
          —based on Isaiah 55:6-7, NRSV

6    The proof of God's amazing love is this:
While we were sinners, Christ died for us.
Because we have faith in him,
we dare to approach God with confidence,
trusting that God will forgive our sin
and cleanse us from every kind of wrong.

Let us confess our sins to almighty God.
—based on Romans 5:8; Hebrews 4:16; 1 John 1:8

7    Remember that our Lord Jesus Christ is able
to sympathize with us in our weaknesses.
In every respect he was tempted as we are, yet without sin.
Let us therefore approach the throne of grace with boldness,
so that we may receive mercy and find grace to help in time of need.

Let us confess our sins to almighty God.
—based on Hebrews 4:15-16, NRSV

8    The very stone that the builders rejected
has become the chief cornerstone.
Come now to Christ, that living stone,
a cornerstone chosen and precious.
Whoever believes in him will not be put to shame.

Trusting in the Lord Jesus Christ,
let us confess our sins before God and one another.
—based on 1 Peter 2:4-7, NRSV

9    If we say that we have no sin,
we deceive ourselves and the truth is not in us.
If we confess our sins, God, who is faithful and just,
will forgive our sins and cleanse us from all unrighteousness.

Let us confess our sins to almighty God.
—based on 1 John 1:8-9, NRSV

10   During his whole life on earth,
but especially at the end,
Christ sustained
in body and soul
the anger of God against the sin of the whole human race.

In response to his sacrifice, let us confess our sins to God.
—based on Heidelberg Catechism, Q&A 37

11   Christ himself bore our sins in his body on the tree
that we might die to sins and live for righteousness.
By his wounds we are healed.

Let us confess our sins.
—based on 1 Peter 2:24, NIV

## J.2.2 Prayers of Confession (see also section 2.2)

**1** *Call to Confession*
From Mount Hor they set out by the way to the Red Sea, to go around the land of Edom; but the people became impatient on the way. The people spoke against God and against Moses, "Why have you brought us up out of Egypt to die in the wilderness? For there is no food and no water, and we detest this miserable food." Then the LORD sent poisonous serpents among the people, and they bit the people, so that many Israelites died. The people came to Moses and said, "We have sinned by speaking against the LORD and against you; pray to the LORD to take away the serpents from us." So Moses prayed for the people. And the LORD said to Moses, "Make a poisonous serpent, and set it on a pole; and everyone who is bitten shall look at it and live." So Moses made a serpent of bronze, and put it upon a pole; and whenever a serpent bit someone, that person would look at the serpent of bronze and live.
—Numbers 21:4-9, NRSV

*Prayer of Confession*
[*spoken by an individual, preferably a child*]
God, we are often impatient like the people of Israel.
We want things our way and we want them in a hurry.
Forgive us when we think this way or say it out loud.
Lord, we are sinful. Please take away our sin.
Help us to seek your way. In Jesus' name, **Amen.**

*Assurance of Pardon*
Just as Moses lifted up the serpent in the wilderness, so must the Son of Man be lifted up, that whoever believes in him may have eternal life. For God so loved the world that he gave his only Son, so that everyone who believes in him may not perish but may have eternal life.
—John 3:14-16, NRSV

**2** If you, O Lord, kept a record of sins,
    O Lord, who could stand?
But with you there is forgiveness;
    therefore you are feared.
I wait for the Lord, my soul waits,
    and in his word I put my hope.
My soul waits for the Lord
    more than watchmen wait for the morning,
    more than watchmen wait for the morning.

Almighty God, our Redeemer,
in our weakness we have failed
to be your messengers of forgiveness and hope.
Renew us by your Holy Spirit,
that we may follow your commands
and proclaim your reign of love,
through Jesus Christ, our Lord,
who lives and reigns with you and the Holy Spirit,
one God, now and forever. **Amen.**
—based on Psalm 130:3-6, NIV

3    Almighty God,
you despise nothing you have made,
and you forgive the sins of all who are penitent.
Create in us new and contrite hearts,
that, truly repenting of our sins
and acknowledging our brokenness,
we may obtain from you, the God of all mercy,
full pardon and forgiveness,
through your Son, Jesus Christ, our Redeemer,
who lives and reigns with you and the Holy Spirit,
one God, now and forever. **Amen.**

4    **Holy and merciful God,**
**we confess to you and to one another,**
**and to the whole communion of saints in heaven and on earth,**
**that we have sinned by our own fault**
**in thought, word, and deed,**
**by what we have done**
**and by what we have left undone.**
We have not loved you with our whole heart and mind and strength.
We have not loved our neighbors as ourselves.
We have not forgiven others as we have been forgiven.
**Have mercy on us, O God.**
We have not listened to your call to serve as Christ served us.
We have not been true to the mind of Christ.
We have grieved your Holy Spirit.
**Have mercy on us, O God.**
We confess to you, O God, all our past unfaithfulness:
the pride, hypocrisy, and impatience in our lives,
**we confess to you, O God.**
Our self-indulgent appetites and ways
and our exploitation of other people,
**we confess to you, O God.**
Our anger at our own frustration
and our envy of those more fortunate than ourselves,
**we confess to you, O God.**
Our intemperate love of worldly goods and comforts
and our dishonesty in daily life and work,
**we confess to you, O God.**
Our negligence in prayer and worship
and our failure to commend the faith that is in us,
**we confess to you, O God.**
Accept our repentance, O God,
for the wrongs we have done.
For our neglect of human need and suffering
and our indifference to injustice and cruelty,
**accept our repentance, O God.**
For all false judgments,

for uncharitable thoughts toward our neighbors,
and for our prejudice and contempt
toward those who differ from us,
**accept our repentance, O God.**
For our waste and pollution of your creation
and our lack of concern for those who come after us,
**accept our repentance, O God.**
Restore us, O God,
and let your anger depart from us.
**Favorably hear us, O God,**
**for your mercy is great. Amen.**

5    O Lord, you desire truth in our inward being;
**teach us wisdom in our secret heart.**
Send out your light, send out your truth,
**and let them lead us to our home.**
Take from us the weight of our sin,
**that room might be made for the spirit of truth.**
If we prepare a dwelling place, that spirit will abide within us,
**and the truth will set our spirits free.**
Then shall we love not only in word or in speech;
then shall we love in deed and in truth,
**and by this know that our service is faithful.**
O Lord, you desire truth in our inward being;
**teach us wisdom in our secret heart. Amen.**

6    God of compassion,
you are slow to anger and full of mercy,
welcoming sinners who return to you with penitent hearts.
Receive in your loving embrace
all who come home to you.
Seat them at your bountiful table of grace,
that, with all your children,
they may feast with delight
on all that satisfies the hungry heart.
We ask this in the name of Jesus Christ, our Savior,
who lives and reigns with you in the unity of the Holy Spirit,
one God, forever and ever. **Amen.**

7    O Christ,
out of your fullness we have all received grace upon grace.
You are our eternal hope;
you are patient and full of mercy;
you are generous to all who call upon you.
**Save us, Lord.**
O Christ, fountain of life and holiness,
you have taken away our sins.
On the cross you were wounded for our transgressions

and were bruised for our iniquities.
**Save us, Lord.**
O Christ, obedient unto death,
source of all comfort,
our life and our resurrection,
our peace and reconciliation:
**Save us, Lord.**
O Christ, Savior of all who trust you,
hope of all who die for you,
and joy of all the saints:
**Save us, Lord.**
Jesus, Lamb of God,
**have mercy on us.**
Jesus, bearer of our sins,
**have mercy on us.**
Jesus, redeemer of the world,
**grant us peace. Amen.**

8    God of comfort and mercy,
you sent your prophets to proclaim,
"Make straight in the wilderness a highway for our God."
We confess we have not done as you asked;
instead, we have sinned in thoughts, words, and deeds
by what we have done and by what we have left undone.
*[silent confession]*
In your mercy, forgive us, O Lord;
help us to proclaim your message.
Equip us to walk more faithfully in the footsteps of Christ,
who lives and reigns with you
in the unity of the Holy Spirit, one God forever. **Amen.**

9    Most merciful God
whose Son, Jesus Christ, was tempted in every way, yet was without sin,
we confess before you our own sinfulness;
we have hungered after that which does not satisfy;
we have compromised with evil;
we have doubted your power to protect us.
Forgive our lack of faith; have mercy on our weakness.
Restore in us such trust and love that we may walk in your ways and delight in doing your will. **Amen.**

10   God of mercy, whose Son, Jesus Christ,
longs to gather us in the wide embrace of his love,
we confess that we have been wayward children.
We have disobeyed your commands;
our ears have been deaf to your call;
our hearts have been cold to your love.
In thought, in word, and in deed
we have hurt others and dishonored your name.

*569*

In your great mercy receive us yet again as your well-beloved children,
not because we are worthy but for the sake of him
who loved us and gave himself for us. **Amen.**

11  Everlasting God,
    fountain of all life and the true home of every heart:
    our hearts are restless until they rest in you.
    Yet we confess that our hearts have been enslaved
    by selfish passion and base desire.
    We have sought after many things
    and have neglected the one thing needful.
    We have not loved you with our whole hearts;
    help us to turn to you and find forgiveness.
    Lead us home, that we may again find in you
    our life and joy and peace. **Amen.**

12  God of compassion,
    in Jesus Christ you did not disdain the company of sinners
    but welcomed them with love.
    Look upon us in mercy, we pray.
    Our sins are more than we can bear;
    our pasts enslave us; our misdeeds are beyond correcting.
    Forgive the wrongs we cannot undo;
    free us from a past we cannot change;
    heal what we can no longer fix.
    Grace our lives with your love and turn the tears of our past
    into the joys of new life with you. **Amen.**

13  Almighty God,
    to you all hearts are open, all desires known,
    and from you no secrets are hid.
    Cleanse the thoughts of our hearts
    by the inspiration of your Holy Spirit,
    that we may perfectly love you
    and worthily magnify your holy name,
    through Christ, our Lord. **Amen.**

14  Lord, we have denied you by refusing to know you.
    We have betrayed you by keeping our distance.
    We have mocked you by pretending we are not yours.
    Lord, we are lost; let your forgiveness find us.
    Welcome us into your strong, forgiving arms
    and let us feel reconciled again. **Amen.**

15  O God, in gracious love
    you promise to care for the creatures of earth;
    in steadfast love you keep your promise.
    But we, who so quickly embrace your covenant,
    just as quickly betray it;

we, from whom you desire worship,
too often offer only scorn.
For making and then keeping your promise
in the greatness of your mercy,
we sing your praise, Lord;
and for accepting and then spurning your covenant
in the greatness of our sin, we ask your forgiveness. **Amen.**

16   O God, our great shepherd,
you tenderly gather us as lambs,
carrying us with your all-embracing love.
Yet, like sheep, we wander from you:
following our own ways, ignoring your voice,
distrusting your provisions.
Forgive our stubborn rebellion, our hardened hearts, our lack of trust.
Refresh us once again by your quiet waters of mercy
and restore our souls by your redeeming love.
Guide our paths, that we might follow you more closely. . . .
[*Silent confession*]
Through Jesus Christ, our good shepherd, we pray. **Amen.**

17   *A prayer especially mindful of children*

God, we make so many mistakes;
we turn away from you so often.
We need you so much.
Thank you that you so loved the world
that you sent Jesus to die on the cross
to save us from our sins. **Amen.**

18   Almighty God,
because of Christ's blood,
do not hold against us, poor sinners that we are,
any of the sins we do
or the evil that constantly clings to us.
Forgive us just as we are fully determined,
as evidence of your grace in us,
to forgive our neighbors.
By ourselves we are too weak
to hold our own even for a moment.
And our sworn enemies—
the devil, the world, and our own flesh—
never stop attacking us.
And so, Lord, uphold us and make us strong
with the strength of your Holy Spirit,
so that we may not go down to defeat
in this spiritual struggle,
but may firmly resist our enemies

until we finally win the complete victory.
Through Jesus Christ, our Lord, **Amen.**

—based on Heidelberg Catechism, Q&A's 126-127

19  **Lamb of God, we are burdened:**
**We do not love you as we should.**
We forget our dependence on you and do not honor you.
Instead of glorifying you, we try to bring ourselves glory.
**Lamb of God, we are burdened:**
**We do not love others as we should.**
We hurry through our days and miss opportunities to be your hands and feet.
We judge quickly and respond thoughtlessly.
**Lamb of God, we are burdened:**
**We do not love ourselves as we should.**
We disparage our appearances, criticize our best efforts, and misuse our bodies.
**Lamb of God, we are burdened:**
**We are weighed down by the bad things that are done to us.**
We hold grudges, harbor bad feelings, and believe lies told about us.
**Lamb of God, we are burdened:**
**We are overwhelmed by sin.**
Man of sorrows, you know our pain and suffering.
By your wounds we are healed.
**Take our burdens, we pray, and free us from sin. Amen.**

20  Word of God Incarnate,
you came to this world to accomplish salvation.
By your grace you call us to repent, to be crucified with you,
that we might be raised as new creations.
But we confess that often we do not live as renewed people.
We confess that often we "go with the flow"
instead of stemming sin's tide.
Forgive us when we do not show evidence of renewal.
Forgive us when we let the fruit of the Spirit
be choked by the weeds of evil.
You have made us your children, members of your kingdom.
Help us to show evidence of that every day
as we work to bring your justice, peace, gentleness,
goodness, love, joy, and hope to all we meet.
For Jesus' sake, **Amen.**

21  God of Abraham, Isaac, and Jacob,
we are your covenant people—one church, drawn from all nations.
Our citizenship is in heaven.
Yet we confess, O Lord, that we sometimes lose sight
of your kingdom and its ways.
We confess that we sometimes live more as citizens of our own land
than as citizens of your kingdom.
By your truth you call all peoples to account.

Forgive us for losing our distinctiveness.
Focus us on the cross and on the salvation
you give through him
who is the Lord and King and Judge of us all,
Jesus, the Christ, in whose name we pray. **Amen.**

22   Righteous God, in Christ you became sin for us.
You took what we are so that we might become what you are.
But we confess that often we ignore our sin.
We confess that too often we do not confess.
We keep silent about the sin that clings to us.
But our sins are too great a burden for us.
Forgive us. In Christ take away our iniquity.
You are our stronghold, our hiding place.
May we confess our sins, that we might then rejoice
and be glad in you and in the righteousness
that flows over us as a mighty stream of grace. In Christ, **Amen.**

23   Almighty God, in Jesus Christ you love us,
but we have not loved you.
You have opened your heart to us,
and in our pride we have spurned your care.
You have given us all things, and we have squandered your gifts.
We have grieved you and caused hurt to others,
and we are not worthy to be called your children.
Have mercy on us, O Lord, for we are ashamed
and sorry for all we have done to displease you.
Cleanse us from our sin and receive us again into your household,
that we might nevermore stray from your love
but always remain within the sound of your voice. **Amen.**

24   God, forgive our doubting, questioning hearts.
Like the scribes who witnessed Jesus' miracles of healing
and heard his proclamation, yet spurned belief,
we too have seen wonders, yet have hardened our hearts.
We confess the many times that our pessimism
has caused others to doubt themselves and your Spirit,
the times that our criticism has wounded others,
the times that our dejection has dampened the enthusiasm
of those inspired by your Word and work.
O God, forgive us and in your mercy renew us,
that with open hearts we may believe
and never pose an obstacle to the faith of others. **Amen.**

### J.2.3 Lament (see also section 2.3)

1   Where are you, O God?
We are lost in the night; have you cast us from your presence?
Temptations surround us; their masks grin through the darkness.
We run from them, but which way should we go?
Where can we hide when all lies in shadow?
Have mercy on us, O God.
Our eyes are swollen from tears; our bones are cold with fear;
our souls have been broken—do you not hear, Lord?
Save us! According to your steadfast love, answer us!
Do not hide your face, but draw near and redeem us!

### J.2.4 Assurance of Pardon (see also section 2.4)

1   Those who love me, I will deliver, says the Lord;
      I will protect those who know my name.
When they call to me, I will answer them;
      I will be with them in trouble,
      I will rescue them and honor them
      and show them my salvation.
Receive the good news of the gospel:
In Jesus Christ we are forgiven.
                    —based on Psalm 91:14-15, NRSV

2   Israel, put your hope in the LORD,
      for with the LORD is unfailing love
      and with him is full redemption.
He himself will redeem Israel
      from all their sins.
                    —Psalm 130:7-8, NIV

3   The Lord God said:
I will give you a new heart and put a new spirit within you;
I will remove from you your heart of stone
and give you a heart of flesh.

Brothers and sisters: In Christ, all God's promises are "Yes."
Hear the good news: Through Christ,
our minds and hearts are cleansed, healed, and renewed!
                    —based on Ezekiel 36:26; 2 Corinthians 1:20, NIV

4   Return to the Lord your God,
for he is gracious and merciful,
slow to anger, and abounding in steadfast love.

In Christ, we are forgiven!
Thanks be to God for his indescribable gift!
                    —based on Joel 2:13; 2 Corinthians 9:15, NRSV

5    Jesus said:
     Come to me, all you that are weary
     and are carrying heavy burdens,
     and I will give you rest.
     Take my yoke upon you, and learn from me;
     for I am gentle and humble in heart,
     and you will find rest for your souls.
     For my yoke is easy, and my burden is light.
          —from Matthew 11:28-30, NRSV

6    Jesus said, "I am the light of the world.
     Whoever follows me will never walk in darkness
     but will have the light of life."
          —from John 8:12, NIV

7    If anyone is in Christ, there is a new creation:
     everything old has passed away; see, everything has become new!
     All this is from God, who reconciled us to himself through Christ,
     and has given us the ministry of reconciliation.

     Receive the good news of the gospel:
     In Jesus Christ we are forgiven.
          —based on 2 Corinthians 5:17-18, NRSV

8    By grace you have been saved through faith,
     and this is not your own doing; it is the gift of God.
          —Ephesians 2:8, NRSV

9    Can a woman forget her nursing child,
          or show no compassion for the child of her womb?
     Even these may forget,
          yet I will not forget you.
     As a mother comforts her child,
          so will I comfort you, says the Lord.
          —from Isaiah 49:15; 66:12-13, NRSV

10   The saying is sure and worthy of full acceptance,
     that Jesus Christ came into the world to save sinners.
     He himself bore our sins in his body on the cross,
     so that we, free from sins, might live for righteousness;
     by his wounds we have been healed.
          —from 1 Timothy 1:15; 1 Peter 2:24, NRSV

11   You are a chosen race, a royal priesthood,
     a holy nation, God's own people,
     in order that you may proclaim the mighty acts of him
     who called you out of darkness into his marvelous light.
     Once you were not a people,
     but now you are God's people;
     once you had not received mercy,
     but now you have received mercy.
          —1 Peter 2:9-10, NRSV

# J.3 PROCLAIMING THE WORD

**J.3.1 Prayers for Illumination** (see also section 3.1)

1   Send your Spirit among us, O God,
    as we meditate on the sacrifice of Jesus Christ.
    Prepare our minds to hear your Word.
    Move our hearts to accept what we hear.
    Purify our will to obey in joy and faith.
    This we pray through Christ, our Savior. **Amen.**

2   O Christ, by remaining faithful till death,
    you show us the road to greater love.
    O Christ, by taking the burden of sin upon yourself,
    you reveal to us the way of generosity.
    O Christ, by praying for those who crucified you,
    you lead us to forgive without counting the cost.
    O Christ, by opening paradise to the repentant thief,
    you awaken hope in us.
    O Christ, come and help our weak faith.
    O Christ, create a pure heart in us;
    renew and strengthen our spirit.
    O Christ, your Word is near;
    may it live within us and protect us always. **Amen.**

3   Through God's Word, O Holy Spirit,
    bring us closer to our Savior.
    And in response, triune God, prompt our hearts
    to offer you sincere thanks for our salvation.
    In the strong name of Jesus, our Lord. **Amen.**

**J.3.6 Profession of Our Church's Faith** (see also section 3.6)

1   During his whole life on earth,
    but especially at the end,
    Christ sustained
    in body and soul
    the wrath of God against the sin of the whole human race.
    This he did in order that,
    by his suffering as the only atoning sacrifice,
    he might deliver us, body and soul,
    from eternal condemnation,
    and gain for us God's grace,
    righteousness, and eternal life.
              —Heidelberg Catechism, Q&A 37

2    By Christ's power
our old selves are crucified, put to death, and buried with him,
so that the evil desires of the flesh
may no longer rule us,
but that instead we may offer ourselves
as a sacrifice of gratitude to him.
       —Heidelberg Catechism, Q&A 43

3    I believe that God,
because of Christ's satisfaction,
will no longer remember
any of my sins
or my sinful nature
which I need to struggle against all my life.
Rather, by grace
God grants me the righteousness of Christ
to free me forever from judgment.
       —Heidelberg Catechism, Q&A 56

# J.4 PRAYERS OF THE PEOPLE

## J.4.4 Complete Model Outlines and Prayers (see also section 4.4)

*Prayer Outlines*

1    *The following is a guide for extemporaneous prayers. The pattern provides a suggested text for the opening and closing of each part of the prayer and calls for extemporaneous prayers of thanksgiving, petition, and intercession.*

God of our salvation,
we praise you for sending your Son, Jesus Christ,
to suffer for our sins so we may be redeemed.
We are thankful for the reminders of that redemption visible in
    creation . . .
    the nations of the world when they . . .
    our nation and those who govern as they . . .
    our own community as it . . .
    the church universal as it seeks to . . .
    our local church as it . . .
    the lives of those near to us . . .
    our own life as we experience your saving grace . . .

We also ask that
as the source of the world's hope and redemption
you hear our prayers on behalf of
    all creation . . .
    the nations of the world . . .
    our nation and those in authority . . .
    the community and those who govern . . .
    the church universal, its mission, and those who minister . . .
    our church and its ministry . . .
    those with particular needs . . .

We pray this in the name of the triune God, our Redeemer and Savior, to whom
belong all glory and honor. **Amen.**


## Complete Prose Prayers

2    Maker of heaven and earth,
    you are our help; we lift our eyes to you.
    As we walk this Lenten journey,
    you watch over our coming and our going
    both now and forevermore.
    You are our shade and our protection;
    you keep us from all harm.
    We ask that you strengthen and guide us
    as we do your work in your world.
    Convict us of our disobedience,
    and enable us to obey your call in our lives.
    Open our ears to the cry of the poor.
    Teach us to seek and to do justice,
    to stay in the path of understanding,
    to pursue righteousness and love
    in the strong name of your Son, our Savior. **Amen.**
        —based on Psalm 121


3    Almighty God,
    your Son fasted forty days in the wilderness
    and was tempted as we are but did not sin.
    Give us grace to direct our lives
    in obedience to your Spirit,
    that as you know our weakness,
    so we may know your power to save
    through Jesus Christ, our Redeemer,
    who lives and reigns with you and the Holy Spirit,
    one God, now and forever. **Amen.**


4    O Lord God,
    you led your people through the wilderness
    and brought them to the promised land.

So guide us that, following our Savior,
we may walk through the wilderness of this world
toward the glory of the world to come,
through your Son, Jesus Christ, our Lord,
who lives and reigns with you and the Holy Spirit,
one God, now and forever. **Amen.**

5   God of the covenant,
as the forty days of deluge
swept away the world's corruption
and watered new beginnings of righteousness and life,
so in the saving flood of baptism
we are washed clean and born again.
Throughout these forty days,
unseal within us the wellspring of your grace,
cleanse our hearts of all that is not holy,
and cause your gift of new life to flourish once again.
Grant this through Jesus Christ, our Redeemer,
who lives and reigns with you in the unity of the Holy Spirit,
one God, forever and ever. **Amen.**

6   O Jesus, you know the anguish of our human lives.
As one who sees the pain of those who suffer,
bring comfort, peace, and strength.
As one who has experienced the agony
and tears of losing loved ones,
comfort all who grieve.
As one who wept over the faithlessness of your people,
send your Spirit to correct us in our unfaithfulness.
As one who understands the agony of those who have been deserted,
stand alongside those who feel alone and abandoned today.
As one who was once forsaken by all others,
give hope and assurance to those who feel rejection.
As one who knows the ravages of violence,
bring peace and healing to those who are tortured by enemies.
You, our Lord, have offered up prayers with loud cries and tears;
hear us when we do the same.
We approach your throne of grace with boldness.
May we receive mercy and grace in our time of need. **Amen.**

7   God of all seasons,
in your pattern of things
there is a time for keeping and a time for losing,
a time for building up and a time for pulling down.
In this season of Lent
as we journey to the cross,
help us to discern in our lives
what we must lay down and what we must take up,

what we must end and what we must begin.
Give us grace to lead a disciplined life,
in glad faithfulness and with the joy
that comes from a closer walk with Christ. **Amen.**

*Prayers in Litany Form*

**8**   God of grace and glory,
in this season of repentance and hope:
Help us to turn away from evil **and turn toward you.**
We pray that your people everywhere
will receive the courage
to turn away from evil **and turn toward you.**
We pray for the leaders of the nations and all people,
that they may turn away from evil **and turn toward you.**
We pray for every ministry of our community,
that as we minister in your name,
we may turn away from evil **and turn toward you.**
We pray for each of us as we live among
neighbors, people whom you love:
help us to turn away from evil **and turn toward you.**
We pray that even now as we worship you,
your Holy Spirit will be at work,
teaching us how to turn away from evil **and turn toward you.**
*[After a brief silence, the leader concludes:]*
Lord Jesus Christ,
in this Lenten season,
we hear your call to repentance.
We pray for a generous outpouring of your Holy Spirit
to help us resist evil in all its forms
in our individual lives and institutions.
Help us turn toward you,
eager to receive the fullness of all you promise. **Amen.**

**9**   Leader:    Remembering that in his life, passion, and death Jesus identified with
the poor, the oppressed, and the marginalized in society, let us join in a
litany of intercession for all for whom Christ suffered and died and for
all for whom he lives today.

Reader 1:   Let us pray for all who commit themselves to God's mission to establish
human relationships based upon freedom and justice.

Reader 2:   Save us from indifference, and give us courage to work for justice and
responsible freedom.

People:    **Lord of all nations, help your servants.**

Reader 1:   We pray for the affluent in developed and developing countries, that
they may not succumb to materialism.

Reader 2:   Help us to discover our worth in terms of what we can become as persons rather than in what we own or consume.

People: **Lord of all nations, help your servants.**
Reader 1: We pray for countries in which there is exploitation of natural resources . . . and the earth is desecrated to satisfy the lust for profit.
Reader 2: Save us from misusing what you have given for all to share.
People: **Lord of all nations, help your servants.**
Reader 1: We pray for all tribal and aboriginal peoples threatened with disposses- sion and the loss of ancestral lands.
Reader 2: Help us to remember that the land is yours and that we hold it in trust for future generations.
People: **Lord of all nations, help your servants.**
Reader 1: We pray for all minority communities faced with the loss of their cul- tural identity.
Reader 2: Help us to respect each person's way of life.
People: **Lord of all nations, help your servants.**
Reader 1: We pray for refugees forcibly uprooted from their homeland to live as aliens in other lands.
Reader 2: Help us to find human solutions to this human tragedy.
People: **Lord of all nations, help your servants.**
Reader 1: We pray for all people separated from one another because of religious or political differences.
Reader 2: Help us to work for tolerance, dialogue, and goodwill among peoples of differing faiths and political convictions.
People: **Lord of all nations, help your servants. Amen.**

10    Jesus the Christ,
       you refused to turn stones into bread.
       **Save us from using our power,**
       **however little,**
       **to satisfy the demands of selfishness**
       **in the face of the greater needs of others.**
       Jesus the Christ,
       you refused to leap from the temple top.
       **Save us from displaying our skills,**
       **however modest,**
       **to win instant popularity**
       **in the face of nobler calls on our abilities.**
       Jesus the Christ,
       you refused to bend the knee to a false god.
       **Save us from offering our devotion,**
       **however weak,**
       **to cheap or easy religion**
       **in the face of the harder path**
       **on which you bid us to follow you.**
       Jesus the Christ,
       **give us wisdom to discern evil,**
       **and in the face of all that is deceptively attractive**
       **help us to choose the will of God. Amen.**

# J.5 OFFERING

**J.5.2 Offering Prayers** (see also section 5.2)

1   Mighty God and Father, you overwhelm us with your great mercy.
    At the time of our greatest need you surprised us with your wondrous love.
    Jesus offered his life for us to remove our dreadful curse.
    As you draw us into this renewing relationship of love,
    may we respond with gratitude
    as we offer the substance of our souls to continue the ministry of Christ.
    For his name and glory we pray and present our gifts. **Amen!**

2   Compassionate God,
    we offer you these gifts as signs of our time and labor.
    Receive the offering of our lives and feed us with your grace,
    that in the midst of death all creation might feast
    on your unending life in Jesus Christ, our Lord. **Amen.**

# J.8 THE LORD'S SUPPER

**J.8.2 Great Prayer of Thanksgiving** (see section 8.2)

*J.8.2.2 Thanksgiving for the Work of God in Creation (see also section 8.2.2)*

*The following prayer offers thanks for the work of God in creation and may be included in the complete Prayer of Thanksgiving as found in section 8.2 of this book.*

1   With joy we praise you, gracious God,
    for you have created heaven and earth,
    made us in your image, and kept covenant with us—
    even when we fell into sin.
    We give you thanks for Jesus Christ, our Lord,
    by whose grace we may triumph over temptation,
    be more fervent in prayer, and be more generous in love.
    Therefore we join our voices
    with all the saints and angels and the whole creation
    to proclaim the glory of your name.

*J.8.2.4 Thanksgiving for the Work of Christ (see also section 8.2.4)*

*The following prayer offers thanks for the work of Jesus Christ and may be included in the complete Prayer of Thanksgiving as found in section 8.2 of this book.*

1    You are holy, O God of majesty,
      and blessed is Jesus Christ, your Son, our Lord.
      He took upon himself the weight of our sin
      and carried the burden of our guilt.
      He shared our life in every way,
      and, though tempted, was sinless to the end.
      Baptized as your own, he went willingly to his death
      and by your power was raised to new life.
      In his dying and rising,
      you gave birth to your church,
      delivered us from slavery to sin and death
      and made with us a new covenant by water and the Spirit.

# J.9 CLOSING OF WORSHIP

## J.9.1 Sending (see also section 9.1)

*Closing Prayers*

1    God of mercy,
      you are full of tenderness and compassion,
      slow to anger, rich in mercy,
      and always ready to forgive.
      Grant us grace to renounce all evil
      and to cling to Christ,
      that in every way we may prove to be your loving children,
      through Jesus Christ, our Lord,
      who lives and reigns with you and the Holy Spirit,
      one God, forever and ever. **Amen.**

2    God of all times and places,
      in Jesus Christ, lifted up on the cross,
      you opened for us the path to eternal life.
      Grant that we, being born again of water and the Spirit,
      may joyfully serve you in newness of life
      and faithfully walk in your holy ways,

through Jesus Christ, our Lord,
who lives and reigns with you in the unity of the Holy Spirit,
one God, now and forever. **Amen.**

3    God of all times and places,
as we leave this place of worship,
help us to know that there is no place we might go
that will separate us from you.
With this sure knowledge,
give us Spirit-inspired courage and imagination
to discern faithful ways of responding
to every person we will meet this week
and to every situation we will encounter.
May our Lenten vows of faithfulness
lead us to joyful obedience all week long. **Amen.**

4    My Father, I abandon myself to you.
Do with me as you will.
Whatever you may do with me, I thank you.
I am prepared for anything; I accept everything,
provided your will is fulfilled in me and in all creatures;
I ask for nothing more, my God.
I place my soul in your hands.
I give it to you, my God, with all the love of my heart,
because I love you. **Amen.**

## J.9.2 Blessing/Benediction (see also section 9.2)

1    Do not live by bread alone, but by the will of God.
May God give the angels charge over you;
may their hands bear you up and keep you from falling. **Amen.**
        —based on Matthew 4:4, 6, 11

2    Grace and peace to you
from God our Father and the Lord Jesus Christ,
who gave himself for our sins to rescue us from the present evil age,
according to the will of our God and Father,
to whom be glory for ever and ever. **Amen.**
        —Galatians 1:2-5, NIV

3    May God himself, the God of peace,
sanctify you through and through.
May your whole spirit, soul and body
be kept blameless
at the coming of our Lord Jesus Christ. **Amen.**
        —1 Thessalonians 5:23, NIV

**4** Sisters and brothers,
let us claim the freedom Christ gives us
by his self-giving on the cross.
May he enable us to serve together
in faith, hope, and love.
Go in peace and serve the Lord.
**Thanks be to God.**

May the God of love, who shared his love,
strengthen us in our love for others.
May the Son who shared his life
grant us grace, that we might share our life.
And may the Holy Spirit dwelling in us
empower us to be only and always for others. **Amen.**

# J.10 Suggested Scripture Readings

**1**  *Baptismal identity and union with Christ*

Romans 6:1-14: United with Christ in baptism
Romans 8:1-11: Living in the realm of the Spirit
2 Corinthians 5:16-21: A new creation, a ministry of reconciliation
Colossians 1:9-15: Buried with Christ, raised with Christ
Ephesians 1:3-14: Every spiritual blessing in Christ
Ephesians 2:1-10: Seated in the heavenly realms with Christ
1 John 5:1-12: Eternal life in God's Son

**2**  *Practices of fasting and repentance*

2 Samuel 12:1-23: David repents of his sin
Job 42:1-6: Job repents
Nehemiah 9: The people of Israel confess their sin
Matthew 4:1-11: Jesus' forty-day fast
Matthew 6:16-18: Jesus encourages secret practices of repentance

**3**  *Repentance leads to forgiveness*

2 Chronicles 7:14-15: Healing for the land
John 3:14-21: Light in the darkness
Luke 7:36-50: Jesus is anointed
Luke 15:11-32: The lost son and the generous father
Acts 26:15-18: Paul sent to the Gentiles

Ephesians 2:1-9: God raised us up in Christ
Romans 6:1-14: From death to life
1 John 1:5-10: Forgiveness and fellowship
Titus 3:1-8: Saved to do good

**4** *Psalms of repentance*

Psalm 6: Have mercy
Psalm 38: Sin is painful
Psalm 50: Call to confession
Psalm 51: Create in me a clean heart, O God
Psalm 106: God's historic forgiveness
Psalm 130: Wait for the Lord
Psalm 143: Hear my prayer

**5** *Prayers of confession*

Psalm 30: Thanksgiving for divine redemption
Psalm 51: Create in me a clean heart
Psalm 130: With God there is forgiveness
Jeremiah 14:7-9: Do not forsake us
Daniel 9:1-19: We are covered with shame

# SECTION K
# PASSION/PALM SUNDAY

The events framed by Jesus' entry into Jerusalem and his resurrection are some of the most dramatic and theologically important of the entire scriptural narrative. These days feature not only the drama of the triumphal entry, trial, last supper, and crucifixion but also poignant prayers and prophetic teachings of our Lord. John's gospel devotes eight of its twenty-one chapters to this week alone! The week begins with Passion/Palm Sunday and ends with the "three days" (also called the *Triduum*, from sunset on Thursday to sunset on Easter Day), the period during which we mark Jesus' trial, death, and resurrection.

The first Sunday of Holy Week is commonly called either "Palm Sunday" or "Passion Sunday." Those who call it "Palm Sunday" tend to focus on the entry of Christ into Jerusalem to shouts of "Hosanna! Blessed is the one who comes in the name of the Lord!" (Mark 11:9). Those who refer to the day as "Passion Sunday" tend to focus on Jesus' suffering. This is

especially appropriate in contexts in which participation in midweek services on Maundy Thursday or Good Friday is difficult or minimal, and, as a result, worshipers would sing "Hosanna" on one Sunday and "Christ arose" on the next, with little attention to Jesus' suffering and death in between.

But even for congregations that celebrate the day as Palm Sunday, it's important to capture the irony of the day. This is the day on which Jesus entered the city in triumph, but as a part of his journey to the cross; this is the week in which the crowd's cries of "Hosanna" would soon turn to "Crucify him!" One helpful approach to Palm Sunday worship is to move through the last week of Jesus' life over the course of the service, beginning with the procession into Jerusalem and concluding with his suffering.

Worship on Passion/Palm Sunday, as well as other Holy Week services, often invites members of the congregation to think of themselves as participants in a kind of dramatic reenactment of scriptural events.

Thus children or perhaps the whole congregation may be invited to process while shouting "Hosanna!" Or, in the reading of the passion narrative, the entire congregation may be invited to speak the words, "Crucify him! Crucify him!" (certainly one of the most unsettling actions in any worship service). The goal of such reenactment is to recount the narratives memorably and to help the congregation sense the significance of the narratives for what they teach us about Jesus' ministry, about God's being and character, and about the nature and scope of redemption in Christ.

---

### Scriptures Applying to the Theme of Passion/Palm Sunday

*The following texts are especially appropriate for supplemental liturgical use.*

*On Christ's procession into Jerusalem:*
Psalm 118:19-29
Zechariah 9:9-12
Matthew 21:1-11
Mark 11:1-11
Luke 19:28-40
John 12:12-19
1 Kings 1:28-40

*On Holy Week and Christ's passion:*
Psalm 31:9-18
Isaiah 50:4-9; 52:13-53:12
Matthew 21-27
Mark 11-15
Luke 19-23
John 12-19
Philippians 2:5-11

---

# K.1 OPENING OF WORSHIP

---

### K.1.1 Preparation for Worship (see also section 1.1)

1    Loving Father,
     as we journey with your Son in this week of remembrance and hope,
     help us to understand you and your love for the world more clearly.

Transform us by the saving knowledge of Jesus Christ
and prepare us for service in your kingdom,
through Christ, our Lord. **Amen.**

2    God of all time,
     as we prepare to worship you today and this week,
     help us to call to mind these past events in Jesus' life
     so that we can sense their significance for our present lives
     and for the future you are preparing for all creation.
     In Jesus' name, **Amen.**

## K.1.2 Call to Worship (see also section 1.2)

1    Blessed is the one who comes in the name of the Lord.
     **Hosanna in the highest!**
          —based on Psalm 118:26, NRSV

2    Rejoice greatly, O daughter Zion!
     **Shout aloud, O daughter Jerusalem!**
     Lo, your king comes to you;
     **triumphant and victorious is he,**
     humble and riding on a donkey,
     **on a colt, the foal of a donkey.**
          —Zechariah 9:9, NRSV

3    King Jesus comes, King Jesus,
     Son of God, Son of Man, Messiah.
     **Hail! King Jesus, King of all!**
     Recall the words of the Scriptures:
     "A great crowd who had come to the feast
     heard that Jesus was coming to Jerusalem.
     So they took branches of palm trees
     and went out to meet him, crying, 'Hosanna!
     Blessed is he who comes in the name of the Lord,
     even the King of Israel!'"
     **In praise we adore you, King Jesus.**
     **Enter our hearts today**
     **as you entered Jerusalem long ago,**
     **and lead us by faith in the way everlasting. Amen.**
          —based on John 12:13

4    People of God, be gathered together!
     **Like a hen with her brood beneath her wings,**
     **God has brought us together!**
     People of God, await Christ's coming!
     **Blessed is the one who comes**
     **in the name of the Lord of heaven!**
          —based on Luke 13:34; 19:38

5     As we are called into worship today,
it is sobering to remember
that when God appeared on earth in the person of Jesus,
most of the world did not recognize him
and therefore did not worship him.
Today we ask for faith that will open our eyes
to see Jesus for who he is,
that we might worship him in truth.
People of God, behold and see your God!

**We open our eyes to see his glory.**
**We open our ears to hear his wisdom.**
**We open our hands to offer him gifts.**
**We open our mouths to sing his praise.**
**We open our hearts to offer him our love.**
**He is Lord!**

## K.1.4 Opening Responses (see also section 1.4)

*Prayers of Adoration*

1     We praise you, O God,
for your redemption of the world through Jesus Christ.
He entered the holy city of Jerusalem in triumph
and was proclaimed Messiah and King
by those who spread garments and branches along his way.
Just as we carry these branches,
may we follow Christ in the way of the cross,
that, dying and rising with him, we may enter into your kingdom,
through Jesus Christ, who lives and reigns
with you and the Holy Spirit, now and forever. **Amen.**

2     O Lord Christ,
as you once entered Jerusalem,
enter our hearts this day afresh.
As you once set your face toward death on a cross,
help us this day to walk with you to victory.
As the children once cried "Hosanna" to bless you,
enable us to confess you openly as Lord and Savior.
Grant us your presence by the power of your Spirit,
that our worship and our lives may truly honor you. **Amen.**

*Prayers of Invocation*

3     Merciful God,
as we enter Holy Week and gather at your house of prayer,
turn our hearts again to Jerusalem,

to the life, death, and resurrection of Jesus Christ
so that, united with Christ and all the faithful,
we may one day enter in triumph
the city not made by human hands,
the new Jerusalem, eternal in the heavens,
where with you and the Holy Spirit,
Christ lives in glory forever. **Amen.**

4    Everlasting God,
in your tender love for the human race
you sent your Son to take our nature and to suffer death upon the cross.
In your mercy enable us to share in his obedience to your will
and in the glorious victory of his resurrection,
through Jesus Christ, our Lord,
who lives and reigns with you and the Holy Spirit,
one God, forever and ever. **Amen.**

5    God of all,
you gave your only Son to take the form of a servant
and to be obedient even to death on a cross.
Give us the same mind of Christ Jesus
so that, sharing in his humility,
we may come to be with him in his glory,
our Lord who lives and reigns with you and the Holy Spirit,
one God, now and forever. **Amen.**
        —based on Philippians 2:5-11

# K.2 CONFESSION AND ASSURANCE

## K.2.1 Call to Confession (see also section 2.1)

1    Like the people who greeted Jesus as he entered Jerusalem
and then later pronounced "Crucify him,"
we are fickle people who often deny Christ
in our thoughts, words, and deeds.
Remembering the events of Jesus' last week
helps us see ourselves for what we are:
sinners in need of a Savior, a Savior—praise God—we have in Christ.
In honesty and hope, we confess now our sins to God.

## K.2.2 Prayers of Confession (see also section 2.2)

1   O King of glory,
    we confess that our praise of your majesty has often been faint,
    our performance as citizens of your kingdom treasonous.
    For we have surrendered to the enemy
    by our secret and our known sins.
    For our treason you died, Lord Jesus.
    For our restoration, you rose again.
    Draw us closer to you in this holy week,
    that our eyes may catch the vision of your tears,
    and our hearts, the wonder of your grace.
    By the Holy Spirit's continuing discipline,
    let us be loyal and loving servants of the King.
    Praise be to you, Father, Son, and Holy Spirit. **Amen.**

2   O Lord, who on this day entered the rebellious city
    that later rejected you,
    we confess that our wills are as rebellious as Jerusalem's,
    that our faith is often more show than substance,
    that our hearts are in need of cleansing.
    Have mercy on us, Son of David, Savior of our lives.
    Help us to lay at your feet all that we have and all that we are,
    trusting you to forgive what is sinful, to heal what is broken,
    to welcome our praises, and to receive us as your own. **Amen.**

3   Loving God,
    you rode a donkey and came in peace,
    humbled yourself and gave yourself for us.
    We confess our lack of humility.
    As you entered Jerusalem,
    the crowds shouted "Hosanna: 'Save us now!'"
    On Good Friday they shouted "Crucify!"
    We confess our praise is often empty.
    We sing "Hosanna," but cry "Crucify."
    As the crowd laid their palms in front of you,
    you took no glory for yourself.
    We confess that we want to be accepted and take the easy way.
    We do not stay true to your will.
    Forgive us, Lord, and help us
    to follow in the way of obedience. **Amen.**

4   O Lord, we confess
    our hands are not clean, our hearts are not pure.
    Forgive our capricious discipleship
    and keep our faith constant, O Lord.
    Lead us always to a deeper experience of your love.
    Enliven us by the familiar

but always new story of shame and triumph,
suffering and hope, that this week reveals.
Mold us to the ways of the Servant whose life we honor this morning.
In the name of Christ, our Lord, **Amen.**

5    Gracious God, having heard your Word,
we thankfully remember the life
of our Lord Jesus Christ on this earth.
Yet we also acknowledge our failure
to respond earnestly and faithfully to his witness.
We often mistake Jesus for a mere earthly king,
friendly companion, or problem-solver,
failing to see him as the ruler of all creation.
We do not appreciate the depth
of his passion and sacrifice on the cross,
failing to acknowledge him as our way of salvation.
Even in this Lenten season, we have not walked faithfully
in the way of Jesus Christ.
Forgive us, we pray, and bring us ever more fully
into the joy of union with Jesus Christ, our Lord. **Amen.**

6    *Confession*
Jesus, our Lord, we shout hosannas to praise you. With eager hands, we place our
cloaks and palms on the path before you. Yet, Lord, we confess that the mouths that
seek to praise you often deny or defy you. And we confess that the hands that seek
to serve you often become fists. Lord, hear us as we confess.
[*Silence*]

*Assurance and Law*
Hosanna to the Son of David!
Blessed is he who comes in the name of the Lord!
**For Christ came into the world not to condemn the world,**
**but that the world through him should be saved.**
Therefore, be imitators of God, as beloved children.
**And walk in love, as Christ loved us and gave himself up for us,**
**a fragrant offering and sacrifice to God.**
**Hosanna! Amen!**
        —based on Matthew 21:8-9; John 3:17; Ephesians 5:1-2

## K.2.4 Assurance of Pardon (see section 2.4)

1    Hear the Word of the Lord from Psalm 118:

Let those who fear the Lord say,
    "His steadfast love endures for ever."
Out of my distress I called on the Lord;
    the Lord answered me and set me free.
The Lord is my strength and my song;
    he has become my salvation.

I shall not die, but I shall live,
and recount the deeds of the Lord.

In Christ, God answers us and sets us free!
In Christ, we are forgiven! Thanks be to God.
—based on Psalm 118:4-5, 14, 17, NRSV

# K.3 PROCLAIMING THE WORD

### K.3.1 Prayers for Illumination (see also section 3.1)

1   Eternal God,
whose Word silences the shouts of the mighty:
Quiet within us every voice but your own.
Speak to us through the suffering and death of Jesus Christ,
that by the power of your Holy Spirit
we may receive grace to show Christ's love
in lives given to your service. **Amen.**

# K.4 PRAYERS OF THE PEOPLE

### K.4.4 Complete Model Outlines and Prayers (see also section 4.4)

*Prayer Outlines*

1   *The following is a guide for extemporaneous prayers. The pattern provides a suggested text
for the opening and closing of each part of the prayer and calls for extemporaneous prayers of
thanksgiving, petition, and intercession.*

Son of David,
you entered Jerusalem with a triumphal procession
that left you alone and in humiliation on the cross.
We thank and praise you
for your selfless sacrifice . . .

for the redemption of creation . . .
for those who offer their lives in Christlike service
    around the world . . .
for your work as it continues in our community . . .
for the sacrificial love of those who serve us in your name . . .
for our redemption . . .

The cries of "Hosanna!" soon turned into cries of "Crucify him!"
Today too there are those who refuse to recognize you as King.
The effects of sin continue to be felt in all of life. So we pray
    for creation . . .
    for the nations of the world . . .
    for our nation and its leaders . . .
    for this community and those who are in authority . . .
    for the church universal as it works on your behalf . . .
    for this local church in its ministry . . .
    for persons with particular needs . . .

With the angels and all of creation we look forward
to the day when we will join in declaring "Hosanna to the Son of David!
Blessed is the one who comes in the name of the Lord!" **Amen.**

*Complete Prose Prayers*

2    God, whose gracious love for us embraced that long and lonely journey to the cross,
gather us close to you in these days when again we make that journey in meditation
and recollection.

Help us to contemplate again the way taken by our Savior: the false charges
against him, the fear and flight of the disciples, the kiss of betrayal, the crown of
thorns, the purple robe—and in such contemplation give us courage to face those
times in our own lives when he received the same at our hands. Yet help us also
remember that you have gone before us, so we look to you for compassion and
forgiveness, knowing you are able to save.

When we are weak, make us strong; when hurt and resentful, make us forgiving;
when defeated and discouraged, make us hopeful. Keep us from asking for mercy
without giving it ourselves, from praying for your kingdom but never working for it.

In this week, deepen our faith by your matchless grace. Deepen the measure of our
gratitude and Christian obedience. Move us, who have so much, to share with others
who have so little. Uphold us when we summon our courage to speak out for the
alien and stranger within our gates and for those long denied dignity and freedom.

Guard and guide us through these days of meditation and remembrance. Guard
and guide us through all our days until we come at last to that day when all our
days and journeys will be gathered into your eternity, and we shall be with you
forever. Glory be to you, O God. **Amen.**

3    You are holy, O God of majesty,
and blessed is Jesus Christ, your Son, our Lord.
As one of us, he knew our joys and sorrows
and our struggles with temptation.
He was like us in every way except sin.
In him we see what you created us to be.
Though blameless, he suffered willingly for our sin.
Though innocent, he accepted death for the guilty.
On the cross he offered himself, a perfect sacrifice, for the life of the world.
By his suffering and death, he freed us from sin and death.
Risen from the grave, he leads us to the joy of new life.
[*Intercessions for the church and the world may be included here.*]

Lead us, O God, in the way of Christ.
Give us courage to take up our cross
and, in full reliance upon your grace, to follow him.
Help us to love you above all else
and to love our neighbor as we love ourselves,
demonstrating that love in deed and word by the power of your Spirit.
Give us strength to serve you faithfully
until the promised day of resurrection,
when, with the redeemed of all the ages,
we will feast with you at your table in glory.
Through Christ, all glory and honor are yours, almighty Father,
with the Holy Spirit in the holy church, now and forever. **Amen.**

# K.8 THE LORD'S SUPPER

## K.8.2 Great Prayer of Thanksgiving (see section 8.2)

### K.8.2.2 Thanksgiving for the Work of God in Creation (see also section 8.2.2)

*The following prayer offers thanks for the work of God in creation and may be included in the complete Prayer of Thanksgiving as found in section 8.2 of this book.*

1    Your Son, Jesus Christ, fulfilled the prophets' words
and entered the city of Jerusalem,
where he was lifted high upon the cross,
that the whole world might be drawn to him.
By his suffering and death
he defeated the power of death,
becoming the source of eternal life.
The tree of defeat became the tree of victory;
where life was lost, life has been restored.

# K.9 CLOSING OF WORSHIP

## K.9.1 Sending (see also section 9.1)

*Call to Service/Discipleship*

1    If any want to become my followers,
let them deny themselves
and take up their cross daily and follow me.
      —Luke 9:23, NRSV

2    Do nothing from selfish ambition or conceit,
but in humility regard others as better than yourselves.
Let each of you look not to your own interests,
but to the interests of others.
Let the same mind be in you that was in Christ Jesus,
    who, though he was in the form of God,
        did not regard equality with God
        as something to be exploited,
    but emptied himself,
        taking the form of a slave,
        being born in human likeness.
    And being found in human form,
        he humbled himself
        and became obedient to the point of death—
        even death on a cross.
      —Philippians 2:3-8, NRSV

*Closing Prayers*

3    God and Father of Jesus Christ,
     we leave this place for a week in which busy activities
     and worshipful remembrance are intertwined.
     Teach us, even now, how to make every day a day of prayer,
     so that each day of our lives is filled with hope
     because of Jesus' death and resurrection.
     Through Jesus we pray. **Amen.**

**K.9.2 Blessing/Benediction** (see also section 9.2)

1    May our Lord, whose arms were spread on the cross
     to embrace the whole world,
     help us this week to take up the cross and follow him. **Amen.**

2    The peace of God, which surpasses all understanding,
     guard your hearts and minds in the knowledge and love of God,
     and of God's Son, Jesus Christ, our Lord;
     and the blessing of God almighty,
     the Father, the Son, and the Holy Spirit,
     remain with you always. **Amen.**
          —based on Philippians 4:7, NRSV

3    May the God who sent his Son
     so that we could be adopted as God's own children,
     send his Spirit into your hearts—
     especially in this week of remembrance and renewal—
     and equip you to live
     as God's own children,
     dearly loved and called to serve a needy world.
          —based on Galatians 4:4-6

# K.10 SUGGESTED SCRIPTURE READINGS

1    *Expectation of and the surprising, countercultural nature of a Messianic ruler*

     Psalm 72: A vision of a righteous Messiah and the coming of peaceful flourishing
     Psalm 118:19-27: Ancient royal psalm of praise and petition for God's redemption
     Isaiah 42:1-9: God's servant as one who brings justice and peace
     Zechariah 9:9-12: The promise of Zion's righteous, humble, peacemaking king

# SECTION L
# MAUNDY THURSDAY

On Maundy Thursday the church remembers the last evening Jesus shared with his disciples in the upper room before his arrest and crucifixion. Maundy Thursday marks three key events in Jesus' last week: his washing of his disciples' feet, his institution of the Lord's Supper, and his new commandment to love one another. This service begins the *Triduum*, the three-day period from sunset on Thursday to sunset on Easter Day. The name "Maundy Thursday" comes from the Latin *mandatum novum*, referring to the "new commandment" Jesus taught his disciples (John 13:34). In other words, this is "new commandment Thursday."

Maundy Thursday worship naturally features the Lord's Supper and, in some traditions, an act of foot washing or another sign of mutual love and dedication. Celebrations of the Lord's Supper can call attention to the many theologically rich dimensions of the Last Supper itself, including its attention to communal love and its clear eschatological orientation (its

focus on hopeful anticipation of the coming kingdom).

In some churches a Maundy Thursday service is the primary or even only midweek service during Holy Week. In this case, the service needs to call attention both to the events in the upper room and to the events of Good Friday (see section M). Because there are so many theologically significant and spiritually nourishing events and themes to be addressed, many congregations find it helpful to have services on both Maundy Thursday and Good Friday.

---

### Scriptures Applying to the Theme of Maundy Thursday

*The following texts are particularly appropriate for sermons or for supplemental liturgical use.*

| | | |
|---|---|---|
| Exodus 12:1-14 | Isaiah 53 | 1 Corinthians 10:1-22 |
| Psalm 23 | Matthew 26:17-46 | 1 Corinthians 11:17-34 |
| Psalm 34 | Mark 14:12-72 | Colossians 3:12-17 |
| Psalm 103 | Luke 22:1-46 | Hebrews 9 |
| Psalm 116 | John 6 | 1 John 4:7-21 |
| Isaiah 25 | John 13-17 | |

# L.1 OPENING OF WORSHIP

---

### L.1.1 Preparation for Worship (see also section 1.1)

1    God of love,
as we prepare to remember the events of this poignant night,
open our eyes to see the beauty of Jesus' self-giving love,
and by your Spirit work in our community a desire and commitment
to serve each other and our hurting world.
In Jesus' name, **Amen.**

2    Covenant God,
we bless and thank you for the gift of the meal
that Jesus commanded us to share.
We thank you for this sign of your presence with us
and your love for the world that Jesus came to redeem.
We long to feast with Jesus in the fullness of the coming kingdom.
May our worship today deepen our anticipation of that glory. **Amen.**

### L.1.2 Call to Worship (see also section 1.2)

1    I will bless the LORD at all times;
    his praise shall continually be in my mouth.
**My soul makes its boast in the LORD;**
    **let the humble hear and be glad.**
O magnify the LORD with me,
    and let us exalt his name together.

**I sought the LORD, and he answered me,**
**and delivered me from all my fears.**
O taste and see that the LORD is good;
**happy are those who take refuge in him.**
—Psalm 34:1-4, 8, NRSV

2   What shall we return to the LORD
    for all his bounty to us?
**We will lift up the cup of salvation**
    **and call on the name of the LORD;**
**we will pay our vows to the LORD**
    **in the presence of all his people.**
—from Psalm 116:12-14, NRSV

3   I give you a new commandment,
    that you love one another.
    Just as I have loved you,
    you also should love one another.

    In worship on this day,
    we testify to God's love shown perfectly in Christ,
    and we recommit ourselves
    to love one another as a community of faith.
—based on John 13:34, NRSV

4   On this day Christ the Lamb of God
    gave himself into the hands of those who would slay him.
    On this day Christ gathered with his disciples in the upper room.
    On this day Christ took a towel and washed his disciples' feet,
    giving us an example that we should do to others as he has done to us.
    On this day Christ our God gave us this holy feast,
    that we who eat this bread and drink this cup
    may here proclaim his holy sacrifice and be partakers of his resurrection
    and at the last day may reign with him in heaven.

## L.1.4 Opening Responses (see also section 1.4)

*Prayers of Adoration*

1   O Lord Jesus Christ,
    you are enthroned in the majesty of heaven,
    yet you gave up that heavenly perfection to become a servant.
    We adore you for laying aside your glory
    and clothing yourself in complete humility as one of us.
    We praise you for the example of washing your disciples' feet.
    Teach us to do as you have done.
    Deliver us from pride, jealousy, and ambition,
    and make us ready to serve one another in lowliness for your sake,
    O Jesus Christ, our Lord and Savior. **Amen.**

**2**  Holy God, your Son Jesus came as a servant
to wash away our pride and feed us with the bread of life.
We praise you for inviting us
to serve one another without pride,
to forgive one another as we have been forgiven,
and to feast at his table as members of one household. **Amen.**

*Additional Resources*

**3**  O living Christ,
this evening as we gather for prayer,
we are reminded of your solitary prayer in the garden.
It must have been hard to break bread with your disciples that night,
knowing that later one would betray you, one would deny you,
and all would sleep out of weariness when you needed them most.
With you, O Christ, we pray that the cup of testing be removed from us.
We pray that God's will be worked in our lives.
Preserve us from the Gethsemane sleep
and the sorrow of those who live without hope.
Keep us vigilant in prayer, steadfast in trust,
and grateful for your risen presence. **Amen.**

**4**  Holy God, we come to worship
in the gathering shadows of Jesus' suffering and death.
We come with his friends,
the men and women who have followed him
in every place and generation,
to live once again this story of service and betrayal,
of weakness and courage.
We come to witness your love in action.
Be with us, we pray, in Jesus' name. **Amen.**

**5**  Infinite, intimate God;
this night you kneel before your friends
and wash our feet.
Bound together in your love,
trembling, we drink your cup
and watch. **Amen.**

**6**  Breath of God,
quiet our hearts,
hush our lips,
open our eyes,
and fill us with holy wonder
as we look to Jesus,
our host, your servant, our Lord. **Amen.**

# L.2 CONFESSION AND ASSURANCE

## L.2.1 Call to Confession (see also section 2.1)

1    The psalmist declares:
I love the Lord, because he has heard
    my voice and my supplications.
Because he inclined his ear to me,
    therefore I will call on him as long as I live.

We gather as a community in need of a Savior.
We offer our honest confession,
in faith and trust in our covenant God,
knowing that God hears our voice.
        —based on Psalm 116:1-2, NRSV

2    Christ shows his self-giving love by washing his disciples' feet.
Surely we do not live up to Christ's example.
We confess now our sin and our need of a Savior.

## L.2.2 Prayers of Confession (see also section 2.2)

1    Merciful God, we have not loved you
with all our heart and mind and strength and soul.
[*Silence*]
Lord, have mercy.
**Lord, have mercy.**

We have not loved our neighbors as you have taught us.
[*Silence*]
Christ, have mercy.
**Christ, have mercy.**

We are indifferent to the saving grace of your Word and life.
[*Silence*]
Lord, have mercy.
**Lord, have mercy.**

Forgive and heal us by your steadfast love made known to us
in the passion, death, and resurrection of Jesus Christ, our Lord. **Amen.**

2    Loving Lord,
you taught us compassion.
You took a servant's role and knelt at the feet of your friends.
You gave us a meal to remind us of your life-giving love.
You called us to love one another too.

Forgive us, Lord, for not practicing the compassion you modeled.
Forgive us, Lord, for wanting to be served rather than to serve.
Forgive us, Lord, for not loving as you called us to love. **Amen.**

3    Eternal God, whose covenant with us is never broken:
We confess that we have failed to fulfill your will for us.
We betray our neighbors, desert our friends,
and run in fear when we should be loyal.
Though you have bound yourself to us,
we have not bound ourselves to you.
God, have mercy on us weak and willful people.
Lead us once again to your table,
and unite us to Christ,
who is the bread of life
and the vine from which we grow in grace.
To Christ be praise forever. **Amen.**

## L.2.4 Assurance of Pardon (see also section 2.4)

1    We have seen and do testify
that the Father has sent his Son as the Savior of the world.
God abides in those who confess
that Jesus is the Son of God, and they abide in God.
So we have known and believe the love that God has for us.
God is love, and those who abide in love abide in God,
and God abides in them.

Brothers and sisters in Christ,
the Jesus we remember tonight is the Savior of the world.
In Christ we are forgiven.
And through him God abides with even us.
Praise God, from whom all blessings flow!
      —based on 1 John 4:14-16, NRSV

## L.2.5 The Peace (see also section 2.5)

*This section contains resources for foot washing as well as for the passing of the peace.*

### Passing of the Peace

*The passing of the peace is an act of mutual love and dedication that may function in a way that symbolizes Jesus' washing of the disciples' feet.*

1    Hear the teaching of Christ:
A new commandment I give to you:
Love one another.
As I have loved you, so you must love one another.

The peace of Christ be with you all.
**And also with you.**
—based on John 13:34

## Foot Washing

*Some Christian traditions regularly practice foot washing as a symbol of mutual love and dedica-*
*tion. Other congregations might consider a culturally sensitive form of foot washing on Maundy*
*Thursday. This may be practiced by the entire congregation or by a representative group. Some*
*simple provisions, such as inviting participants to wear sandals and having small sponges avail-*
*able to minimize water use, can help reduce some of the worshipers' discomfort or concerns. The*
*point of the celebration is to depict in a simple, memorable way the dramatic action of Jesus, to*
*sense the power and beauty of seeing Christ's power expressed through service, and to practice the*
*kind of self-giving love to which the entire Christian community is called.*

2    We have an example of humility.
     In God's name let each of us humble our heart
     at the sight of the high majesty
     who washes the feet of the fishermen.
     The most honored one among us is the most humble.

3    Lord Christ, our Servant and Savior,
     on earth you washed the feet of your disciples,
     and now through your cross and resurrection
     you always live to make intercession for us:
     Give us grace to be your faithful disciples
     and servants to our lives' end.
     For your name's sake, **Amen.**

4    Your Word, O Lord, commands us:
     "In humility consider others better than yourselves."
     Jesus, our Savior and Lord, taught us what you command
     when he dropped to his knees
     to wash his followers' smelly, dirty feet.
     Focus our eyes to see others' needs.
     Ready our hands to bring them help.
     Bend our wills—and our knees—to humbly serve.
     In Jesus' name we pray. **Amen.**

5    May this symbolic act
     not only teach us
     but also form in us
     a deeper desire
     to follow Jesus,
     to embody his love,
     to practice his humility.
     Lord Jesus, teach us what it means
     to live as members of your body. **Amen.**

# L.4 PRAYERS OF THE PEOPLE

### L.4.4 Complete Model Outlines and Prayers (see also section 4.4)

*Prayer Outlines*

1   *The following is a guide for extemporaneous prayers. The pattern provides a suggested text for the opening and closing of each part of the prayer and calls for extemporaneous prayers of thanksgiving, petition, and intercession.*

God of love,
it is because of your immense love for us that
you stooped to be our servant and willingly suffered to give us life.
For that love we give you thanks.
We also praise you for the way that love is evidenced
    in creation . . .
    in our community . . .
    in our church . . .
    in our lives . . .
    in the events of this Holy Week . . .

God of love,
you have given us a new command to love each other.
Help us to show that love
    in our care of creation . . .
    to the nations of the world . . .
    to our nation and its leaders . . .
    in this community . . .
    through the church universal . . .
    through this local church in its ministry . . .
    to persons with particular needs . . .

In all our thoughts and actions
may we be your servants and reflect your love.
We pray this in the name of your servant Son, Jesus Christ,
who lives and reigns with you forever. **Amen.**

# L.8 THE LORD'S SUPPER

1    *This model liturgy for the Lord's Supper features a structure similar to the traditional Jewish Passover celebration, in which a young child asks the adults in the community about the meaning of the ritual action.*

Children:    Why do we give thanks and praise before this table?

All:    **We give thanks for God's work of creation, liberation, and salvation.**

Minister:    It is indeed right, our duty and delight, that we should at all times and in all places give thanks to you, O holy Lord, eternal God. You created the heavens and the earth and all that is in them; you made us in your own image; and in countless ways you show us your mercy. Therefore, with choirs of angels and the whole company of heaven, we worship and adore your glorious name, joining our voices in their unending praise:

All [*sung or spoken*]:    **Holy, holy, holy Lord, God of power and might,**
**heaven and earth are full of your glory.**
**Hosanna in the highest.**
**Blessed is the one who comes in the name of the Lord.**
**Hosanna in the highest.**

Minister:    All glory and blessing are yours, O holy God, for in your mercy you gave your only Son, Jesus Christ. He took our human nature and suffered death on the cross for our redemption. There he made a perfect sacrifice for the sins for the whole world. We praise you that before he suffered and died, our Savior gave us this holy sacrament and commanded us to continue it until he comes again.

Children:    Why do we eat bread at this table?

Minister:    On the night before he died, Jesus took bread. After giving thanks, he broke it and gave it to his disciples, saying, "Take, eat. This is my body, given for you. Do this in remembrance of me."

Children:    Why do we drink from the cup at this table?

Minister:    The same night Jesus took the cup, saying, "This cup is the new covenant sealed in my blood, shed for you for the forgiveness of sins. Do this in remembrance of me."

Children:    What do we remember at this table?

Minister:    We remember God's gracious love for us, Christ's death and resurrection for us, and the Spirit's tender care for us. Let us proclaim the mystery of faith:

All [*sung or spoken*]: **Dying, you destroyed our death;
rising, you restored our life.
Lord Jesus, come in glory.**

Minister: Merciful God, pour out your Holy Spirit on these gifts of bread
and wine, that in eating and drinking we may be made one
with Christ and one another.

All: **Amen.**

Minister: Through Christ, with Christ, in Christ, now and forever.

All: **Amen. Our Father in heaven . . .**

—based on 1 Corinthians 11:23-26

## L.8.2 Great Prayer of Thanksgiving (see section 8.2)

*L.8.2.2 Thanksgiving for the Work of God in Creation (see also section 8.2.2)*

*The following prayer offers thanks for the work of God in creation and may be included in the
complete Prayer of Thanksgiving as found in section 8.2 of this book.*

1    With joy we praise you, gracious God,
for you have created heaven and earth,
made us in your image, and kept covenant with us—
even when we fell into sin.
We give you thanks for Jesus Christ, our Lord,
who became the true paschal Lamb
that was sacrificed for our salvation.
Therefore we join our voices
with all the saints and angels and the whole creation
to proclaim the glory of your name.

# L.9 CLOSING OF WORSHIP

## L.9.1 Sending (see also section 9.1)

*Call to Service/Discipleship*

1    Beloved, let us love one another, because love is from God;
everyone who loves is born of God and knows God.
Whoever does not love does not know God, for God is love.
God's love was revealed among us in this way:
God sent his only Son into the world so that we might live through him.

In this is love, not that we loved God
but that he loved us and sent his Son to be the atoning sacrifice for our sins.
Beloved, since God loved us so much, we also ought to love one another.
　　　—1 John 4:7-11, NRSV

## Closing Prayers

2　　God of love, truly we see your glory in the face of Jesus Christ,
who offered himself in humble service to his disciples
even on the night he was betrayed.
Truly you shine in our hearts
when we show your love to others
in Christlike acts of service and fellowship.
**We leave this place eager to reflect the glory of Christ,**
**our source of hope and life, our Teacher and Lord,**
**who laid down his life so that we might live. Amen.**

3　　Lord Jesus Christ,
you stretched out your arms of love on the hard wood of the cross
that everyone might come within the reach of your saving embrace:
So clothe us in your Spirit that we, reaching forth our hands in love,
may bring those who do not know you to the knowledge and love of you,
for the honor of your name. **Amen.**

4　　O Jesus, our ever-living Teacher, Friend, and Master:
　　we have heard your new command to love one another;
　　we have seen your example of how to serve humbly—you, their leader and Lord,
　　　　bent down to wash your disciples' feet;
　　we have received bread and wine, signs of your presence and power within us.
By your Spirit, prompt us now, we pray,
　　to do as you command, to imitate your willingness to serve,
　　and to live as your children, fed and nourished for the journey by Jesus, our Lord.
**Draw us closer and closer, our Savior, to your cross.**
**Help us to ponder with wonder your great sacrifice.**
**Move our hearts to love you more and more. Amen.**

## L.9.2 Blessing/Benediction (see also section 9.2)

1　　May our Lord Jesus Christ himself and God our Father,
who loved us and through grace gave us
eternal comfort and good hope,
comfort your hearts and strengthen them
in every good work and word. **Amen.**
　　　　—from 2 Thessalonians 2:16-17, NRSV

**2** The peace of God,
which passes all understanding,
keep your hearts and minds
in the knowledge and love of God,
and of God's Son, Jesus Christ, our Lord;
and the blessing of God almighty,
the Father, the Son, and the Holy Spirit,
remain with you always. **Amen.**
—based on Philippians 4:7

**3** *The following text includes both a prayer of blessing, spoken by the people to God, and a word of blessing, spoken as God's Word to the people.*

We bless you, God our Father, that on this night your Son, Jesus,
humbled himself to wash his disciples' feet
and modeled the servant way of your kingdom for our life.
**We bless you, Lord Christ, that on this night you set before us**
**a table of the finest wheat and abundant wine,**
**that we may taste your goodness all the days of our life.**
We bless you, Spirit of God, that on this night you help us to pray,
"Not ours, but your will be done,"
in all the public and private places of our life.
**We bless you, triune God, that on this night you lead us**
**from the upper room to Calvary,**
**and from death to resurrected life. Amen.**
And now may this God—Father, Son, and Holy Spirit—
bless you and keep you,
make his face to shine upon you, and be gracious to you.
May this God—Father, Son, and Holy Spirit—
turn his face to you and give you peace. **Amen.**

# L.10 SUGGESTED SCRIPTURE READINGS

**1** *Christian fellowship and servanthood*

Luke 22:24-27: The first and the last
John 13:1-17: Jesus washes feet
John 15:1-17: Love each other and bear fruit
Acts 2:42-47: Everything in common
Ephesians 4-5: Walk in love
Philippians 2:1-18: Be humble as Christ
Galatians 3:23-29: One in Christ
Colossians 3: Set your hearts on things above
Hebrews 10:19-25: Spur one another on toward love
1 John 4:7-21: Let us love one another

# SECTION M
# GOOD FRIDAY

Good Friday marks the death of Jesus Christ. It's called "good" because of what Jesus' death means for the redemption of the world. Worship on this day may focus on three aims: (1) to narrate and remember the events of Jesus' death, (2) to open up the meaning of these events for our understanding of God and the redemption accomplished by the cross, and (3) to invite worshipers to renewed prayer and dedication.

First, the historical remembrance is often best accomplished through a dramatic reading of the gospel account of Jesus' passion. (The account in John 18-19 is perhaps the most commonly used.) In some churches the reading is structured to follow the "seven last words of Christ" or to take the shape of a Tenebrae service of deepening shadows, in which each portion of the passion narrative is marked by extinguishing a candle or darkening the worship space in some way. Many Good Friday services are somber because of this historical remembrance.

Second, the theological interpretation of these events may highlight the complementary metaphors and images that the New Testament uses to convey the mystery, power, and significance of Jesus' death—simultaneously an atoning sacrifice for sin; a picture of divine glory; an example of perfect, self-giving love; a surprising means of conquering evil; and a means for redeeming all creation. This interpretive aspect of Good Friday worship may happen through preaching or through hymnody or other music that explores these themes and images. While the historical remembrance dimension may well give the service a somber feel, this interpretive dimension should not in any way lead people to be sad. Profound wonder and gratitude are more appropriate responses! Worshipers gather not only to remember the suffering of the dying Savior but also to rejoice in the purposes of God, who wills to redeem his children, and to offer profound gratitude for God's greatest gift.

Third, Good Friday is also appropriately marked by intercessory prayer. In some traditions dating back to the early church, Good Friday worship includes the longest intercessory prayer of the entire year (traditionally called the "solemn intercessions"). Prompted by Hebrews 4:14-16, these prayers feature sustained intercessions for the needs of the world, of the church, and of the local community.

Some Christian traditions also mark Good Friday with a celebration of the Lord's Supper, focusing on how the supper "proclaims the Lord's death until he comes." In other traditions Good Friday is the one day of the year on which the Lord's Supper is not celebrated.

The worship space for this day may be simple and stark, including only visuals that remind us of the cross and its purpose. A cross may be displayed prominently.

---

### Scriptures and Statements of Faith Applying to the Theme of Good Friday

*The following texts are particularly appropriate for sermons or for supplemental liturgical use.*

| | | |
|---|---|---|
| Genesis 3:14-19 | Lamentations 3:1-9, 19-33 | Philippians 2:5-11 |
| Genesis 22:1-14 | Zechariah 12:10-13:9 | Colossians 1:19-23 |
| Numbers 21:4-9 | Matthew 26:47-27:66 | Colossians 2:13-15 |
| Deuteronomy 21:22-23 | Luke 22:39-23:56 | Hebrews 2:5-9 |
| Psalm 22:1-18 | John 3:13-21 | Hebrews 4:14-5:10 |
| Psalm 43 | John 10:14-18 | Hebrews 10:1-25 |
| Psalm 49 | John 18-19 | Hebrews 12:1-3 |
| Psalm 51 | Acts 13:16-41 | 1 Peter 1:10-20 |
| Psalm 105 | Romans 3:21-26 | 1 Peter 2:19-25 |
| Psalm 130 | Romans 8:1-17 | 1 Peter 3:13-22 |
| Psalm 143 | 1 Corinthians 1:17-21 | 1 John 3:16 |
| Isaiah 50:4-9 | Galatians 3:1-14 | 1 John 4:7-21 |
| Isaiah 52:13-53:12 | Ephesians 2:13-22 | Revelation 5:6-14 |

Belgic Confession, Art. 20-21
Heidelberg Catechism, Q&A's 37-44
Canons of Dort, Pt. II, Art. 3-4, 8; Rej. 2, 7
*Our Song of Hope*, st. 4
*Our World Belongs to God*, st. 25

# M.1 OPENING OF WORSHIP

## M.1.1 Preparation for Worship (see also section 1.1)

1    Holy and loving God,
    as we prepare to set aside our busyness
    and to focus intently on Jesus' suffering and death,
    we ask for eyes to see all of the amazing things that Jesus' death
    means for understanding you, your love, and our salvation.
    In Jesus' name we pray. **Amen.**

2    Loving God,
    we know that you seek the lost and wandering sheep.
    May our worship today be a means through which many come to know you
    and to trust in Jesus as their Savior. **Amen.**

## M.1.2 Call to Worship (see also section 1.2)

1    Who has believed what we have heard?
        And to whom has the arm of the LORD been revealed?
    **Surely he has borne our infirmities**
        **and carried our diseases;**
    **yet we account him stricken,**
        **struck down by God and afflicted.**
    But he was wounded for our transgressions,
        crushed for our iniquities;
    upon him was the punishment that made us whole,
        **and by his bruises we are healed.**
        —from Isaiah 53:1, 4-5, NRSV

2    Today we remember Jesus was crucified.
    He was pierced for our transgressions.
    He suffered and died for our iniquities.
    We remember the sacrifice of our Lord with gratitude
    because his death gives us life and brings redemption to the world.
    Let us worship our Savior.

3    God so loved the world that he gave his own dearly beloved Son
    so that everyone who believes in him
    will not perish but have everlasting life.
    On this day of remembrance and hope, we declare with joy:
    **God did not send his Son into the world**
    **to condemn the world but to save it.**
    Let us worship God.
        —based on John 3:16-17

## M.1.4 Opening Responses (see also section 1.4)

### *Prayers of Adoration*

1    King of glory,
     we adore you, our Savior and Lord.
     You suffered on the cross
     and gave your life as a ransom for many.
     We bless and thank you for the outpouring of your love
     and offer our worship today out of unspeakable gratitude. **Amen.**

### *Prayers of Invocation*

2    O Christ, who forsook no one
     but was forsaken by the closest of friends,
     and who committed no crime yet was sentenced to a criminal's death,
     we enter your presence in awe and adoration.
     On this day, centuries ago, you could have saved your life,
     but you refused to betray the purpose for which you had been born.
     You had come into the world to love God and neighbor as yourself,
     and when that love required you to shoulder a cross,
     you summoned the strength to bear it.
     Today, O Christ, as we sing and pray about the cross,
     teach us its meaning once again
     and help us to take up our cross and follow you. **Amen.**

3    Assist us mercifully with your help,
     O Lord God of our salvation,
     that we may enter with joy
     upon the contemplation of those mighty acts,
     whereby you have given us life
     through Jesus Christ, our Lord. **Amen.**

4    O God,
     who for our redemption gave
     your only Son to the death of the cross,
     and by his glorious resurrection
     delivered us from the power of our enemy:
     Grant us so to die daily to sin,
     that we may evermore live with him
     in the joy of his resurrection,
     now and for ever. **Amen.**

*Additional Resources*

5    Let us remember Jesus,
     who, though rich, became poor and dwelt among us;
     who was mighty indeed, healing the sick and the troubled;
     who, as a teacher to his disciples, was their companion and servant.
     **May we ever be grateful for Jesus the Christ**
     **and what he has done for us.**

     Let us remember Jesus,
     who prayed for the forgiveness of those who rejected him
     and for the perfecting of those who received him;
     who loved all people and prayed for them,
     even if they denied and rejected him;
     who hated sin because he knew the cost of pride and selfishness,
     of cruelty and hatred, both to people and to God.
     **May we ever be grateful for Jesus the Christ**
     **and what he has done for us.**

     Let us remember Jesus,
     who humbled himself, obedient unto the cross.
     God has exalted him who has redeemed us
     from the bondage of sin and given us new freedom.
     **May we ever be grateful for Jesus the Christ**
     **and what he has done for us and continues to do for us.**
     [*Silence of remembrance*]

# M.2 CONFESSION AND ASSURANCE

## M.2.2 Prayers of Confession (see also section 2.2)

1    O crucified Jesus, Son of the Father,
     conceived by the Holy Spirit,
     born of the virgin Mary, eternal Word of God,
     **we worship you.**

     O crucified Jesus, holy temple of God,
     dwelling place of the Most High,
     gate of heaven, burning flame of love,
     **we worship you.**

     O crucified Jesus, sanctuary of justice and love,
     full of kindness, source of all faithfulness,
     **we worship you.**

O crucified Jesus, ruler of every heart,
in you are the treasures of wisdom and knowledge,
in you dwells all the fullness of the Godhead,
**we worship you.**

Jesus, Lamb of God,
**have mercy on us.**
Jesus, bearer of our sins,
**have mercy on us.**
Jesus, redeemer of the world,
**grant us peace.**

[*After a brief silence, the leader concludes the litany:*]
Almighty God, look with mercy on your family
for whom our Lord Jesus Christ was willing to be betrayed
and to be given over to the hands of sinners
and to suffer death on the cross;
through him who now lives and reigns
with you and the Holy Spirit, one God, forever and ever. **Amen.**

2    Great God, our Father:
As we remember Christ's suffering in Gethsemane,
our hearts are filled with shame that we foolishly waste our time in idleness
and that we make little to no progress in the Christian life from day to day.
We lament that war and lust flourish and grow more rampant every day.
Forgive us for our cruel indifference to the cross.
Teach us the good news of your forgiveness.
Allow humanity, degenerate as it is, to live anew,
and hasten the day when the whole world shall be born again. **Amen.**

3    Merciful God,
we meet each other today at the foot of the cross,
as inhabitants of one world.
We wait with each other as those who inflict wounds on one another:
**be merciful to us.**
As those who deny justice to others:
**be merciful to us.**
As those who put our trust in power:
**be merciful to us.**
As those who are greedy:
**be merciful to us.**
As those who put others on trial:
**be merciful to us.**
As those who refuse to receive:
**be merciful to us.**
As those who are afraid of the world's torment:
**be merciful to us. Amen.**

4    Loving God, we know that you love us,
     so we confess that we have let you down.
     Every day we betray you, deny you, misunderstand you, crucify you.
     We betray you when we are selfish or unkind.
     We deny you when we do not speak out for justice and truth.
     We misunderstand you when we justify our actions
     by misquoting your teaching.
     We are truly sorry, and we wait for your word of love.
     Through Christ, our Lord. **Amen.**

## M.2.3 Lament (see also section 2.3)

1    *Jesus expressed his own lament on the cross with the words of Psalm 22:1. The Psalms also
     provide us language in which to express honest lament, as well as trust and hope. The fol-
     lowing rendering of Psalm 22:1-11, 22-31 (NRSV) helps us to remember Jesus' lament, to
     express our own experiences of pain, to sense Jesus' identification with us in our suffering,
     and to conclude by offering words of trust and praise.*

     We hear Jesus say:
     "My God, my God, why have you forsaken me?"

     And we too at times pray:
     **"Why are you so far from helping me,**
     **   from the words of my groaning?**
     O my God, I cry by day, but you do not answer;
        and by night, but find no rest.
     Yet you are holy,
        enthroned on the praises of Israel.
     **In you our ancestors trusted;**
     **   they trusted, and you delivered them.**
     **To you they cried and were saved;**
     **   in you they trusted and were not put to shame."**

     We hear the words of the ancient psalm even as we see Jesus:
     "But I am a worm and not human;
        scorned by others, and despised by the people.
     All who see me mock at me;
        they make mouths at me, they shake their heads;
     'Commit your cause to the LORD; let him deliver—
        let him rescue the one in whom he delights!'"

     And we too pray:
     **"Yet it was you who took me from the womb;**
     **   you kept me safe on my mother's breast.**
     **On you I was cast from my birth,**
     **   and since my mother bore me you have been my God.**
     **Do not be far from me,**
     **   for trouble is near and there is no one to help."**

[*Silent reflection or individual laments*]

Remembering Jesus, we make bold
even in our lament to offer words of trust and praise:
**"I will tell of your name to my brothers and sisters;**
    **in the midst of the congregation I will praise you:**
**You who fear the LORD, praise him!**
    **All you offspring of Jacob, glorify him;**
    **stand in awe of him, all you offspring of Israel!**
**For he did not despise or abhor**
    **the affliction of the afflicted;**
**he did not hide his face from me,**
    **but heard when I cried to him.**
**From you comes my praise in the great congregation;**
    **my vows I will pay before those who fear him.**
The poor shall eat and be satisfied;
    those who seek him shall praise the LORD.
    May your hearts live forever!
All the ends of the earth shall remember
    and turn to the LORD;
and all the families of the nations
    shall worship before him.
**For dominion belongs to the LORD,**
    **and he rules over the nations.**
**To him, indeed, shall all who sleep in the earth bow down;**
    **before him shall bow all who go down to the dust,**
    **and I shall live for him.**
**Posterity will serve him;**
    **future generations will be told about the Lord,**
**and proclaim his deliverance to a people yet unborn,**
    **saying that he has done it."**

## M.2.4 Assurance of Pardon (see also section 2.4)

1    In Christ all the fullness of God was pleased to dwell,
    and through him God was pleased to reconcile to himself all things,
    whether on earth or in heaven,
    by making peace through the blood of his cross.
    And you who were once estranged and hostile in mind, doing evil deeds,
    he has now reconciled in his fleshly body through death,
    so as to present you holy and blameless and irreproachable before him.

    Brothers and sisters: through the cross of Christ
    we are forgiven and reconciled to God. Praise be to God!
        —based on Colossians 1:19-22, NRSV

2 When you were dead in trespasses
and the uncircumcision of your flesh,
God made you alive together with him,
when he forgave us all our trespasses,
erasing the record that stood against us with its legal demands.
He set this aside, nailing it to the cross.
He disarmed the rulers and authorities
and made a public example of them,
triumphing over them in it.

Brothers and sisters: through the cross of Christ
we are forgiven, and the power of evil is broken. Praise be to God!
—based on Colossians 2:13-15, NRSV

3 Jesus himself bore our sins in his body on the cross,
so that, free from sins, we might live for righteousness;
by his wounds you have been healed.
—from 1 Peter 2:24, NRSV

## M.2.5 The Peace (see also section 2.5)

1 Jesus Christ is our peace;
in his flesh he has broken down the dividing wall,
that is, the hostility between us.
He has abolished the law with its commandments and ordinances,
that he might create in himself one new humanity
in place of the two, thus making peace,
and might reconcile both groups to God
in one body through the cross,
thus putting to death that hostility through it.
So he came and proclaimed peace to you who were far off
and peace to those who were near;
for through him both of us have access in one Spirit to the Father.

Christ is the sure source of our peace.
May Christ's peace be always with you.
**And also with you.**
—based on Ephesians 2:14-18, NRSV

## M.2.8 Dedication (see also section 2.8)

1 May I never boast of anything
except the cross of our Lord Jesus Christ,
by which the world has been crucified to me, and I to the world.
—Galatians 6:14, NRSV

# M.3 PROCLAIMING THE WORD

1   *The following is a script for a dramatic reading of a portion of the passion narrative. Ideally Good Friday worship can include the entire passion narrative from John 18-19, which can easily be used as a dramatic reading, following this model. The reading itself may be simple and stark.*

**Narrator:**    They took Jesus; and carrying the cross by himself, he went out to what is called The Place of the Skull, which in Hebrew is called Golgotha. There they crucified him, and with him two others, one on either side, with Jesus between them. Pilate also had an inscription written and put on the cross. It read, "Jesus of Nazareth, the King of the Jews." Many of the Jews read this inscription, because the place where Jesus was crucified was near the city; and it was written in Hebrew, in Latin, and in Greek. Then the chief priests of the Jews said to Pilate,

**Chief Priests:**  Do not write, "The King of the Jews," but, "This man said, I am King of the Jews."

**Narrator:**    Pilate answered,

**Pilate:**     What I have written I have written.

**Narrator:**    When the soldiers had crucified Jesus, they took his clothes and divided them into four parts, one for each soldier. They also took his tunic; now the tunic was seamless, woven in one piece from the top. So they said to one another,

**Soldiers:**    Let us not tear it, but cast lots for it to see who will get it.

**Narrator:**    This was to fulfill what the scripture says, "They divided my clothes among themselves, and for my clothing they cast lots." And that is what the soldiers did. Meanwhile, standing near the cross of Jesus were his mother, and his mother's sister, Mary the wife of Clopas, and Mary Magdalene. When Jesus saw his mother and the disciple whom he loved standing beside her, he said to his mother,

**Jesus:**      Woman, here is your son.

**Narrator:**    Then he said to the disciple,

**Jesus:**      Here is your mother.

**Narrator:**    And from that hour the disciple took her into his own home. After this, when Jesus knew that all was now finished, he said (in order to fulfill the scripture),

**Jesus:**      I am thirsty.

**Narrator:**    A jar full of sour wine was standing there. So they put a sponge full of the wine on a branch of hyssop and held it to his mouth. When Jesus had received the wine, he said,

**Jesus:**      It is finished.

**Narrator:**    Then he bowed his head and gave up his spirit.
        —from John 19:16-30, NRSV

# M.4 PRAYERS OF THE PEOPLE

## M.4.1 Invitations to Prayer (see also section 4.1)

1  From the throne of grace, O God of mercy,
   at the hour your Son gave himself to death,
   hear the devout prayer of your people.

2  We stand beneath the cross of Jesus,
   and we see there his dying form.
   Witnessing his suffering and his great love for us
   compels us to come before him in prayer.

## M.4.4 Complete Model Outlines and Prayers (see also section 4.4)

*Prayer Outlines*

1  *The following is a guide for extemporaneous prayers. The pattern provides a suggested text
   for the opening and closing of each part of the prayer and calls for extemporaneous prayers of
   thanksgiving, petition, and intercession.*

   Lamb of God,
   being human, you knew the pain the cross would inflict;
   being divine, you knew it was the only way we could be redeemed.
   We praise you for willingly suffering a cruel death so that we may experience the
   glories of heaven. And so we thank you
       for the redemption of creation . . .
       for the sacrifice of your servants around the world . . .
       for your work as it continues in our community . . .
       for the sacrifice of those who serve us in your name . . .
       for our redemption . . .

   While your death and resurrection assure us of your victory
   over evil, we have yet to experience that reality in its fullest.
   And so today we pray
       for creation and its care . . .
       for the nations of the world . . .
       for our nation and its leaders . . .
       for this community and those who are in authority . . .
       for the church universal as it works on your behalf . . .
       for this local church in its ministry . . .
       for persons with particular needs . . .

With the angels and those encircling your throne
we join in proclaiming, "Worthy is the lamb that was slaughtered
to receive power and wealth and wisdom and might and honor
and glory and blessing" forever and ever. **Amen.**
  —based on Revelation 5:12, NRSV

*Complete Prose Prayers*

2 We thank you, heavenly Father,
  that you have delivered us from the dominion of sin and death
  and brought us into the kingdom of your Son;
  and we pray that, as by his death he has recalled us to life,
  so by his love he may raise us to eternal joys;
  who lives and reigns with you, in the unity of the Holy Spirit,
  one God, now and forever. **Amen.**

3 *The following extended prayer is the traditional text for the "solemn intercessions." In some*
  *traditions Good Friday is the day for the longest and most wide-ranging intercessory prayer*
  *of the entire year. As we sense Christ's identification with the suffering of the world, we are*
  *bold to pray (on the basis of Hebrews 4:14-16).*

Dear people of God,
God sent Jesus into the world,
not to condemn the world,
but that the world through him might be saved,
that all who believe in him
might be delivered from the power of sin and death
and become heirs with him of eternal life.

Let us pray for the one holy catholic
and apostolic church of Christ throughout the world:
for its unity in witness and service,
for all church leaders and ministers
and the people whom they serve,
for all the people of this presbytery,
for all Christians in this community,
for those about to be baptized [*particularly name(s)*],
that God will confirm the church in faith,
increase it in love,
and preserve it in peace.

[*Silence*]

Eternal God,
by your Spirit the whole body of your faithful people
is governed and sanctified.
Receive our prayers,
which we offer before you
for all members of your holy church,
that in our vocation and ministry

we may truly and devoutly serve you,
through our Lord and Savior, Jesus Christ. **Amen.**

Let us pray for all nations and peoples of the earth,
and for those in authority among them:
for the president/prime minister,
for the legislative bodies and the courts,
for the members and representatives of the United Nations,
for all who serve the common good,
that by God's help
they may seek justice and truth,
and live in peace and concord.

[*Silence*]

Almighty God,
kindle, we pray, in every heart
the true love of peace,
and guide with your wisdom
those who take counsel for the nations of the earth,
that justice and peace may increase,
until the earth is filled
with the knowledge of your love,
through Jesus Christ, our Lord. **Amen.**

Let us pray for all who suffer
and are afflicted in body or in mind:
for the hungry and homeless,
the destitute and the oppressed,
and all who suffer persecution, doubt, and despair;
for the sorrowful and bereaved;
for prisoners and captives
and those in mortal danger;
that God will comfort and relieve them
and grant them the knowledge of God's love,
and stir up in us the will and patience
to minister to their needs.

[*Silence*]

Gracious God,
the comfort of all who sorrow,
the strength of all who suffer,
hear the cry of those in misery and need.
In their afflictions show them your mercy,
and give us, we pray, the strength to serve them,
for the sake of him who suffered for us,
your Son, Jesus Christ, our Lord. **Amen.**

Let us pray for all who have not received the gospel of Christ:
for all who have not heard the words of salvation,
for all who have lost their faith,

for all whose sin has made them indifferent to Christ,
for all who actively oppose Christ by word or deed,
for all who are enemies of the cross of Christ
and persecutors of his disciples,
for all who in the name of Christ have persecuted others,
that God will open their hearts to the truth
and lead them to faith and obedience.

[*Silence*]

Merciful God,
creator of the peoples of the earth and lover of souls,
have compassion on all who do not know you
as you are revealed in your Son, Jesus Christ.
Let your gospel be preached with grace and power
to those who have not heard it.
Turn the hearts of those who resist it
and bring home to your fold those who have gone astray,
that there may be one flock under one shepherd,
Jesus Christ, our Lord. **Amen.**

Let us commit ourselves to God
and pray for the grace of a holy life,
that with all who have departed this life
and have died in the peace of Christ,
and those whose faith is known to God alone,
we may be accounted worthy
to enter into the fullness of the joy of our Lord
and receive the crown of life in the day of resurrection.

[*Silence*]

Eternal God of unchanging power and light,
look with mercy on your whole church.
Bring to completion your saving work
so that the whole world may see
the fallen lifted up,
the old made new,
and all things brought to perfection
by him through whom all things were made,
our Lord Jesus Christ,
who lives and reigns with you,
in the unity of the Holy Spirit,
one God, forever and ever. **Amen.**

Finally, let us pray for all those things
for which our Lord would have us ask:
**Our Father in heaven . . .**

*Prayers in Litany Form*

**4**   Giver of life, we wait with you to offer the hope
that comes from the cross to earth's darkest places.
Where pain is deep and affection is denied:
**let love break through.**
Where justice is destroyed,
**let sensitivity to right spring up.**
Where hope is crucified,
**let faith persist.**
Where peace has no chance,
**let passion live on.**
Where truth is trampled underfoot,
**let the struggle continue.**
Where fear paralyzes,
**let forgiveness break through.**
Eternal God, reach into the silent darkness of our souls
with the radiance of the cross.
O you who are the bearer of all pain,
**have mercy on us.**
Giver of life,
**have mercy on us.**
Merciful God,
**have mercy on us. Amen.**

**5**   *This resource provides a prayer to correspond with the words of Christ from the cross. These prayers may be spoken together as part of the prayers of the people, or they may be spoken during the reading of the passion narrative, with each prayer following the reading of Jesus' words in the context of the entire narrative.*

"Father, forgive them, for they know not what they do."
**Loving Father, to whom your crucified Son prayed**
**for the forgiveness of those who did not know what they were doing,**
**grant that we too may be included in that prayer.**
**Whether we sin out of ignorance or intention,**
**be merciful to us and grant us your acceptance and peace**
**in the name of Jesus Christ, our suffering Savior. Amen.**

"Truly I say to you, today you will be with me in Paradise."
**O Lord Jesus Christ, who promised**
**to the repentant the joy of paradise,**
**enable us by the Holy Spirit to repent and to receive**
**your grace in this world and in the world to come. Amen.**

"Woman, behold your son. . . . Behold your mother."
**O blessed Savior, in your hour of greatest suffering**
**you expressed compassion for your mother**
**and made arrangements for her care;**
**grant that we who seek to follow your example**
**may show our concern for the needs of others,**

reaching out to provide for those who suffer in our human family.
Hear this our prayer for your mercy's sake. Amen.

*"Eloi, Eloi, lama sabachthani?"* ("My God, my God, why have you forsaken me?")
O Lord, I call for help by day,
and in the night I still must cry.
Regard me, listen to my prayer.

My soul is troubled; I am weak,
cut off as one whom you forsake,
forgotten near the pit of death.

Your wrath weighs heavy on me here.
Your angry waves upon me break.
Friends watch in horror from afar.

I am shut in without escape.
My eyes are dim because I weep.
My hands are lifted up to you.

Do you work wonders for the dead?
Can graves tell out your mighty deeds?
There, who can know that you can save?

Lord, do not hide your face from me.
You have afflicted me from youth.
Your anger is destroying me.

Your flood of anger closes in.
The darkness is my closest friend—
shunned and forsaken, all alone. Amen.

"I thirst."
O blessed Savior, whose lips were dry
and whose throat was parched,
grant us the water of life,
that we who thirst after righteousness
may find it quenched by your love and mercy,
leading us to bring this same relief to others. Amen.

"It is finished."
O Lord Jesus Christ, you finished
the work that you were sent to do;
enable us by your Holy Spirit to be faithful to our call.
Grant us strength to bear our crosses
and endure our sufferings, even unto death.
Enable us to live and love so faithfully
that we also become good news to the world, joining your witness,
O Christ, in whose name we pray. Amen.

"Father, into your hands I commit my spirit."
Father, into whose hands your Son, Jesus Christ,
commended his spirit,
grant that we too, following his example,

**may in all of life and at the moment of our death
entrust our lives into your faithful hands of love.
In the name of Jesus, who gave his life for us all. Amen.**
—based on Psalm 88; Mark 15:34; Luke 23:34, 43, 46; John 19:26-30

# M.9 CLOSING OF WORSHIP

## M.9.1 Sending (see also section 9.1)

*Call to Service/Discipleship*

1   Do nothing from selfish ambition or conceit,
     but in humility regard others as better than yourselves.
     Let each of you look not to your own interests,
     but to the interests of others.
     Let the same mind be in you that was in Christ Jesus,
          who, though he was in the form of God,
               did not regard equality with God
               as something to be exploited,
          but emptied himself,
               taking the form of a slave,
               being born in human likeness.
     And being found in human form,
          he humbled himself
          and became obedient to the point of death—
          even death on a cross.
          —Philippians 2:3-8, NRSV

2   Since we are surrounded by so great a cloud of witnesses,
     let us also lay aside every weight and the sin that clings so closely,
     and let us run with perseverance the race that is set before us,
     looking to Jesus the pioneer and perfecter of our faith,
     who for the sake of the joy that was set before him
     endured the cross, disregarding its shame,
     and has taken his seat at the right hand of the throne of God.
     Consider him who endured such hostility against himself
     from sinners, so that you may not grow weary or lose heart.
     —Hebrews 12:1-3, NRSV

3   We know love by this, that he laid down his life for us—
    and we ought to lay down our lives for one another.
        —1 John 3:16, NRSV

*Acclamations/Doxologies*

4   To Christ, our Lord, who loves us and freed us
    from our sins by his blood, and made us to be a kingdom,
    priests serving his God and Father,
    to him be glory and dominion forever and ever. **Amen.**
        —from Revelation 1:5-6, NRSV

5   Worthy is the Lamb that was slaughtered
    to receive power and wealth and wisdom and might
    and honor and glory and blessing!
        —Revelation 5:12, NRSV

*Closing Prayers*

6   Thank you, loving God, for sending to us your Son, Jesus,
    for his redeeming death that we commemorate this night,
    that we might stand forgiven at the cross.
    Thank you, loving God, for sending to us your Son, Jesus,
    to whom we belong—body and soul, in life and in death—
    and who bore our infirmities, carried our sorrows.
    Thank you, loving God, for sending to us your Son, Jesus,
    who became sin for us and suffered the punishment due to us,
    that we might stand forgiven at the cross. **Amen.**

7   O Lord Jesus Christ, suffering Son of God,
    our minds do not grasp
    the length and breadth, the height and depth
    of your love for us sinners,
    poured out in your precious blood.
    Our minds do not grasp your unfathomable love,
    but our hearts hold it; our hearts do hold it. **Amen.**

## M.9.2 Blessing/Benediction (see also section 9.2)

1   May you find in the cross a sure ground for faith,
    a firm support for hope, and the assurance of sins forgiven.
    And may the blessing of God go with you,
    now and forevermore. **Amen.**

2   May God, who gives us a new vision of life through the cross,
    enlighten our understanding, inflame our affections,
    and enable us to walk the way of the cross.
    And may the love of God—the Father, Son, and the Holy Spirit—
    surround us as we seek to discern that love. **Amen.**

3   May Jesus Christ, who was obedient to death,
    even death on a cross,
    guide, encourage, and protect you. **Amen.**

4   May the Christ who walks on wounded feet
    walk with you on the road.
    May the Christ who serves with wounded hands
    stretch out your hands to serve.
    May the Christ who loves with a wounded heart
    open your hearts to love.
    May you see the face of Christ in everyone you meet,
    and may everyone you meet see the face of Christ in you. **Amen.**

5   Brothers and sisters,
    go out in the knowledge
    that the one who thought
    we needed dying for,
    also thought we were worth dying for,
    and gave himself up for us,
    a terrible and thrilling sacrifice.
    Let this blessed assurance be upon you as you leave,
    that Jesus Christ, the Lord of the universe,
    died for you, out of love for you, in order to bless you now and always. **Amen.**

6   Do not hurry away from the cross.
    Linger near
        to survey,
        to stand,
        to ponder our Savior's suffering and death.
    Consider, carefully and well,
        the preciousness of his sacrifice for you,
        the greatness of his mercy toward you.

    Then depart from Golgotha confidently,
    knowing that the Spirit
        will keep you in your crucified Savior's strong embrace
        and prompt you to trust and obey him always.

    The God of peace will go with you. **Amen.**

7   May God the Father, who so loved our world
    that he gave his only Son;
    may Jesus Christ, whose love for us
    made him obedient to death, even death on a cross;

and may the Holy Spirit,
who enables us to love God and each other,
comfort, encourage, and protect you.

8     May we be thankful for the great gifts we have been offered.
May we respond to the grace we have been given
with grace-filled gestures to those we meet this day and this week.
May we know that our sin does not condemn us
but that our Savior's sacrifice has set us free.
May we who have encountered Christ
now be Christlike to those we encounter,
feeding the hungry, clothing the naked, visiting the prisoners.
And may the great love of our glorious God
equip us and feed us and enable us
in all that we do to love and serve in his holy name.
**Amen.**

# M.10 SUGGESTED SCRIPTURE READINGS

1     *The passion narrative: One of the richest traditions of Christian worship involves the reading of complete passion narratives from one of the four gospels each year, interspersed with songs and prayers of reflection. The following suggestions divide the passion narrative of each gospel book into nine sections.*

Matthew 26:30-46, 47-56, 57-75; 27:1-5, 6-23, 24-31, 32-44, 45-50, 51-54
Mark 14:26-42, 43-50, 51-72; 15:1-5, 6-15, 16-20, 21-32, 33-37, 38-39
Luke 22:39-46, 47-53, 54-62, 63-71; 23:1-12, 13-25, 26-38, 39-46, 47-56a
John 18:1-11, 12-24, 25-27, 28-38a, 38b-19:16a, 16b-25a, 25b-27, 28-37, 38-41

2     *Old Testament readings for Good Friday*

Genesis 3:8-15: Striking the serpent's head
Numbers 21:4-9; John 3:13-15: Lifted up in the desert
Numbers 19:1-10; Hebrews 9:14: Sacrifice without blemish
Psalm 22: Why have you forsaken me
Psalm 31: Into your hands I commit my spirit
Psalm 69: Vinegar to drink
Isaiah 53:4-9 [52:13-53:12]: The Suffering Servant

# SECTION N
# EASTER

All the hopes and expectations of Christians are realized in the resurrection of Jesus Christ from the dead, making Easter the most celebrative day of the church year.

Some traditions begin their Easter celebration with an Easter Vigil service, either late Saturday evening or very early Sunday morning. The vigil recapitulates the biblical theme of redemption history through readings, helping worshipers see the powerful sweep of God's actions throughout history. In this way it provides the entrance into Easter. The vigil usually begins outside, in darkness, and opens with a processional into the worship space. Historically baptism of persons instructed in the faith took place (and still does) as part of this vigil. (*Note:* Each part of the traditional Easter Vigil service is included in this section: see N.1.2.12 for the call to worship; see N.1.4.4-5 for the Easter hymn of praise known as the *Exultet;* see the list of Scriptures on page 626 for traditional vigil readings; see pages 636, 647-648 for liturgies for

baptism or baptism renewal; and see N.8 for resources for celebrating the Easter Lord's Supper.)

The Easter morning service is a time of joy, celebration, and renewal. Even churches that do not customarily follow the church year celebrate this day as the culmination of all that the gospel is about. The liturgical colors are white and gold. In contrast to the somber starkness of Holy Week, on Easter the worship space should be bright and celebratory. Music and songs reflect the full joy of the victorious Christian faith because of Christ's resurrection.

Because the good news of Easter can hardly be contained in a single day's celebration, Easter is only the first of fifty days of Eastertide, the "Great Fifty Days" that lead up to Pentecost. This season is designed for extended celebration, for exploring the ramifications of Easter for the redemption of all creation, and for joyful Christian living.

---

### Scriptures and Statements of Faith Applying to the Theme of Easter

*Traditional readings for Easter Vigil services include passages from the Old Testament that recount the history of salvation (Gen. 1:1-2:2; 7:1-5; 8:6-18; 9:8-13; 22:1-18; Ex. 14:10-15:1; Isa. 54:5-14; 55:1-11; Ezek. 36:24-28; 37:1-14; Zeph. 3:14-20) as well as Psalm 114 and Romans 6:3-11 and one of the gospel accounts of the resurrection (Matt. 28:1-10; Mark 16:1-8; or Luke 24:1-12).*

*The following texts are particularly appropriate for Easter sermons or for supplemental liturgical use.*

| | | |
|---|---|---|
| Job 19:23-29 | Isaiah 51:9-11 | John 11:17-32 |
| Psalm 49 | Isaiah 65:17-25 | John 20:1-23 |
| Psalm 93 | Jeremiah 31:1-6 | Acts 10:34-43 |
| Psalm 107 | Daniel 7:13-14 | Romans 6:1-11 |
| Psalm 117 | Zechariah 3 | Romans 8 |
| Psalm 118 | Matthew 28:1-10 | 1 Corinthians 15 |
| Psalm 136 | Mark 16:1-8 | Colossians 2:6-3:4 |
| Psalm 149 | Luke 24:1-35 | 1 Peter 1:3-12 |
| Isaiah 25:6-9 | John 2:13-25 | |

Heidelberg Catechism, Q&A 45
Westminster Confession, Chap. VIII, Sec. 4-5, 8; Chap. XIII, Sec. 1
*Our Song of Hope,* st. 4
*Our World Belongs to God,* st. 25

---

# N.1 OPENING OF WORSHIP

## N.1.1 Preparation for Worship (see also section 1.1)

1   Loving God,
    on this celebrative day, many may join us for worship
    who do not regularly join with your people.
    We pray for the gift of hospitality today,
    that our community will welcome them with open arms.
    May each worshiper sense the power of the gospel today
    and be drawn closer to you, by the power of your Spirit. **Amen.**

2   God of life,
    we praise you for the miracle of Easter.
    We pray for great joy for ourselves and for all who come
    to worship today to celebrate Jesus' resurrection.
    We pray especially for those who will join us for worship
    and whose lives are filled with pain, loss, or deep sadness.
    May they sense how the resurrection is a source of great hope. **Amen.**

## N.1.2 Call to Worship (see also section 1.2)

1   Awake, O harp and lyre!
        I will awake the dawn.
    I will give thanks to you, O Lord, among the peoples,
        I will sing praises to you among the nations.
    For your steadfast love is as high as the heavens;
        your faithfulness extends to the clouds.
    Be exalted, O God, above the heavens.
        Let your glory be over all the earth.
            —Psalm 57:8-11, NRSV

2   Give thanks to the LORD, for he is good;
        **his love endures forever.**
    In our anguish we cried to the LORD,
        and he answered by setting us free.
    Give thanks to the LORD, for he is good;
        **his love endures forever.**
    The LORD is our strength and our song;
        he has become our salvation.
    Give thanks to the LORD, for he is good;
        **his love endures forever.**
    We will not die but live,
        and will proclaim what the LORD has done.

Give thanks to the LORD, for he is good;
**his love endures forever.**
The stone the builders rejected
has become the capstone;
**The LORD has done this;**
**and it is marvelous in our eyes.**
This is the day the LORD has made;
**let us rejoice and be glad in it.**
—from Psalm 118:1, 5, 14, 17, 22-24, NIV

3    Alleluia! Christ is risen!
**The Lord is risen indeed! Alleluia!**
—based on Luke 24:34

4    Jesus said, "I have come that they may have life,
and may have it to the full."
—from John 10:10, NIV

5    Alleluia! Christ, our Passover lamb, is sacrificed for us;
**therefore let us keep the feast. Alleluia!**
—based on 1 Corinthians 5:7-8

6    Worthy is the Lamb that was slaughtered
to receive power and wealth and wisdom and might
and honor and glory and blessing!
—Revelation 5:12, NRSV

7    This is the good news—
the grave is empty;
Christ is risen.
**Hallelujah!**
This is the good news—
the light shines in the darkness,
and the darkness can never put it out.
**Hallelujah!**
This is the good news—
once we were no people;
now we are God's people.
**Hallelujah!**
Christ is our peace,
the indestructible peace
we now share with each other.
**Hallelujah!**

8    Christ is risen from the dead. Alleluia!

We know that since Christ was raised from the dead,
he cannot die again; death no longer has mastery over him.
The death he died, he died to sin once for all;
but the life he lives, he lives to God.
—based on Romans 6:9-10, NIV

9 The Lord who calls us to worship today is the same Jesus
who refused the temptation to worship the evil one.
Rather than receive the glorious kingdoms of this world,
he endured the shame of the cross,
and today is Lord of lords and King of kings.
Now are gathered in him
all the treasures of wisdom and knowledge,
glory and power.
With the saints of all ages we say,
**"Worthy is the Lamb, who was slain,**
**to receive power and wealth and wisdom**
**and strength and honor and glory and praise!"**
<br>   —based on Colossians 2:3; Revelation 5:12, NIV

10 Alleluia! Christ is risen.
**He is risen indeed. Alleluia!**
Praise the God and Father of our Lord Jesus Christ.
**He has given us new life and hope.**
**He has raised Jesus from the dead.**
God has claimed us as his own.
**He has brought us out of darkness.**
**He has made us light to the world.**
Alleluia! Christ is risen.
**He is risen indeed. Alleluia!**
<br>   —based on 1 Peter 1:3-5

11 Joyful is the sound we make this morning!
**For this day liberates us from doubt and fear.**
Thankful is the song we sing!
**For this day moves us past darkness and despair.**
Hopeful is the prayer upon our lips!
**For this day awakens in us long-awaited new life.**
Jesus said, "Where two or more are gathered in my name,
I am there among them."
**Christ lives here and now.**
**He is among us at this and every moment!**
May his peace and presence be known to you.
**And also to you.**
Let us greet one another with expressions of Christian love.
<br>   —based on Matthew 18:20

12 *The following may be used at the beginning of an Easter Vigil service. It may also be further*
*adapted for other occasions of Easter worship.*

The Lord be with you.
**And also with you.**
Sisters and brothers in Jesus Christ,
on this most holy night
when Jesus, our Lord, passed from death to life,

we gather, united with the church throughout the world,
to rehearse again all that God has promised
and to celebrate how all those promises are "Yes" in Jesus Christ, our Lord.
This is the Passover of Jesus Christ.
As people of this Passover,
we tell the whole story of God's covenanting love.
We celebrate that by God's grace this story is our story:
that God has grafted us into his Easter people,
helping us to share in Christ's triumph over sin and death.
On this Passover night, we declare with joy:
"In the beginning was the Word,
and the Word was with God,
and the Word was God.
In him was life,
and the life was the light of all people.
The light shines in the darkness,
and the darkness has not overcome it."
—based on John 1:1, 4-5

## N.1.4 Opening Responses (see also section 1.4)

*Prayers of Adoration*

1    We give you thanks, great God,
for the hope we have in Jesus,
who died but is risen and rules over all.
We praise you for his presence with us.
Because he lives, we look for eternal life,
knowing that nothing past, present, or yet to come
can separate us from your great love
made known in Jesus Christ, our Lord. **Amen.**

2    **Glory to you, O God:**
On this day you won victory over death,
raising Jesus from the grave
and giving us eternal life.
**Glory to you, O Christ:**
For us and for our salvation you overcame death
and opened the gate to everlasting life.
**Glory to you, O Holy Spirit:**
You lead us into the truth.
**Glory to you, O blessed Trinity,
now and forever. Amen.**

3    Lord God,
early in the morning,
when the world was young,

you made life in all its beauty;
you gave birth to all that we know.
Hallowed be your name.
**Hallowed be your name.**
Early in the morning,
when the world least expected it,
a newborn child crying in a manger
announced that you had come among us,
that you were one of us.
Hallowed be your name.
**Hallowed be your name.**
Early in the morning,
surrounded by respectable liars,
religious leaders,
anxious statesmen,
and silent friends,
you accepted the penalty for doing good,
for being God:
You shouldered and suffered the cross.
Hallowed be your name.
**Hallowed be your name.**
Early in the morning,
a voice in a guarded graveyard
and footsteps in the dew
proved that you had risen,
that you had come back
to those and for those
who had forgotten, denied, and executed you.
Hallowed be your name.
**Hallowed be your name.**
This morning,
in the multicolored company
of your church on earth and in heaven,
we celebrate your creation, your life,
your death and resurrection,
your interest in us,
and your redemption of all creation!
**Hallowed be God's name, now and forever. Amen.**

*The following two resources are versions of an ancient Easter hymn of praise known as the* Exultet.

4    Rejoice, heavenly powers! Sing, choirs of angels!
     Exult, all creation around God's throne!
     Jesus Christ, our King, is risen!
     Sound the trumpet of salvation!
     **Rejoice, heavenly powers!**
     **Sing, choirs of angels!**
     **Jesus Christ, our King, is risen!**

Rejoice, O earth, in shining splendor,
radiant in the brightness of your King!
Christ has conquered! Glory fills you!
Darkness vanishes forever!
**Rejoice, heavenly powers!**
**Sing, choirs of angels!**
**Jesus Christ, our King, is risen!**
Rejoice, O mother church! Exult in glory!
The risen Savior shines upon you!
Let this place resound with joy,
echoing the mighty song of all God's people!
**Rejoice, heavenly powers!**
**Sing, choirs of angels!**
**Jesus Christ, our King, is risen! Amen.**

5 The Lord be with you.
**And also with you.**
Lift up your hearts.
**We lift them to the Lord.**
Let us give thanks to the Lord our God.
**It is right to give our thanks and praise.**
It is truly right that with full hearts and minds
and voices we should praise you,
the unseen God, the all-powerful creator,
and your only Son, our Lord Jesus Christ.
For Christ has ransomed us with his blood
and paid for us the debt of Adam's sin.
**Rejoice, heavenly powers!**
**Sing, choirs of angels!**
**Jesus Christ, our King, is risen!**
This is our Passover feast,
when Christ, the true Lamb, is slain,
whose blood consecrates the homes of all believers.
This is the night [*day*] when first you saved our forebears:
You freed the people of Israel from their slavery
and led them dry-shod through the sea.
This is the night [*day*] when Christians everywhere,
washed clean from sin and freed from all defilement,
are restored to grace and grow together in holiness.
This is the night [*day*] when Jesus Christ broke the chains of death
and rose triumphant from the grave.
**Rejoice, heavenly powers!**
**Sing, choirs of angels!**
**Jesus Christ, our King, is risen!**
Lord God, how wonderful your care for us!
How boundless your merciful love!
To ransom a slave, you gave away your Son.
Most blessed of all nights [*days*],

chosen by God to see Christ rising from the dead!
The power of this holy night [*day*]
dispels all evil, washes guilt away,
restores lost innocence, brings mourners joy;
it casts out hatred, brings us peace,
and humbles earthly pride.
Night [*day*] truly blessed, when heaven is wedded to earth,
and we are reconciled with God!
Therefore, gracious God, in the joy of this night [*day*],
receive our evening [*morning*] sacrifice of praise,
your church's solemn offering.
May this Easter candle always dispel the darkness of night!
May the Morning Star that never sets
find this flame still burning—
Christ, that Morning Star,
who came back from the dead
and shed his peaceful light on all creation,
your Son, who lives and reigns forever and ever. Amen.
**Rejoice, heavenly powers!**
**Sing, choirs of angels! Amen.**

## Prayers of Invocation

6  O Father God of the risen Christ,
in whose resurrection we find new life,
send your Spirit to dwell among us in this day of worship.
O risen Christ, Son of the Father,
may we hear your word of peace today.
O Spirit of the living God,
teach us once more to live in the power of Christ's resurrection,
in whose name we pray. **Amen.**

7  Holy God, creator of all,
the risen Christ taught from Scripture
of his death, resurrection,
and ascension into your glorious presence.
May the living Lord
breathe on us his peace,
that our eyes may be opened to recognize him in breaking bread
and to follow wherever he leads,
who lives and reigns with you and the Holy Spirit,
one God, forever and ever. **Amen.**

8  O God, worker of wonders,
you made this day for joy and gladness.
Let the risen Lord abide with us this evening [*day*],
opening the Scriptures to us

and breaking bread in our midst.
Set our hearts aflame and open our eyes
so that we may see in his sufferings
all that the prophets foretold
and recognize him at this table
as the Christ, now entered into his glory,
who lives and reigns with you and the Holy Spirit,
one God, forever and ever. **Amen.**

9   O living Lord,
on the first Easter Day you stood in the midst of your disciples
as the conqueror of sin and death and spoke to them your peace.
Come to us, we pray, in your risen power
and make us glad with your presence,
and so breathe your Holy Spirit into our hearts
that we may be strong to serve you
and spread abroad your good news,
for the glory of your great name. **Amen.**

10  Glorious Lord of life,
by the mighty resurrection of your Son
you overcame the old order of sin and death
to make all things new in him.
Grant that we who celebrate with joy
Christ's rising from the dead
may be raised from the death of sin
to the life of righteousness,
through him who lives and reigns with you and the Holy Spirit,
one God, now and forever. **Amen.**

11  Brightness of God's glory and exact image of God's person,
whom death could not conquer nor the tomb imprison,
as you have shared our frailty in human flesh,
help us to share your immortality in the Spirit.
Let no shadow of the grave terrify us
and no fear of darkness turn our hearts from you.
Reveal yourself to us this day and all our days,
as the first and the last, the living one,
our immortal Savior and Lord. **Amen.**

12  O God, whose presence is veiled from our eyes:
Grant that when we do not recognize you,
our hearts may burn within us,
and that when feeling is lost,
we may cling in faith to your Word
and the power of bread broken
in the name of Jesus Christ, our Lord,
who lives and reigns with you and the Holy Spirit,
one God, forever and ever. **Amen.**

13   O Christ,
     who lived to show what life is like,
     who died to show that sin is death,
     who rose to raise us up to life eternal,
     help us to follow you and love you forever. **Amen.**

14   *The following is particularly appropriate for the opening of an evening service focusing on
     the Emmaus text (Luke 24:13-35).*

     Stay with us, Lord Jesus, for the day is almost over.
     Like the disciples on the road to Emmaus,
     we face times of depression, hopelessness, and fear.
     Just when we think we understand your plan,
     we are again baffled by an unforeseen series of events.
     Dwell with us. Teach us more about you.
     Feed us with your holy bread. Reveal yourself to us.
     Lead us with your light and truth to such exceeding joy
     that we respond in praise
     and eagerly proclaim your good news.
     In your holy name and in the power of your Spirit we pray. **Amen.**

*Additional Resources*

15   **This is the feast of victory for our God.**
     **Hallelujah, hallelujah, hallelujah!**
     **Worthy is Christ, the Lamb who was slain.**

     Worthy is Christ, the Lamb who was slain,
     whose blood set us free to be people of God.

     **This is the feast of victory for our God.**
     **Hallelujah, hallelujah, hallelujah!**
     **Worthy is Christ, the Lamb who was slain.**

     Power, riches, wisdom and strength
     and honor, and blessing and glory are his.

     **This is the feast of victory for our God.**
     **Hallelujah, hallelujah, hallelujah!**
     **Worthy is Christ, the Lamb who was slain.**

     Sing with all the people of God,
     and join in the hymn of all creation.

     **This is the feast of victory for our God.**
     **Hallelujah, hallelujah, hallelujah!**
     **Worthy is Christ, the Lamb who was slain.**

     Blessing, honor, glory, and might
     be to God and the Lamb forever. Amen.

**This is the feast of victory for our God.**
**Hallelujah, hallelujah, hallelujah!**
**Worthy is Christ, the Lamb who was slain.**

For the Lamb who was slain has begun his reign.
Hallelujah!

**This is the feast of victory for our God.**
**Hallelujah, hallelujah, hallelujah!**
**Worthy is Christ, the Lamb who was slain.**

16   If Christ is not risen, nothing matters.
     Our preaching is then useless
     and our faith too.
     We are false witnesses about God,
     for we have testified that God raised Christ from the dead.
     We are still in our sins.
     Those who have died are as dead as ever.
     We who have pinned our hopes on Jesus
     are then the most pitiable of all human beings.

But if Christ is risen, nothing else matters.
     Though in Adam all may have died,
     in Christ all will then be made alive.
     He will destroy every dominion, power, and authority
     and put every enemy under his feet.
     Nothing will be able to separate us from the love of Christ—
        trouble, hardship, persecution, famine,
        nakedness, peril, sword,
        angels, demons,
        the present, the future, nor any powers.
     Nothing whatsoever, in fact,
     nothing in all creation,
     neither height nor depth,
     nothing either in life
        or in death.

Christ, our Lord, is risen indeed!

Therefore, sisters and brothers, stand firm, let nothing move you.
Always give yourselves wholly to the Lord's work. **Amen!**
    —based on 1 Corinthians 15; Romans 8

17   *For Easter worship during times of need or sorrow*

O Risen Christ,
even as you appeared to despondent disciples
in the garden, at your tomb, and on the road to Emmaus,
assure us now of your presence and power
during this time of need and sorrow. **Amen.**

# N.2 CONFESSION AND ASSURANCE

## N.2.2 Prayers of Confession (see also section 2.2)

1   Almighty God,
    in raising Jesus from the grave,
    you shattered the power of sin and death.
    We confess that we remain captive to doubt and fear,
    bound by the ways that lead to death.
    We overlook the poor and the hungry
    and pass by those who mourn;
    we are deaf to the cries of the oppressed
    and indifferent to calls for peace;
    we despise the weak
    and abuse the earth you made.
    Forgive us, God of mercy.
    Help us to trust your power
    to change our lives and make us new,
    that we may know the joy of life abundant
    given in Jesus Christ, the risen Lord. **Amen.**

2   If, at times, we deny you, God forgive.
    When the risks of discipleship are high,
    and we are nowhere to be found:
    **God forgive.**
    When we wash our hands of responsibility:
    **God forgive.**
    When we cast our lot with powerful oppressors
    and seek to buy freedom with silver:
    **God forgive.**
    When fear keeps us from witnessing to your truth,
    or prejudice keeps us from believing it:
    **God forgive.**
    In the bright light of Easter morning, O God,
    our sin is exposed,
    and your grace is revealed.
    **Tender God,**
    **raise us in your love so that, with joy,**
    **we may witness to your awesome deeds,**
    **in the name of Jesus, the risen one. Amen.**

3   Lord, bring new life where we are worn and tired;
    new love where we have turned hard-hearted;
    forgiveness where we feel hurt and where we have wounded;

and the joy and freedom of your Holy Spirit where
we are prisoners of ourselves.

[*Silence*]
To all and to each,
on his community and on his friends,
where regret is real,
Jesus pronounces his pardon
and grants us the right to begin again.
Thanks be to God!
**Amen.**

4    Almighty God, you have raised Jesus from the grave
and crowned him Lord of all.
We confess that we have not bowed before him
or acknowledged his rule in our lives.
We have gone along with the way of the world
and failed to give him glory.
Forgive us and raise us from sin,
that we may be your faithful people,
obeying the commands of our Lord Jesus Christ,
who rules the world and is head of the church, his body. **Amen.**

## N.2.4 Assurance of Pardon (see also section 2.4)

1    You are not in the flesh;
you are in the Spirit, since the Spirit of God dwells in you.
Anyone who does not have the Spirit of Christ does not belong to him.
But if Christ is in you, though the body is dead because of sin,
the Spirit is life because of righteousness.
If the Spirit of him who raised Jesus from the dead dwells in you,
he who raised Christ from the dead will give life to your mortal bodies
also through his Spirit that dwells in you.
            —Romans 8:9-11, NRSV

2    "Death has been swallowed up in victory."
"Where, O death, is your victory?
Where, O death, is your sting?"
The sting of death is sin, and the power of sin is the law.
But thanks be to God, who gives us the victory
through our Lord Jesus Christ.
            —1 Corinthians 15:54-57, NRSV

3    Christ has been raised from the dead,
the first fruits of those who have died.
For since death came through a human being,
the resurrection of the dead has also come through a human being;
for as all die in Adam, so all will be made alive in Christ.
            —1 Corinthians 15:20-22, NRSV

4    God, who is rich in mercy,
     out of the great love with which he loved us
     even when we were dead through our trespasses,
     made us alive together with Christ—by grace you have been saved—
     and raised us up with him and seated us with him
     in the heavenly places in Christ Jesus,
     so that in the ages to come he might show
     the immeasurable riches of his grace
     in kindness toward us in Christ Jesus.
          —Ephesians 2:4-7, NRSV

5    When you were dead in trespasses,
     God made you alive together with him,
     when he forgave us all our trespasses,
     erasing the record that stood against us with its legal demands.
     He set this aside, nailing it to the cross.
     He disarmed the rulers and authorities
     and made a public example of them, triumphing over them in it.
          —from Colossians 2:13-15, NRSV

6    You know that you were ransomed
     from the futile ways inherited from your ancestors,
     not with perishable things like silver or gold,
     but with the precious blood of Christ,
     like that of a lamb without defect or blemish.
     He was destined before the foundation of the world,
     but was revealed at the end of the ages for your sake.
     Through him you have come to trust in God,
     who raised him from the dead and gave him glory,
     so that your faith and hope are set on God.
          —1 Peter 1:18-21, NRSV

# N.3 PROCLAIMING THE WORD

## N.3.1 Prayers for Illumination (see also section 3.1)

1    God of life,
     your Spirit raised Jesus from dead.
     Your Spirit inspired the prophets and writers of Scripture.
     Your Spirit draws us to Christ
     and helps us to acknowledge him as Lord.

We ask that you will send your Spirit now
to give us deeper insight, encouragement, faith, and hope
through the proclamation of the Easter gospel. **Amen.**

2    Lord, you have been our dwelling place throughout all generations.
From everlasting to everlasting you are God.
Speak to us now as you have spoken to us throughout the ages.
On this glorious Easter, reveal yourself and your will for our lives,
that we might live as your Easter people.
We seek your face, O Lord; hear our prayer through Jesus, our Lord. **Amen.**
—based on Psalm 90

## N.3.6 Profession of Our Church's Faith (see also section 3.6)

*On Easter the Apostles' Creed and the Nicene Creed are particularly appropriate as ecumenical
summaries of the Christian faith. The following texts are provided for supplemental use.*

1    On this mountain the LORD of hosts will make for all peoples
    a feast of rich food, a feast of well-aged wines,
    of rich food filled with marrow, of well-aged wines strained clear.
**And he will destroy on this mountain**
    **the shroud that is cast over all peoples,**
    **the sheet that is spread over all nations;**
    **he will swallow up death forever.**
Then the LORD GOD will wipe away the tears from all faces,
    and the disgrace of his people he will take away from all the earth,
    for the LORD has spoken.
It will be said on that day,
**Lo, this is our God;**
    **we have waited for him, so that he might save us.**
**This is the LORD for whom we have waited;**
    **let us be glad and rejoice in his salvation.**
—Isaiah 25:6-9, NRSV

2    **If we confess with our lips that Jesus is Lord**
**and believe in our hearts that God raised him from the dead,**
**we will be saved.**
**Thanks be to God. Amen.**
—based on Romans 10:9, NRSV

3    For us there is one God, the Father,
from whom are all things and for whom we exist,
and one Lord, Jesus Christ,
through whom are all things and through whom we exist.
—1 Corinthians 8:6, NRSV

4    Jesus Christ is the image of the invisible God,
the firstborn of all creation;
for in him all things in heaven and on earth were created,

things visible and invisible,
whether thrones or dominions or rulers or powers—
all things have been created through him and for him.
He himself is before all things, and in him all things hold together.
He is the head of the body, the church;
he is the beginning, the firstborn from the dead,
so that he might come to have first place in everything.
For in him all the fullness of God was pleased to dwell,
and through him God was pleased to reconcile to himself all things,
whether on earth or in heaven,
by making peace through the blood of his cross.

      —from Colossians 1:15-20, NRSV

5    This is the good news that we have received,
in which we stand, and by which we are saved:
**Christ died for our sins, was buried,**
**was raised on the third day,**
**and appeared first to the women,**
**then to Peter and the Twelve,**
**and then to many faithful witnesses.**
**We believe Jesus is the Christ,**
**the Anointed One of God,**
**the firstborn of all creation,**
**the firstborn from the dead,**
**in whom all things hold together,**
**in whom the fullness of God**
**was pleased to dwell**
**by the power of the Spirit.**
**Christ is the head of the body, the church,**
**and by the blood of the cross reconciles all things to God. Amen.**

      —based on 1 Corinthians 15:3-7; Colossians 1:15-20

6    **Christ has died!**
**Christ has risen!**
**Christ will come again!**

7    By his resurrection he has overcome death,
so that he might make us share in the righteousness
he obtained for us by his death.
By his power we too are already raised to a new life.
Christ's resurrection is a sure pledge to us of our blessed resurrection.

      —from Heidelberg Catechism, Q&A 45

8    He walked out of the grave,
conqueror of sin and death—Lord of life!
We are set right with God, given new life,
and called to walk with him
in freedom from sin's dominion.

      *—Our World Belongs to God*, st. 25

9    Jesus Christ is the hope of God's world.
     In his death,
     the justice of God is established;
     forgiveness of sin is proclaimed.
     On the day of his resurrection,
     the tomb was empty; his disciples saw him;
     death was defeated; new life had come.
     God's purpose for the world was sealed.
           —from *Our Song of Hope*, st. 4

10   In life and in death we belong to God.
     Through the grace of our Lord Jesus Christ,
     the love of God,
     and the communion of the Holy Spirit,
     we trust in the one triune God, the Holy One of Israel,
     whom alone we worship and serve.
     We trust in Jesus Christ,
     fully human, fully God.
     Jesus proclaimed the reign of God:
     preaching good news to the poor
     and release to the captives,
     forgiving sinners,
     and calling all to repent and believe the gospel.
     Unjustly condemned for blasphemy and sedition,
     Jesus was crucified,
     suffering the depths of human pain
     and giving his life for the sins of the world.
     God raised Jesus from the dead,
     vindicating his sinless life,
     breaking the power of sin and evil,
     delivering us from death to life eternal.
     With believers in every time and place,
     we rejoice that nothing in life or in death
     can separate us from the love of God in Christ Jesus, our Lord.
     Glory be to the Father, and to the Son, and to the Holy Spirit. **Amen.**
           —from *A Brief Statement of Faith*

11   I believe in the Jesus who healed
     and the Jesus who was arrested.
     I believe in the Jesus who was abused
     and the Jesus who abused not in return.
     I believe in the Jesus who was called a traitor
     and the Jesus who was a peacemaker.
     I believe in the Jesus who was falsely accused
     and the Jesus who turned those accusations back on his accusers.
     I believe in the Jesus who was crucified
     and the Jesus who forgave his crucifiers
     as they watched the breath of life leave him.

*648*

I believe that the Jesus who was buried on Friday
is the Christ who arose on Sunday,
and because I believe this,
I affirm Jesus to be the Christ, Son of the living God, Savior,
liberator, long-awaited Messiah, King of kings and Lord of lords.
I gladly proclaim the day of Christ's resurrection
to be the Easter for all generations.
Glory to God—our Savior lives!

12   By his resurrection Christ broke apart the gates of death
and opened to us the way of life,
announced victory to the women and apostles
and brought salvation to the whole world,
annihilated the power of death and renewed the entire creation,
gave us the promise of resurrection
so that we might rise with him in new life.

13   This office the Lord Jesus most willingly undertook,
and in order to discharge its obligations
he was born under the law and perfectly fulfilled it.
He endured most grievous torments in his soul
and most painful sufferings in his body;
he was crucified, died, and was buried;
he remained under the power of death,
yet his body did not undergo decay;
and he arose from the dead on the third day
with the same body in which he had suffered.
In this body he ascended into heaven,
where he sits at the right hand of his Father, making intercession,
and he shall return to judge men and angels at the end of the age.
The Lord Jesus, by his perfect obedience and sacrifice of himself—
which he through the eternal Spirit once offered up to God—
has fully satisfied the justice of his Father.
He purchased not only reconciliation
but also an everlasting inheritance in the kingdom of heaven
for all whom the Father has given to him.
        —from Westminster Confession (MESV), Chap. VIII, Sec. 4-5

14   We declare with joy and trust:
Christ is risen.
We declare with joy and trust:
Christ has conquered sin and death.
We declare with joy and trust:
Christ is Lord of all creation.
We declare with joy and trust:
Christ, our risen Lord, is coming.
We declare with joy and trust:
The ends of the earth shall see the salvation of our God.

# N.4 Prayers of the People

## N.4.4 Complete Model Outlines and Prayers (see also section 4.4)

*Prayer Outlines*

1   *The following is a guide for extemporaneous prayers. The pattern provides a suggested text for the opening and closing of each part of the prayer and calls for extemporaneous prayers of thanksgiving, petition, and intercession.*

God of life,
we rejoice in the resurrection of your Son,
his defeat over death, and his gift of new life.
We praise you for the reflections of that new life
    in creation . . .
    in nations and governments around the world . . .
    in the ministry of the church universal . . .
    in our community as it . . .
    in the sacrifice of those who serve . . .
    in our new life in Christ . . .

To you as the giver of new life and renewed hope
we bring our prayers
    for creation and its care . . .
    for the nations of the world . . .
    for our nation and its leaders . . .
    for this community and those who are in authority . . .
    for the church universal as it works on your behalf . . .
    for this local church in its ministry . . .
    for persons with particular needs . . .

We pray all this in your name, the Lord and giver of life. **Amen.**

*Complete Prose Prayers*

2   O Holy God, beyond our imagining and yet near to us as flesh to fingernails, we come before you this Easter day in gratitude. We confess, O God, that we like to think of Easter as a sunny and warm day, full of light and sweetness, redolent of all that is fragrant in springtime. Yet no matter what the weather outside, on this day your world remains in so many corners a dark and stormy place, sunk deep into the cold winter of sin and evil. Those who first witnessed your Son's resurrection found it to be a fearful and fearsome event. For you, O great God of surprises, crashed into our reality with something new and unexpected. But on this morning we do not want to forget the darkness of last Friday afternoon and the way by which the Easter victory, about which we so happily sing this day, came about. We cannot

forget the sacrifice, the bloody death, the God-forsaken pain of it all. This clash between your kingdom and this world was fierce.

Today we do praise you for all the might, power, and creativity by which you won the victory, Father. We praise you for raising from the dead our Lord and Savior, Jesus Christ, the great shepherd now of all of us sheep who follow him. But because we cannot and must not forget also the darkness of sin that even still is around us, we make petition this morning for all people anywhere and everywhere who continue to feel crucified by a cruel world and yet do not perceive any Easter.

We pray for refugees, for tortured prisoners, for the innocent victims of war. We pray for abused children and battered women, for stricken families from whom a loved one has disappeared without a trace. We pray for the homeless poor and those victimized and diminished by racism, discrimination, and oppression of all kinds. We pray for all those who can see no Easter light because all that is good and lovely has been eclipsed by a depression that will not lift, by chronic pain that will not abate, by a stretch of unemployment with no end in sight, or by a job that is slaying the spirit day by day because the work seems so meaningless. O Lord, the things that led Jesus to the cross have not yet disappeared from the face of the earth. The need for resurrection remains stubbornly present in the lives of millions. Make us, O Spirit of the living God, life-giving spirits to minister to those in need this Easter Sunday and always.

Right here in this congregation there are also needs aplenty. So we make petition for the widow or widower who marks this Easter for the first time without a beloved spouse who died since last we observed this holy day. Be with anyone who feels that he or she needs to believe in the resurrection more than ever but is finding it more and more difficult because the absence of that dear person is too real to deny, too total to grasp. We pray for those who are sick this day or who are worried about a loved one who is very ill.

And be with each of us gathered for this service. Thank you for friends and family who are our guests this morning, and grant them a special blessing by your Spirit. We bless you, Father God, for gracing us with musicians who spend their talents thoughtfully and well in this place so that all of us may be edified and, through the mystery of music, be drawn closer to you. But above all we thank you for the presence of the Spirit of the living Lord, Christ Jesus. As we encounter nothing short of your very self here this morning, may we know for sure that we have indeed been in your sacred presence, and may this encounter in turn embolden us to live an Easter life not only now but also in the days to come and forevermore. Help us to take what we experience and learn here and to allow it to set a holy tone for us always and everywhere. We pray in the name of Jesus, the Christ. **Amen.**

3    Let us give thanks to the Lord our God.
**It is right to give our thanks and praise.**
Eternal God,
we praise you that your glory has dawned on us
and brought us into this day of resurrection.
We rejoice that the grave could not hold your Son
and that he has conquered death,
risen to rule over all powers of this earth.

We praise you that he summons us into new life,
to follow him with joy and gladness.
By your Spirit
lift us from doubt and despair
and set our feet in Christ's holy way,
that our lives may be signs of his life
and that all we have may show forth his love.
Praise, glory, and thanksgiving to you, our God,
forever and ever. **Amen.**

4 Let us give thanks to the Lord our God.
**It is right to give our thanks and praise.**
Eternal and ever-blessed God,
Lord of heaven and earth:
We praise your glorious majesty.
We see your wisdom in all your works;
your grace and truth are revealed in Jesus Christ, your Son;
your power and presence are given to us through your Holy Spirit;
we adore your holy name, O blessed Trinity,
forever and ever. **Amen.**

5 Let us give thanks to the Lord our God.
**It is right to give our thanks and praise.**
We give you thanks, great God,
for the hope we have in Jesus,
who died but is risen and rules over all.
We praise you for his presence with us.
Because he lives, we look for eternal life,
knowing that nothing past, present, or yet to come
can separate us from your great love
made known in Jesus Christ, our Lord. **Amen.**

6 We worship you, Jesus, our Savior;
you conquered death by your cross:
you are the stone rejected by the builders;
you have become the cornerstone:
make all of us living stones in your church.
We pray to you for Christians:
may they live in the joy of the resurrection
and be a visible sign of your presence by their mutual love.
We pray to you for the leaders of your church:
as they celebrate your resurrection with all your servants,
may they be strengthened for your service.
We pray to you for the leaders of the nations:
may they exercise their office as servants of justice and peace.
We pray to you for all who are suffering
from illness, grief, old age, and exile:
may your resurrection be a source of comfort and aid for them. **Amen.**

*Prayers in Litany Form*

7    Risen and reigning Lord,
truly you are a high priest
who has passed through the heavens.
Truly you were tested as we are,
and yet were without sin.
With boldness we approach your throne,
deeply assured of your mercy and grace
in our time of need.
And so we pray, **O Lord of glory.**

Your rising and your reigning
give hope to your people.
May all who live without hope today
taste and see that you are good.
So we pray, **O Lord of glory.**

Your rising and your reigning call us, your people,
to testify to your goodness.
Equip each of us today
to be bold witnesses of Easter news.
So we pray, **O Lord of glory.**

Your rising and your reigning
call all the nations of the world
to stop their scheming and seek your peace.
May your Spirit convict all people
to submit to your rule and to pursue true peace.
So we pray, **O Lord of glory.**

Your rising and your reigning
call each of us to turn from the path of death
to the path of obedience and life.
Send your Spirit to strengthen our resolve,
and help us to live as people of life and light.
So we pray, **O Lord of glory.**

Your rising and your reigning
bring life and light and healing.
May all who suffer in the valley of the shadow of death and disease
know your healing presence.
So we pray, **O Lord of glory.**

Your rising and your reigning
are firstfruits of all that is to come:
justice, joy, and peace in the Holy Spirit.
May your kingdom come quickly.
So we pray, **O Lord of glory.**

May we, your Easter people,
never fail to bless and thank you

for your immeasurable love and sure promises.
All praise to you, risen Christ,
who with the Father and the Spirit lives
in perfect communion forever and ever. **Amen.**

8    You, O Christ, are Lord of all creation.
You are exalted above all.
Every knee will bow,
and every tongue will confess that you are Lord!
We join with all creation
and sing of your glory: "Alleluia, Amen!"
By your death and resurrection you conquered evil.
**By your Spirit sustain us in our struggle with the powers of evil.**
By your resurrection you lead us from death to life.
**By your Spirit unite us to you,**
**and help us turn away from sin**
**and toward life everlasting.**
By your resurrection you evoked worship from astonished guards
and gave your disciples joy and peace that surpass understanding.
**By your Spirit help us to live our lives**
**in resurrection-shaped gratitude, joy, and peace.**

*[After a brief silence, the leader continues the prayer:]*

God of grace and glory,
whether we are weak or strong,
old or young,
struggling or flourishing,
help us to see Jesus, our risen Lord.
Give us joy in the knowledge that
your Spirit unites us with Jesus,
helps us cross over from death to life,
and strengthens us to live an Easter life
both now and forever.
We pray through Jesus Christ, our Lord,
who lives and reigns with you and the Holy Spirit. **Amen.**

9    O Christ, born of the Father before all ages,
you took upon yourself our humanity and you rose for us:
we worship you.
**Glory to you, O Lord.**
Son of God, source of life, we invoke your goodness
upon us and upon the entire human family.
**Hear us, Lord of glory.**
Allow us to live by your life
and to walk as children of light in the joy of Easter.
**Hear us, Lord of glory.**
Increase the faith of your church;
may it faithfully bear witness to your resurrection.

**Hear us, Lord of glory.**
Comfort all who are burdened
and engrave in their hearts your words of eternal life.
**Hear us, Lord of glory.**
Strengthen those who are weak in faith
and reveal yourself to doubting hearts.
**Hear us, Lord of glory.**
Give strength to the sick, support the elderly,
and reassure the dying by your saving presence.
**Hear us, Lord of glory. Amen.**

10    By the love with which you drew near to your disciples
as they went to Emmaus and talked together of your passion,
draw near to us and join yourself to us
and give us the knowledge of yourself.
**Hear us, blessed Jesus.**

By the mercy with which at first their eyes were closed,
that they should not know you,
be merciful to those that are slow of heart to believe.
**Hear us, blessed Jesus.**

By the compassion with which,
amid the joy of your resurrection, you sought out those who were sad,
console the fainthearted who have not yet learned to rejoice in you.
**Hear us, blessed Jesus.**

By the patience with which you opened to them the Scriptures,
open our understanding and insight.
**Hear us, blessed Jesus.**

By the fire with which you made their hearts burn
within them as you talked with them by the way,
inflame with devotion every heart
that is not already burning with love for you
and consume with zeal those that you have kindled.
**Hear us, blessed Jesus.**

By the wisdom with which
you made as though you would have gone farther,
inviting them to constrain you to tarry with them,
may no one depart this place until all have received
from you the blessing you are ready to give.
**Hear us, blessed Jesus.**

By the loyalty with which you went in
and tarried with the disciples when the day was far spent,
fulfill in every soul your promise that says,
"I will come to him and sup with him and he with me."
**Hear us, blessed Jesus.**

By the blessing in which you made yourself known
to the disciples in the breaking of the bread,
may every act of yours be to us a revelation,
opening our eyes in faith, making you more fully known to us.
**Hear us, blessed Jesus.**

By the power by which you vanished out of their sight,
that their faith in the mystery of your resurrection might be increased,
strengthen and confirm this faith in us.
**Hear us, blessed Jesus.**

O blessed Jesus, who,
when the doors were shut where the disciples were gathered,
came and stood in the midst and said, "Peace be unto you,"
may no fear ever place a barrier between our souls and you
or hinder us from the peace which the world cannot give.
**May the peace that you gave your apostles,
sending them forth in your Father's name as you yourself were sent,
be also upon us and remain with us always. Amen!**

# N.5 OFFERING

## N.5.2 Offering Prayers (see also section 5.2)

1   *A prayer especially mindful of children*

Living God, you have given us so much in Jesus Christ:
hope, joy, and peace.
Above all, you have given us life!
What can we give in return?
If the whole world were ours, it would not be enough.
What little we have we humbly offer to you.
Thousand, thousand thanks are due,
dearest Jesus, unto you. **Amen.**

2   Good Shepherd, you spread a table before us.
We offer you our gifts,
signs of your gracious love and tokens of our grateful hearts.
Nourish us at the feast of the Lamb,
that we may proclaim to all the world
your triumphant love in Jesus Christ, our Lord. **Amen.**

# N.8 THE LORD'S SUPPER

**N.8.2 Great Prayer of Thanksgiving** (see section 8.2)

*N.8.2.2 Thanksgiving for the Work of God in Creation (see also section 8.2.2)*
*The following prayers offer thanks for the work of God in creation and may be included in the complete Prayer of Thanksgiving as found in section 8.2 of this book.*

1      You are holy, O God of majesty,
       and blessed is Jesus Christ, your Son, our Lord,
       whom you sent to save us.
       He came with healing in his touch
       and was wounded for our sins.
       He came with mercy in his voice
       and was mocked as one despised.
       He came with peace in his heart
       and met with violence and death.
       By your power he broke free from the prison of the tomb,
       and at his command the gates of hell were opened.
       The one who was dead now lives.
       The one who humbled himself is raised to rule over all creation,
       the Lamb upon the throne.
       The one ascended on high is with us always, as he promised.

2      Nourished at this table, O God,
       may we know Christ's redemptive love
       and live a new life in him.
       Help us who recognize our Lord in the breaking of bread
       to see and serve him in all whose lives are broken.
       Give us who are fed at his hand
       grace to share our bread with the hungry
       and with the hungry of heart.
       Keep us faithful in your service
       until Christ comes in final victory,
       and we shall feast with all your saints
       in the joy of your eternal realm.
       Through Christ,
       all glory and honor are yours, almighty Father,
       with the Holy Spirit in the holy church,
       now and forever. **Amen.**

**3** Gracious God,
pour out your Holy Spirit upon us,
that the bread we break and the cup we bless
may be the communion of the body and blood of Christ.
By your Spirit make us one with Christ,
that we may be one with all who share this feast,
united in ministry in every place.
As this bread is Christ's body for us,
send us out to be the body of Christ in the world.

**4** With joy we praise you, gracious God,
for you have created heaven and earth,
made us in your image, and kept covenant with us—
even when we fell into sin.
We give you thanks for Jesus Christ, our Lord,
who by his glorious resurrection
overcame the power of sin and gave us new life.
Therefore we join our voices
with all the saints and angels and the whole creation
to proclaim the glory of your name.

**5** By your power you raised Jesus from death to life.
Through his victory over the grave
we are set free from the bonds of sin and the fear of death
to share the glorious freedom of the children of God.
In his rising to life you promise eternal life to all who believe in him.
We praise you that as we break bread in faith,
we shall know the risen Christ among us.

# N.9 CLOSING OF WORSHIP

## N.9.1 Sending (see also section 9.1)

*Call to Service/Discipleship*

**1** As Christ burst forth from the tomb,
may new life burst forth from us
and show itself in acts of love and healing to a hurting world.
And may that same Christ, who lives forever
and is the source of our new life,
keep your hearts rejoicing and grant you peace
this day and always. **Amen.**

*Acclamations/Doxologies*

2    Now to him who by the power at work within us
     is able to accomplish abundantly far more
     than all we can ask or imagine,
     to him be glory in the church and in Christ Jesus
     to all generations, forever and ever. **Amen.**
          —Ephesians 3:20-21, NRSV

3    Now to the King eternal,
     immortal, invisible, the only God,
     be honor and glory for ever and ever. **Amen.**
          —1 Timothy 1:17, NIV

*Closing Prayers*

4    O Lord, though you were rich,
     for our sakes you became poor.
     You have promised in your gospel
     that whatever is done to the least,
     you will receive as done to you.
     Give us grace, we humbly ask you,
     to be ever willing and ready to minister, as you enable us,
     to the necessities of our brothers and sisters,
     and to extend the blessings of your kingdom
     over all the world, to your praise and glory,
     God over all, blessed forever. **Amen.**

5    God of our salvation,
     you have restored us to life,
     you have brought us back again into your love
     by the triumphant death and resurrection of Christ:
     continue to heal us
     as we go to live and work
     in the power of your Spirit,
     to your praise and glory. **Amen.**

6    You have given yourself to us, Lord.
     **Now we give ourselves for others.**
     You have raised us with Christ and made us a new people.
     **As people of the resurrection, we will serve you with joy.**
     Your glory has filled our hearts.
     **Help us to glorify you in all things. Amen.**

## N.9.2 Blessing/Benediction (see also section 9.2)

1    Grace to you and peace
     from him who is and who was and who is to come,

and from the seven spirits who are before his throne,
and from Jesus Christ, the faithful witness, the firstborn of the dead,
and the ruler of the kings of the earth.
To him who loves us and freed us from our sins by his blood,
and made us to be a kingdom, priests serving his God and Father,
to him be glory and dominion forever and ever. **Amen.**
—Revelation 1:4-6, NRSV

2   Go forth in joy to love and serve God in all that you do.
**We are sent in the name of the risen Christ.**
Let us bless our Lord.
**Thanks be to God. Alleluia!**

May the God of peace,
who raised to life the great shepherd of the sheep,
make us ready to do his will in every good thing,
through Jesus Christ, to whom be glory forever and ever.
**Alleluia! Amen.**
—based on Hebrews 13:20-21

# N.10 SUGGESTED SCRIPTURE READINGS

*The following readings are associated with traditional Easter Vigil services, tracing the whole sweep of the narrative of God's creating and saving work. Each narrative text is paired with a psalm or biblical canticle. Taken together, these texts present a symphonic vision of Easter glory, both in length and in the profound interplay of images, themes, and metaphors that later New Testament writers draw upon to unfold the meaning of Jesus' resurrection.*

1   *Easter Vigil*

Genesis 1:1-2:4a; Psalm 136: God creates the world and rests
Genesis 7:1-18; 8:6-18; 9:8-13; Psalm 46: God's covenant with the earth
Genesis 22:1-8; Psalm 16: Abraham's obedience
Exodus 14:10-31; 15:20-21; Exodus 15:1-18: God's deliverance of Israel
Isaiah 54:1-10; Psalm 30: The eternal covenant of peace
Isaiah 55:1-11; Isaiah 12: Salvation freely offered
Proverbs 8:1-8, 19-21; 9:4b-6; Psalm 19: A vision of divine wisdom
Ezekiel 36:24-26; Psalm 42-43: A new heart and spirit
Ezekiel 37:1-14; Psalm 143: New life for God's people
Zephaniah 3:14-20; Psalm 98: The gathering of God's people

*For supplemental or alternative texts, consider also additional texts used in the Byzantine tradition:*

Isaiah 60:1-16; Exodus 12:1-11; Jonah 1:1-4:11; Joshua 5:10-15; Zephaniah 3:8-15; Isaiah 61:10-62:5; Isaiah 63:11-64:5; Jeremiah 31:31-34; Daniel 3:1-68

# SECTION O
# ASCENSION OF OUR LORD

Ascension Day, the fortieth day after Easter, marks the day on which Jesus went to the Mount of Olives with his disciples and ascended to heaven before their eyes (Acts 1:1-12).

Though often overlooked, the ascension of Christ is filled with theological significance. Christ's ascension means that in heaven there is one who, knowing first-hand the experience of suffering and temptation, prays for us and perfects our prayers. The ascension is a witness and guarantee of our own bodily resurrection, as well as an invitation for us to set our hearts and minds "on things above, where Christ is seated at the right hand of God" (Col. 3:1-2) to rule over all things in heaven and throughout the universe (Eph. 1:10, 20-23). Finally, the ascension of Jesus serves as the prelude to Pentecost, when the power of the risen Christ came upon all believers through the Holy Spirit.

Some churches observe Ascension Day with a service on the actual day of ascension, which is always a Thursday. Others observe Jesus' ascension on the preceding or following Sunday. As during the celebration of Easter, the liturgical colors are white and gold.

**Scriptures and Statements of Faith Applying to the Theme of the Ascension**

*The following texts are particularly appropriate for sermons or for supplemental liturgical use.*

| | | |
|---|---|---|
| 2 Kings 2:1-18 | Luke 24:44-53 | Colossians 3:1-4 |
| Psalm 47 | John 14:1-14 | Hebrews 2:5-18 |
| Psalm 68 | Acts 1 | Hebrews 4:14-5:10 |
| Psalm 97 | Acts 3:17-26 | Hebrews 6:13-20 |
| Psalm 110 | Romans 8:34 | Hebrews 8 |
| Psalm 113 | Ephesians 1:15-23 | Hebrews 9:23-28 |
| Daniel 7:9-14 | Ephesians 2:4-7 | 1 Peter 3:18-22 |
| Matthew 28:16-20 | Ephesians 4:7-16 | 1 John 2:1-6 |
| Mark 16:15-20 | Colossians 1:15-23 | Revelation 5 |

Belgic Confession, Art. 26
Heidelberg Catechism, Q&A's 46-52
Canons of Dort, Pt. V, Art. 1-15
Westminster Confession, Chap. VIII, Sec. 4-5
*Our Song of Hope,* st. 5
*Our World Belongs to God,* st. 27

# O.1 OPENING OF WORSHIP

### O.1.1 Preparation for Worship (see also section 1.1)

1    Almighty God,
as we prepare to worship today,
we ask that you will stretch our imaginations
to sense the majesty and mystery of your ascension.
Help us perceive how Jesus' presence in heaven
can give us confidence in our praying
and hope for the future.
Through Jesus, our Lord. **Amen.**

2    Ascended and reigning Christ,
help all of us who struggle to worship you as Lord
perceive the beauty and glory of your sovereign rule.
Help all of us who struggle to worship you as heavenly priest
discover the beauty and power of your ongoing prayer for us and with us. **Amen.**

**O.1.2 Call to Worship** (see also section 1.2)

1    The earth is the LORD's and all that is in it,
        the world, and those who live in it;
    for he has founded it on the seas,
        and established it on the rivers.
    **Who shall ascend the hill of the LORD?**
        **And who shall stand in his holy place?**
    Those who have clean hands and pure hearts,
        who do not lift up their souls to what is false,
        and do not swear deceitfully.
    They will receive blessing from the LORD,
        and vindication from the God of their salvation.
    Such is the company of those who seek him,
        who seek the face of the God of Jacob.

    **Lift up your heads, O gates!**
        **and be lifted up, O ancient doors!**
        **that the King of glory may come in.**
    Who is the King of glory?
        **The LORD, strong and mighty,**
        **the LORD, mighty in battle.**
    Lift up your heads, O gates!
        and be lifted up, O ancient doors!
        that the King of glory may come in.
    Who is this King of glory?
        **The LORD of hosts,**
        **he is the King of glory.**
            —Psalm 24, NRSV

2    Clap your hands, all you peoples;
        shout to God with loud songs of joy.
    **For the LORD, the Most High, is awesome,**
        **a great king over all the earth.**
    The LORD is king, he is robed in majesty;
        the LORD is robed, he is girded with strength.
    **He has established the world; it shall never be moved.**
    Since, then, we have a great high priest
    who has passed through the heavens,
    Jesus, the Son of God,
    let us hold fast to our confession.
    **Let us therefore approach the throne of grace with boldness,**
    **so that we may receive mercy**
    **and find grace to help in time of need.**
            —Psalm 47:1-2; 93:1; Hebrews 4:14, 16, NRSV

3    **Worthy is the Lamb, who was slain,**
        **to receive power and wealth and wisdom and strength**
        **and honor and glory and praise!**

Then every creature in heaven and on earth and under the earth
and on the sea, and all that is in them, sang,
**"To the one who sits on the throne and to the Lamb**
**be praise and honor and glory and power**
**for ever and ever!" Amen.**
—from Revelation 5:12-13, NIV

4　　God has ascended amid shouts of joy,
**the LORD amid the sounding of trumpets.**
Sing praises to God, sing praises;
**sing praises to our King, sing praises.**
For God is the King of all the earth;
**sing to him a psalm of praise.**
God reigns over the nations;
**God is seated on his holy throne.**
—Psalm 47:5-8, NIV

5　　Jesus ascended in triumph,
raising our humanity to the heavenly throne.
All authority, glory, and sovereign power are given to him.
There he hears our prayers and pleads our cause before the Father.
Blessed are all who take refuge in him.
**Come, let us worship and bow down.**
—from *Our World Belongs to God*, st. 27

6　　People of God,
the Lord of glory, Jesus Christ, sends his greeting to you.
And his greeting is this:
Grace to you and peace from God our Father and the Lord Jesus Christ,
through the working of the Holy Spirit.
This is the greeting of Christ, who arose from the grave.
**He died and rose that we might have eternal life.**
**All thanks be to him!**
This same Christ has ascended to the Father.
**He ascended that we might experience God's presence and power.**
**All praise be to him!**

7　　Jesus Christ has come into heaven and is at God's right hand—
with angels, authorities, and powers in submission to him.
**Since we have a great high priest who has gone into heaven—**
**Jesus, the Son of God—let us hold firmly to the faith we profess.**
**Let us praise his holy name!**
Salvation belongs to our God, who sits on the throne, and to the Lamb!
**Blessing, glory, wisdom, thanks, honor, power, and strength**
**be to our God forevermore!**
Alleluia, Amen!
**Alleluia!**
—based on Hebrews 4:14; Revelation 5:10, 12

**O.1.4 Opening Responses** (see also section 1.4)

*Prayers of Adoration*

1    We give thanks to you, Lord God Almighty,
     the one who is and who was,
     for you have taken your great power
     and have begun to reign.
     **Now have come the salvation and the power**
     **and the kingdom of our God,**
     **and the authority of his Christ.**
     Great and amazing are your deeds, Lord God the Almighty.
     **Just and true are your ways, King of the nations.**
     Lord, who will not fear and glorify your name?
     **For you alone are holy.**
     **All nations will come and worship before you,**
     **for your judgments have been revealed. Amen.**
                —from Revelation 11:17; 12:10, NIV; 15:3-4, NRSV


2    Eternal God, mighty in the heavens,
     you brought back from the dead our Lord Jesus Christ,
     lifting him to life and drawing him up
     into the glory he shares with you and the Holy Spirit.
     Stretch our minds and hearts toward your majestic love.
     Raise our eyes, lift our heads,
     expand our vision of you
     and your sovereign purposes in the world
     that rest upon the strength
     of our ascended Lord. **Amen.**


3    Almighty God,
     we thank you that you have highly exalted
     your Son, Jesus Christ.
     Before him every knee shall bow
     and every tongue confess
     that Jesus Christ is Lord.
     He has made captivity itself a captive;
     and has given gifts to his people.
     We rejoice that Jesus Christ,
     the pioneer and perfecter of our faith,
     has triumphed most gloriously
     and is our Lord.
     Bring us at last into your presence,
     so that we can live and praise you
     together with all the saints
     forever and ever. **Amen.**
                —based on Ephesians 4:8; Philippians 2:10-11; Hebrews 12:2

**4**  Father, O God most high,
who dwells in the highest of heavens,
**we praise you.**
Father, O Lord most exalted,
beyond our thoughts and imaginations,
**we praise you.**
We celebrate the victory of your Son,
who has overcome death
and saved us from the power of sin.
We rejoice in his exaltation!
Our great high priest
has gone before,
has entered into the Holy of Holies,
and has opened up a way for us to follow.
In his name, we too would enter into your eternal presence,
for he is our priest forever
after the order of Melchizedek.
**To him be all praise,**
**together with you, O Father,**
**and the Holy Spirit,**
**one Lord, the same in every age.**
**Amen and Amen.**

**5**  O God of all power and majesty,
you created the heavens and stretched them out.
You formed the earth and all that comes from it.
You give the breath of life to all who walk on the face of the earth.
Jesus, you conquered sin and death and now reign victorious.
You are Lord; glory is due your name.
The former things have come to pass;
we now await the new things you will bring through the Holy Spirit.
**We rejoice to be gathered in your name.**
**Alleluia! Accept our praises and petitions. Amen.**

**6**  All-powerful God,
your only Son came to earth in the form of a slave
and is now enthroned at your right hand,
where he rules in glory.
As he reigns as King in our hearts,
may we rejoice in his peace,
glory in his justice,
and live in his love.
For with you and the Holy Spirit he rules now and for ever. **Amen.**

*Prayers of Invocation*

7    Eternal God, the King of glory,
     you have exalted your only Son
     with great triumph to be Lord of all;
     leave us not comfortless
     but send your Holy Spirit to strengthen us,
     that we may labor for the coming of your kingdom,
     through Jesus Christ, our Lord,
     who lives and reigns with you and the Spirit,
     one God now and for ever.
     Jesus Christ, you left your disciples,
     that you might send the Holy Spirit
     to be our advocate.
     Grant us the Spirit of truth
     to convince the world
     that you are risen from the dead.
     Eternal God,
     you have given your Son authority
     in heaven and on earth;
     grant that we may never lose
     the vision of his kingdom
     but serve him with hope and joy. **Amen.**

8    Almighty God,
     grant that, as your only Son, our Lord Jesus Christ,
     ascended into the heavens,
     so may we also set our minds on things above, where Christ is,
     who lives and reigns with you and the Holy Spirit,
     one God, world without end. **Amen.**

9    God of power and love,
     you raised Jesus from death to life,
     resplendent in glory to rule over all creation.
     Free the world to rejoice in his peace,
     to glory in his justice,
     and to live in his love.
     Unite all humankind in Jesus Christ, your Son,
     who lives and reigns with you and the Holy Spirit,
     one God, forever and ever. **Amen.**

*Additional Resources*

10   Loving God,
     the heavens are open wide
     since Jesus, our Redeemer,
     has entered through the veil.
     We thank you for his new and living way,

by which we join the unnumbered millions
who are with you forever.
Eternal God,
by raising Jesus from the dead
you proclaimed his victory,
and by his ascension
you declared him King.
Lift up our hearts to heaven,
that we may live and reign with him.
Eternal and gracious God,
we believe your Son, our Savior, Jesus Christ,
to have ascended with triumph
into your kingdom in heaven;
may we also continually dwell with him
who lives and reigns with you and the Holy Spirit,
one God, now and forever. **Amen.**

# O.2 CONFESSION AND ASSURANCE

### O.2.2 Prayers of Confession (see also section 2.2)

1    Almighty God,
     you have raised Jesus from death to life
     and crowned him Lord of all.
     We confess that we have not bowed before him
     or acknowledged his rule in our lives.
     We have gone along with the ways of the world
     and failed to give him glory.
     Forgive us
     and raise us from sin,
     that we may be your faithful people,
     obeying the commands of our Lord Jesus Christ,
     who rules the world
     and is head of the church, his body. **Amen.**

2    *Call to Confession*
     While we claim to celebrate the ascension of our Lord,
     the way we live proclaims our lack of faith
     in his power to deal with the world.
     Let us confess the incongruity between our faith and practice.
     Let us pray.

*Prayer of Confession*
**We come, O Lord, on this day of glory to confess our lack of trust.**
**While we sing of your lordship over all creation,**
**we have too often acted as though you are powerless**
**in the face of today's events.**
**Help us to live with confidence in your presence today**
**and in hope for life with you forever. Amen.**

## O.2.4 Assurance of Pardon (see also section 2.4)

1    Hear the good news of the gospel:
     God, who is rich in mercy,
     out of the great love with which he loved us
     even when we were dead through our trespasses,
     made us alive together with Christ—
     by grace you have been saved—
     and raised us up with him and seated us with him
     in the heavenly places in Christ Jesus,
     so that in the ages to come he might show
     the immeasurable riches of his grace
     in kindness toward us in Christ Jesus.
     In Christ, by God's grace, we are saved.
     Praise God, from whom all blessings flow!
             —based on Ephesians 2:4-7, NRSV

2    Hear the good news of the gospel:
     If anyone does sin, we have an advocate with the Father,
     Jesus Christ the righteous;
     and he is the atoning sacrifice for our sins,
     and not for ours only but also for the sins of the whole world.
     In Christ, we are forgiven! Thanks be to God.
             —based on 1 John 2:1-2, NRSV

3    Hear the good news: "For Christ also suffered once for sins,
     the righteous for the unrighteous, to bring you to God.
     He was put to death in the body but made alive in the Spirit.
     After being made alive, he went and made proclamation
     to the imprisoned spirits—to those who were disobedient long ago
     when God waited patiently in the days of Noah while the ark was being built.
     In it only a few people, eight in all, were saved through water,
     and this water symbolizes baptism that now saves you also—
     not the removal of dirt from the body
     but the pledge of a clear conscience toward God.
     It saves you by the resurrection of Jesus Christ,
     who has gone into heaven and is at God's right hand—
     with angels, authorities and powers in submission to him."
             —1 Peter 3:18-22, NIV

# O.3 PROCLAIMING THE WORD

## O.3.1 Prayers for Illumination (see also section 3.1)

1    Blessed are you, Lord God,
     King of all creation:
     You have taught us by your Word.
     Open our hearts to your Spirit
     and lead us on the paths of Christ, your Son.
     All praise and glory be yours forever. **Amen.**

## O.3.6 Profession of our Church's Faith (see also section 3.6)

1    Child 1:          The Word of the Lord from Philippians 2.
                       Christ Jesus, though he was in the form of God
     Child 2:          did not regard equality with God
     Child 3:          as something to be exploited,
     Child 4:          but emptied himself,
     Child 5:          taking the form of a slave,
                       being born in human likeness.
     Child 6:          And being found in human form, he humbled himself
     Child 7:          and became obedient to the point of death—even death on a cross.
     All Children:     Therefore,
     Child 7:          God also highly exalted him
     Child 6:          and gave him the name that is above every name,
     Child 5:          so that at the name of Jesus, every knee should bend,
                       in heaven and on earth and under the earth,
     Child 4:          and every tongue should confess
     Child 3:          that Jesus Christ is Lord,
     Child 2:          to the glory of God the Father.
     Child 1:          The Word of the Lord.
     Congregation:     **Thanks be to God.**
               —based on Philippians 2:5-11, NRSV

2    We believe that we have no access to God
     except through the one and only Mediator and Intercessor:
     "Jesus Christ the righteous,"
     who therefore was made human,
     uniting together the divine and human natures,
     so that we human beings might have access to the divine majesty.
               —from Belgic Confession, Art. 26

3    Our hope for a new creation
     is not tied to what humans can do,
     for we believe that one day
     every challenge to God's rule
     will be crushed.
     His kingdom will fully come,
     and the Lord will rule.
     We long for that day
     when our bodies are raised,
     the Lord wipes away our tears,
     and we dwell forever
     in the presence of God.
     We will take our place
     in the new creation,
     where there will be
     no more death
     or mourning
     or crying
     or pain,
     and the Lord will be our light.
     Come, Lord Jesus, come.
          —from *Our World Belongs to God*, st. 55-56

4    Christ, while his disciples watched,
     was taken up from the earth into heaven.
     **He remains there on our behalf until he comes again**
     **to judge the living and the dead.**

     Christ is true human and true God.
     **In his human nature Christ is not now on earth;**
     **but in his divinity, majesty, grace, and Spirit**
     **he is never absent from us.**

     Christ is our advocate in heaven in the presence of his Father.
     **We have our own flesh in heaven**
     **as a sure pledge that Christ our head**
     **will also take us, his members, up to himself.**

     Christ sends his Spirit to us on earth as a corresponding pledge.
     **By the Spirit's power we seek not earthly things**
     **but the things above, where Christ is,**
     **sitting at God's right hand.**

     Christ is seated at the right hand of God
     to show there that he is head of his church,
     the one through whom the Father rules all things.
     **Through his Holy Spirit he pours out gifts**
     **from heaven upon us his members,**
     **and by his power he defends us and keeps us safe**
     **from all enemies.**

In all distress and persecution,
with uplifted head,
we confidently await the very judge
who has already offered himself to the judgment of God
in our place and removed the whole curse from us.
**Christ will cast all his enemies and ours
into everlasting condemnation,
but will take all his chosen ones to himself
into the joy and glory of heaven.**
—from Heidelberg Catechism, Q&A's 46-47, 49-52

5    Our ascended Lord gives hope for two ages.
In the age to come, Christ is the judge,
rejecting unrighteousness,
isolating God's enemies to hell,
blessing the new creation in Christ.
In this age, the Holy Spirit is with us,
calling nations to follow God's path,
uniting people through Christ in love.
—from *Our Song of Hope*, st. 5

6    This saying is sure and worthy of full acceptance:
**that Christ Jesus came into the world to save sinners.**
There is one God; there is one mediator
between God and humankind, Christ Jesus,
**who gave himself as a ransom for all, to whom we testify.**
Great indeed is the mystery of our religion:
**He was revealed in flesh,
vindicated in spirit,
seen by angels,
proclaimed among the nations,
believed in throughout the world,
taken up in glory.**
—based on 1 Timothy 1:15; 2:5-6; 3:16, NRSV

7    We declare with joy:
Christ suffered once for sins,
the righteous for the unrighteous,
to bring us to God.
He was put to death in the body
but made alive in the Spirit.
Now he has gone into heaven
and is at God's right hand—
with angels, authorities, and powers in submission to him.
—based on 1 Peter 3:18, 22

# O.4 PRAYERS OF THE PEOPLE

## O.4.4 Complete Model Outlines and Prayers (see also section 4.4)

*Prayer Outlines*

1  *The following is a guide for extemporaneous prayers. The pattern provides a suggested text for the opening and closing of each part of the prayer and calls for extemporaneous prayers of thanksgiving, petition, and intercession.*

Jesus Christ, mediator and high priest,
we thank you for becoming human and for experiencing
the joys and sorrows of life, which assures us that you are able
to sympathize and rejoice with us. We praise you for the many joys of life:
    for the beauty of creation, especially . . .
    for your work in this world . . .
    for the growth of your kingdom . . .
for the greatest source of our happiness, the gift of eternal life . . .

As our mediator, you stand before God, petitioning him on our behalf, so we boldly
bring before you our prayers for
    creation and its care . . .
    the nations of the world . . .
    our nation and its leaders . . .
    this community and those in authority . . .
    the church universal as it works on your behalf . . .
    this local church in its ministry . . .
    persons with particular needs. . . .

We pray this in your strong name, O Christ,
our mediator and high priest. **Amen.**

*Complete Prose Prayers*

2  Ascended Lord Jesus, help us to turn our thoughts toward you. We confess to you this Ascension Day that we so often fail to take you into account. Sometimes we do *not* set our minds upon you because of sheer laziness—it's easier just to go with society's flow. Sometimes we do not take you into account because of simple inattention—we just forget to look for ways in which we could serve your gospel in a given situation. At other times we have not turned *toward* you because we have actively and willfully decided to turn *away* from you.

When and where we fail to be transparent to your cosmic lordship, please forgive us. By your Spirit of Pentecost, sent to us precisely because you are reigning on high, help us to see this world the way you see it. From your exalted throne you are able to see us and this world and its many hurting people clearly and well. Help us to open our own eyes. Grant us vision and insight to view the people around us through the lens of your own compassion.

Sometimes, O God, we conceive of your lordship as regal, powerful, and perhaps a bit distant. We think your sovereign rule involves mostly quashing evil, pursuing justice, and judging sin. Remind us by your Spirit that your lordship is also about being close to people in need. Prod us to recall that in your kingdom, rulership comes through servanthood and that the hands that uphold our world are the pierced and tender hands of Jesus. Help us to remember (so that we may imitate this ourselves) that you see not just evil that needs judging but also suffering that needs ministry.

For you, O Lord, see the tears of the widowed, the sobs that overtake them when the rest of us are not looking. You see the disorientation in which so many people live every day—confusion borne of war, poverty, abuse, or chronic illness. You see the people in dead-end jobs who trudge to work every day filled with so much despair that they can hardly breathe. You see those who search a loved one's eyes for traces of love but find only an empty stare. As Lord of the earth, you spy every instance of one person cutting another to the quick, every place where a child lives in fear, every bar where someone tries to drown their sorrows.

Yet you are our world's every hope. You are tender enough to weep with those who weep and yet strong enough to lend comfort and not be consumed with the sorrows that overwhelm us. You are discerning enough to see where our lives run off the rails and yet gracious enough to forgive our foolishness and open again the better path that leads into your kingdom. You are the bright center to all of life, O God! Your lordship helps us glimpse our future with you in your kingdom, even as it points the way home.

Make us into people of the ascension, Christ Jesus! Make us your hands of mercy, your voice of grace, your presence of love. Whatever we do, whether in word or deed; whatever we see, whether sinful or salacious; whatever we hear, whether uplifting or depressing; whatever we face in this world, help us to face it in your power and with the knowledge of your grace and goodness. Help us to be gentle with prodigal children. Help us to be stalwart in the truth with people in love with lies. Help us to be radiant with hope with people who fear death. Help us to be your people, Lord God.

For today, as always, this world needs your shalom-filled presence. Bring peace to war-torn places and help people everywhere to see in one another your image. May those who delight in the paths of suicide and destruction be turned instead to delight in life and in mutual flourishing. End the terror in which so many live, and thwart the dreams of those who plot still more terror on the unsuspecting. Where there is hunger, bring bread; where there is drought and thirst, send refreshing rains; where there is hatred, bring your peace; where there is greed, bring your own fullness and so turn appetites run amok away from short-term pleasures toward things that last and that foster richness and plenty for all.

We are the people of your ascension and reign, Holy Christ of God. Whatever we do, help us never to forget who we are, whose we are, and where true joy may be found.

In the power and blessing of your name we pray. **Amen.**

3   Ascended Lord, we praise you.
    In your death you utterly wiped out the damning evidence
    of broken laws and commandments that always hung over our heads.
    You completely annulled it by nailing it over your head on the cross.
    In your resurrection you gave us new life, free life, full of new possibilities.
    In your ascension you paraded sin and death behind you
    in your triumphal procession.
    You are our guarantee of victory.
    You are our guarantee because you went through everything
    we struggle with and triumphed over all evil.
    What you did, you promised to help us do.
    You will always be with us—not merely with sympathy but also with power.
    You are our guarantee because it is truly "one of us"
    who now governs as ruler of time and space.
    This too gives us confidence and courage for the future.
    You are our guarantee because, in going away,
    you released the Spirit on us.
    You are not distant from us but closer to us than ever before.
    The current of the Spirit works over and through us endlessly.
    It seeps and trickles into all the depths of heart and mind and will
    so that truly we are like trees planted by water.
    We bear fruit in season, our leaves do not wither,
    and all that we do turns out well.
    We bring our hopes, our needs, our desires to you.
    We are confident of access because you are "one of us."
    We are confident of answers because you are the ruler of the universe.
    Yours is the name above every other name,
    the name before which every knee bows and every tongue confesses,
    "You are Lord," to the glory of God.
    Hear our prayers and accept our praises.
    May they rise like sweet-smelling incense before you
    from lives that are like altars set ablaze by the fire of the Spirit. **Amen.**
        —based on Psalm 1:3; Ephesians 2:5-6; Colossians 2:12-15; Philippians 2:10-11

4   Ascended Christ,
    how grateful we are that you ever live to pray for us,
    even now at God's right hand.
    We pray to you as Lord, and with you to the Father:
    Hallowed be your name.
    May your kingdom come.
    May your will be done.
    May all people have bread to nourish body and soul.
    May your people walk in the way of forgiveness
    and stand firm in the time of trial.
    May you, with the Father and the Spirit, receive all the glory. **Amen.**

# O.8 THE LORD'S SUPPER

**O.8.2 Great Prayer of Thanksgiving** (see section 8.2)

*O.8.2.2 Thanksgiving for the Work of God in Creation (see also section 8.2.2)*
*The following prayers offer thanks for the work of God in creation and may be included in the complete Prayer of Thanksgiving as found in section 8.2 of this book.*

1   With joy we praise you, gracious God,
    for you have created heaven and earth,
    made us in your image, and kept covenant with us—
    even when we fell into sin.
    We give you thanks for Jesus Christ, our Lord,
    who was exalted as King of the universe,
    that at the name of Jesus every knee shall bow.
    Therefore we join our voices
    with all the saints and angels and the whole creation
    to proclaim the glory of your name.

2   You raised up Christ to rule over all creation,
    giving him the name that is above all other names,
    that at the name of Jesus every knee shall bow.
    We praise you that, lifted in power,
    he lives and reigns forever in your glory
    and so fulfills his promise to be with us always
    to the end of time.

# O.9 CLOSING OF WORSHIP

**O.9.1 Sending** (see also section 9.1)

*Call to Service/Discipleship*

1   Why do you stand looking up toward heaven?
    This Jesus will come in the same way as you saw him go into heaven.
    **Alleluia!**

    Go and make disciples of all nations, says the Lord;
    I am with you always,
    to the end of time.
    **Alleluia!**
        —based on Matthew 28:19-20; Acts 1:11

*Closing Prayers*

2   Lord, help us not to dwell too much on the past,
    holding you to the Galilean hills and the streets of Jerusalem,
    but to know you more and more
    as our Lord and Savior,
    risen, ascended, and always present with us
    through the power of the Holy Spirit. **Amen.**

3   You said, "Peace be with you." And you breathed on your disciples,
    that they might receive the Holy Spirit and be able to go in peace.
    And so, victorious Lord, we pray to you:
    **Lord, hear us and give us your peace.**

    O Christ, after your resurrection you sent out your disciples to teach the nations,
    to baptize them in the name of the Father, the Son, and the Holy Spirit.
    You said you would be with them always, to the end of the age.
    And so, victorious Lord, we pray to you:
    **Lord, hear us, and send us out with your promise.**

    O Christ, exalted one, through your resurrection you have lifted us up,
    you have given gifts to us, you have sent your Spirit to us,
    that we might be equipped for service to a world that knows you not.
    And so, victorious Lord, we pray to you:
    **Lord, hear us, and distribute your gifts among us.**

    O Christ, exalted one, you are glorified by angels in heaven,
    you are honored and worshiped on earth,
    and all of history stands on tip-toe, eagerly awaiting the final day
    of your return, when you will make all things new.
    And so, victorious Lord, we pray to you:
    **Lord, hear us, and come again soon.**

    Our Father, grant that we may evermore
    live in the fullness of your power, filled with your peace,
    directed by your Spirit, and sent as Christ was sent.
    We ask this through Christ, our Lord,
    who lives and reigns with you and the Holy Spirit,
    one God, now and forever. **Amen.**

## O.9.2 Blessing/Benediction (see also section 9.2)

1   Grace and peace to you
    from him who is, and who was, and who is to come,
    and from the seven spirits before his throne,
    and from Jesus Christ, who is the faithful witness,
    the firstborn from the dead, and the ruler of the kings of the earth.
    To him who loves us and has freed us from our sins by his blood,
    and has made us to be a kingdom and priests to serve his God and Father—
    to him be glory and power for ever and ever! **Amen.**
        —Revelation 1:4-6, NIV

2    May the love of the cross,
the power of the resurrection,
and the presence of the living Lord
be with you always.
And the blessing of the eternal God,
creator and sustainer,
risen and ascended Lord and Savior,
giver of holiness and love,
be upon you now and evermore. **Amen.**

3    People of God, go now in peace, knowing that
if we suffer with Christ, we shall also rejoice with him;
if we die with Christ, we shall also rise with him.
Go in peace, letting your old self die with Christ,
and your new self, glorious with purpose and strength,
prepare for the great day of our ascended Lord's return.
Go in peace to love and serve the Lord. **Amen.**

# O.10 SUGGESTED SCRIPTURE READINGS

1    *Christ, the ascended Lord, as Prophet, Priest, King*

Hebrews 1:1-4: Jesus as prophet
John 14:5-21: Jesus shows the way to the Father
Acts 3:11-24: Peter testifies that Jesus is a prophet

Psalm 110: God's Anointed as Priest
Hebrews 4:14-5:10: Jesus intercedes on our behalf
Hebrews 7:11-29: Jesus, our High Priest

John 18:33-37: Jesus is King
Romans 10:5-13: Jesus is Lord
Philippians 2:1-11: Our humble King raised and exalted

# SECTION P
# CHRIST THE KING

Christ the King Sunday focuses our worship on the cosmic character of Christ's reign over the world. It is a proclamation to all that everything in creation and culture must submit to Christ and an invitation to actively and joyfully submit to his rule.

The day is celebrated widely in some traditions and is normally scheduled on the last Sunday before Advent. It therefore serves as a transitional Sunday leading directly into Advent, the Christmas cycle, and the new Christian year. The day fits well with the eschatological emphasis and anticipation of Christ's second coming highlighted during Advent. It also helps worshipers, who are already thinking about Christmas, to remember that Christmas is about much more than a baby in a manger—it is about a sovereign Christ who came to be the "Prince of Peace."

Whether or not this day is celebrated annually, the theme of Christ's lordship is central to the New Testament and to the faithful practice of Christian worship. The texts in this section are appropri-

ate for any service focusing on the lordship of Christ.

White is the customary color for Christ the King Sunday. Gold or some purple may also be appropriate to represent royalty. Symbols of royalty may be used, especially when combined with a cross.

*Note:* This section appears in this volume "out of order" in relation to the traditional structure of the Christian year because we are here following the structure of the Nicene Creed.

**Scriptures and Statements of Faith Applying to the Theme of Christ the King**

*The following texts are particularly appropriate for sermons or for supplemental liturgical use.*

| | | |
|---|---|---|
| 2 Samuel 23:1-7 | Psalm 100 | Ephesians 1:15-23 |
| Psalm 2 | Psalm 110 | Colossians 1:10-20 |
| Psalm 24 | Jeremiah 23:1-6 | 1 Timothy 6:11-16 |
| Psalm 93 | Daniel 7:9-10, 13-14 | 1 Peter 3:21-22 |
| Psalm 95 | Luke 1:68-79 | Revelation 1:4-8 |
| Psalm 97 | John 18:33-37 | Revelation 5 |
| Psalm 99 | 1 Corinthians 15:20-28 | Revelation 19:1-16 |

Belgic Confession, Art. 26, 37
Heidelberg Catechism, Q&A's 50-52
Westminster Confession, Chap. VIII, Sec. 7-8; Chap. XX, Sec. 4; Chap. XXXIII, Sec. 1-3
*Our Song of Hope,* st. 20-21
*Our World Belongs to God,* st. 1-2, 6, 27, 43, 55-58

# P.1 OPENING OF WORSHIP

### P.1.1 Preparation for Worship (see also section 1.1)

1 Lord God,
the words "Jesus is King" come easily to our lips,
yet we often fail to grasp the significance of what they mean for us.
In this service, help us worship you in spirit and truth,
and give us a vision for how we may live in homage to you
every day of our lives, through Christ, our Lord. **Amen.**

2 Lord God,
when we struggle to worship you as Lord,
show us again the beauty and power of your rule.
Teach us again that serving you is the path to true freedom.
May your Holy Spirit strengthen us today,
leading us to honor and worship you more deeply,
not only with the words we sing
but also with the lives we lead before your face,
through Jesus, our reigning Lord. **Amen.**

## P.1.2 Call to Worship (see also section 1.2)

1    Lift up your heads, you gates;
        be lifted up, you ancient doors,
        that the King of glory may come in.
    **Who is this King of glory?**
        **The LORD Almighty—**
        **he is the King of glory.**
           —Psalm 24:7-8, 10, NIV

2    O come, let us sing to the LORD;
        let us make a joyful noise to the rock of our salvation!
    **Let us come into his presence with thanksgiving;**
        **let us make a joyful noise to him with songs of praise!**
    **For the LORD is a great God,**
        **and a great King above all gods.**
    In his hand are the depths of the earth;
        the heights of the mountains are his also.
    The sea is his, for he made it,
        and the dry land, which his hands have formed.
    **O come, let us worship and bow down,**
        **let us kneel before the LORD, our Maker!**
    **For he is our God,**
        **and we are the people of his pasture,**
        **and the sheep of his hand.**
           —Psalm 95:1-7, NRSV

## P.1.4 Opening Responses (see also section 1.4)

*Prayers of Adoration*

1    You are worthy, our Lord and God,
        to receive glory and honor and power,
    for you created all things,
        and by your will they were created
        and have their being.
    Worthy is the Lamb, who was slain,
    to receive power and wealth and wisdom and strength
    and honor and glory and praise!
    To him who sits on the throne and to the Lamb
    be praise and honor and glory and power,
        for ever and ever! **Amen.**
           —Revelation 4:11; 5:12-13, NIV

2   Let us give thanks to the Lord our God.
    **It is right to give our thanks and praise.**
    We praise you, great God,
    for you are ruler of the universe
    and have sent your Son to be King of kings.
    We rejoice that he has triumphed over all the powers of this world
    and governs the nations in justice and righteousness.
    We celebrate his victory in his life, death, resurrection,
    and ascension to honor and might at your side.
    By your Spirit, claim our complete loyalty,
    establish Christ's rule in every land and in every heart.
    Accept our homage as we offer our lives
    in the service of Christ's kingdom.
    He is Lord forever and ever. **Amen.**

*Prayers of Invocation*

3   Almighty and everlasting God,
    you have willed to restore all things
    in your well-beloved Son, our Lord and King.
    Grant that the people of earth,
    now divided and enslaved by sin,
    may be freed and brought together
    under the gentle and loving rule of Christ,
    who lives and reigns with you and the Holy Spirit,
    one God, now and forever. **Amen.**

4   Eternal God,
    you set Jesus Christ to rule over all things
    and made us servants in your kingdom.
    By your Spirit empower us to love the unloved
    and to minister to all in need.
    Then at the last bring us into your eternal realm,
    where we may worship and adore you
    and be welcomed into your everlasting joy,
    through Jesus Christ, our Lord,
    who lives and reigns with you in the unity of the Holy Spirit,
    one God, forever and ever. **Amen.**

5   God and Father of our Lord Jesus Christ,
    you gave us your Son,
    the beloved one who was rejected,
    the Savior who appeared defeated.
    Yet the mystery of his kingship illumines our lives.
    Show us in his death the victory that crowns the ages,
    and in his broken body the love that unites heaven and earth.
    We ask this through your Son, our Lord Jesus Christ,

who lives and reigns with you in the unity of the Holy Spirit,
one God, forever and ever. **Amen.**

*Additional Resources*

6    The LORD reigns, he is robed in majesty;
         **the LORD is robed in majesty**
         **and armed with strength;**
     indeed, the world is established,
         firm and secure.
     **Your throne was established long ago;**
         **you are from all eternity.**
     Your statutes, LORD, stand firm;
         **holiness adorns your house**
         **for endless days**.
             —Psalm 93:1-2, 5, NIV

7    Mighty and tender God,
     voice of the voiceless,
     power of the powerless:
     we praise you for your vision
     of a community of wholeness,
     a realm of peace,
     in which all who hunger and thirst are nourished,
     in which the stranger is welcomed,
     the hurting are healed,
     and the captive is set free.
     Guide us by your truth and love
     until we and all your people
     make manifest your reign of justice and compassion.
     We pray in the name of your anointed one, our servant-king,
     to whom with you and the Spirit, one Holy God,
     be honor, glory, and blessing,
     this day and forever. **Amen.**

8    Grace and peace to you
     from him who is and who was and who is to come.
     **All praise to you, God of all, for your blessing upon us now,**
     **for your blessing upon us in what has been**
     **and for the gifts of grace and peace you wait to give us.**
     To him who loves us and has freed us from our sins by his blood,
     and made us to be a kingdom, priests serving his God and Father,
     to him be glory and dominion forever and ever.
     **All praise to you, Jesus Christ, for your great love for us,**
     **for giving yourself to us, and for bringing us back to the Father.**
     Look! He is coming with the clouds; every eye will see him.
     **Lord Jesus, we look in expectant hope**

to the day of your great glory
and wait with eager breath
to join with all creation in your praise.
"I am the Alpha and Omega," says the Lord God, "who is and who was and who is
to come, the Almighty."
Amen! Blessing and glory and wisdom and thanksgiving and honor and power
and might be to our God forever and ever! Amen.
—based on Revelation 1:4-8; 7:12

9    We give you thanks, O God, for revealing your love in creation:
we bless your holy name.
For human beings made in your image
and called to live in your communion,
we bless your holy name.
For the promise of your reign in justice and peace, in holiness and charity,
we bless your holy name.
For the revelation of your kingdom in our midst
through your Son, Jesus Christ,
we bless your holy name.
For his humble birth and his holy life, for his words and his miracles,
we bless your holy name.
For his sufferings and his death, for his resurrection and his entry into glory,
we bless your holy name.
For your church, called to be a place of communion for every human being,
we bless your holy name.
For the coming of your kingdom within us by the gift of the Holy Spirit,
we bless your holy name.
By the coming of your kingdom at the end of time,
when you will be all in all,
we bless your holy name.

# P.2 CONFESSION AND ASSURANCE

## P.2.2 Prayers of Confession (see also section 2.2)

1    Righteous God,
you have crowned Jesus Christ as Lord of all.
We confess that we have not bowed before him
and are slow to acknowledge his rule.
We give allegiance to the powers of this world
and fail to be governed by justice and love.

In your mercy, forgive us.
Raise us to acclaim him as ruler of all,
that we may be loyal ambassadors,
obeying the commands of our Lord Jesus Christ.

## P.2.4 Assurance of Pardon (see also section 2.4)

1    Do not weep!
See, the Lion of the tribe of Judah, the Root of David, has triumphed.
With his blood he has purchased people for God
     from every tribe and language and people and nation.
He has made them to be a kingdom and priests to serve our God,
     and they will reign on the earth.
**Thanks be to God!**
       —based on Revelation 5:5, 9-10, NIV

# P.3 PROCLAIMING THE WORD

## P.3.1 Prayers for Illumination (see also section 3.1)

1    O God Most High!
Everlasting Lord, mighty and lifted up!
Grant to us your Holy Spirit,
that in these words of Holy Scripture
our hearts might be lifted up
and our minds set on heavenly realities,
that contemplating the reign of our ascended Lord
we might long to be with him
and enter into the joy of his eternal kingdom.
Through Jesus Christ our Lord, **Amen.**

## P.3.6 Profession of Our Church's Faith (see also section 3.6)

1    Jesus Christ has been ordained by God the Father
and has been anointed with the Holy Spirit
to be our chief prophet and teacher
     who fully reveals to us
     the secret counsel and will of God concerning our deliverance;
our only high priest

who has delivered us by the one sacrifice of his body,
and who continually pleads our cause with the Father;
and our eternal king
who governs us by his Word and Spirit,
and who guards us and keeps us in the freedom he has won for us.
He ascended to heaven
to show there that he is head of his church,
the one through whom the Father rules all things.

In all distress and persecution,
with uplifted head,
we confidently await the very judge
who has already offered himself to the judgment of God
in our place and removed the whole curse from us.
Christ will cast all his enemies and ours
into everlasting condemnation,
but will take all his chosen ones to himself
into the joy and glory of heaven.

> —from Heidelberg Catechism, Q&A's 31, 50, 52

2   As followers of Jesus Christ,
living in this world—
which some seek to control,
and others view with despair—
we declare with joy and trust:
Our world belongs to God!

From the beginning,
through all the crises of our times,
until the kingdom fully comes,
God keeps covenant forever:
Our world belongs to God!
God is King! Let the earth be glad!
Christ is victor: his rule has begun!
The Spirit is at work: creation is renewed!
Hallelujah! Praise the Lord!

Jesus ascended in triumph,
raising our humanity to the heavenly throne.
All authority, glory, and sovereign power are given to him.
There he hears our prayers
and pleads our cause before the Father.
Blessed are all who take refuge in him.

Our hope for a new creation is not tied
to what humans can do,
for we believe that one day
every challenge to God's rule will be crushed.
His kingdom will fully come,
and our Lord will rule.
Come, Lord Jesus, come.

> —*Our World Belongs to God*, st. 1-2, 27, 55

# P.4 PRAYERS OF THE PEOPLE

**P.4.4 Complete Model Outlines and Prayers** (see also section 4.4)

*Prayer Outlines*

1   *The following is a guide for extemporaneous prayers. The pattern provides a suggested text for the opening and closing of each part of the prayer and calls for extemporaneous prayers of thanksgiving, petition, and intercession.*

Sovereign King,
we praise you for your just and righteous reign over the cosmos:
    for the order you give to creation . . .
    for your sovereign rule over the nations . . .
    for your faithfulness to your church . . .
    for your lordship in our lives . . .

You are at once King and servant, willing to give your life
and caring even for what we might count as insignificant.
So we approach your throne knowing you will listen to our prayers
    for creation and its care . . .
    for the nations of the world . . .
    for our nation and its leaders . . .
    for this community and those who are in authority . . .
    for the church universal as it works on your behalf . . .
    for this local church in its ministry . . .
    for persons with particular needs . . .

We pray in your name, O Christ, our sovereign servant King. **Amen.**

*Prayers in Litany Form*

2   That each of us will understand
that our ordinary lives are pleasing to Christ, our King,
Lord in your mercy,
**hear our prayer.**
That all leaders in government will realize
that the ordinary people in our country are important,
Lord in your mercy,
**hear our prayer.**
For all those people who are very ordinary but also are extraordinary
because of the way they care for God's people,
Lord in your mercy,
**hear our prayer.**
For people who are sick
and unable to do the ordinary things they used to do,

that they will be patient with themselves and with those who care for them,
Lord in your mercy,
**hear our prayer.**
For people whose lives are recorded in our newspapers and magazines,
Lord in your mercy,
**hear our prayer.**
Father, hear our prayers and the prayers of all your people.
Help us to be faithful in ordinary ways,
loving and caring for your people whom we meet every day.
We ask this through Jesus, your Son and our King. **Amen.**

# P.5 OFFERING

## P.5.2 Offering Prayers (see also section 5.2)

1    Lord God, heavenly King,
we offer these our gifts
as a sign of love, devotion, and praise.
Through these, as through our praises,
we acknowledge that you are our Lord.
In your name we pray. **Amen.**

# P.8 THE LORD'S SUPPER

## P.8.2 Great Prayer of Thanksgiving (see section 8.2)

*P.8.2.2 Thanksgiving for the Work of God in Creation (see also section 8.2.2)*
*The following prayer offers thanks for the work of God in creation and may be included in the complete Prayer of Thanksgiving as found in section 8.2 of this book.*

1    Lead us, O God, to conform this world
to your kingdom of love, justice, and peace.

Help us to live as the Lord requires:
to do justice,
to love kindness,
and to walk humbly with you, our God.
Keep us faithful in your service
until Christ comes in final victory
and we shall feast with all your saints
in the joy of your eternal realm.
Through Christ, with Christ, in Christ,
in the unity of the Holy Spirit,
all glory and honor are yours, almighty God,
now and forever. **Amen.**

# P.9 CLOSING OF WORSHIP

## P.9.1 Sending (see also section 9.1)

*Call to Service/Discipleship*

1   Jesus says:
    "All authority in heaven and on earth has been given to me.
    Therefore go and make disciples of all nations, baptizing them
    in the name of the Father and of the Son and of the Holy Spirit,
    and teaching them to obey everything I have commanded you.
    And surely I will be with you always, to the very end of the age." **Amen.**
        —from Matthew 28:18-20, NIV

2   In the presence of God, who gives life to all things,
    and of Christ Jesus, who in his testimony
    before Pontius Pilate made the good confession,
    I charge you to keep the commandment without spot or blame
    until the manifestation of our Lord Jesus Christ,
    which he will bring about at the right time—
    he who is the blessed and only Sovereign,
    the King of kings and Lord of lords.
    It is he alone who has immortality and dwells in unapproachable light,
    whom no one has ever seen or can see;
    to him be honor and eternal dominion. **Amen.**
        —1 Timothy 6:13-16, NRSV

## Acclamations/Doxologies

3 Now to the King eternal,
immortal, invisible, the only God,
be honor and glory for ever and ever. **Amen.**
—1 Timothy 1:17, NIV

4 To him who is able to keep you from stumbling
and to present you before his glorious presence
without fault and with great joy—
to the only God our Savior be glory, majesty, power and authority,
through Jesus Christ our Lord,
before all ages, now and forevermore! **Amen.**
—Jude 24-25, NIV

## Closing Prayers

5 Almighty and merciful God,
through your well-beloved Son, Jesus Christ,
the King of kings and Lord of lords,
you have willed to make all things new.
Grant that we may be renewed by your Holy Spirit
and may come at last to that heavenly country
where your people hunger and thirst no more
and the tears are wiped away from every eye,
through Jesus Christ, our Lord. **Amen.**

6 All-powerful God,
your only Son came to earth in the form of a slave
and is now enthroned at your right hand,
where he rules in glory.
As he reigns as King in our hearts,
may we rejoice in his peace,
glory in his justice, and live in his love.
For with you and the Holy Spirit
he rules now and for ever. **Amen.**

## P.9.2 Blessing/Benediction (see also section 9.2)

1 Grace to you and peace
from him who is and who was and who is to come,
and from the seven spirits who are before his throne,
and from Jesus Christ, the faithful witness,
the firstborn of the dead, and the ruler of the kings of the earth.
To him who loves us and freed us from our sins by his blood,
and made us to be a kingdom, priests serving his God and Father,
to him be glory and dominion forever and ever. **Amen.**
—Revelation 1:4-6, NRSV

# P.10 SUGGESTED SCRIPTURE READINGS

1   *Lordship of Christ*

Psalm 24: King of glory
Isaiah 9: Prince of Peace
Daniel 7:9-10, 13-14: Son of Man
Colossians 1:11-20: Firstborn over all creation
Revelation 1:4-8: Ruler of the kings of the earth

2   *The kingdom of our Lord*

Psalm 72: A kingdom of blessing
Isaiah 11: A peaceable kingdom
John 18:33-37: A kingdom not of this world
Romans 14:17: A kingdom of righteousness, peace, and joy in the Holy Spirit
Revelation 21:1-27: No more mourning, crying, pain

3   *Jesus reigning and praying at God's right hand*

Psalm 110; Matthew 22:41-46: Praise for the messianic ruler
Daniel 7:9-10, 13-14: The Son of Man with the "Ancient of Days"
Matthew 26:59-66: Jesus' prophecy of his session at God's right hand
Acts 7:55: Stephen's vision of the ascended Lord
Romans 8:34: Jesus intercedes for us
Hebrews 7:25: Jesus ever lives to pray for us
Hebrews 10:11-14: The Priest at God's right hand
1 Peter 3:18-22: Every authority and power submits to Christ

4   *Psalms of praise to both the God of Israel and Jesus Christ, the King*

Psalm 95: Come, let us sing for joy
Psalm 96: Sing to the LORD a new song
Psalm 97: The LORD reigns
Psalm 98: The LORD judges the world in righteousness
Psalm 99: The mighty King who loves justice
Psalm 100: Praise for the shepherd King

# PENTECOST

Ten days after the ascension of Christ and fifty days after his resurrection, the Holy Spirit descended on the disciples on the day of Pentecost. Pentecost was an established Jewish festival also known as the Feast of Weeks, which drew people from many nations back to Jerusalem (Lev. 23:15-21; Deut. 16:16).

Pentecost symbolizes a new beginning. It celebrates the unleashing of the Holy Spirit on the world and the empowering of the church to reach the world with the gospel. In celebrating Pentecost, the church expresses its gratitude for the faithfulness of Christ in fulfilling his promise to send "another counselor" (John 14:16); celebrates the work of the Spirit in renewing all of creation; professes its confidence and security in knowing the Spirit's power is available for its

mission; and grows in awareness of the immensity of its calling to reach the world with the gospel.

The traditional color for Pentecost is red, after the flames described in Acts 2:3.

**Scriptures and Statements of Faith Applying to the Theme of Pentecost**

*The following texts are particularly appropriate for sermons or for supplemental liturgical use.*

| | | |
|---|---|---|
| Genesis 1:1-2 | John 3 | Romans 5:1-5 |
| Numbers 11:24-30 | John 7:37-39 | Romans 8 |
| Psalm 51 | John 14:8-27 | Romans 15:13 |
| Psalm 104 | John 15:18-16:4 | 1 Corinthians 2 |
| Isaiah 61:1-4 | John 16:4-15 | 1 Corinthians 6:12-20 |
| Ezekiel 37:1-14 | John 20:19-23 | 1 Corinthians 12:1-13 |
| Joel 2 | Acts 2:1-41 | Galatians 4:1-7 |
| Luke 11:9-13 | Acts 4:23-31 | Ephesians 1:13-14 |

Belgic Confession, Art. 11
Heidelberg Catechism, Q&A's 49, 51, 53
Canons of Dort, Pt. III/IV, Art. 11-12
*Our Song of Hope,* st. 6-14
*Our World Belongs to God,* st. 28-30

# Q.1 OPENING OF WORSHIP

### Q.1.1 Preparation for Worship (see also section 1.1)

1   God of life,
    as we prepare for worship today,
    help us not to take lightly the highly charged message we proclaim.
    Help us sense the power, beauty, and mission of your Spirit.
    Through Christ, our Lord, **Amen.**

2   Lord God,
    especially today as we remember the coming of your Spirit,
    teach those of us who lead worship not to rely on our own strength
    to make worship meaningful and inspiring.
    Rather, give us joy and freedom in knowing that worship is a gift
    made possible by the work of your Holy Spirit.
    Through Christ, our Lord, **Amen.**

## Q.1.2 Call to Worship (see also section 1.2)

1    God will pour out the Spirit on all flesh,
and our daughters and sons shall prophesy.
Our old ones shall dream dreams,
and our young ones shall see visions;
and all who call upon the name of the Lord shall be delivered.
**Come, let us call upon the name of the Lord.**
       —based on Acts 2:17-21

2    *A text particularly mindful of children*

This is the day that the Lord has made.
**Let us rejoice and be glad in it!**
This is the day when the Spirit came.
**Let us rejoice and be glad in it!**
And again I say—
**Rejoice!**
       —based on Psalm 118:24; Philippians 4:4

3    The love of God has been poured into our hearts
through the Holy Spirit who has been given to us;
**we dwell in him and he in us.**
Give thanks to the Lord and call upon his name;
**make known his deeds among the peoples.**
Sing to him, sing praises to him,
**and speak of all his marvelous works.**
Holy, holy, holy is the Lord God Almighty,
**who was and is and is to come!**
       —based on Psalm 105:1-2; Romans 5:5; Revelation 4:8

4    By sending down a confusion of languages,
the Most High scattered the nations.
By distributing the tongues of fire,
God calls all peoples into unity.
**In harmony we glorify the Holy Spirit.**
In the sound of a mighty wind rushing from the heavens,
the Most High trumpets good news over the earth.
And those who once cast nets to fish in the sea
now cast your Word to fish among people.
**We worship and glorify the Holy Spirit.**
**May the Savior who opens the gates of paradise**
**open our hearts to wisdom and truth.**

5    The God of the whirlwind and fire
sweeps into our presence in this hour.
Glory be to God, who strengthens us
**and blesses all people with peace.**
God, who called all the world into being,
calls forth new life in us today.

**Glory be to God, in whose creative
purpose we are claimed and empowered.**
God, whose Spirit unites all people in a common language of love,
confirms God's gifts in us as we gather here.
**Glory be to God, who created light in which
we can walk in confident expectation.**

6    The Spirit gathers us to worship God
     and builds us up in faith, hope, and love
     so that we may go into the world to proclaim the gospel
     and work for justice and peace.
     Let us worship God together.

## Q.1.4 Opening Responses (see also section 1.4)

*Prayers of Invocation*

1    Come, Creator Spirit, and move over this chaotic world.
     **Come, Creator Spirit, and bring life to this world.**
     Come, Creator Spirit, and move over the chaos of our lives.
     **Come, Creator Spirit, and bring us new life. Amen.**

2    Spirit of the living God, visit us again on this day of Pentecost.
     **Come, Holy Spirit.**
     Like a rushing wind that sweeps away all barriers,
     **come, Holy Spirit.**
     Like tongues of fire that set our hearts aflame,
     **come, Holy Spirit.**
     With speech that unites the Babel of our tongues,
     **come, Holy Spirit.**
     With love that overlaps the boundaries of race and nation,
     **come, Holy Spirit.**
     With power from above to make our weakness strong,
     **come, Holy Spirit. Amen.**

3    Holy Spirit, Lord and giver of life:
     At the beginning of time you moved over the face of the waters;
     you gave every living thing the breath of life.
     **Come, Creator Spirit, and renew the whole creation.**
     Holy Spirit, voice of the prophets:
     You enflame men and women with a passion for your truth,
     and through them you call your people
     to the ways of justice and compassion.
     **Come, Spirit of righteousness, and burn in our hearts.**
     Holy Spirit, Spirit of Jesus:
     By your power Jesus came to bring good news to the poor
     and release to those held captive.

Come, liberating Spirit, and free us
from the powers of sin and death.
Holy Spirit, Advocate, Teacher:
You speak to us of our Lord
and show us the depth of his love.
Come, Spirit of truth, abide in us
and lead us in the way of Jesus Christ.
Holy Spirit, wind and flame:
You filled disciples with joy and courage,
empowering them to preach your Word
and to share your good news.
Come, Spirit of power, make us bold witnesses
of your redeeming love.
Holy Spirit, Spirit of peace:
You break down barriers of language, race, and culture
and heal the divisions that separate us.
Come, reconciling Spirit, and unite us all in the love of Christ.
Holy Spirit, Lord and giver of life:
At the close of the age
all creation will be renewed to sing your praises.
Come, Creator Spirit, and make us new creations
in Jesus Christ. Amen.

4    Come, Holy Spirit, renew the whole creation.
Send the wind and flame of your transforming life
to lift up the church in this day.
Give us wisdom and faith, that we may know
the great hope to which we are called.
Come, Holy Spirit.
Giver of life, sustain your creation.
Confront us with our greedy consuming of your gifts.
Stand before us as we pillage and destroy.
Call us forth into new harmonies of care
for all who live and breathe and have their being.
Come, Holy Spirit.
Spirit of truth, set us free to emerge as the children of God.
Open our ears, that we may hear the weeping of the world.
Open our mouths, that we may be a voice for the voiceless.
Open our eyes, that we may see your vision of peace and justice.
Make us alive with the courage and faith of your prophetic truth.
Come, Holy Spirit.
Spirit of unity, reconcile your people.
Give us the wisdom to hold to what we need to be your church.
Give us the grace to lay down those things that you can do without.
Give us a vision of your breadth and length and height
to challenge our smallness of heart and bring us humbly together.
Come, Holy Spirit.

Holy Spirit, transform us and sanctify us
as we take up this task in your name.
Give us the gifts we need to be your church in spirit and truth.
**Come, Holy Spirit. Amen.**

5    Loving God and Father of our Lord Jesus Christ,
we thank and praise you for raising Jesus from the dead,
the firstfruits of your new creation,
and for sending your Spirit, that we too
may have new life in Christ.
**Thank you for giving us your Spirit.**

We thank and praise you
for the power and promise of your Holy Spirit
to lead and guide us in all our ways.
Help us live in accordance with your Spirit,
setting our minds on what the Spirit desires,
so that we may be joyfully alive in Christ.
**Thank you for giving us your Spirit.**

We thank and praise you that the Spirit testifies to us
that we are your children and that through the Spirit
we can approach you in confidence as our compassionate Father.
Thank you that as co-heirs with Christ, we will share in his glory.
Comfort us with the knowledge that your Spirit also helps us in our weakness
and intercedes for us according to your will.
**Thank you for giving us your Spirit.**

In the name of Jesus Christ,
who lives and reigns with you and the Spirit,
one God, now and forever, **Amen.**

6    Blessed be our God at all times,
now and always and forever and ever. Amen.

**Glory to you, our God! Glory to you!**
**Holy Spirit, Lord and Comforter,**
**Spirit of truth everywhere present, filling all that exists,**
**treasury of good gifts and source of life, come and dwell in us;**
**cleanse us from all sin and in your love bring us to salvation:**
**God, holy; God, strong and holy;**
**God, holy and immortal; have pity on us. Amen.**

7    *A prayer especially mindful of children*

God in heaven,
you surprised and amazed your disciples at Pentecost
with the gift of the Holy Spirit.
We praise you for the Spirit
who still fills our lives and hearts.
Send your mighty Spirit on us as we worship;
fill us with joy and excitement. **Amen.**

8    Holy Spirit, Creator,
     at the beginning you hovered over the waters;
     you breathe life into all creatures.
     **Come into us, Holy Spirit.**
     Holy Spirit, Comforter,
     by you we are born again as children of God;
     you make us living temples of your presence;
     you pray within us with prayers too deep for words.
     **Come into us, Holy Spirit.**
     Holy Spirit, Lord and giver of life,
     you are light, you bring us light;
     you are goodness and the source of all goodness.
     **Come into us, Holy Spirit.**
     Holy Spirit, breath of life,
     you sanctify and breathe life into the whole body of the church;
     you dwell in each one of its members,
     and you will one day give new life to our mortal bodies.
     **Come into us, Holy Spirit. Amen.**

9    Come, Spirit God, Creator blest,
     and in our hearts take up your rest;
     come with your grace and heavenly aid
     to fill the lives which you have made.

     O Comforter, to you we cry,
     O heavenly gift of God Most High,
     O fount of life and spark of love,
     anoint us with fire from above.

     You bless us with gifts sevenfold,
     inspiring Christians to be bold,
     for you, the promised breath of God,
     help us to speak Christ's name abroad.

     Kindle our senses from above,
     and make our hearts o'erflow with love;
     with patience firm and virtue high
     the weakness of our flesh supply.

     Drive far from us the foe we dread,
     and grant to us your peace instead;
     so shall we not, with you as guide,
     turn from the path of life aside.

     O Spirit God, through you alone
     know we the Father and the Son;
     for we confess in ancient creed
     that you from both of them proceed.

     Praise to the Father and the Son
     and Holy Spirit with them one;

to whom all honor, glory be
for now and for eternity. **Amen.**

> —based on "Veni Creator Spiritus"; the entire text may be sung to OLD HUNDRETH or other LM [Long Meter] tunes, identified in most hymnals in a metrical tune index.

**10** The Spirit of the Lord shall rest upon us:
a spirit of wisdom and understanding.
**Strengthen us with your gifts**
**of wisdom and understanding, Holy Spirit.**
The Spirit of the Lord shall rest upon us:
a spirit of right judgment and courage.
**Strengthen us with your gifts**
**of right judgment and courage, Holy Spirit.**
The Spirit of the Lord shall rest upon us:
a spirit of knowledge and reverence.
**Strengthen us with your gifts**
**of knowledge and reverence, Holy Spirit.**
The Spirit of the Lord shall rest upon us:
a spirit of wonder and awe in the presence of the living God.
**Strengthen us with your gifts**
**of wonder and awe, Holy Spirit. Amen.**

> —based on Isaiah 11:2

**11** Wind of God, blow far from us
   all dark despair,
   all deep distress,
   all groundless fears,
   all sinful desires,
   all Satan's snares,
   all false values,
   all selfish wishes,
   all wasteful worries.
Blow into us
   your holy presence,
   your living love,
   your healing touch,
   your splendid courage,
   your mighty strength,
   your perfect peace,
   your caring concern,
   your divine grace,
   your boundless joy.
Wind of God, blow strong, blow fresh, blow now. **Amen.**

**12** Holy Spirit, you are the fire of holiness
that surrounds the throne of God.
You burn away our sin and blindness;
you fill us with the beauty and purity of Jesus, our Lord. **Amen.**

13 Almighty and Holy Spirit, our Comforter,
pure, living, true—illumine, govern, sanctify us,
and confirm our hearts and minds
in the faith and in all genuine consolation;
preserve and rule over us so that,
dwelling in the house of the Lord all the days of our lives,
we may behold the Lord and praise him with joyful spirit,
in union with all the heavenly church. **Amen.**

# Q.2 CONFESSION AND ASSURANCE

## Q.2.1 Call to Confession (see also section 2.1)

1 Jesus said, "If you love me, you will obey what I command.
and I will ask the Father, and he will give you another Counselor
to be with you forever—the Spirit of truth.
Whoever has my commands and obeys them,
he is the one who loves me.
He who loves me will be loved by my Father,
and I too will love him and show myself to him."
Let us confess our sin to God.
—based on John 14:15-17, 21, NIV

2 Do not marvel that Jesus says to us, "You must be born again."
What is born of the flesh is flesh, and what is born of the Spirit is spirit.
The wind blows where it wills, and you hear the sound of it,
but you do not know where it comes from or where it goes;
so it is with everyone who is born of the Spirit,
who convicts us of sin and leads us into all righteousness.
Let us confess our sin to God.
—based on John 3:6-8; 16:8, NRSV

3 The Spirit of the Lord fills the world
and knows our every word and deed.
Let us then open ourselves to the Lord
and confess our sins in penitence and faith.

### Q.2.2 Prayers of Confession (see also section 2.2)

1    Almighty God,
to you all hearts are open, all desires known,
and from you no secrets are hid.
Cleanse the thoughts of our hearts
by the inspiration of your Holy Spirit,
that we may perfectly love you
and worthily magnify your holy name,
through Christ, our Lord. **Amen.**

2    *A prayer especially mindful of children*

Holy Spirit,
you are so full of energy
you are like fire.
And like fire
you came upon the disciples at Pentecost.
But our lives this past week
have not blazed with your Spirit.
Forgive us, we pray,
and fill us with your Spirit.
Come down, O Spirit,
fill us and set us on fire. **Amen.**

3    Come, Holy Spirit!
Rain upon our dry and dusty lives.
Wash away our sin
and heal our wounded spirits.
Kindle within us the fire of your love
to burn away our apathy.
With your warmth bend our rigidity
and guide our wandering feet. **Amen.**

4    The Spirit of the Lord fills the world
and knows our every word and deed.
Let us then open ourselves to the Lord
and confess our sins in penitence and faith.
You raise the dead to life in the Spirit:
Lord, have mercy.
**Lord, have mercy.**
You bring pardon and peace to the broken in heart:
Christ, have mercy.
**Christ, have mercy.**
You make one by your Spirit the torn and divided:
Lord, have mercy.
**Lord, have mercy. Amen.**

5    Generous God,
     you send us the Spirit of courage,
     but we have been afraid.
     You send us the Spirit of truth,
     but we cling to our illusions.
     You send us the Spirit of healing,
     but we cannot let go of our hurts.
     Holy Spirit of forgiveness, come to us again:
     shake our hearts,
     set our souls on fire with your love:
     send us out into the world
     rejoicing in your power.
     We hold out to you
     all our particular burdens of guilt and sin,
     and we ask for your help
     to live the way of your justice and love. **Amen.**

6    Sovereign Lord,
     you have anointed us with your Spirit,
     yet we have not shared your great gift.
     **Create in us a clean heart, O God.**
     **Restore to us the joy of your salvation.**
     We have not proclaimed your good news to the poor.
     We have not bound up the brokenhearted.
     **Create in us a clean heart, O God.**
     **Restore to us the joy of your salvation.**
     We have not proclaimed your freedom to the captives.
     We have not comforted those who mourn.
     **Create in us a clean heart, O God.**
     **Restore to us the joy of your salvation.**
     Forgive us for closing our eyes to the needs of others.
     Forgive us for limiting your abundance.
     **Create in us a clean heart, O God.**
     **Restore to us the joy of your salvation.**
     Open our minds, Lord. Open our hearts, Lord.
     Open our hands, Lord. Open our lips, Lord.
     **Give us a willing spirit to show your love to your world. Amen.**
       —based on Psalm 51; Isaiah 61

7    Gracious God,
     who pours out freely the gift of your Holy Spirit:
     we confess before you and to each other
     that we have failed to recognize this most precious gift.
     We have been satisfied with ordinary things,
     suspicious of unfamiliar things,
     and blind to spiritual things.
     Cleanse us, O God, with your celestial fire.

Burn away our presumptuous self-sufficiency,
and open us in faith to receive the renewing touch of your hand. **Amen.**

8    Burn in us this morning, Holy Spirit.
We give you the places of our hearts
that have been choked by the cares of this world.
We give you our tiredness, our sin, our struggles with apathy.
We await your fiery cleansing. **Amen.**

9    Our God, we come in humility, confessing who and what we are.
We are often unresponsive, for we are afraid.
When your Spirit speaks, we turn deaf ears,
for we fear what you might call us to do.
When your Spirit touches our lips,
we close our mouths,
embarrassed to speak your Word.
When the wind of your Spirit blows,
we close the windows of our hearts,
afraid the breeze will disrupt our ordered lives.
When the fire of your Spirit touches us,
we quench the flame, afraid of the new life it might bring.
Forgive us, O Lord. **Amen.**

10   Almighty God,
who sent the promised power of the Holy Spirit
to fill disciples with willing faith:
We confess that we resist the force of your Spirit among us,
that we are slow to serve you
and reluctant to spread the good news of your love.
God, have mercy on us.
Forgive our divisions
and by your Spirit draw us together.
Inflame us with a desire to do your will
and be your faithful people
for the sake of your Son, our Lord, Jesus Christ. **Amen.**

11   Almighty God, you poured out your Spirit upon gathered disciples
creating bold tongues, open ears, and a new community of faith.
We confess that we hold back the force of your Spirit among us.
We do not listen for your word of grace,
speak the good news of your love,
or live as a people made one in Christ.
Have mercy on us, O God.
Transform our timid lives by the power of your Spirit
and fill us with a flaming desire to be your faithful people,
doing your will for the sake of Jesus Christ, our Lord. **Amen.**

## Q.2.4 Assurance of Pardon (see also section 2.4)

1    "I will take you out of the nations;
I will gather you from all the countries.
I will sprinkle clean water on you, and you will be clean.
I will give you a new heart and put a new spirit in you;
I will remove from you your heart of stone and give you a heart of flesh.
And I will put my Spirit in you and move you to follow my decrees.
You will be my people, and I will be your God."

Friends in Christ: by the power of the Spirit,
we are united with Christ and given a new spirit.
Live in the joy and peace of that assurance.
> —based on Ezekiel 36:24-28, NIV

2    Since we have been justified through faith,
we have peace with God through our Lord Jesus Christ,
through whom we have gained access by faith
into this grace in which we now stand.
And we boast in the hope of the glory of God.
And hope does not put us to shame,
because God's love has been poured out into our hearts
through the Holy Spirit, who has been given to us.
> —Romans 5:1-2, 5, NIV

3    There is now no condemnation for those who are in Christ Jesus,
because through Christ Jesus the law of the Spirit of life
sets us free from the law of sin and death.
And if the Spirit of God who raised Jesus from the dead lives in us,
God who raised Christ from the dead will also give life to our mortal bodies
through the Spirit, who lives in us.
> —from Romans 8:1-2, 11, NIV

4    All the promises of God find their "Yes" in Christ.
That is why we utter the "Amen" through him, to the glory of God.
It is God who has put his seal upon us
and given us his Spirit in our hearts as a guarantee.

In Christ, by the power of the Spirit, we are redeemed.
Praise God, from whom all blessings flow!
> —based on 2 Corinthians 1:20-22

5    In Christ you were marked with the Holy Spirit,
a seal of our redemption in Christ.
By the power of the Holy Spirit
we become dead in sin and alive anew in Christ.
May you be filled with the Holy Spirit
so that you may have hope of new life,
may grow in your knowledge of the God of our Lord Jesus Christ,
and may experience the incomparable power of God
that raised our Lord Jesus Christ from the dead.

# Q.3 PROCLAIMING THE WORD

### Q.3.1 Prayers for Illumination (see also section 3.1)

1    Lord, open our hearts and minds
     by the power of your Holy Spirit,
     that as the Scriptures are read
     and your Word is proclaimed,
     we may hear with joy what you say to us today. **Amen.**

2    Lord of heaven and earth,
     pour out on us the abundant gifts of your Holy Spirit.
     May the work begun by the Spirit on the day of Pentecost
     continue in us as we hear your Word and do your will. **Amen.**

3    O God whom we long to know,
     burning fire within our souls,
     grant to us the tongues like fire,
     the sound of rushing wind, your descending Holy Spirit,
     that in knowing your Word we might know your presence,
     that in following your ways we might live in your light.
     Through Jesus Christ, our Lord. **Amen.**

4    Grant us, Lord, the spirit of wisdom and insight,
     the spirit of counsel and power,
     the spirit of knowledge and of the fear of the Lord;
     to make us quick in understanding and true in judgment,
     according to the example of Christ and by his grace. **Amen.**
        —based on Isaiah 11:2

5    Lord of heaven and earth,
     may these words from long ago,
     fulfilled by your Son, our Savior,
     be once again made present in us today
     by the power and persuasion of your Spirit,
     and may we live in the assurance they provide. **Amen.**

6    May the Word of God this morning
     burn in our minds, our wills, our feelings,
     as we sense the light and heat of your presence in that Word.
     Speak to us, O burning power of God! **Amen.**

7    Eternal God,
     your Spirit inspired those who wrote the Bible
     and enlightens us to hear your Word fresh each day.

Help us to rely always on your promises in Scripture.
In Jesus' name we pray. **Amen.**

8    Empowering God,
     we pray that you will send your Holy Spirit
     to move us to understanding;
     to help us to believe the gospel;
     to give us strength and wisdom to live by it. **Amen.**

## Q.3.6 Profession of Our Church's Faith (see also section 3.6)

1    In his divinity, majesty, grace, and Spirit,
     Christ is not absent from us for a moment.
     By the Spirit's power
     we make the goal of our lives not earthly things
     but the things above where Christ is,
     sitting at God's right hand.
     Through the Holy Spirit
     Christ pours out his gifts from heaven upon us his members.
     The Spirit, as well as the Father and the Son, is eternal God.
     The Spirit has been given to us personally
     so that by true faith
     the Spirit makes us share in Christ and all his blessings,
     comforts us, and remains with us forever.
     —from Heidelberg Catechism, Q&A's 47, 49, 51, 53

2    We trust in God the Holy Spirit,
     everywhere the giver and renewer of life.

     The Spirit justifies us by grace through faith,
     sets us free to accept ourselves and to love God and neighbor,
     and binds us together with all believers
     in the one body of Christ, the church.

     The same Spirit
     who inspired the prophets and apostles
     rules our faith and life in Christ through Scripture,
     engages us through the Word proclaimed,
     claims us in the waters of baptism,
     feeds us with the bread of life and the cup of salvation,
     and calls women and men to all ministries of the church.

     In a broken and fearful world
     the Spirit gives us courage
     to pray without ceasing,
     to witness among all peoples to Christ as Lord and Savior,
     to unmask idolatries in church and culture,
     to hear the voices of peoples long silenced,
     and to work with others for justice, freedom, and peace.

In gratitude to God, empowered by the Spirit,
we strive to serve Christ in our daily tasks
and to live holy and joyful lives,
even as we watch for God's new heaven and new earth,
praying, Come, Lord Jesus!

With believers in every time and place,
we rejoice that nothing in life or in death
can separate us from the love of God in Christ Jesus, our Lord.
Glory be to the Father, and to the Son, and to the Holy Spirit. Amen.
—from *A Brief Statement of Faith*

3    The Holy Spirit builds one church,
     united in one Lord and one hope,
     with one ministry around one table.
     The Spirit calls all believers in Jesus
     to respond in worship together,
     to accept all the gifts from the Spirit,
     to learn from each other's traditions,
     to make unity visible on earth.
     —from *Our Song of Hope*, st. 17

4    We believe in the Holy Spirit,
     who establishes the holy catholic church.
     We are the church:
     the people who believe the good news about Jesus,
     who are baptized, and who share in the Lord's Supper.
     Through these means of grace, the Spirit renews us
     so that we may serve God in love.
     All those who live in union with Christ,
     whether on earth or with God in heaven, are saints.
     Our communion with Christ makes us members one of another.
     As by his death Christ removed our separation from God,
     so by his Spirit Christ removes all that divides us from each other.
     Breaking down every wall of hostility,
     the Spirit makes us, who are many, one body in Christ.
     God does not will to be God without us,
     but instead grants to us creatures eternal life.
     Communion with Jesus is eternal life itself.
     By the Holy Spirit we are joined to Christ through faith
     and adopted as children, the sons and daughters of God.
     Through Christ we are raised from death to new life.
     For Christ we shall live to all eternity.

# Q.4 PRAYERS OF THE PEOPLE

## Q.4.4 Complete Model Outlines and Prayers (see also section 4.4)

*Prayer Outlines*

1   *The following is a guide for extemporaneous prayers. The pattern provides a suggested text for the opening and closing of each part of the prayer and calls for extemporaneous prayers of thanksgiving, petition, and intercession.*

Spirit of fire,
who came as a rushing wind breathing life and hope
into dead bones and cold hearts,
we praise you for the comfort and guidance
you have given the church throughout the ages:
    for your presence in creation, especially . . .
    for changing hearts and guiding decisions as evidenced in . . .
    for your work through the church universal . . .
    for your presence in our worship . . .
    for your sanctifying work in our lives . . .

Holy Spirit, we pray for your comfort and guidance
    as we care for creation . . .
    for the nations of the world . . .
    for our nation and its leaders . . .
    for this community and those who are in authority . . .
    for the church universal as it works on your behalf . . .
    for this local church in its ministry . . .
    for persons with particular needs . . .

We pray in the name of the Father and the Son,
who live and reign together with you,
one God forever and ever. **Amen.**

*Complete Prose Prayers*

2   Creator Spirit, create in us eagerness
to care for the world.
Spirit of Christ, fill us with urgency
to share our joy in our Savior and Lord.
Spirit of holiness, transform our lives
to be beacons in a world of shadows.
Spirit of truth, compel us to see the truth
and make us advocates of justice.
Spirit of wisdom, shower us with wisdom,
that we may best discern how to serve the world.

Advocate, intercede on our behalf for these and other unspoken requests
that weigh heavy on our hearts and minds. **Amen.**

*Prayers in Litany Form*

**3**  O Spirit of God,
you are a fire cleansing and consuming;
**you are a dove coming from on high;**
you are a still, small voice;
**you are everywhere;**
you are in us and about us;
**you have prompted our faith;**
you have suggested our good works;
**you have formed us into your people;**
you have built the church on earth.
**You are a fire;**
you are a dove;
**you are a still, small voice—**
and we listen for you and we follow you,
lest we turn aside into the ways of darkness.
**Move in and through your church.**
**Set it to the preaching of the gospel**
**and the doing of your will.**
**Where it is narrow, enlarge its vision.**
**Where it is weary, restore its strength.**
**Where it is wrong, give it sense.**

Surge within the lives of your people in every place.
Spur them to visit the sick and the imprisoned,
to care for the needy and the underprivileged,
to right the wrongs done by the accidents of life,
to encourage each other in the doing of love.
**Even when people refuse to believe,**
**work within them to the good of others.**
**Be the power behind all thrones**
**and offices and headquarters.**
**Be the thrust of society,**
**a force for the virtues of our race.**
And set us, God,
to reaching for high goals,
to noble and helpful purposes,
to the improvement of our world
and the improvement of our lives.
Prevent us from being discouraged,
and let us see visions of the world as it could be,
in peace and prosperity
by commitment to Jesus Christ,
who lives and rules with you and the Father,
one God forever. **Amen.**

4   Eternal God, our Father, you are the source of our being,
the breath of our life, and the joy of our living.
We know that you delight in the worship of your children
and that you eagerly send your Holy Spirit upon us.

**As your Spirit came upon your people of old,
giving them understanding and the knowledge of truth,
so send your Spirit today,
that we may speak in words not taught by human wisdom,
but taught by the Spirit.**

Your Spirit came upon the prophets.
You sent your Spirit to your Son and your church,
giving them each power and wisdom to follow your ways,
speak your truth, and accomplish your purposes.

**So grant us your Spirit with all fruit and equipping gifts,
that we may reflect your glory
and the world might believe,
for the honor of your holy name. Amen.**

5   Gracious God, your Holy Spirit hovered over the waters at creation.
You made a world that was breathtaking and life-giving.
Sin invaded this world and shattered it.
Pollution, disease, and natural disasters plague our world.
God, our provider, heal the sick, give peace to the dying,
shelter the homeless, and protect the vulnerable.
**With your Holy Spirit, renew your creation.**
When you formed humanity, you breathed your spirit into us.
You walked in the garden. You wanted fellowship with us.
Our sin separated us from you, so we live in a world of pain and hurt.
Some are hungry. Some are lonely. Some are empty.
Almighty God, giver of strength, feed the hungry, quench the thirsty,
support the orphans, uplift the depressed, and free the downtrodden.
**With your Holy Spirit, point us to new life in Christ.**
You called a people to be your own and to be a light to the world.
Throughout the world your church suffers.
Some are mocked for professing your name. Some are killed for praying to you.
Some pursue personal preferences rather than loving unity.
God, our refuge, shield from harm those who love you,
surround us with your mercy, and gird your church with the fruit of your Spirit.
**With your Holy Spirit, empower your church to witness to your glory.
Through the grace of Jesus Christ and the power of the Holy Spirit we pray.
Amen.**

6   God of rushing wind,
coming from where it wants
and going to where it wants,
**pour out your Spirit upon us.**

God of fire,
flaring on gathered disciples
and burning away their stubborn pride,
**pour out your Spirit upon us.**
God of miraculous speaking and hearing,
amazing the faithful
and riveting their attention to what is about to happen,
**pour out your Spirit upon us.**
God of the young who see visions,
of the old who dream dreams,
of male prophets and female prophets,
**pour out your Spirit upon us.**
God of wonders above and signs below,
God of blood and fire and billowing smoke,
God of blackened sun and bloodied moon,
**pour out your Spirit upon us.**
You raised up Peter to prophesy on Pentecost,
Peter to preach straight truth to a crooked generation,
Peter to accuse people he loved of complicity in the death of Jesus;
**pour out your Spirit upon us.**
God of wind and fire and tongues,
God of visions and dreams and prophecies,
God of signs and wonders,
**pour out your Spirit upon us.**
You raised up Peter to preach Jesus to a skeptical audience,
and with the two-edged sword of Peter's word
you cut through the armor of a crooked generation,
you pricked their hearts and saved them.
**Great God, send your Spirit to save us too.**
You sent your Spirit to assail hard hearts.
You sent repentance and faith,
baptism and forgiveness,
teaching and fellowship, communion and prayer.
**Great God, send your Spirit to save us too. Amen.**

# Q.5 OFFERING

### Q.5.2 Offering Prayers (see also section 5.2)

1    God of abundant love,
    we thank you for the gift of your Spirit,
    poured out on all who live in Christ.

May these gifts be our response of abundant love;
use them to bless others [*name the specific cause*],
through Christ, our Lord, in the power of the Holy Spirit. **Amen.**

2    God of wind, word, and fire,
we bless your name this day for sending
the light and strength of your Holy Spirit.
We give you thanks for all the gifts, great and small,
that have been poured out upon your children.
Accept us with our gifts to be living praise and witness
to your love throughout all the earth,
through Jesus Christ, who lives with you
in the unity of the Holy Spirit,
one God, forever. **Amen.**

# Q.8 THE LORD'S SUPPER

## Q.8.2 Great Prayer of Thanksgiving (see section 8.2)

### Q.8.2.2 Thanksgiving for the Work of God in Creation (see also section 8.2.2)

*The following prayers offer thanks for the work of God in creation and may be included in the complete Prayer of Thanksgiving as found in section 8.2 of this book.*

1    It is right, and a good and joyful thing,
always and everywhere to give thanks to you,
Father almighty, creator of heaven and earth.
In the beginning
your Spirit moved over the face of the waters.
You formed us in your image and breathed into us the breath of life.
When we turned away and our love failed,
your love remained steadfast.
Your Spirit came upon prophets and teachers,
anointing them to speak your Word.

And so, with your people on earth
and all the company of heaven,
we praise your name and join their unending hymn:
[*Sanctus*]
Holy are you, and blessed is your Son, Jesus Christ.
At his baptism in the Jordan your Spirit descended upon him
and declared him your beloved Son.

With your Spirit upon him
he turned away the temptation of sin.
Your Spirit anointed him
to preach good news to the poor,
to proclaim release to the captives
and recovery of sight to the blind,
to set at liberty those who are oppressed,
and to announce that the time had come
when you would save your people.
He healed the sick, fed the hungry, and ate with sinners.
By the baptism of his suffering, death, and resurrection
you gave birth to your church,
delivered us from slavery to sin and death,
and made with us a new covenant by water and the Spirit.
When the Lord Jesus ascended,
he promised to be with us always,
baptizing us with the Holy Spirit and with fire,
as on the day of Pentecost.

2    Blessed you are, Lord God, King of the universe.
Blessed you are, ruler of all being,
God from the beginning and God in the end.

You are Lord of creation,
sending your Spirit to brood upon the deep
and giving to Adam the breath of life.

We bless you for the human spirit,
for the intelligence you have granted to us and to all humankind,
for the energy of our bodies, the strength of our arms,
for the determination of our wills, the power of our imagination.

We bless you that even in our fallen state we have a thirst for you.
We cry out for you.
Our spirits crave the anointing of your Spirit.

Blessed you are, Lord God of Israel,
calling the patriarchs and speaking through the prophets,
enlightening their visions, kindling their hope, teaching them wisdom.

Praise be to you, O Shepherd of the flock of Jacob.

How blessed you are, eternal Lord,
for giving us a Savior,
conceived of the Spirit, born of a virgin.
We bless you for his baptism,
for the descent of the dove,
the anointing of the Spirit,
for his divine empowering,
for his illumination by the Spirit of truth.
We bless you for his ministry of mighty works and tender mercies.
We praise you for his obedient suffering,

for his sacrifice on the cross,
for his rest in the tomb,
for his glorious resurrection and ascension into heaven.
How thankful we are, great God.
To you be eternal praise.

Blessed you are, O Father,
that on the day of Pentecost
Christ poured out the fire of his Spirit on his disciples
and made them one body,
that in this last day
your Spirit is being poured out on all flesh,
making us a holy people and a royal priesthood.

It is in the unity of that same Spirit
that we pray, saying, **Our Father . . .**

3    How right and fitting it is, almighty and loving God,
to give you all thanks and praise.
We bless you in this day of celebration and hope
for the gift of your Spirit.
In the beginning your Spirit moved over the face of the waters,
bringing forth light and life.
Throughout history your Spirit moved over the world you love,
renewing the face of the earth.
In the fullness of time, you sent your Spirit-filled Son
to be our Savior, full of grace and truth.
Then you sent the Spirit of your Son into our hearts,
teaching us to pray to you as your adopted children.
With gratitude and delight, we savor these lavish gifts,
confident that your Spirit is the first fruit of the age to come,
where we will join, with undivided hearts, all your saints and angels
who forever sing your praise: [*conclude with "Holy, Holy, Holy" or another song of praise.*]

# Q.9 CLOSING OF WORSHIP

## Q.9.1 Sending (see also section 9.1)

*Call to Service/Discipleship*

1    Now may the God of hope fill you
with all joy and peace in believing

so that by the power of the Holy Spirit
you overflow with love and hope.
**Thanks be to God.**
Remember that the harvest of the Spirit is
love, joy, peace, patience, kindness, goodness,
faithfulness, gentleness, and self-control.
The Spirit is our source of life.
Let us therefore walk by the Spirit. **Amen.**
> —based on Romans 15:13; Galatians 5:22-23, 25

2    Go forth into the world,
rejoicing in the power of the Holy Spirit. **Amen.**

3    The Holy Spirit sends the church
to call sinners to repentance,
to proclaim the good news
that Jesus is personal Savior and Lord.
The Spirit sends us out in ministry
to preach good news to the poor,
righteousness to the nations,
and peace among all people. **Amen.**
> —from *Our Song of Hope*, st. 16

4    You have given yourself to us, Lord.
**Now we give ourselves for others.**
You have sent your Holy Spirit and made us a gifted people.
**As people of Pentecost,**
**we will serve you and proclaim your good news with joy.**
Your glory has filled our hearts.
**Help us to glorify you in all things. Amen.**

## Closing Prayers

5    Almighty God,
you sent your only Son, Jesus Christ, to die for our sins.
You sent your Holy Spirit to empower the disciples
on the day of Pentecost.
Send us out as your witnesses, filled with the Holy Spirit,
to proclaim the gospel to all nations,
carrying out the great commission
in obedience to the teaching of your Son, Jesus Christ, our Lord. **Amen.**

6    Lord Jesus, after giving your life on the cross,
you entered the glory of the Father.
Allow all people to share in your risen life.
In you, Jesus, God made a new covenant with us.
You are with us always, until the end of time.
Jesus, you appeared to your disciples after your passion.

Strengthen our faith by your presence in our midst.
Jesus, you promised the Holy Spirit to the apostles.
May the Spirit of consolation renew our faithfulness to you.
Jesus, you sent your apostles to proclaim good news
to the ends of the earth.
May the Holy Spirit make us witnesses to your love. **Amen.**

7    Almighty God,
send us out filled with your life-giving Holy Spirit,
that we may proclaim your gospel through our words and deeds.
May your Spirit lead, equip, and empower us to
bring you glory now and always. **Amen.**

8    We praise you, Jesus Christ, our risen and reigning Lord,
that you kept your promise not to leave us as orphans in this world:
    You sent us your Spirit to abide with us always.
As we depart from this time and place of worship,
we ask you, O Spirit of Jesus:
    Protect us from the evil one and from our sinful selves,
    help us to live daily for our Lord,
    prompt us to bless and serve others, and
    open our mouths to bear witness to the gospel.
And, our earthly journeys ended, bring us home at last
        to enjoy fellowship with the saints
        and to worship and adore you, O Triune God, forever and ever. **Amen.**

9    *Reader 1:* "Lord God, we hear your Word today:
*Reader 2:* "When the day of Pentecost came, they were together in one place,
and those disciples heard a violent wind and saw tongues of fire upon each of them.
Filled with the Holy Spirit, they spoke in strange tongues,
and the people around them thought they were drunk!
But Peter quieted the crowd,
reminding them of the prophet Joel's words from long ago,
that our God would pour out his Spirit,
and that everyone who calls on the name of the Lord will be saved."
*Reader 1:* "So now too, Lord, may we, your people,
speak your name and trust your Spirit;
may we see your Son at your right hand and not be shaken.
With glad hearts and rejoicing tongues, may we call upon your name."
        —based on Acts 2

## Q.9.2 Blessing/Benediction (see also section 9.2)

1    May the God of hope fill you
with all joy and peace in believing
so that you may abound in hope
by the power of the Holy Spirit. **Amen.**
        —from Romans 15:13, NRSV

2    May the love of the Father enfold us,
     the wisdom of the Son enlighten us,
     and the fire of the Spirit kindle us;
     and may the blessing of the Lord God
     come down upon us
     and remain with us always. **Amen.**

3    May the Spirit of truth lead you into all truth,
     giving you grace to confess that Jesus Christ is Lord
     and to proclaim the wonderful works of God;
     and the blessing of God Almighty,
     the Father, the Son, and the Holy Spirit,
     be among you and remain with you always. **Amen.**

4    *Blessing in multiple languages for Pentecost*

     *This blessing may be spoken first by the pastor in the common language of the congregation and then by any worshipers who know other languages, to demonstrate the gift of the Holy Spirit at Pentecost, so that each might hear the gospel in his or her own tongue.*

     May the grace of the Lord Jesus Christ, and the love of God,
     and the fellowship of the Holy Spirit be with you all. **Amen.**

5    May the Holy Spirit fall upon you, encompass you, and support you.
     May the Holy Spirit transform you, lead you, and equip you.
     May the Holy Spirit give you encouragement, strength, and comfort
     to serve and worship our triune God both now and forever. Amen.

# Q.10 SUGGESTED SCRIPTURE READINGS

1    *God's Spirit ("breath") throughout the Old Testament*

     Genesis 1-2: The breath of God at work in creation
     Numbers 11:17-29: God's Spirit rests on the chosen leaders
     Psalm 104: God's Spirit renews the face of the earth
     Isaiah 61:1-4: The Spirit of the Lord at work through God's anointed
     Ezekiel 37: The breath of God brings new life to dry bones
     Joel 2:28-29: The promise of God's Spirit

# SECTION R
# TRINITY SUNDAY

While every Christian worship service is a celebration of the Trinity, Trinity Sunday focuses explicitly on the mystery, power, and beauty of the triune God. Our Christian identity and mission are given to us as we are baptized in the name of the Father, the Son, and the Holy Spirit (Matt. 28:19). Our worship is not only directed to the triune God but is also enabled by the prompting of the Holy Spirit and the mediation of Jesus Christ. At its best, our worship is also an expression of the unity and common purpose of the church, which Jesus prayed would reflect the unity between himself and God (John 17:20-21).

Trinity Sunday, which is traditionally celebrated one week after Pentecost, marks the acknowledgment that all three persons of the Trinity exist together from eternity to eternity. Whereas other special services, such as Christmas, Good Friday, and Pentecost, are tied to specific events, this celebration is linked with a doctrine, which is itself a summary of scriptural teaching about God's being. The

texts in this section may also be used for any worship service that focuses especially on God's triune nature.

The visual environment should be conducive to adoration and praise before the mystery of the holy Trinity. Though green is the color of Ordinary Time, the season following Pentecost, white or gold is appropriate for Trinity Sunday. The use of trinitarian creeds is especially appropriate for worship on this day.

719

Scriptures and Statements of Faith Applying to the Theme of
Trinity Sunday

*The following texts are particularly appropriate for sermons or for supplemental liturgical use.*

| | | |
|---|---|---|
| Deuteronomy 4:32-40 | Isaiah 6:1-8 | Romans 5:1-5 |
| Psalm 8 | Matthew 3:13-17 | Romans 8:12-17 |
| Psalm 29 | Matthew 28:16-20 | 2 Corinthians 1:21-22 |
| Psalm 33:1-12 | John 3:1-17 | 2 Corinthians 13:5-13 [14] |
| Proverbs 8:22-31 | John 16:12-15 | Ephesians 4:4-6 |

# R.1 OPENING OF WORSHIP

### R.1.1 Preparation for Worship (see also section 1.1)

1    Holy, holy, holy God,
     we worship and adore you—Father, Son, and Holy Spirit.
     Today in our worship we long for a glimpse of your glory,
     seen perfectly in Christ, our Lord.
     As we worship, may we gain new insight
     about the mystery and wonder of your love.
     And may we sense new ways to mirror that love in our world,
     through Christ, our Lord. **Amen.**

### R.1.2 Call to Worship (see also section 1.2)

1    Jesus prayed that we, the church, would be one,
     just as he and the Father are one.
     Today we offer our praise and prayer together,
     as one body, in Christ, through the power of the Holy Spirit.
     In harmony, let us glorify God—Father, Son, and Spirit.

2    Since we are justified by faith,
     we have peace with God through our Lord Jesus Christ,
     through whom we have obtained access to this grace in which we stand;
     and we boast in our hope of sharing the glory of God.
     And not only that, but we also boast in our sufferings,
     knowing that suffering produces endurance,
     and endurance produces character, and character produces hope,

and hope does not disappoint us,
because God's love has been poured into our hearts
through the Holy Spirit that has been given to us.

In the shadow of God's peace,
in the powerful name of Jesus,
and with the hope of the Holy Spirit, let us worship God.
    —based on Romans 5:1-5, NRSV

### R.1.3 Greeting (see also section 1.3)

1    In the name of the Father, and the Son, and the Holy Spirit.
     **Our help is in the name of the Lord,**
     **who made heaven and earth.**
     Grace be to you and peace
     from God our Father and our Lord Jesus Christ. **Amen.**

### R.1.4 Opening Responses (see also section 1.4)

*Prayers of Adoration*

1    We have known you;
     we have loved you;
     we worship you, the triune God.
     To you we pray,
     upon you rests all our hope of salvation.
     Have mercy on us according to your great mercy,
     and save us in your heavenly kingdom. **Amen.**

2    The poor and the needy will praise you, O Lord.
     Glory to the Father,
     glory to the Son,
     glory to the Holy Spirit, who spoke through the prophets.
     God is my hope,
     Christ is my refuge,
     the Holy Spirit is my shelter. **Amen.**

3    Father, we praise you;
     through your Word and Holy Spirit you created all things.
     You reveal your salvation in all the world
     by sending to us Jesus Christ, the Word made flesh.
     Through your Holy Spirit
     you give us a share in your life and love.
     Fill us with the vision of your glory,
     that we may always serve and praise you,
     Father, Son, and Holy Spirit,
     one God, forever and ever. **Amen.**

4    Blessed are you, Lord our God,
     Father, Son, and Holy Spirit.
     Your glory is beyond our comprehension.
     Your mercy is greater than our sinfulness.
     Your love is more than we can measure.
     Your wisdom is more than we can fathom.
     To you, Father, Son, and Holy Spirit,
     be all glory, honor, and praise
     now and forevermore. **Amen.**

5    Praise to you, triune God—Father, Son, and Holy Spirit.
     God our Father, we praise and adore you,
     the origin of all things and our loving provider.
     Jesus Christ, our Savior and Lord, we praise and adore you,
     the living Word, Wisdom, and the exact image of the Father.
     Holy Spirit, we praise you and adore you,
     the eternal power and might, our Comforter and Advocate.
     Loving God, we acknowledge the mystery of your being
     and bow before you in awe and gratitude,
     for you have drawn us into your communion of love,
     through Christ, our Lord, and the fellowship of the Holy Spirit. **Amen.**

*Prayers of Invocation*

6    O blessed Trinity,
     in whom we know the maker of all things seen and unseen,
     the Savior of all both near and far:
     By your Spirit enable us so to worship your divine majesty
     that with all the company of heaven
     we may magnify your glorious name, saying,
     **Holy, holy, holy.**
     **Glory to you, O Lord Most High. Amen.**

7    Holy Father of our Lord Jesus Christ,
     send your Holy Spirit to awaken us.
     Send your grace to forgive us,
     your truth to instruct us,
     your mercy to relieve us.
     Holy Father, you created the world
     through your mediating Son and brooding Spirit.
     Lord Jesus Christ, on the Father's mission
     you redeemed the world your Father loves.
     Holy Spirit of Father and Son,
     you blew power into the church and sent her out to the world.
     Majestic God, triune from all ages,
     brimming with life upon life in triplicate verve,
     you poured out life to create, save, and inspire.
     And so we worship and adore you. **Amen.**

**8**    Come, almighty King,
and help us your name to sing,
for you are a God of love.
Come, incarnate Word,
and make known your wonders to our souls,
for you are a God of grace.
Come, holy Comforter,
and bear witness within every heart that we belong to you,
for you are a God who creates fellowship.
Come, triune God, that we might love
and adore you all the days of our lives. **Amen.**

**9**    Father, you sent your Word to bring us truth
and your Spirit to make us holy.
Through them we come to know
the mystery of your life.
Help us to worship you, one God in three persons,
by proclaiming and living our faith in you.
Grant this through our Lord Jesus Christ, your Son,
who lives and reigns with you and the Holy Spirit,
one God, for ever and ever. **Amen.**

**10**    Almighty God, our Father,
dwelling in majesty and mystery,
renewing and fulfilling creation by your eternal Spirit,
and revealing your glory through our Lord, Jesus Christ:
Cleanse us from doubt and fear
and enable us to worship you,
with your Son and the Holy Spirit, one God,
living and reigning, now and forever. **Amen.**

**11**    O God, who created us in love,
**create us anew in love as we worship you.**
O Jesus Christ, who redeemed this world in love,
**reclaim our hearts as we worship you.**
O Holy Spirit, who moves this world toward its God-appointed end,
**move within us as we worship you. Amen.**

## Additional Resources

**12**    We praise you, Holy Father,
for sending your Son to be our Savior.
We praise you, Holy Jesus,
for the promise of sending us a Comforter,
so that you would be with us always.
We praise you for the abundant life we have in you,
Father, Son, and Holy Spirit,
one God, now and forevermore. **Amen.**

13  O God of greatness and goodness,
    not only did you set us apart from the rest of creation,
    but you made us in your own image.
    **O Lord, give us grateful hearts**
    **and let us rejoice in the presence of our Creator.**
    O God of might and mercy,
    not only did you follow your people into the far country,
    but you took up the cross to set them free.
    **O Lord, give us grateful hearts**
    **and let us rejoice in the presence of our Redeemer.**
    O God of consolation and comfort,
    not only did you bring us together in one place,
    but you called us to be your witnesses.
    **O Lord, give us grateful hearts**
    **and let us rejoice in the presence of our Sustainer.**
    Gracious God, you have revealed yourself to us
    in more ways than we can recall or recount.
    **O Lord, give us grateful hearts**
    **and let us rejoice in the love that will not let us go. Amen.**

14  Almighty God, before you angels sang for joy
    when you created with your voice the heavens and the earth.
    **Hear our voice this day and accept our praise**
    **and thanksgiving for the gifts of speech and song,**
    **which we on earth share with the heavenly host.**
    O Jesus Christ, you are the Word made flesh,
    the firstborn of many children in the family of God
    who have heard your music in their hearts.
    **Open the ears of our hearts this day, that all we say**
    **and all we sing may reveal you in us and us in you,**
    **whose body and voice we are in this world.**
    O Holy Spirit, with tongues as of fire you have inspired
    the speech and song of evangelists, preachers, poets, and musicians.
    **Visit us this day to kindle anew the fire of love**
    **and the light of understanding, that your church**
    **may live in the counterpoint of community.**
    O Creator, Redeemer, Sustainer, you are three persons
    in one God living in harmony.
    As your church, our many voices, our many lives
    become one chorus to praise your holy name.
    **Bless our coming together now**
    **so that we, in communion with your saints,**
    **may hear your voice and sing your words**
    **this day and always. Amen.**

# R.2 CONFESSION AND ASSURANCE

## R.2.2 Prayers of Confession (see also section 2.2)

1   Father, you have come to meet us as we return to you:
Lord, have mercy.
**Lord, have mercy.**
Jesus, you died on the cross for our sins.
Christ, have mercy.
**Christ, have mercy.**
Spirit, you give us life and peace.
Lord, have mercy.
**Lord, have mercy. Amen.**

2   Let us pray our confession to the all-holy Trinity:
Father God, have mercy; Christ, have mercy; Spirit, have mercy!
**Surely it is God who saves us;**
**because we trust in you, we make our confession to you.**
[*silence for personal prayers confessing sins of commission*]
Father God, have mercy; Christ, have mercy; Spirit, have mercy!
**For the Lord is our stronghold and our sure defense;**
**You are our Savior, and thus we confess to you.**
[*silence for personal prayers confessing sins of omission*]
Father God, have mercy; Christ, have mercy; Spirit, have mercy! **Amen.**
      —based on Isaiah 12:2

3   Triune God,
we praise you as the God of love and life.
Though Jesus prayed that we would be one,
we confess that we fail to live in unity with each other and with you.
We break our communion through hostile words and unkind actions.
We long for your Spirit to heal us and to correct us.
We long for you to help us experience communion
with you and with each other
as we gather around your Word [*and table*].
Even now, dependent on your grace, we commit ourselves
to live more fully in the unity you desire.
Through Christ, our Lord, **Amen.**

## R.2.4 Assurance of Pardon (see also section 2.4)

1   You did not receive a spirit of slavery to fall back into fear,
but you have received a spirit of adoption.
When you cry, "Abba! Father!"

it is that very Spirit bearing witness with our spirit
that we are children of God,
and if children, then heirs,
heirs of God and joint heirs with Christ.

In Christ, by the power of the Spirit, we are forgiven.
Thanks be to the triune God.
—based on Romans 8:15-17, NRSV

# R.3 PROCLAIMING THE WORD

### R.3.1 Prayers for Illumination (see section 3.1)

1    God, our Father, you made us, you love us,
and you invite us to be in community with you.
Jesus, you rescued us, you made us holy,
and you enabled us to be in community.
Holy Spirit, you inspired these words of Scripture,
you guide the words of the message, and you transform us.
Triune God, thank you for your Word to us.
May it deepen our faith, comfort us, and challenge us
so that we may grow in our love for you and each other.
In the name of Jesus, through the power of the Holy Spirit, we pray. **Amen.**

### R.3.6 Profession of Our Church's Faith (see also section 3.6)

1    In keeping with this truth and Word of God
we believe in one God, who is one single essence,
in whom there are three persons,
really, truly, and eternally distinct
according to their incommunicable properties—
namely, Father, Son, and Holy Spirit.
The Father is the cause, origin,
and source of all things, visible as well as invisible.
The Son is the Word, the Wisdom, and the image of the Father.
The Holy Spirit is the eternal power and might,
proceeding from the Father and the Son.
Nevertheless, this distinction does not divide God into three,
since Scripture teaches us that the Father, the Son, and the Holy Spirit
each has his own subsistence distinguished by characteristics—

yet in such a way that these three persons are only one God.
It is evident then that the Father is not the Son
and that the Son is not the Father,
and that likewise the Holy Spirit is neither the Father nor the Son.
Nevertheless, these persons, thus distinct, are neither divided
nor fused or mixed together.
For the Father did not take on flesh, nor did the Spirit, but only the Son.
The Father was never without his Son, nor without his Holy Spirit,
since all these are equal from eternity, in one and the same essence.
There is neither a first nor a last, for all three are one
in truth and power, in goodness and mercy.

    —Belgic Confession, Art. 8

2    I bind unto myself today
the strong name of the Trinity,
by invocation of the same,
the Three in One, and One in Three.

I bind this day to me forever,
by power of faith, Christ's incarnation;
his baptism in the Jordan river;
his death on the cross for my salvation.
His bursting from the spiced tomb;
his riding up the heavenly way;
his coming at the day of doom
I bind unto myself today.

I bind unto myself today
the virtues of the star-lit heaven,
the glorious sun's life-giving ray,
the whiteness of the moon at even,
the flashing of the lightning free,
the whirling wind's tempestuous shocks,
the stable earth, the deep salt sea
around the old eternal rocks.

I bind unto myself today
the power of God to hold and lead,
God's eye to watch, God's might to stay,
God's ear to hearken to my need,
the wisdom of my God to teach,
God's hand to guide, God's shield to ward,
the Word of God to give me speech,
God's heavenly host to be my guard.

Christ be with me, Christ within me,
Christ behind me, Christ before me,
Christ beside me, Christ to win me,
Christ to comfort and restore me,
Christ beneath me, Christ above me,
Christ in quiet, Christ in danger,

Christ in hearts of all that love me,
Christ in mouth of friend and stranger.

I bind unto myself the name,
the strong name of the Trinity,
by invocation of the same,
the Three in One, the One in Three,
of whom all nature has creation,
eternal Father, Spirit, Word.
Praise to the Lord of my salvation,
salvation is of Christ, the Lord. **Amen.**

# R.4 PRAYERS OF THE PEOPLE

## R.4.4 Complete Model Outlines and Prayers (see section 4.4)

*Prayer Outlines*

1   *The following is a guide for extemporaneous prayers. The pattern provides a suggested text
    for the opening and closing of each part of the prayer and calls for extemporaneous prayers of
    thanksgiving, petition, and intercession.*

Triune God,
Father, Son, and Holy Spirit,
we adore you for your threeness and oneness, a holy mystery.
We are in awe of that same unfathomable mystery reflected in
        the creation around us . . .
        the complexity of an atom . . .
        the birth of a child . . .
        your work in our lives . . .

Your ways are higher than our ways,
your thoughts greater than our thoughts,
so although we acknowledge
that we do not always understand your ways,
we continue to offer you our prayers for
        creation and its care . . .
        the nations of the world . . .
        our nation and its leaders . . .
        this community and those in authority . . .
        the church universal as it works on your behalf . . .

this local church in its ministry . . .
persons with particular needs . . .

We pray in the name of the triune God,
three in one, from eternity to eternity. **Amen.**


*Prayers in Litany Form*

2    Let us give thanks to the Lord our God.
**It is right to give our thanks and praise.**
Gracious Father,
giver of all good things:
For our home on earth
and for your unfailing mercy,
**we give you thanks.**
Christ, our Redeemer:
For your sacrifice on the cross
and for rising from death so that we might live,
**we give you thanks and praise.**
Holy Spirit, giver of life:
For your abiding presence in our lives
and for comforting and guiding us,
**we give you thanks, praise, and glory.**
O triune God:
To you be glory and praise
now and forever. **Amen.**

3    Triune God, in a world of division and despair:
may we be one, **as you are one.**
In a church of brokenness and hurt:
may we be one, **as you are one.**
In families so often divided:
may we be one, **as you are one.**
In lives so often lived in isolation:
may we be one, **as you are one.**
Through Jesus Christ, our Lord. **Amen.**

# R.8 THE LORD'S SUPPER

## R.8.2 Great Prayer of Thanksgiving (see section 8.2)

### R.8.2.2 Thanksgiving for the Work of God in Creation (see also section 8.2.2)

*The following prayer offers thanks for the work of God in creation and for the work of Christ and may be included in the complete Prayer of Thanksgiving as found in section 8.2 of this book.*

1    Holy God, Creator of each of us,
      we exclaim with the psalmist:
           "O LORD, you have searched me and you know me.
           You created my inmost being;
           you knit me together in my mother's womb.
           I praise you because I am fearfully and wonderfully made."

      With thanksgiving and delight we acknowledge that
      none of us is the mindless product of arbitrary forces of nature.
      We are persons created by you with Fatherly care.

      You could have made each of us different—
           located at a different time and place,
           and possessing different features and different gifts.
      You remind us that in our uniqueness
           each of us is loved and willed by you,
           and the details of our lives matter to you.

      Humbly we say thanks for making us who we are.

      We bless you and give thanks too
           for your Son, Jesus Christ, our Savior from sin,
           and for his Spirit,
                our Lord's continuing presence and power among us.

      We ask for one thing more:
           Swell our hearts with gratitude
           and open our mouths to exclaim:

                "How precious are your thoughts toward us, O God;
                how vast the sum of them.
                Were we to count them,
                they would outnumber the grains of sand."
                —based on Psalm 139:1, 13-14, 17-18

# R.9 CLOSING OF WORSHIP

## R.9.1 Sending (see also section 9.1)

*Call to Service/Discipleship*

1   Go forth to greet the world at work,
    as here the Lord has greeted us in worship.
    Go forth in the name of God the Creator,
    whose strength empowers us;
    in the name of Christ the Redeemer,
    whose love transforms us;
    and in the name of the Holy Spirit,
    whose presence guides us. **Amen.**

## R.9.2 Blessing/Benediction (see also section 9.2)

1   The grace of the Lord Jesus Christ,
    the love of God,
    and the communion of the Holy Spirit
    be with all of you. **Amen.**
        —from 2 Corinthians 13:13, NRSV

2   May God, the Holy Trinity,
    make you strong in faith and love,
    defend you on every side,
    and guide you in truth and peace;
    and the blessing of God Almighty,
    the Father, the Son and the Holy Spirit,
    be among you and remain with you always. **Amen.**

3   The peace of God,
    which passes all understanding,
    keep your hearts and minds
    in the knowledge and love of God,
    and of our Savior, Jesus Christ;
    and the blessing of God Almighty,
    Father, Son, and Holy Spirit,
    be among you and remain with you always. **Amen.**

# R.10 SUGGESTED SCRIPTURE READINGS

1    *Father, Son, and Spirit in the unfolding drama of Scripture*

Genesis 1:1-2; John 1:1-4: Word and Spirit in creation
Matthew 3:16-17: Father and Spirit blessing Jesus at his baptism
John 14-15: Jesus, the way to the Father, promises the Spirit
Acts 7:55: Stephen's Spirit-given vision of Jesus at God's right hand
Romans 8:11-27: The Holy Spirit and union with Christ
Ephesians 2: We are made alive in Christ, and God's Spirit lives in us
Galatians 4:4-6: God sent the Spirit of the Son into our hearts
Hebrews 9:11-15: Blood of Christ through the Spirit makes us clean before God

# SECTION S
# UNITY OF THE CHURCH

Though not a specific day on the calendar of the Christian year, the unity of the church is a theme that needs constant attention. In a day of embarrassing fractures, congregations must step back from their own local concerns and highlight the unity of the body for which Jesus himself prayed (John 17:20-21). Such observances also give the church an opportunity to recommit itself to a life of unity.

The unity of the church needs to be observed and valued on several levels. Local unity sees worshipers of a local community experiencing their oneness in Christ without regard to their diverse experiences, ethnicity, opinions, or gender. Generational unity sees worshipers of all age levels sharing their oneness in Christ and encouraging one another. Historical unity sees the worshipers of today affirming their oneness with those who have gone before, perhaps many centuries before. Global unity sees God's people of a variety of cultures and traditions affirming one another's value, praying for

one another, and joining in service together. Each of these dimensions demonstrates that unity does not imply uniformity.

Though this theme may be highlighted often during the Christian year, two occasions are especially appropriate. Worldwide Communion Sunday in October gives local churches the opportunity to come to the Lord's table with the awareness

733

of brothers and sisters of many churches and cultures who are doing the same. Pentecost Sunday, when the apostles proclaimed the gospel in every language, is a time for the church to celebrate the Spirit's work in calling us together as Christ's body. These times of worship may include scriptural texts that emphasize the importance of solidarity in Christ; creeds and confessional statements that point to our unity; prayers of thanksgiving and intercession for the entire body of Christ; and sensitivity toward those parts of the body of Christ that are suffering.

---

**Scriptures and Statements of Faith Applying to the Theme of the Unity of the Church**

*The following texts are particularly appropriate for sermons or for supplemental liturgical use.*

| | | |
|---|---|---|
| Psalm 87 | Acts 15:1-35 | Ephesians 4:1-6 |
| Psalm 102:18-22 | Romans 12:3-21 | Philippians 2:1-5 |
| Psalm 122 | 1 Corinthians 3 | Colossians 1:15-20 |
| Psalm 133 | 1 Corinthians 10:16-17 | Colossians 3:12-17 |
| Isaiah 45:22-23 | 1 Corinthians 12:12-26 | 1 Peter 2:4-12 |
| Ezekiel 37:15-24 | Ephesians 1:22-23 | Revelation 7:9-12 |
| John 10:11-16 | Ephesians 2:11-22 | Revelation 21:9-14, 22-27 |
| John 17:20-24 | | |

Belgic Confession, Art. 27-29
Heidelberg Catechism, Q&A's 54-55
Canons of Dort, Pt. II, Art. 9; Pt. V, Art. 9
Westminster Confession, Chap. XXV, Sec. 1-4
*Our Song of Hope,* st. 15-19
*Our World Belongs to God,* st. 28, 34-42

---

# S.1 OPENING OF WORSHIP

---

### S.1.1 Preparation for Worship (see also section 1.1)

1   Triune God,
    you have called us to live in unity with each other
    and with our brothers and sisters around the world.
    Help us to sense that our love for Jesus binds us together.
    May our worship today be a witness

to the kind of unity that comes only
through Christ, our Lord. **Amen.**

2    God of life,
     thank you for calling us to belong to something
     so much bigger than ourselves.
     Thank you for your church in all times and places.
     We pray that all who come to worship today
     may sense that the gospel of Christ
     is so much bigger than this congregation.
     In Jesus' name, **Amen.**

## S.1.2 Call to Worship (see also section 1.2)

1    How very good and pleasant it is
         when kindred live together in unity!
     It is like the precious oil on the head,
         running down upon the beard, on the beard of Aaron,
         running down over the collar of his robes.
     It is like the dew of Hermon,
         which falls on the mountains of Zion.
     For there the LORD ordained his blessing,
         life forevermore.

     Come, let us all worship and bow down together,
         **let us kneel together before the LORD, our maker.**
     **For he is our God,**
         **and we are the people of his pasture,**
         **and the sheep of his hand.**
         —from Psalm 95:6-7; 133, NRSV

2    The God of creation makes us one in body!
     **Let us join hearts and voices in praise of the Lord!**
     The God of Christ makes us one in the Spirit!
     **Let us join hearts and voices in praise of the Lord!**

3    Let us acknowledge the company in which we meet:
     the church on earth and in heaven;
     the faithful who worshiped here before us;
     the hundreds of thousands
     of every place and language
     who, on the Lord's day, seek to set their lives
     within the atmosphere of renewing grace.
     As we think of them,
     let us take deliberate encouragement
     from our unity with them all.

## S.1.4 Opening Responses (see also section 1.4)

*Prayers of Adoration*

1    O God of all creation,
      you alone are God.
      And you alone can satisfy our longing
      for a support that earth cannot give
      and that heaven will not take away.
      Help us, in recognition of our common dependence on you,
      to acknowledge our need of one another.
      Let the oneness of our worship
      make us one in love and service. **Amen.**

2    Our great and gracious God,
      you have called us to this place; **we are grateful.**
      You have called us to live together in unity; **we are grateful.**
      You have fulfilled your promises to us; **we are grateful.**
      You have given us a Savior and your Spirit; **we are grateful.**
      Now, from a deep well of gratitude,
      help us to teach the next generation of your great and glorious deeds.
      In response to our sin and your salvation,
      helps us to live lives of service to you.
      You are merciful and faithful beyond our comprehension.
      We fail to forgive, yet you sent your Son to save us.
      Our feet stumble and fall,
      but you created the very ground we walk upon.
      Humbly we praise you, God, this day and every day. **Amen.**

3    Almighty God,
      your love for us and for all people is powerful beyond measure.
      Your love is so vast that nothing will prevail against it.
      We know this love is trustworthy because of Jesus Christ:
      his life of compassion, death on the cross,
      and resurrection from the dead.
      In life and death we belong to you,
      holy triune God—Father, Son, and Holy Spirit. **Amen.**

*Prayers of Invocation*
*The following prayers are appropriate for services that include the Lord's Supper.*

4    We, your people, Lord,
      are scattered around the world today.
      Yet when we gather at your table, we become one.
      Like grain from many fields becomes one loaf,
      and grapes from many vines become one cup,
      so we become one body here today.

For as we partake of one bread
and drink from one cup,
we are united together.
Remove the divisions that separate us,
heal the brokenness that too often marks us.
Make this time of sacrament
a celebration of our oneness with Christ
and with one another,
that the world may believe. **Amen.**

5    O risen Christ, you made yourself known to the disciples
in the breaking of the bread at Emmaus;
through our sharing in the bread of life
in our many Christian communions,
open our eyes and hands to the needs of all people.
Let our hearts burn to share your gifts
and help us to go forth with one another with bread:
bread of hope, bread of life, bread of peace. **Amen.**

# S.2 CONFESSION AND ASSURANCE

## S.2.2 Prayers of Confession (see also section 2.2)

1    Gracious God,
you have called us to be a new community in Christ,
and yet we remain divided.
Forgive us our fear, anxiety, prejudice, and misunderstandings.
Strengthen our common bonds and deepen our resolve
to promote the unity of your church. **Amen.**

2    Across the barriers that divide race from race:
**reconcile us, O Christ, by your cross.**
Across the barriers that divide rich from poor:
**reconcile us, O Christ, by your cross.**
Across the barriers that divide people of different cultures:
**reconcile us, O Christ, by your cross.**
Across the barriers that divide Christians:
**reconcile us, O Christ, by your cross.**
Across the barriers that divide men and women, young and old:
**reconcile us, O Christ, by your cross.**
**Confront us, O Christ, with the hidden prejudices and fears**

that deny and betray our prayers.
**Enable us to see the causes of strife,**
**remove from us all senses of superiority.**
**Teach us to grow in unity with all God's children. Amen.**

3      Forgive us the sins of disunity, O Lord:
       pride and jealousy and narrow-mindedness.
       Forgive us the sins of false unity:
       lack of imagination, apathy, and indifference.
       Make us one in genuine love and mutual trust.
       Make us many in gifts and talents and vision. **Amen.**

4      God of all nations, God of all children,
       we ask for your mercy on behalf of all the children
       who do not run in the sunshine
       but live out their lives in dark corners.
       Forgive us for not seeing; forgive us for not looking.
       Be with us as we search for new beginnings
       in caring for these children.
       We pray that one day every child
       might sleep through the night in peace. **Amen.**

5      Dear friends, let us love one another,
       because love comes from God.
       Whoever loves is a child of God and knows God.
       **Jesus Christ, life of the world and of all creation,**
       **forgive our separation and grant us peace and unity.**
       The peace that Christ gives is to guide us in the decisions we make,
       for it is to this peace that God has called us together into one body.
       **Jesus Christ, life of the world and of all creation,**
       **forgive our separation and grant us peace and unity.**
       With his own body he broke down the walls of separation.
       By his death on the cross Christ destroyed our divisions.
       **Jesus Christ, life of the world and of all creation,**
       **forgive our separation and grant us peace and unity.**
             —based on Ephesians 2:14-22; 4:3-6; Colossians 3:15; 1 John 4:7

6      Almighty God,
       we confess that we are often swept up in the tide of our generation.
       We have failed in our calling to be your holy people,
       a people set apart for your divine purpose.
       We live more in apathy born of fatalism than in passion born of hope.
       We are moved more by private ambition than by social justice.
       We dream more of privilege and benefits than of service and sacrifice.
       We try to speak in your name without relinquishing our glories,
       without nourishing our souls, without relying wholly on your grace.
       Help us to make room in our hearts and lives for you.
       By your Holy Spirit, forgive us, revive us,
       and reshape us in your image. **Amen.**

7    God of all flesh,
in Jesus Christ you have immersed divine splendor
and wisdom into human life.
He is not repelled by the shabbiness and shamefulness of our lives
but seeks to redeem us.
We confess our repulsion from those whose actions bewilder us,
whose sorrow burdens us,
or whose good fortune somehow detracts from our lives.
Our compassion is limited to those like ourselves.
Our kindness is reserved for those kind to us.
Our passionate concern remains silent
until our own little kingdoms are threatened.
O God, forgive us.
Cleanse us of self-centeredness
and open us to the whole breadth and length,
height and depth of your love, manifest in all creation. **Amen.**

8    God of grace, we grieve that the church,
which shares one Spirit, one faith, one hope, and one calling,
has become a broken communion in a broken world.
The one body spans all time, place, race, and language,
but in our fear we have fled from and fought one another,
and in our pride we have mistaken our part for the whole.
Yet we marvel that you gather the broken pieces to do your work,
that you bless us with joy, with growth, and with signs of unity.
Forgive our sins and help us to commit ourselves
to seeking and showing the unity of the body of Christ.
In his name, **Amen.**

       —based on *Our World Belongs to God,* st. 40

9    O God, your will is that
all your children should be one in Christ.
We pray for the unity of your church.
Pardon all our pride and our lack of faith,
of understanding and of charity,
which are the causes of our divisions.
Deliver us from our narrow-mindedness,
from our bitterness, from our prejudices.
Save us from considering as normal
that which is a scandal to the world
and an offense to your love.
Teach us to recognize the gifts of grace
among all who call upon you
and confess faith in Jesus Christ, our Lord. **Amen.**

**S.2.4 Assurance of Pardon** (see also section 2.4)

1    You are a chosen race,
     a royal priesthood, a holy nation, God's own people,
     in order that you may proclaim the mighty acts of him
     who called you out of darkness into his marvelous light.
     Once you were not a people, but now you are God's people;
     once you had not received mercy, but now you have received mercy.

     People of God,
     all of us together have received God's mercy in Christ.
     In Christ we are forgiven, redeemed,
     and made to be a community united in faith.
     Thanks be to God.
          —based on 1 Peter 2:9-10, NRSV

# S.3 PROCLAIMING THE WORD

**S.3.1 Prayers for Illumination** (see also section 3.1)

1    Pour out your Spirit on us again,
     as your Word is proclaimed,
     that we may be faithful to our baptismal calling,
     ardently desire the communion of Christ's body and blood,
     and serve the poor of your people and all who need your love,
     **through Jesus Christ, our Lord,**
     **who lives and reigns with you,**
     **in the unity of the Holy Spirit,**
     **ever one God, world without end. Amen.**

**S.3.6 Profession of Our Church's Faith** (see also section 3.6)

1    What do you believe concerning "the holy catholic church"?
     **I believe that the Son of God**
          **through his Spirit and Word,**
          **out of the entire human race,**
          **from the beginning of the world to its end,**
     **gathers, protects, and preserves for himself**
          **a community chosen for eternal life**
          **and united in true faith.**
     **And of this community I am and always will be**
          **a living member.**
          —Heidelberg Catechism, Q&A 54

740

# S.4 PRAYERS OF THE PEOPLE

## S.4.4 Complete Model Outlines and Prayers (see also section 4.4)

*Prayer Outlines*

1   *The following is a guide for extemporaneous prayers. The pattern provides a suggested text for the opening and closing of each part of the prayer and calls for extemporaneous prayers of thanksgiving, petition, and intercession.*

God of our salvation,
we rejoice that in you there is no Jew or Greek, slave or free,
male or female, for we all belong as one in Christ Jesus.
We praise you for the evidence of that unity in
    the church of past generations . . .
    the church of all places . . .
    the cooperation between missionaries . . .
    the corporate work of the churches in this community . . .
    our baptisms, which make us a part of your body, the church . . .

As one body we lift our common prayers
    for creation and its care . . .
    for the nations of the world . . .
    for our nation and its leaders . . .
    for this community and those in authority . . .
    for the church universal as it works on your behalf . . .
    for this local church in its ministry . . .
    for persons with particular needs . . .

We pray this in the name of the one God and Father of all,
who is above all and through all and in all. **Amen.**
       —based on Galatians 3:28; Ephesians 4:6

*Complete Prose Prayers*

2   Almighty Father,
whose blessed Son before his passion prayed
that his disciples might be one, as you and he are one:
Grant that your church,
being bound together in love and obedience to you,
may be united in one body by the one Spirit,
that the world may believe in him whom you have sent,
your Son, Jesus Christ, our Lord;
who lives and reigns with you,
in the unity of the Holy Spirit, one God, now and forever. **Amen.**

3    Bless your church throughout the world by your Holy Spirit,
     draw the scattered flock of Christ into a visible unity,
     and make your church a sign of hope to our divided world.
     Grant that we who bear your Son's name
     may be instruments of your peace,
     bringing peace to our homes, our communities,
     our nation, and our world. **Amen.**

4    Lord God,
     we thank you for calling us
     into the company of those who trust in Christ
     and seek to obey his will.
     You have made us strangers no longer
     but pilgrims together on the way to your kingdom.
     Guide us closer to you and to one another
     in the unity of the Spirit and the bond of peace,
     and strengthen us together
     in mission and service to your world,
     through Jesus Christ, our Lord. **Amen.**

5    Almighty God,
     you have built your church
     on the foundation of the apostles and prophets,
     Jesus Christ himself being the chief cornerstone.
     Join us together in unity of spirit by their teaching,
     that we may become a holy temple, acceptable to you,
     through Jesus Christ, our Lord, who lives and reigns
     with you and the Holy Spirit, one God, now and forever. **Amen.**

6    Lord, we pray for the unity of your church.
     Help us to see ourselves as rays from the one sun,
     branches of a single tree,
     and streams flowing from one river.
     May we remain united to you and to each other
     because you are our common source of life,
     and may we send out your light
     and pour forth your flowing streams over all the earth,
     drawing our inspiration and joy from you. **Amen.**

7    Too often, far too often, O Lord Jesus Christ,
     what should most unite us does in fact most divide us:
          We turn our own interpretations of common Christian creeds and convictions
          into weapons to belittle and insult, to despise and to bludgeon
          our Christian sisters and brothers whose interpretations differ from ours.
     Put to death our contentious spirits, O Lord.
     Open our hearts to welcome one another as you have welcomed us. **Amen.**

8    Lord, make our hearts places of peace
     and our minds harbors of tranquility.
     Sow in our souls true love for you and for one another,
     and root deeply within us friendship and unity
     and concord with reverence.
     So may we give peace to each other sincerely
     and receive it beautifully. **In Christ, Amen.**

9    Gather us or scatter us, O Lord,
     according to your will.
     Build us into one church:
     a church with open doors and large windows,
     a church that takes the world seriously,
     ready to work and to suffer and even to bleed for it. **Amen.**

10   O Lord our God, listening to us here,
     you accept also the prayers of our sisters and brothers
     in Africa, Asia, the Pacific, the Americas, and Europe.
     We are all one in prayer. So may we, as one,
     rightly carry out your commission to witness and to love
     in the church and throughout the world.
     Accept our prayers graciously, even when they are somewhat strange.
     We offer them in Jesus' name. **Amen.**

11   Lord God of mission,
     grant that the mission of Christ in the world
     may be fully accomplished through your church.
     Inspire your servants to discover windows in different cultures
     through which the light of the gospel may shine,
     that we may be able to share this precious treasure
     with others in languages they fully understand.
     We pray for the work of Bible translation into many human tongues
     and for the work of writers articulating the same faith,
     that Christ may be fully incarnated into many cultures
     and your church be established all over the world,
     through the risen Savior, Jesus Christ. **Amen.**

12   God,
     good beyond all that is good,
     fair beyond all that is fair,
     in you is calmness, peace, and concord.
     Heal the dissensions that divide us from one another,
     and bring us back to a unity of love
     bearing some likeness to your divine nature.
     Through the embrace of love
     and the bonds of godly affection,
     make us one in the Spirit by your peace,
     which makes all things peaceful.

We ask this through the grace, mercy, and tenderness
of your Son, Jesus Christ, our Lord. **Amen.**

13  Tender and compassionate God,
we thank you for inviting all your children into your kingdom.
Let us see each other with your eyes.
Too often we are afraid
to examine ways in which we fall short of your kingdom purpose
for our lives as individuals and as a community,
to accept without reservation those who are disabled in body or mind.
Forgive our apathy, our narrow-mindedness,
our misunderstandings.
Forgive our laziness of effort to be inclusive,
to love spontaneously, to welcome genuinely.
Call forth our best selves and help us to lift each other up.
Bless those among us with disabilities,
those who are still outside looking in,
those who long to feel included.
Prepare our hearts to set about the work of being one people,
the inclusive body of Christ, ministers of unconditional love.
May we follow the example of Christ, who opened himself to all,
the powerful and powerless alike.
Through his name we pray. **Amen.**

14  Almighty God,
bless all in every place who call on the name of our Lord Jesus Christ.
May the grace and power of the Holy Spirit fill every member
so that all the company of your faithful people
may bear witness to you on the earth.
Heal the outward divisions of your people,
inclining the wills of all to unity in the truth,
for the work of the one Lord.
Above all we pray for the unity of the Spirit,
through whom alone we are guided into all truth,
through the same Jesus Christ, our Lord. **Amen.**

15  Almighty God, in Jesus Christ you called disciples
and prayed for them to be joined in faith.
We pray for Christian churches from which we are separated.
Let us never be so sure of ourselves
that we condemn the faith of others or refuse reunion with them,
but make us ever ready to reach out for more truth
so that your church may be one in the Spirit,
through Jesus Christ, our Lord. **Amen.**

16  Triune God, we pray for the church you love.
We pray for its unity:
Make us one as you are one.

We pray for its holiness:
Make us holy as you are holy.
We pray for the church in all its universal breadth:
Strengthen your church in all places, nearby and very far away.
We pray for its mission:
Make us joyful and effective ambassadors for our Lord Jesus Christ.
In the name of Jesus Christ,
who lives and reigns with you and the Spirit,
one God, now and forever, **Amen.**

17    God of the church, your Son prayed that we might be one—
the one body of Christ throughout the whole world.
Fill us with your love, we pray,
that we may be brought to complete unity,
so all may know that you sent Christ
and that you have loved us even as you loved Christ.
We long to see your glory in the church. **Amen.**

18    O God, the giver of life,
we pray for the church throughout the world.
Sanctify its life, renew its worship,
empower its witness, restore its unity.
Remove from your people all pride
and every prejudice that dulls their will for unity.
Strengthen the work of all who strive to seek
the common obedience that binds us together.
Heal the divisions that separate your children from one another,
that they may keep the unity of the Spirit in the bond of peace. **Amen.**

19    *Sections of this prayer may be spoken in various languages.*

Sovereign God,
we give you thanks for calling us your children
and for entrusting us with the care of your creation.
**Help us to feel the many textures of your global tapestry.**
**Unstop our ears, that we may hear**
**your Word spoken in many languages.**
**Breathe into us the sweet aromas of life,**
**that we may taste the fruits of your reign.**

Even now, Lord, even in Asia,
so vast, so deeply rooted in tradition;
where your church is small, but where religion is great,
**Lord, teach us respect.**
**Help us learn from those who express faith in you in different ways.**
**Deepen our understanding of customs that are unfamiliar.**
**Help us discover new ways to witness in this ancient land.**

Even now, Lord, even in the Middle East,
the cradle of the church, the land many faiths call holy,

and now the place where the pain of the cross is so vivid,
where the dry earth is watered by the tears of suffering,
**free your people from their warring madness.**
**Teach us mutual respect, that the captives might be freed**
**and the frightened might be comforted.**

Even now, Lord, even in Latin America,
where your church stands faithfully with the weak and the poor,
where martyrs are made and drugs dictate,
where we are paying for the sins of our past,
**bring peace to our neighbors, O Lord.**
**Tear down the barriers that divide**
**and build bridges that bring people together for the common good.**

Even now, Lord, even in Africa,
where your church grows rapidly,
where faith is exuberant, but where there is famine and oppression,
**break the cycle of suffering among our sisters and brothers**
**and help us to respond to their needs in ways**
**that bring your message of hope to those who languish in despair.**

Even now, Lord, even in North America,
where so much affluence causes so much indifference—
North America, the land with so much to give
yet a land held prisoner by its possessions—
**help us to assume the role of a servant, as Jesus did.**
**Open our eyes to all parts of your creation**
**even now, Lord, even if what we see frightens us.**
**And help us to trust you to guide us as we act faithfully. Amen.**

20  Almighty Lord of the church, we pray to you
from rural meeting houses and downtown cathedrals,
from ranch homes and thatched-roof huts,
from factories, hospitals, and classrooms:
**Make your people one!**

Almighty Lord of the church, we pray to you
with saints of old and newborn disciples,
with your church around the world,
with men, women, and children:
**Make your people one!**

Almighty Lord of the church, we pray to you:
Fulfill in us the prayer of Jesus to make your people one. **Amen.**

*Prayers in Litany Form*

21  That we may manifest the unity of the Spirit in the bond of peace
and together confess that there is only one body and one spirit,
one Lord, one faith, one baptism,
let us pray to the Lord:

**Lord, have mercy upon us.**
That we may soon achieve visible communion in the body of Christ
by breaking the bread and blessing the cup around the same table,
let us pray to the Lord:
**Lord, have mercy upon us.**
That having been reconciled to God through Christ
we may be united in one ministry of reconciliation,
let us pray to the Lord:
**Lord, have mercy upon us. Amen.**

> —based on 2 Corinthians 5:18-19; Ephesians 4:4-6

22   O God, the heavens are yours and the earth is yours.
All our life belongs to you.
**Make us your messengers of peace and justice.**
May your kingdom come and your will be done on earth,
as it is in heaven.
**Make us your messengers of peace and justice.**
May all injustice, violence, and oppression give way
to fairness, mercy, and goodwill.
**Make us your messengers of peace and justice.**
Teach us to use the manifold resources of the earth
so that none may waste and none may want.
**Make us your messengers of peace and justice.**
In all our labors, may cooperation triumph over conflict;
may all people find their reward in work that serves the good of all.
**Make us your messengers of peace and justice.**
Keep alive the holy fire within the hearts
of all who dare to be the voices of unwelcome wisdom.
Make us willing to hear hard demands.
**Make us your messengers of peace and justice.**
Fill us with a passion for righteousness
and a zeal to serve where there is need.
Fill us with a purpose that is holy and right and just.
Help us to love the noblest and best.
**Make us your messengers of peace and justice.**
**Unto you, O God, be all might and majesty,**
**dominion and power, both now and evermore. Amen.**

23   **Bearer of all pain,**
**you shoulder the burden of all this world's suffering.**
In the refugee camp:
**grant us your peace.**
At the door of the torture chamber:
**grant us your peace.**
In the shanty town:
**grant us your peace.**
Among the broken street children:
**grant us your peace.**

In the oppressor's court:
**grant us your peace.**
In the devastated city:
**grant us your peace.**
On earth soaked with blood:
**grant us your peace. Amen.**

24   We pray for the churches
in which many suffer for the sake of freedom and justice.
**Servant Lord, lead us to be the willing servants of all.**
We pray for the churches
in which there is success in terms of wealth, prestige, and influence.
**Servant Lord, lead us to be the willing servants of all.**
We pray for the churches
working closely with peoples' movements for peace for the good of all.
**Servant Lord, lead us to be the willing servants of all.**
O God, our creator,
who gave us all that we are and have,
release us from self-love to be able to share
what we are, what we know, what we have
with one another and in the world that you love,
in the name of Christ, who makes this a possibility. **Amen.**

# S.5 OFFERING

## S.5.2 Offering Prayers (see also section 5.2)

1   Lord of life, you promise abundant life to all who live together in Christ.
We offer these gifts as a sign of our desire to share
our resources for the common good and building of your kingdom.
We humbly ask that you use them to strengthen our unity
and deepen our witness and healing presence in this needy world. **Amen.**

2   God of life,
we pray that our unity will be seen not only in what we believe
but also in how we work together to be salt and light in this world.
May our gifts today be a sign for each other and the world,
that we pledge to work together in your name
for the healing of this broken and hurting world.
Through Christ, our Lord. **Amen.**

# S.8 THE LORD'S SUPPER

**S.8.5 Response of Praise and Prayer** (see also section 8.5)

*S.8.5.2 Prayer*

1    God, who nourishes us for the journey,
it is strengthening to know that
as we have gathered at your table today,
your people throughout the world
are offering praise and thanksgiving
as bread and wine are shared.
May the mystery of your presence, experienced in our worship,
bind us together into one worldwide community. **Amen.**

2    God of unfailing love, in your holy mysteries
you have graciously fed us with the body and blood of your dear Son.
We pray that we and all who faithfully receive him
may grow together in the communion of the body of Christ
and finally attain to the glory of the resurrection,
through Christ, our Lord. **Amen.**

3    Lord Jesus Christ,
head of the body, your church:
How grateful we are to be members of your body,
joined with you, our head.
How grateful we are to commune with you and each other—
with all those, in every time and place, that are united with you.
Encourage us now with your Spirit
so that we may live as your body in this world,
serving as your hands and your feet,
to meet the needs of the world you so love. **Amen.**

# S.9 Closing of Worship

**S.9.1 Sending** (see also section 9.1)

*Call to Service/Discipleship*

1   People of God,
    not only in our common worship but also in our daily lives
    may we live in obedience to this invitation:

    Come to him, a living stone,
    though rejected by mortals yet chosen and precious in God's sight,
    and like living stones, let yourselves be built into a spiritual house,
    to be a holy priesthood, to offer spiritual sacrifices
    acceptable to God through Jesus Christ.
        —based on 1 Peter 2:4-5, NRSV

*Closing Prayers*

2   O Lord our God,
    we give you thanks for uniting us by baptism in the body of Christ
    and for filling us with joy in the sacrament.
    Lead us toward the full visible unity of your church
    and help us to treasure all the signs of reconciliation you have granted us.
    Now that we have tasted the banquet
    you have prepared for us in the world to come,
    may we all one day share together the inheritance of the saints
    in the life of the heavenly city,
    **through Jesus Christ, our Lord,**
    **who lives and reigns with you in the unity of the Holy Spirit,**
    **ever one God, world without end. Amen.**

3   Almighty God, you sent your Son, Jesus Christ,
    to reconcile the world to yourself.
    We praise and bless you
    for those whom you have sent in the power of the Spirit
    to preach the gospel to all nations.
    We thank you that in all parts of the earth
    a community of love has been gathered together
    through their prayers and labors,
    and that in every place your servants call upon your name,
    for the kingdom and the power and the glory
    are yours forever. **Amen.**

4   God of our lives,
    by the power of your Holy Spirit
    we have been drawn together by one baptism into one faith,
    serving one Lord and Savior.
    Do not let us tear away from one another
    through division or bad argument.
    May your peace embrace our differences,
    preserving us in unity,
    as one body of Jesus Christ, our Lord. **Amen.**

5   Loving God,
    we have heard your call to live as one body.
    We thank you for your Son, the head of the body.
    We praise you for your Spirit, who works to make us one.
    Now as we leave to worship you
    in our work, fellowship, and leisure,
    we pray for the grace to live together in harmony.
    We pray for imagination
    to find ways to strengthen our unity in Christ.
    We also pray for courage
    to carry out these commitments in a spirit of joy,
    through Jesus Christ, our Lord,
    who lives and reigns with you and the Spirit,
    one God, now and forever. **Amen.**

6   Almighty God,
    we thank you for having renewed your church
    at various times and in various ways
    by rekindling the fire of love for you
    through the work of your Holy Spirit.
    Rekindle your love in our hearts and renew us
    to fulfill the great commission
    that your Son committed to us
    so that, individually and collectively,
    as members of your church we may help many
    to know Jesus Christ as their Lord and Savior.
    Empower us by your Spirit to share
    with our neighbors and friends
    our human stories in the context of your divine story,
    through Jesus Christ, our Lord. **Amen.**

7   Lord,
    in these times when we are about to lose hope
    and our efforts seem futile,
    grant that we may perceive in our hearts and minds
    the image of your resurrection,
    which remains our only source of courage and strength,
    so that we may continue to face challenges
    and struggle against hardship and oppression born of injustice. **Amen.**

**S.9.2 Blessing/Benediction** (see also section 9.2)

1   May the God who makes everything holy and whole,
    make you holy and whole, put you together—
    spirit, soul, and body—
    and keep you fit for the coming of our Master, Jesus Christ.
    The one who called you is completely dependable.
    If he said it, he will do it! **Amen.**
            —from 1 Thessalonians 5:23-24, TM

2   May our Lord Jesus Christ,
    who prayed that we would be one,
    even as he and the Father are one,
    so grace you with his Spirit
    that you may grow in grace and fellowship
    and discover joy in walking together as part of Christ's body—
    so that the world may know of God's love for us in Christ.

3   Go from this place united in heart and thought,
    strong to serve the Lord of the church,
    ready to face and battle the foes of the Lord,
    ready to find and join the friends of the Lord,
    always vigilant, always faithful.
    And may the blessing of God—
    the Father, the Son, and the Holy Spirit—
    come upon you and stay with you always. **Amen.**

# S.10 SUGGESTED SCRIPTURE READINGS

1   *The unity of God's people*

    Ezekiel 37:15-24: A vision of a resurrected people
    Psalm 133: Picturing the beauty of God's united people
    John 17:20-24: Jesus prays for the unity of believers
    Ephesians 4:1-6: The singular unity of God and God's people

2   *The marks of the church: "We believe one holy catholic and apostolic church"*

    1 Corinthians 12:12-13: God's people are one body through the Spirit
    1 Peter 2:4-10; Ephesians 5: God's people are holy
    Matthew 28:18-20: God's people are from all nations
    Ephesians 2:11-22: God's people are built together on the apostles and prophets

# SECTION T
# COMMUNION
# OF THE SAINTS

In every time and place, imperfect and broken people who have been made saints through Jesus Christ are called to offer their gifts readily and cheerfully for the service and enrichment of the body of Christ. In this way we all share in the treasures and gifts so lavishly given by Christ to the church (Heidelberg Catechism, Q&A 55).

Christian worship is an occasion for expressing communion of the saints as well as for calling attention to the profound gifts God gives us through others in the body of Christ. Worship on such occasions involves reflection on and thanksgiving for the gifts of all who have given witness to Christ's love and demonstrated the fruits of the Spirit. It also calls for recognition of Christ's continued work in the church through imperfect people who are nevertheless "called to be saints" (Rom. 1:7).

This theme may be celebrated at any time during the year. Many churches have focused on this theme on All Saints' Day (November 1), appropriating this

day not as an occasion to invoke the saints but to give thanks for all who have gone before and to celebrate Christian unity with the "great cloud of witnesses" that precedes us (Heb. 12:1). The focus on All Saints' Day should not be on extraordinary achievements of particular Christians but on the grace and work of God through ordinary people. Other congregations have focused on this theme on the last Sunday of the calendar year, giving thanks for the gift of God expressed through all members of the congregation, including those who died during the past year. Whenever the theme of the communion of the saints is celebrated, it is important to remember that all who are united in Christ, whether dead or alive, are saints ("sanctified," made holy, to serve God) because—and only because—of the unmerited work of Christ through the power of the Holy Spirit.

---

**Scriptures and Statements of Faith Applying to the Theme of the Communion of the Saints**

*The following texts are particularly appropriate for sermons or for supplemental liturgical use.*

| | | |
|---|---|---|
| Psalm 23 | Matthew 5:1-12 | Ephesians 1:11-23 |
| Psalm 24 | Luke 6:20-31 | Ephesians 4:1-16 |
| Psalm 34:1-10, 22 | Romans 8:37-39 | Hebrews 11:1-12:13 |
| Psalm 116:12-15 | Romans 12:4-8 | 1 John 3:1-3 |
| Psalm 149 | 1 Corinthians 12:20-27; | Revelation 7:9-17 |
| Isaiah 25:6-9 | 13:1-7 | Revelation 21:1-7 |
| Daniel 7:1-3, 15-18 | | |

Belgic Confession, Art. 27-28, 33-35
Heidelberg Catechism, Q&A's 55, 76-77
Westminster Confession, Chap. XXVI, 1-3
*Our Song of Hope*, st. 15-19
*Our World Belongs to God*, st. 34-39

---

# T.1 OPENING OF WORSHIP

---

### T.1.1 Preparation for Worship (see also section 1.1)

1      Almighty and loving God,
         we thank and bless you for the encouragement you have given us
         through teachers and mentors and witnesses of your love.
         We pray that as we lead worship today,
         you will use our words and actions to encourage others.
         May this worship service truly enable us to sense our communion
         with all the people of God in every time and place—
         to the glory and praise of you alone,
         through Christ, in the power of the Holy Spirit. **Amen.**

2    God of life,
     thank you for each person you have placed in this congregation
     and for the gifts you have given them.
     We pray that everyone here—
     rich and poor, men and women, young and old—
     will find effective ways to use their gifts for the common good.
     May our worship today encourage and challenge
     all who come to know and use the gifts
     you have them given for your purposes in this world.
     Through Christ we pray. **Amen.**

3    God of our salvation,
     we bless and thank you for calling us to be saints
     and to share every good gift with other members of your body.
     We pray that today's worship service
     will be a lavish sharing of these gifts.
     We pray for generous and open hearts
     for all who lead and all who offer worship.
     We pray for the active and powerful work of your Spirit
     in this gathering so that everyone here will experience
     the kind of fellowship that is only possible
     because of what Jesus has done for us. In Jesus' name, **Amen.**

## T.1.2 Call to Worship (see also section 1.2)

1    Great is the Lord, and greatly to be praised;
         **there is no end to his greatness.**
     One generation shall praise your works to another
         **and shall declare your power.**
     All your works praise you, Lord,
         **and your faithful servants bless you.**
     They make known the glory of your kingdom
         **and speak of your power.**
     My mouth shall speak the praise of the Lord:
         **Let all flesh bless his holy name for ever and ever.**
         —based on Psalm 145:3-4, 10-11, 21

2    Since we are surrounded by so great a cloud of witnesses,
     let us lay aside every weight and the sin that clings so closely,
     and let us run with perseverance the race that is set before us.
     In the name of Jesus, our one Lord and Savior, let us worship God.
         —based on Hebrews 12:1, NRSV

3    I looked, and there was a great multitude
     that no one could count, from every nation,
     from all tribes and peoples and languages,
     standing before the throne and before the Lamb,
     robed in white, with palm branches in their hands.

They cried out in a loud voice, saying,
**"Salvation belongs to our God**
**who is seated on the throne,**
**and to the Lamb!"**
Today our voices join this ongoing heavenly hymn of praise.
In Jesus' name, let us worship God.
—based on Revelation 7:9-10, NRSV

## T.1.3 Greeting (see also section 1.3)

*Scriptural Greeting*

1   To those who are sanctified in Christ Jesus,
called to be saints,
together with all those who in every place
call on the name of our Lord Jesus Christ,
both their Lord and ours:
Grace to you and peace
from God our Father and the Lord Jesus Christ.
—1 Corinthians 1:2-3, NRSV

2   Grace to you and peace from God,
who is and who was and who is to come,
and from Jesus Christ, the faithful witness,
the firstborn of the dead,
and the ruler of the kings of the earth. **Amen.**
—from Revelation 1:4-5, NRSV

## T.1.4 Opening Responses (see also section 1.4)

*Prayers of Adoration*

1   God of grace and glory,
whom saints and angels
delight to worship in heaven,
we bless you,
we magnify you,
we adore you
as Lord of heaven and earth.
We bless and thank you
for all those made saints
through Jesus Christ,
who have testified to your love,
and shared the gifts with which you graced them.
May your Spirit be powerfully at work
through the communion of your saints

to build us all up in faith and love,
for loving service to each other
and to the world you so love,
through Jesus Christ, our Lord. **Amen.**

2    God of all ages:
we thank you for the faithful witness
of your apostles, prophets, and martyrs
throughout the history of your church
and throughout the world even today.
Through their witness we see and hear your truth.
We bless you for all who bless your name
through their writing, speaking, art, and music.
Through their work we glimpse your beauty.
We praise you for all who serve you without recognition or honor,
offering encouragement to the lonely, the sick, and the fearful.
Through their lives we see your faithfulness and sense your comfort.
Now we pray that you will use even us
to reflect the glory we see in Christ.
May the voices of all your saints, made holy in Christ,
swell in joyous praise to you, the giver of all good gifts,
through Christ, our Lord, who lives and reigns
with you and the Holy Spirit, one God, now and forever. **Amen.**

3    *This text is based on the anonymous fourth-century Latin hymn* Te Deum Laudamus.

We praise you, O God;
we acclaim you as Lord;
all creation worships you,
the Father everlasting.
To you all angels, all the powers of heaven,
the cherubim and seraphim, sing in endless praise:
    **Holy, holy, holy Lord, God of power and might,**
    **heaven and earth are full of your glory.**
The glorious company of apostles praise you.
The noble fellowship of prophets praise you.
The white-robed army of martyrs praise you.
Throughout the world the holy church acclaims you:
    **Father, of majesty unbounded;**
    **your true and only Son, worthy of all praise;**
    **the Holy Spirit, advocate and guide.**

You, Christ, are the King of glory,
the eternal Son of the Father.
When you took our flesh to set us free,
you humbly chose the virgin's womb.
You overcame the sting of death
and opened the kingdom of heaven to all believers.
You are seated at God's right hand in glory.

We believe that you will come to be our judge.
Come, then, Lord, and help your people,
bought with the price of your own blood,
and bring us with your saints
to glory everlasting. **Amen.**

4    God of the ages,
we praise you for all your servants
who have done justice, loved mercy,
and walked humbly with their God.
We praise you for all who have sought your new creation,
and who, by their steadfast faith,
have shown their discipleship in Christ Jesus.
We praise you for those we have known and loved,
and pray that we, with them,
may follow in the way of Christ,
and, at the last, dwell in your holy city,
sharing the inheritance of the saints in light,
through your Son, our Savior, Jesus Christ. **Amen.**

## Prayers of Invocation

5    Our Lord Jesus Christ, who by your Word and Spirit
has been gathering your people out of the entire human race
from the beginning of the world to its end:
Keep your church strong and add to it.
Destroy every force that conspires against you and your people.
Empower your church
to keep faith, hope, and love alive;
to declare your Word's promises and commands;
to bless and enrich the lives of others;
to worship and bring delight to you.
O Triune God, prompt your people eagerly to await the day
when they shall fellowship with one another forever
and unite to sing you their undying thanks and praise. **Amen.**

6    God of the universe,
hear our prayer this day, as we gather together in this place.
Send your Spirit to prompt our prayers.
May our voices join the voices of those scattered far from here
so that in all that we are,
and wherever we might be,
we may join with the saints throughout the ages
in serving and praising your holy name. **Amen.**

7    Almighty God,
      whose people are knit together in one holy church,
      the body of Christ, our Lord:
      Grant us grace to follow your blessed saints
      in lives of faith and commitment
      and to know the inexpressible joys
      you have prepared for those who love you,
      through your Son, Jesus Christ, our Lord,
      who lives and reigns with you and the Holy Spirit,
      one God, now and forever. **Amen.**

8    We give you thanks, our God and Father,
      for all those who have formed us in the faith,
      for those near to us who have instructed us,
      for those in public roles who have inspired us,
      for those in generations past who have gone before us.
      For all these may you receive glory,
      through Jesus Christ, our Lord. **Amen.**

# T.2 CONFESSION AND ASSURANCE

## T.2.1 Call to Confession (see also section 2.1)

1    Christ calls us to share the heavenly banquet of his love
      with all the saints in earth and heaven.
      Knowing our unworthiness and sin,
      let us ask from him both mercy and forgiveness.

## T.2.2 Prayers of Confession (see also section 2.2)

1    Eternal God, in every age
      you have raised up men and women to live and die in faith.
      Forgive our indifference to your will.
      You have commanded us to speak, but we have been silent.
      You have called us to do what is just, but we have been fearful.
      Have mercy on us, your faithless servants.
      Keep before us faithful people for us to follow
      so that, by the power of your Holy Spirit,
      we may grow in the knowledge of our Lord and Savior Jesus Christ,
      to the praise of your holy name. **Amen.**

**T.2.4 Assurance of Pardon** (see also section 2.4)

1    You are no longer strangers and aliens,
but you are citizens with the saints
and also members of the household of God,
built upon the foundation of the apostles and prophets,
with Christ Jesus himself as the cornerstone.
In him the whole structure is joined together
and grows into a holy temple in the Lord;
in whom you also are built together spiritually
into a dwelling place for God.
      —Ephesians 2:19-22, NRSV

# T.3 PROCLAIMING THE WORD

**T.3.6 Profession of Our Church's Faith** (see also section 3.6)

1    I believe that the Son of God,
through his Spirit and Word,
out of the entire human race,
from the beginning of the world to its end,
gathers, protects, and preserves for himself
a community chosen for eternal life
and united in true faith.
And of this community I am and always will be a living member.
The communion of saints—
believers one and all—as members of this community,
share in Christ and in all his treasures and gifts.
Each member should consider it a duty
to use these gifts readily and joyfully
for the service and enrichment of the other members.
      —from Heidelberg Catechism, Q&A's 54-55

2    We believe and confess
one single catholic or universal church—
a holy congregation and gathering of true Christian believers,
awaiting their entire salvation in Jesus Christ,
being washed by his blood, and sanctified and sealed by the Holy Spirit.
This church has existed from the beginning of the world
and will last until the end, as appears from the fact
that Christ is eternal King who cannot be without subjects.
And this holy church is preserved by God

against the rage of the whole world,
even though for a time it may appear very small to human eyes—
as though it were snuffed out.
And so this holy church is not confined, bound,
or limited to a certain place or certain people.
But it is spread and dispersed throughout the entire world,
though still joined and united in heart and will,
in one and the same Spirit, by the power of faith.

—from Belgic Confession, Art. 27

3    All saints—who are united to Jesus Christ their head
by his Spirit and by faith—have fellowship with him in his graces, sufferings, death,
        resurrection, and glory.
And, being united to one another in love,
they participate in each other's gifts and graces
and are obligated to perform those public and private duties
that lead to their mutual good, both inwardly and outwardly.

It is the duty of professing saints to maintain
a holy fellowship and communion in the worship of God
and in performing such other spiritual services
as help them to edify one another.
It is their duty also to come to the aid of one another
in material things according to their various abilities and necessities.
As God affords opportunity, this communion is to be extended
to all those in every place who call on the name of the Lord Jesus.

—from Westminster Confession (MESV), Chap. XXVI, Sec. 1-2

4    The church is a gathering of forgiven sinners called to be holy.
Saved by the patient grace of God, we deal patiently with others
and together confess our need for grace and forgiveness.
Restored in Christ's presence, shaped by his life,
this new community lives out
the ongoing story of God's reconciling love,
announces the new creation,
and works for a world of justice and peace.

We grieve that the church,
which shares one Spirit, one faith, one hope,
and spans all time, place, race, and language,
has become a broken communion in a broken world.
When we struggle for the truth of the gospel
and for the righteousness God demands,
we pray for wisdom and courage.
When our pride or blindness
hinders the unity of God's household, we seek forgiveness.
We marvel that the Lord gathers the broken pieces to do his work
and that he blesses us still with joy, new members,
and surprising evidences of unity.
We commit ourselves to seeking and expressing

the oneness of all who follow Jesus,
and we pray for brothers and sisters who suffer for the faith.

We long for that day
when our bodies are raised,
the Lord wipes away our tears,
and we dwell forever in the presence of God.
We will take our place in the new creation,
where there will be no more death
or mourning or crying or pain,
and the Lord will be our light.
Come, Lord Jesus, come.

On that day we will see our Savior face to face,
sacrificed Lamb and triumphant King, just and gracious.
He will set all things right,
judge evil, and condemn the wicked.
We face that day without fear,
for the Judge is our Savior,
whose shed blood declares us righteous.
We live confidently, anticipating his coming,
offering him our daily lives—our acts of kindness,
our loyalty, and our love—knowing that he will weave
even our sins and sorrows into his sovereign purpose.
Come, Lord Jesus, come.

—from Our World Belongs to God, st. 39-40, 56-57

# T.4 PRAYERS OF THE PEOPLE

## T.4.4 Complete Model Outlines and Prayers (see also section 4.4)

*Prayer Outlines*

*The following are guides for extemporaneous prayers. The patterns provide suggested texts for the opening and closing of each part and call for extemporaneous prayers of thanksgiving, petition, and intercession.*

1   Eternal God,
    in all times and places you have provided your church
    with individuals who have been used to point others to you.
    We are grateful for the testimony of the great cloud of witnesses
    who surround your throne:

for the apostles and first believers . . .
for those in the early church . . .
for the martyrs of all ages . . .
for those who have reformed the church in every age . . .
for those who have ministered to us . . .
For these great examples of the faith we give you praise.

As we join this communion of saints,
we pray that we too may be worthy witnesses for you
    in our care of creation . . .
    in our interaction with people of other nations and ethnicities . . .
    in our respect for those in authority . . .
    in our care for those in our broader community . . .
    in our support of Christians around the world . . .
    in our daily lives of ministry . . .
    as we support persons with particular needs, especially . . .

In all of this we look forward to the day
when we will join those who have gone before us in praising you,
the one eternal God, forever and ever. **Amen.**

2    Loving and faithful God,
we bless you for calling us to be a holy people,
living for you in service to each other for the sake of your world.
We pray that our congregation will experience
a rich and free sharing of the gifts you have generously given us.
Knowing that we are called to be saints,
we humbly ask that you will work powerfully through us
to accomplish your purposes in the world.
We pray for the courage, the patience, and the generosity of spirit
that comes from imitating the love you have shown us in Christ.
We long for your Spirit's power to make us more Christlike
in our thoughts, words, and deeds.
Help us to think of others and their needs even now as we pray for
    creation, in its groaning . . .
    the world, in its suffering . . .
    our nation and city, in their need of healing . . .
We pray in the name of Jesus, the author and finisher of our faith,
who lives and reigns with you and the Holy Spirit,
one God, now and forever. **Amen.**

*Complete Prose Prayers*

3    God of grace,
we thank you for the saints whom we ourselves have known and loved.
It does not come easily to us to call them saints;
it seems as if ordinary mortals are not good enough or great enough,
but you have given your people this name

and invited us into your company,
and you know how much we have loved them.
So for these good companions,
whom we name before you for their love
and for our love of them, we give you grateful thanks [*name(s)*].
In the mystery of your love, in the power of your Spirit,
we are one with them. We give great thanks. **Amen.**

## Prayers in Litany Form

**4**   Remembering those who have gone ahead . . .

[*This may be a time of reflecting on the lives and contributions
of historical saints and/or remembering members of the congregation
who have died in the past year.*]

Let us give thanks to the Lord our God.
**It is right to give our thanks and praise.**
God of the ages, we praise you for all your servants,
who have done justice, loved mercy,
and walked humbly with their God.
For apostles and martyrs and saints of every time and place,
who in life and death have witnessed to your truth,
**we praise you, O God.**
For all your servants who have faithfully served you,
witnessed bravely, and died in faith,
who are still shining lights in the world,
**we praise you, O God.**
For those we have known and loved,
for teachers and colleagues and friends,
for parents and grandparents, husbands and wives, brothers and sisters,
for all who by their faithful obedience and steadfast hope
have shown the same mind that was in Christ Jesus,
**we praise you, O God.**
Keep us grateful for their witness, and, like them,
eager to follow in the way of Christ.
Then at last, bring us together
to share in the inheritance of the saints in light,
**through Jesus Christ, our Savior. Amen.**

**5**   I looked, and there was a great multitude
that no one could count, from every nation,
from all tribes and peoples and languages,
standing before the throne and before the Lamb,
robed in white, with palm branches in their hands.
They cried out in a loud voice, saying,
"Salvation belongs to our God
who is seated on the throne, and to the Lamb!"
**We praise you, O God, for all your saints in heaven.**

How grateful we are of the life and witness of . . .
[A list of names may be read.]
**We also praise you for all those whose names are held in your loving memory,**
**the vast company of voices who acclaim you as Lord.**
We are grateful for this vast company of witnesses.
**Strengthen us as we follow their lead.**
Help us to keep our eyes on Jesus,
forerunner in faith, Lord of all.
**Strengthen us in the hope that we with them**
**will taste and see your goodness in the land of the living.**
By your Spirit, teach us even now
to sing the song of heaven:
**"Salvation belongs to our God,**
**who sits on the throne,**
**and to the Lamb. Amen!**
**Praise and glory**
**and wisdom and thanks and honor**
**and power and strength**
**be to our God for ever and ever. Amen!"**
　　　　—based on 1 Corinthians 2:9; Hebrews 12:1-2; Revelation 7:9-12

6　　O Lord our God, we thank you
for the many people throughout the ages
who have followed your way of life joyfully:
for the many saints and martyrs, men and women,
who have offered up their very lives
so that your life abundant may become manifest
and your kingdom may advance.
**For your love and faithfulness**
**we will at all times praise your name.**
O Lord, we thank you for those
who chose the way of your Son, our brother Jesus Christ.
In the midst of trial, they held out hope;
in the midst of hatred, they kindled love;
in the midst of persecutions, they witnessed to your power;
in the midst of despair, they clung to your promise.
**For your love and faithfulness**
**we will at all times praise your name.**
O Lord, we thank you for the truth they learned and passed on to us:
that it is by giving that we shall receive;
it is by becoming weak that we shall be strong;
it is by loving others that we shall be loved;
it is by offering ourselves that the kingdom will unfold;
it is by dying that we shall inherit life everlasting.
Lord, give us courage to follow your way of life.
**For your love and faithfulness**
**we will at all times praise your name. Amen.**

7    Eternal God,
      we give you thanks for the founders of your church,
      for those whom you called and formed in the image of your Son,
      for those who suffered and died for their faith.
      **We thank you for the cloud of witnesses.**

      We give you thanks for the reformers of your church:
      for their rediscovery of truth,
      for their eagerness to live simply,
      for their faithful study of your Word,
      for their endeavor to serve their neighbors.
      **We thank you for the cloud of witnesses.**

      **God of our forebears,**
      **give us the courage and wisdom**
      **of the saints who have gone before us;**
      **form us in the image of your Son;**
      **renew your Holy Spirit's work in our generation.**
      **May we live and serve under the rule of Jesus Christ**
      **until your reign comes. Amen.**

8    Eternal God,
      your Word declares that the life that is laid down in faith
      will be raised and produce a great harvest.
      This we celebrate as we proclaim:
      **Christ has died, Christ is risen, Christ will come again.**
      We remember and praise you
      for the saints and martyrs of this and every age.
      We name them before you now [*aloud or in silence*].
      These lives, like seeds, dropped to the ground,
      yet their witness has borne fruit and enables us to say:
      **Christ has died, Christ is risen, Christ will come again.**
      We pray for your church throughout the world
      and for that part to which we belong,
      that it may be ready to spend and to be spent in your service,
      that the love of self-preservation may be set aside,
      that the deaths you demand of it may be embraced joyfully,
      and that through all it may proclaim:
      **Christ has died, Christ is risen, Christ will come again.**
      In silence we surrender to your will and purpose
      ourselves and all that we count important.
      For we cannot know the glory of Christ's resurrection
      if we do not have the fellowship of sufferings.
      And we cannot expect to gather the kingdom's harvest
      if we do not sow the kingdom's seed.
      In us and through us, may your Spirit proclaim:
      **Christ has died, Christ is risen, Christ will come again. Amen.**

# T.9 CLOSING OF WORSHIP

**T.9.1 Sending** (see also section 9.1)

*Call to Service/Discipleship*

1   Lead a life worthy of the calling
    to which you have been called,
    with all humility and gentleness,
    with patience, bearing with one another in love,
    making every effort to maintain
    the unity of the Spirit in the bond of peace.
    There is one body and one Spirit,
    just as you were called to the one hope of your calling,
    one Lord, one faith, one baptism, one God and Father of all,
    who is above all and through all and in all.
       —Ephesians 4:1-6, NRSV

*Closing Prayers*

2   Almighty God,
    you have knit together your elect
    in one communion and fellowship
    in the body of your Son, Christ, our Lord:
    Give us grace so to follow your blessed saints
    in all virtuous and godly living
    that we may come to those ineffable joys
    that you have prepared for those who truly love you,
    through Jesus Christ our Lord,
    who with you and the Holy Spirit lives and reigns,
    one God, in glory everlasting. **Amen.**

**T.9.2 Blessing/Benediction** (see also section 9.2)

1   May God, who has given us, in the lives of his saints,
    patterns of holy living and victorious dying,
    strengthen your faith and devotion
    and enable you to bear witness to the truth
    against all adversity. **Amen.**

**2**    United as one body in Christ, our Lord,
turn your minds and hearts toward each other in love
so that you may rest in God's eternal love,
    at peace with those who have gone before us,
    at peace with those around us,
    and trusting in God's peace for those yet to come.
Receive now this blessing from our God,
the God of the past, the present, and the future:

Grace and peace to you,
from him who is, who was, and who is to come,
and from the seven spirits before his throne,
and from Jesus Christ, the faithful witness,
the firstborn of the dead,
and the ruler of the kings of the earth.
    —based on Revelation 1:4-5

# T.10 SUGGESTED SCRIPTURE READINGS

**1**    *Sharing gifts within the body of Christ*

1 Corinthians 12:12-27: One body, many parts
Ephesians 4:1-16: The body, united in Christ, grows in love
Colossians 3:1-17: Called to peace as members of one body
Romans 12: We belong to each other

# APPENDIX

## WORSHIPING THE TRIUNE GOD
### Receiving and Sharing Christian Wisdom
### across Continents and Centuries
Adopted in 2010 by the World Communion of Reformed Churches

*For more information and a study guide, see* Wise Church, *available through Faith Alive Christian Resources (www.faithaliveresources.org; 1-800-333-8300).*

## I. A Called and Forgiven People: Assembling in Jesus' Name

### 1.1 Called by the Triune God

Blessed are the people of God
who are deeply aware
that they are both called by and address the triune God,
Father, Son, and Holy Spirit,
who gathers, protects, and cares for the church
through Word and Spirit—[1]
a God of splendour and majesty
perfectly revealed in Jesus Christ,
the "image of the invisible God" (Col. 1:15).

Blessed is the community
that gratefully acknowledges
that the triune God not only receives our worship,
but also makes our worship possible,
prompting us through the Holy Spirit,
and sanctifying our offerings
through the perfect priesthood of Jesus Christ,
who during his life on earth offered
praise "to the Father," "full of joy in the Holy Spirit" (Luke 10:21),
and even now "ever lives to pray for us" (Heb. 7:25).

Blessed is the congregation
that insists that believers gather to worship God
not first of all in order that God might bless them,
but because God has already blessed them.

Blessed is the congregation that then discovers
that God does indeed bless them

---

1    Heidelberg Catechism, Q&A 54; Belhar Confession, Art. 1

as they worship the triune God
who nourishes, teaches, convicts, and corrects them,
and strengthens bonds
that unite believers with Jesus Christ and with each other
through the sanctifying actions
of the proclamation of the Word and corporate prayer,
through baptism and the Lord's Supper,
through fellowship, offerings, and testimony.

### 1.2 *Corporate Assembly, the Whole People of God*

Wise is the worshiping community
that "does not neglect meeting together" (Heb. 10:25),
but joyfully gathers in Jesus' name,
eager to proclaim the Word of God,
to offer praise and prayer,
and to celebrate the sacraments,
each of which are actions of the whole people of God,
"the royal priesthood" (1 Pet. 2:9).

Blessed is the congregation
that invites all worshipers—
including those which our cultures
may label in different ways as "disabled"—
to full, conscious, and active participation in corporate worship,
engaging heart, soul, and mind in devotion to God,
deeply aware of how their own personal worship
participates in a much larger chorus of praise to God.

Blessed is the congregation
that expresses in its worship
the communion in the body of Christ,
the unity of the Spirit in the bond of peace,
and the oneness that is the gift and calling of God
that unites the young and old
and believers of every time and place
who share a common calling by the Spirit of God in Jesus Christ.[2]

### 1.3 *The Holy Spirit*

Wise is the worshiping community
that recognizes how the Holy Spirit works
through both reason and emotion,
through both spiritual disciplines and surprising events,
through both services that are prayerfully planned
and through moments of spontaneous discovery.

Wise is the worshiping community that recognizes that
the lasting value or spiritual power of worship

---

[2] from WCRC materials for the inaugural assembly in Grand Rapids, Michigan.

does not depend upon our own creativity,
imagination, intellect, or emotions,
but comes from the Holy Spirit,
who may choose to use any or all of these things.
For, truly, worship is a gift to receive,
not an accomplishment to achieve.

## 1.4 Affirming and Resisting Culture

Wise is the church
that seeks to be "in" but not "of" the world (John 15:19),
resisting aspects of the culture
that compromise the integrity of the gospel,
and eagerly engaging its culture
with the good news of the gospel of Jesus Christ
who comes to each culture, but is not bound by any culture.

Wise, then, is the church
that is grateful that the gospel of Jesus
is at once transcultural, contextual,
cross-cultural, and counter-cultural.[3]

## 1.5 The Goodness of the Redeemed Creation

Wise is the congregation
that makes clear that its worship
participates in the song of praise
that is offered by all creation.

Wise is the congregation that
celebrates worship as an embodied reality,
grateful for the gestures and postures
that express our praise and prayer,
and the book, water, bread, and wine
that God ordains for our use—
the gifts of God for the people of God.

## 1.6 Leading God's People

Wise is the community that
calls, trains, affirms, and responds to
those gifted for leadership in all genders, ages, races, and abilities,
providing formative training and mentorship for them
in the theology and practices of worship.

Wise are leaders in worship
who equip all the members of the community
for full, conscious, and active participation (cf. Vatican II)
taking care to express hospitality
to those who are not yet a part of Christ's body, the church.

---

3    Cf. the Lutheran World Federation's Nairobi Statement on Worship and Culture

*1.7 Artistic Expression*

Blessed is the congregation in which the Word is proclaimed
and prayers and praise are offered
not only through words,
but also through artistic expression:
through gifts God has given
to each local community
in music and dance,
in speech and silence,
in visual art and architecture.
Blessed are the artists
who offer and discipline their gifts
so God's people may
testify to the goodness of God,
offer thanks, and express repentance.

Wise are artists who are grateful
both for the limitations offered by the second commandment,
and also for the example of the biblical artists called by God
and equipped by God's people for service
according to God's commands. (Ex. 35:30ff)

Wise is the church
that gratefully receives
the gifts of faithful songs and artworks
from other centuries and other cultures,
celebrating the catholicity of the church
and cultivating creativity
through new songs and works for worship.

## II. Joyfully Proclaiming God's Word

*2.1 Word and Spirit*

Blessed is the congregation
in which the Word of God is proclaimed
with conviction and joy,
surrounded by expectant prayers
and profound gratitude
for the Holy Spirit's work
to illuminate the hearts and minds of God's people.

*2.2 The Breadth of the Christ-Centered Word*

Wise is the congregation
that nourishes believers
with readings and sermons that engage the breadth and depth of God's Word,

Old Testament and New Testament,
always proclaiming the fullness of the gospel of Jesus Christ.

## 2.3 Calling Forth Rest and Witness, Justice and Peace

Blessed is the congregation
in which the proclamation of God's Word
comforts those who mourn
and confronts those who oppose God's reign.

Wise is the preacher
who invites hearers to receive God's lavish grace,
to repent from sin and evil,
to turn toward Christ,
to proclaim peace,
"to do justice, to love kindness and to walk humbly with God" (Mic. 6:8).

## 2.4 Resisting Idolatry

Wise is the congregation
that proclaims the Word of God
in ways that actively expose and resist
both the idols that we are tempted to worship instead of God
and also the idols of our distorted understandings of God.

Blessed is the congregation
that challenges these distortions
by contemplating the person and work of Jesus Christ,
"the radiance of God's glory and the exact representation of God's being" (Heb. 1:3).

## 2.5 Credo: The Response of Faith

Wise is the congregation
in which the proclamation of the gospel
is accepted as the Word of God,
which is at work in you who believe (1 Thess. 2:13),
leading to both confession and praise,
both repentance and a commitment to service,
both compassion and a passion for justice,
both personal and communal actions,
both new obedience and profound gratitude.

Blessed is the congregation
that invites believers to testify to the goodness of God
by expressing the faith of the church
that transcends and forms our individual experiences
and unites us with believers across cultures and centuries,
and by testifying to the work of God in the life of the local community.

## III. Responding to God in Prayer and Offerings

### 3.1 *Praise and Gratitude*

> Blessed is the church that
> offers praise and thanksgiving (cf. Ps. 50:14; Heb. 13:15),
> not only extolling the beauty and glory of God,
> but also contemplating, reciting,
> and celebrating all that God has done
> throughout history.

> Wise is the congregation
> that draws upon and learns from
> the Bible's own narratively-shaped prayers
> of praise and thanksgiving (e.g., Ps. 136)
> as it gives form to its own prayer.

### 3.2 *Praying in Jesus' Name, through the Spirit*

> Blessed is the church that prays in Jesus' name,
> acknowledging our union with our ascended and ever-present Lord.

> Blessed is the worshiping community
> that prays in and through the Holy Spirit,
> desiring the gifts of the Holy Spirit,
> and acknowledging that as we pray
> the Holy Spirit helps us in our weakness,
> interceding for us according to the will of God (Rom. 8:26, 27)
> and resisting the "cosmic powers of this present darkness" (Eph. 6:12).

### 3.3 *Full Range of Human Experience*

> Wise is the church that,
> following the example of the psalms,
> encourages honest and trusting prayers to God
> that express the full range of human experience—
> the "anatomy of the soul"—[4]
> spoken, sung, or silent,
> danced, dramatized, or visualized—
> prayers of celebration and lament,
> trust and desperation,
> supplication and intercession,
> thanksgiving and confession,
> healing and hope.

> Blessed is the church that prays not only for its own needs,
> but also for the needs of the world that God so loves.

---

[4]  The phrase "anatomy of the soul" is from John Calvin's commentary on the psalms.

## 3.4 Gifts and Offerings

Wise is the church that gratefully practices
the giving of gifts, time, and talent,
as an act of dedication and worship.

Wise is the church which affirms
that all of life is lived in service to God and neighbor,
and that believers are called to be stewards of every gift of God.

## IV. Baptizing and Feasting

### 4.1 Jesus' Commands to Baptize and Celebrate the Lord's Supper

Blessed is the church
that faithfully obeys Jesus' commands
"to make disciples,
baptizing them
in the name of the Father, Son, and Holy Spirit
and teaching them to obey
everything Jesus has commanded (Matt. 28:20)
and to "eat and drink in remembrance of me" (Luke 22: 19-20),
receiving these signs
as occasions in which God
works to nourish and sustain,
comfort and challenge,
teach and transform us.

### 4.2 Baptism

Blessed is the congregation
that announces that their true identity
is found in Jesus Christ.

Blessed is the congregation
that proclaims how the waters of baptism
are a sign and seal
of God's promises
to wash us clean,
to adopt us into the body of Christ,
to send the Holy Spirit to renew, empower,
and resurrect us to new life in Christ.

Blessed is the congregation
that proclaims how the waters of baptism
are also a sign and seal of God's call to renounce sin and evil,
to embrace Christ and our new identity in him,
and to live a renewed and holy life.

Wise is the community
who celebrates baptism joyfully

and remembers that baptism
as a means of grace and encouragement
to live out our vows of covenant faithfulness.

## 4.3 Lord's Supper

Blessed is the church
that regularly celebrates the Lord's Supper
as a feast of thanksgiving, communion, and hope.

Blessed is the congregation
that not only gratefully remembers God's
creating and redeeming work in Jesus Christ,
knowing his presence in the breaking of the bread,
but also gratefully receives the gift of union
with Jesus Christ and Christ's body,
and looks forward to the feast of the coming kingdom.

Blessed is the congregation
that shares this meal
by "discerning the body of Christ" in its manifold oneness,
by expressing hospitality for one another
with grace and truth (1 Cor. 11:29-33),
and by reflecting God's hospitality for us
in ministries of hospitality in the world.

## V. A Blessed and Commissioned People Serving in Jesus' Name

### 5.1 God's Sending

Blessed is the congregation
in which believers are
encouraged by God's gracious blessing
and challenged by God's gracious call
to proclaim the good news of Jesus
and to live as a healing presence in the world
in the name of Jesus.

### 5.2 Daily Worship

Wise is the community
that nourishes faith
by encouraging daily worship for all believers,
with emphasis on reading and meditating on God's Word,
seeking the guidance of the Holy Spirit,
offering prayers of praise and petition,
singing psalms, hymns, and spiritual songs,
listening for God in "sheer silence" (1 Kings 19:12),
and living every moment before the face of God.

## 5.3 Hospitality and Evangelization

Blessed are communities
in which hospitality is practiced
in both public worship and in personal lives,
where strangers and guests are welcomed and embraced,
where the poor and marginalized, diseased and forsaken,
can find refuge under the shadow of God's wings.

Blessed are communities
in which all people are invited and challenged
to become disciples of Jesus,
receiving baptism and formation in the faith (cf. Matt. 28:19)

## 5.4 Formation for Worship

Wise are congregations
that invite and challenge believers
of all ages and abilities
to "grow in the grace and knowledge
of our Lord and Savior Jesus Christ" (2 Pet. 3:18).

Blessed are congregations
that nurture the faithful interplay
of Scripture, doctrines, practices, and the fruit of the Spirit.

Wise are congregations that deepen worship
through reflection on and teaching about
the meaning of worship practices.

## 5.5 Worship, Compassion, and Justice

Blessed are congregations
whose public worship points to Jesus Christ,
and Jesus' message about the
kingdom of God.

Blessed are congregations
whose corporate worship and public witness
are consistent with each other
and faithful to God's Word,
whose worship and witness are
a testimony to the work of the Holy Spirit.

Blessed are congregations who seek to receive
the liberating work of the Holy Spirit
who alone can break though hypocrisy
and through whom
justice and peace, worship and witness,
can truly embrace.

## 5.6 Maranatha: Worship and Christian Hope

> Blessed are congregations
> who are not content
> to live only in the present moment,
> but whose worship expresses
> the groaning of all creation
> for the fullness of God's reign
> in Jesus Christ.
>
> Blessed are congregations whose
> life together is summed up
> in the certain hope of the prayer "Maranatha"—
> "come, Lord Jesus" (Rev. 22:20).

# INDEXES

# ACKNOWLEDGMENTS

## Permissions

Brief portions of this book may be reproduced without special permission for one-time use only, for worship and educational purposes, in an order of service for use by a congregation, or in a special program or lesson resource, provided that no part of such reproduction is sold, directly or indirectly, and that the following acknowledgment is included: "Reprinted by permission from *The Worship Sourcebook*, Second Edition © 2013, Faith Alive Christian Resources." This notice can appear in small print preferably on the same page on which the resource is reprinted. For all other uses, please contact the copyright holder of each resource used.

Every effort has been made to trace the owner or holder of each copyright. If any required acknowledgment has been omitted, the publisher asks that the omission be excused and agrees to make necessary corrections in subsequent printings.

Please address questions about rights and reproductions to Permissions, Faith Alive Christian Resources, 2850 Kalamazoo Ave. SE, Grand Rapids, MI 49560; phone: 800-333-8300; fax: 616-726-1164; e-mail: permissions@faithaliveresources.org.

## Scripture Versions and Paraphrases

Scriptural texts in this book are from a variety of Bible versions and paraphrases (used by permission and indicated below) and are referenced as exact quotations, as slight adaptations (noted as "from" a particular text), or as paraphrases or quotations coupled with additional phrasing (noted as "based on" a particular text). Abbreviations referring to the sources of scriptural texts are indicated in the left column below. An index of Scripture references (p. 832) offers additional Scripture source information as an aid to worship planning.

NIV  *Holy Bible*, New International Version. © 1973, 1978, 1984, 2011, International Bible Society. Used by permission of Zondervan Bible Publishers.

NJB  *The New Jerusalem Bible.* © 1985, Darton, Longman, and Todd, Ltd., and Doubleday, a division of Bantam Doubleday Dell Publishing Group, Inc. All rights reserved.

NLT  *Holy Bible*, New Living Translation. © 1996, Tyndale Charitable Trust. Used by permission of Tyndale House Publishers, Inc., Wheaton, IL 60189. All rights reserved.

NRSV    *Holy Bible,* New Revised Standard Version. © 1989, Division of Christian Education of the National Council of the Churches of Christ in the United States of America. Used by permission. All rights reserved.

TEV     *Good News Bible with Deuterocanonicals/Apocrypha,* Today's English Version, Second Edition. © 1992, American Bible Society.

TM      *The Message: The Bible in Contemporary Language.* Eugene H. Peterson. © 1993, 1994, 1995, 1996, 2000, 2001, 2002. Used by permission of NavPress Publishing Group.

TP      *The Psalter,* a faithful and inclusive rendering from the Hebrew into contemporary English poetry, intended primarily for communal song and recitation. International Commission on English in the Liturgy (ICEL). © 1994, International Commission on English in the Liturgy, Inc. All rights reserved. Third printing, 1998. © 1995, Archdiocese of Chicago: Liturgy Training Publications, 1800 North Hermitage Avenue, Chicago, IL 60622-1101; 1-800-933-1800. All rights reserved.

## Confessions and Statements of Faith

The various confessions and statements of faith used in this book are listed here in chronological order.

Apostles' Creed, translated from the fourth-century Latin text. © 1988, CRC Publications, Grand Rapids, Mich.

Nicene Creed, translated from the Greek text approved at the Council of Chalcedon in 451, revised in 589. © 1988, CRC Publications, Grand Rapids, Mich.

Belgic Confession (1561), translated from the French text of 1619 adopted at Synod of Dort (1618-1619). © 2011, Faith Alive Christian Resources, Grand Rapids, Mich.

Heidelberg Catechism (1563), translated from the first edition of the German text. © 2011, Faith Alive Christian Resources, Grand Rapids, Mich.

Westminster Confession (MESV), the Modern English Study Version of the Westminster Confession of Faith (1647). © 1993, Committee on Christian Education of The Orthodox Presbyterian Church, Box P, Willow Grove, PA 19090.

Westminster Shorter Catechism, a confession of faith adopted by the Westminster Assembly of 1647. Public domain.

*Our Song of Hope,* approved in 1978 by the General Synod of the Reformed Church in America as a statement of the church's faith for use in its ministry of witness, teaching, and worship. © 1975, Wm. B. Eerdmans Publishing Co., Grand Rapids, Mich.

*Our World Belongs to God: A Contemporary Testimony,* Second Edition, adopted by the Christian Reformed Church in North America in 2008. © 2008, Faith Alive Christian Resources, Grand Rapids, Mich.

*A Brief Statement of Faith.* © 1991 by the Office of the General Assembly, Presbyterian Church (U.S.A.) as part of the Book of Confessions, which is in turn Part I of the Constitution of the Presbyterian Church (U.S.A.). Reprinted with permission of the Office of the General Assembly, Presbyterian Church (U.S.A.).

## Other Sources

This list identifies the numerous other sources used in this book. These sources are arranged alphabetically according to their identifying abbreviations used in the next subsection, titled Sources of Specific Texts (see p. 791).

| | |
|---|---|
| AC | *Alternative Collects 1985.* © 1985, The Anglican Church of Australia Trust Corporation. Reproduced with permission. |
| AESP | *And Everyone Shall Praise: Resources for Multicultural Worship.* R. Mark Liebenow. United Church Press, 1999. © 1999, R. Mark Liebenow. |
| AFS-1994 | *Agenda for Synod 1994.* © 1994, Christian Reformed Church in North America. |
| ANZPB-HKMOA | *A New Zealand Prayer Book: "He Karakia Mihinare o Aotearoa."* William Collins Publishers, Ltd., 1989. Distributed in North America by HarperCollinsSanFrancisco. © 1989, The General Secretary, The Anglican Church in Aotearoa, New Zealand, and Polynesia. |
| AOS-1976 | *Acts of Synod 1976.* © 1976, Christian Reformed Church. |
| AOS-1981 | *Acts of Synod 1981.* © 1981, Christian Reformed Church. |
| APB | *An African Prayer Book,* selected and with introductions by Desmond Tutu. Doubleday, 1995. © 1995, Desmond Tutu. |
| AS | *An Advent Sourcebook.* Edited by Thomas J. O'Gorman. Liturgy Training Publications, 1988. © 1988, Archdiocese of Chicago. |
| ASB | *The Alternative Service Book 1980,* services authorized for use in the Church of England in conjunction with *The Book of Common Prayer* (1662). Cambridge University Press, William Clowes Publishers, Ltd., and SPCK, 1980. © 1980, The Central Board of Finance of the Church of England; © 1999, The Archbishops' Council. |
| ASM | *All the Seasons of Mercy.* Diane Karay. Westminster Press, 1987. © by Diane Karay. Used by permission of Westminster John Knox Press. |
| BAS | *The Book of Alternative Services of the Anglican Church of Canada.* Anglican Book Centre, 1985. © 1985, General Synod of the Anglican Church of Canada. Used with permission. |
| BCO | *Book of Common Order of the Church of Scotland.* Saint Andrew Press, 1994. © 1994, Panel on Worship of the Church of Scotland. |
| BCO-1940 | *The Book of Common Order.* © 1940, Church of Scotland. |
| BCP | *The Book of Common Prayer,* according to the use of the Episcopal Church in the United States of America. © 1977, Charles Mortimer Guilbert as custodian; public domain. |
| BCW | *Book of Common Worship* (Presbyterian Church, U.S.A.). © 1993, Westminster John Knox Press. |
| BCW-1932 | *The Book of Common Worship.* © 1932, Presbyterian Church (U.S.A.). |
| BCW-1946 | *The Book of Common Worship.* © 1946, Presbyterian Church (U.S.A.). |

BCWP              *The Book of Common Worship: Provisional Services* (United
                  Presbyterian Church, U.S.A.). © 1966, Westminster Press.

BCW-PCC           *The Book of Common Worship* (Presbyterian Church in Canada).
                  © 1991, The Presbyterian Church in Canada.

BFJ               *Bread for the Journey: Resources for Worship.* Edited by Ruth C. Duck.
                  © 1981, Pilgrim Press.

BOS-1994          *The Book of Occasional Services 1994.* © 1995, The Church Pension
                  Fund. All rights reserved. Used by permission of Church Publishing
                  Inc., New York, New York.

BRP               *A Book of Reformed Prayers.* Edited by Howard L. Rice and Lamar
                  Williamson, Jr. © 1998, Westminster John Knox Press.

BSBL              *Breaking Silence Before the Lord: Worship Prayers.* E. Lee Phillips.
                  © 1986, Baker Books, a division of Baker Book House Company.

BTG               *Belonging to God: Catechism Resources for Worship.* Geneva Press,
                  2003. © 2003, Office of Theology and Worship, Presbyterian Church
                  (U.S.A). Used by permission. A collection of liturgical resources
                  compiled of statements of faith adopted by the Presbyterian Church
                  (U.S.A.). Each entry in BTG traces the exact references to earlier
                  confessional documents.

BW-1944           *The Book of Worship.* © 1944, renewed 1971, 1972, Abingdon Press.

BW-1964           *The Book of Worship.* © 1965, Methodist Publishing House. Used by
                  permission.

BWFC              *A Book of Worship for Free Churches.* © 1948, renewed 1976, United
                  Church Press.

BWH               *Baker's Worship Handbook: Traditional and Contemporary Service
                  Resources.* Paul E. Engle. Baker Books, a division of Baker Book
                  House Company, 1998. © 1998, Paul E. Engle.

BW-UCC            *Book of Worship, United Church of Christ.* © 1986, United Church of
                  Christ, Office for Church Life and Leadership; reprinted, © 2002,
                  United Church of Christ, Local Church Ministries, Worship and
                  Education Ministry Team, Cleveland, Ohio. All rights reserved.

CB                *A Celebration of Baptism.* Consultation on Common Texts (CCT).
                  Abingdon Press, 1988. © by Consultation on Common Texts. All
                  rights reserved. Used by permission.

CBCP              *The Complete Book of Christian Prayer.* © 2000, The Continuum
                  International Publishing Group, Inc. Excerpts reprinted by permis-
                  sion of the publisher.

CC                *Celebrating Community: Prayers and Songs of Unity.* Janet Crawford,
                  et al. World Council of Churches, 1993.

CGP               *Celebrate God's Presence: A Book of Services for The United Church of
                  Canada.* United Church Publishing House, 2000.

CH-1973           *Covenant Hymnal 1973.* Covenant Press, 1973. © 1973, Covenant
                  Publications.

CH-1996           *The Covenant Hymnal: A Worshipbook.* © 1996, Covenant Publications.

| CIGIP | *The Church in Germany in Prayer.* Compiled by Conrad Ameln, et al. Oxford: A. R. Mowbray, 1937. Reprinted by permission of The Continuum International Publishing Group, Inc. |
| CL-A | *A Children's Lectionary: Cycle A.* John Behnke. © 1974, Paulist Press, Inc., New York/Mahwah, N.J. Used with permission of Paulist Press. www.paulistpress.com. |
| CLCW | *The Complete Library of Christian Worship.* Edited by Robert E. Webber. Star Song Publishing Group, a division of Jubilee Communications, Inc., 1994. © 1994, Star Song; transferred to Hendrickson Publishers, Peabody, Mass. Used by permission of Robert E. Webber.<br>Volume 4, Books 1-2. *Music and the Arts in Christian Worship.*<br>Volume 5. *The Services of the Christian Year.* |
| CLUWG | *Come, Let Us Worship God: A Handbook of Prayers for Leaders of Worship.* David M. Currie. Westminster Press, 1977. Used by permission of Westminster John Knox Press. |
| CRCL-3 | *Companion to the Revised Common Lectionary.* Volume 3. *All Age Worship, Year B.* Edited by Judy Jarvis and Donald Pickard. Epworth Press, 1999. © 1999, Judy Jarvis and Donald Pickard. |
| CSL | *A Child Shall Lead: Children in Worship. A Sourcebook for Christian Educators, Musicians, and Clergy.* Edited by John D. Witvliet. Choristers Guild and Calvin Institute of Christian Worship, 1999. © 1999, Choristers Guild. |
| CTW | *Call to Worship: Liturgy, Music, Preaching, and the Arts. Year A Lectionary Aids for 2001-2002.* Edited by Theodore A. Gill, Jr. © 2001, Office of Theology and Worship, Presbyterian Church (U.S.A.) and Geneva Press. Used by permission. |
| CW | *Chalice Worship.* Edited and compiled by Colbert S. Cartwright and O. I. Cricket Harrison. © 1997, Chalice Press. |
| ECY | *Enriching the Christian Year.* Compiled by Michael Perham, et al. The Liturgical Press, 1993; first published by SPCK, 1993. Compilation © 1993, Michael Perham. |
| ELL | Eucharistic Liturgy of Lima. Faith and Order Commission of the World Council of Churches, 1982. |
| FAF | *From Ashes to Fire,* services of worship for the seasons of Lent and Easter with introduction and commentary. © 1979, Abingdon Press. Used by permission. |
| FAWM | *For All Who Minister: A Worship Manual for the Church of the Brethren.* © 1993, Brethren Press. |
| FHEG | *For His Excellent Greatness.* Louis Lotz. Reformed Church in America Northern Regional Center. |
| FS | *Flames of the Spirit.* Edited by Ruth C. Duck. © 1985, Pilgrim Press. |
| FWS | *Fresh Winds of the Spirit.* Book 2. *Liturgical Resources for Year A.* Lavon Baylor. © 1992, Pilgrim Press. |

GMC                 *Gifts of Many Cultures: Worship Resources for the Global Community.* Maren C. Tirabassi and Kathy Wonson Eddy. Pilgrim Press, 1995. © 1995, Maren C. Tirabassi and Kathy Wonson Eddy.

HWB               *Hymnal: A Worship Book,* prepared by Churches in the Believers Church Tradition. © 1992, Brethren Press, Faith and Life Press, and Mennonite Publishing House.

ICEL                International Commission on English in the Liturgy, Inc., also sometimes referred to as International Committee on English in the Liturgy, Inc.

ICP                  *Intercessions for the Christian People: Prayers of the People for Cycles A, B, and C of the Roman, Episcopal, and Lutheran Lectionaries.* Edited by Gail Ramshaw. © 1988, Pueblo Publishing Co., Inc.; © 1990, The Order of St. Benedict, Inc.; The Liturgical Press.

ILID                *In Life and in Death: A Pastoral Guide for Funerals.* Compiled by Leonard J. Vander Zee. © 1992, CRC Publications.

IPB                  *An Iona Prayer Book.* Compiled by Peter W. Millar. The Canterbury Press, 1998, a publishing imprint of Hymns Ancient and Modern, Limited, a registered charity. © 1998, Peter W. Millar.

IPF                   *In Penitence and Faith.* David Silk. Mowbray, 1988. Reprinted by permission of The Continuum International Publishing Group, Inc.

JCLW              *Jesus Christ—the Life of the World: A Worship Book for the Sixth Assembly of the World Council of Churches.* © 1983, World Council of Churches.

JPWT              *Jerusalem Prayers for the World Today.* George Appleton. SPCK, 1974.

LBW               *Lutheran Book of Worship.* Augsburg Publishing House and Board of Publication, Lutheran Church in America, 1978. © 1978, Augsburg. Used by permission of Augsburg Fortress.

LH                    English translation of *The Divine Office: The Liturgy of the Hours According to the Roman Rite.* © 1974, International Committee on English in the Liturgy, Inc. (ICEL). All rights reserved.

LLJ                  *Liturgy as Life-Journey.* William B. Oden. Acton House, Inc., 1976. © by William B. Oden.

LOP-A            *Litanies and Other Prayers: For the Revised Common Lectionary, Year A.* Phyllis Cole and Everett Tilson. © 1989, 1992, Abingdon Press. Used by permission.

LOP-B            *Litanies and Other Prayers: For the Revised Common Lectionary, Year B.* Phyllis Cole and Everett Tilson. © 1990, 1993, Abingdon Press. Used by permission.

LOP-C            *Litanies and Other Prayers: For the Revised Common Lectionary, Year C.* Phyllis Cole and Everett Tilson. © 1991, 1994, Abingdon Press. Used by permission.

LP                    *Leading in Prayer: A Workbook for Ministers.* Hughes Oliphant Old. © 1995, William B. Eerdmans Publishing Co.

LUP             *Let Us Pray: Reformed Prayers for Christian Worship.* Edited by Martha S. Gilliss. © 2002, Geneva Press.

LUYH         *Lift Up Your Hearts.* Walter Russell Bowie. © 1951, renewed 1984, Abingdon Press. Used by permission.

MCL           *More Children's Liturgies.* Edited by Maria Bruck. © 1981, Paulist Press, Inc., New York/Mahwah, N.J. Used with permission of Paulist Press. www.paulistpress.com.

MPS           *More Prayers for Sundays: On Themes for Any Lectionary.* Edited by Michael Counsell. HarperCollins Publishers, Ltd., 1997. Compilation © by Michael Counsell.

NHCY         *The New Handbook of the Christian Year.* Hoyt L. Hickman, et al. © 1986, 1992, Abingdon Press. Used by permission.

OS              *Occasional Services: A Companion to the Lutheran Book of Worship.* © 1982, administered by Augsburg Fortress. Used by permission.

PCY           *Prayers for the Christian Year.* Revised edition. Oxford University Press, 1952. © by The Committee on Public Worship and Aids to Devotion of the Church of Scotland.

PE              *Prayers for Everyday.* Compiled by Elaine Sommers Rich. Faith and Life Press, 1990. © by Elaine Sommers Rich.

PED           *Prayer for Each Day.* Taizé. GIA Publications, Inc., and Cassell, 1997. © 1997, 1998, Ateliers et Presses de Taizé, 71250 Taizé Community, France.

PEO           *Prayers for Every Occasion.* Compiled and edited by Frank Colquhoun. Morehouse-Barlow Co., 1974. © by The Morehouse Group.

PEW          *Prayers Encircling the World: An International Anthology of 300 Prayers.* Edited by Robin Keeley. Westminster John Knox Press, 1999. © 1998, SPCK.

PHG          *The Promise of His Glory: Services and Prayers for the Season from All Saints to Candlemas.* Continuum, 1991. Reprinted by permission of The Continuum International Publishing Group, Inc.

PL              *Pray to the Lord: Prayers for Corporate Worship.* The Commission on Worship, Reformed Church in America. Reformed Church Press, 1988.

POD           *The Pattern of Our Days: Worship in the Celtic Tradition from the Iona Community.* Edited by Kathy Galloway. © 1996 by the Authors, Paulist Press, Inc., New York/Mahwah, N.J. Used with permission of Paulist Press. www.paulistpress.com.

PP              *A Procession of Prayers: Prayers and Meditations from Around the World.* Edited by John Carden. Morehouse, 1998. © 1998, John Carden.

PPW          *Prayers for Public Worship.* Carl T. Uehling. © 1972, Fortress Press, administered by Augsburg Fortress. Used by permission.

| | |
|---|---|
| PRT | *Prayers from the Reformed Tradition: In the Company of a Great Cloud of Witnesses.* Edited and compiled by Diane Karay Tripp. © 2001, Witherspoon Press, Presbyterian Church (U.S.A.). |
| PsH | *Psalter Hymnal.* © 1987, 1988, CRC Publications. |
| PTC | *Prayers for Today's Church.* Edited by Dick Williams. Augsburg Publishing House, 1977. © 1972, R. H. L. Williams. Used by permission of Falcon Press c/o Christian Pastoral Aid Society. |
| PT-ELLC | *Praying Together.* English translation of the Lord's Prayer, *Agnus Dei, Gloria in Excelsis, Sursum Corda, Sanctus, Benedictus, Gloria Patri,* and *Te Deum Laudamus,* prepared by the English Language Liturgical Consultation (ELLC). Abingdon Press, 1988. © 1988, ELLC. All rights reserved. |
| PUAS | *Prayers for Use at the Alternative Services.* David Silk. © 1980, revised 1986, 1992, Mowbray, an imprint of Cassell. © 2000, The Continuum International Publishing Group, Inc. Reprinted by permission of the publisher. |
| PWL | *Prayers for Worship Leaders.* Arnold Kenseth and Richard P. Unsworth. © 1978, Fortress Press, administered by Augsburg Fortress. Used by permission. |
| RCA-OPF | *Reformed Church in America General Synod, Order for Profession of Faith.* © by Reformed Church Press. |
| RCA-OSB | *Reformed Church in America General Synod, Order for the Sacrament of Baptism.* © by Reformed Church Press. |
| RCA-OW | *Reformed Church in America General Synod, Order of Worship: The Lord's Day.* © by Reformed Church Press. |
| RCLP | *Revised Common Lectionary Prayers,* proposed by the Consultation on Common Texts (CCT). Augsburg Fortress Publishers, 2002. © 2002, Consultation on Common Texts. All rights reserved. Used by permission. |
| RFR | *Reaching for Rainbows.* Ann Weems. Westminster Press, 1980. Used by permission of Westminster John Knox Press. |
| RH | *A Restless Hope.* Edited by Kate Compston. The United Reformed Church, 1995. © by Kate Compston. |
| RM | English translation of the Roman Missal. © 1973, International Committee on English in the Liturgy, Inc. (ICEL). All rights reserved. |
| RW | *Reformed Worship,* a quarterly journal. CRC Publications, 1986-present. Most service resources published in RW are submitted by individual churches that write their own prayers and are hereby declared to be in public domain; no further permission is required for use of these items. The only request is that *Reformed Worship* be acknowledged in any future publication. (Items from RW that are adapted or adopted from other published resources under copyright are identified by the earlier published source.) |

*787*

SAS             *Sundays and Seasons, Cycle B.* © 1996, Augsburg Fortress. Used by permission.

SBCY            *Saint Bernard on the Christian Year.* Translated by Sister Penelope. A. R. Mowbray and Co., 1954. © by Community of St. Mary the Virgin. Reprinted by permission of The Continuum International Publishing Group, Inc.

SBK-92          *Sourcebook for Sundays and Seasons: An Almanac of Parish Liturgy, 1992, Year C.* G. Thomas Ryan, et al. International Commission on English in the Liturgy, Inc. (ICEL). Liturgical Training Publications, 1992.

SB-UCC          *Service Book for Use of Ministers Conducting Public Worship.* United Church Publishing House, 1969.

SFS             *Searching for Shalom.* Ann Weems. © 1991, Ann Barr Weems. Used by permission of Westminster John Knox Press.

SLDL            *Service for the Lord's Day and Lectionary for the Christian Year.* © 1964, Westminster Press.

SLR-1           *The Service for the Lord's Day. The Worship of God: Supplemental Liturgical Resource 1.* Presbyterian Church (U.S.A.), 1984.

SLR-2           *Holy Baptism and Services for the Renewal of Baptism. The Worship of God: Supplemental Liturgical Resource 2.* Presbyterian Church (U.S.A.), 1985.

SLR-5           *Daily Prayer. The Worship of God: Supplemental Liturgical Resource 5.* Presbyterian Church (U.S.A.), 1987.

SLR-7           *Liturgical Year. The Worship of God: Supplemental Liturgical Resource 7.* Presbyterian Church (U.S.A.), 1992.

SNC             *Sing! A New Creation.* The Calvin Institute of Christian Worship, Faith Alive Christian Resources, and Reformed Church in America, 2001. © 2001, CRC Publications.

SO              *Sinfonia Oecumenica: Worship with the Churches in the World.* Second edition. Edited by Dietrich Werner, et al. Commissioned by Evangelischen Missionswerks and Basler Mission. © 1998, Gütersloher Verlagshaus, Gütersloh.

SP              *Seasons of Prayer: Resources for Worship.* Lisa R. Withrow. SPCK, 1995. © by Lisa R. Withrow. Used by permission of SPCK.

SPCK            Society for Promoting Christian Knowledge, London, UK.

SW              *Stages on the Way: Worship Resources for Lent, Holy Week and Easter.* Wild Goose Worship Group. Wild Goose Publications, 1998. © by Wild Goose Resource Group.

TAF             *The Adventurous Future.* Edited by Paul H. Bowman. © 1959, Brethren Press.

TCBCW           *The Companion to the Book of Common Worship.* Edited by Peter C. Bower. Geneva Press, 2003. © 2003, Office of Theology and Worship, Presbyterian Church (U.S.A). Used by permission.

| TFF | *This Far by Faith: An African American Resource for Worship.* © 1999, Augsburg Fortress. Used by permission. |
| TH | *Touch Holiness.* Edited by Ruth C. Duck and Maren C. Tirabassi. © 1990, Pilgrim Press. |
| TSP | *Taizé: Songs for Prayer.* © 1998, Ateliers et Presses de Taizé, 71250 Taizé Community, France. |
| TTP | *There's a Time and Place: Prayers for the Christian Year.* Jamie Wallace. Collins Liturgical Publications, 1982. © HarperCollins Publishers, Ltd. |
| TWS | *The Worship Sourcebook.* Second Edition. Calvin Institute of Christian Worship, Faith Alive Christian Resources, Baker Books, 2013. © 2013, Faith Alive Christian Resources. Individual prayers and resources prepared specifically for *The Worship Sourcebook* are hereby declared to be in public domain. The only request is that *The Worship Sourcebook* be acknowledged in any future publication (see note under Permissions, p. 789). |
| UMBW | *The United Methodist Book of Worship.* © 1992, The United Methodist Publishing House. Used by permission. |
| UW-LB | *Uniting in Worship,* leader's book. National Commission on Liturgy, Uniting Church Press, 1988. © 1988, The Uniting Church in Australia Assembly Commission on Liturgy. Used by permission. |
| VU | *Voices United: The Hymn and Worship Book of the United Church of Canada.* United Church Publishing House, 1996. |
| WAGP | *With All God's People: The New Ecumenical Prayer Cycle.* Compiled by John Carden. © 1989, WCC Publications, World Council of Churches. |
| WAGP-OS | *With All God's People: The New Ecumenical Prayer Cycle. Orders of Service.* Compiled by John Carden. © 1989, WCC Publications, World Council of Churches. |
| WAS-1 | *Worship for All Seasons.* Volume 1. *Selections from* Gathering *for Advent, Christmas, Epiphany.* Edited by Thomas Harding. United Church Publishing House, 1993. |
| WAS-2 | *Worship for All Seasons.* Volume 2. *Selections from* Gathering *for Lent, Holy Week, Easter.* Edited by Thomas Harding. United Church Publishing House, 1993. |
| WAS-3 | *Worship for All Seasons.* Volume 3. *Selections from* Gathering *for Pentecost, Summer, Autumn.* Edited by Thomas Harding. United Church Publishing House, 1994. |
| WBK | *The Worshipbook — Services.* Prepared by the Joint Committee on Worship for Cumberland Presbyterian Church, Presbyterian Church in the United States, the United Presbyterian Church in the U.S.A. © 1970, Westminster Press. |
| WBK-SH | *The Worshipbook — Services and Hymns.* Prepared by the Joint Committee on Worship for Cumberland Presbyterian Church, |

Presbyterian Church in the United States, the United Presbyterian Church in the U.S.A. © 1972, Westminster Press.

WE   *Worshipping Ecumenically: Orders of Service from Global Meetings with Suggestions for Local Use.* Edited by Per Harling. © 1995, WCC Publications, World Council of Churches.

WFW  *Words for Worship.* Edited by Arlene M. Mark. © 1996, Herald Press.

WG   *Whispers of God.* Lavon Bayler. © 1987, Pilgrim Press.

WGT  *We Gather Together.* © 1979, Brethren Press.

WL   *Worship the Lord.* Edited by James R. Esther and Donald J. Bruggink. Wm. B. Eerdmans Publishing Co., 1987. © by Reformed Church in America.

WN   *Worship Now.* Compiled by David Cairns, et. al. © 1972, Saint Andrew Press.

WN-II  *Worship Now—Book II: A Collection of Services and Prayers for Public Worship.* Compiled by Duncan B. Forrester, et al. © 1989, Saint Andrew Press.

WNYHL  *We Need You Here, Lord: Prayers from the City.* Andrew W. Blackwood, Jr. Baker Books, a division of Baker Book House Company. © 1969, Andrew W. Blackwood, Jr.

WR-UMH *The Worship Resources of the United Methodist Hymnal.* Edited by Hoyt Hickman. © 1989, United Methodist Publishing House. Used by permission.

WV   *Worship Vessels: Resources for Renewal.* F. Russell Mitman. Harper and Row, Publishers, 1987. © by F. Russell Mitman.

WWB  *A Wee Worship Book.* Wild Goose Worship Group. GIA Publications, Inc., 1999, fourth incarnation. © 1999, Wild Goose Resource Group.

WWG-C  *When We Gather: A Book of Prayers for Worship, Year C.* James G. Kirk. © 1985, Geneva Press. Used by permission.

## Sources of Specific Texts

The following table lists sources of specific texts used in this book, arranged by item number and including abbreviations of original sources (such as BCW-1946, BCP, PE, and so on) as identified in the preceding subsection, Other Sources (pp. 782-90).

For example, to find the source information for resource number 3 in section 1.1 (Preparation for-Worship), see resource 1.1.3 below. Various standard abbreviations are also included in this table and are identified in the box above.

| Abbreviations Used in This Table | |
|---|---|
| alt. | altered |
| attrib. | attributed to |
| b. | born |
| c. | circa (around) |
| ed. | edited by |
| p., pp. | page, pages |
| PD | public domain |
| rev. | revised by |
| tr. | translation, translated by |

| Resource | Incipit | Source |
|---|---|---|
| 1.1.3 | (Almighty God, we . . .) | BCW-1946, pp. 3, 109, alt., PD |
| 1.1.4 | (Almighty God, to . . .) | 11th cent., in BCP, p. 355, PD |
| 1.1.5 | (O God, you . . .) | from *Ancient Collects and Other Prayers Selected for Devotional Use from Various Rituals* (J. H. and Has. Parker, 1862), alt., PD |
| 1.1.6 | (Blessed are you. . .) | TWS |
| 1.1.7 | (This is the day . . .) | James R. Hawkinson in CH-1996 866, © 1973, 1996, Covenant Publications |
| 1.1.8 | (Dear God, we . . .) | HWB 674, © 1992, The Hymnal Project, Brethren Press |
| 1.1.9 | (Dear God, silence . . .) | RW 19:31 |
| 1.1.10 | (Holy God, we . . .) | TWS |
| 1.1.11 | (Loving God, for . . .) | TWS |
| 1.2.5 | (Let us worship . . .) | RW 34:17 |
| 1.2.17 | (Our hearts are . . .) | RW 16:46 |
| 1.2.22 | (Great and marvelous . . .) | RW 16:46 |
| 1.2.23 | (Sing a new song . . .) | PED, p. 41 |
| 1.2.24 | (The earth is . . .) | BCP, p. 81, PD |
| 1.2.25 | (All who thirst . . .) | WE, p. 83 |
| 1.2.26 | (Let us worship . . .) | Ruth Duck in TH, p. 93 |
| 1.2.27 | (God invites us . . .) | RW 27:43 |
| 1.2.28 | (God calls us . . .) | TWS |
| 1.2.29 | (The eternal Father . . .) | RW 27:41 |
| 1.2.30 | (The Lord Jesus . . .) | RW 27:40 |
| 1.2.31 | (People of God . . .) | RW 27:39 |
| 1.2.32 | (Let us worship . . .) | RW 34:16 |
| 1.2.33 | (Our help is . . .) | BTG, p. 4 [7] |
| 1.2.34 | (When Moses gathered . . .) | BTG, p. 5 [9] |
| 1.2.35 | (In Christ, the . . .) | RW 66:19 |
| 1.2.36 | (In your wisdom . . .) | RW 57:20 |
| 1.3.18 | (Welcome in the . . .) | TWS |
| 1.3.19 | (Welcome to . . .) | TWS |
| 1.3.20 | (Whether we are . . .) | TWS |
| 1.3.21 | (Those who love . . .) | TWS |
| 1.3.22 | (If you are . . .) | RW 59:16 |
| 1.3.23 | (We welcome to . . .) | TWS |
| 1.4.7 | (All glorious God . . .) | Desmond Tutu in APB, p. 69, PD |

| 1.4.8 | (We praise you . . .) | TWS |
|---|---|---|
| 1.4.9 | (God, our creator . . .) | TWS |
| 1.4.10 | (God of light . . .) | SLR-1, p. 42, with phrases from SB-UCC, p. 224 |
| 1.4.11 | (We praise you . . .) | CIGIP, alt. |
| 1.4.12 | (Creator God . . .) | Douglas Galbraith in POD, p. 102 [16], © Douglas Galbraith |
| 1.4.13 | (You are the . . .) | WWG-C p. 58, alt. |
| 1.4.14 | (O God, you . . .) | WWB, p. 25, alt. |
| 1.4.15 | (Mighty God, we . . .) | CRCL-3, p. 62, alt. |
| 1.4.16 | (Loving God, we . . .) | CRCL-3, p. 68 |
| 1.4.17 | (We give thanks . . .) | WBK, p. 142 |
| 1.4.18 | (Our Father . . .) | LP, p. 18 |
| 1.4.19 | (Let us join . . .) | BWH, p. 72 |
| 1.4.20 | (You, O God . . .) | adapted from a first-century daily Jewish liturgy, PD |
| 1.4.21 | (God our Father . . .) | BTG, p. 6 [3] |
| 1.4.22 | (We are very . . .) | TWS |
| 1.4.23 | (Loving God, we . . .) | HWB 674, © 1992, The Hymnal Project, Brethren Press |
| 1.4.24 | (Too often, O God, . . .) | TWS |
| 1.4.25 | (O gracious and . . .) | attrib. Benedict of Nursia (6th cent.), PD |
| 1.4.26 | (O most merciful . . .) | Richard, bishop of Chichester (12th cent.), PD |
| 1.4.27 | (Eternal God, you . . .) | SLDL, p. 11, alt., PD |
| 1.4.28 | (Everlasting God . . .) | BCO-1940, pp. 38, 259, alt.; lines 3-4 derived from St. Augustine (*Confessions* 1:1) |
| 1.4.29 | (God of grace . . .) | SLDL, p. 12, with opening lines from BCW-1946, p. 5, alt., PD |
| 1.4.30 | (Eternal Light . . .) | Alcuin of Tours (8th cent.), PD |
| 1.4.31 | (God of goodness . . .) | TWS |
| 1.4.32 | (Praise the Lord. . . .) | WBK, p. 16, PD |
| 1.4.33 | (O God, our . . .) | BW-1964, p. 94, PD |
| 1.4.34 | (O Lord, our . . .) | BCP, p. 234, alt., PD |
| 1.4.35 | (Sing praises to . . .) | Jann C. Weaver in FS, p. 67 |
| 1.4.36 | (Almighty and . . .) | adapted from a prayer by Chandran Devanesen, India, in IPB, p. 6, © Chandran Devanesen. Permission sought. |
| 1.4.37 | (Lord, open to . . .) | from the Syrian Church, in IPB, p. 14 |
| 1.4.38 | (O Lord, our . . .) | from Ashanti, Ghana, in APB, p. 59, alt., PD |
| 1.4.39 | (Show us the . . .) | Dorothy Kramer in MCL, p. 108 |
| 1.4.40 | (Jesus Christ, you . . .) | PED, p. 43 |
| 1.4.41 | (God of all . . .) | CRCL-3, p. 34 |
| 1.4.42 | (Loving God, we . . .) | CRCL-3, p. 46 |
| 1.4.43 | (Lord, our God, . . .) | TWS |
| 1.4.44 | (O God, our . . .) | Christopher Idle in PTC, p. 65 [140], alt. |
| 1.4.45 | (Christ, in this . . .) | AESP, p. 35, alt. |
| 1.4.46 | (Holy and loving . . .) | TWS |
| 1.4.47 | (With you, gracious . . .) | TWS |
| 1.4.48 | (Great and loving . . .) | BSBL, p. 27 [2], alt. |
| 1.4.49 | (God, our Rock . . .) | Margaret Richer Smith in WFW 120 |
| 1.4.50 | (Ever present God . . .) | TWS |
| 1.4.51 | (Spirit divine, inspire . . .) | TWS |
| 1.4.52 | (O God, who . . .) | RW 35:23 |
| 1.4.53 | (O Lord God . . .) | RW 3:29 |
| 1.4.54 | (Dear God, help . . .) | TWS |

| | | |
|---|---|---|
| 1.4.60 | (In holy splendor . . .) | Lara J. Hall in WFW 110 |
| 1.4.61 | (We will bless . . .) | PED, p. 133, alt. |
| 1.4.62 | (If today we . . .) | CL-A, p. 78, alt. |
| 1.4.63 | (This is the day . . .) | Roy Umble in WFW 111 |
| 1.4.64 | (For rebirth and . . .) | from Cape Town, South Africa, in APB, p. 58, alt., PD |
| 1.4.65 | (You are the . . .) | Xhosa, from South Africa, in APB, p. 12, PD |
| 1.4.66 | (God of the . . .) | Ruth Burgess in POD, p. 92 [3], alt., © Ruth Burgess |
| 1.4.67 | (We come to . . .) | Ruth Burgess in POD, p. 33, alt., © Ruth Burgess |
| 1.4.68 | (God, who has . . .) | BWH, p. 84 |
| 1.4.69 | (Our worship is . . .) | WV, p. 34, alt. |
| 1.4.70 | (Lord God, we . . .) | TWS |
| 1.4.71 | (Lord, you are . . .) | TWS |
| 1.4.72 | (O Lord, our . . .) | TWS |
| 2.1.14 | (We cannot come . . .) | AESP, p. 41 |
| 2.1.15 | (When we see . . .) | TWS |
| 2.1.16 | (When we gather . . .) | LLJ, p. 38 |
| 2.1.17 | (In spite of . . .) | BTG, p. 7 [2] |
| 2.2.5 | (Lamb of God, you . . .) | *Agnus Dei* from PT-ELLC, p. 37 |
| 2.2.10 | (O Lord, great . . .) | LP, pp. 94-95 |
| 2.2.11 | (Merciful God, we . . .) | derived from John Hunter, *Devotional Services for Public Worship*, p. 52 (London: Dent, 1901); rev. from BCW-1946, p. 39, the Joint Liturgical Group of Great Britain, and from BCP, p. 79, PD |
| 2.2.12 | (Almighty and . . .) | *Book of Common Prayer* (1552), alt., PD |
| 2.2.13 | (Holy and merciful . . .) | Henry van Dyke in *Book of Common Worship* (Presbyterian, 1906), pp. 20-21, alt., PD |
| 2.2.14 | (Merciful God, you . . .) | BCW-1946, p. 26, alt., PD |
| 2.2.15 | (Gracious God, our . . .) | BW-UCC, p. 211 |
| 2.2.16 | (Merciful God, in . . .) | BCW-PCC, p. 28, alt. |
| 2.2.17 | (O gracious and . . .) | Johann Arndt (1555-1621) in CBCP, p. 246 [631], alt. |
| 2.2.18 | (Awesome and . . .) | RW 52:17 |
| 2.2.19 | (Eternal and merciful . . .) | RW 52:18 |
| 2.2.20 | (Almighty God, we . . .) | PL, General Confession 3 |
| 2.2.21 | (Lord, you showed . . .) | TWS |
| 2.2.22 | (Often, O holy . . .) | TWS |
| 2.2.23 | (Father, we are . . .) | Dorothy Akey in MCL, p. 18, alt. |
| 2.2.24 | (O God of . . .) | Michael J. O'Donnell in UMBW 493 |
| 2.2.25 | (Wondrous God, who . . .) | WV, p. 55 |
| 2.2.26 | (Holy God, we . . .) | TWS |
| 2.2.27 | (O Lord, our . . .) | TWS |
| 2.2.28 | (To you, Holy God . . .) | TWS |
| 2.2.29 | (O Lord our God. . .) | TWS |
| 2.2.30 | (Merciful God, for . . .) | Kate McIlhagga in POD, p. 39, © Kate McIlhagga |
| 2.2.31 | (Forgive us our . . .) | Lancelot Andrewes (1555-1626) in CBCP, p. 244 [628], alt. |
| 2.2.32 | (Gracious God, you . . .) | Ruth C. Duck in BFJ, p. 37 |
| 2.2.33 | (God of birth . . .) | Paul J. Flucke in BFJ, p. 45 |
| 2.2.34 | (For the times . . .) | Anne Macksoud in MCL, p. 41, alt. |
| 2.2.35 | (Loving God, we . . .) | TWS |
| 2.2.36 | (Lord, we cry . . .) | TWS |
| 2.2.37 | (Eternal God, we . . .) | LLJ, p. 38 |
| 2.2.38 | (Holy and merciful . . .) | TWS |

| | | |
|---|---|---|
| 2.2.39 | (Almighty God . . .) | TWS |
| 2.2.40 | (Righteous Father . . .) | BSBL, p. 68 [7] |
| 2.2.41 | (Jesus, friend of sinners . . .) | TWS |
| 2.2.42 | (God of love . . .) | ANZPB-HKMOA, p. 407, alt. |
| 2.2.43 | (For self-righteousness . . .) | source unknown |
| 2.2.44 | (Merciful God, you. . .) | BCO, p. 13 |
| 2.2.45 | (Lord, sometimes our . . .) | TWS |
| 2.2.46 | (God of love . . .) | Ruth C. Duck in FS, p. 45, alt. |
| 2.2.47 | (Holy God, we confess . . .) | TWS |
| 2.2.48 | (Our Father, forgive . . .) | RW 27:42 |
| 2.2.49 | (There are many . . .) | RW 27:41 |
| 2.2.50 | (Lord, in your . . .) | RW 27:40 |
| 2.2.51 | (God of everlasting . . .) | BTG, p. 11 [5] |
| 2.2.52 | (God of grace . . .) | BTG, p. 12 [7] |
| 2.2.53 | (O God, you . . .) | adapted from the Covenant Service of John Wesley (1703-1791) as found in NHCY, p. 81 |
| 2.2.54 | (When we have . . .) | WE, p. 132 |
| 2.2.55 | (O God, in . . .) | TWS |
| 2.2.56 | (God of all nations . . .) | Ruth Duck in BFJ, p. 46 |
| 2.2.57 | (Father, you tell . . .) | RW 27:39 |
| 2.2.58 | (Eternal God, you . . .) | RW 34:16 |
| 2.2.59 | (Lord, you have . . .) | RW 56:32 |
| 2.2.60 | (Gracious Father, the . . .) | TWS |
| 2.2.61 | (Gracious Father and . . .) | TWS |
| 2.2.62 | (Almighty God and . . .) | TWS |
| 2.2.63 | (Great Creator, we . . .) | TWS |
| 2.2.64 | (Loving God, you call . . .) | TWS |
| 2.2.65 | (Lord Jesus Christ . . .) | A.R.C. McLellan in WN-II, p. 25 [20], alt. |
| 2.2.66 | (Lord, you said . . .) | RW 64:24 |
| 2.2.67 | (O Lord, we . . .) | James W. Weir (1805-1878) in PRT, p. 52 [57], alt., PD |
| 2.2.68 | (God blesses those . . .) | BWH, pp. 23-25 |
| 2.2.69 | (Dear Jesus, I want . . .) | TWS |
| 2.2.70 | (Lord, you are . . .) | CSL, p. 85 |
| 2.2.71 | (Lord, we are . . .) | CSL, p. 84 |
| 2.3.6 | (Why, Lord, must . . .) | Calvin Seerveld in PsH 576, © 1986, Calvin Seerveld |
| 2.4.1 | (Hear the good news . . .) | TWS |
| 2.4.30 | (Hear the good news . . .) | BCW, p. 56 [2], PD |
| 2.4.31 | (Here are words . . .) | CW, p. 319 [310] |
| 2.4.32 | (While it is true . . .) | BCW-PCC, pp. 27, 56 |
| 2.4.33 | (Hear these comforting . . .) | BW-UCC, p. 82 |
| 2.4.34 | (Christ is our . . .) | reprinted from Twenty-fourth Assembly Closing Service of the United Congregational Church of Southern Africa (Oct. 2, 1990), 2-3, in GMC, p. 19, PD |
| 2.4.35 | (God the Creator . . .) | ANZPB-HKMOA, p. 460 |
| 2.4.36 | (Take comfort in . . .) | BW-UCC, p. 302 |
| 2.4.37 | (In the life . . .) | Don Daniels in WAS-3, p. 31. Adapted with permission. |
| 2.4.38 | (The God who . . .) | William Steadman in WAS-2, p. 23. Reprinted with permission. |
| 2.4.39 | (To all who . . .) | Paul Fayter in WAS-1, p. 40. Reprinted with permission. |
| 2.4.40 | (Hear the good news . . .) | *A Service of Healing I* and *A Service of Healing II*, © 1992, |

| | | |
|---|---|---|
| | | United Methodist Publishing House. Used by permission. |
| 2.4.41 | (Through the blood . . .) | TWS |
| 2.4.42 | (Our God pardons . . .) | TWS |
| 2.4.48 | (May almighty God . . .) | BW-1944, p. 10 |
| 2.4.49 | (May the God of . . .) | BCP, p. 360, alt., PD |
| 2.5.1 | (Since God has . . .) | BCW, p. 57, PD |
| 2.5.2 | (Hear the teaching . . .) | BCW, p. 57, PD |
| 2.5.3 | (As God has given . . .) | TWS |
| 2.5.4 | (In his abundant . . .) | TWS |
| 2.6.4 | (Glory to God . . .) | PT-ELLC, p. 19, alt. |
| 2.6.5 | (Glory to the Father . . .) | PT-ELLC, p. 39, alt. |
| 2.7.16 | (You shall have no . . .) | Responsive Reading of the Law: (2) From the Epistles, in PsH, p. 1014 |
| 2.7.17 | (Hear, O people . . .) | Responsive Reading of the Law: (5) As a Rule of Gratitude, in PsH, p. 1017 |
| 2.7.19 | (God gave us . . .) | TWS |
| 2.7.21 | (As we are . . .) | RW 3:29 |
| 3.1.7 | (Lord, to whom . . .) | TWS |
| 3.1.10 | (Lord, open our . . .) | *A Service of Word and Table I*, alt., © 1972, The Methodist Publishing House; © 1980, 1985, 1989, 1992, United Methodist Publishing House |
| 3.1.11 | (Prepare our hearts . . .) | SLDL, p. 15, alt., PD |
| 3.1.12 | (Guide us, O God . . .) | SB-UCC, p. 133, alt. |
| 3.1.13 | (Lord, before this . . .) | TWS |
| 3.1.14 | (O God, our guide . . .) | TWS |
| 3.1.15 | (Living God, help . . .) | Huldrych Zwingli (1484-1531), alt., PD |
| 3.1.16 | (God, source of . . .) | ancient collect, source unknown, alt., PD |
| 3.1.17 | (Holy Spirit, pour . . .) | ancient collect, source unknown, alt., PD |
| 3.1.18 | (Come, Holy Spirit . . .) | TWS |
| 3.1.19 | (Our Lord and . . .) | Epiphany liturgy, Church of the Servant, Grand Rapids, Michigan |
| 3.1.20 | (Lord Jesus Christ . . .) | TSP, p. 31, alt. |
| 3.1.21 | (We pray, Lord . . .) | prayer by Chinese Christian women (prayer when opening a door), PD |
| 3.1.22 | (Lord God, thank . . .) | TWS |
| 3.1.23 | (O Lord, you . . .) | Jerome (c. 342-420), PD |
| 3.1.24 | (Lord God, you . . .) | WWB, p. 17, alt. |
| 3.1.25 | (O God, on earth's . . .) | TWS |
| 3.1.26 | (Blessed are you . . .) | CRCL-3, p. 27, alt. |
| 3.1.27 | (Almighty God, you . . .) | BWH, p. 29 |
| 3.1.28 | (Loving God, you provide . . .) | TWS |
| 3.1.29 | (Eternal God, in . . .) | BW-UCC, p. 114, alt. |
| 3.1.30 | (O gracious God . . .) | Geneva Bible (1560), PD |
| 3.1.31 | (Open our eyes . . .) | WV, p. 82 |
| 3.1.32 | (Lord, our God . . .) | TWS |
| 3.1.33 | (Almighty, gracious Father . . .) | based on Geneva Liturgy, PD |
| 3.1.34 | (God of all history . . .) | TWS |
| 3.1.35 | (Blessed you are . . .) | LP, p. 153, alt. |
| 3.1.36 | (Lord, our God . . .) | TWS |
| 3.1.37 | (Blessed are you . . .) | TWS |
| 3.2.1 | (The Word of . . .) | PD |

| | | |
|---|---|---|
| 3.2.2 | (A reading from . . .) | PD |
| 3.2.3 | (The gospel . . .) | PD |
| 3.2.4 | (Listen to the . . .) | PD |
| 3.2.5 | (Hear what the . . .) | PD |
| 3.2.6 | (Attend to the . . .) | PD |
| 3.2.7 | (Let us hear . . .) | PD |
| 3.3.1 | (The Word of . . .) | PD |
| 3.3.2 | (This is the . . .) | PD |
| 3.3.3 | (The gospel of our . . .) | PD |
| 3.3.4 | (The gospel of the . . .) | PD |
| 3.3.7 | (May God bless . . .) | CGP, p. 46, alt. Reprinted with permission. |
| 3.3.8 | (Herein is wisdom. . . .) | CGP, p. 46, PD |
| 3.3.9 | (God's Word is full . . .) | TWS |
| 3.3.10 | (God has spoken . . .) | TWS |
| 3.3.11 | (God, we thank . . .) | Pentecost liturgy, Church of the Servant, Grand Rapids, Michigan |
| 3.4.8 | (Lord God, by . . .) | TWS |
| 3.4.9 | (Almighty and loving . . .) | TWS |
| 3.4.10 | (O Lord, our God . . .) | Frank Colquhoun in PEO, p. 116 [463], alt. |
| 3.4.11 | (O Lord, we give . . .) | TWS |
| 3.5.1 | (Let us together . . .) | TWS |
| 3.5.2 | (Let us affirm . . .) | TWS |
| 3.5.3 | (Let us profess . . .) | TWS |
| 3.5.4 | (Let us join . . .) | TWS |
| 3.5.5 | (Let us together . . .) | TWS |
| 3.5.6 | (Let us express . . .) | TWS |
| 3.5.7 | (Let us join . . .) | TWS |
| 3.5.8 | (Together, we state . . .) | TWS |
| 3.6.9 | (This is the good . . .) | BCWP, p. 26, alt., PD |
| 3.6.26 | (The Lord is my . . .) | CL-A, p. 80 |
| 3.6.48 | (We believe in . . .) | TWS |
| 4.1.1 | (We offer now . . .) | TWS |
| 4.1.2 | (We join our . . .) | TWS |
| 4.1.3 | (We pray together . . .) | TWS |
| 4.1.4 | (We offer our . . .) | TWS |
| 4.1.5 | (Let us join . . .) | TWS |
| 4.1.6 | (Let us bring . . .) | TWS |
| 4.1.7 | (Let us pray . . .) | TWS |
| 4.1.8 | (God calls us . . .) | excerpt from "Invitations to Prayer" in WAS-3, p. 64. Reprinted with permission. |
| 4.1.16 | (The prayer our . . .) | TWS |
| 4.1.17 | (God is the one . . .) | excerpt from "Invitations to Prayer" in WAS-3, p. 64. Adapted with permission. |
| 4.1.18 | (Nothing in all creation . . .) | TWS |
| 4.3.9 | (Lord, in your . . .) | PD |
| 4.3.10 | (Let us pray . . .) | PD |
| 4.3.11 | (Gracious God, hear . . .) | PD |
| 4.3.12 | (For your love and . . .) | PD |
| 4.3.13 | (God of grace . . .) | PD |
| 4.3.14 | (Heavenly Father . . .) | PD |
| 4.3.15 | (O God, hear . . .) | PD |
| 4.3.16 | (Holy Spirit, our . . .) | PD |

| 4.3.17 | (Holy Spirit, act . . .) | PD |
|---|---|---|
| 4.3.18 | (Healing Spirit . . .) | PD |
| 4.3.22 | (In the strong name . . .) | TWS |
| 4.3.23 | (In the name of . . .) | PD |
| 4.3.26 | (To your holy name . . .) | PD |
| 4.3.27 | (Loving God, we . . .) | TWS |
| 4.3.28 | (Ever-faithful God, . . .) | BCW-PCC, p. 33, alt. |
| 4.3.29 | (Almighty God, Father . . .) | BCP, pp. 101, 125, PD |
| 4.3.30 | (Almighty God, you . . .) | attrib. St. John Chrysostom (c. 347-407), PD |
| 4.3.31 | (Gracious God . . .) | TWS |
| 4.4.1 | (Address to God . . .) | TWS |
| 4.4.2 | (We praise you. . .) | TWS; last paragraph from ANZPB- HKMOA, p. 60 |
| 4.4.3 | (We praise and . . .) | RCA-OW, alt. |
| 4.4.4 | (Sovereign God, King . . .) | TWS |
| 4.4.5 | (O Lord and Father . . .) | LP, pp. 194-195, alt. |
| 4.4.6 | (Almighty God . . .) | Andrew B. Doig in WN-II, p. 51 [39], alt. |
| 4.4.7 | (O great God . . .) | TWS, by Scott Hoezee, director of Center for Excellence in Preaching, Calvin Theological Seminary, Grand Rapids, Michigan |
| 4.4.8 | (O God, whom . . .) | TWS, by Scott Hoezee, director of Center for Excellence in Preaching, Calvin Theological Seminary, Grand Rapids, Michigan |
| 4.4.9 | (Lord of creation . . .) | TWS, by Scott Hoezee, director of Center for Excellence in Preaching, Calvin Theological Seminary, Grand Rapids, Michigan |
| 4.4.12 | (Our Father in . . .) | TWS |
| 4.4.13 | (Lord, our Lord . . .) | TWS |
| 4.4.14 | (O Lord, we . . .) | TWS |
| 4.4.15 | (No matter where . . .) | TWS |
| 4.4.16 | (Praise the Lord! . . .) | TWS |
| 4.4.17 | (Lord Jesus, you . . .) | Edith Bajema in CLCW, vol. 4, bk. 2, pp. 810-811, alt. |
| 4.4.18 | (Gracious God, we . . .) | Louise Mangan in WAS-1, p. 43. Reprinted with permission. |
| 4.4.19 | (Let us bring . . .) | Harold M. Daniels in BCW, p. 111 [94], alt., PD |
| 4.4.20 | (In peace, let us . . .) | from Eastern liturgies of St. Basil and St. John Chrysostom (4th cent.), PD |
| 4.4.21 | (Lord God, because . . .) | WWB, pp. 16-17 |
| 4.4.22 | (Let us pray for . . .) | BCP, pp. 388-389, 394 [3], alt., PD |
| 4.4.23 | (Bound together in . . .) | ICP, p. 30, alt. |
| 4.4.24 | (Almighty God, in . . .) | SLDL, pp. 17-19; WBK, pp. 31-33; BCWP, p. 33, PD |
| 4.4.25 | (Lord, draw near . . .) | WWB, pp. 61-62, alt. |
| 4.4.26 | (Eternal God, whom . . .) | WWB, pp. 77-79, alt. |
| 4.4.27 | (In the brief. . .) | TWS |
| 4.4.28 | (Loving God: We . . .) | TWS |
| 4.4.29 | (Lord God, thank. . .) | TWS |
| 4.4.30 | (Loving God, thank . . .) | TWS |
| 4.5.1 | (Lover of all . . .) | SB-UCC, p. 288 [403]. Adapted with permission. |
| 4.5.2 | (Creator God, convenience. . .) | TWS |
| 4.5.3 | (How crooked is. . .) | TWS |
| 4.5.5 | (Father, we give . . .) | WNYHL, p. 43 |
| 4.5.6 | (Almighty God, you . . .) | RW 43:41 |
| 4.5.7 | (We pray to you . . .) | from a prayer for use on Rogation Sunday, |

|          |                                |                                                                                                                                                                                             |
|----------|--------------------------------|---------------------------------------------------------------------------------------------------------------------------------------------------------------------------------------------|
|          |                                | Evangelical Church of the River Plate, Argentina; from "Confessing Our Faith Around the World IV: South America" (p. 10), 1985 World Council of Churches Publications, Geneva                 |
| 4.5.8    | (From many places...)          | TWS                                                                                                                                                                                          |
| 4.5.9    | (Let us pray ...)              | adapted from part of a prayer in WWB, p. 105                                                                                                                                                 |
| 4.5.10   | (Most merciful God ...)        | Ministry with Persons with AIDS, Ministry with Persons with Life-Threatening Illness, and Ministry with Persons in Coma or Unable to Communicate, © 1992, United Methodist Publishing House. Used by permission. |
| 4.5.11   | (Lord Jesus Christ ...)        | Ministry with Persons with AIDS, Ministry with Persons with Life-Threatening Illness, and Ministry with Persons in Coma or Unable to Communicate, © 1992, United Methodist Publishing House. Used by permission. |
| 4.5.12   | (Eternal God, you ...)         | Ministry with Persons with AIDS, Ministry with Persons with Life-Threatening Illness, and Ministry with Persons in Coma or Unable to Communicate, © 1992, United Methodist Publishing House. Used by permission. |
| 4.5.13   | (O Christ, our ...)            | adapted from part of a prayer in WWB, p. 105                                                                                                                                                 |
| 4.5.14   | (Almighty and ...)             | *A Service of Healing I* and *A Service of Healing II*, © 1992, United Methodist Publishing House. Used by permission.                                                                       |
| 4.5.15   | (God the Father ...)           | BOS-1994, pp. 167-168, adapted                                                                                                                                                               |
| 4.5.16   | (O God, the strength ...)      | BCP, p. 458, alt., PD                                                                                                                                                                        |
| 4.5.17   | (Eternal God, shepherd ...)    | ILID, p. 90                                                                                                                                                                                  |
| 4.5.18   | (Merciful God, you ...)        | TWS                                                                                                                                                                                          |
| 4.5.19   | (God of compassion ...)        | OS, p. 106, alt.                                                                                                                                                                             |
| 4.5.20   | (Jesus, Lamb of God ...)       | TWS                                                                                                                                                                                          |
| 4.5.21   | (Man of sorrows...)            | TWS                                                                                                                                                                                          |
| 4.5.22   | (To you, O...)                 | TWS                                                                                                                                                                                          |
| 4.5.26   | (Why, Lord, must ...)          | Calvin Seerveld in PsH 576, © 1986, Calvin Seerveld                                                                                                                                          |
| 4.5.27   | (God of life ...)              | TWS                                                                                                                                                                                          |
| 4.5.28   | (O God, whose...)              | TWS                                                                                                                                                                                          |
| 4.5.29   | (O God, your ...)              | RW 56:36                                                                                                                                                                                     |
| 4.5.30   | (We are tired, Lord ...)       | T.A. Patterson, Presbyterian pastor (N. Ireland) in WAGP, p. 79, alt.                                                                                                                        |
| 4.5.31   | (O God, resting ...)           | TWS                                                                                                                                                                                          |
| 4.6.1    | (God of the promise ...)       | TWS                                                                                                                                                                                          |
| 4.6.2    | (Lord God, as you ...)         | TWS                                                                                                                                                                                          |
| 4.6.3    | (Triune God—Father ...)        | TWS                                                                                                                                                                                          |
| 4.6.4    | (Lord, our God ...)            | TWS                                                                                                                                                                                          |
| 4.6.5    | (Lord God, we ... )            | TWS                                                                                                                                                                                          |
| 4.6.6    | (Lord, our God ...)            | TWS                                                                                                                                                                                          |
| 4.6.7    | (God of justice ... )          | TWS                                                                                                                                                                                          |
| 4.6.8    | (God of justice ...)           | TWS                                                                                                                                                                                          |
| 4.6.9    | (Loving God, we ...)           | TWS                                                                                                                                                                                          |
| 5.1.4    | (Let us give thanks ...)       | WFW 214 [15]                                                                                                                                                                                 |
| 5.1.16   | (As we come...)                | TWS                                                                                                                                                                                          |
| 5.1.17   | (Give to the Lord ...)         | Arlene M. Mark in WFW 207                                                                                                                                                                    |

| | | |
|---|---|---|
| 5.1.18 | (God has shown . . .) | Anne B. Day in TH, p. 213, alt. |
| 5.1.19 | (The willingness . . .) | Earl W. Fike, Jr., in FAWM |
| 5.1.20 | (Let us be faithful . . .) | Arlene M. Mark in WFW 212, alt. |
| 5.1.21 | (With thankfulness . . .) | BSBL, p. 110 [4] |
| 5.1.22 | (With joy, we . . .) | TWS |
| 5.1.23 | (As recipients of . . .) | TWS |
| 5.1.24 | (With gladness . . .) | BCP, p. 377, alt., PD |
| 5.1.25 | (Responding to God's . . .) | TWS |
| 5.1.26 | (We are very . . .) | TWS |
| 5.1.27 | (Our offering is . . .) | TWS |
| 5.2.2 | (Blessed are you . . .) | ANZPB-HKMOA, p. 420 |
| 5.2.3 | (Merciful Father, we . . .) | LBW, p. 67 [239] |
| 5.2.4 | (Blessed are you . . .) | LBW p. 68 [240] |
| 5.2.5 | (Lord God, we . . .) | TWS |
| 5.2.6 | (Gracious God, everything . . .) | TWS |
| 5.2.7 | (Gracious God, we . . .) | FWS, p. 125, alt. |
| 5.2.8 | (We are not . . .) | TWS |
| 5.2.9 | (Ever-giving God . . .) | Arlene M. Mark in WFW 220 |
| 5.2.10 | (Generous God . . .) | source unknown; adapted by Theodore W. Loder in WFW 222 |
| 5.2.11 | (Dear God, wherever . . .) | TWS |
| 5.2.12 | (Almighty God, you . . .) | TWS |
| 5.2.13 | (Almighty and most . . .) | BW-1964, p. 183, alt. |
| 5.2.14 | (All good things . . .) | Hoyt L. Hickman in WR-UMH, p. 51 |
| 5.2.15 | (O Lord our God . . .) | BCO-1940, p. 25, alt. |
| 5.2.16 | (O God of. . .) | TWS |
| 5.2.17 | (Almighty God, giver . . .) | BW-1964, alt. |
| 5.2.18 | (O Mighty One . . .) | SAS |
| 5.2.19 | (God of wonder . . .) | SAS |
| 5.2.20 | (God of glory . . .) | SAS |
| 5.2.21 | (Giving God, just. . .) | TWS |
| 5.2.22 | (Our Father in. . .) | TWS |
| 5.2.23 | (In the name . . .) | BCO, p. 78, alt. |
| 5.2.24 | (Merciful God, always . . .) | TWS |
| 5.2.25 | (Ever-present God . . .) | Peter Wyatt in WAS-3, p. 32. Adapted with permission. |
| 5.2.26 | (God of every . . .) | LLJ, p. 97 |
| 5.2.27 | (Lord, you give . . .) | TWS |
| 5.2.28 | (We bring you . . .) | TWS |
| 5.2.29 | (Dear God, we . . .) | HWB 748, alt., © 1992, The Hymnal Project, Brethren Press |
| 5.2.30 | (Gracious God, we . . .) | Kenneth I. Morse in WGT |
| 5.2.31 | (Generous God, we . . .) | TWS |
| 5.2.32 | (We thank you . . .) | RW 47:39 |
| 5.2.33 | (Blessed you are . . .) | LP, p. 305, alt. |
| 5.2.35 | (Good shepherd, you . . .) | TWS |
| 5.2.36 | (As you received . . .) | Pentecost liturgy, Church of the Servant, Grand Rapids, Michigan |
| 5.2.37 | (God of the harvest . . .) | SAS |
| 5.2.38 | (Creating God, all . . .) | TWS |
| 5.2.39 | (Giver of every…) | TWS |
| 6.1.1 | (Hear these words . . .) | TWS; AFS-1994, pp. 170-171, alt. |
| 6.1.2.15 | (Our gracious God . . .) | AFS-1994, pp. 170-171 [1] |

| | | |
|---|---|---|
| 6.1.2.16 | (In the sacrament . . .) | AFS-1994, p. 171 [2] |
| 6.1.2.17 | (By baptism God . . .) | AFS-1994, pp. 171-172 [3] |
| 6.1.2.18 | (Let us hear . . .) | AOS-1976, pp. 345-346, alt. |
| 6.1.2.19 | (Let us recall . . .) | AOS-1976, p. 346, alt. |
| 6.1.2.22 | (Obeying the word . . .) | SLR-2, p. 26, alt. |
| 6.1.2.23 | (Christ is present . . .) | BCO, pp. 86-87, alt. |
| 6.1.2.24 | (Before we celebrate . . .) | AOS-1981, p. 329, alt. |
| 6.2.1.1 | (Having heard God's . . .) | TWS |
| 6.2.1.2 | (In presenting your . . .) | TWS |
| 6.2.1.3 | (Who presents . . .) | TWS |
| 6.2.1.4 | (Having heard . . .) | TWS |
| 6.2.1.5 | (In presenting yourself . . .) | TWS |
| 6.2.1.6 | (Having heard . . .) | TWS |
| 6.2.2.1 | (With all God's . . .) | TWS |
| 6.2.2.2 | (Since you are . . .) | AFS-1994, p. 174, alt. |
| 6.2.2.3 | (In presenting your . . .) | BCO, p. 87, alt. |
| 6.2.2.4 | (Do you renounce . . .) | AFS-1994, p. 174 |
| 6.2.2.5 | (Trusting in the . . .) | BCW, p. 407 [1]; third question from WBK, p. 44, alt., PD |
| 6.2.2.6 | (Do you renounce . . .) | SLR-2, p. 28, alt. |
| 6.2.2.7 | (Beloved of God . . .) | RCA-OSB, alt. |
| 6.2.3.1 | (Since you have . . .) | AFS-1994, p. 174 |
| 6.2.3.2 | ([Names(s)], will you . . .) | AOS-1981, pp. 334-335 |
| 6.2.3.3 | ([Names(s)], will you . . .) | AFS-1994, p. 174 |
| 6.2.3.4 | (Will you be . . .) | BCW, p. 409, PD |
| 6.2.3.5 | (Will you devote . . .) | BCP, p. 304, alt., PD |
| 6.3.1 | (A. Address of God . . .) | TWS |
| 6.3.2 | (Father in heaven . . .) | AOS-1976, pp. 346-347, alt. |
| 6.3.3 | (We thank you . . .) | AFS-1994, p. 173 |
| 6.3.4 | (Blessed are you . . .) | TFF, pp. 65-66, alt. |
| 6.3.5 | (Blessed are you . . .) | CB, pp. 14-16 |
| 6.4.1.1 | ([Name], for you . . .) | French Reformed Church liturgy, alt. |
| 6.4.1.2 | (Our Lord said . . .) | AFS-1994, p. 175 |
| 6.4.2.3 | ([Name], child of . . .) | AFS-1994, p. 175 |
| 6.4.2.4 | (O Lord, uphold . . .) | based on a prayer from the early church, PD |
| 6.5.1.1 | (Brothers and sisters . . .) | AFS-1994, p. 176 |
| 6.5.1.2 | (Brothers and sisters . . .) | AFS-1994, p. 176 |
| 6.5.1.3 | ([Name(s)] have been . . .) | SLR-2, p. 32, alt. |
| 6.5.1.4 | (You who are . . .) | BCO, pp. 91-92, alt. |
| 6.5.1.6 | (On the strength . . .) | AFS-1994, p. 174 |
| 6.5.1.7 | (On the strength . . .) | BCW, p. 409, alt., PD |
| 6.5.1.8 | (On the strength . . .) | BCP, p. 304, alt., PD |
| 6.5.2.1 | (Gracious God . . .) | AFS-1994, pp. 175-176 |
| 6.5.2.2 | (Lord our God . . .) | AOS-1976, pp. 347-348, alt. |
| 6.5.2.3 | (Our Father . . .) | AOS-1976, p. 351 |
| 6.5.2.4 | (Ever-living God . . .) | SLR-2, p. 43 |
| 6.5.2.5 | (Gracious God . . .) | SLR-2, pp. 42-43 |
| 6.5.2.6 | (Merciful God . . .) | SLR-2, p. 42 |
| 6.5.2.7 | (Loving God . . .) | SLR-2, p. 43 |
| 6.5.2.8 | (O God, as a . . .) | BW-UCC, p. 248, alt. |
| 6.5.2.9 | (Loving God, in . . .) | TWS |
| 6.5.2.10 | (Our loving God . . .) | TWS |

| 6.5.2.11 | (God our Father . . .) | TWS |
| 6.5.2.12 | (Thank you, O God . . .) | TWS |
| 7.1.1.1 | (Congregation of our . . .) | AOS-1976, p. 352, alt. |
| 7.1.1.2 | ([*Name(s)*] are presented . . .) | SLR-2, pp. 73-74, alt. |
| 7.1.1.3 | (The elders of . . .) | RCA-OPF [cf. EN10] |
| 7.1.2.1 | (Brothers and sisters, from . . .) | from *A Celebration of New Beginnings in Faith* in UW-LB, p. 433, alt. |
| 7.1.3.1 | (Brothers and sisters, we . . .) | TWS |
| 7.1.4.1 | (Brothers and sisters in . . .) | TWS |
| 7.1.4.2 | (Brothers and sisters in . . .) | TWS |
| 7.2.2.1 | (Through baptism God . . .) | from "Sacrament of Baptism" (Reformed Church Press, 1994) in RCA-OPF, alt. |
| 7.3.1.1 | (I invite you now . . .) | TWS |
| 7.3.1.2 | (Now, as you . . .) | TWS |
| 7.3.1.3 | (We ask you now . . .) | from *Liturgy* (Reformed Church Press, 1987) in RCA-OPF, alt. |
| 7.3.1.4 | (Sisters and brothers . . .) | SLR-2, pp. 82-83, alt. |
| 7.3.1.5 | (The faith we . . .) | TWS |
| 7.3.2.1 | (Do you renounce . . .) | AFS-1994, p. 174 |
| 7.3.4.1 | ([*Name(s)*], will you . . .) | AOS-1976, pp. 352-352, alt. |
| 7.3.4.2 | (You have publicly . . .) | BCP, p. 304, alt., PD |
| 7.3.4.3 | (You have publicly . . .) | BCW, p. 409, alt., PD |
| 7.3.4.4 | (Will you promise . . .) | from *Liturgy* (Reformed Church Press, 1968, 1987) in RCA-OPF, alt. |
| 7.4.1 | (Lord, our God . . .) | AOS-1976, pp. 353-354, alt. |
| 7.4.2 | (Gracious God . . .) | SLR-2, p. 76, alt. |
| 7.4.3 | (Almighty God, thank . . .) | TWS |
| 7.4.4 | (Defend, O Lord . . .) | *Book of Common Prayer* (1552), alt., PD |
| 7.4.5 | (Ever-living God . . .) | SLR-2, p. 77 |
| 7.4.6 | (Holy God, we . . .) | WBK, pp. 50, 52, PD |
| 7.4.7 | (Faithful God, you . . .) | SLR-2 p. 80, alt. |
| 7.4.8 | (Faithful God, in . . .) | BCW, p. 443 [423], PD |
| 7.4.9 | (Covenant God, we . . .) | TWS |
| 7.4.10 | (The Lord be with . . .) | John Paarlberg in SNC 240-241, alt.; adapted from the liturgy of the sacrament of baptism of the Reformed Church in America, 2001 |
| 7.4.11 | (We praise you . . .) | TWS |
| 7.4.12 | (The Lord be. . .) | TWS |
| 7.5.1 | (In the name of . . .) | AOS-1976, p. 353, alt. |
| 7.5.2 | ([*Name(s)*], by publicly . . .) | SLR-2, p. 32, alt. |
| 7.5.3 | (Welcome our . . .) | RCA-OPF |
| 7.5.4 | (Welcome to . . .) | SLR-2, p. 97, alt. |
| 7.5.5 | (By the Holy Spirit . . .) | from "Provisional Order for the Ordination of a Minister of Word and Sacrament" (Reformed Church Press, 1998) in RCA-OPF, alt. |
| 7.5.6 | (Do you promise . . .) | from *Liturgy* (Reformed Church Press, 1968, 1987) in RCA-OPF, alt. |
| 7.6.1.4 | (You are disciples . . .) | SLR-2, p. 91, alt. |
| 7.6.1.5 | (Remember your . . .) | SLR-2, p. 84 |
| 7.6.2.2 | (The peace of . . .) | PD |
| 8.1.1.1 | (Hear the words . . .) | BCW, pp. 68-69, PD |
| 8.1.1.3 | (Friends, this is . . .) | WBK, p. 34, alt., PD |
| 8.1.1.5 | (Now let us hear . . .) | WWB, p. 96, alt. |
| 8.1.2.4 | (Beloved in the Lord . . .) | RCA-OW, alt. |

| | | |
|---|---|---|
| 8.1.3.5 | (Brothers and sisters . . .) | AOS-1981, p. 295 |
| 8.1.3.6 | (He was always . . .) | WWB, p. 84, alt. |
| 8.1.3.7 | (Come to this table . . .) | WWB, p. 95, alt. |
| 8.1.3.8 | (Congregation of Jesus . . .) | AFS-1994, p. 182, alt. |
| 8.1.3.9 | (Congregation of our . . .) | AFS-1994, p. 181, alt. |
| 8.1.3.10 | (Professing members . . .) | from Church of the Servant, Grand Rapids, Michigan |
| 8.1.3.11 | (We welcome all . . .) | TWS |
| 8.2.1.2 | (As the Lord Jesus . . .) | TWS |
| 8.2.2.1 | (It is truly right . . .) | Alexandrine liturgy of St. Basil (4th cent.), PD |
| 8.2.2.2 | (Generous God, overflowing . . .) | TWS |
| 8.2.2.3 | (With joy we praise . . .) | AFS-1994, p. 178, alt. |
| 8.2.3.1 | (Holy, holy, holy Lord . . .) | *Sanctus* from PT-ELLC, p. 35 |
| 8.2.3.2 | (Holy, holy, holy! . . .) | Reginald Heber (1872), alt., PD |
| 8.2.4.1 | (We acclaim you . . .) | Alexandrine liturgy of St. Basil (4th cent.), PD |
| 8.2.4.2 | (Holy God, you . . .) | TWS |
| 8.2.4.3 | (We give thanks . . .) | AFS-1994, p. 180 |
| 8.2.5.1 | (We shall do as . . .) | AOS-1981, p. 296 |
| 8.2.5.2 | (Therefore we proclaim . . .) | AFS-1994, p. 181, and ancient Eastern liturgies |
| 8.2.5.3 | (Praise to you. . .) | from ancient Eastern liturgies in RM, and proposed revisions of the liturgy of the Mass prepared by ICEL |
| 8.2.5.4 | (We profess our . . .) | TWS |
| 8.2.5.5 | (Christ is the bread . . .) | in RM, and proposed revisions of the liturgy of the Mass prepared by ICEL |
| 8.2.6.1 | (Heavenly Father . . .) | AOS-1981, p. 296, alt. |
| 8.2.6.2 | (Send your Holy Spirit . . .) | RCA-OW, alt. |
| 8.2.6.3 | (Living God, send . . .) | TWS |
| 8.2.6.4 | (God of all power . . .) | Advent liturgy, Church of the Servant, Grand Rapids, Michigan |
| 8.2.6.5 | (Creator God, be . . .) | Christmas liturgy, Church of the Servant, Grand Rapids, Michigan |
| 8.2.6.6 | (Lord, our God . . .) | AFS-1994, p. 181 |
| 8.2.7.2 | (Our Father . . .) | PT-ELLC, p. 13, alt. |
| 8.2.8.1 | (Thanks be to God . . .) | TWS |
| 8.2.8.2 | (Lord Jesus Christ . . .) | TWS |
| 8.2.8.3 | (On the evening . . .) | BCO, p. 140, alt. |
| 8.2.9.1 | (Thankful praise . . .) | BCW, pp. 42-43, alt., PD |
| 8.2.9.2 | (Lift up your . . .) | AOS-1981, pp. 973-974, alt. |
| 8.2.9.3 | (The Lord be with . . .) | RCA-OW, alt. |
| 8.2.9.4 | (The Lord be with . . .) | BCW, pp. 153-155 [122], alt.; from common elements of other eucharistic prayers in BCW with rubrics based on the Directory for Worship in the *Book of Order of the Presbyterian Church (U.S.A)*, W-2.4003, 4, 5, 6, 7, and W-3.3613, PD |
| 8.2.9.5 | (The Lord be with . . .) | based on English tr. of *Eucharistic Prayer of Hippolytus: Text for Consultation,* © 1983, International Committee on English in the Liturgy, Inc. (ICEL). All rights reserved. |
| 8.2.9.6 | (The Lord be with . . .) | Trinity Season liturgy, Church of the Servant, Grand Rapids, Michigan |
| 8.2.9.7 | (The Lord be with . . .) | WWB, pp. 86-88, alt. |
| 8.2.9.8 | (The Lord be with . . .) | BCO, pp. 131-134, alt. |
| 8.2.9.9 | (The Lord be with . . .) | from *Genevan Service Book,* alt., PD |

| 8.2.9.10 | (The Lord be with . . .) | BCO, pp. 131-138, alt. |
|---|---|---|
| 8.2.9.11 | (The Lord be with . . .) | BCO, pp. 169-170, alt. |
| 8.3.1 | (Is not the bread . . .) | AOS-1981, pp. 296-297, alt. |
| 8.3.2 | (We celebrate this . . .) | PD |
| 8.4.1.3 | (Come then, for . . .) | Advent liturgy, Church of the Servant, Grand Rapids, Michigan |
| 8.4.1.4 | (Hear the words . . .) | Lenten liturgy, Church of the Servant, Grand Rapids, Michigan |
| 8.4.1.5 | (Come then, for . . .) | Easter liturgy, Church of the Servant, Grand Rapids, Michigan |
| 8.4.1.6 | (Congregation of . . .) | AFS-1994, p. 181, alt. |
| 8.4.1.7 | (The gifts of God . . .) | BCP, p. 338, PD |
| 8.4.1.8 | (The gifts of God . . .) | BCP, p. 338, PD |
| 8.4.2.1 | (Take, eat, . . .) | AOS-1981, p. 297, alt. |
| 8.4.2.2 | (Take and eat . . .) | BCO, p. 140 |
| 8.4.2.3 | (The body of Christ, given . . .) | ancient source, PD |
| 8.4.2.4 | (The body of Christ, the. . .) | ancient source, PD |
| 8.5.2.2 | (O Lord, our God . . .) | ELL |
| 8.5.2.3 | (Lord God, in . . .) | WWB, pp. 89-90 |
| 8.5.2.4 | (We thank and . . .) | TWS |
| 8.5.2.5 | (We bless you . . .) | TWS |
| 8.5.2.6 | (Gracious God, we . . .) | BCO, p. 141, alt. |
| 8.5.2.7 | (Glory to God . . .) | BCO, pp. 141-142 |
| 8.5.2.8 | (Lord, you have put . . .) | BCO, p. 193, alt. |
| 8.5.2.9 | (Loving God, we . . .) | UW-LB, p. 655, alt. Permission sought. |
| 8.5.2.10 | (You have fed . . .) | TWS |
| 8.5.2.11 | (Most gracious God . . .) | TWS |
| 8.5.2.12 | (Eternal God, you . . .) | Leo Malania in BCP, p. 365, PD |
| 8.5.2.13 | (Loving God, you . . .) | from the Liturgy of Malabar (5th cent.), alt., PD |
| 8.5.2.14 | (Loving God, you have . . .) | RM, alt. |
| 8.5.2.15 | (O God, you have . . .) | prayer used by Westminster Assembly of Divines in 1647, PD |
| 8.5.2.16 | (God of grace . . .) | RM, alt. |
| 8.5.2.17 | (God of all . . .) | TWS |
| 8.5.2.18 | (O amazing God . . .) | "Into the Ordinary," reproduced from SFS, p. 81 |
| 8.5.2.19 | (Generous God, you...) | TWS |
| 8.5.2.20 | (Most holy and...) | TWS |
| 8.5.2.21 | (Loving, glorious, gracious...) | TWS |
| 9.1.10 | (Go in peace to . . .) | BCP, p. 366, PD |
| 9.1.12 | (Go in peace, in . . .) | CRCL-3, p. 75 |
| 9.1.13 | (Go into the world . . .) | CGP, p. 73, alt.; from the Commission for Mission, Uniting Church in Australia. Used by permission. |
| 9.1.14 | (Go forth, remembering . . .) | CGP, p. 73. Reprinted with permission. |
| 9.1.15 | (God be in your . . .) | Sarum Liturgy, England, late medieval period, PD |
| 9.1.16 | (Let us go forth in . . .) | BCP, p. 366, PD |
| 9.1.17 | (Go in peace to . . .) | BCP, p. 366, PD |
| 9.1.18 | (Let us go forth into . . .) | BCP, p. 366, PD |
| 9.1.19 | (Let us bless . . .) | BCP, p. 366, PD |
| 9.1.20 | (As you have been . . .) | Kate McIlhagga in POD, p. 158 [75], alt., © Kate McIlhagga |
| 9.1.21 | (Go in peace as . . .) | LLJ, p. 88, alt. |
| 9.1.23 | (Go out into . . .) | CH-1973, alt. |

| 9.1.24 | (As you leave . . .) | RW 11:23 |
|---|---|---|
| 9.1.25 | (Watch now . . .) | BCP, p. 134, alt., PD |
| 9.1.37 | (Grant, O Lord . . .) | John Hunter, Scotland (19th cent.), PD |
| 9.1.38 | (O Creator and . . .) | Pakistan, source unknown; based on a poem by Annie Johnson Flint |
| 9.1.39 | (Lord, we have . . .) | David Vroege in CSL, p. 89, alt. |
| 9.1.40 | (Grant us, Lord God . . .) | Church in Australia in PEW, p. 104 [119]. Used by permission of Anglican Consultative Council. |
| 9.1.41 | (Almighty God . . .) | Church of the West Indies in PEW, p. 71 [75]. Used by permission of Anglican Consultative Council. |
| 9.1.42 | (God the Sender . . .) | Church in Wales in PEW, p. 246 [299]. Used by permission of Anglican Consultative Council. |
| 9.1.43 | (Grant to us . . .) | Thomas à Kempis (15th cent.), PD |
| 9.1.44 | (With you, wondrous . . .) | TWS |
| 9.1.45 | (Loving God, together . . .) | TWS |
| 9.1.46 | (Bless to us . . .) | Kate McIlhagga in POD, p. 158 [73], © Kate McIlhagga |
| 9.1.47 | (Tender and . . .) | HWB 746, © 1992, The Hymnal Project, Brethren Press |
| 9.1.48 | (Lord, dismiss us . . .) | TWS |
| 9.2.4 | (May the grace of Christ . . .) | CH-1973, alt. |
| 9.2.11 | (The peace of God . . .) | BCP, p. 339, alt., PD |
| 9.2.12 | (May the love . . .) | TWS |
| 9.2.13 | (May you, people . . .) | TWS |
| 9.2.14 | (The love of God . . .) | Kate McIlhagga in POD, p. 158 [74], © Kate McIlhagga |
| 9.2.15 | (May our Lord Jesus . . .) | TWS |
| 9.2.16 | (May the love of God . . .) | WE, p. 33, © Wild Goose Resource Group, The Iona Community, Pearce Institute, Govan, Glasgow G51 3UU, United Kingdom |
| 9.2.17 | (May God the Father . . .) | BOS-1994, p. 171 |
| 9.2.18 | (As you leave . . .) | TWS |
| 9.2.19 | (May the grace. . .) | TWS |
| 9.2.20 | (May the blessing . . .) | Peter Wyatt in WAS-3, p. 40. Adapted with permission. |
| 9.2.21 | (The grace of Christ . . .) | SB-UCC, p. 72. Reprinted with permission. |
| 9.2.22 | (May God go...) | TWS |
| 9.2.23 | (May the omniscient...) | TWS |
| A.1.2.3 | (Who is this God. . .) | BTG, p. 3 [5] |
| A.1.2.4 | (This is the day . . .) | TWS |
| A.1.4.1 | (We praise you, God . . .) | R.C. Thorp in PTC, p. 36 [55] |
| A.1.4.2 | (O God, our . . .) | Patricia Mitchell in PTC, p. 111 [259] |
| A.1.4.3 | (Creator God, you . . .) | BTG, p. 6 [2] |
| A.1.4.4 | (How magnificent for . . .) | TWS |
| A.1.4.5 | (Creator God, whose . . .) | John Paarlberg in RW 35:26 |
| A.1.4.6 | (Creator God, who . . .) | John Paarlberg in RW 35:27 |
| A.1.4.7 | (Creator God, who . . .) | John Paarlberg in RW 35:27 |
| A.1.4.8 | (On this day of . . .) | RCLP, p. 70 |
| A.1.4.9 | (O Lord, our Lord . . .) | TWS |
| A.1.4.10 | (We gather in . . .) | TWS |
| A.1.4.11 | (At the beginning . . .) | RW 40:24 |
| A.1.4.12 | (In you, infinite . . .) | TWS |
| A.1.4.13 | (Creator God, we. . .) | TWS |
| A.2.2.1 | (Lord God, you . . .) | TWS |
| A.2.2.2 | (God of all creation . . .) | TWS |

| A.2.2.3 | (Creator God, we . . .) | RW 10:24 |
| A.2.2.4 | (Great God, you. . .) | TWS |
| A.2.2.5 | (Creator God, breathing . . .) | World Council of Churches Assembly Worship Committee in JCLW, p. 6 [4] |
| A.2.2.6 | (O God, the earth . . .) | LOP-C, p. 105, alt. |
| A.2.2.7 | (God of all creation . . .) | Janet Cawley in CGP, p. 32 |
| A.3.1.1 | (Lord God, at the . . .) | TWS |
| A.3.6.2 | (We believe in God . . .) | BTG, p. 18 [2], based on first article of Apostles' Creed |
| A.4.4.1 | (Creator God, we . . .) | TWS |
| A.4.4.2 | (Lord, you make . . .) | RW 14:39 |
| A.4.4.3 | (Lord, you saw . . .) | RW 14:39 |
| A.4.4.4 | (God of beauty . . .) | TWS |
| A.4.4.5 | (The heavens declare . . .) | TWS |
| A.4.4.6 | (For the earth and . . .) | RW 10:25 |
| A.9.1.1 | (God, our creator . . .) | TWS |
| A.9.2.1 | (May God, the . . .) | from Sarum Missal |
| B.1.2.3 | (God makes the . . .) | TWS |
| B.1.4.1 | (Loving God, you . . .) | TWS |
| B.1.4.3 | (God of new . . .) | RCLP, p. 45 |
| B.1.4.4 | (God of our life . . .) | Hugh Thomson Kerr, 1916, alt.; a hymn sung to the tune SANDON [*Presbyterian Hymnal* 275], from *The Hymnal for Youth* (Westminster Press), © 1928, F. M. Braselman, renewed 1956, Presbyterian Board of Christian Education |
| B.1.4.5 | (For all the . . .) | John Charles Vockler in CBCP, p. 365 [938], alt. |
| B.2.2.1 | (As we draw . . .) | RW 17:42 |
| B.2.2.2 | (Loving Father, we . . .) | TWS |
| B.4.4.1 | (Lord of heaven . . .) | TWS |
| B.4.4.2 | (Eternal God, a . . .) | John T. Ames in LUP, p. 24, alt. |
| B.5.2.1 | (Lord, you have . . .) | TWS |
| B.5.2.2 | (Generous God . . .) | TWS |
| B.9.1.1 | (Lord of time . . .) | Susan Williams in PTC, p. 32 [48] |
| B.9.1.2 | (Eternal God . . .) | TWS |
| B.9.1.3 | (Covenant God . . .) | TWS |
| C.1.2.4 | (O give thanks . . .) | TWS |
| C.1.2.6 | (Our help is in . . .) | RW 8:44 |
| C.1.4.1 | (Father in heaven . . .) | TWS |
| C.1.4.2 | (Great God, King . . .) | TWS |
| C.1.4.3 | (Gracious God, your . . .) | Arlene M. Mark in WFW 72 |
| C.1.4.4 | (Loving God, you . . .) | TWS |
| C.1.4.5 | (Give us, our Father . . .) | Frank Colquhoun in CBCP, p. 341 [882] |
| C.1.4.6 | (Almighty God . . .) | John Cosin (1594-1672) in CBCP, p. 420 [1065], alt. |
| C.1.4.7 | (Lord our God . . .) | NHCY, p. 271 |
| C.1.4.8 | (Praise is due to . . .) | Julia C. Cory, 1902, alt., in RW 36:42 |
| C.1.4.9 | (Let us give thanks . . .) | RW 1:19 |
| C.1.4.10 | (Let us give thanks . . .) | RW 1:19 |
| C.1.4.11 | (Great God of our . . .) | RW 43:41 |
| C.1.4.12 | (Gracious God, for . . .) | TWS |
| C.2.2.1 | (Loving God, we . . .) | RW 8:44 |
| C.2.2.2 | (Holy God, you . . .) | TWS |
| C.2.2.3 | (Almighty God, giver . . .) | TWS |
| C.4.4.1 | (God of all good . . .) | TWS |

| | | |
|---|---|---|
| C.4.4.3 | (Loving God: Thank you . . .) | TWS |
| C.4.4.4 | (We thank you . . .) | E. LaVern Epp in WFW 73 |
| C.4.4.5 | (Mighty God of . . .) | Donald Wilson Stake in SLR-5, p. 279 |
| C.4.4.6 | (Almighty God . . .) | TWS |
| C.4.4.7 | (Almighty and . . .) | BCW, p. 81 [66], based on an adaptation by Louis F. Benson from a prayer in the Church of Scotland's *Prayers for Social and Family Worship* (1859), PD |
| C.4.4.8 | (God, giver of . . .) | BWFC, alt. |
| C.4.4.9 | (Give thanks to . . .) | WBK, pp. 114-115, alt. |
| C.4.4.10 | (Make a joyful . . .) | Louis Lotz in FHEG, alt. |
| C.4.4.11 | (Gracious God, you . . .) | Arlene M. Mark in WFW 75 |
| C.4.4.12 | (Let us give thanks . . .) | RW 40:25 |
| C.4.4.13 | (Give thanks to . . .) | Ron Rienstra in *Reformed Review* (Winter 1995-96), Vol. 49, No. 2, pp. 129-131, alt. |
| C.4.4.14 | (Almighty God, we thank . . .) | TWS |
| C.4.4.15 | (Caring God, we . . .) | ANZPB-HKMOA, p. 463 |
| C.5.2.1 | (All good things . . .) | Hoyt L. Hickman in WR-UMH, p. 51, alt. Adapted by permission. |
| C.9.1.1 | (Almighty and gracious . . .) | NHCY, p. 271 |
| C.9.2.1 | (May God the Creator . . .) | TWS |
| C.9.2.2 | (Almighty God, the one . . .) | TWS |
| C.9.2.3 | (May our great God . . .) | TWS |
| D.1.2.6 | (I wait for the . . .) | WAGP-OS, p. 5 |
| D.1.2.7 | (We gather in . . .) | LLJ, p. 23, alt. |
| D.1.2.8 | (The mighty God . . .) | RW 57:4 |
| D.1.2.9 | (The Lord has done . . .) | RW 57:6 |
| D.1.2.10 | (Our souls magnify . . .) | RW 57:10 |
| D.1.2.11 | (Show us your . . .) | RW 57:8 |
| D.1.2.12 | (The Lord whom . . .) | Advent liturgy, Church of the Servant, Grand Rapids, Michigan |
| D.1.2.13 | (Let us praise our . . .) | TWS |
| D.1.3.1 | (The Lord be with . . .) | RW 57:4 |
| D.1.4.1 | (Lord God Almighty . . .) | PCY |
| D.1.4.2 | (Father, all-powerful . . .) | RM |
| D.1.4.3 | (Blessed are you . . .) | from Jewish prayerbook in AS, p. 73, alt., PD |
| D.1.4.4 | (King of glory . . .) | TWS |
| D.1.4.6 | (God of Israel . . .) | NHCY, p. 58 |
| D.1.4.7 | (Father in heaven . . .) | RM, alt. |
| D.1.4.8 | (Faithful God, we . . .) | TWS |
| D.1.4.9 | (The Lord is glorious . . .) | RW 9:23 |
| D.1.4.10 | (Covenant God, you heard . . .) | TWS |
| D.1.4.11 | (God of all hope . . .) | ANZPB-HKMOA, p. 554 |
| D.1.4.12 | (If our lives are . . .) | RW 9:22 |
| D.1.4.13 | (O God, whose will . . .) | RM |
| D.1.4.14 | (In this Advent . . .) | RW 9:22 |
| D.1.4.15 | (O Lord Jesus . . .) | TWS |
| D.1.4.16 | (All-powerful God . . .) | RM |
| D.1.4.17 | (In the psalms of . . .) | RM |
| D.1.4.18 | (Above the clamor . . .) | RM |
| D.1.4.19 | (Father of our Lord . . .) | RM |
| D.1.4.20 | (Lord of hope . . .) | TWS |
| D.1.4.21 | (O God, you have . . .) | Christopher Idle in PTC, p. 17 [3] |

| D.1.4.22 | (God of power and . . .) | BAS, p. 270, alt. |
| D.1.4.23 | (In anticipation we . . .) | AESP, p. 38, alt. |
| D.1.4.24 | (God of timeless . . .) | RCLP, p. 30 |
| D.1.4.25 | (God of hope . . .) | RCLP, p. 31, alt. |
| D.1.4.27 | (Jesus said, "I am . . .) | TWS |
| D.1.4.28 | (We light [these . . .) | Peter C. Bower in SLR-7, pp. 61-62, alt. |
| D.1.4.29 | (We light [these . . .) | John Paarlberg in SNC 94, © 2000, John Paarlberg |
| D.1.4.33 | (In the beginning . . .) | RW 29:19 |
| D.1.4.34 | (Prepare the way . . .) | David Vroege in CSL, p. 86, alt. |
| D.1.4.35 | (The Advent wreath . . .) | RW 65:10 |
| D.2.1.1 | (Prepare the way . . .) | CGP, p. 84, PD |
| D.2.2.2 | (Lord God, our lives . . .) | David Vroege in CSL, p. 86 |
| D.2.2.3 | (O promised Christ . . .) | adapted from TTP, p. 15, with the kind permission of Collins Liturgical Publications. |
| D.2.2.4 | (Arise, shine: for . . .) | PL, Advent Confession [3], alt. |
| D.2.2.5 | (Lord Christ, we . . .) | PL, Advent Confession [4] |
| D.2.2.6 | (Merciful God, always . . .) | Janet Cawley in CGP, p. 85 |
| D.2.2.7 | (Lord, we have not . . .) | CRCL-3, p. 4 |
| D.2.2.8 | (While we ask, Lord . . .) | RW 33:9 |
| D.2.2.9 | (Almighty God, you . . .) | RW 33:10 |
| D.2.2.10 | (God of salvation . . .) | RW 34:20 |
| D.2.2.11 | (O God, you give . . .) | RW 37:7 |
| D.2.2.12 | (It is Advent . . .) | Susan R. Tomlinson in LUP, p. 14 |
| D.2.2.13 | (If we look at . . .) | RW 9:23 |
| D.2.2.14 | (O Holy Child of . . .) | "O Little Town of Bethlehem," Phillips Brooks (1835-1893), PD |
| D.2.4.2 | (Comfort, comfort my . . .) | CGP, p. 86. Reprinted with permission. |
| D.2.4.6 | (As we hear . . .) | TWS |
| D.2.4.7 | (Almighty God, by . . .) | BOS-1994, p. 22, adapted |
| D.2.4.8 | (Jesus, the long-expected . . .) | TWS |
| D.3.1.2 | (Creator God, you . . .) | Tom Schwanda in CLCW, vol. 5, p. 123 |
| D.3.1.3 | (God of love and . . .) | John D. Witvliet in CLCW, vol. 5, p. 140 |
| D.3.1.4 | (God of the universe . . .) | PL, Advent Illumination [1], alt. |
| D.3.1.5 | (Gracious God, sometimes . . .) | TWS |
| D.3.1.6 | (O God, our beginning . . .) | PUAS |
| D.3.1.7 | (Immanuel, as we . . .) | TWS |
| D.3.6.2 | (In love you came . . .) | PL, Advent Confession [4], alt. |
| D.3.6.4 | (We are called . . .) | TWS |
| D.4.4.1 | (God, our hope, we . . .) | TWS |
| D.4.4.2 | (God of the future . . .) | TWS |
| D.4.4.3 | (To God we pray . . .) | John A. Dalles in RW 35:39, © 1994, CRC Publications |
| D.4.4.4 | (Eternal God, for . . .) | John T. Ames in LUP, pp. 16-17, alt. |
| D.4.4.5 | (Remember your church . . .) | ecumenical prayer from France |
| D.4.4.6 | (O Immanuel, child . . .) | RW 21:37 |
| D.4.4.7 | (O Wisdom, Divine . . .) | TWS |
| D.4.5.1 | (Lord God, we long . . .) | RW 45:23 |
| D.5.2.1 | (What can I give . . .) | "In the Bleak Midwinter," Christina Rossetti (1830-1894), PD |
| D.5.2.2 | (O Mighty One, you . . .) | SAS |
| D.5.2.3 | (God of hope . . .) | TWS |
| D.8.2.2.1 | (With joy we praise . . .) | AFS-1994, pp. 178-179 |
| D.8.2.4.1 | (You are holy . . .) | Donald Wilson Stake and Harold M. Daniels in |

| | | |
|---|---|---|
| D.8.5.2.1 | (Strengthen us, O God . . .) | SLR-7, pp. 63-65; rev. Marney Ault Wasserman, alt. Donald Wilson Stake and Harold M. Daniels in SLR-7, pp. 63-65; rev. Marney Ault Wasserman, alt. |
| D.9.1.5 | (May Jesus Christ . . .) | TWS, adapted from Psalm 72 |
| D.9.1.7 | (Eternal God, you . . .) | BCW, p. 173 [137], based on WBK, p. 135, PD |
| D.9.1.8 | (O King of nations . . .) | RW 21:37 |
| D.9.1.9 | (Lord, in these . . .) | TWS |
| D.9.2.4 | (God the Father . . .) | Michael Perham in CBCP, p. 375 [959], alt., © Michael Perham |
| E.1.2.2 | (All God's people . . .) | TWS |
| E.1.2.3 | (Let us go, in . . .) | CRCL-3, p. 11, alt. |
| E.1.2.4 | (Lift up your hearts . . .) | WAGP-OS, p. 14 |
| E.1.2.5 | (God is here! . . .) | RW 13:13 |
| E.1.4.1 | (Jesus, Son of the . . .) | PED, pp. 46-47 |
| E.1.4.2 | (Everlasting God, your Son . . .) | TWS |
| E.1.4.3 | (Almighty God, you . . .) | BCP, p. 214, alt., PD |
| E.1.4.4 | (All glory to you . . .) | WBK-SH, p. 137, alt. |
| E.1.4.5 | (God of glory . . .) | RCLP, p. 38, alt. |
| E.1.4.6 | (Come and stand . . .) | medieval Dutch carol, trans. Klaas Hart, rev CRC Publications, © 1987, CRC Publications |
| E.1.4.7 | (Glory be to God . . .) | Thomas Ken (1637-1711) in CBCP, p. 378 [965], alt. |
| E.1.4.8 | (O Immanuel, O Wisdom . . .) | TWS, based on the "O" antiphons |
| E.1.4.9 | (Be near us, Lord . . .) | Tom Schwanda in CLCW, vol. 5, p. 166 [189] |
| E.1.4.10 | (We pray, O Lord . . .) | William Temple (1881-1944) in PEO, p. 35 [65], alt. |
| E.1.4.11 | (O God, our Father . . .) | Church of Ceylon (Sri Lanka) in PEW, p. 44 [45]. Used by permission of Anglican Consultative Council. |
| E.1.4.12 | (He came as baby . . .) | TWS |
| E.1.4.13 | (Emmanuel, God with us. . .) | TWS |
| E.1.4.14 | (You came in . . .) | TWS |
| E.1.4.15 | (O God, our loving . . .) | Robert Louis Stevenson (1850-1894) |
| E.1.4.16 | (O God, you have . . .) | BCP, p. 212, PD |
| E.1.4.17 | (O God, who made . . .) | ancient Western rite, PD |
| E.1.4.18 | (Let your goodness . . .) | SBCY |
| E.1.4.19 | (God of power . . .) | TWS |
| E.1.4.20 | (O Lord, our God . . .) | Stephen S. Smalley in CBCP, p. 379 [970], © Stephen Smalley |
| E.1.4.21 | (God of love, open . . .) | WN, alt. |
| E.1.4.22 | (Good Christian friends . . .) | TWS, based on the medieval hymn *In dulci jubilo* ("Good Christian Friends, Rejoice") |
| E.1.4.23 | (Almighty and everlasting . . .) | David Silk in CBCP, p. 379 [969], alt., © David Silk |
| E.1.4.24 | (You surprised a world . . .) | WV, p. 93 |
| E.1.4.25 | (Lord Jesus, you . . .) | Michael Counsell in MPS |
| E.2.1.1 | (Today we celebrate . . .) | TWS |
| E.2.2.1 | (God of love . . .) | TWS |
| E.2.2.2 | (O God, in the . . .) | PL, Christmas Confession [1], alt. |
| E.2.2.3 | (O God, we need . . .) | PL, Christmas Confession [2], alt. |
| E.2.2.4 | (Generous God, you . . .) | Janet Cawley in CGP, p. 115 |
| E.2.2.5 | (Holy God, you sent . . .) | WBK-SH, p. 137, alt. |
| E.2.2.6 | (When we allow . . .) | LLJ, p. 26, alt. |
| E.2.2.7 | (Almighty God who . . .) | Christmas liturgy, Church of the Servant, Grand Rapids, Michigan |

| | | |
|---|---|---|
| E.2.4.1 | (Break forth together . . .) | TWS |
| E.2.4.2 | (Go through, go through . . .) | TWS |
| E.2.4.8 | (The saying is sure . . .) | TWS |
| E.2.4.12 | (In the past . . .) | TWS |
| E.2.4.11 | (The Lord's grace is . . .) | David Vroege in CSL, p. 87 |
| E.3.1.1 | (Mighty God, the . . .) | Tom Schwanda in CLCW, vol. 5, p. 167 [189] |
| E.3.1.2 | (O Christ, the prophets . . .) | PED, p. 43, alt. |
| E.3.6.2 | (I believe the Word . . .) | CLCW, vol. 5, p. 168 [190] |
| E.3.6.12 | (Jesus is our Savior! . . .) | TWS |
| E.4.4.1 | (Incarnate God, with . . .) | TWS |
| E.4.4.2 | ("This is what will . . .) | Wesley Ariarajah in WAGP-OS, p. 16, alt. |
| E.4.4.3 | (All the ends of . . .) | ecumenical prayer from France |
| E.5.2.1 | (What can I give . . .) | "In the Bleak Midwinter," Christina Rossetti (1830-1894), PD |
| E.5.2.2 | (God of wonder . . .) | SAS |
| E.5.2.3 | (Gracious God, you . . .) | Mary Marple Thies in LUP, p. 21, alt. |
| E.8.2.2.1 | (With joy we praise . . .) | AFS-1994, p. 179 |
| E.8.2.2.2 | (O God, in the . . .) | SLR-1, p. 88, and ancient source, alt. |
| E.8.2.4.1 | (This feast for which . . .) | TWS |
| E.9.1.2 | (Go now into the . . .) | RFR, p. 90 |
| E.9.1.3 | (O God, you have . . .) | BCP, p. 212, PD |
| E.9.1.4 | (God of all grace . . .) | TWS |
| E.9.1.5 | (Almighty God, you . . .) | BCP, p. 213, PD |
| E.9.1.6 | (O God, you make . . .) | BCP, p. 212, alt., PD |
| E.9.2.1 | (The joy of the . . .) | PHG, p. 189 |
| E.9.2.2 | (Jesus is the Word . . .) | TFF, p. 91, alt. |
| E.9.2.3 | (May God, who sent . . .) | BOS-1994, p. 23, adapted |
| E.9.2.4 | (May Jesus Christ . . .) | TWS |
| F.1.2.5 | (Arise, shine, for . . .) | TWS |
| F.1.2.6 | (The Christ child . . .) | ASM, p. 28 |
| F.1.2.7 | (Long ago, God . . .) | RW 21:29 |
| F.1.2.8 | (O come, let us . . .) | LOP-C, p. 183, alt. Adapted by permission. |
| F.1.2.9 | (The mystery from . . .) | TWS |
| F.1.2.10 | (Give the king your . . .) | CTW, p. 106, alt. |
| F.1.2.11 | (May the light of . . .) | RW 63:10 |
| F.1.4.1 | (Almighty Lord God . . .) | James M. Todd in PEO, p. 41 [96], alt. |
| F.1.4.2 | (God, you have made . . .) | CRCL-3, p. 18 |
| F.1.4.3 | (Perfect Light of . . .) | RCLP, p. 50 |
| F.1.4.4 | (O God, you spoke . . .) | RCLP, p. 50 |
| F.1.4.5 | (Everlasting God, you . . .) | from ancient sources, alt. |
| F.1.4.6 | (O God who quickens . . .) | LOP-C, p. 184, alt. Adapted by permission. |
| F.1.4.7 | (God of Advent . . .) | CRCL-3, p. 19 |
| F.1.4.8 | (Father, you revealed . . .) | LH |
| F.1.4.9 | (Eternal God, by a . . .) | ASB, p. 460, alt. |
| F.1.4.10 | (O God, our Father . . .) | Church of Ceylon (Sri Lanka) in PEW, p. 44 [45]. Used by permission of Anglican Consultative Council. |
| F.1.4.11 | (Almighty Father, in . . .) | Piers Nash-Williams in PTC, p. 27 [34] |
| F.1.4.12 | (O God, by the . . .) | BOS-1994, p. 48 |
| F.1.4.13 | (God, whom we . . .) | CLUWG, p. 88, alt. |
| F.1.4.14 | (Gracious God, you . . .) | TWS |
| F.2.2.1 | (God of the Bethlehem . . .) | ASM, p. 35 |
| F.2.2.2 | (O God, our guide . . .) | PL, Epiphany Confession |

| F.2.2.3 | (God of grace . . .) | WBK-SH, p. 139, alt. |
|---|---|---|
| F.2.2.4 | (Jesus, the Magi saw . . .) | David Vroege in CSL, p. 87, alt. |
| F.2.2.5 | (Eternal Light, shine . . .) | Alcuin of Tours (8th cent.), PD |
| F.2.2.6 | (Almighty and merciful . . .) | Christmas liturgy, Church of the Servant, Grand Rapids, Michigan |
| F.2.2.7 | (God of light, we . . .) | BSBL, p. 69 [8] |
| F.3.1.1 | (Lord God of the . . .) | SBK-92, p. 44, alt. |
| F.3.1.2 | (God of light . . .) | TWS |
| F.3.1.3 | (Shine your truth . . .) | WG, p. 26 |
| F.3.1.4 | (Guide us, O God . . .) | SB-UCC, p. 133, alt. |
| F.3.1.5 | (We pray, Lord . . .) | TWS |
| F.3.1.6 | (Our Lord and our . . .) | RW 5:39 |
| F. 3.1.7 | (We praise you . . .) | TWS |
| F.4.4.1 | (God of light, we . . .) | TWS |
| F.4.4.2 | (God of new beginnings . . .) | TWS |
| F.4.4.3 | (God of glory, we . . .) | Jan Berry in CBCP, p. 381 [975], alt., © Jan Berry |
| F.4.4.4 | (O Jesus, light of . . .) | RW 42:30 |
| F.4.4.5 | (Let us pray for . . .) | NHCY, p. 85 |
| F.4.4.6 | (God has called us . . .) | ICP, p. 81, alt. |
| F.4.4.7 | (All the ends of . . .) | ecumenical prayer from France |
| F.4.4.8 | (Let us praise God . . .) | RW 13:39 |
| F.4.4.9 | (Where ignorance, self-love . . .) | WE, p. 44 |
| F.5.2.1 | (Bright Morning Star . . .) | RCLP, p. 53 |
| F.5.2.2 | (Lord, you were born . . .) | David Vroege in CSL, p. 87 |
| F.5.2.3 | (Emmanuel, God with us . . .) | TWS |
| F.5.2.4 | (O God, from whom . . .) | WG, p. 26, alt. |
| F.8.1.3.1 | (Brothers and sisters . . .) | Christmas liturgy, Church of the Servant, Grand Rapids, Michigan |
| F.8.2.2.1 | (With joy we praise . . .) | AFS-1994, p. 179 |
| F.8.2.2.2 | (We thank you, God, . . .) | BTG, pp. 76-77 |
| F.8.2.4.1 | (In sending Christ . . .) | SLR-1, p. 89, alt. |
| F.8.2.4.2 | (God of wisdom . . .) | SP, p. 13 |
| F.8.2.4.3 | (With the coming of . . .) | BTG, pp. 76-77 |
| F.9.1.1 | (The light of God's . . .) | WG, p. 26 |
| F.9.1.2 | (Our risen Lord . . .) | TWS |
| F.9.1.4 | (God of goodness . . .) | TWS |
| F.9.1.5 | (As sages from the . . .) | BW-UCC, p. 489, alt. |
| F.9.1.6 | (O God, who in . . .) | WL, p. 38, alt. |
| F.9.1.7 | (God of blazing light . . .) | RCLP, p. 58 |
| F.9.2.1 | (May the light of . . .) | BCO, p. 599, alt. |
| F.9.2.2 | (In response to what . . .) | LLJ, p. 31, alt. |
| F.9.2.3 | (May Christ, the Son . . .) | BOS-1994, p. 24 |
| F.9.2.4 | (As we leave . . .) | TWS |
| F.9.2.5 | (Almighty God has . . .) | TWS |
| G.1.2.3 | (God said, "This is . . .) | LOP-A, pp. 30-31, alt. Adapted by permission. |
| G.1.2.4 | (God anointed Christ . . .) | LOP-C, p. 34 |
| G.1.2.5 | (All who thirst, come . . .) | WE, p. 83, alt. |
| G.1.4.1 | (God of majesty . . .) | Donald Wilson Stake in SLR-7, p. 89, alt. |
| G.1.4.2 | (Lord God, gracious . . .) | ELL |
| G.1.4.3 | (Eternal God, at the . . .) | Charles M. Guilbert in BCP, p. 214, alt., based on ancient collects, PD |
| G.1.4.4 | (Glory be to you . . .) | WG, p. 27 |

| G.1.4.5 | (God of grace and . . .) | RCLP, p. 54 |
| G.1.4.6 | (Holy God, you sent . . .) | WBK, p. 140, alt. |
| G.1.4.7 | (Let us give thanks . . .) | Donald Wilson Stake in SLR-7, p. 97, alt. |
| G.1.4.8 | (Your voice, O God . . .) | TWS |
| G.2.2.1 | (God of all mercy . . .) | TWS |
| G.2.2.2 | (Creator of all worlds . . .) | WG, p. 28 |
| G.2.2.3 | (Merciful God, in . . .) | SLR-7, p. 94 [34], alt. |
| G.2.4.2 | (Friends, hear the . . .) | TWS |
| G.4.4.1 | (Triune God, at . . .) | TWS |
| G.4.4.2 | (O Lord Jesus . . .) | TWS |
| G.4.4.3 | (In the waters of . . .) | ICP, p. 82, alt. |
| G.8.2.2.1 | (In being baptized . . .) | SLR-1, p. 89, alt. |
| G.8.2.4.1 | (You are holy . . .) | Donald Wilson Stake and Harold M. Daniels in SLR-7, pp. 94-96; rev. Marney Ault Wasserman, alt. |
| G.8.2.4.2 | (O God, as you . . .) | Donald Wilson Stake and Harold M. Daniels in SLR-7, pp. 94-96; rev. Marney Ault Wasserman, alt. |
| G.9.1.1 | (Spirit of God . . .) | TWS |
| G.9.2.1 | (God the Father . . .) | CLCW, vol. 5, p. 213 [212], alt. |
| G.9.2.2 | (The peace of God . . .) | WG, p. 28, alt. |
| G.9.2.3 | (May the Holy . . .) | TWS |
| H.1.2.1 | (The Lord is Sovereign . . .) | NHCY, p. 97 |
| H.1.2.2 | (Great is the Lord . . .) | TWS |
| H.1.4.1 | (Holy God, mighty . . .) | RCLP, p. 72, alt. |
| H.1.4.2 | (God of power . . .) | Jane V. Doull in WAS-1, p. 106. Reprinted with permission. |
| H.1.4.3 | (Jesus, today we . . .) | TWS |
| H.1.4.4 | (O God of the . . .) | RCLP, p. 73 |
| H.1.4.5 | (God of glory and . . .) | NHCY, p. 98, alt. Adapted by permission. |
| H.1.4.6 | (Lord Jesus Christ . . .) | BCO, p. 435, alt. |
| H.2.2.1 | (Eternal God, we . . .) | Ruth C. Duck in BFJ, p. 29 |
| H.2.2.2 | (Most amazing God . . .) | ASM, p. 37, alt. |
| H.2.2.3 | (Almighty God, we . . .) | John D. Witvliet in CLCW, vol. 5, p. 202 [209], alt. |
| H.2.2.4 | (Eternal God, we . . .) | PWL, p. 30, alt. |
| H.2.2.5 | (God of transfiguration . . .) | CGP, p. 128. Reprinted with permission. |
| H.2.2.6 | (God of compassion . . .) | SLR-7, p. 109 |
| H.3.1.1 | (Holy God, you . . .) | RCLP, p. 73 |
| H.3.1.2 | (Lord Jesus, your . . .) | TWS |
| H.4.4.1 | (Jesus Christ, glorified . . .) | TWS |
| H.4.4.2 | (The word of God . . .) | ICP, p. 91, alt. |
| H.4.4.3 | (O God, as your . . .) | RCLP, p. 72 |
| H.8.2.4.1 | (On the holy mountain . . .) | SLR-1, p. 89 |
| H.8.2.4.2 | (In splendor and . . .) | TWS |
| H.9.1.1 | (O God, before the . . .) | BCP, p. 217, alt., PD |
| H.9.2.2 | (May the glory . . .) | TWS |
| H.9.2.3 | (May our covenant . . .) | TWS |
| I.1.2.2 | (Brothers and sisters . . .) | TWS |
| I.1.4.3 | (Lord, our God . . .) | TWS |
| I.1.4.4 | (Merciful God, we . . .) | AESP, p. 104, alt. |
| I.1.4.5 | (Covenant God of . . .) | TWS |
| I.1.4.6 | (Faithful and loving God . . .) | TWS |
| I.2.1.1 | (Our congregation . . .) | TWS |
| I.2.1.2 | (Lent is a journey . . .) | CGP, p. 144. Reprinted with permission. |

| I.2.2.2 | (Lord God, it is hard . . .) | TWS |
| I.2.4.3 | (May God the Father . . .) | Michael Perham in CBCP, p. 384 [986], alt., © Michael Perham |
| I.4.4.1 | (God of new birth . . .) | TWS |
| I.4.4.2 | (We begin our journey . . .) | TWS |
| I.4.4.3 | (Gracious God, out of . . .) | TWS |
| I.9.1.1 | (Jesus Christ, we want . . .) | TWS |
| I.9.1.2 | (God of compassion . . .) | BAS, p. 286, alt. |
| I.9.2.2 | (May God the Father . . .) | Michael Perham in CBCP, p. 384 [986], alt., © Michael Perham |
| I.9.2.3 | (May God, who . . .) | TWS |
| I.9.2.4 | (May the Lord . . .) | TWS |
| I.9.2.5 | (Hear these words . . .) | TWS |
| I.9.2.6 | (Penitent and forgiven . . .) | TWS |
| J.1.1.1 | (Holy and loving God . . .) | TWS |
| J.1.1.2 | (Lord God, in this . . .) | TWS |
| J.1.2.1 | (Let us worship God . . .) | RW 34:20 |
| J.1.2.2 | (Let us worship God . . .) | RW 34:19 |
| J.1.2.3 | (Let us worship God . . .) | RW 34:18 |
| J.1.2.5 | (Let us contemplate . . .) | PED, pp. 84-85, alt. |
| J.1.2.6 | (Come to the Lord . . .) | Lenten liturgy, Church of the Servant, Grand Rapids, Michigan |
| J.1.2.7 | (The trumpet of the . . .) | LOP-B, p. 58 |
| J.1.2.8 | (The day of the Lord . . .) | LOP-C, p. 58 |
| J.1.4.1 | (O Christ, Savior . . .) | PED, pp. 79-80, alt. |
| J.1.4.2 | (All-knowing and . . .) | Tom Schwanda in CLCW, vol. 5, p. 235 [222] |
| J.1.4.3 | (O God, in creation . . .) | LOP-B, p. 61, alt. Adapted by permission. |
| J.1.4.4 | (From Bethlehem to . . .) | SW, p. 39 |
| J.1.4.5 | (Gracious God, out . . .) | Peter C. Bower in SLR-7, p. 116, alt. |
| J.1.4.6 | (Journey with us . . .) | Tom Schwanda in CLCW, vol. 5, p. 235 [222] |
| J.1.4.7 | (Lord God, we . . .) | TWS |
| J.1.4.8 | (Lord Jesus, we . . .) | bulletin of Eastern Avenue Christian Reformed Church, Grand Rapids, Michigan |
| J.1.4.9 | (God of all hope . . .) | TWS |
| J.2.1.5 | (Seek the Lord . . .) | John Paarlberg in RW 34:7 |
| J.2.1.6 | (The proof of God's . . .) | BCW, p. 52 [2], alt., PD |
| J.2.1.7 | (Remember that our . . .) | BCW, p. 53 [3], alt., PD |
| J.2.1.8 | (The very stone . . .) | John Paarlberg in RW 34:8 |
| J.2.1.9 | (If we say that . . .) | BCW, p. 52 [1], alt., PD |
| J.2.1.11 | (Christ himself bore . . .) | IPF |
| J.2.2.1 | (From Mount Hor they . . .) | David Vroege in CSL, p. 85 [26], alt. |
| J.2.2.2 | (If you, O Lord . . .) | LBW, p. 133 (30), alt. |
| J.2.2.3 | (Almighty God, you . . .) | prayer written by Thomas Cranmer for the *Book of Common Prayer* (1549), alt., PD |
| J.2.2.4 | (Holy and merciful . . .) | Massey H. Shepherd, Jr., in BCP, pp. 267- 268, alt., PD |
| J.2.2.5 | (O Lord, you desire . . .) | LOP-C, pp. 58-59, alt. Adapted by permission. |
| J.2.2.6 | (God of compassion . . .) | Harold M. Daniels in BCW, p. 248 [231], PD |
| J.2.2.7 | (O Christ, out of . . .) | ecumenical prayer from France |
| J.2.2.8 | (God of comfort . . .) | TWS |
| J.2.2.9 | (Most merciful God . . .) | John Paarlberg in RW 34:6 |
| J.2.2.10 | (God of mercy . . .) | John Paarlberg in RW 34:6 |
| J.2.2.11 | (Everlasting God . . .) | John Paarlberg in RW 34:7, alt. |

| J.2.2.12 | (God of compassion . . .) | John Paarlberg in RW 34:8 |
| J.2.2.13 | (Almighty God, to . . .) | BCP, p. 355, alt., PD |
| J.2.2.14 | (Lord, we have denied . . .) | Arlene M. Mark in WFW 35, alt. |
| J.2.2.15 | (O God, in gracious . . .) | LOP-C, pp. 64-65 |
| J.2.2.16 | (O God, our great . . .) | Tom Schwanda in CLCW, vol. 5, p. 236 [222] |
| J.2.2.17 | (God, we make so . . .) | David Vroege in CSL, p. 87 [27] |
| J.2.2.19 | (Lamb of God . . .) | TWS |
| J.2.2.20 | (Word of God Incarnate . . .) | RW 34:18 |
| J.2.2.21 | (God of Abraham . . .) | RW 34:17 |
| J.2.2.22 | (Righteous God, in . . .) | RW 34:19 |
| J.2.2.23 | (Almighty God, in . . .) | John Paarlberg in RW 34:7 |
| J.2.2.24 | (God, forgive our . . .) | ASM, p. 36 [6], alt. |
| J.2.3.1 | (Where are you . . .) | LOP-C, p. 58 |
| J.3.1.1 | (Send your Spirit . . .) | Lenten liturgy, Church of the Servant, Grand Rapids, Michigan |
| J.3.1.2 | (O Christ, by . . .) | PED, p. 70 |
| J.3.1.3 | (Through God's Word . . .) | TWS |
| J.4.4.1 | (God of our salvation . . .) | TWS |
| J.4.4.2 | (Maker of Heaven . . .) | TWS |
| J.4.4.3 | (Almighty God, your . . .) | BAS, pp. 286-287, alt. |
| J.4.4.4 | (O Lord God, you . . .) | LBW, p. 131 (24), alt. |
| J.4.4.5 | (God of the covenant . . .) | ICEL, Second Progress Report on the Revision of the Roman Missal, p. 53, alt. |
| J.4.4.6 | (O Jesus, you . . .) | TWS |
| J.4.4.7 | (God of all seasons . . .) | BCO, pp. 431-432, alt. |
| J.4.4.8 | (God of grace . . .) | TWS |
| J.4.4.9 | (Remembering that in . . .) | from the *Worship Handbook of the Seventh Assembly of the Christian Conference of Asia* (CCA), Bangalore, 1981, in WAGP-OS, p. 33, alt. Permission sought. |
| J.4.4.10 | (Jesus the Christ, you . . .) | BCO, p. 434, alt. |
| J.5.2.1 | (Mighty God and Father . . .) | Tom Schwanda in CLCW, vol. 5, p. 236 [222] |
| J.5.2.2 | (Compassionate God, we . . .) | SAS |
| J.8.2.2.1 | (With joy we praise . . .) | AFS-1994, p. 179 |
| J.8.2.4.1 | (You are holy . . .) | Donald Wilson Stake and Harold M. Daniels in SLR-7, pp. 128-131; rev. Marney Ault Wasserman, alt. |
| J.9.1.1 | (God of mercy . . .) | UW-LB, p. 241, alt. |
| J.9.1.2 | (God of all times . . .) | UW-LB, p. 170, alt. |
| J.9.1.3 | (God of all times . . .) | TWS |
| J.9.1.4 | (My Father, I abandon . . .) | Charles de Foucauld (1858-1916), PD |
| J.9.2.4 | (Sisters and brothers . . .) | source unknown |
| K.1.1.1 | (Loving Father, as we . . .) | TWS |
| K.1.1.2 | (God of all time . . .) | TWS |
| K.1.2.3 | (King Jesus comes . . .) | BSBL, p. 59, alt. |
| K.1.2.4 | (People of God, be . . .) | LOP-C, pp. 63-64 |
| K.1.2.5 | (As we are called . . .) | RW 27:42 |
| K.1.4.1 | (We praise you, O God . . .) | BCP, p. 271, based on ancient sources, alt., PD |
| K.1.4.2 | (O Lord Christ . . .) | TWS |
| K.1.4.3 | (Merciful God, as we . . .) | BW-UCC pp. 187-188 |
| K.1.4.4 | (Everlasting God, in . . .) | from ancient sources in BCP, p. 219, with alterations from LBW, p. 19 (31) |
| K.1.4.5 | (God of all, you . . .) | AC, p. 26, alt., based on *Book of Common Prayer* (1662) |
| K.2.1.1 | (Like the people who . . .) | TWS |

| K.2.2.1 | (O King of glory . . .) | bulletin of Rochester Christian Reformed Church, Rochester, New York |
| K.2.2.2 | (O Lord, who on . . .) | John Paarlberg in RW 34:8 |
| K.2.2.3 | (Loving God, you rode . . .) | CRCL-3, pp. 48-49, alt. |
| K.2.2.4 | (O Lord, we confess . . .) | PL, Palm Sunday Confession [2], alt. |
| K.2.2.5 | (Gracious God, having . . .) | John D. Witvliet in CLCW, vol. 5, pp. 299-300 [247] |
| K.2.2.6 | (Jesus, our Lord, we . . .) | PL, Palm Sunday Confession [1], alt. |
| K.3.1.1 | (Eternal God, whose . . .) | BW-UCC, p. 190 |
| K.4.4.1 | (Son of David, you . . .) | TWS |
| K.4.4.2 | (God, whose gracious . . .) | PL, Holy Week Thanksgiving and Intercession, alt. |
| K.4.4.3 | (You are holy . . .) | Donald Wilson Stake and Harold M. Daniels in SLR-7, pp. 145-148; rev. Marney Ault Wasserman, alt. |
| K.8.2.2.1 | (Your Son, Jesus . . .) | BCP, p. 379, alt., PD; "The tree of defeat . . ." in RM, from a sermon of Leo the Great (5th cent.), alt. |
| K.9.1.3 | (God and Father of . . .) | TWS |
| K.9.2.1 | (May our Lord . . .) | CRCL-3, p. 49 |
| K.9.2.3 | (May the God . . .) | TWS |
| L.1.1.1 | (God of love, as . . .) | TWS |
| L.1.1.2 | (Covenant God, we . . .) | TWS |
| L.1.2.4 | (On this day Christ . . .) | BAS, p. 304, alt. |
| L.1.4.1 | (O Lord Jesus Christ . . .) | PCY |
| L.1.4.2 | (Holy God, your Son . . .) | WBK, p. 41, alt. |
| L.1.4.3 | (O living Christ, this . . .) | ASM, p. 51 [12] |
| L.1.4.4 | (Holy God, we come . . .) | Janet Cawley in CGP, p. 172 |
| L.1.4.5 | (Infinite, intimate God . . .) | ANZPB-HKMOA, p. 585 |
| L.1.4.6 | (Breath of God . . .) | TWS |
| L.2.1.1 | (The psalmist declares . . .) | TWS |
| L.2.1.2 | (Christ shows his . . .) | TWS |
| L.2.2.1 | (Merciful God, we . . .) | FAF. Adapted by permission. |
| L.2.2.2 | (Loving Lord, you taught . . .) | TWS |
| L.2.2.3 | (Eternal God, whose . . .) | WBK-SH, p. 146, alt. |
| L.2.4.1 | (We have seen and . . .) | TWS |
| L.2.5.2 | (We have an example . . .) | Italian lauda, 14th cent. |
| L.2.5.3 | (Lord Christ, our Servant . . .) | Stephen S. Smalley in CBCP, p. 390 [1003], alt., © Stephen S. Smalley |
| L.2.5.4 | (Your Word, O Lord . . .) | TWS |
| L.2.5.5 | (May this symbolic . . .) | TWS |
| L.4.4.1 | (God of love, it is . . .) | TWS |
| L.8.1 | (Why do we give . . .) | TCBCW, pp. 62-63 |
| L.8.2.2.1 | (With joy we praise . . .) | AFS-1994, p. 179 |
| L.9.1.2 | (God of love, truly . . .) | TWS |
| L.9.1.3 | (Lord Jesus Christ, you . . .) | BCP, p. 101, alt., PD |
| L.9.1.4 | (O Jesus, our . . .) | TWS |
| L.9.2.3 | (We bless you . . .) | TWS |
| M.1.1.1 | (Holy and loving God . . .) | TWS |
| M.1.1.2 | (Loving God, we know . . .) | TWS |
| M.1.2.2 | (Today we remember . . .) | TWS |
| M.1.2.3 | (God so loved . . .) | TWS |
| M.1.4.1 | (King of glory, we . . .) | TWS |
| M.1.4.2 | (O Christ, who forsook . . .) | LOP-A, p. 70, alt. Adapted by permission. |
| M.1.4.3 | (Assist us mercifully . . .) | from Church of the Servant, Grand Rapids, Michigan |
| M.1.4.4 | (O God, who for . . .) | BCP, p. 222, alt., PD |

| | | |
|---|---|---|
| M.1.4.5 | (Let us remember . . .) | RW 18:15 |
| M.2.2.1 | (O crucified Jesus . . .) | ecumenical prayer from France; concluding collect from ancient sources in BCP, p. 276, alt., PD |
| M.2.2.2 | (Great God, our Father . . .) | Toyohiko Kagawa (1888-1960) in CBCP, p. 393 [1012] |
| M.2.2.3 | (Merciful God, we . . .) | SO, p. 690 |
| M.2.2.4 | (Loving God, we know . . .) | CRCL-3, p. 47, alt. |
| M.2.3.1 | (We hear Jesus say . . .) | TWS |
| M.4.1.1 | (From the throne of . . .) | RM |
| M.4.1.2 | (We stand beneath . . .) | TWS |
| M.4.4.1 | (Lamb of God, being . . .) | TWS |
| M.4.4.2 | (We thank you, heavenly . . .) | from Church of the Servant, Grand Rapids, Michigan |
| M.4.4.3 | (Dear people of God . . .) | from ancient sources in BCP, pp. 277- 280, alt., PD; with concluding prayer from RM, alt. |
| M.4.4.4 | (Giver of life, we . . .) | SO, p. 694 |
| M.4.4.5 | ("Father, forgive them . . .) | RW 18.15, alt.; seven stanzas under "Eloi, eloi" by Stanley Wiersma in PsH 88:1-7 |
| M.9.1.6 | (Thank you, loving God . . .) | TWS |
| M.9.1.7 | (O Lord Jesus . . .) | TWS |
| M.9.2.1 | (May you find in the . . .) | ANZPB-HKMOA, p. 536 |
| M.9.2.2 | (May God, who gives . . .) | SO, p. 694 |
| M.9.2.3 | (May Jesus Christ, who . . .) | TWS |
| M.9.2.4 | (May the Christ who . . .) | traditional Celtic prayer |
| M.9.2.5 | (Brothers and sisters . . .) | TWS |
| M.9.2.6 | (Do not hurry . . .) | TWS |
| M.9.2.7 | (May God the Father . . .) | TWS |
| M.9.2.8 | (May we be thankful . . .) | TWS |
| N.1.1.1 | (Loving God, on this . . .) | TWS |
| N.1.1.2 | (God of life, we . . .) | TWS |
| N.1.2.3 | (Alleluia! Christ is . . .) | BCP, p. 294, PD |
| N.1.2.5 | (Alleluia! Christ, our . . .) | BCP, pp. 337, 364, alt., PD |
| N.1.2.7 | (This is the good . . .) | SW, p. 183 |
| N.1.2.9 | (The Lord who calls . . .) | RW 27:40 |
| N.1.2.10 | (Alleluia! Christ is . . .) | BAS, p. 98 |
| N.1.2.11 | (Joyful is the sound . . .) | RW 58:19 |
| N.1.2.12 | (The Lord be . . .) | TWS |
| N.1.4.1 | (We give you thanks . . .) | WBK-SH, p. 148, alt. |
| N.1.4.2 | (Glory to you, O God . . .) | BCW-1946, p. 304, alt., PD |
| N.1.4.3 | (Lord God, early in . . .) | SW, pp.184-185, alt. |
| N.1.4.4 | (Rejoice, heavenly powers . . .) | RM, alt. |
| N.1.4.5 | (The Lord be with you . . .) | *Sursum Corda* from PT-ELLC, p. 33; RM, alt. |
| N.1.4.6 | (O Father God . . .) | TWS |
| N.1.4.7 | (Holy God, creator . . .) | source unknown |
| N.1.4.8 | (O God, worker . . .) | SBK-92, p. 157, alt. |
| N.1.4.9 | (O living Lord, on . . .) | Frank Colquhoun in PEO, p. 86 [317], alt. |
| N.1.4.10 | (Glorious Lord of life . . .) | from BAS, p. 335; SLR-7, p. 209, alt.; ANZPB-HKMOA, p. 592, alt. |
| N.1.4.11 | (Brightness of God's . . .) | Henry van Dyke in BCW-1932, pp. 166- 167, alt., PD |
| N.1.4.12 | (O God, whose presence . . .) | Diane Karay Tripp in BCW, p. 325 [281], PD |
| N.1.4.13 | (O Christ, who lived . . .) | Dick Williams in PTC, p. 53 [102] |
| N.1.4.14 | (Stay with us . . .) | TWS |
| N.1.4.15 | (This is the feast of . . .) | John W. Arthur, "Worthy Is Christ," in LBW, pp. 60-61, 81-82, 102 |

| | | |
|---|---|---|
| N.1.4.16 | (If Christ is . . .) | TWS |
| N.1.4.17 | (O Risen Christ . . .) | TWS |
| N.2.2.1 | (Almighty God, in raising . . .) | BCW, p. 317 [271], alt., PD |
| N.2.2.2 | (If, at times, we deny . . .) | BW-UCC, pp. 495-496, alt. |
| N.2.2.3 | (Lord, bring new life . . .) | SW, p. 185 |
| N.2.2.4 | (Almighty God, you . . .) | WBK-SH, p. 150, alt. |
| N.3.1.1 | (God of life, your . . .) | TWS |
| N.3.1.2 | (Lord, you have . . .) | TWS |
| N.3.6.6 | (Christ has died! . . .) | ancient source, PD |
| N.3.6.11 | (I believe in the . . .) | BSBL, pp. 117-118 |
| N.3.6.12 | (By his resurrection . . .) | from Church of the Servant, Grand Rapids, Michigan |
| N.3.6.14 | (We declare with joy . . .) | TWS |
| N.4.4.1 | (God of life, we . . .) | TWS |
| N.4.4.2 | (O Holy God, beyond . . .) | TWS |
| N.4.4.3 | (Let us give thanks . . .) | Donald Wilson Stake in SLR-7, pp. 207- 208, alt. |
| N.4.4.4 | (Let us give thanks . . .) | BCW-1946, p. 26, alt., PD |
| N.4.4.5 | (Let us give thanks . . .) | WBK, p. 148, PD |
| N.4.4.6 | (We worship you . . .) | PED, p. 95, alt. |
| N.4.4.7 | (Risen and reigning . . .) | TWS |
| N.4.4.8 | (You, O Christ . . .) | TWS |
| N.4.4.9 | (O Christ, born of . . .) | PED, pp. 101-102, alt. |
| N.4.4.10 | (By the love with . . .) | RW 18:29 |
| N.5.2.1 | (Living God, you have . . .) | David Vroege in CSL, p. 88, alt. |
| N.5.2.2 | (Good Shepherd, you . . .) | SAS |
| N.8.2.2.1 | (You are holy . . .) | Donald Wilson Stake and Harold M. Daniels in SLR-7, pp. 204-207; rev. Marney Ault Wasserman, alt. |
| N.8.2.2.2 | (Nourished at this . . .) | Donald Wilson Stake and Harold M. Daniels in SLR-7, pp. 204-207; rev. Marney Ault Wasserman, alt. |
| N.8.2.2.3 | (Gracious God, pour . . .) | BCW, p. 321 [272], alt., PD |
| N.8.2.2.4 | (With joy we praise . . .) | AFS-1994, p. 180 |
| N.8.2.2.5 | (By your power you . . .) | WBK, p. 41, alt. |
| N.9.1.1 | (As Christ burst forth . . .) | Carol A. Wise in FAWM |
| N.9.1.4 | (O Lord, though you . . .) | Augustine of Hippo (354-430), PD |
| N.9.1.5 | (God of our salvation . . .) | ANZPB-HKMOA, p. 535 |
| N.9.1.6 | (You have given yourself . . .) | FAF. Adapted by permission. |
| O.1.1.1 | (Almighty God, as we . . .) | TWS |
| O.1.1.2 | (Ascended and reigning . . .) | TWS |
| O.1.2.6 | (People of God, the . . .) | RW 23:40 |
| O.1.2.7 | (Jesus Christ has come . . .) | RW 23:41 |
| O.1.4.2 | (Eternal God, mighty . . .) | TWS |
| O.1.4.3 | (Almighty God, we . . .) | Arlene M. Mark in WFW, 54 |
| O.1.4.4 | (Father, O God Most High . . .) | LP, p. 53, alt. |
| O.1.4.5 | (O God of all power . . .) | RW 39:28 |
| O.1.4.6 | (All-powerful God . . .) | NHCY, p. 253 |
| O.1.4.7 | (Eternal God, the king . . .) | ANZPB-HKMOA, p. 603 |
| O.1.4.8 | (Almighty God, grant . . .) | BCP, p. 226, alt., PD |
| O.1.4.9 | (God of power and . . .) | RM, alt. |
| O.1.4.10 | (Loving God, the heavens . . .) | ANZPB-HKMOA, pp. 601-602 |
| O.2.2.1 | (Almighty God, you . . .) | WBK, p. 150, alt. |
| O.2.2.2 | (While we claim to . . .) | RW 11:22 |
| O.2.4.3 | (Hear the good news . . .) | TWS |
| O.3.1.1 | (Blessed are you, Lord . . .) | RW 39:29 |

| | | |
|---|---|---|
| O.3.6.1 | (The Word of the Lord . . .) | CSL, pp. 81-82 |
| O.3.6.7 | (We declare with joy . . .) | TWS |
| O.4.4.1 | (Jesus Christ, mediator . . .) | TWS |
| O.4.4.2 | (Ascended Lord Jesus . . .) | TWS |
| O.4.4.3 | (Ascended Lord, we . . .) | RW 15:34 |
| O.4.4.4 | (Ascended Christ, how . . .) | TWS |
| O.8.2.2.1 | (With joy we praise . . .) | AFS-1994, p. 180 |
| O.8.2.2.2 | (You raised up Christ . . .) | SLR-1, p. 91, alt. |
| O.9.1.1 | (Why do you stand . . .) | BCW, p. 332 [3], [2], PD |
| O.9.1.2 | (Lord, help us not to . . .) | Lady Coggan in PP, p. 312 [9], alt. |
| O.9.1.3 | (You said, "Peace . . .) | TWS |
| O.9.2.2 | (May the love of the . . .) | JPWT 95, alt. |
| O.9.2.3 | (Brothers and sisters . . .) | TWS |
| O.9.2.4 | (People of God . . .) | TWS |
| P.1.1.1 | (Lord God, the words . . .) | TWS |
| P.1.1.2 | (Lord God, when we . . .) | TWS |
| P.1.4.2 | (Let us give thanks . . .) | Donald Wilson Stake in SLR-7, p. 270, alt. |
| P.1.4.3 | (Almighty and everlasting . . .) | Howard E. Galley in BCP, p. 236, alt., based on ancient collect, PD |
| P.1.4.4 | (Eternal God, you set . . .) | SLR-7, p. 267, alt. |
| P.1.4.5 | (God and Father of . . .) | SBK-92, p. 208 |
| P.1.4.7 | (Mighty and tender God . . .) | Paul Fayter, "A Prayer for the Reign of Christ," in VU 214, alt. Reprinted with permission. |
| P.1.4.8 | (Grace and peace to . . .) | CRCL-3, p. 120, alt. |
| P.1.4.9 | (We give you thanks . . .) | PED, pp. 25-26 |
| P.2.2.1 | (Righteous God, you . . .) | Harold M. Daniels in BCW, p. 396 [408], alt., PD |
| P.3.1.1 | (O God Most High! . . .) | LP, p. 173, alt. |
| P.4.4.1 | (Sovereign King, we . . .) | TWS |
| P.4.4.2 | (That each of us will . . .) | MCL, pp. 140-141 [65], alt. |
| P.5.2.1 | (Lord God, heavenly . . .) | TWS |
| P.8.2.2.1 | (Lead us, O God . . .) | Donald Wilson Stake in SLR-7, pp. 267- 269; rev. Marney Ault Wasserman, alt. |
| P.9.1.5 | (Almighty and merciful . . .) | BOS-1994, p. 45 |
| P.9.1.6 | (All-powerful God . . .) | NHCY, p. 253 |
| Q.1.1.1 | (God of life, as . . .) | TWS |
| Q.1.1.2 | (Lord God, especially . . .) | TWS |
| Q.1.2.2 | (This is the day . . .) | David Vroege in CSL, p. 88, alt. |
| Q.1.2.3 | (The love of God . . .) | BAS, p. 99, alt. |
| Q.1.2.4 | (By sending down a . . .) | Pentecost liturgy, Church of the Servant, Grand Rapids, Michigan |
| Q.1.2.5 | (The God of the . . .) | WG, p. 27, alt. |
| Q.1.2.6 | (The Spirit gathers us . . .) | BTG, p. 5 [11], alt. |
| Q.1.4.1 | (Come, Creator Spirit . . .) | RW 35:20 |
| Q.1.4.2 | (Spirit of the living . . .) | RW 39:32 |
| Q.1.4.3 | (Holy Spirit, Lord and . . .) | John Paarlberg in RW 55:39 |
| Q.1.4.4 | (Come, Holy Spirit, renew . . .) | WE, pp. 148-149, alt. |
| Q.1.4.5 | (Loving God and Father . . .) | TWS |
| Q.1.4.6 | (Blessed be our God . . .) | ecumenical prayer from France |
| Q.1.4.7 | (God in heaven, you . . .) | David Vroege in CSL, p. 88, alt. |
| Q.1.4.8 | (Holy Spirit, Creator . . .) | ecumenical prayer from France |
| Q.1.4.9 | (Come, Spirit God . . .) | TWS |
| Q.1.4.10 | (The Spirit of the Lord . . .) | MCL, p. 113 [50] |

| | | |
|---|---|---|
| Q.1.4.11 | (Wind of God, blow . . .) | Pamela Wilding, Kenya, in PEW, p. 63 [62], © SPCK |
| Q.1.4.12 | (Holy Spirit, you are . . .) | RW 31:4 |
| Q.1.4.13 | (Almighty and Holy Spirit . . .) | Philipp Melanchthon (1497-1560) |
| Q.2.1.2 | (Do not marvel that . . .) | AOS-1981, p. 304, alt. |
| Q.2.1.3 | (The Spirit of the Lord . . .) | IPF |
| Q.2.2.1 | (Almighty God, to you . . .) | BCP, p. 355, alt., PD |
| Q.2.2.2 | (Holy Spirit, you are . . .) | David Vroege in CSL, p. 88, alt. |
| Q.2.2.3 | (Come, Holy Spirit! . . .) | SLR-5, p. 186 |
| Q.2.2.4 | (The Spirit of the Lord . . .) | invitation to confession, IPF; *Kyrie* by David Stancliffe for Portsmouth Cathedral |
| Q.2.2.5 | (Generous God, you send . . .) | Janet Cawley in CGP, p. 205, alt. |
| Q.2.2.6 | (Sovereign Lord, you . . .) | TWS |
| Q.2.2.7 | (Gracious God, who . . .) | WV, p. 56 |
| Q.2.2.8 | (Burn in us this . . .) | RW 31:4 |
| Q.2.2.9 | (Our God, we come . . .) | RW 39:33 |
| Q.2.2.10 | (Almighty God, who . . .) | WBK-SH, p. 152, alt. |
| Q.2.2.11 | (Almighty God, you . . .) | Joseph D. Small III in BCW, p. 343 [319], alt., with phrases from WBK, p. 152 |
| Q.2.4.5 | (In Christ you . . .) | TWS |
| Q.3.1.1 | (Lord, open our hearts . . .) | *A Service of Word and Table I*, alt., © 1972, The Methodist Publishing House, © 1980, 1985, 1989, 1992, United Methodist Publishing House |
| Q.3.1.2 | (Lord of heaven and . . .) | from Church of the Servant, Grand Rapids, Michigan |
| Q.3.1.3 | (O God whom we . . .) | LP, p. 158, alt. |
| Q.3.1.4 | (Grant us, Lord, the . . .) | TWS |
| Q.3.1.5 | (Lord of heaven . . .) | TWS |
| Q.3.1.6 | (May the Word of God . . .) | RW 31:4 |
| Q.3.1.7 | (Eternal God, your . . .) | BTG, p. 17 [1] |
| Q.3.1.8 | (Empowering God, we . . .) | BTG, p. 17 [2], alt. |
| Q.3.6.4 | (We believe in the . . .) | BTG, p. 20 [4], alt. |
| Q.4.4.1 | (Spirit of fire, who . . .) | TWS |
| Q.4.4.2 | (Creator Spirit, create . . .) | TWS |
| Q.4.4.3 | (O Spirit of God . . .) | PPW, pp. 76-77 |
| Q.4.4.4 | (Eternal God, our Father . . .) | TWS |
| Q.4.4.5 | (Gracious God, your. . .) | TWS |
| Q.4.4.6 | (God of rushing wind . . .) | TWS |
| Q.5.2.1 | (God of abundant love . . .) | TWS |
| Q.5.2.2 | (God of wind, word . . .) | FAF |
| Q.8.2.2.1 | (It is right, and . . .) | first eight lines from BCP, PD; remaining lines from FAF |
| Q.8.2.2.2 | (Blessed you are . . .) | LP, pp. 286-287, alt. |
| Q.8.2.2.3 | (How right and fitting. . .) | TWS |
| Q.9.1.1 | (Now may the God . . .) | from Church of the Servant, Grand Rapids, Michigan |
| Q.9.1.2 | (Go forth into the . . .) | BCP, p. 366, alt., PD |
| Q.9.1.4 | (You have given . . .) | RW 39:34 |
| Q.9.1.5 | (Almighty God, you sent . . .) | Church in Singapore, in PEW, p. 103 [116]. Used by permission of Anglican Consultative Council. |
| Q.9.1.6 | (Lord Jesus, after . . .) | PED, pp. 113-114, alt. |
| Q.9.1.7 | (Almighty God, send . . .) | TWS |
| Q.9.1.8 | (We praise you . . .) | TWS |
| Q.9.1.9 | (Lord God, we hear . . .) | TWS |
| Q.9.2.2 | (May the love of the . . .) | PUAS |

| | | |
|---|---|---|
| Q.9.2.3 | (May the Spirit of . . .) | BOS-1994, p. 27 |
| R.1.1.1 | (Holy, holy, holy God . . .) | TWS |
| R.1.2.1 | (Jesus prayed that we . . .) | TWS |
| R.1.3.1 | (In the name of the . . .) | Trinity Season liturgy, Church of the Servant, Grand Rapids, Michigan |
| R.1.4.1 | (We have known you . . .) | St. John Chrysostom (c. 347-407) |
| R.1.4.2 | (The poor and the . . .) | St. Auxentios (third cent.) |
| R.1.4.3 | (Father, we praise you . . .) | BAS, p. 346, alt. |
| R.1.4.4 | (Blessed are you . . .) | TWS |
| R.1.4.5 | (Praise to you . . .) | TWS |
| R.1.4.6 | (O blessed Trinity . . .) | BCW-1946, p. 311, alt., PD |
| R.1.4.7 | (Holy Father of . . .) | TWS |
| R.1.4.8 | (Come, almighty King . . .) | Tom Schwanda in CLCW, vol. 5, p. 470 [311] |
| R.1.4.9 | (Father, you sent your . . .) | NHCY, p. 237 |
| R.1.4.10 | (Almighty God, our . . .) | LBW, p. 24 (77), alt. |
| R.1.4.11 | (O God, who created . . .) | RW 35:23 |
| R.1.4.12 | (We praise you. . .) | TWS |
| R.1.4.13 | (O God of greatness . . .) | LOP-A, pp. 93-94 |
| R.1.4.14 | (Almighty God, before . . .) | RW 47:36 |
| R.2.2.1 | (Father, you have come . . .) | Michael Perham in ECY, p. 68, alt., PD |
| R.2.2.2 | (Let us pray . . .) | TWS |
| R.2.2.3 | (Triune God, we praise . . .) | TWS |
| R.2.4.1 | (You did not receive . . .) | TWS |
| R.3.1.1 | (God, our Father . . .) | TWS |
| R.3.6.2 | (I bind unto myself . . .) | St. Patrick of Ireland (389-461), tr. Cecil Frances Alexander (1818-1895), alt.; this prayer is known as "St. Patrick's Breastplate," as is the tune to which it is sung |
| R.4.4.1 | (Triune God, Father . . .) | TWS |
| R.4.4.2 | (Let us give thanks . . .) | SLR-7, p. 235, alt. |
| R.4.4.3 | (Triune God, in . . .) | TWS |
| R.8.2.2.1 | (Holy God, Creator . . .) | TWS |
| R.9.1.1 | (Go forth to greet . . .) | LOP-A, p. 95 |
| R.9.2.2 | (May God, the Holy . . .) | BOS-1994, p. 28 |
| R.9.2.3 | (The peace of God . . .) | Trinity Season liturgy, Church of the Servant, Grand Rapids, Michigan |
| S.1.1.1 | (Triune God, you have . . .) | TWS |
| S.1.1.2 | (God of life, thank you . . .) | TWS |
| S.1.2.2 | (The God of creation . . .) | LOP-A, p. 158, alt. Adapted by permission. |
| S.1.2.3 | (Let us acknowledge . . .) | BCO, p. 63 |
| S.1.4.1 | (O God of all creation . . .) | LOP-A, p. 158, alt. Adapted by permission. |
| S.1.4.2 | (Our great and gracious . . .) | TWS |
| S.1.4.3 | (Almighty God, your . . .) | BTG, p. 6 [1] |
| S.1.4.4 | (We, your people . . .) | TWS |
| S.1.4.5 | (O risen Christ, you . . .) | JCLW, p. 100 [46], alt. |
| S.2.2.1 | (Gracious God, you . . .) | CC, p. 24 [10] |
| S.2.2.2 | (Across the barriers . . .) | WN, alt. |
| S.2.2.3 | (Forgive us the sins . . .) | Simon H. Baynes in PTC, p. 88 [207], alt. |
| S.2.2.4 | (God of all nations . . .) | RFR, pp. 127-128 |
| S.2.2.5 | (Dear friends, let us . . .) | World Council of Churches Assembly Worship Committee in JCLW, p. 64 [28], alt. |
| S.2.2.6 | (Almighty God, we . . .) | Lydia S. Martinez in 1987 *United Methodist* |

*Clergywomen's Consultation Resource Book,* p. 57, alt. Used by permission.

| | | |
|---|---|---|
| S.2.2.7 | (God of all flesh . . .) | ASM, p. 35, alt. |
| S.2.2.9 | (O God, your will . . .) | French Reformed Church liturgy in CBCP, p. 440 [1122], alt. |
| S.3.1.1 | (Pour out your Spirit . . .) | ELL |
| S.4.4.1 | (God of our salvation . . .) | TWS |
| S.4.4.2 | (Almighty Father, whose . . .) | BCP, p. 255, alt., PD |
| S.4.4.3 | (Bless your church . . .) | BCO, p. 419, alt. |
| S.4.4.4 | (Lord God, we thank . . .) | BCO, p. 479 |
| S.4.4.5 | (Almighty God, you . . .) | BCO, p. 684, alt. |
| S.4.4.6 | (Lord, we pray for . . .) | after St. Cyprian of Carthage (c. 200-258) |
| S.4.4.7 | (Too often, far . . .) | TWS |
| S.4.4.8 | (Lord, make our hearts . . .) | Native American in WWB, p. 38, alt. |
| S.4.4.9 | (Gather us or scatter . . .) | Church in Hungary in WWB, p. 40, alt. |
| S.4.4.10 | (O Lord our God . . .) | Church in Ghana in WWB, p. 41, alt. |
| S.4.4.11 | (Lord God of mission . . .) | Naftali Okello Siwa, Kenya, in PEW, p. 101 [122], alt., © SPCK |
| S.4.4.12 | (God, good beyond all . . .) | Dionysius of Alexandria (d. 264), PD |
| S.4.4.13 | (Tender and compassionate . . .) | Arlene M. Mark in WFW 93, based on a Mennonite Central Committee "Disability Awareness Prayer." |
| S.4.4.14 | (Almighty God, bless . . .) | Handley C. G. Moule in PEO, p. 317 [1328], alt. |
| S.4.4.15 | (Almighty God, in Jesus . . .) | WBK, p. 201, alt. |
| S.4.4.16 | (Triune God, one . . .) | TWS |
| S.4.4.17 | (God of the church . . .) | TWS |
| S.4.4.18 | (O God, the giver of . . .) | WAGP, p. 311, alt. |
| S.4.4.19 | (Sovereign God, we . . .) | RW 16:40 |
| S.4.4.20 | (Almighty Lord of . . .) | TWS |
| S.4.4.21 | (That we may manifest . . .) | ELL |
| S.4.4.22 | (O God, the heavens . . .) | LUYH, pp. 83-85, alt. Adapted by permission. |
| S.4.4.23 | (Bearer of all pain . . .) | SO, p. 692, alt. |
| S.4.4.24 | (We pray for the . . .) | prayer used at the Eighth Assembly of the Christian Conference of Asia (CCA), Seoul, Korea, 1985, in WAGP, p. 193, alt. Permission sought. |
| S.5.2.1 | (Lord of life, you . . .) | TWS |
| S.5.2.2 | (God of life, we . . .) | TWS |
| S.8.5.2.1 | (God, who nourishes . . .) | Camillia LaRouche in WAS-3, p. 71. Reprinted with permission. |
| S.8.5.2.2 | (God of unfailing love . . .) | BCO, p. 194, alt. |
| S.8.5.2.3 | (Lord Jesus Christ . . .) | TWS |
| S.9.1.2 | (O Lord our God . . .) | ELL |
| S.9.1.3 | (Almighty God, you . . .) | Caroline Rose in BCP, p. 838, PD |
| S.9.1.4 | (God of our lives . . .) | WBK, p. 200 |
| S.9.1.5 | (Loving God, we have . . .) | TWS |
| S.9.1.6 | (Almighty God, we . . .) | Church in West Malaysia in PEW, p. 103 [117], alt. Used by permission of Anglican Consultative Council. |
| S.9.1.7 | (Lord, in these times . . .) | from a liturgy created for the people of one of the poorest slum areas in Manila, the Philippines, alt.; source unknown |
| S.9.2.2 | (May our Lord . . .) | TWS |
| S.9.2.3 | (Go from this . . .) | TWS |
| T.1.1.1 | (Almighty and loving . . .) | TWS |

| T.1.1.2 | (God of life, thank you . . .) | TWS |
| T.1.1.3 | (God of our salvation . . .) | TWS |
| T.1.2.1 | (Great is the Lord . . .) | BAS, p. 99 |
| T.1.4.1 | (God of grace . . .) | TWS |
| T.1.4.2 | (God of all ages . . .) | TWS |
| T.1.4.3 | (We praise you, O God . . .) | PT-ELLC, p. 41 |
| T.1.4.4 | (God of the ages . . .) | SLR-7, pp. 264-265, alt. |
| T.1.4.5 | (Our Lord Jesus . . .) | TWS |
| T.1.4.6 | (God of the universe . . .) | TWS |
| T.1.4.7 | (Almighty God, whose . . .) | LBW, p. 36 (136) |
| T.1.4.8 | (We give you thanks . . .) | TWS |
| T.2.1.1 | (Christ calls us to . . .) | PHG |
| T.2.2.1 | (Eternal God, in every . . .) | from Report of the Special Joint Committee on *The Worshipbook* (Minutes of the 186th General Assembly [1974] of the United Presbyterian Church in the U.S.A., Part I, Journal) in SLR-7, p. 262, alt. Reprinted with permission of the Office of the General Assembly, Presbyterian Church (U.S.A.). |
| T.4.4.1 | (Eternal God, in all . . .) | TWS |
| T.4.4.2 | (Loving and faithful . . .) | TWS |
| T.4.4.3 | (God of grace, we . . .) | Kathy Galloway in POD, p. 147 [61], alt., © Kathy Galloway |
| T.4.4.4 | (Remembering those . . .) | SLR-7, p. 264, alt. |
| T.4.4.5 | (I looked, and there . . .) | TWS |
| T.4.4.6 | (O Lord our God . . .) | World Council of Churches Assembly Worship Committee in JCLW, pp. 49-50 [21], alt. |
| T.4.4.7 | (Eternal God, we give . . .) | Edward K. Ziegler in TAF, alt. |
| T.4.4.8 | (Eternal God, your Word . . .) | WE, pp. 38-39, alt. |
| T.9.1.2 | (Almighty God, you . . .) | BCP, p. 245, alt., PD |
| T.9.2.1 | (May God, who has . . .) | BOS-1994, p. 29 |
| T.9.2.2 | (United as one . . .) | TWS |

# CENTRAL THEMES IN STATEMENTS OF FAITH

| Theme | Belgic Confession | Heidelberg Catechism | Canons of Dort | Westminster Confession of Faith | Our Song of Hope | Our World Belongs to God |
|---|---|---|---|---|---|---|
| Creation | Art. 2, 12, 14, 15 | Q&A's 6, 9 | Pts. III/IV, Art. 1 | Chap. IV, Sec. 1, 2 | st. 2 | st. 7-11, 13-17 |
| Providence | Art. 13 | Q&A's 1, 27, 28 | | Chap. V, Sec. 1-7 | | st. 4-5, 12 |
| Thanksgiving | | Q&A's 86, 116 | Pts. III/IV, Art. 15 | | | st. 6, 44 |
| Advent | Art. 10, 18 | Q&A's 29-36 | | Chap. VIII, Sec. 2 | st. 1-2 | st. 5, 23 |
| Christmas | Art. 18-19 | Q&A's 35-36 | | Chap. VIII, Sec. 3 | st. 3 | st. 23 |
| Epiphany | Art. 19 | | | | | st. 24 |
| Baptism of Our Lord | | Q&A's 31, 32 | | | | |
| Transfiguration | | | | | | |
| Ash Wednesday | | Q&A's 3-11, 88-89 | | | | |
| Lent | Art. 21 | Q&A's 37-39 | Pt. II, Art. 2-5, 8 | Chap. VIII, Sec. 4; Chap. XV, Sec. 1-6 | | st. 24-26 |
| Passion/ Palm Sunday | | | | | | |
| Maundy Thursday | | | | | | |
| Good Friday | Art. 20-21 | Q&A's 37-44 | Pt. II, Art. 3-4, 8; Rej. 7 | | st. 4 | st. 25 |
| Easter | | Q&A 45 | | Chap. VIII, Sec. 4-5, 8; Chap. XIII, Sec. 1 | st. 4 | st. 25 |
| Ascension | Art. 26 | Q&A's 46-52 | Pt. V, Art. 1-15 | Chap. VIII, Sec. 4-5 | st. 5 | st. 27 |
| Christ the King | Art. 26, 37 | Q&A's 50-52 | | Chap. VIII, Sec. 7-8; Chap. XX, Sec. 4; Chap. XXXIII, Sec. 1-3 | st. 20-21 | st. 1-2, 6, 27, 43, 55-58 |
| Pentecost | Art. 11 | Q&A's 49, 51, 53 | Pt. III/IV, Art. 11-12 | | st. 6-14 | st. 28-30 |
| Trinity Sunday | Art. 8-9, 11 | Q&A's 24-25 | | Chap. II, Sec. 1-3 | st. 1 | |
| Unity of the Church | Art. 27-29 | Q&A's 54-55 | Pt. II, Art. 9; | Chap. XXV, Sec. 1-4 | st. 15-19 | st. 28, 34-42 |
| Communion of the Saints | Art. 27-28, 33-35 | Q&A's 55, 76-77 | Pt. V, Art. 9 | Chap. XXVI, Sec. 1-3 | st. 15-19 | st. 34-39 |

# THE *REVISED COMMON LECTIONARY*

A lectionary is a schedule of Scripture readings arranged and intended for proclamation during worship. The *Revised Common Lectionary* is a three-year schedule prepared by the Consultation on Common Texts (*www.commontexts.org*), an ecumenical consultation of liturgical scholars and denominational representatives from the United States and Canada who produce liturgical texts for use in common by North American Christian churches. The lectionary presented here is adapted from the *Revised Common Lectionary*, © 1992 by the Consultation on Common Texts and used with permission.

The three years (designated A, B, and C) include several Scripture readings for each Sunday: an Old Testament reading; a psalm, preferably sung, which serves as a congregational response to the Old Testament reading; a reading from one of the New Testament epistles; and, finally, a reading from one of the four gospels—Matthew in Year A, Mark in Year B, and Luke in Year C. Readings from the gospel of John are included in all three years. Over the three years, at least one reading from each book of the Bible is included. When used regularly, the lectionary functions in a way similar to the historic Reformed use of the Heidelberg Catechism: a disciplined approach to covering the range of Scripture.

A table highlighting important dates in the liturgical calendar for Years A, B, and C until the year 2040 is included on page 831.

| Sunday or Festival | Year A | Year B | Year C |
|---|---|---|---|
| **Season of Advent** | | | |
| 1st Sunday of Advent | Isa. 2:1-5 | Isa. 64:1-9 | Jer. 33:14-16 |
| | Ps. 122 | Ps. 80:1-7, 17-19 | Ps. 25:1-10 |
| | Rom. 13:11-14 | 1 Cor. 1:3-9 | 1 Thess. 3:9-13 |
| | Matt. 24:36-44 | Mark 13:24-37 | Luke 21:25-36 |
| 2nd Sunday of Advent | Isa. 11:1-10 | Isa. 40:1-11 | Mal. 3:1-4 |
| | Ps. 72:1-7, 18-19 | Ps. 85:1-2, 8-13 | Luke 1:68-79 |
| | Rom. 15:4-13 | 2 Pet. 3:8-15a | Phil. 1:3-11 |
| | Matt. 3:1-12 | Mark 1:1-8 | Luke 3:1-6 |
| 3rd Sunday of Advent | Isa. 35:1-10 | Isa. 61:1-4, 8-11 | Zeph. 3:14-20 |
| | Ps. 146:5-10 | Ps. 126 | Isa. 12:2-6 |
| | or Luke 1:47-55 | or Luke 1:47-55 | |
| | James 5:7-10 | 1 Thess. 5:16-24 | Phil. 4:4-7 |
| | Matt. 11:2-11 | John 1:6-8, 19-28 | Luke 3:7-18 |

| 4th Sunday of Advent | Isa. 7:10-16 | 2 Sam. 7:1-11, 16 | Mic. 5:2-5a |
| | Ps. 80:1-7, 17-19 | Luke 1:47-55 or | Luke 1:47-55 |
| | | Ps. 89:1-4, 19-26 | or Ps. 80:1-7 |
| | Rom. 1:1-7 | Rom. 16:25-27 | Heb. 10:5-10 |
| | Matt. 1:18-25 | Luke 1:26-38 | Luke 1:39-45 |
| | | | (46-55) |

## Season of Christmas

| Christmas Eve | Isa. 9:2-7 | Isa. 9:2-7 | Isa. 9:2-7 |
| (Dec. 24) | Ps. 96 | Ps. 96 | Ps. 96 |
| | Titus 2:11-14 | Titus 2:11-14 | Titus 2:11-14 |
| | Luke 2:1-14 (15-20) | Luke 2:1-14 (15-20) | Luke 2:1-14 (15-20) |
| Nativity of | Isa. 62:6-12 | Isa. 62:6-12 | Isa. 62:6-12 |
| Jesus Christ/ | Ps. 97 | Ps. 97 | Ps. 97 |
| Christmas Day | Titus 3:4-7 | Titus 3:4-7 | Titus 3:4-7 |
| (at dawn) | Luke 2:(1-7) 8-20 | Luke 2:(1-7) 8-20 | Luke 2:(1-7) 8-20 |
| Nativity of | Isa. 52:7-10 | Isa. 52:7-10 | Isa. 52:7-10 |
| Jesus Christ/ | Ps. 98 | Ps. 98 | Ps. 98 |
| Christmas Day | Heb. 1:1-4 (5-12) | Heb. 1:1-4 (5-12) | Heb. 1:1-4 (5-12) |
| (Dec. 25) | John 1:1-14 | John 1:1-14 | John 1:1-14 |
| 1st Sunday after | Isa. 63:7-9 | Isa. 61:10-62:3 | 1 Sam. 2:18-20, 26 |
| Christmas Day | Ps. 148 | Ps. 148 | Ps. 148 |
| | Heb. 2:10-18 | Gal. 4:4-7 | Col. 3:12-17 |
| | Matt. 2:13-23 | Luke 2:22-40 | Luke 2:41-52 |
| 2nd Sunday after | Jer. 31:7-14 | Jer. 31:7-14 | Jer. 31:7-14 |
| Christmas Day | Ps. 147:12-20 | Ps. 147:12-20 | Ps. 147:12-20 |
| | Eph. 1:3-14 | Eph. 1:3-14 | Eph. 1:3-14 |
| | John 1:(1-9) 10-18 | John 1:(1-9) 10-18 | John 1:(1-9) 10-18 |
| Epiphany | Isa. 60:1-6 | Isa. 60:1-6 | Isa. 60:1-6 |
| (Jan. 6 or | Ps. 72:1-7, 10-14 | Ps. 72:1-7, 10-14 | Ps. 72:1-7, 10-14 |
| Sunday before | Eph. 3:1-12 | Eph. 3:1-12 | Eph. 3:1-12 |
| Epiphany) | Matt. 2:1-12 | Matt. 2:1-12 | Matt. 2:1-12 |

## Season of Epiphany/Ordinary Time

| Baptism | Isa. 42:1-9 | Gen. 1:1-5 | Isa. 43:1-7 |
| of Our Lord | Ps. 29 | Ps. 29 | Ps. 29 |
| (Jan. 7-13) | Acts 10:34-43 | Acts 19:1-17 | Acts 8:14-17 |
| | Matt. 3:13-17 | Mark 1:4-11 | Luke 3:15-17, 21-22 |
| 2nd Sunday in | Isa. 49:1-7 | 1 Sam. 3:1-10 (11-20) | Isa. 62:1-5 |
| Ordinary Time | Ps. 40:1-11 | Ps. 139:1-6, 13-18 | Ps. 36:5-10 |
| (Jan. 14-20) | 1 Cor. 1:1-9 | 1 Cor. 6:12-20 | 1 Cor. 12:1-11 |
| | John 1:29-42 | John 1:43-51 | John 2:1-11 |
| 3rd Sunday in | Isa. 9:1-4 | Jon. 3:1-5, 10 | Neh. 8:1-3, 5-6, 8-10 |
| Ordinary Time | Ps. 27:1, 4-9 | Ps. 62:5-12 | Ps. 19 |
| (Jan. 21-27) | 1 Cor. 1:10-18 | 1 Cor. 7:29-31 | 1 Cor. 12:12-31a |
| | Matt. 4:12-23 | Mark 1:14-20 | Luke 4:14-21 |
| 4th Sunday in | Mic. 6:1-8 | Deut. 18:15-20 | Jer. 1:4-10 |
| Ordinary Time | Ps. 15 | Ps. 111 | Ps. 71:1-6 |
| (Jan. 28-Feb. 3) | 1 Cor. 1:18-31 | 1 Cor. 8:1-13 | 1 Cor. 13:1-13 |
| | Matt. 5:1-12 | Mark 1:21-28 | Luke 4:21-30 |

| | | | |
|---|---|---|---|
| 5th Sunday in Ordinary Time (Feb. 4-10) | Isa. 58:1-9a (9b-12) Ps. 112:1-9 (10) 1 Cor. 2:1-12 (13-16) Matt. 5:13-20 | Isa. 40:21-31 Ps. 147:1-11, 20c 1 Cor. 9:16-23 Mark 1:29-39 | Isa. 6:1-8 (9-13) Ps. 138 1 Cor. 15:1-11 Luke 5:1-11 |
| 6th Sunday in Ordinary Time (Feb. 11-17) | Deut. 30:15-20 Ps. 119:1-8 1 Cor. 3:1-9 Matt. 5:21-37 | 2 Kings 5:1-14 Ps. 30 1 Cor. 9:24-27 Mark 1:40-45 | Jer. 17:5-10 Ps. 1 1 Cor. 15:12-20 Luke 6:17-26 |
| 7th Sunday in Ordinary Time (Feb. 18-24) | Lev. 19:1-2, 9-18 Ps. 119:33-40 1 Cor. 3:10-11, 16-23 Matt. 5:38-48 | Isa. 43:18-25 Ps. 41 2 Cor. 1:18-22 Mark 2:1-12 | Gen. 45:3-11, 15 Ps. 37:1-11, 39-40 1 Cor. 15:35-38, 42-50 Luke 6:27-38 |
| 8th Sunday in Ordinary Time (Feb. 25-29) | Isa. 49:8-16a Ps. 131 1 Cor. 4:1-5 Matt. 6:24-34 | Hos. 2:14-20 Ps. 103:1-13, 22 2 Cor. 3:1-6 Mark 2:13-22 | Isa. 55:10-13 Ps. 92:1-4, 12-15 1 Cor. 15:51-58 Luke 6:39-49 |
| Transfiguration of Our Lord (Sunday preceding Lent) | Ex. 24:12-18 Ps. 2 or 99 2 Pet. 1:16-21 Matt. 17:1-9 | 2 Kings 2:1-12 Ps. 50:1-6 2 Cor. 4:3-6 Mark 9:2-9 | Ex. 34:29-35 Ps. 99 2 Cor. 3:12-4:2 Luke 9:28-36 (37-43) |

**Season of Lent**

| | | | |
|---|---|---|---|
| Ash Wednesday | Joel 2:1-2, 12-17 or Isa. 58:1-12 Ps. 51:1-17 2 Cor. 5:20b-6:10 Matt. 6:1-6, 16-21 | Joel 2:1-2, 12-17 or Isa. 58:1-12 Ps. 51:1-17 2 Cor. 5:20b-6:10 Matt. 6:1-6, 16-21 | Joel 2:1-2, 12-17 or Isa. 58:1-12 Ps. 51:1-17 2 Cor. 5:20b-6:10 Matt. 6:1-6, 16-21 |
| 1st Sunday in Lent | Gen. 2:15-17; 3:1-7 Ps. 32 Rom. 5:12-19 Matt. 4:1-11 | Gen. 9:8-17 Ps. 25:1-10 1 Pet. 3:18-22 Mark 1:9-15 | Deut. 26:1-11 Ps. 91:1-2, 9-16 Rom. 10:8b-13 Luke 4:1-13 |
| 2nd Sunday in Lent | Gen. 12:1-4a Ps. 121 Rom. 4:1-5, 13-17 John 3:1-17 | Gen. 17:1-7, 15-16 Ps. 22: 23-31 Rom. 4:13-25 Mark 8:31-38 | Gen. 15:1-12, 17-18 Ps. 27 Phil. 3:17-4:1 Luke 13:31-35 |
| 3rd Sunday in Lent | Ex. 17:1-7 Ps. 95 Rom. 5:1-11 John 4:5-42 | Ex. 20:1-17 Ps. 19 1 Cor. 1:18-25 John 2:13-22 | Isa. 55:1-9 Ps. 63:1-8 1 Cor. 10:1-13 Luke 13:1-9 |
| 4th Sunday in Lent | 1 Sam. 16:1-13 Ps. 23 Eph. 5:8-14 John 9:1-41 | Num. 21:4-9 Ps. 107:1-3, 17-22 Eph. 2:1-10 John 3:14-21 | Josh. 5:9-12 Ps. 32 2 Cor. 5:16-21 Luke 15:1-3, 11b-32 |
| 5th Sunday in Lent | Ezek. 37:1-14 Ps. 130 Rom. 8:6-11 John 11:1-45 | Jer. 31:31-34 Ps. 51:1-12 or 119:9-16 Heb. 5:5-10 John 12:20-33 | Isa. 43:16-21 Ps. 126 Phil. 3:4b-14 John 12:1-8 |

**Holy Week**

| Passion/Palm Sunday (6th Sunday in Lent) | *Liturgy of the Palms:*<br>Matt. 21:1-11<br><br>Ps. 118:1-2, 19-29 | *Liturgy of the Palms:*<br>Mark 11:1-11<br>or John 12:12-16<br>Ps. 118:1-2, 19-29 | *Liturgy of the Palms:*<br>Luke 19:28-40<br><br>Ps. 118:1-2, 19-29 |
|---|---|---|---|
| | *Liturgy of the Passion:*<br>Isa. 50:4-9a<br>Ps. 31:9-16<br>Phil. 2:5-11<br>Matt. 26:14-27:66<br>or Matt. 27:11-54 | *Liturgy of the Passion:*<br>Isa. 50:4-9a<br>Ps. 31:9-16<br>Phil. 2:5-11<br>Mark 14:1-15:47<br>or Mark 15:1-39 (40-47) | *Liturgy of the Passion:*<br>Isa. 50:4-9a<br>Ps. 31:9-16<br>Phil. 2:5-11<br>Luke 22:14-23:56<br>or Luke 23:1-49 |
| Monday of Holy Week | Isa. 42:1-9<br>Ps. 36:5-11<br>Heb. 9:11-15<br>John 12:1-11 | Isa. 42:1-9<br>Ps. 36:5-11<br>Heb. 9:11-15<br>John 12:1-11 | Isa. 42:1-9<br>Ps. 36:5-11<br>Heb. 9:11-15<br>John 12:1-11 |
| Tuesday of Holy Week | Isa. 49:1-7<br>Ps. 71:1-14<br>1 Cor. 1:18-31<br>John 12:20-36 | Isa. 49:1-7<br>Ps. 71:1-14<br>1 Cor. 1:18-31<br>John 12:20-36 | Isa. 49:1-7<br>Ps. 71:1-14<br>1 Cor. 1:18-31<br>John 12:20-36 |
| Wednesday of Holy Week | Isa. 50:4-9a<br>Ps. 70<br>Heb. 12:1-3<br>John 13:21-32 | Isa. 50:4-9a<br>Ps. 70<br>Heb. 12:1-3<br>John 13:21-23 | Isa. 50:4-9a<br>Ps. 70<br>Heb. 12:1-3<br>John 13:21-32 |
| Maundy Thursday | Ex. 12:1-4 (5-10), 11-14<br>Ps. 116:1-2, 12-19<br>1 Cor. 11:23-26<br>John 13:1-17, 31b-35 | Ex. 12:1-4 (5-10), 11-14<br>Ps. 116:1-2, 12-19<br>1 Cor. 11:23-26<br>John 13:1-17, 31b-35 | Ex. 12:1-4 (5-10), 11-14<br>Ps. 116:1-2, 12-19<br>1 Cor. 11:23-26<br>John 13:1-17, 31b-35 |
| Good Friday | Isa. 52:13-53:12<br>Ps. 22<br>Heb. 10:16-25<br>or 4:14-16; 5:7-9<br>John 18:1-19:42 | Isa. 52:13-53:12<br>Ps. 22<br>Heb. 10:16-25<br>or 4:14-16; 5:7-9<br>John 18:1-19:42 | Isa. 52:13-53:12<br>Ps. 22<br>Heb. 10:16-25<br>or 4:14-16; 5:7-9<br>John 18:1-19:42 |

**Season of Easter**

| Easter Vigil (First service of Easter) | Gen. 1:1-2:4a<br>Ps. 136:1-9, 23-26<br>Gen. 7:1-5, 11-18;<br>8:6-18; 9:8-13<br>Ps. 46<br>Gen. 22:1-18<br>Ps. 16<br>Ex. 14:10-31;<br>15:20-21<br>Ex. 15:1b-13, 17-18<br>Isa. 55:1-11<br>Isa. 12:2-6<br>Prov. 8:1-8, 19-21;<br>9:4b-6<br>Ps. 19<br>Ezek. 36:24-28<br>Ps. 42 and 43<br>Ezek. 37:1-14<br>Ps. 143 | Gen. 1:1-2:4a<br>Ps. 136:1-9, 23-26<br>Gen. 7:1-5, 11-18;<br>8:6-18; 9:8-13<br>Ps. 46<br>Gen. 22:1-18<br>Ps. 16<br>Ex. 14:10-31;<br>15:20-21<br>Ex. 15:1b-13, 17-18<br>Isa. 55:1-11<br>Isa. 12:2-6<br>Prov. 8:1-8, 19-21;<br>9:4b-6<br>Ps. 19<br>Ezek. 36:24-28<br>Ps. 42 and 43<br>Ezek. 37:1-14<br>Ps. 143 | Gen. 1:1-2:4a<br>Ps. 136:1-9, 23-26<br>Gen. 7:1-5, 11-18;<br>8:6-18; 9:8-13<br>Ps. 46<br>Gen. 22:1-18<br>Ps. 16<br>Ex. 14:10-31;<br>15:20-21<br>Ex. 15:1b-13, 17-18<br>Isa. 55:1-11<br>Isa. 12:2-6<br>Prov. 8:1-8, 19-21;<br>9:4b-6<br>Ps. 19<br>Ezek. 36:24-28<br>Ps. 42 and 43<br>Ezek. 37:1-14<br>Ps. 143 |
|---|---|---|---|

|  | | | |
|---|---|---|---|
|  | Zeph. 3:14-20<br>Ps. 98<br>Rom. 6:3-11<br>Ps. 114<br>Matt. 28:1-10 | Zeph. 3:14-20<br>Ps. 98<br>Rom. 6:3-11<br>Ps. 114<br>Mark 16:1-8 | Zeph. 3:14-20<br>Ps. 98<br>Rom. 6:3-11<br>Ps. 114<br>Luke 24:1-12 |
| Easter /<br>Resurrection<br>of Our Lord | Acts 10:34-43<br>or Jer. 31:1-6<br>Ps. 118:1-2, 14-24<br>Col. 3:1-4<br>or Acts 10:34-43<br>John 20:1-18<br>or Matt. 28:1-10 | Acts 10:34-43<br>or Isa. 25:6-9<br>Ps. 118:1-2, 14-24<br>1 Cor. 15:1-11<br>or Acts 10:34-43<br>John 20:1-18<br>or Mark 16:1-8 | Acts 10:34-43<br>or Isa. 65:17-25<br>Ps. 118:1-2, 14-24<br>1 Cor. 15:19-26<br>or Acts 10:34-43<br>John 20:1-18<br>or Luke 24:1-12 |
| Easter evening | Isa. 25: 6-9<br>Ps. 114<br>1 Cor. 5:6b-8<br>Luke 24:13-49 | Isa. 25: 6-9<br>Ps. 114<br>1 Cor. 5:6b-8<br>Luke 24:13-49 | Isa. 25: 6-9<br>Ps. 114<br>1 Cor. 5:6b-8<br>Luke 24:13-49 |
| 2nd Sunday<br>of Easter | Acts 2:14a, 22-32<br>Ps. 16<br>1 Pet. 1:3-9<br>John 20:19-31 | Acts 4:32-35<br>Ps. 133<br>1 John 1:1-2:2<br>John 20:19-31 | Acts 5:27-32<br>Ps. 118:14-29 or 150<br>Rev. 1:4-8<br>John 20:19-31 |
| 3rd Sunday<br>of Easter | Acts 2:14a, 36-41<br>Ps. 116:1-4, 12-19<br>1 Pet. 1:17-23<br>Luke 24:13-25 | Acts 3:12-19<br>Ps. 4<br>1 John 3:1-7<br>Luke 24:36b-48 | Acts 9:1-6 (7-20)<br>Ps. 30<br>Rev. 5:11-14<br>John 21:1-19 |
| 4th Sunday<br>of Easter | Acts 2:42-47<br>Ps. 23<br>1 Pet. 2:19-25<br>John 10:1-10 | Acts 4:5-12<br>Ps. 23<br>1 John 3:16-24<br>John 10:11-18 | Acts 9:36-43<br>Ps. 23<br>Rev. 7:9-17<br>John 10:22-30 |
| 5th Sunday<br>of Easter | Acts 7:55-60<br>Ps. 31:1-5, 15-16<br>1 Pet. 2:2-10<br>John 14:1-14 | Acts 8:26-40<br>Ps. 22:25-31<br>1 John 4:7-21<br>John 15:1-8 | Acts 11:1-18<br>Ps. 148<br>Rev. 21:1-6<br>John 13:31-35 |
| 6th Sunday<br>of Easter | Acts 17:22-31<br>Ps. 66:8-20<br>1 Pet. 3:13-22<br>John 14:15-21 | Acts 10:44-48<br>Ps. 98<br>1 John 5:1-6<br>John 15:9-17 | Acts 16:9-15<br>Ps. 67<br>Rev. 21:10, 22-22:5<br>John 14:23-29 or 5:1-9 |
| Ascension of<br>Our Lord<br>(for Thurs. or 7th<br>Sunday of Easter) | Acts 1:1-11<br>Ps. 47 or 93<br>Eph. 1:15-23<br>Luke 24:44-53 | Acts 1:1-11<br>Ps. 47 or 93<br>Eph. 1:15-23<br>Luke 24:44-53 | Acts 1:1-11<br>Ps. 47 or 93<br>Eph. 1:15-23<br>Luke 24:44-53 |
| 7th Sunday<br>of Easter | Acts 1:6-14<br>Ps. 68:1-10, 32-35<br>1 Pet. 4:12-14; 5:6-11<br><br>John 17:1-11 | Acts 1:15-17, 21-26<br>Ps. 1<br>1 John 5:9-13<br><br>John 17:6-19 | Acts 16:16-34<br>Ps. 97<br>Rev. 22:12-14,<br>16-17, 20-21<br>John 17:20-26 |
| Day of<br>Pentecost | Acts 2:1-21<br>or Num. 11:24-30<br>Ps. 104:24-34, 35b<br>1 Cor. 12:3b-13<br>or Acts 2:1-21<br>John 20:19-23<br>or John 7:37-39 | Acts 2:1-21<br>or Ezek. 37:1-14<br>Ps. 104:24-34, 35b<br>Rom. 8:22-27<br>or Acts 2:1-21<br>John 15:26-27;<br>16:4b-15 | Acts 2:1-21<br>or Gen. 11:1-9<br>Ps. 104:24-34, 35b<br>Rom. 8:14-17<br>or Acts 2:1-21<br>John 14:8-17 (25-27) |

**Season After Pentecost / Ordinary Time**

| | | | |
|---|---|---|---|
| Trinity Sunday | Gen. 1:1-2:4a<br>Ps. 8<br>2 Cor. 13:11-13<br>Matt. 28:16-20 | Isa. 6:1-8<br>Ps. 29<br>Rom. 8:12-17<br>John 3:1-17 | Prov. 8:1-4, 22-31<br>Ps. 8<br>Rom. 5:1-5<br>John 16:12-15 |
| 9th Sunday in<br>Ordinary Time<br>(May 29-June 4,<br>if after Trinity<br>Sunday) | Gen. 6:9-22; 7:24;<br>8:14-19<br>Ps. 46<br>Rom. 1:16-17;<br>3:22b-28 (29-31)<br>Matt. 7:21-29 | 1 Sam. 3:1-10<br>(11-20)<br>Ps. 139:1-6, 13-18<br>2 Cor. 4:5-12<br><br>Mark 2:23-3:6 | 1 Kings 18:20-21<br>(22-29), 30-39<br>Ps. 96<br>Gal. 1:1-12<br><br>Luke 7:1-10 |
| 10th Sunday in<br>Ordinary Time<br>(June 5-11,<br>if after Trinity<br>Sunday) | Gen. 12:1-9<br><br>Ps. 33:1-12<br>Rom. 4:13-25<br>Matt. 9:9-13, 18-26 | 1 Sam. 8:4-11 (12-15),<br>16-20 (11:14-15)<br>Ps. 138<br>2 Cor. 4:13-5:1<br>Mark 3:20-35 | 1 Kings 17:8-16<br>(17-24)<br>Ps. 146<br>Gal. 1:11-24<br>Luke 7:11-17 |
| 11th Sunday in<br>Ordinary Time<br>(June 12-18,<br>if after Trinity<br>Sunday) | Gen. 18:1-15<br>(21:1-7)<br>Ps. 116:1-2, 12-19<br>Rom. 5:1-8<br><br>Matt. 9:35-10:8 (9-23) | 1 Sam. 15:34-16:13<br><br>Ps. 20<br>2 Cor. 5:6-10<br>(11-13), 14-17<br>Mark 4:26-34 | 1 Kings 21:1-10<br>(11-14), 15-21a<br>Ps. 5:1-8<br>Gal. 2:15-21<br><br>Luke 7:36-8:3 |
| 12th Sunday in<br>Ordinary Time<br>(June 19-25,<br>if after Trinity<br>Sunday) | Gen. 21:8-21<br><br>Ps. 86:1-10, 16-17<br><br><br>Rom. 6:1b-11<br>Matt. 10:24-39 | 1 Sam. 17:(1a, 4-11,<br>19-23) 32-39 and<br>Ps. 9:9-20; or<br>1 Sam. 17:57-18:5,<br>10-16 and Ps. 133<br>2 Cor. 6:1-13<br>Mark 4:35-41 | 1 Kings 19:1-4<br>(5-7), 8-15a<br>Ps. 42-43<br><br><br>Gal. 3:23-29<br>Luke 8:26-39 |
| 13th Sunday in<br>Ordinary Time<br>(June 26-July2) | Gen. 22:1-14<br>Ps. 13<br>Rom. 6:12-23<br>Matt. 10:40-42 | 2 Sam. 1:1, 17-27<br>Ps. 130<br>2 Cor. 8:7-15<br>Mark 5:21-43 | 2 Kings 2:1-2, 6-14<br>Ps. 77:1-2, 11-20<br>Gal. 5:1, 13-25<br>Luke 9:51-62 |
| 14th Sunday in<br>Ordinary Time<br>(July 3-9) | Gen. 24:34-38, 42-49,<br>58-67<br>Ps. 45:10-17 or<br>Song of Songs 2:8-13<br>Rom. 7:15-25a<br>Matt. 11:16-19, 25-30 | 2 Sam. 5:1-5, 9-10<br><br>Ps. 48<br><br>2 Cor. 12:2-10<br>Mark 6:1-13 | 2 Kings 5:1-14<br><br>Ps. 30<br><br>Gal. 6:(1-6) 7-16<br>Luke 10:1-11, 16-20 |
| 15th Sunday in<br>Ordinary Time<br>(July 10-16) | Gen. 25:19-34<br>Ps. 119:105-112<br>Rom. 8:1-11<br>Matt. 13:1-9, 18-23 | 2 Sam. 6:1-5, 12b-19<br>Ps. 24<br>Eph. 1:3-14<br>Mark 6:14-29 | Amos 7:7-17<br>Ps. 82<br>Col. 1:1-14<br>Luke 10:25-37 |
| 16th Sunday in<br>Ordinary Time<br>(July 17-23) | Gen. 28:10-19a<br>Ps. 139:1-12, 23-24<br>Rom. 8:12-25<br>Matt. 13:24-30, 36-43 | 2 Sam. 7:1-14a<br>Ps. 89:20-37<br>Eph. 2:11-22<br>Mark 6:30-34, 53-56 | Amos 8:1-12<br>Ps. 52<br>Col. 1:15-28<br>Luke 10:38-42 |
| 17th Sunday in<br>Ordinary Time<br>(July 24-30) | Gen. 29:15-28<br>Ps. 105:1-11, 45b<br>or Ps. 128<br>Rom. 8:26-39<br>Matt. 13:31-33, 44-52 | 2 Sam. 11:1-15<br>Ps. 14<br><br>Eph. 3:14-21<br>John 6:1-21 | Hos. 1:2-10<br>Ps. 85<br><br>Col. 2:6-15 (16-19)<br>Luke 11:1-13 |

*828*

| | | | |
|---|---|---|---|
| 18th Sunday in Ordinary Time (July 31-Aug. 6) | Gen. 32:22-31<br>Ps. 17:1-7, 15<br>Rom. 9:1-5<br>Matt. 14:13-21 | 2 Sam. 11:26-12:13a<br>Ps. 51:1-12<br>Eph. 4:1-16<br>John 6:24-35 | Hos. 11:1-11<br>Ps. 107:1-9, 43<br>Col. 3:1-11<br>Luke 12:13-21 |
| 19th Sunday in Ordinary Time (Aug. 7-13) | Gen. 37:1-4, 12-28<br>Ps. 105:1-6, 16-22, 45b<br>Rom. 10:5-15<br>Matt. 14:22-33 | 2 Sam. 18:5-9, 15, 31-33<br>Ps. 130<br>Eph. 4:25-5:2<br>John 6:35, 41-51 | Isa. 1:1, 10-20<br>Ps. 50:1-8, 22-23<br>Heb. 11:1-3, 8-16<br>Luke 12:32-40 |
| 20th Sunday in Ordinary Time (Aug. 14-20) | Gen. 45:1-15<br>Ps. 133<br>Rom. 11:1-2a, 29-32<br>Matt. 15: (10-20) 21-28 | 1 Kings 2:10-12; 3:3-14<br>Ps. 111<br>Eph. 5:15-20<br>John 6:51-58 | Isa. 5:1-7<br>Ps. 80:1-2, 8-19<br>Heb. 11:29-12:2<br>Luke 12:49-56 |
| 21st Sunday in Ordinary Time (Aug. 21-27) | Ex. 1:8-2:10<br><br>Ps. 124<br>Rom. 12:1-8<br>Matt. 16:13-20 | 1 Kings 8: (1, 6, 10-11) 22-30, 41-43<br>Ps. 84<br>Eph. 6:10-20<br>John 6:56-69 | Jer. 1:4-10<br><br>Ps. 71:1-6<br>Heb. 12:18-29<br>Luke 13:10-17 |
| 22nd Sunday in Ordinary Time (Aug. 28-Sept. 3) | Ex. 3:1-15<br>Ps. 105:1-6, 23-26, 45c<br>Rom. 12:9-21<br>Matt. 16:21-28 | Song of Songs 2:8-13<br>Ps. 45:1-2, 6-9<br>James 1:17-27<br>Mark 7:1-8, 14-15, 21-23 | Jer. 2:4-13<br>Ps. 81:1, 10-16<br>Heb. 13:1-8, 15-16<br>Luke 14:1, 7-14 |
| 23rd Sunday in Ordinary Time (Sept. 4-10) | Ex. 12:1-14<br>Ps. 149<br>Rom. 13:8-14<br><br>Matt. 18:15-20 | Prov. 22:1-2, 8-9, 22-23<br>Ps. 125<br>James 2:1-10 (11-13), 14-17<br>Mark 7:24-37 | Jer. 18:1-11<br>Ps. 139:1-6, 13-18<br>Philem. 1-21<br><br>Luke 14:25-33 |
| 24th Sunday in Ordinary Time (Sept. 11-17) | Ex. 14:19-31<br>Ps. 114 or<br>Ex. 15:1b-11, 20-21<br>Rom. 14:1-12<br>Matt. 18:21-35 | Prov. 1:20-33<br>Ps. 19<br><br>James 3:1-12<br>Mark 8:27-38 | Jer. 4:11-12, 22-28<br>Ps. 14<br><br>1 Tim. 1:12-17<br>Luke 15:1-10 |
| 25th Sunday in Ordinary Time (Sept. 18-24) | Ex. 16:2-15<br>Ps. 105:1-6, 37-45<br>Phil. 1:21-30<br>Matt. 20:1-16 | Prov. 31:10-31<br>Ps. 1<br>James 3:13-4:3, 7-8a<br>Mark 9:30-37 | Jer. 8:18-9:1<br>Ps. 79:1-9<br>1 Tim. 2:1-7<br>Luke 16:1-13 |
| 26th Sunday in Ordinary Time (Sept. 25-Oct. 1) | Ex. 17:1-7<br><br>Ps. 78:1-4, 12-16<br>Phil. 2:1-13<br>Matt. 21:23-32 | Esther 7:1-6, 9-10; 9:20-22<br>Ps. 124<br>James 5:13-20<br>Mark 9:38-50 | Jer. 32:1-3a, 6-15<br><br>Ps. 91:1-6, 14-16<br>1 Tim. 6:6-19<br>Luke 16:19-31 |
| 27th Sunday in Ordinary Time (Oct. 2-8) | Ex. 20:1-4, 7-9, 12-20<br>Ps. 19<br>Phil. 3:4b-14<br>Matt. 21:33-46 | Job 1:1; 2:1-10<br>Ps. 26<br>Heb. 1:1-4; 2:5-12<br>Mark 10:2-16 | Lam. 1:1-6; 3:19-26<br>or Ps. 137<br>2 Tim. 1:1-14<br>Luke 17:5-10 |
| 28th Sunday in Ordinary Time (Oct. 9-15) | Ex. 32:1-14<br>Ps. 106:1-6, 19-23<br>Phil. 4:1-9<br>Matt. 22:1-14 | Job 23:1-9, 16-17<br>Ps. 22:1-15<br>Heb. 4:12-16<br>Mark 10:17-31 | Jer. 29:1, 4-7<br>Ps. 66:1-12<br>2 Tim. 2:8-15<br>Luke 17:11-19 |

| | | | |
|---|---|---|---|
| 29th Sunday in<br>Ordinary Time<br>(Oct. 16-22) | Ex. 33:12-23<br>Ps. 99<br>1 Thess. 1:1-10<br>Matt. 22:15-22 | Job 38:1-7 (34-41)<br>Ps. 104:1-9, 24, 35c<br>Heb. 5:1-10<br>Mark 10:35-45 | Jer. 31:27-34<br>Ps. 119:97-104<br>2 Tim. 3:14-4:5<br>Luke 18:1-8 |
| 30th Sunday in<br>Ordinary Time<br>(Oct. 23-29) | Deut. 34:1-12<br>Ps. 90:1-6, 13-17<br>1 Thess. 2:1-8<br>Matt. 22:34-35 | Job 42:1-6, 10-17<br>Ps. 34:1-8 (19-22)<br>Heb. 7:23-28<br>Mark 10:46-52 | Joel 2:23-32<br>Ps. 65<br>2 Tim. 4:6-8, 16-18<br>Luke 18:9-14 |
| 31st Sunday in<br>Ordinary Time<br>(Oct. 30-Nov. 5) | Josh. 3:7-17<br>Ps. 107:1-7, 33-37<br>1 Thess. 2:9-13<br>Matt. 23:1-12 | Ruth 1:1-18<br>Ps. 146<br>Heb. 9:11-14<br>Mark 12:28-34 | Hab. 1:1-4; 2:1-4<br>Ps. 119:137-144<br>2 Thess. 1:1-4, 11-12<br>Luke 19:1-10 |
| All Saints' Day<br>(Nov. 1 or<br>1st Sunday in<br>November) | Rev. 7:9-17<br>Ps. 34:1-10, 22<br>1 John 3:1-3<br>Matt. 5:1-12 | Isa. 25:6-9<br>Ps. 24<br>Rev. 21:1-6a<br>John 11:32-44 | Dan. 7:1-3, 15-18<br>Ps. 149<br>Eph. 1:11-23<br>Luke 6:20-31 |
| 32nd Sunday in<br>Ordinary Time<br>(Nov. 6-12) | Josh. 24:1-3a, 14-25<br>Ps. 78:1-7<br><br>1 Thess. 4:13-18<br>Matt. 25:1-13 | Ruth 3:1-5; 4:13-17<br>Ps. 127<br><br>Heb. 9:24-28<br>Mark 12:38-44 | Hag. 1:15b-2:9<br>Ps. 145:1-5, 17-21<br>or Ps. 98<br>2 Thess. 2:1-5, 13-17<br>Luke 20:27-38 |
| 33rd Sunday in<br>Ordinary Time<br>(Nov. 13-19) | Judg. 4:1-7<br>Ps. 123<br>1 Thess. 5:1-11<br><br>Matt. 25:14-30 | 1 Sam. 1:4-20<br>1 Sam. 2:1-10<br>Heb. 10:11-14<br>(15-18), 19-25<br>Mark 13:1-8 | Isa. 65:17-25<br>Isa. 12<br>2 Thess. 3:6-13<br><br>Luke 21:5-19 |
| Christ the King/<br>Reign of Christ<br>(Nov. 20-26) | Ezek. 34:11-16, 20-24<br>Ps. 100<br>Eph. 1:15-23<br>Matt. 25:31-46 | 2 Sam. 23:1-7<br>Ps. 132:1-12 (13-18)<br>Rev. 1:4b-8<br>John 18:33-37 | Jer. 23:1-6<br>Luke 1:68-79<br>Col. 1:11-20<br>Luke 23:33-43 |

# DATES IN THE LITURGICAL CALENDAR

| Year | First Sunday of Advent | Ash Wednesday | Easter | Ascension | Pentecost |
|------|------------------------|---------------|--------|-----------|-----------|
| A | Dec. 1, 2013 | Mar. 5, 2014 | Apr. 20, 2014 | May 29, 2014 | June 8, 2014 |
| B | Nov. 30, 2014 | Feb. 18, 2015 | Apr. 5, 2015 | May 14, 2015 | May 24, 2015 |
| C | Nov. 29, 2015 | Feb. 10, 2016 | Mar. 27, 2016 | May 5, 2016 | May 15, 2016 |
| A | Nov. 27, 2016 | Mar. 1, 2017 | Apr. 16, 2017 | May 25, 2017 | June 4, 2017 |
| B | Dec. 3, 2017 | Feb. 14, 2018 | Apr. 1, 2018 | May 10, 2018 | May 20, 2018 |
| C | Dec. 2, 2018 | Mar. 6, 2019 | Apr. 21, 2019 | May 30, 2019 | June 9, 2019 |
| A | Dec. 1, 2019 | Feb. 26, 2020 | Apr. 12, 2020 | May 21, 2020 | May 31, 2020 |
| B | Nov. 29, 2020 | Feb. 17, 2021 | Apr. 4, 2021 | May 13, 2021 | May 23, 2021 |
| C | Nov. 28, 2021 | Mar. 2, 2022 | Apr. 17, 2022 | May 26, 2022 | June 5, 2022 |
| A | Nov. 27, 2022 | Feb. 22, 2023 | Apr. 9, 2023 | May 18, 2023 | May 28, 2023 |
| B | Dec. 3, 2023 | Feb. 14, 2024 | Mar. 31, 2024 | May 9, 2024 | May 19, 2024 |
| C | Dec. 1, 2024 | Mar. 5, 2025 | Apr. 20, 2025 | May 29, 2025 | June 8, 2025 |
| A | Nov. 30, 2025 | Feb. 18, 2026 | Apr. 5, 2026 | May 14, 2026 | May 24, 2026 |
| B | Nov. 29, 2026 | Feb. 10, 2027 | Mar. 28, 2027 | May 6, 2027 | May 16, 2027 |
| C | Nov. 28, 2027 | Mar. 2, 2028 | Apr. 16, 2028 | May 25, 2028 | June 4, 2028 |
| A | Dec. 3, 2028 | Feb. 14, 2029 | Apr. 1, 2029 | May 10, 2029 | May 20, 2029 |
| B | Dec. 2, 2029 | Mar. 6, 2030 | Apr. 21, 2030 | May 30, 2030 | June 9, 2030 |
| C | Dec. 1, 2030 | Feb. 26, 2031 | Apr. 13, 2031 | May 22, 2031 | June 1, 2031 |
| A | Nov. 30, 2031 | Feb. 11, 2032 | Mar. 28, 2032 | May 6, 2032 | May 16, 2032 |
| B | Nov. 28, 2032 | Mar. 2, 2033 | Apr. 17, 2033 | May 26, 2033 | June 5, 2033 |
| C | Nov. 27, 2033 | Feb. 22, 2034 | Apr. 9, 2034 | May 18, 2034 | May 28, 2034 |
| A | Dec. 3, 2034 | Feb. 7, 2035 | Mar. 25, 2035 | May 3, 2035 | May 13, 2035 |
| B | Dec. 2, 2035 | Feb. 27, 2036 | Apr. 13, 2036 | May 22, 2036 | June 1, 2036 |
| C | Nov. 30, 2036 | Feb. 18, 2037 | Apr. 5, 2037 | May 14, 2037 | May 24, 2037 |
| A | Nov. 29, 2037 | Mar. 10, 2038 | Apr. 25, 2038 | June 3, 2038 | June 13, 2038 |
| B | Nov. 28, 2038 | Feb. 23, 2039 | Apr. 10, 2039 | May 19, 2039 | May 29, 2039 |
| C | Nov. 27, 2039 | Feb. 15, 2040 | Apr. 1, 2040 | May 10, 2040 | May 20, 2040 |
| A | Dec. 2, 2040 | Mar. 6, 2041 | Apr. 21, 2041 | May 30, 2041 | June 9, 2041 |
| B | Dec. 1, 2041 | Feb. 19, 2042 | Apr. 6, 2042 | May 15, 2042 | May 25, 2042 |
| C | Nov. 30, 2042 | Feb. 11, 2043 | Mar. 29, 2043 | May 7, 2043 | May 17, 2043 |
| A | Nov. 29, 2043 | Mar. 2, 2044 | Apr. 17, 2044 | May 26, 2044 | June 5, 2044 |
| B | Nov. 27, 2044 | Feb. 22, 2045 | Apr. 9, 2045 | May 18, 2045 | May 28, 2045 |
| C | Dec. 3, 2045 | Feb. 7, 2046 | Mar. 25, 2046 | May 3, 2046 | May 13, 2046 |
| A | Dec. 2, 2046 | Feb. 27, 2047 | Apr. 14, 2047 | May 23, 2047 | June 2, 2047 |
| B | Dec. 1, 2047 | Feb. 19, 2048 | Apr. 5, 2048 | May 14, 2048 | May 24, 2048 |
| C | Nov. 29, 2048 | Mar. 3, 2049 | Apr. 18, 2049 | May 27, 2049 | June 6, 2049 |

# SCRIPTURE REFERENCES